Managing IT Human Resources:

Considerations for Organizations and Personnel

Jerry Luftman
Stevens Institute of Technology, USA

Senior Editorial Director:	Kristin Klinger
Director of Book Publications:	Julia Mosemann
Editorial Director:	Lindsay Johnston
Acquisitions Editor:	Erika Carter
Development Editor:	Christine Bufton
Production Coordinator:	Jamie Snavely
Typesetters:	Keith Glazewski, Natalie Pronio and Milan Vracarich, Jr.
Cover Design:	Nick Newcomer

Published in the United States of America by
Business Science Reference (an imprint of IGI Global)
701 E. Chocolate Avenue
Hershey PA 17033
Tel: 717-533-8845
Fax: 717-533-8661
E-mail: cust@igi-global.com
Web site: http://www.igi-global.com/reference

Library of Congress Cataloging-in-Publication Data

Managing IT human resources: considerations for organizations and personnel /
Jerry Luftman, editor.
    p. cm.
  Includes bibliographical references and index.
  Summary: "This book provides a comprehensive presentation of current and
emerging perspectives focusing on all aspects of managing IT HR from the view
of both practitioners and academics located around the globe"--Provided by
publisher.
  ISBN 978-1-60960-535-3 (hbk.) -- ISBN 978-1-60960-536-0 (ebook) 1.
Information technology--Management. 2. Personnel management. 3. Electronic
data processing departments--Management. 4. Electronic data processing
personnel. I. Luftman, Jerry N.
  HD30.2.M36417 2011
  004.068'3--dc22
                          2011001303

British Cataloguing in Publication Data
A Cataloguing in Publication record for this book is available from the British Library.

Wow - This book provides a global perspective on IT HR issues for the coming decade. As IT pervades all aspects of business and society, HR organizations must adapt and this book provides a much needed guide for practitioners and researchers.

Dr. James C. Spohrer
Innovation Champion and Director
IBM University Programs World-Wide (IBM UP), IBM Almaden Research Center
San Jose, CA USA

This book provides an important contribution to education and re-skilling of the CIO for the 21st century. Any CIO who aspires to a business leader and change agent, must master the people aspect of their role or be doomed to remain in the engine room.

It has been said that there are three legs to CIO's 'knowledge stool': technology, business, and people. The first is universally understood and there have been great advances in IT leaders developing their business experience and acumen. However, far too many of us are more comfortable working with things rather than with and through people. That has to change if we are really are going to make the sort of contribution that our companies, and society, needs. This book is an outstanding way to learn, refresh or re-enforce those skills, and successfully balances real work experience with current research and leading academic thinking.

Peter Whatnell
CIO
Sunoco
Philadelphia, PA USA

As a global CIO, I regard the management of our IT human resources as the most rewarding as well as the most challenging aspect of my job. Without expert help, such as found in this book, my ability to make important human capital resourcing and deployment decisions is likely to suffer from limited thinking and perspective. As a member of the 'baby boom' generation, I find myself managing through an accelerating retirement-turnover-succession cycle that will persist well into the next decade. Combine this with the challenges of: finding replacement talent; optimizing global sourcing; and acquiring people who possess the adaptive behaviors and skills necessary in our always-on world, and you understand the 'must have' nature of this text.

The topics covered by this book, such as IT talent requirements in the 21st Century, all aspects of Recruiting 2.0, and understanding the new generation of IT professionals, speak directly to my current agenda and challenges. However much the world is changing, the book reminds us of what remains constant, by covering topics including: Building Great Talent and Effective Teams, Aligning business and technology as a Leadership imperative. Importantly, the book presents case studies illustrating the best people practices of IT leaders in providing an excellent balance of challenge, reward and quality work life. I consider this book an essential tool for today's IT executives and leaders.

Warren C. Fristensky
Senior Vice President and Chief Information Officer
John Wiley & Sons, Inc
New Jersey USA

The past decade has shown enormous changes in how we run and govern IT. Also the role of the CIO has transformed. Under the influence of technological and societal change, the role of the IT organization will diminish in the years to come where the role of IT will increase even more. Cloud Computing and consumerization in IT will change the way we will think about architecture, governance, service management, collaboration and communication and ultimately our thinking about business IT alignment.

However one of the areas that we will need to change most drastically is competences in IT. In a globalized world with the next generation knocking on the doors of organizations, retained and developing knowledge to survive will be vital. This book will prove to be one of the leading publications and a must read for future oriented IT executives and managers. It is a beautiful mix of topics, some driven by organizational needs, some by generational developments and some by the technological push.

Dr. Herman E. van Bolhuis
Director CIOnet
Managing Partner bITa Center
The Netherlands

The extensive real world research that is incorporated into Luftman's work make it an invaluable resource for IT practitioners and leaders. To me the most valuable insight provided by "Managing IT Human Resources" is that it is an extremely timely topic that provides the holistic analysis of the IT human resource discipline that is critical to an Information Technology organization if it strives to 1) Escape Outsourcing and 2) Be a Business enabler.

The insights on relevant topics such as "The four characteristics of the new generations of IT professionals" is invaluable to Old Guard IT leaders, such as myself, who have limited understanding of the goals and objectives of these generations which is critical to developing corporate hiring and retention strategies.

John J Tugman
President EPS Network Solutions
Eatontown, NJ USA

A must read for CIO's, CTO's, and HR professionals, this timely book recognizes that new and different methods will be necessary for companies to meet the emerging challenges of hiring, developing, and retaining IT talent. As the economy goes into high gear, IT resources will once again be at a premium.

The book addresses the problem completely and provides both strategic and tactical solutions that are practical and well referenced. The arguments are always backed up by the latest research and real organizational case studies. The writing is straight forward and to the point. It will make a great desk top reference.

Roy S. Nicolosi
Former CIO, CTO and SVP for ISO and Verisk Analytics Inc.
New York USA

This book combines comprehensive research with a wealth of practical experience gained by IT leaders. A must read for leaders seeking to enable their organizations to respond and excel in a rapidly changing business environment.

Ralph Schonenbach, CEO
Trestle Group
Germany

This is a comprehensive book on one of the key factors for the success of Information Technology in realizing business strategies: the human capital!

It offers a complete perspective on contemporary research, trends and insights for recruiting, developing, and retaining IT professionals that can make a significant difference for the success of an organization.

In this exciting new era of changing business models, with challenges in outsourcing and offshoring, this book transforms the already revolutionary concept of "peopleware" of the last century into a professional view of human management in IT for the next century.

Peter Vruggink
Principal Management Consultant
Logica
The Netherlands

We all have loved Jerry's perspectives on Technology and Processes over the years. Through this work he completes the trifecta with his wisdom on the people aspect of the equation.

Frank Kovaks
Former CTO McGraw Hill
Senior Manager Advisory Services Ernst & Young

Technology, sourcing policies and business strategy are highly dynamic and regularly ask new questions about the management of IT talent. This book is comprehensive, right up to date and draws on evidence and hard won insights from the latest academic research, and senior practitioner experiences. I highly recommend it.

Leslie Willcocks
Professor London School of Economics and Political Science
Editor in Chief, Journal of Information Technology
London, UK

Recruiting, retaining and developing talent has never been as complex, or as important, as it is now. This area is literally a battleground, with professional services organizations, technology vendors and the companies they serve competing for the best and brightest. Doctor Luftman has provided leaders in IT with an approachable handbook that should be read and embraced for its insightful, succinct, illuminating and actionable advice. I wouldn't go into this battle without it!

Frank Wander
Chief Information Officer
Guardian Life Insurance Company

Editorial Advisory Board

John Oglesby, *Buckman Laboratories, USA*
Lisa Meisenbacher, *ADP, USA*
Donald Brown, *Prudential, USA*
Angela Brodbeck, *UFRGS, Brazil*
Henrique Brodbeck, *UFRGS, Brazil*
Andreas Eckhardt, *Goethe University Frankfurt, Germany*
Wolfgang Brickwedde, *ICR Institute for Competitive Recruiting, Germany*
Sven Laumer, *Bamberg University, Germany*
Tim Weitzel, *Bamberg University, Germany*
Jim Spohrer, *IBM, USA*
Harvey Koeppel, *IBM, USA*
Paul Gray, *Claremont University, USA*
Martin Santana, *ESAN University, Peru*
Ed Trainor, *Amtrak, USA*

Table of Contents

Section 1
Trends in Skills/Careers and Development

Chapter 1

Christine V. Bullen, Stevens Institute of Technology, USA
Thomas Abraham, Kean University, USA

Chapter 2

Benn Konsynski, Emory University, USA

Chapter 3

Vijay K. Agrawal, University of Nebraska at Kearney, USA
Vipin K. Agrawal, California State University – Fullerton, USA
Ross Taylor, University of Nebraska at Kearney, USA
Frank Tenkorang, University of Nebraska at Kearney, USA

Section 2
Recruiting

Section 3
Retaining

Section 4
Executive Perspectives

Detailed Table of Contents

Section 1
Trends in Skills/Careers and Development

Traditionally the role of IT was to provide technical support to the business; most frequently, this was just in support of back office processes (e.g., accounting, payroll, email). Over time, IT roles have evolved to a key enabler/driver of front office services including direct support to important business partners and customers/clients. Significant emphasis is now on aligning IT and business strategies that increase revenues and productivity.

Chapter 1
Christine V. Bullen, Stevens Institute of Technology, USA
Thomas Abraham, Kean University, USA

The authors have highlighted, in Chapter 1, the shift in demand of the skills required by individuals pursuing a successful career in IT. Their extensive research in understanding the new skills patterns required by IT professionals indicates that just possessing technical skills and domain specific knowledge is not sufficient; instead a combination of technical, business, ability to learn and comprehend new technologies, and having the right attitude are considered of prime importance.

Chapter 2
Benn Konsynski, Emory University, USA

Chapter 2 presents the evolving role of managers and the challenges they encounter with technological advances, hiring diverse new candidates, making recommendations on IT Sourcing (Insourcing/Outsourcing), retaining quality professionals, and having effective employee career development plans. All of these considerations are the driving force behind the trends in Information Technology jobs in the future.

Chapter 3

Vijay K. Agrawal, University of Nebraska at Kearney, USA
Vipin K. Agrawal, California State University – Fullerton, USA
Ross Taylor, University of Nebraska at Kearney, USA
Frank Tenkorang, University of Nebraska at Kearney, USA

Chapter 3, "Trends in IT Human Resources and its Determinants" (The authors Vijay Agrawal, Vipin Agrawal, Allen Taylor, and Frank Tenkorang) introduces a new framework, described in Figure 4 of Chapter 3, which has proven to be valuable when developing IT-hiring, retaining, and career developing plans.

Section 2
Recruiting

In today's highly competitive environment, there are several considerations which organizations need to deliberate before/during the recruiting process, including the: (1) talent Management approach, (2) human resource life cycle, (3) sourcing framework, (4) role of human resource departments in Sourcing Decisions

Chapter 4

Phil Schneidermeyer, Heidrick & Struggles, USA

In Chapter 4, "IT Human Resources: Experts at Talent Management & Critical Partners to the CIO," Phil Schneidermeyer describes the important phases and their significance in increasing the performance of IT human resources. The phases involved in managing IT talent reflect all considerations of effective talent management. Initially, it begins with identifying and attracting new workers/students by making a presentation about the company's strategic goals, its growth, and services provided by them.

Chapter 5

Jo Ellen Moore, Southern Illinois University Edwardsville, USA
Clay K. Williams, Southern Illinois University Edwardsville, USA

The first step of the IT human resource life cycle is the selection process which is discussed in Chapter 5, "Selection: the Crux of IT HR Management," by Moore and Williams. Candidate selection can be considered as completing a simple application form followed by a brief interview, and/or a more complex process like situational structured interviews, simulations, performance tests, and other techniques which may be required for certain job openings.

In Chapter 6, "IT Hiring Criteria versus Valued IT Competencies" Jo Ann Starkweather and Deborah H. Stevenson present best practices for IT recruitment. Their analysis determined that knowledge, skills, and abilities are core competencies viewed by hiring, IT-recruiters, and IT-executives.

Derek Sedlack in Chapter 7 describes the the use of an expert systems as a valuable step in filtering prospective candidates. The biggest advantage of having this system is that it provides 24/7 inter/extra-organizational access and it can serve as a single reference vehicle for the job postings (for the hiring manager and applicant).

According to Anna Frazzetto, to make the best possible IT sourcing decisions, the IT-HR team must be ready to provide real-world facts on human capital data, in four core areas, described in Chapter 8: (1) Talent Cost, (2) Skill Roster and skill need, (3) Timing, (4) Workload balance & strain. Frazzetto discusses these core considerations in detail along with the specific tasks that organizations make regarding Outsourcing versus Insourcing.

In Chapter 9, Kristen Lamoreaux & Dibi Varghese discuss the role of women as an important rising workforce in IT. The chapter focuses on several factors including work life balance, gender schema, female role models, mentoring challenges, visibility, and recognition programs which will help organizations leverage their female employees.

Section 3
Retaining

Retaining IT personnel is crucial when it comes to developing the respective career building and motivational strategies necessary to maintain the IT workforce. Concerns about turnover have led firms to create formal employee retention programs. These programs are designed to focus on what IT employees are seeking to keep them satisfied and thus avoid the disruption and expense of a high turnover rate.

In Chapter 10, "Retaining IT Professionals," Gina Pipoli and Rosa María Fuchs discuss the best practices for keeping people in organizations and analyzing important retention issues. The chapter evaluates the six factor model developed by Julia Naggiar.

The four characteristics of the new generations of IT professionals, described by Jannie M. Buitenhuis in Chapter 11, "In the Pipeline: The New Generations of IT Professionals," are having a set of shared responsibilities, optimized use of technology, space for knowledge creation, and addressing corporate social responsibility by contributing to environmental friendly and non wasteful technologies. Organizations need to consider the generational differences when recruiting and retaining candidates.

In Chapter 12, Deepak Khazanchi and Dawn Owens elaborate on these characteristics (monetary/non-monetary) and their implications. It can be observed that not all employees are attracted by monetary incentives, and thus, for them non-monetary retention practices are more important. For example, non-monetary incentives like job characteristics, work culture, and team and community building have an influencing effect in retaining IT employees. Managers must be able to identify what motivates each employee.

In Chapter 13, the research conducted by authors Cesar Akira Yokomizo and Lina Eiko Nakata identifies the expectations of IT professionals. As summarized in Table 4 from Chapter 13, learning and development is considered most important by IT professional in ICT and in non-ICT companies. The chapter also provides different considerations based on gender, which is significant considering the rise in women in the IT workforce. As discussed, it is imperative to consider gender when deriving and deploying retention policies

Chapter 14

Adrián Hernández-López, Universidad Carlos III Madrid, Spain
Ricardo Colomo-Palacios, Universidad Carlos III Madrid, Spain
Ángel García-Crespo, Universidad Carlos III Madrid, Spain
Fernando Cabezas-Isla, Universidad Carlos III Madrid, Spain

Chapter 14, "Present, Past and Future of IT Careers, a Review: From the Local Pyramid to the Flat World" (authors Ricardo Colomo-Palacios, Adrián Hernández-López, Ángel García-Crespo, Fernando Cabezas-Isla) describe emerging career models including Boundaryless, Symbiotic, and Portfolio.

Section 4
Executive Perspectives

In this section of the book, we have an opportunity to hear the experience from IT leaders.

Chapter 15

Marianne Broadbent, EWK International, Australia & Arbiter Leadership Technologies, Australia

Effective talent and team management is a necessity as discussed by Marianne Broadbent in Chapter 15, "Building Great talent and Effective Team." She presents the benefits approach to talent management, as well as focusing on team dynamics and mutual accountabilities. Every organization should strive to bring out the best from each employee. For the CIO to be successful, it is important to build and stimulate effective teams.

Chapter 16

Mary Jo Greil, Carson Greil Group, LLC, USA
Elaine Millam, WorkWise Coaching and Consulting, USA

Another important consideration is the leadership development process as conveyed in Chapter 16, "Building IT Capacity for Leadership in a New Age," by Mary Jo Greil and Elaine Millam. Organizations must unleash the talent of those people who have the skills and capabilities to maximize organizational performance.

After leading IT Organizations for over twenty years John Stevenson, in Chapter 17 "Developing A players," introduces the team "A-Player". These are employees who have demonstrated leadership skills, project management skills, core IT technical skills, and have made a strong impact in challenging situations. Organizations should look for these A-players across the staff and create an environment where talent grows and stays to benefit the organization. He discusses the state of the art in identifying such talent, especially when teams are not co-located in the same geographic area.

In Chapter 18, "The Critical Five People Practices of IT Leaders," the founder of CIO Service Group, John Oglesby, shares the activities that are most likely to motivate and make employees be loyal to their organization. They are, to give people: (1) Interesting and challenging work, (2) The freedom to do it their way, (3) Things they can "own", (4) An environment in which they can excel, (5) Recognition for their efforts and accomplishments

Lisa Meisenbacher, in Chapter 19, "Considerations for Organizations and Personnel," discusses the long-term career opportunities in the IT industry and the immediate paradigm shift in the whole recruiting process. The author is optimistic that the networked organizations will provide a breeding ground for developing the skills that have been lacking in the IT industry.

In Chapter 20, "IT HR and the Perceived Value of Networking Organizations," the issues, controversies, and problems experienced by IT professionals are identified, as well as valuable recommendation to address them. The author, Donald Brown, derives these solutions based on the synergies between networked organizations and the human resource organization

Section 5
Cases

The successful organization of the future will be the ones with a prepared motivated team. The successful team will be comprised of people with the appropriate balance of skills who have taken charge of their future.

Chapter 21

Ângela F. Brodbeck, Federal University of Rio Grande do Sul (UFRGS), Brazil
Henrique J. Brodbeck, Federal University of Rio Grande do Sul (UFRGS), Brazil

In Chapter 21, the authors Ângela F. Brodbeck and Henrique J. Brodbeck discuss the Information Technology (IT) structure for two Brazilian companies, identifying their similarities and differences with respect to organizational culture and interpersonal relations, in the form of managing and motivating IT departments.

Chapter 22

Andreas Eckhardt, University of Frankfurt a. Main, Germany
Wolfgang Brickwedde, Institute for Competitive Recruiting, Germany
Sven Laumer, University of Bamberg, Germany
Tim Weitzel, University of Bamberg, Germany

In Chapter 22, Andreas Eckhardt, Wolfgang Brickwedd, Sven Laumer, and Tim Weitzel present the implications that social networking is making on recruiting. This case highlights the need for IT to go beyond conventional recruiting and to use new social networking tools (e.g., LinkedIn and Facebook). This case study introduces the need and challenge for transforming recruiting.

Foreword

Successful businesses of all kinds have one common denominator: the ability to attract, develop, and retain top talent. This is especially true in Information Technology (IT), where top-drawer talent properly applied to solving business problems differentiates the winners from the also-rans, and where decisions about IT talent impact the ability of companies to compete effectively in their respective marketplaces. For this reason, the most important skill an executive or manager can possess is effective IT human resource management.

Human resources management is "the art and science of allocating human resources among various projects or business units; maximizing the utilization of available personnel resources to achieve business goals; and performing the activities that are necessary in the maintenance of that workforce through identification of staffing requirements, planning and oversight, education and professional development, and administering their work-life needs" (Wikipedia). If you think about it, this really describes the core attributes of success in almost any endeavor. However, it has particular relevance for the IT knowledge worker, due in part to the unique needs of IT professionals, but also because successful application of these principles correlates with the success of the enterprise.

Just as people are different, so are enterprises. Readers whose enterprise's rely directly on technology to successfully compete in the marketplace will find greater importance in what Dr. Luftman and his colleagues have to say in "Managing Information Technology Human Resources." Executives and managers in companies that compete on the basis of technology, use technology to differentiate themselves in the marketplace, and/or rely on technology to achieve efficiency will find this book to be extraordinarily valuable. Companies who do not materially rely on technology to compete, differentiate and/or achieve efficiencies will find this book less valuable, but fewer and fewer successful companies today that fall into that category.

IT personnel are generally highly skilled, very marketable knowledge workers with unique needs and motivations, while sharing many of the same general needs as other people in the workforce. Dr. Luftman and his colleagues help readers decipher the unique needs of the IT knowledge worker and give us the key insights necessary to apply them to the demanding business problems of today. Nothing else that we can do or learn will provide a bigger payback than the efficient and effective management of IT human resources.

I have spent 25 years managing large IT departments in four different industries (railroad, airline, utility, and entertainment), and I have found that the single common denominator for success in these diverse environments is, without a doubt, the efficient and effective management of human resources. I have also had the pleasure of knowing and working closely with Dr. Luftman during much of that time, and I have developed a great deal of respect for the knowledge and insights that he has brought to the IT profession over the years. His extensive, informed insights and those of his colleagues are now available to all of us in his latest book.

"Managing Information Technology Human Resources" is a seminal work in the modern philosophy and practice of managing people, the most important of all IT resources. Starting with trends in skills/careers and development, moving through various aspects of recruiting and retaining talent, and finishing with contemporary executive perspectives, it provides practitioners and researchers with the insights and knowledge required for success. Highly relevant case studies illustrate the application of the core principles advocated by the impressive list of contributors to this book.

Dr. Luftman and the colleagues who have collaborated with him on this essential guide are all experienced IT professionals with many years of experience in IT and industry. Their collective wisdom should make this book essential reading for managers at all levels and in all fields, and their expertise is particularly applicable to IT professionals. I highly recommend this guide to those of us in IT and other fields who work with and manage people—and that means just about all of us!

Ed Trainor
Amtrak, USA

Ed Trainor has been a Chief Information Officer (CIO) for over 25 years for large companies in the airline, utility, entertainment and railroad industries. In these roles he has led information technology (IT) teams through numerous mergers, acquisitions and business transformation efforts. Mr. Trainor is a past national President of the Society for Information Management (SIM) and is also the co-author of two books on information strategy.

Introduction

Attracting and retaining top IT (Information Technology) talent is a major concern for most organizations. As we transitioned into the new millennium, the dot com boom turned to a bust, Y2K was over, and the recession hit, everything came to a dramatic halt. The economy then improved and was struck again with the more severe recession of 2008. The economy is now improving and the hiring of IT staff is expected to rebound. It will not likely grow at the breakneck speed of the 90s, but it is anticipated to grow. It is a continuous cycle that must be addressed, as the demand for IT grows.

Today, new skills are required to compete in a global economy where organizations have new opportunities to leverage IT, all of which present new alternatives to consider. In the next ten years as baby boomers retire, even more skills gaps will have to be reconciled. Finding and keeping IT professionals with appropriate skills is no easy feat. Today's IT professionals require not only strong technical skills, but also excellent business, management, industry, and interpersonal (e.g., speaking and written communications, negotiating, marketing, teaming) abilities. Additionally the choices for meeting the skills demand include more than just hiring the best candidate(s). Considerations like training/educating existing staff, outsourcing, partnering/collaborating, and acquiring new organizations each provide unique alternatives to the hiring conundrum.

This book will be a comprehensive presentation of current and emerging perspectives focusing on all aspects of managing IT human resources from the view of both leading practitioners and academics located around the globe. It will focus on the results of recent research (from exemplar practitioners and academics) and their implications to IT human resource considerations. It presents what IT professionals are seeking in a position, characteristics of the IT environment that contributes to the HR complexity, the retention of IT talent, stress in the workplace, IT career development, and the impact of IT outsourcing. Real world examples are presented to illustrate these important insights.

This book will introduce the state of human resources within the IT organization and review the critical elements that must be effectively managed by every CIO, IT manager, and Human Resource professional. It also provides important insights that all IT professionals should consider. With senior business executives acknowledging the important role IT has to play when it comes to integrating and delivering results (e.g., increased profits, revenues, and productivity, and reduced expenses) across a company in cost effective and efficient ways, there is greater need to have the right people doing the right job.

IT organizations must ensure that they have the right personnel for the respective positions, develop new IT strategies in accordance with the dynamic environment, nurture and develop talent, assist senior executives in sourcing decisions, and have a career advancement process for every employee which will allow them to excel in their professional career.

At the same time, the Information Technology work force is experiencing the migration of many skills offshore due to the visibility of global sourcing, the reduced pipeline of skills in high-income locations due to several years of lowered enrollments in IT-related university programs, and the impact of the largest retirement bubble in history (the retirement of baby boomers).

The skill set required for a successful career in IT has also evolved overtime from a more technical focus to a more balanced focus (including business management, industry, and interpersonal skills). The book presents the transformation of IT talent requirements in the 21st Century.

It is also important to understand the perspectives of the diverse workforce (geographic, cultural, sex, and age) that must effectively work in cohesive teams.

The above important considerations will be elaborated on in this chapter as the respective chapters of the book are introduced.

SECTION 1: TRENDS IN SKILLS/CAREERS AND DEVELOPMENT

Traditionally the role of IT was to provide technical support to the business; most frequently, this was just in support of back office processes (e.g., accounting, payroll, email). Over time, IT roles have evolved to a key enabler/driver of front office services including direct support to important business partners and customers/clients. Significant emphasis is now on aligning IT and business strategies that increase revenues and productivity.

In 2009, the results of the Society for Information Management (SIM) sponsored research facilitated by the author with results from CIOs located around the world ranked business productivity and cost reduction as the number one concern; slightly above IT and business alignment which has been a persistent chart topper. The implications of these findings are significant for both industry hiring and career development, and for planning IT curricula in colleges and universities. Understanding the appropriate skills required to attain the productivity and cost reduction demands during the recession while ensuring IT-business alignment to meet future demands is essential.

The top IT skills and capabilities that are required, in consideration of hiring and career development, and in decisions on IT outsourcing (listed in Table 1 of Chapter 1, "Patterns of Skills and Careers in the Information Technology Workforce," by Christine Bullen and Thomas Abraham) include:

- Technical
- Project management
- Business domain knowledge
- Sourcing-Selling
- Sourcing-Buying

These skills are required by both the client (internal IT organization) and provider (outsourcing vendor) of IT services. For example, a sound technical background with project management skills and overall business knowledge is required by IT client and IT provider companies. These skill sets are different from what was seen in the past (prior to 2000) wherein a desirable IT graduate was one with deep technical skills and a foundation in math and programming.

The authors have highlighted, in Chapter 1, the shift in demand of the skills required by individuals pursuing a successful career in IT. Their extensive research in understanding the new skills patterns required by IT professionals indicates that just possessing technical skills and domain specific knowledge is not sufficient; instead a combination of technical, business, ability to learn and comprehend new technologies, and having the right attitude are considered of prime importance.

The future in-house critical skills illustrated in Table 4 of Chapter 1 are the result of careful consideration of both client and provider IT service providers. The following section elaborates on the recruiting guidelines that all IT and HR professionals should be cognizant of. Clearly, the appropriate balance of technology, business/management, and interpersonal skills is considered to be fundamental.

Often, it is the human resources (HR) organization that emerges as the focus of many of these demands as new skill sets and new talent portfolio requirements emerge in organizations faced with a wide range of management and technology challenges with growing economic pressures, necessity for global expansion, shifting demographics and generational complexities, and constantly varying competitive pressures.

There are several technological influences which have lead to the transformation of the IT talent requirement of the 21st century. These technological factors are described by Benn Konsynski in Chapter 2, "Changing Capabilities and Capacities: Key Technology Influences in the Transformation of IT Talent Requirements in the 21st Century". It presents the evolving role of managers and the challenges they encounter with technological advances, hiring diverse new candidates, making recommendations on IT Sourcing (Insourcing/Outsourcing), retaining quality professionals, and having effective employee career development plans. All of these considerations are the driving force behind the trends in Information Technology jobs in the future.

Chapter 3, "Trends in IT Human Resources and its Determinants" (The authors Vijay Agrawal, Vipin Agrawal, Allen Taylor, and Frank Tenkorang) introduces a new framework, described in Figure 4 of Chapter 3, which has proven to be valuable when developing IT-hiring, retaining, and career developing plans.

SECTION 2: RECRUITING

In today's highly competitive environment, there are several considerations which organizations need to deliberate before/during the recruiting process, including the:

- talent Management approach
- human resource life cycle
- sourcing framework
- role of human resource departments in Sourcing Decisions

In Chapter 4, "IT Human Resources: Experts at Talent Management & Critical Partners to the CIO," Phil Schneidermeyer describes the important phases and their significance in increasing the performance of IT human resources. The phases involved in managing IT talent reflect all considerations of effective talent management. Initially, it begins with identifying and attracting new workers/students by making a presentation about the company's strategic goals, its growth, and services provided by them.

The next step is recruiting and hiring, followed by on-boarding and integration. Continuous learning and development experience is a dynamic process where experienced employees share/interact their experiences in a way that it becomes learning and developing experiences for all employees. Constant feedback for supporting employee aspirations is addressed during the engaging and retaining phase.

Once the talent has been identified and developed, it is then promoted and made available for other job opportunities within the organization.

The remaining phases focus on developing leadership skills to manage new teams, succession planning, and finally termination. This process continues to evolve, successfully managing the talent and leveraging high potential employee skills to benefit the organization in the most effective way.

Within talent management, performance management and leadership development are interconnected. The success of an IT organization depends upon the quality of its leadership which is achieved via leadership development and performance management, both which should be based on talent management strategies. Organizations should grow their internal staff capabilities by continuous recognition of the skills required, talent development, retention and promotion programs, and creating a leadership pipeline that ensures management and staff succession.

The HR lifecycle has five phases described as follows (Luftman, 2010):

1. **Determine Personnel Needs (Selection)**: The purpose of this phase is to analyze and identify personnel gaps, and staffing strategies to close the gaps to derive a sourcing plan.
2. **Sourcing**: This phase performs sourcing for permanent and contract candidates. It undertakes screening for permanent hires, usually working in collaboration with agencies and technical recruiters.
3. **Interviewing**: This process applies best practices for individual or group discussions. Evaluating candidates (internal and external) helps in establishing a long term relationship with the best possible employee.
4. **Hiring**: Finalizing the selected candidate, including due diligence, and reconciling responsibilities, salary, benefits, and reporting.
5. **Managing**: Includes preparing for staff retention/attrition, compensation, benefits, performance measurement, handling layoffs, and IT staff career development.

The first step of the IT human resource life cycle is the selection process which is discussed in Chapter 5, "Selection: the Crux of IT HR Management," by Moore and Williams. They elaborate on two key inputs:

1. Result (information) of the job analysis
2. Pool of applicants generated through recruitment strategy

Candidate selection can be considered as completing a simple application form followed by a brief interview, and/or a more complex process like situational structured interviews, simulations, performance tests, and other techniques which may be required for certain job openings.

Luftman's SIM survey identified attracting, developing and retaining IT staff as another pressing issue for CIOs. It is important to address the relationship between IT recruiters and IT executives (CIO, Director of IT, IT executives) in the hiring process, especially when it comes to the hiring of project managers or experienced IT personnel. There is often disparity in the valuation of IT hiring criteria used by IT recruiters and the valuation of criteria used by the IT executives.

In Chapter 6, "IT Hiring Criteria versus Valued IT Competencies" Jo Ann Starkweather and Deborah H. Stevenson present best practices for IT recruitment. Their analysis determined that knowledge, skills, and abilities are core competencies viewed by hiring, IT-recruiters, and IT-executives. Table-1 and Table-2 in Chapter 8 provide the details of the hiring criteria preferences by IT-recruiters and IT executives respectively, while Table-4 compares their hiring criteria preferences. Finally, they recommend that IT management needs to teach their recruiters how to understand and recognize the demands of IT and how to "speak IT". They should be considered an important part of the team that helps the senior IT executives with the entire sourcing process.

Derek Sedlack in Chapter 7 describes the the use of an expert systems as a valuable step in filtering prospective candidates. The biggest advantage of having this system is that it provides 24/7 inter/extra-organizational access and it can serve as a single reference vehicle for the job postings (for the hiring manager and applicant).

To outsource or insource an IT initiative is an important business decision that IT executives need to make by considering things like the costs to be saved, skills to be attained, intellectual capital to be protected, and standards to be maintained. According to Anna Frazzetto, to make the best possible IT sourcing decisions, the IT-HR team must be ready to provide real-world facts on human capital data, in four core areas, described in Chapter 8:

1. Talent Cost
2. Skill Roster and skill need
3. Timing
4. Workload balance & strain

Frazzetto discusses these core considerations in detail along with the specific tasks that organizations make regarding Outsourcing versus Insourcing.

The recession has relegated the priority of IT human resource concerns, though we expect them to raise up the management agenda once the recession is over. The current recession has exposed the critical role of executives in leading their companies, and IT is no different—CIOs serve as leaders and role models to their IT staff. This role becomes extremely important in downturns when employees look up to their leadership. Concerns about CIO leadership will probably continue to be important, as CIOs with the appropriate leadership skills become more difficult to find.

Given the persistently high ranking of management concerns in previous SIM surveys, and our expectation that they will climb back up the management agenda after the recession, the 2009 survey asked respondents to rank their time priorities for IT human resource issues. In first place was "developing interpersonal skills" (e.g., communicating, collaborating), with 45% of U.S. respondents indicating its importance. Second was "developing business skills in IT," mentioned by 35% of the respondents. "Developing technical skills" (8%), Retaining (7%) and Recruiting (5%) staff were far behind. However, when asked as part of the question on time priorities allocated to IT and business alignment, the time devoted to skills was in last place, with only 7% of organizations ranking it as a priority. Again, this was being asked during the economic recession.

In Chapter 9, Kristen Lamoreaux & Dibi Varghese discuss the role of women as an important rising workforce in IT. The chapter focuses on several factors including work life balance, gender schema, female role models, mentoring challenges, visibility, and recognition programs which will help organizations leverage their female employees.

SECTION 3: RETAINING

Retaining IT personnel is crucial when it comes to developing the respective career building and motivational strategies necessary to maintain the IT workforce. Concerns about turnover have led firms to create formal employee retention programs. These programs are designed to focus on what IT employees are seeking to keep them satisfied and thus avoid the disruption and expense of a high turnover rate.

Luftman's SIM research identified the following six vehicles for retaining IT professionals:

1. Open and honest communication
2. Good worker-supervisor relationship
3. Trust among co-workers
4. Challenging work experience
5. Opportunity for advancement
6. Balance between work and outside life

The recommended guidelines for a successful retention program are as follows. First, organizations need to adequately compensate their IT workers. Competitive salaries should be within 10% of market rates. Naturally, employees should be provided with health (including dental and vision) insurance benefits. Some companies include financial benefits, such as matching 401K plans, pensions, employee stock purchase plans, and tuition/education reimbursement. Lifestyle benefits are a bonus. These include casual dress, telecommuting, flexible hours, and sabbaticals.

Employee training/education has long been recognized as key in not only preparing employees for the challenges of the job, but also in improving morale. Organizations that invest less than 3 percent of payroll expense on training often see twice the staff turnover rate compared to those that invest 10%. Since the early 90's, IT organizations typically allocate between 15-18% of their operating budget on training.

A positive work environment goes a long way in ensuring employee contentment and retention. One effective way is to provide IT professionals with a chance to work with new technologies through job-rotation programs. Some organizations even attempt to make the work environment fun by using innovative benefits such as "walk-up massages" and "napping tents".

Employee burnout can be reduced by allowing time-off for employees that have put in long hours over an extended period to work on a project. Providing challenging work to deserving employees is fundamental. More mundane tasks such as Help Desk or End User Support can sometimes be outsourced or co-opted out.

As described in Section 2, hiring the right people is paramount. Managers need to analyze an individual's cultural fit within the organization and the role the individual might be best suited for in the long-term. Aggressive go-getters can "go get" the next best employment opportunity for themselves.

Mentoring is another important factor. Individuals who are able to play well in the roles of both "mentor" and "mentee" are especially favorable for the organizations in which continuous learning and innovation is advocated.

Important characteristics of a mentor are to be one who is trustworthy and approachable. Many mentees like their mentors to have a good sense of humor, be a good listener, admit mistakes, and share failures. The more comfortable you are in giving and receiving feedback the better it is for the mentor and mentee to understand each other.

Good mentors emphasize "coaching" rather than "consulting". They should be able to create an environment of mutual respect and trust that encourages the mentee to learn and grow. Such "mentorship" fosters an environment of sharing and has become another major source of job satisfaction in the IT industry, besides competitive compensation packages.

That being said, employees should be polled at least annually to determine their satisfaction levels and/or concerns. Some firms use a 360-degree review process so that managers can better understand how their staffs perceive them.

In Chapter 10, "Retaining IT Professionals," Gina Pipoli and Rosa María Fuchs discuss the best practices for keeping people in organizations and analyzing important retention issues. The chapter evaluates the six factor model developed by Julia Naggiar (2001):

1. Motivation
2. Career development
3. Compensation
4. Orientation
5. Training
6. Feedback and evaluation

Based on their extensive research, career development and compensation are considered to be the top two most effective practices for employee retention.

The turnover rate of IT personnel (Luftman SIM research) has typically been 7-8.5% of the total IT staff. It is relatively low in comparison to the rates of five-ten years ago. In 2009, the IT staff turnover rate was 6.90; very low in comparison to 2008 (Average 8.40) and 2007 (Average 8.20).There are several reasons why management needs to avoid a high turnover rate. First, it is difficult to anticipate human resource demands without knowing what skills are required. Second, losing employees is very disruptive to the organization as a whole. The loss of knowledge severely impacts the organization.

These costs are hard to pin down, because different firms value the retention of employees differently. However, the costs generally come from a combination of the direct costs associated with recruiting (e.g., advertising, recruiting, selecting, training, recruiter fees) and indirect costs, such as low employee morale and/or organizational satisfaction. Dysfunctional turnover occurs when effective performers leave an organization that does not want to see them go. Exit interviews help to identify the reasons for leaving a company which will help identify employees' requirements, desires, and needs to retain their most qualified staff. Recognize that the most important factor is to keep employees comfortable and happy.

It is important to have a vision and strategy addressing what and how the organization wants employees to perform. It should define the methods to achieve these goals and provide guidelines for reconciling obstacles. An effective review process that has clearly defined objectives and provides valuable direction to employees is essential.

Luftman (2007) identified that it is important that companies update their retention programs and regularly communicate to their employees about job satisfaction, advancement opportunities, new challenges, leadership changes, ability to use new technologies, job security, and faith in the organization's financial security, location changes, retirement plans, and bonus plans.

With Baby-boomers (born 1946-1964) retiring and Generation X (born 1965-1980) workforce aging, Generation Y (born 1981-1999) is starting to enter the IT job market. The four characteristics of the new generations of IT professionals, described by Jannie M. Buitenhuis in Chapter 11, "In the Pipeline:

The New Generations of IT Professionals," are having a set of shared responsibilities, optimized use of technology, space for knowledge creation, and addressing corporate social responsibility by contributing to environmental friendly and non wasteful technologies. Organizations need to consider the generational differences when recruiting and retaining candidates.

An important function of the IT manager is to ensure the personal career development of IT employees through education and training. The Conference Board reports that workplace education programs improve employee morale and esteem. In fact, this was the number one benefit according to 87% of the companies which provide such programs.

Other benefits include:

- Increased quality of work – 82%
- Improved capacity to solve problems – 82%
- Better team performance – 82%
- Improved capacity to cope with change in the workplace – 75%
- Higher success rates in promoting employees within the organization – 71%
- Increased output of products and services – 65%
- Increased employee retention – 40%

These results suggest that education programs have beneficial effects far beyond the education itself. And, perhaps even more importantly, the programs appear to counteract some of the stress-induced problems and enhance employee retention.

IT managers must evaluate education programs to determine the right amount to be invested in and the right mix of delivery mechanisms. The delivery mechanism varies from computer-based training, in-house training, to outside classes at professional and academic institutions.

Different types of education can be handled effectively in different ways. Individuals respond differently to various forms of education. Therefore, the IT manager needs to customize educational opportunities to the individual IT employee. In addition, there should be a formal evaluation programs that measure the effectiveness of the educational programs.

As mentioned previously, education should encompass the full range of information that each IT professional needs for their personal career development. This includes general managerial skills, communication skills, and technical skills. Many companies provide tuition reimbursement for individuals seeking higher degrees such as Masters Degrees in IS or Business Administration as well as Doctoral degrees in these areas. It is not uncommon for firms to require a commitment of several years of employment in exchange for providing tuition reimbursement. Most IT staff members are willing to make this commitment to gain the higher degree, which will be important for their careers.

Understanding the needs and desires of IT employees or their reason for dissatisfaction will always help organizations develop employee retention programs. The ranges of methods used to obtain employee feedback used include:

- Exit interviews
- Informal conversation between employee and supervisors
- Annual employee performance review
- Periodic formal conversation between employee and executives
- Periodic formal conversation between employee and mentors

- Information employee surveys

There are monetary and non-monetary characteristics which have an influencing effect on IT employee retention. In Figure 1 of Chapter 12, Deepak Khazanchi and Dawn Owens elaborate on these characteristics (monetary/non-monetary) and their implications. It can be observed that not all employees are attracted by monetary incentives, and thus, for them non-monetary retention practices are more important. For example, non-monetary incentives like job characteristics, work culture, and team and community building have an influencing effect in retaining IT employees. Managers must be able to identify what motivates each employee.

One effective attraction and retention strategy is to base compensation on performance. Another is to effectively communicate to IT employees the career path that they can pursue, which is in alignment with the organizational goals and individual interest. Employees also need to understand what they need to do to attain these career goals. Personnel Decision (2008) found that over 90% of IT professionals indicated that career path understanding is the most important reason for staying in their positions.

In Chapter 13, the research conducted by authors Cesar Akira Yokomizo and Lina Eiko Nakata identifies the expectations of IT professionals. As summarized in Table 4 from Chapter 13, learning and development is considered most important by IT professional in ICT and in non-ICT companies. The chapter also provides different considerations based on gender, which is significant considering the rise in women in the IT workforce. As discussed, it is imperative to consider gender when deriving and deploying retention policies.

In the past, an upward linear progression within the same industry was considered as stable employment; in IT, the path began as Junior Programmer to Project Manager, First Line Manager, Middle Manager, to CIO. Chapter 14, "Present, Past and Future of IT Careers, a Review: From the Local Pyramid to the Flat World" (authors Ricardo Colomo-Palacios, Adrián Hernández-López, Ángel García-Crespo, Fernando Cabezas-Isla) describe emerging career models including Boundaryless, Symbiotic, and Portfolio.

SECTION 4: EXECUTIVE PERSPECTIVES

In this section of the book, we have an opportunity to hear the experience from IT leaders.

Effective talent and team management is a necessity as discussed by Marianne Broadbent in Chapter 15, "Building Great talent and Effective Team." She presents the benefits approach to talent management, as well as focusing on team dynamics and mutual accountabilities. Every organization should strive to bring out the best from each employee. For the CIO to be successful, it is important to build and stimulate effective teams.

Another important consideration is the leadership development process as conveyed in Chapter 16, "Building IT Capacity for Leadership in a New Age," by Mary Jo Greil and Elaine Millam. Organizations must unleash the talent of those people who have the skills and capabilities to maximize organizational performance.

After leading IT Organizations for over twenty years John Stevenson, in Chapter 17 "Developing A players," introduces the team "A-Player". These are employees who have demonstrated leadership skills, project management skills, core IT technical skills, and have made a strong impact in challenging situations. Organizations should look for these A-players across the staff and create an environment where talent grows and stays to benefit the organization. He discusses the state of the art in identifying such talent, especially when teams are not co-located in the same geographic area.

In Chapter 18, "The Critical Five People Practices of IT Leaders," the founder of CIO Service Group, John Oglesby, shares the activities that are most likely to motivate and make employees be loyal to their organization. They are, to give people:

1. Interesting and challenging work
2. The freedom to do it their way
3. Things they can "own"
4. An environment in which they can excel
5. Recognition for their efforts and accomplishments

Luftman's Strategic alignment maturity assessment discusses the following six components which help in bridging the gap between IT and the business:

1. Communication
2. Competency/Value measurement
3. Governance
4. Partnership
5. Scope and Architecture
6. Skills

Each component focuses on core competencies which will serve as guidelines for IT-HR recruiting and team development. With over 1/3 of the Global 1,000 companies participating in assessments, the Strategic Alignment Maturity (SAM) assessment has helped organizations to not only improve the relationship between IT and the business, the Skills Maturity component helps organizations identify opportunities to enhance IT-HR considerations.

SAM assessments carefully consider the key components of the Skills maturity including:

- the extent to which an innovative environment is facilitated for individuals
- having a balanced culture and locus of power in decision making
- organizations ability to manage change
- Opportunities for career crossover
- Effectiveness of programs such as cross training and job rotation

Building of interpersonal skills across IT and business units is fundamental.

Lisa Meisenbacher, in Chapter 19, "Considerations for Organizations and Personnel," discusses the long-term career opportunities in the IT industry and the immediate paradigm shift in the whole recruiting process. The author is optimistic that the networked organizations will provide a breeding ground for developing the skills that have been lacking in the IT industry.

In Chapter 20, "IT HR and the Perceived Value of Networking Organizations," the issues, controversies, and problems experienced by IT professionals are identified, as well as valuable recommendation to address them. The author, Donald Brown, derives these solutions based on the synergies between networked organizations and the human resource organization

SECTION 5: CASES

The Brazilian Cases

In Chapter 21, the authors Ângela F. Brodbeck and Henrique J. Brodbeck discuss the Information Technology (IT) structure for two Brazilian companies, identifying their similarities and differences with respect to organizational culture and interpersonal relations, in the form of managing and motivating IT departments.

The German Software Manufacturer Case

In Chapter 22, Andreas Eckhardt, Wolfgang Brickwedd, Sven Laumer, and Tim Weitzel present the implications that social networking is making on recruiting. This case highlights the need for IT to go beyond conventional recruiting and to use new social networking tools (e.g., LinkedIn and Facebook). This case study introduces the need and challenge for transforming recruiting.

CONCLUSION

An organizations ability to manage change in this dynamic environment is a constant challenge. Finding, developing, leveraging, and retaining them is a daunting task, but a necessity for organizations to master. Talent management is one of the phases in the human resource life cycle that helps define the needs of the employees and allows them to achieve their career aspirations. The successful organization of the future will be the ones with a prepared motivated team. The successful team will be comprised of people with the appropriate balance of skills who have taken charge of their future.

Jerry Luftman
Stevens Institute of Technology, USA

REFERENCES

Chesebrough, P. H., & Davis, G. B. (1983). Planning a career path in Information Systems. *Journal of Systems Management, 34*(1), 6–13.

Levinson, D. J. (1978). *The seasons of a man's life.* New York: Ballantine Books.

Luftman, J. (in press). Managing Information Technology resources. *HR Consideration.*

Luftman, J., & Kempaiah, R. (2007). The IS organization of the future: The IT talent challenge. *Information Systems Management, 24*, 129–138. doi:10.1080/10580530701221023

Naggiar, J. (2001). *An exploration of retention practices in the IT industry.* Concordia University, Montreal, Quebec, Canada. Luftman, J. & Ben-Zvi, T. (2010). Key issues for IT executives 2009. *MIS Quarterly Executive, 9*(1).

PersonnelDecision.com. (2008). *Keeping good talent during bad times*: How to retain key employees during an economic downturn. Retrieved on November 12, 2008, from http://www.personneldecisions. com/uploadedFiles/China/Nov2008_Newsletter/Retention_PDIpulseFINALEng.pdf

Schein, E. H. (1978). *Career dynamics: Matching individual and organizational needs*. Reading, MA: Addison-Wesley.

KEY TERMS AND DEFINITIONS

360-Degree Review: Is review process allows each individual to review his or her supervisor as well as be reviewed by them.

Boundaryless Career: Boundaryless career represents the globalization of career, that is, individual transcending psychical and psychological boundaries, establishing new career opportunities.

Preface

Everyone knows the old adage, "those who can, do; and those who can't, teach." After a notable twenty-two year career at IBM that combined the experience of practitioner (including being a CIO), consultant (including being a manager of consultants), and the last fifteen+ years at Stevens Institute as an academic (including being a Professor, Program Director, Associate Dean, and researcher), I can comfortably say that I have familiarity with all aspects of an IT career. I trust that there might even be some who would say I was a good CIO, consultant, and Professor. My roles as an Executive Vice President of SIM (Society of Information Management) International and an active member of The Conference Board have provided additional insights regarding the challenges facing Information Technology (IT) organizations.

Whether you are a CIO, Information Technology (IT) manager, Human Resource (HR) manager, HR staff member, consultant to IT organizations, recruiter, academic, or in pursuit of enhancing your IT career, you will find the need to appreciate the fundamental Information Technology human resource considerations. These considerations include understanding the trends in:

- skills/careers and development
- recruiting
- retaining

Given the importance of IT HR considerations, it is perplexing why there has not previously been a book available to address this essential area. This book is based on grounded academic research and executive experiences. The insights and examples provided in this balanced perspective make this book a valuable asset for experienced professionals, academics, and students.

In investigating the importance that IT executives have placed on IT HR over the years, my Society for Information Management (SIM) trends research suggests that prior to the new millennium, attracting and retaining IT professionals was not among the top executive considerations, even with Y2K and the dot com boom. In reviewing the top twenty considerations since 1980, IT executives ranked HR considerations between 6 and 19, and more typically in the high end (low is considered more important). Since 2000, and prior to the economic conundrum, attracting and retaining IT professionals was typically ranked first or second among all considerations. With the economy in recession, IT HR considerations fell back to the pre-millennium rankings. However, with the growth in leveraging IT throughout the business, anticipated retirement of the Baby Boomer generation, and the dip in students graduating with Computer Science/Information Systems Degrees, all indications suggest that IT HR will once again move towards the top of the list after the recession.

Today, new skills are required to compete in a global economy where organizations have new challenges to meet and new alternatives to choose from. Finding and keeping IT professionals with the appropriate skills is no easy feat. Today's job skills require not only strong technical skills, but also excellent business, industry, communications, marketing, and negotiating abilities. Additionally, the choices for meeting the skills demand include more than just hiring the best candidate(s). Considerations like training/educating existing staff, outsourcing, partnering/collaborating, and acquiring new organizations each provide unique alternatives to the hiring conundrum.

This book provides a comprehensive presentation of current and emerging perspectives focusing on all aspects of managing IT HR from the view of both practitioners and academics located around the globe. It focuses on the results of recent research (from leading practitioners and academics) and their implications to IT human resource considerations. It presents what IT professionals are seeking in a position, characteristics of the IT environment that contributes to the HR complexity, the retention of IT talent, stress in the workplace, IT career development, and the impact of IT outsourcing. Real world examples are presented to illustrate these important insights.

This is a critical subject for IT management and human resource management programs, as well as for all practitioners from IT and HR organizations, and academics seeking to identify program content. This book will also benefit all prospective IT candidates applying for jobs and the recruiters for the hiring companies by presenting them with recruiting guidelines, employee retaining strategies, inputs on developing great talent and recruiting skills, and developing key players to become future leaders. It is paramount to recognize that as technology and business environments change, skills will be required to change; however, it is not just the technical skills that will lead to a successful IT career or IT organization, it is the appropriate balance of technical, business, management, industry, and interpersonal skills.

Among the most important IT management responsibilities is to ensure that the organization has the right personnel for the respective services that they provide, develop new IT strategies in accordance with the dynamic business and technical environment, nurture and develop talent, assist senior executives in sourcing decisions, and have a career advancement process for every employee which will allow them to excel in their professional career.

The purpose of this book is to provide a set of practical and powerful tools to facilitate the understanding of the strategic, tactical, and operational human resource responsibilities for IT management. We have learned a lot from applying the tools and approaches presented in this book. Our experiences have helped identify and measure the key elements that lead to a successful IT career and successful IT organization. Defining what will be demanded of managers and firms to survive and succeed in the information age remains a major challenge. This book prepares IT professionals to meet the challenge.

Jerry Luftman
Stevens Institute of Technology, USA July 2010

Acknowledgment

This book has its origins in research that began in 1980. Much of the original work has been published and presented around the world. A great deal has changed, and will continue to change. A lot has been learned, and will continue to be learned. The chapters in this book present an outstanding balance of experience from leading academics and executive practitioners.

While researching, writing, and editing this book, I have become indebted to a large number of individuals and organizations, only a few of whom can be mentioned here. I am greatly appreciative to The Society of Information Systems (SIM) for sponsoring a large part of the important research that stimulated a lot of the insights presented. Recognition is due to Stevens Institute of Technology for giving me time to research and teach these important ideas to the future leaders of industry, including the participants in the executive information management programs.

Of course a large degree of thanks is due to the hundreds of organizations that have been used in creating, developing, and advancing the insights presented. This includes the thousands of students attending the Stevens graduate programs where thought-provoking discussion has led to many of the new insights.

This book is dedicated to the families of all of the contributors. A major responsibility of a Professor is to prepare the leaders of the future. I especially want to dedicate this book to Michael, Melissa, Marcy, Jayden, and Jesse who are well on their way to being the kind of leaders we had always dreamed they would become. I especially want to dedicate it to my Vivian who has been my best friend for over 40 years.

Jerry Luftman
Stevens Institute of Technology, USA

Section 1
Trends in Skills/Careers and Development

Traditionally the role of IT was to provide technical support to the business; most frequently, this was just in support of back office processes (e.g., accounting, payroll, email). Over time, IT roles have evolved to a key enabler/driver of front office services including direct support to important business partners and customers/clients. Significant emphasis is now on aligning IT and business strategies that increase revenues and productivity.

Chapter 1
Patterns of Skills and Careers in the Information Technology Workforce

Christine V. Bullen
Stevens Institute of Technology, USA

Thomas Abraham
Kean University, USA

ABSTRACT

There are a number of significant forces shaping the Information Technology (IT) work force: the migration of skills due to global sourcing, the thin pipeline of skills in high-income locations due to several years of lowered enrollments in IT-related university programs, and the impact of the largest retirement bubble in history, that is, the retirement of baby boomers. The impact of these forces was investigated through interviews and surveys with companies that purchase IT global sourcing (clients) and those that deliver IT services (providers). The results of this research indicate a new pattern of skills and capabilities that will be required by individuals pursuing a successful career in Information Technology. Business skills and client facing skills showed up at the top of the rankings. They also indicate the need for industry to develop a new approach to hiring and retaining IT professionals. The traditional career path of programmer-analyst-manager will need to be replaced by new paths.

INTRODUCTION

This chapter will provide an overview of the results of this work, which has been supported by the Society for Information Management

DOI: 10.4018/978-1-60960-535-3.ch001

(SIM), and carried out by a team of academics and practitioners located around the world (see acknowledgements section). The implications of these findings are significant for both industry hiring and career development, and for planning IT curricula in colleges and universities. The initial phase was a study of workforce trends in IT client companies. Results from phase one revealed a shift in the mission of the information system function from delivering technology-based solutions to managing the process of delivering solutions. Client-facing capabilities were found to be critical to this mission as well as business and project-management capabilities.

Phase two examined workforce trends in IT provider companies. Results indicate that provider firms are also seeking client-facing capabilities, project management and business domain knowledge over technical capabilities. Comparing the results of the two phases reveals implications for hiring, curriculum design, and corporate training practices.

The results of this research underline a looming crisis in several areas: (1) graduates who are not trained in areas that the marketplace is seeking; (2) thin pipeline for specific technical skills; (3) increasing pressure to source IT capability; (4) lag in university responsiveness to the needs of the marketplace; and (5) lag in industry practice regarding hiring and retention.

BACKGROUND

The IT community has focused on staffing and workforce issues as a critical topic in the management of the function for the past thirty years (Ball & Harris, 1982; Brancheau & Wetherbe, 1987; Leitheiser, 1992; Luftman and Kempaiah, 2008; Niederman and Mandviwalla, 2004). The work described here specifically examines what firms consider critical when hiring and developing their own IT professionals. In addition, there has been very little investigation into the capabilities sought by IT service providers. Therefore this study represents a view into previously overlooked research areas.

Kaplan and Lerouge (2007) review the human resource management literature for IT workers and make some recommendations including

- Creating boundary spanning jobs, practicing effective performance management, and increasing participation in decision making.
- Providing concrete resources such as research time, opportunities to attend courses, and physical facilities that facilitate trial and error.
- Augmenting generalized technical knowledge and skills with organization-specific ones.

King (2008) indicates traditional IT job titles such as programmer and systems analyst are disappearing and these jobs are being embedded in the business.

Ingervaldson (2008) recommends establishing separate technical and managerial career paths that enable workers to remain technical and achieve higher pay and status within the organization. This is the only way to retain top technical people who have no interest in managing others.

The literature demonstrates that interest in the IT workforce and career paths has been a research issue for many years. Management has struggled with understanding how to motivate and reward IT professionals. But the IT workforce is a proverbial "moving target" as specific technical areas gain and then loses popularity, as market forces such as IT outsourcing influence the hiring and development decisions, and as market supply and demand varies.

The research described here addresses the evolution of what has been a strictly technical position to one which blends technical and business expertise. The new set of blended skills goes beyond previously described need for specific business knowledge and also brings the requirements to the entry-level position and thereby affects the academic program curricula.

Table 1. IS skills and capabilities

TECHNICAL
Systems Analysis
Systems Design
Programming
System Testing
Database Design / Management
IT Architecture/Standards
Voice/Data Telecommunications
Operating Systems
Server Hosting
Security
Mainframe/Legacy
Operations
Continuity/Disaster Recovery
Desktop Support/Help Desk
PROJECT MANAGEMENT
Project Planning, Budgeting and Scheduling
Project Risk Management
Negotiation
Project Leadership
User Relationship Management
Working with Virtual Teams

Working Globally
Capability Maturity Model Utilization
BUSINESS DOMAIN
Industry Knowledge
Company Specific Knowledge
Functional Area Process Knowledge
Business Process Design and Reengineering
Change Management/Organizational Readiness
Managing Stakeholder Expectations
Communication
SOURCING – SELLING (only Phase two)
Customer/Product/Service Go-to-Market Strategy
Customer Selection or Qualification
Contracting and Legal
Managing Customer Relationships
SOURCING – BUYING (only phase 2)
Sourcing Strategy
Third-Party Provider Selection
Contracting and Legal
Managing Third Party Providers

OVERVIEW OF RESEARCH RESULTS

The respondents in both phases of the study were asked to use the following list of skills and capabilities (in Table 1) to indicate their importance in a variety of questions related to the critical nature of the skills currently, in the future, in considerations of hiring and career development, and in decisions on IT outsourcing. We use the phrase "skills and capabilities" because some of the items in the list represent specific skills (e.g. Project Leadership), while others represent a general category of capability (e.g., Programming).

The phase one results from IT client companies included a wide range of industry and sizes as shown in Table 2. A comprehensive discussion of phase one can be found in Zwieg et. al. (2006) and will be summarized here.

The phase two companies were all in the services providing marketplace, therefore they are shown by geographic distribution and revenue in Table 3. A comprehensive discussion of the phase two results can be found in Kaiser et.al. (2008) and will be summarized here.

Both sets of respondents provided a range of organizations resulting in a good distribution of demographic characteristics allowing the analysis to be carried out by looking at a variety of patterns, for example, by size, by location, by industry, etc.

Table 2. Phase one sample firms

Industry	% of Sample
Professional Services	21%
Financial Services	21%
Heavy Industry	26%
Other Services	33%
Revenue	
Fortune 500+ *(over $3 billion)*	41%
Large *($500 million - $3 billion)*	22%
SME *(less than $500 million)*	37%

Table 3. Phase two sample firms

Geographical Distribution	% of Sample
North & South America	66%
W. Europe, E. Europe/CIS	17%
Australia, India	16%
Revenue	
Fortune 500+ *(over $3 billion)*	14%
Large *($500 million - $3 billion)*	15%
SME *(less than $500 million)*	71%

In addition to basic demographic information for analysis purposes, a variety of questions were asked (in both phases) about current and future skills needs, hiring at entry (new college graduates) and mid (minimum of five years experience) levels, missing skills in IT professionals, etc.

Skills that the two groups consider important to retain in the future are summarized in Table 4. These skills are grouped by type of skill and include the top ten skills for each type of respondent.

While, at first glance the top skills seem different, there are important overlaps. For example,

providers value managing relationships with customers, while clients value the corresponding engagement skills related to managing providers Neither includes many technical skills among the most highly rated critical or emerging skills. In both cases only two technical skills ranked among the top ten critical skills. Provider firms place greater emphasis on project management skills, while client firms place greater emphasis on business-oriented skills, possibly related to the different nature of their corporate missions.

Clients rate company knowledge, BPR, and change management among the leading critical

Table 4. IT client and provider future in-house critical skills

Skill	Type of Skill	Client	Provider
Systems Analysis	Technical	x	x
Systems Design	Technical	x	
Architecture/Standards	Technical		x
Project Leadership	Project Management	x	x
Project Planning	Project Management	x	x
Project Risk Management	Project Management		x
Working Globally	Project Management		x
Industry Knowledge	Business Domain	x	x
Process Knowledge	Business Domain	x	x
Company Knowledge	Business Domain	x	
Business Process Reengineering (BPR)	Business Domain	x	
Change Management	Business Domain	x	
Customer Relationship Management	Sourcing		x
User Relationship Management	Sourcing		x
Managing Third-party Providers	Sourcing	x	

Table 5. Major client and provider differences

Type of Skill	Client	Provider
Technical	Desired in entry-level hires	Less important at entry level
Sourcing – Relationship Management	Only important in future. Not emphasized in hiring	Critical now and in the future. Emphasized in hiring
Project management	Desired in mid level	Desired in entry and mid level
Sourcing – Global Delivery	Not highly rated	Highly rated
Industry & Process Knowledge	Highly rated	Highly rated

skills. Both clients and providers consider industry and process knowledge critical to keep in house. For providers, company knowledge is useful for a specific client but is less applicable across clients. On the other hand, industry and process knowledge provide a valuable base that can be leveraged across multiple customers.

When asked about skill needs at entry level and mid level, perhaps the most striking difference between client and provider responses is the importance that clients give to technical skills at entry level. Nine out of the eleven entry-level skills desired by clients are technical. IT providers seek a more diverse set of skills, with seven of the eleven most desired entry-level skills being non-technical. Table 5 summarizes this and other major differences.

The results of these interviews and surveys describe the need for anyone pursuing a career as an IT professional, with either client or provider organizations to look for opportunities through education and experience to develop a set of skills that includes both technical and business capabilities.

ISSUES, CONTROVERSIES AND PROBLEMS

Several interesting questions are raised by these results:

1. If clients are depending on providers for the bulk of their technical work, then why are the providers not indicating a critical need for a wide range of technical skills?
2. If the university pipeline is thin in high-income locations, where will organizations find the talent they need?
3. If clients are hiring entry-level IT staff without the general business skills that they value for the future, then how will those employees gain the required experience?

Some partial answers to the first question have been provided in the interviews with participants. The large providers have strategic plans that expand beyond the commodity-level work they have traditionally carried out. As a result they want to build a workforce of talent in managerial-level areas like project management and relationship management. At the same time they are looking for low-income locations (often lower than their own locations) to create captive centers and partnerships for carrying out the commodity-level work. This strategy will allow them to continue to offer the best value to their clients, despite changes in their own income levels and foreign exchange rates. There is an additional factor that commodity-level work will become increasingly automated and therefore carried out by fewer IS staff. Both of these factors help to explain how the providers will continue to fulfill the business needs of their clients.

The second question is part of the dilemma that organizations looking to hire entry-level IT students are not finding the skills they seek and therefore are driven to outsourcing jobs to other locations. The combination of the economic pressures and thin pipeline make it difficult for organizations to solve their IT staffing needs through hiring. In addition, as companies have become more experienced in outsourcing IT work, more comfortable with managing outsourced work, and accustomed to the value they are getting from quality work done in lower-income locations, the impetus to hire locally weakens. Both experienced IT professionals and graduates from IT and computer science-related programs will need to present an attractive value package to find employment. Understanding the blend of skills that organizations deem valuable is an important step in a successful career in IT.

The third question poses a challenge to organizations to develop career paths and educational opportunities to develop their in-house talent in the directions they have chosen for the future of their IT professional staff. Moreover, with the impending baby-boomer retirement bubble, valuable professionals will be leaving the workplace without adequate new ones coming up the ranks.

LESSONS LEARNED

The marketplace demands a set of skills and capabilities for long-term success in the world of an IT professional. This set is different from what was seen in the past. Previously the desirable IT graduate was one with deep technical skills and a foundation in math and programming. The respondents to our survey indicate an interest in entry-level candidates who have business skills as well as technical foundational skills. They are asking for someone who has mastered programming, but also studied project management and has had an opportunity to gain knowledge of business processes and industry domains.

This blend of technology and business skills is described as a T-shaped person: the deep technical skills represented by the vertical bar of the T and the broad business skills by the horizontal bar. This combination is highly valued by both clients and providers and provides a roadmap for individuals in planning their careers and one for organizations in developing their staff.

Our data indicates that another highly valued version would be a person with broad technical skills and deep business skills. In particular, the data on mid-level positions shows a real need for project management and business skills. Our provider data also shows that respondents listed several business and project management skills as missing in entry level hires. The top three missing skills were managing stakeholder expectations, process knowledge, and business process reengineering.

Currently, most computer science programs provide deep technical skills. They need to incorporate business applications of those skills and to foster such general skills as team work and communication. Information Systems (IS) or Information Technology (IT) programs, on the other hand, are often housed in business schools. Core requirements include accounting, finance, marketing and operations courses that build deep business skills and capabilities. They also provide a broad technical education that includes programming, systems analysis and telecommunications courses. These programs could be strengthened by exposing students to cross functional courses and projects that emphasize supporting business processes. These curriculum prescriptions are reflected in the ACM draft IT curriculum and the ACM/AIS task force on curriculum. The draft IT curriculum addresses the need for social and professional development, experiential learning and working in teams. The task force emphasizes enterprise systems, business process management, project management, collaboration, communication, and functional specialization.

Specifically, we recommend additional changes in curriculum to support what the respondents in both groups are looking for in their entry-level hiring:

- **Improving language diversity and cultural appreciation** – today's graduates will have global careers. This will be true whether they work for a client or a provider. It is important to master several languages and develop an appreciation for cultures of the world.
- **Internships for students and faculty** – undergraduate programs should endeavor to create *meaningful* internships for students. Specifically, this means work experience that will help them to learn about business processes and different industries. At the same time, there is value in faculty internships. Faculty instructors should take time to work in industry to be current with the business world.
- **Cooperation of universities/ industry/ government to determine incentives to get people into STEM programs** – Incentives must be created (as is being done in many countries) to attract students STEM (Science/Technology/Engineering/Math) programs and related careers. Examples of incentives include extended repayment of educational loans, income tax holidays for 8-10 years for those employed in IT positions, cash payments to organizations that hire STEM graduates.
- **Industry career path planning** – Organizations should develop clear career paths for IT professionals indicating various positions and the educational and experiential route to achieving the various levels.

To elaborate on the last point, these four categories are typical mid-level positions: developer, analyst, technical specialist, and project manager. As a result of our data analysis, we recommend that alternate career paths should be created for these positions rather than forcing all new hires to start as programmers. We also suggest that IT programs may better prepare students for some

of these new paths. Some companies are already doing this. At Chubb Insurance, new hires may start in quality assurance to learn business rules and get on a path to business analyst positions. Other new hires start at the service desk on a career path to IT operations manager. At L'Oreal, new recruits are rotated through several departments to understand the business and develop contacts. These companies also recruit from a variety of programs including computer science, information systems and business.[1]

Our recommendations can be summarized in the simple statement that anyone choosing a career as an IT professional in most client and provider organizations will need a balance of technical and managerial skills to meet the demands of the marketplace. The technical skills will vary widely depending on the company and industry needs; however, in light of increasing sourcing of IT services, the managerial skills in the categories of project management and business domain knowledge are becoming increasingly critical in practice.

FUTURE RESEARCH DIRECTIONS

Industry trends based on increasing growth in the global sourcing marketplace will have a significant effect on careers in the IT workforce. The following are some general trends that will be important:

Clients and Providers

- **Rethinking career paths and sourcing strategies in client companies** – discussed previously, it is important for companies to develop strategies to keep client-facing IT skills in house.
- **Shift in strategy of big providers to higher-level work** – discussed previously, this is a key strategic direction for large service providers and will increasingly affect the careers for IT professionals

- **Consolidation in provider market vs. increase in specialized niche players** – While medium to large providers are undergoing some consolidation to strengthen their market positions, there is also a growth in specialized niche providers. The specialization ranges from industry expertise to technical expertise. These smaller providers are looking for IT staff with a blend of skills since the smaller the organization, the more the need for new hires who can "hit the ground running" and handle a wide range of client engagements.

IT Professionals and University Programs

- • **Career paths that include global experience** – The growth of global sourcing is consistent with a growth in global business in many areas. The future workforce will be one with vastly more experience with global business and managing worldwide teams. IT careers will be consistent with this trend and therefore experience and education in global business will be valuable. At the undergraduate level there has always been opportunities for programs such as "junior year abroad" however these have been more common in liberal arts programs and less so in STEM programs. This aspect of undergraduate education must be expanded to STEM programs. At the graduate level, universities in the US are seeing many more international students as they recognize the value of global experience in their careers. This trend will increase and include students from high-income locations attending programs in low-income locations.

- **Managing at a distance** – As global work increases, so does the management of worldwide teams. Managers are becoming more experienced with collaboration and management of teams with diversity in location, culture and work ethics. Managing at a distance will increase and the development of skills in this area should become part of educational programs and part of industry career training.

- **Managing securely, sustainably and serviceably** - Some specific observations from, our research results suggest that security and IT service management are also emerging as key areas where business and technology intersect. Many universities' IT programs are adding courses or modules that discuss the Information Technology Infrastructure Library (ITIL) prescriptions for standardizing IT operations and SaaS (software as a service). In addition, we are seeing the topic of how to implement "green IT" gaining in importance as a new business/IT area. Organizations are looking to IT to implement environmental measures that have an impact on the entire organization, e g., new electronics that conserve power and are recyclable, using new technologies such as ground water cooling systems in place of traditional air conditioning in data centers, and so on.

The future of this research is to continue surveying clients and providers to track developments in the marketplace and changes in skill needs. To a large extent management research is influenced by the current economic and political environments. It is therefore critical to follow the issues of the IT workforce on a continuing basis.

CONCLUSION

The IT workforce research has gathered information through interviews and surveys from both client and provider organizations to better understand the skills and capabilities that organizations rate as critical to their strategies for the hiring and development of IT professionals. The results of this research to date define a clear picture of IT professionals of the future who have a blend of technical and business skills which will ensure their success in the marketplace. This differs from the historical IT professional who was valued primarily for his or her deep technical knowledge. A key factor in this change is the growth of the IT global sourcing market allowing client organizations to fulfill their needs for some IT skills outside their own organizations. In addition, the growth of IT global sourcing has supported the success of service providers around the globe who also seek the blend of technical and business skills to support their future business strategies.

ACKNOWLEDGMENT

We would like to acknowledge our current research team members, all of whom contributed to the data collection and analysis reported in this chapter: Cynthia Beath, University of Texas Austin; Keith Frampton, RMIT University; Kevin Gallagher, Northern Kentucky University; Tim Goles, Texas A&M International University; Stephen Hawk, University of Wisconsin-Parkside; Kate Kaiser, Marquette University; Judith Simon, University of Memphis.

REFERENCES

Ball, L., & Harris, R. (1982). SMIS members: A membership analysis. *Management Information Systems Quarterly, 61*(1), 19–38. doi:10.2307/248752

Brancheau, J. C., & Wetherbe, J. C. (1987). Key issues in Information Systems management. *Management Information Systems Quarterly, 11*(1), 23–45. doi:10.2307/248822

Bullen, C. V., Abraham, T., Gallagher, K., Simon, J. C., & Zwieg, P. (2009). IT workforce trends: Implications for curriculum and hiring. *Communications of the Association for Information Systems, 24*(9).

Ingervaldson, P. M. (2008). Top 10 qualities of a great IT shop. *Computerworld, 42*(50), 17.

Kaiser, K.M., Abraham, T., Beath, C., Bullen, C.V., Frampton, K., Gallagher, K.P., et al. (2008). *The Information Technology workforce: IT provider trends and implications 2006-2009.*

Kaplan, D. M., & Lerouge, C. (2007). Managing on the edge of change: Human resource management of Information Technology employees. *Human Resource Management, 46*(3), 325–330. doi:10.1002/hrm.20166

King, J. (2008, February 19). Career paths you never dreamed of. *ComputerWorld.*

Leitheiser, R. L. (1992). MIS skills for the 1990s: A survey of MIS managers' perceptions. *Journal of Management Information Systems, 9*(1), 69–91.

Luftman, J. & Kempaiah, R. (2008). Key issues for IT executives 2007. *MIS Quarterly Executive, 7*(2).

Neiderman, F., & Mandviwall, M. (2004). The evolution of IT (computer) personnel research: More theory, more understanding, more questions. *ACM SIGMIS, 35*(3), 6–8.

Zweig, P., Kaiser, K.M., Beath, C.M., Bullen, C.V., Gallgher, K., Goles, T., et al. (2006). The Information Technology workforce: Trends and implications 2005-2008. *MIS Quarterly Executive, 5*(2).

ENDNOTE

[1] Information is from personal interviews with the authors

Chapter 2
Changing Capabilities and Capacities:
Key Technology Influences in the Transformation of IT Talent Requirements in the 21st Century

Benn Konsynski
Emory University, USA

ABSTRACT

Few would doubt that companies face a wide range of management and technology challenges with growing economic pressures, necessity for global expansion, shifting demographics and generational complexities, and constantly varying competitive pressures. Often, it is the human resources (HR) organization that emerges as the focus of many of these needs as new skill sets and new talent portfolio requirements emerge.

Increasingly, the management of human capital management emerges as a key differentiator in the competitive marketplace. The talent pool and inventory of capabilities is a critical source of competitive differentiation, and also a key to accomplishing many of the strategic objectives essential for success of the competitive enterprise in the 21st century. Product and service innovation and process and practice improvement are essential in the modern market.

DOI: 10.4018/978-1-60960-535-3.ch002

If you are in a shipwreck and all the boats are gone, a piano top... that comes along makes a fortuitous life preserver. But this is not to say that the best way to design a life preserver is in the form of a piano top. I think that we are clinging to a great many piano tops in accepting yesterday's fortuitous contriving. – Buckminster Fuller

INTRODUCTION

When asked to present some observations related to challenges faced by the ever-changing IT talent role, I thought first to tell some anecdotes of recent cases in enterprise and market transformation. Rather, I want to raise the horizon to the emerging environment. Here I offer some macro trends that suggest some direction for evolution of the attention and consideration of the changing pool of IT talent and HR responsibilities.

Serious assessment of operational and organizational design of the IT organization needs to be made by a new kind of leadership. It is doubtful that piecemeal fixes, small "band-aids", or incremental solutions will suffice. Rather serious rethinking of how the IT organization might operate. There is a realization that the global environment in which the IT organization operates is radically changing and so, too, might serious thought be necessary to re-align the functions of the IT organization to address this challenging environment.

Rather than offer a verbose narrative of examination of a leading employment of information technologies talent, I will offer a spectrum of thoughts on trends that influence the management of the human capital in the IT organization. The objective is to identify key questions that the IT HR managers needs to ask themselves related to their positioning and leverage of the talent pool. My horizon is the five to ten year window. The items relate to trends and considerations that I expect will be important to the effective talent managers in the contemporary enterprise.

The themes discussed below represent a broad spectrum of issues and questions that are interconnected factors that will influence the evolving role of the human resource manager. The list is not intended to be comprehensive, merely representative.

From Development to Integration

The most dramatic trend is a shifting in the skill sets in the portfolio needed by the effective IT organization. With the architecture and infrastructure changes taking place in the enterprise and the market, the skill set in the portfolio of IT services evolves from mainly *development* to mainly *integration*. The skill mix has been there all the time; it is merely the emphasis that is changing. Service orientation, outsourcing, syndication and cloud migration speak to the need for agile provisioning of services – with a diminishing emphasis on development.

The budget and resource management shifts from a CapEx focus to one of OpEx. Prioritization of feature-set provisioning and managing an extended pool of leveraged talent (much of it *on-demand*) are a growing element in the management practice in the IT organization.

Are my talent rosters adequate for my shifting attention from capital oriented initiatives to those that are more operationally oriented? Do I need to adjust the talent pool, or change the incentives systems to acknowledge these changes in focus?

The Incredible Shrinking Legacy Environment

Few would doubt the value and service of the legacy environments that well served the enterprise in the waning days of the 20th century. The challenge to many an enterprise is that legacy systems are seldom ready for the facile and mobile environments emerging in the early days of the 21st century. The skill sets required in development and maintenance of the legacy environments of ERP, CRM and other systems differs from those needed beyond the API extensions and "bolt-on" elements that characterize the traditional monolithic systems environments of the 20th century. New skills for new architectures that more heavily involve Web services, SaaS and cloud infrastructures.

How shall we balance the skill portfolio needed to maintain the essential legacy environments in the architecture migration toward cloud–like environments that are highly syndicated and service oriented?

Getting Real about Real-Time - Again

I, for one, have long hated the term "real-time". As one who has been involved with computing since the 1960s, we have long proffered that term as a meaningful direction for information capture and employment. The term rises from the ground levels every decade. Most often, we fail to test the meaning of real-time in the context of the application domain. Nonetheless, the term "real-time" has arisen in recent discourse. Let us hope that this time we will employ it in the context of the application environment.

Having said this, there is a growing interest in shrinking the horizon of service to decision with rich and timely information. Timely insight for situation assessment and *en vivo* decision support are more readily available and do-able. Skill requirements need renewal on both the provision side and the consumption side – meaning that it is incumbent on the IT organization to assist management in leveraging the emerging information capabilities.

How will the growing capabilities and interest in real-time information change the skills and capabilities needed in design and operation of the IT environment? What staffing and skill require-

ments emerge as increasingly real-time decision demands change the "face" and "interface" of our systems?

Continuous Analytics

Our traditional approach to data and analysis has been to treat data as warehouse item – worthy of storage, retention, organization and eventual employment by "query". Yet the network driven world and growing real-time demands suggest the warehouse approach is not adequate for the pace of timely relevance demanded by the modern market or enterprise. Demands of operations, advertising, mobility, and other domains call for a *continuous analytics* involving many data sources. Massive amounts of historical and contemporary information need to be constantly employed in active decision support.

Continuous Analytics approaches eliminate the need to batch, store, organize, and retrieve data before it is analyzed. It enables organizations to instantly query large volumes of both live and stored data to provide actionable insight in time for real-time effect. Expectations for leverage of historical and live data to provide immediate insight are growing. Scalability and granularity at the same time are essential principles in the modern architecture. Continuous analytics infrastructure must also support personal "lenses" via dashboard and visualization tools.

The skills of the manager and the skills of the system designers require a new posture as information is subject to review, assessment and analysis on a continuous basis. A culture of both user and designer that tolerates the high velocity and volume associated with these environments raises a challenge to the HR function in hiring and training the worker/manager of the future.

How will the skills of the developers and users of systems supporting continuous analytics evolve as all information is under continuous review and subject to challenge and assessment? How does data, put to work on entry, raise the need for context analysis and constant semantic "scrubbing"?

The Small and the Mobile

As the architecture changes, so too should the skill portfolio and capabilities evolve accordingly. Where development and integration skills adjust to the architecture of "the small and the many", the "many" are also *mobile* assets.

Software is being sold and delivered in small chunks, or "*snacklets.*" Mobile apps, widgets, gizmos, bots, gadgets and, of course, Web delivered apps. Stores then emerge as important context providers – where we find the content. Apple App Store, which launched last year, is such an example on the mobile store – extending the iTunes Store model. Apple is not the only player offering markets for snack-sized applications: Research In Motion (BlackBerry's App World), Palm (App Catalog) Google (Android Market), Microsoft (Window's Marketplace For Mobile), and Nokia (Ovi) all offer an application distribution platform or have them in the works.

The "small and the mobile" speaks to sourcing of system assets as much as the architecture of the systems themselves. What are the implications for staffing, sourcing and quality control as more and more functions are delivered from, or by, outside entities? The IT enterprise role, once again, shifts from a regulated monopoly to one of regulating a free market of tools, data sources, syndicated content, services and provisioned Web/cloud services. Traditional issues of integrity and security re-emerge as a new model of a disciplined market emerges for provision of essential information and analytic services.

Information Refineries

There is a growing need for information refineries – engines that process and assess the veracity and viability of the oceans of information that might be relevant to decision makers in the enterprise. Ironically, twenty years ago, I had an article with John Clippinger in Computerworld on the advent of information refineries. We need them more than ever with the oceans of information that surround, and run through, the enterprise.

We see exponential growth in the capture and accessibility to information on activities in our world. Little happens that is not observable, sense-able or recordable. To this point, we have ignored neglected or deemed most of what can be observed as unworthy of our investment in observation. Google and others have begun to educate us to recognize that the cost and capabilities now suggest a shift to observation and record of even the meanest of activities, especially online. The volume and velocity of new information underscore the need for active scanners and filters that assess the relevance and target the distribution and employment of information to our systems and people.

In the past, the majority of historical information and expertise lay in the heads of the employees. With dynamic job shifting and increasing volume and velocity or potentially relevant information, what means are being used in your enterprise to "tolerate" and "thrive" in an environment where more and more of the folks have shorter tenure with the organization? How then shall the enterprise of the future maintain, and leverage its relevant history?

Asset Monitoring

Few would doubt the growing demands for greater efficiency, improved availability and effective leverage and performance of assets in the enterprise. With CapEx shifting to OpEx, the attention to asset management is an increasing concern. Asset monitoring, coupled with effective analytics, is required for efficiency and effectiveness of ongoing investment. Service levels, operations and reduction in total cost of ownership accompany the central focus of strategic leverage of investment and employment of capital assets.

In the name of sustainability, more of the enterprise assets are being monitored on a continuous basis. While many an enterprise has had employees report on time allocation and accounting, few have watched asset employment as closely. With the advent of IP access, we may readily expect that both human and non-human assets will be increasingly monitored.

Gartner says that PCs and peripherals are responsible for 31% of the overall energy consumption of a corporation. Fraunhofer Institute says that power consumption will increase by 40% by 2020 – even if we invest in more efficient hardware. Most enterprise sustainability goals challenge their companies to take measures to reduce or minimize their environmental impact. One provider, Greenology, states that effective smart controls may result in 30 – 60% reduction in power consumption.

Aligned with staffing decisions, what productivity assets align with the working culture? How do the human and non-human assets operate together to effect the performance and sustainability goals of the enterprise? It has been a long time since the HR manager was independent of the nature of the work environment decisions. What is the role of HR management in decisions on asset allocation, employment and performance assessment?

Head in the Clouds

Cloud computing has emerged as an important business model of computing resource allocation. The promise of cloud computing is appealing because it may reduce total business costs and provide significantly greater flexibility and scalability of services throughout the enterprise. Hosting, Web services, SOA, grid models, RAID storage, mashups, syndicated content, and many

other indicators lead to the inevitable migration to public and private cloud mechanisms.

At the same time, many firms' perception of risks regarding the cloud computing such as security, performance and availability of the cloud services or legal compliance challenges hinders a wider adoption of cloud services by enterprises. Some of these concerns will be resolved as corporations have the knowledge about the market architecture and the general market characteristics of cloud computing. Therefore, it is critical to explore the cloud computing market and understand the market attributes to promote cloud computing.

Cloud initiatives raise the very real issues of ownership and control in the inter- and extra-organizational settings. Building trust, while increasing reliance on externally sourced data and services is no small challenge. The HR community needs to consider relations of engagement that are well beyond employment or contractual association.

- How secure the cloud services are – both in motion and at rest
- Whether the cloud operating performance is adequate to stakeholder requirements,
- Whether the company is managing the essential human resources,
- Role of HR in managing the extended portfolio of human resources both inside and outside the enterprise
- What risk transfer options associated with human resources employed outside the enterprise.

Many factors need consideration by the IT HR management. Are all responsible parties subject to effective identity and authority challenge and review? Are third parties engaged in the data, processes and services well credentialed as they might be in your enterprise? How are limits on damages controlled when human resources beyond the boundary of the enterprise are engaged? Are there adequate and proper incentives for positive behavior and disincentives for risky behavior by such individuals?

Security Incentives and Perceptions

Security is not just the purview of the technical, legal and operational aspects of our systems environments. Most threats to, and defense of, security and integrity are within the human resource of the enterprise. Technologies and procedures for securing the enterprise in cyberspace exist, but are largely neglected. One reason for this is that organizational reward systems lack the proper incentives for allocation of resources. One can identify numerous characteristics of differing stakeholder perceptions of security and privacy risks and incorporate them in a decision-making framework. We need a methodology for identification of perverse incentives---situations where the interests of a manager or employee are not aligned with those of the organization; and how the policies and reward system may be modified to correct this misalignment.

While most of the attention has been placed on control mechanisms and systems and the technologies for governance of operations, many of the remedies are not being utilized due to the problems that are endemic to the human dimension. Adoption and employment of essential security technologies and practice are often neglected or delayed as a result of fears or assumptions of risk to operation, employee morale, or exposure of reputation/brand. Attention is paid to assessment of damages and evaluation of risk vulnerability, yet the powerful leverage of perceptions and incentives is often neglected.

Incentives for proper behavior and disincentives for risky or hazardous behavior are often fitted in the later stages of security technology adoption. A key factor in the alignment of security and privacy risk initiatives with the strategic objectives of the enterprise is that variance in the perceptions of level of threat and ownership of the risk responsibility by key managerial stakeholders in the enterprise.

Recognition of these differences is important to effective investment in security measures that align with enterprise strategic objectives. These inform HR issues of hiring, training, incentives and setting expectations. There is a need for a logical and coordinated process that aligns an organization's risk management programs with its key business drivers and initiatives.

Information security is more than a mere responsibility of the technology infrastructure and is an ongoing process, dynamic to the situation and context of threats, both real and perceived. Information systems deal with a large set of potential risks, with an equally large (or larger) set of possible losses. Losses can include damage to or loss of physical systems, employee time, subtle corruption of data, loss of privacy, and loss of an organization's reputation for care and accuracy, etc. Management seeking to mitigate the full set of risks must assess the system for all of these potential losses. HR management must also address the perceptions of risk that may be held by all stakeholders that could be different. It is important to align the assessed and perceived risks.

It is true that, in business, valuation and values dominate most other measures of performance. We provide incentives to build value, so must we also invest to protect our value and valuation. Few can doubt that the most powerful incentive for an organization in the private sector to invest in cyber-security activities is the motivation to sustain the enterprise value to shareholders.

A key factor in the alignment of security and privacy risk initiatives with the strategic objectives of the enterprise is the considerable variance in the *perceptions* of threat and acceptance of the risk responsibility in the enterprise. Threats carry a burden of potential hazard and probability in conditions of occurrence. Perception is a reality to markets that constantly make a judgment on the viability of an ongoing concern.

Personal risks require little communication and special attention. As experience shapes user perceptions they become proxies of actual risk. It is the institutional risk that transcends individual risk that often requires special consideration in the hiring, training and performance incentives that are a critical part of the HR responsibility.

It is incumbent on the management team and HR community to consider possible security risk threats, means and controls for prevention of breaches, isolation and minimization of damage and recovery and renewal of operational stability. The result of misdirected perceptions, ill-advised allocation of decision rights and failure to assess the mix of controls are significant exposure for the enterprise.

Proper incentives will bring the complex issues to light as decisions are made regarding information security options. HR plays a significant role. It is the understanding of the incentives and desired outcomes that permit the allocation of decision rights and authorities to deal with the daily decisions of management. The HR position plays no small role in achieving the desired level of risk control.

The need to increase information security literacy is a high priority in the increasingly technology-based environment. The IT HR management needs to insure increasing literacy and awareness, training, and education programs. With the ever-changing nature of the network environments, questions arise that transcend any current network technologies. It is incumbent on our studies of organization, networks and inter-organizational practice to facilitate secure environments for commerce. HR management must balance the interests that are technical, social and organizational. These issues matter to the HR community, their comfort and trust in the employment and engagement of the network environment, procedures, and practice.

The IT HR community needs to consider: What are the perceived information security risks held by members of the community? What are the

perceived benefits that the IT community believes are associated with reducing those risks? What are the roles that incentives play in aligning the stakeholder interests and effective and proper behavior?

Immersion Technologies, Virtual Worlds and Avatars

Virtual worlds are now a reality. They permit everyone to create a digital avatar - characters representing themselves and interact with other computer-generated individuals, landscapes, and even virtually-run global businesses in real-time. Fascinatingly, both endogenously produced economies and social orders are emerging in these virtual worlds. Though seldom seen in the business environment, we have decades of history with these environments. There is a strong reflection and expectation both the past and present of virtual worlds, in the promise of relevance to future electronic commerce and governance issues.

Virtual environments permit interaction, collaboration, learning, exploration and modeling. Visualization and navigation are a growing importance as these technologies permit immersion and gesture based navigation. Augmented reality techniques permit the co-existence and mashup of the real and the rendered. New commerce possibilities arise as we mix the real world capture and sensors with the analytic capabilities and rendered visualizations.

These "*toys* are becoming *tools*" as they are leveraged for conferencing, training, visualization, and new forms of collaboration. Avatars are models that represent our roles and responsibilities, sometimes in exaggeration, or caricature, of a role. We might expect more of this adoption of representation as we move forward.

Are there training and meeting applications suited to the leverage of immersive forums in both the IT organization (distributed) and in the external and extra-enterprise interactions? What are the limits of effective leverage and employment of avatars, representations and surrogates in both intra and extra-organizational settings?

Getting Real about Collaboration

Collaboration is extending well beyond mere group patterns of work. Many transactions of the past, especially in inter-organizational settings, are being reassessed as a pursuit of collaborative practice. As many have said – "markets are a conversation". Work is being transformed by new means and capabilities of collaboration. Industries are subject to disruption by new forms of communication and collaboration - for example, *news* is now being recognized as a process not product. New communication platforms offer new possibilities for enterprise and market behavior.

Without a doubt, Collective Intelligence is a critical part of emerging organizational practice. From early hunter-gatherer societies working together for greater benefit to ancient Greeks practicing democracy, collective intelligence has existed for a long time in human history. What has recently changed is the ability to employ internet technologies for extremely cheap asynchronous communications across vast distances with large numbers of participants. Digitally speaking, time and distance no longer should serve as constraints for what the IT organization can do when employing the collective intelligence of its personnel. New tools lead to new relations between the IT community and the functional and user communities.

Let me indulge in one example of new and emerging platforms that speak to this new environment. How Google Wave should be used is not immediately obvious, but is "email + IM + Twitter + wiki" accurate?

In Google Wave we see unbundled, the common elements of communication. Individuals, teams and communities can shape and reshape and align their communication services for each community activity. Messages, mail, SMS/IM/Twitter, video/voice, gadgets/robots, content syn-

dication, dynamic "groups", etc. all are available on a hybrid basis.

In my view - this is not the end, just the beginning. Many will reject Wave as either too complicated or a "hassle" to do things in light of the familiar, specific tools – email, RSS, stand alone wiki, etc. We should rather think of Wave as a platform - templates and new "bundles" of services will be made to facilitate communication in different communities. Powerful "skins" will provide simple contexts for group work. Extensible and adaptable libraries of functions and capabilities will emerge to serve different communities

For decades we have added new templates - email, IM, Twitter, etc. Here we are presented with a shapeable and adaptable communication innovation forum. We might expect no less that the emergence of apps that provide new lenses in the platform that serve specific communities. This has been the case for SMTP through Twitter as operating communications platforms.

Whole new forms of collaboration are possible. Living wikis and popup gizmos let you shape the interaction to the needs of the teams and communities. What tools fit the emerging culture in your enterprise?

March of the Millennials

It is doubtful, even in the IT arena, that many HR managers will deny that there are particular challenges in hiring and retaining the so-called millennials, or Gen-Y community. Questions, positive and negative, arise related to the skills, values and expectations. Talent pools are changing and many an enterprise has expressed frustration when dealing with a community of these tech savvy, global minded, reward seeking, individuals. As a growing percentage of the workforce, it is imperative that the proper alignment of skills, values and objectives are established for the effective employment of these employees. C-levels of all dimensions have expressed recognition of these challenges and a necessity to account for the growing percentage of the working population that are millennials. Given the general classification of those born after 1982, millennials are workers and employees who joined the workforce in or after the year 2000.

Millennials have a reputation of being tech skilled, social values-oriented, globally aware, and bring high expectation of acknowledgement and reward. They are told to expect many job/career transitions (4-5 times that of previous generations) and are thus often perceived as potentially disloyal and always at the ready to hop jobs and demanding of special considerations. As we might expect, few of these characterizations hold more than a hint or reflection of the culture and media representation.

The economic times have educated them to expect less trust in enterprise employment as the pathway to secure retirement or retention as an expected reward for loyal association. One wonders if it is they who have brought a distrust of the expected benefits of enterprise association, or have we so changed the rules and processes that we have earned that "hesitation to association." It is little wonder that many see self-employment and entrepreneurship as less risky than large enterprise employment.

While most do not have unique demands for work flexibility, many are more vocal than past managerial apprenticeships in discussing their work environment. Most do not view numerous short-term employments as an aspiration or a desired career path. And most do have a strong loyalty where values are aligned for ethical and equitable practice and social responsibility.

Training, personal development and proper incentives go a long way in making millennials productive and collaborative in the work environment. As many are attracted to the technology of the IT world, growing attention is placed in the specific actions in the IT environment to demonstrate the effective leverage of the skill sets of these young individuals.

While not always the "digital natives" portrayed in popular writings, most are more than comfortable, and sometimes dependent on the technology *appendages* of the modern world.

Are we geared up as employers to embrace the millenials? Is our culture tuned to make best use of the skills and interests of this population? Do we have the control elements in place to engage the skill sets of this community – recruiting processes, reward systems, and career in individual development processes? Retention of members of this generation may be based on an alignment of the enterprise goals and the skills and capabilities of the differing sets of employees. It is said that Boomers get along well with Millennials, but Gen Xers do not. Broad-brush statements are always wrong. Still, echoes from the HR folks I have interviewed suggest that there is an element of truth in the tension of the Gen X and Gen Y generations.

Lessons Learned

The IT HR manager role has gone through significant evolution in the last four decades. Management and control of a rare and often unique skill set in the development of large capital projects has taken new form. The centralized, regulated monopoly of the mainframe days with monolithic software systems and limited, well-trained users changed. It evolved into a free market with technology capabilities available to all. This gave rise to the need for control and regulation in the name of security and integrity as individual datasets and inter-organizational settings emerged. Now the strict hierarchy of owned assets has given way to a marketplace of independent sources for services. It is little wonder that there would be frustration in the IT HR community related the management of these transitions. As we see – many more changes are around the corner.

The improvisational nature of the emerging IT organization and infrastructure is just in its early stages. The need to simultaneously achieve operational efficiency, while accommodating a continuous morphing of alliances and network arrangements, is a key challenge in the contemporary enterprise and market. Inter-enterprise interdependence and unpredictable market shifts heighten the need to establish an architecture and governance arrangement that permits rapid adaptation. Fully integrated firms have increasingly morphed into networks of collaborators. The demand for efficient and effective inter-firm coordination is no longer a desired condition, but essential for competitive position.

The future enterprise operates more like a market. Market trends demand an ability to improvise in the marketplace – converge execution with planning – while being simultaneously efficient. Efficiency need not come at a high cost in attaining the ability to be adaptive and spontaneous. The human resource management of the IT capacities and capabilities has a significant responsibility.

Challenges and Opportunities

It has been my purpose to raise issues and questions of the extra-normal considerations faced by

IT HR management as the environment rapidly changes. The issues raised are, by no means, a cover set for the broad spectrum of considerations. Rather, they are a sample of challenges and possibilities – often considered to be outside the scope of the historic HR function. It has been my intent to raise the horizon to the emerging environment by indentifying certain macro trends.

The volatility of social, market, and technology directions change the global competitive landscape in dramatic ways. The staffing, skilling and employment of IT talent is no longer merely an intra-organizational issue. The need for effective and attentive HR management has never been greater – and never been more complex. The "skill set required" to manage the "skill sets required" increasingly invoke the image of an HR management with super social, economic and technical understanding. The Information Technology Human Resource manager of the 21st century can be no limited dimensional manager.

Chapter 3
Trends in IT Human Resources and its Determinants

Vijay K. Agrawal
University of Nebraska at Kearney, USA

Vipin K. Agrawal
California State University – Fullerton, USA

Ross Taylor
University of Nebraska at Kearney, USA

Frank Tenkorang
University of Nebraska at Kearney, USA

ABSTRACT

This chapter discusses the driving forces behind the trends in Information Technology (IT) that are likely to influence the number of available IT jobs in the future. One advantage of focusing on industry trends as opposed to the current job market is that long term trends are more likely to be useful for strategic planning. Institutions of higher education (IHE) want to provide their graduates with the knowledge and skills needed by employers, but given the rapid change within the IT industry, chasing short term trends as part of a multi-year degree is a fool's errand.

The purpose of this chapter is to examine the various, sometimes contradictory, factors influencing the demand for IT professionals and to build a simple framework that can be used to predict demand. The ability to predict the demand for IT professionals with a reasonable degree of accuracy is important for IHE's and businesses to correctly identify where their scarce resources should be allocated to develop a curriculum for the 21st century workforce.

INTRODUCTION

When one of the authors was in a doctoral program, the PhD students from the business school would occasionally gather in a local drinking establishment and engage in an attempt at scholarly banter over various fun topics. One of the topics that emerged on several occasions was which

DOI: 10.4018/978-1-60960-535-3.ch003

business discipline is the most important for a successful business.

The accounting students might point out that without accounting you would not be able to effectively keep track of your money. Management students might counter that without operations you would not be able to effectively make products. Marketing would try to sell us on the idea that without marketing a firm could not effectively sell products and thus there would be no need for any of the other disciplines. All the other disciplines would pitch

in with why their area was the most important area of study and so the conversation would go. There was one exception to the arguments. It emerged during those conversations that nearly every discipline admitted that an understanding of Information Technology was essential for a complete understanding of their discipline. Correspondingly, an understanding of other disciplines was essential for most Information Technology students and practitioners.

The emergence of IT as a discipline has been recent and has evolved rapidly. Topics such as Business Intelligence, Data Mining, and Software Development were once mainly topics that Information Technology researchers discussed and only a few large businesses experimented with using a small fraction of their budgets. Now IT has become essential for most businesses and is becoming more integrated into the way businesses function each year. IT areas such as software development have also become much more of a process driven endeavor and have moved away from the days of an individual or small team working in isolation to produce spaghetti code that resulted in software that seemed to be produced by magic to the end user. Modern business software tends to be very complex and to span multiple business functions. Because it is beyond the capability and an individual to be able to build software in isolation project teams are formed. These teams have functions that can largely be broken down into three areas, management, technology expertise,

and domain expertise in area such as accounting, marketing, or consumer psychology to give a few examples. Each of the team members contributes toward the design and implementation of application that would be beyond the ability of even the most capable person to produce in isolation.

Officers and managers of a firm no longer have the luxury of an army of data analyst at their disposal to find data, analyze it and then present the findings to the executives. Because of the IT revolution management has had to embrace the use of technology and learn how to use the firm's IT tools to utilize the data resources for more efficient and effective operations across all areas. The digital revolution has caused IT to go from being something a firm might use to being a core part of most organizations.

IT cannot exist in isolation because it is integrated throughout the firm. In fact, IT has become so pervasive that most jobs now require interacting with IT. To have competent IT performance, firms need an adequate supply of IT professionals and many of these professionals will need to be provided by institutions of higher education. The challenge for institutions of higher education is how to balance the need for rigorously teaching students the underlying theory of a field, needed skills, and how to engage in the type of continuous life-long learning that will be needed to keep them up to date after completion of their degree. These goals should be accomplished within a curriculum that provides students with relevant knowledge and skills that are in demand by employers. One of the reasons it is difficult to develop such a curriculum is that the technology field is in a period of tremendous change.

According to futurist George Gilder (2002) the amount of technical knowledge is doubling every two years and it is expected that the pace of growth will continue to increase. Because of this rate of rapid change, institutions of higher education that offer degrees in the Information Technology fields will have difficult choices to make regarding how their curriculum should be structured. Schools will have to be willing to adapt quickly to the needs of their key stakeholders to remain viable (Fleming, 2008). Some scholars question whether it is even possible for business schools to adequately prepare their graduates for the workforce given the current structure of the schools (Mintzberg, 2004; McKenna, Cotton, & Van Auken, 1995; Bennis & O'Toole, 2005; McNamara, 2006).

As a result an increasing number of businesses are choosing to train their employees in-house through corporate universities (Gerdes, 2005). Corporate University Xchange estimates that the number of corporate universities totals 2000 which is up from only 400 about 15 years ago and they predict that the number will grow to 3,700 by 2010 (AACSB, 2002).

This chapter reviews trends in IT human resources (HR) and postulates some factors that are likely to impact the number of IT jobs, filled or vacant. One advantage of looking at industry trends as opposed to current jobs is that long term trends are more likely to be detected since the short term vagrancies of the job market are filtered out. Another advantage of looking at industry trends is that we can develop a framework that is generic enough so that human resources departments can use the frame work to better communicate with IT departments at educational institutions for the purpose of developing a customized curriculum. It is imperative that businesses and IHE's work together to develop students into graduates who are exceptionally well qualified and can contribute value to an organization quickly. This collaboration will also enable IHE and businesses to correctly identify where their scarce resources should be allocated to develop employees for the 21st century workforce. IT graduates face a highly competitive job market while businesses face a competitive global marketplace so any efforts to produce market ready graduates and to increase productivity should be explored.

Curriculum committees can conduct curriculum reviews to indentify niches that are available for their particular institution by considering the framework presented in this paper. Gerdes (2005) reported that for mid-tier MBA programs, focusing on niche areas has led to growth in their programs. While no research could be found that examined niche undergraduate programs, it is not unreasonable to believe that a curriculum that is employer friendly and results in more job offers for graduates would also be welcomed by students. For example, if an environmental scan reveals that many businesses who are key stakeholders of the educational institution are involved in the use of business intelligence (BI) then the curriculum can be developed so that more graduates will have knowledge and skills that are valued for that application of IT. A different institution might find that they are located in an area where their key stakeholders rarely use BI but there is a huge demand for graduates with programming and system analysis and design knowledge, in which case the curriculum could be adapted to produce well rounded graduates who have a concentration of courses in that area.

It is in the best interest of businesses and IHE's to work together to help determine what skills and abilities are likely to be in demand. Human Resource departments are tasked with finding the right personnel for the available positions. By working with IHE's HR departments can increase the number of qualified applicants and decrease the amount of time needed for newly hired employees to provide value.

BACKGROUND

Bureau of Labor Statistics Projected Growth Rate

Bureau of Labor Statistics (BLS) data indicates that one of the fastest-growing sectors in the U.S. economy is the IT sector (Dohm & Shniper, 2007). Ten year employment rolling forecasts of IT labor demand have been made every other year since

Figure 1. BLS 10-year labor projections

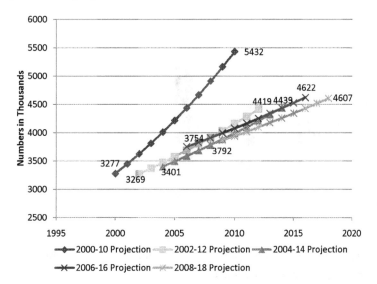

2000 (Dohm & Shniper, 2007; Hecker, 2006; Hecker, 2004; Hecker, 2001). These forecasts are published biennially and each biennium the future growth rates are revised. Based on projections it is anticipated that the increase in demand for IT professionals will continue but it will do so at a decreasing rate. Figure 1 shows a plot of these projections.

Each revised projection is getting flatter indicating that the growth rate of IT related jobs is being revised down with each new report. One possible explanation that we will explore in this chapter is that the nature of who performs the business processes is transitioning from IT specialist to more general knowledge workers in other functional areas.

The BLS has a reputation for nonpartisan research and does an excellent job. However, all projections are necessarily subject to error by their very nature. Figure 2 compares actual IT professional jobs to BLS projections. The intent is not to in anyway criticize the BLS projections but rather to gain some insights into what type of errors may be occurring in order to consider possible sources for the nature of the error. In 2002, BLS was very optimistic about the IT labor

market which is reflected in the more than 10% projection over actual number of jobs. In 2004, the difference reduced drastically to 2.1%, and in 2006 BLS was pessimistic about the market, with the projected number of jobs being 4.4% less than the predicted jobs. Although the latest projection (2008) is greater than the actual, the difference in percentage points is one third that of 2002. As the IT field matures and is incorporated into other functional areas it is anticipated that the BLS projections will continue to become more accurate as errors generated by the evolutionary nature of IT enabled business practices diminishes.

From examining Figure 2 it would appear that the increase in demand for IT professionals is actually present. One shortcoming with the forecast as presented so far is that skills sets for IT professionals are not easily transferable. That is to say for example, a programmer is generally not equipped to perform well as a business analyst or vice versa. Knowing if there are particular job categories that are net winners and losers in the job creation process would be more useful.

From 2000 until 2008 there was a positive overall growth rate for the development and adoption of IT applications but the growth was

Figure 2. Actual jobs compared to projected

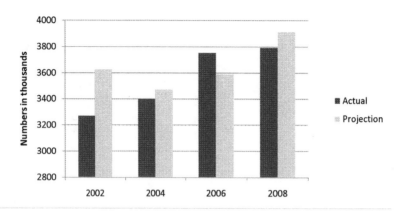

not across all categories. Two out of the eleven IT professional job categories experienced declines between 2000 and 2008 as shown in Figure 3. The categories are computer and Information Systems managers and computer programmers. The fastest growing IT jobs include network systems and data communications analyst (145%) and network and computer systems administrators (48%). Computer software engineers accounts for the highest proportion of all IT professional jobs (over 21%).

One complicating factor that makes the BLS data of very limited value for predicting HR needs is that the job growth rates across different industry segments and geographic regions are not likely to have a uniform demand for different knowledge sets. As an example, the demand for

a systems analyst might be high in an urban area or an area where there are a lot of software development firms but it is likely that in some rural areas those skills would not be in high demand because of the lack of larger companies or software development houses.

That does not indicate an absence of need for courses that develop students for other IT areas such as business analyst. Instead it is an indicator that while a standardized approach such as that put forth by the Association for Computing Machinery is a very valuable guide for developing a core curriculum that covers the knowledge all IT majors need in their respective broad subject areas, it will not be sufficient to produce an agile IT workforce that is able to become productive quickly after employment. In areas where there

Figure 3. IT jobs by category

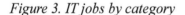

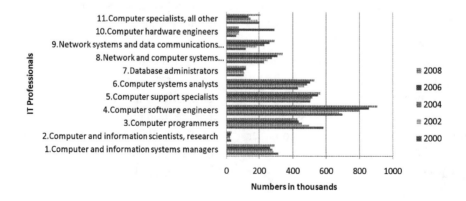

is a thriving vibrant business environment that needs a certain IT niche there is an opportunity for businesses and institutions of higher learning to partner together to serve that community's needs by developing and emphasizing an area of study that will increase the value of IT graduates.

Therefore, the needed framework is one that can serve as a lens through which trends in the community can be viewed so that areas of emphasis can be identified. Toward that end, we have identified the key factors that are likely to influence the demand for IT professionals and allow for the prediction of which areas are likely to be in most demand.

FACTORS CONTRIBUTING OR INHIBITING GROWTH IN IT HUMAN RESOURCES

Demand for IT Applications

The average IT investment by U.S. organizations is approximately 3.5 to 7.0% of their sales revenue (Network World, 2009) and contributes up to 50% in total capital costs (Applegate et. al. 2007). IT is essential to survival for most businesses but while IT jobs have not been spared from the economic downturn currently impacting the global economy they have not been as hard hit as the overall economy in the United States. According to an analysis of Bureau of Labor Statistics data conducted by GovInfoSecurity.com the unemployment rate for IT professionals was 4.1 percent for the second quarter of 2009. While that was up substantially from the 2.3 percent unemployment of a year earlier it was still far better than the overall jobless rate of 9.3 percent (BLS, 2010). There are also some signs of recovery on the IT front. President Obama has requested an increase of 1.2 percent in spending for IT projects for fiscal year 2011 bringing total requested IT spending for the United States Government to $79.4 billion. Global spending on IT was down

4.6 percent in 2009 but it is expected to rebound to $3.4 trillion in 2010 (Gartner, 2010). This increase is likely to be driven by demand for new technologies such as cloud computing, software as a service (SaaS) and Enterprise Resource Planning packages among others.

Reliance upon Information Technology is pervasive and is likely to become more so in the future. The acquisition of new software can be broken down into two categories. The first category is software that a company acquires primarily from another source. This includes common applications such as Microsoft Office, Quickbooks, and more complex applications such as Peoplesoft which have to be extensively customized during implementation. For the purpose of discussion we will refer to software made by other companies that is not for one particular client as Commercial Off-The-Shelf (COTS) applications. The second category is software that a company largely develops on their own and for their own use. Software developed largely in-house and not for sale will be considered proprietary software.

The skill set needed to manage an IT infrastructure consisting primarily of COTS software is different than the skill set needed to build and maintain proprietary software. In order to predict the demand for different types of software professionals we need to understand the trends in COTS and proprietary software development.

Businesses are moving toward great use of software solutions to satisfy customer demand, increase effectiveness, and become more efficient. This is leading to an overall growth in demand for IT applications that is driving the greater need for both proprietary and COTS software. As an example, customers increasingly want to utilize their mobile communications devices, such as smart phones, netbooks, and tablet computers, to check their account information online. This creates a demand for a service that many businesses have to satisfy. In looking for a solution they might need to purchase a COTS solution from a vendor or they might decide to build a proprietary

Figure 4. Framework

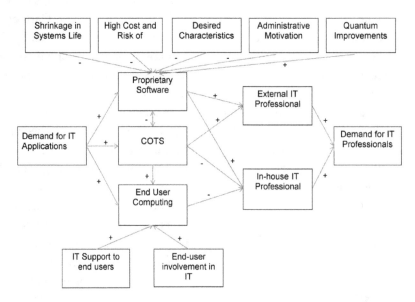

system. Whichever choice they make will influence the skill set needed to implement, manage, and maintain the solution The trends could be explained with the framework depicted in Figure 4. The framework is developed based on the model suggested by Agrawal, Tenkorang, Agrawal and Taylor (2009) and Agrawal (2005 a, b).

Components of the Framework

The growth in demand for IT applications is driving the greater need for proprietary software and COTS software. However, assuming constant demand for IT applications, increase in demand for proprietary software will have a negative impact on COTS and end user computing. A detailed discussion of the framework components is presented below.

Proprietary Software

The shifting role of IT as a strategic necessity will affect strategic decisions regarding the level of corporate investment in IT (Carr, 2003). When organizations have a possibility of strategic advantage, the organizations will maximize investments and develop proprietary application packages,

maintaining control of the software development and the flexibility in the packages.

In a free market, it is very difficult to get and maintain a sustainable competitive advantage (Porter, 1980). This goes for using IT as a competitive advantage as well. When a competitive advantage is achieved the time to duplicate the advantage is very short (months not years) once a rival's IT is understood.

Organizations such as Wal-Mart, Dell, and Jet-Blue have used proprietary IT to gain a competitive advantage in the marketplace (Wailgum, 2007). By using proprietary software these companies and others have been able to add capabilities that were hard for their competitors to copy as long as the capabilities remained confidential. However, because of factors associated with developing customized software companies have begun to use less proprietary software in favor of COTS software. Even companies such as Wal-Mart that have traditionally believed that technology should be built to support best practice business procedures have started to adopt best of breed commercial application for business intelligence and other infrastructural technological needs (Wailgum, 2007) while at the same time building new custom applications when there is a potential to gain a large strategic advantage. The observed decline in proprietary software use is attributed to four major trends.

These trends are shrinkage in systems life cycle (faster development time), high cost and risk-prone tendency of the needed software (more complex projects), desired characteristics of the software solution (ease of use and predictability), and administrative motivation (desire of management to avoid risks and to focus on core competencies.

Each of these serves to make the development of proprietary software more risky and of less incremental value than using commercial off the shelf software. One countervailing force is when quantum improvements, improvements that radically change existing business practices, in software are desired in order to get a competitive advantage. The overall decrease in dependence of firms on proprietary software is seen in their shift to COTS software for an increasing percentage of their applications. We will consider each of the trends in turn with respective to its impact on COTS.

Commercial-Off-The-Shelf Software (COTS)

As a result of the trends previously mentioned human resource departments need to identify which strategy their company is likely to predominantly employ so the skill sets of employees will meet the needs of the business. In order for human resource professionals to understand which strategy their business is likely to adopt we will consider each of these in turn. This overview is not intended to be exhaustive but is instead designed to serve as a primer to enable the reader to converse with senior management regarding areas of long-term strategic alignment of HR resources with business needs.

The *systems life cycle is shrinking* as software development advances. With blurring national boundaries, the numbers of competing organizations and knowledge workers have been

increasing. Additionally, the environment is turbulent, changing rapidly, and in an unpredictable manner (Applegate, 2007, Scott-Morton, 1991; Turban et al., 2001). The characteristics of this environment identified by El Sawy et al. (1999) include time-compression, short product life cycles, strategic discontinuity, increase in knowledge intensity, and a customer-focused approach. The environmental trends will make organizational processes and resulting software applications vulnerable to frequent changes. The faster obsolescence of packages will result in an increase in the cost of the IT applications. Li and Ye (1999) also contend that it is an era of time-based competition. The same strategy will not work for a prolonged period of time. The changes in strategy will lead to alteration in the processes and the resulting software. Matheson and Tarjan (1998) and Nidumolu and Knotts (1998) found that software firms have very short development time cycles since technology changes very rapidly. Brancheau et al. (1996) asserted that the effectiveness of software development has been a key management Information Systems issue since the 1980s. Agrawal (2005d) asserted that the higher rate of product obsolescence will lead to increased adoption of Enterprise Resource Planning (ERP) packages and decrease in usage of off-the-shelf applications (other than ERP packages). Under such circumstances organizations are expected to invest a minimum amount of time and money on the software by using traditional off-the-shelf solutions, cloud computing, software as a service, Enterprise Resource Planning packages, and other COTS solutions as appropriate.

Software development is expensive and risky due to the complexity of modern systems and high project failure rates. A report by Standish Group International on the success of software projects reveals that in the United States 31.1% of projects are not completed; while 52.7% are completed, but with an average cost overrun of 189%, and many of these did not contain all the functionalities of original specifications. Only 16.2% of projects are completed in-time and on-budget (Hays, 1997; Turban et al. 2001). Since the early 1980s the estimated failure rate of large-scale software development is 85% (Ambler, 1999). According to Laudon and Laudon (1999), a complex package is one which contains more than 400 programs and 500,000 lines of codes. Jeong and Klein (1999) note that more complex systems are susceptible to high failure. Most integrated packages can be considered large and complex, and therefore have an inherent risk of failure. Turban et al. (2001) have stated that because of associated risks, some managers refuse to develop systems that require budgets over $1 million, take more than one year, or require more than ten people for completing the project. Agrawal (2005a) stated that the higher costs and risks are associated in development of organization specific software and therefore, organizations are using off-the-shelf/ERP packages in higher proportion compared to proprietary packages. In the past, in-house development was popular due to the flexibility needed in the packages and the control on the development cycle. Because of the reusability of codes and customizability, the object oriented approach results in higher software development productivity. It will also lead to increased flexibility, increased predictability, and few errors (Nidumolu & Knotts, 1998). However, the faster rate of obsolescence, high cost, and risk factor will make the in-house development option unattractive for all but the simplest projects unless the functionality required is such that COTS is not a viable option.

Desired characteristics of software that favor a transition to COTS are ease of use and predictability of cost and outcome. In order to reduce training costs and improve user satisfaction firms want software that is easy to use. A simpler user interface and improved artificial intelligence are factors that are leading many COTS systems to be usable with little or no training. To avoid some of the risk factors mentioned earlier firms want predictability. By using an established COTS solution firms are able to know the approximate costs,

requirements, and functionality before committing to a product. In the case of the off-the-shelf/ERP solutions, it is possible to get reliable predictions of costs of acquisition, implementation, and use (Heikkila et al., 1991; Laudon and Laudon, 1999). Furthermore, these software packages are available without delay and can save up to 50% or more in development efforts. In addition, organizations can save high maintenance costs associated with in-house developed packages. The maintenance costs of in-house developed packages are as high as 80% of the corporate IT budget (Turban et al. 2001).

The *administrative motivation* for moving to COTS includes many of the factors mentioned previously. Some reasons for administrative motivation include the continuing growth in software and the outsourcing market that can be attributed to the reliability of services provided by these sources and to the role of IT as a commodity. Because management is not satisfied with the performance of IT departments they are replacing in-house development with COTS (Turban et al. 2001). The shift to the COTS or outsourcing helps organizations survive in an increasingly competitive environment.

Agrawal, et al. (2001) argued that a move from proprietary to COTS packages will reduce cost at the expense of flexibility. If IT's role is only a strategic necessity and not a source of competitive advantage, then the substantial risks and high investments associated with proprietary packages are not desirable. In a turbulent environment with faster obsolescence in product/services, the combination of limited time available for development and the need for frequent changes will also make the option of proprietary packages infeasible and unattractive (Agrawal, 2005d) and the uses of commercial off-the-shelf/ERP packages will be in higher proportion compared to proprietary/customized packages (Agrawal, 2005a). Thus, it does not seem possible in a short period for organizations to develop the complex and integrated large size packages which can be used for a short amount of time. Additionally, such projects may require a very large in-house IT department with continuous training and upgrades of technology. Under this situation the organizations will tend to rely more on commercial off-the-shelf packages/ERP solutions and outsourcing.

Continuous improvements/quantum improvements: Intense competition leads to uncertainty and stimulates higher innovation and adoption rates that will, in turn, increase competition (Ettlie, 1983; Lewin et al., 1987). Porter (1980) argued that in a competitive market with free entry, firms cannot earn sustainable supernormal profit. While in the short-run it may be possible to earn such profits, in the long-run the accounting profit will be just enough to pay for the cost of capital and compensation to the owner for any unique inputs to production (i.e. management expertise). It is possible to achieve a short-term competitive advantage with IT if secrecy is maintained. However, the time to duplicate applications is months, not years, and new innovations (which are very fast and rapid) will make the old ones obsolete (Porter, 1996; Turban et al., 2001), raising doubts about the role of IT in gaining competitive advantages. Conversely, there are a number of arguments identifying IT mostly as a commodity or a strategic necessity for the organization. Thus, IT cannot be a source of sustainable competitive advantage (Brynjolfsson, 1996; Clemons 1990, 1991; Clemons & Kimbrough, 1986; Emery, 1990; Kermer & Sosa, 1991; McNurlin, 1991).

Further, most businesses in the industrial world could not compete, and many could not even survive without computers and software (Jones, 1994). The shifting role of IT as a strategic necessity will affect strategic decisions regarding the level of corporate investment in IT. Considering IT's role as a strategic necessity, the organizations will invest minimally on application packages by using off-the-shelf/ERP solutions with a policy of continuous improvements. On the contrary, with a possibility of strategic advantage, the corporations will maximize investments and develop proprietary application packages, maintaining the control on the software development and the flexibility in the packages.

The increase in usage of COTS software will lead to lesser demand for programmers and higher demand for system analysts including project managers. It is important for HR planning professionals to keep in mind that these changes are macroeconomic and apply to the United States. Individual labor markets may vary. In the cases where a labor demand in a local market is markedly different from the national market it is important that partners in higher education be advised of the differences so appropriate strategic planning can occur.

Generally, COTS involves point-and-click and/or very simple commands to solve problems, hence it has led to increase in end-user computing.

End-User Computing

The growth in the importance of Information Technology as part of an enterprise's basic infrastructure is augmented by evolutions in hardware, software, and the graphic user interface (GUI) which facilitates the use of IT applications by many end-users. The growth in the usefulness and the ease of use of software applications has greatly increased demand for the number of people who are knowledge workers and this growth is expected to continue. The radical transformation of business processes from IT centric computing to increased adoption of end-user computing (EUC) has fundamentally changed the way businesses operate. This trend accelerated in the 1980's when the effectiveness of software development became a key management Information Systems issue. As executives wanted access to information to make better decision and companies needed more IT applications developed by IT professionals there was not enough capacity to get things done in a timely manner. The growth in end-user computing is one of the solutions to handle such a backlog of information demand. Trends in hardware and software such as miniaturization, speed, connectivity, interactivity, multimedia, and affordability (Sawyer and William, 2003) have contributed to the growth of end-users computing by providing more ***support to end-users from the technical component of IT.*** The control of Information Systems departments on their manpower and IT budget has been decreasing and has shifted to end-users (Edberg & Bowman, 1996; He et al., 1998; Lucas, 2000). These and other factors are ***drivers working toward involving end-users in the IT functions.***

The end-users are taking more and more responsibilities of Information Systems applications, and their involvement is also positively correlated with the success of Information Systems (Doll & Torkzaddah, 1988; McLean et al., 1993; Winter et al., 1997). Turban et al. (2001) claimed that many of the user requirements are smaller in size and can be developed by end-users themselves.

The modular approach in an object-oriented system makes some programming jobs much less complex, and allows end users to accomplish some functions that formerly required professional programmers.

Furthermore, because of the reusability of codes and customizability, the object oriented approach results in higher software development productivity. Agrawal et al. (2001) claimed that the object-oriented approach would make the development process simple, enhancing customizability and contributing to the growth of EUC. These projections have been largely born out and are expected to continue.

Expert systems and other forms of artificial intelligence (AI) hastened the trend toward end-user computing. The use of AI helps businesses make decision better and faster. As these tools have spread throughout businesses their use has become common and continues to spread to jobs throughout the corporate hierarchy. Examples range from executives using applications that utilize artificial intelligence to build complex risk

analysis models to cashiers using AI to identify produce (Sadahiro, Checkley, & Trivedi, 2001).

The natural language processing will lead to simple user interface. It will also lead to increased flexibility, increased predictability, and fewer errors (Nidumolu & Knotts, 1998). The graphical user-interface (GUI) makes software user friendly and allows end-users to communicate with the application more effectively in their familiar vocabulary. These trends have lead to the development and adoption of Web 2.0 applications that allow the user to customize the way they interact with the virtual world. Customers expect businesses to be able to provide an interactive experience for viewing bills, shopping, and getting support among other traditional activities. This trend has important implications for the type of employees human resource departments need to hire. Employees who are technology illiterate will not have the needed skills to provide maximum benefit in the Web 2.0 world. Employees who have extensive technical skills will have some benefit but in order to be of maximum value to the firm they will need to learn business processes and how to interact with customers.

Agrawal and Kotcherlakota (2006) asserted that in a stable IT environment end-users will make more use of the technical component of IT. Contrarily, in an unstable environment the end-users will not be able to work effectively with IT and will thus be required to look for tools and/or skills that are not IT based in order to meet their functional requirements. This reduction in the use of IT would also lead to a corresponding reduction in the need for end-user support but the enterprise would have a competitive disadvantage in regards to their technological infrastructure.

The trends seen in proprietary software, COTS, and end-user computing have implications for both external and in-house IT professionals.

The trend toward more end-user computing will reduce the number of tasks that are required of in-house IT professionals as end users are increasingly able to accomplish tasks that formerly required an IT professional. This trend will be across industries. Some companies will see a growth in the number of IT professionals required to support functions not previously offered so the human resource professionals at those companies will need to work closely with the firms IT department to identify areas of need. Since the overall trend should be toward a reduction of in-house personnel dedicated to IT infrastructure demand it is important that sources for the entry level personal who will be needed should be identified.

External and In-House IT Professionals

When firms decide to build their own proprietary software applications they can either build the applications in-house or they can outsource the development of the application. If the application is built in-house the demand for in-house software developers will increase. If the application is built by a professional software development shop the demand for software developers will increase. Hence, in both scenarios there will be an increased demand for more programming for potential employees.

External IT Professionals

Outsourcers, application service providers, and software houses using their economies of scale can meet their requirements economically. The current declining trends (compared to the projections of BLS) in the requirements of IT professionals, in addition to the earlier discussion, leads one to believe that the concentration of IT professionals will shift heavily from in-house IT departments to software houses, outsourcers, and application service providers. Moreover, it implies that the current declining trend in the requirement of IT professionals is the symptom of the higher use of readily available solutions, i.e. production and usage of more and more COTS/ERP solutions.

In-House IT Professionals Demand

The shift to COTS and subsequently to more end-users control has led Information Systems departments to reduce control of their manpower and IT budget (Edberg & Bowman, 1996; He et al., 1998; Lucas, 2000). The main reason for this shift is credited to the availability of user-friendly software, knowledgeable end-users and extensive company support to EUC (Turban et al., 2001). The end-users are taking more and more responsibilities for Information Systems applications, and their involvement is also positively correlated with the success of Information Systems (Doll & Torkzaddah, 1988; McLean et al., 1993; Winter et al., 1997). Agrawal (2005b) stated that the growth in EUC will increase the requirements of help desk support. Furthermore, the faster obsolescence in products/services and turbulent environment will lead to higher involvement of end-users in implementation and maintenance of software packages (Agrawal, 2005c). As end-users start to become more involved in areas that were once exclusively within the purview of IT departments, a decline in the requirements of in-house software developers is likely to occur (Agrawal, 2005b)). It should also be pointed out that the increased demand for COTS will have some positive impact on in-house IT professionals required. However the net overall effect will be a reduction since the usage of COTS/ERP packages in higher proportion will further lead to a decline in the requirements of in-house IT professionals. Lazowska (2008) asserted that 70% of all IT jobs are with "IT consumers" (companies that use it) rather than with "IT producers" (companies that invent it). The increased usage in COTS/ERP packages will lead to a growth in 30% segment and shrinkages in 70% segment.

Projected Demand for External IT Professionals

We predict that the demand for external IT professionals will increase. This will be driven by a shift toward more commercial off-the-shelf software applications, increased utilization of application service providers (ASPs), as well as mainstream outsourcing arrangements. Commercial off–the-shelf solutions include ERP applications and other packages that allow for customization. The advantages that specialized developers have in areas such as scale, experience, and specialization are difficult for an in-house team to compete against on a consistent basis (Klepper & Jones, 1998). Companies that develop software as their primary business also have the added advantage of being able to more easily introduce the latest technologies and skills into their labor force without a disruption of their business.

Implications of Growth in IT Human Resources in Curriculum Design

This chapter has discussed the various drivers of demand for IT professionals and the impact to IT HR. While there are macroeconomic factors at work the microeconomic considerations are paramount considering the difference in demand among firms and regional industries. In the absence of careful planning and the development of proactive solutions for future IT needs firms are facing a sustained shortage of IT professionals and knowledge workers who work outside of the IT functional area but who do many of the jobs that have traditionally been within the province of IT professionals. Human resource professionals and IHE's should work together to plan for changes in curriculum and course offerings that will allow graduates to be productive in the shortest possible time while also equipping the graduates with a knowledge of theoretical principles that with enable lifelong learning.

LESSONS LEARNED

The role of IT is a strategic necessity but is unlikely to be a source of sustained competitive advantage. Because of this management is likely to focus on strengthening their products and services and forego development of proprietary software. In most cases current IT requirements can be met by complex and integrated high volume off-the-shelf/ERP software without the need for the problems associated with proprietary software, such as risk associated with time pressure and very high costs. This will lead to a higher dependency on outsourcers and software vendors as well as consulting services for professional assistance. The shift toward more reliance on outsourcers, software vendors, and consultants will lead to organizations adapting be reducing IT manpower for implementation and increasing support to end-users. Few senior IT executives will be needed in the organization for IT strategy and planning; maintenance and development of IT architecture. The trends will lead to growth in IT manpower for technical positions such as programmers and systems analyst at outsourcers and software houses, but the in-house departments dedicated solely to IT may start to shrink. Furthermore, the growth in end-users computing and faster obsolescence in technology would lead an increased demand for employees to integrate the use of technology throughout their job functions. This will lead to a need for human resource departments to revise their hiring practices to increasingly look for employees who not only have the expertise needed in the functional area being filled but who can also demonstrate proficiency in IT through course work and/or experience. Human resource professionals will also need to manage the training and development of end-users to keep them current in the IT skills needed to be productive. The needed training could be obtained from the in-house IT department or from outsourcers.

CONCLUSION

IT curriculum committees are faced with an ever more difficult challenge as they try to retain a curriculum core of knowledge that should be universally understood by all graduates in their departmental areas. At the same time, these committees are trying to predict what knowledge is most needed by the rapidly changing society so that students can have both the depth and breadth of knowledge they will need upon graduation. To facilitate the planning process we have developed a conceptual framework that is based upon a review of megatrends within the IT area that will drive the market.

The framework was developed by looking at macro level trends. One trend found is that some industry experts are strongly predicting the demise of corporate IT departments allowing business users the capability to take on operational-level technical tasks, freeing a small core of IT staffers to focus on analytical and strategic issues. Because technology is becoming easier for end users, and considering IT function as problematic to manage, a lot of IT processes will move to outsourcers. The cost and risk of developing applications in-house will also prompt some organizations to rely more on customized or off-the-shelf packages, including ERP software. However, each IHE has its own unique group of stakeholders to be served so each school will need to review the model looking at the environment for their school and determine the effects of the short and long term trends upon their program viability. The framework presented in the paper is general and can be used as a template by human resource professionals to help shape their mental model when developing a staffing strategy plan.

REFERENCES

AACSB. (2002). Business schools at risk. *BizEd,* May/June, 48-54.

Agrawal, V. K. (2005a). From proprietary software to off-the-shelf/ERP solutions: Identifications of critical factors. *National Social Science Journal, 23*(2), 9–32.

Agrawal, V. K. (2005b). Critical factors influencing the requirements of human resources engaged in IT applications. *National Social Science Journal, 24*(1), 1–32.

Agrawal, V. K. (2005c). Implications of environmental and cultural factors on the growth in end-users computing. *National Social Science Journal, 24*(2), 1–14.

Agrawal, V. K. (2005d). Implications of environmental and cultural factors on the trends in usage of various categories of software. *National Social Science Journal, 25*(1), 1–15.

Agrawal, V.K., Haleem, A. & Sushil. (2001). Trends in the demand for different categories of software and human resources. *Proceedings of the Annual Conference of Midwest Decision Sciences Institute,* (p. 4).

Agrawal, V.K., & Kotcherlakota, V. (2006). Impact of environmental pressures and culture on factors influencing the requirements of human resources engaged in IT applications. *Indian Journal of Business and Economics, 5*(1), 15–40.

Agrawal, V. K., Tenkorang, F., Agrawal, V. K., & Taylor, A. R. (2009). Trends in IT human resources and its impact on curriculum design. *Review of Business Information Systems, 13*(4), 67–78.

Ambler, S. (1999). Comprehensive approach cuts project failure. *Computing Canada, 25*(1), 15–16.

Applegate, L. M., Austin, R. D., & McFarlan, F. W. (2007). *Corporate information strategy and management: Text and cases.* New York: McGraw Hill/Irwin.

Bartels, A. (2009). *US IT market outlook: Q1 2009. Our bleak alternative view moves closer to reality.* Cambridge, MA: Forrester Research Incorporated.

Bennis, W. G., & O'Toole, J. (2005). How business schools lost their way. *Harvard Business Review, 83*(5).

Brancheau, J. C., Janz, B. D., & Wetherbe, J. C. (1996). Key issues in Information Systems management: 1994-95, SIM delphi results. *Management Information Systems Quarterly, 20*(2), 225–242. doi:10.2307/249479

Broadbent, M., & Weil, P. (1997). Management by maxim: How business and IT managers can create IT infrastructures. *Sloan Management Review, 38*(3), 77–92.

Brynjolfsson, E. (1996). The contribution of Information Technology to consumer welfare. *Information Systems Research, 7*(3), 281–300. doi:10.1287/isre.7.3.281

Carr, N.G. (May 2003). IT doesn't matter. *Harvard Business Review*. Boston: Harvard Business School Press.

Chabrow, E. (2010, April 2). *IT employment gains in first quarter*. Retrieved from http://www.govinfosecurity.com/ articles.php ?art_id =2372

Clemons, E. K. (1990). MAC-Philadelphia national banks strategic venture in shared ATM networks. *Journal of Management Information Systems, 7*(1), 5–25.

Clemons, E. K. (1991). Evaluation of strategic investments in Information Technology. *Communications of the ACM, 34*(1), 22–36. doi:10.1145/99977.99985

Clemons, E. K., & Kimbrough, S. O. (1986). Information Systems, telecommunications, and their effects on industrial organizations. In L. Maggi, R. Zmud & J. Wetherbe (Eds.), *Proceedings of the Seventh International Conference on Information Systems,* San Diego, CA, (pp. 99-108).

Dohm, A., & Shniper, L. (2007). Occupational employment projections to 2016, *Monthly Labor Review*. Retrieved on February 12, 2009, from http://www.bls.gov/opub/mlr/ 2007/11/ art5 full. pdf

Doll, W. J., & Torkzaddeh, G. (1988). The measurement of end-user computing satisfaction. *Management Information Systems Quarterly*, 259–274. doi:10.2307/248851

Edberg, D. T., & Bowman, B. J. (1996). User-developed applications: An empirical study of application quality and developer productivity. *Journal of Management Information Systems, 13*(1), 167.

El Sawy, O. A., Malhotra, A., Gosain, S., & Young, K. M. (1999). IT-intensive value innovation in the electronic economy: Insights from Marshall Industries. *Management Information Systems Quarterly, 23*(3), 309–335.

Emery, J. C. (1990). Misconception about strategic Information Systems. *Management Information Systems Quarterly, 14*(2), vii–viii.

Ettlie, J. E. (1983). Organizational policy and innovation among suppliers to the food processing sector. *Academy of Management Journal, 26*(1), 27–44. doi:10.2307/256133

Fleming, D. L. (2008). Building bridges to connect the disconnects: An analysis of business program design processes. *American Journal of Business Education, 1*(2), 21–46.

Gartner. (2010). *Gartner says worldwide IT spending to grow 4.6 percent in 2010*. Retrieved from http://www.gartner.com/it/ page.jsp?id= 1284813

Gerdes, L. (2005, September 5). B-School with a niche. *Business Week*, 70-72.

Gilder, G. (2002). *Telecosm: The world after bandwidth abundance*. Touchstone.

Hayes, F. (1997). Managing user expectation. *Computerworld, 31*(4), 8–9.

He, Z. M., Kusy, K. M., & Zhao, T. (1998). A survey study of the current IS usage in the Chinese manufacturing industry. *Information & Management, 34*, 285–294. doi:10.1016/S0378-7206(98)00063-9

Hecker, D. (2001). Occupational employment projections to 2010. *Monthly Labor Review*, 57-84. Retrieved February 10, 2009, from http://www.bls.gov/opub/mlr/ 2001/ 11/ art4full.pdf

Hecker, D. (2004). Occupational employment projections to 2012. *Monthly Labor Review*, 80-105. Retrieved February 10, 2009, from http://www.bls.gov/opub/mlr/ 2004/ 02/art5 full.pdf

Hecker, D. (2006). Occupational employment projections to 2014. *Monthly Labor Review*, 70-101. Retrieved February 10, 2009, from http://www.bls.gov/opub/mlr/ 2005/ 11/art 5full.pdf

Heikkilä, J. T., Saarinen, T., & Sääksjärvi, M. (1991). Success of software packages in small businesses: An exploratory study. *European Journal of Information Systems, 1*(3), 159–169. doi:10.1057/ejis.1991.31

Hof, R. (2003, August 17). We can't even glimpse the potential. *Business Week*. Retrieved from http://www.businessweek.com/ @@Gov-uBoUQaQmEPwkA/ magazine/ content/03_34/ b384 6612.htm

Jeong, J. J., & Klein, G. (1999). Risks to different aspects of system success. *Information & Management, 36*, 263–272. doi:10.1016/S0378-7206(99)00024-5

Jones, M. (1994). Don't emancipate, exaggerate: Rhetoric, reality and reengineering. In R. Baskerville, S. Smithson, C. Ngwenyama & J.I. DeGross (Eds.), *Transforming organization with Information Technology*. (pp. 357-378). North Holland: Elseiver Science.

Kemerer, C. F., & Sosa, G. L. (1991). Systems development risks in strategic Information Systems. *Information and Software Technology, 33*(3), 212–223. doi:10.1016/0950-5849(91)90136-Y

Klepper, R., & Jones, W. O. (1998). *Outsourcing Information Technology, systems, & services*. Upper Saddle River, NJ: Prentice Hall.

Laudon, K. C., & Laudon, J. P. (1999). *Essentials of management Information Systems: Transforming business and management*. Upper Saddle River, NJ: Prentice Hall.

Lazowska, E. (2008, July 11). Computer Science enrollment: The real news. *Computer Community Consortium*. Retrieved from http://www.cccblog.org/ 2008/07/11/ computer-science-enroll ment-the-real-news/

Lewin, S. G., Lewin, S. L., & Meisel, J. B. (1987). A dynamic analysis of the adoption of a new technology: The case of optical scanners. *The Review of Economics and Statistics, 69*(1), 12–17. doi:10.2307/1937895

Li, M. F., & Ye, R. L. (1999). Information Technology and firm performance: Linking with environmental strategic managerial contexts. *Information & Management, 35*, 53–51. doi:10.1016/S0378-7206(98)00075-5

Lucas, H. C. (2000). *Information Technology for management* (7th ed.). New York: McGraw-Hill, Inc.

Mahmood, M. A., & Mann, G. (1993). Measuring the organizational impact of Information Technology investment: An exploratory study. *Journal of Management Information Systems, 10*(1), 97–122.

Mann, J. (2010, February 2). Obama requests $80 billion in IT spending for 2011. *ExecutiveGov*. Retrieved from http://www.executivegov.com/ 2010/02/ obama-requests-80-billion-in- it-spending- for-2011/

Matheson, L., & Tarjan, R. (1998). Culturally induced information impactedness: A prescription for failure in software ventures. *Journal of Management Information Systems, 15*(2).

McKenna, J. F., Cotton, C. C., & Van Auken, S. (1995). Business school emphasis on teaching, research, and service to industry: Does where you sit determine where you stand? *Journal of Organizational Change Management, 8*(2), 3–16. doi:10.1108/09534819510084319

McLean, E. R., Kappelman, L. A., & Thompson, J. P. (1993). Converging end-user computing and corporate computing. *Communications of the ACM, 36*(12), 79–92. doi:10.1145/163298.163314

McNamara, D. E. (2006). The relevance of business school education, what do you think? *Journal of College Teaching & Learning, 3*(11), 1–14.

McNurlin, B. (Ed.). (1991). *Trends in Information Technology*. Chicago: Anderson Consulting.

Mintzberg, H. (2004). *Managers not MBAs: A hard look at the soft practice of managing and management development*. San Francisco: Berrett-Koehler.

Network World. (2009). IT spending as a percentage of corporate revenue. *New World (New Orleans, La.), 26*(1), 27.

Nidumolu, S. R., & Knotts, G. W. (1998). The effect of customizability and reusability on perceived process and competitive performance of software firms. *Management Information Systems Quarterly*, 105–137. doi:10.2307/249392

Porter, M. (1980). *Competitive strategy*. New York: Free Press.

Porter, M. E. (1996). *What is a strategy? Harvard Business Review*. November/December.

Porter, M.E. (2001). Strategy and the Internet. *Harvard Business Review*.

Sadahiro, I., Checkley, D., & Trivedi, M. (2001, August). REFLICS: Real-time flow imaging and classification system. *Machine Vision and Applications, 13*(1).

Sawyer, S., & Williams, B. (2003). *Using Information Technology: A practical introduction to computers and communications* (5th ed.). New York: McGraw-Hill.

Scott Morton, M. S. (1991). *The corporation of the 1990s: Information Technology and organizational transformation*. Oxford University Press.

Turban, E., McLean, E., & Whetherbe, J. (2001). *Information Technology for management: Making connections for strategic advantages* (2nd ed.). New York: John Wiley and Sons, Inc.

Wailgum, T. (October 2007). How Wal-Mart lost its technology edge. *CIO*. Retrieved February 10, 2009, from http://www.cio.com/ article /print / 143451

Winter, S. J., Chudoba, K. M., & Gutek, B. A. (1997). Misplaced resources? Factors associated with computer literacy among end-users. *Information & Management, 32*, 29–42. doi:10.1016/S0378-7206(96)01086-5

Section 2
Recruiting

In today's highly competitive environment, there are several considerations which organizations need to deliberate before/during the recruiting process, including the: (1) talent Management approach, (2) human resource life cycle, (3) sourcing framework, (4) role of human resource departments in Sourcing Decisions.

Chapter 4
IT Human Resources:
Experts at Talent Management & Critical Partners to the CIO

Phil Schneidermeyer
Heidrick & Struggles, USA

ABSTRACT

In this chapter, IT human recourse professionals will find confirmation of the important role that they play in ensuring the creation of a high performance department. They develop, recommend, and then lead the talent management strategy. As leadership needs arise, HR works with IT leadership to assess internal candidates, and if they do not fit, then they can assess and recommend external staffing firms with the appropriate expertise and reach. The human resources/CIO partnership will include leading the effort to develop a position specification, managing the candidates through the interview process, and negotiating an offer that often times must be customized to attract the ideal candidate. Finally, once selected, human resources will manage the on-boarding process to ensure that the recent hire has the support they need and can get up to speed quickly.

INTRODUCTION

The success of an IT organization is dependent upon the quality of its leadership. Leadership quality is assessed by human resources professionals supporting the IT organization, but assessment cannot take place in a vacuum. The human resources professionals need to start with a Talent Strategy. This roadmap will include the Chief Information Officer, the CIO's direct reports and the staff below them, and therefore will need to be customized to fit each level. As this is being developed a clear understanding of the company's culture and, if it exists, the sub-culture within IT

DOI: 10.4018/978-1-60960-535-3.ch004

must be defined. Without understanding the culture an appropriate fit and assessment of personal characteristics cannot be made. On the other hand, while qualifications and experience are critical they are fairly straight forward to assess.

Developing a Talent Strategy

Talent management has been a point of discussion for companies of all sizes and across all industries for many years. Human resource organizations play a critical role, but all managers and business leaders must commit time and resources to the process.

A talent strategy has many components that when tied together create a cycle. To be successful companies must follow the defined path and aggressively support the respective processes. Different points in the cycle emphasize external talent, while others focus on internal talent that may have been recently hired or have been with the company for some time. To begin, the talent management process the organization must have the capacity to target and be attractive to the relevant pools of talent. At the entry level where technical skills are critical this can mean offering an opportunity to work with leading edge technologies, continuous education and training programs, and flexible work hours.

As human resources moves forward with the selection, recruitment and hiring of talent behavioral characteristics and technical skills must be aligned. Next, on boarding is the induction process for new hires. Going forward, to maintain a competitive advantage, organizations must have a talent management strategy that offers continuous learning. Best of breed companies offer not only training but have formal mentoring programs as well. Defining roles that leverage an individual's competencies, communicating a career track and providing performance feedback is known to engage and retain talent. Through promotion and rotation the organization creates a leadership pipeline. Hiring at the technical, manager and

Vice President level gives the CIO an external benchmark against the internal team.

Following the identification of future leaders, the talent strategy cycle comes full circle establishing process to secure effective and smooth successions. Finally it is generally accepted that to be successful the talent management strategy must be employee centric. An annual review with a formal 360 evaluation is a tool, but this tool must be part of a broader talent management strategy.

For example, in Compensation Today, Barry MacLean (2009) writes that a Talent Strategy is employee-centric and is focused on recruiting, training, aligning performance, planning for growth and development and identifying high-potential employees, and charting a course for their career growth. However to be comprehensive, measurable, and have impact the Talent Strategy must also include compensation management "which by contrast is all about jobs: wkat grades or bands they fall into, and what target incentives are associated with varying levels of jobs within the company." To retain and attract the strongest talent, a good Talent Strategy will go beyond the internal comparison of jobs and will include a market valuation of individual employees.

There are many approaches to determining market valuation and some require more resources (e.g., time, money, staff, etc.) than others. For managers and directors, entry level management, job posting and career web sites can provide quick but un-scrubbed data. Recruiting firms (generally contingency) will also have helpful data points and should be willing to offer an opinion based on their current view of the market. Do not look to online resources for data at the senior management level (Vice President and above). If the organization has a relationship with an executive search firm (retainer-based) consultant specializing in IT they will offer an opinion. While this may be at no cost, a fee will be charged for a more detailed study and human resource consulting firms such as Towers Watson & Co. and Hewitt Associates are specialists. Further discussion of market valuation follows in Compensation Management section.

Recruiting

As the Talent Management strategy identifying and recruiting, whether IT HR is assisting with the recruitment of a new CIO or direct reports and their staff, they must take a lead role in defining the selection process, aligning technical skills with behavioral characteristics, understanding and setting expectations, and measuring outcomes; each goes hand in hand to create a recruiting cycle within the talent management cycle. If for example the expectations are for a very tight job specification (narrowly defined qualifications) then, since there are fewer qualified candidates, the search will likely take longer and success can depend on available, affordable, qualified talent – either internal or external. While the position specification outlines day to day responsibilities it should also be the roadmap for the search and represent the ideal candidate however the HR business partner should counsel their IT client that trade-offs will need to be made. Should the ideal candidate not be available an upfront understanding of the trade-offs or flexibility in the position specification will be a time saver. IT recruiters will provide examples of how other companies have approached the market, what they found and the trade-offs they made.

Trade-offs are a natural and therefore expected aspect of the recruiting process. When a media company recently went to market to recruit an applications team leader, the first requirement was for experience in this specific application. The question, is this truly a "must have" or is it an "ideal". In this case it was the later as individual team members were experts in the application and therefore the leader needed to bring process, mentoring and communication skills.

The internal recruiting process should also emphasize the importance of managing the scheduling and handling of candidates as they interview with the company. One person should be the lead on setting up the schedules of the interviewers. It takes someone on the "inside" with access to calendars and support staff to bring several people together on the same day. The recruiter will provide the candidate's availability and work with them on travel when necessary. The interviewers will have the candidate's resume and need to know what position the candidate is coming in for as many organizations have multiple positions to fill. Both candidate and interviewer should be aligned. The company is not viewed well by candidates when there is confusion on their end. Also biographical information on the interviewers should be provided to the candidate in advance. At a minimum a title should be included and where possible the recruiter will use public sources like LinkedIn and Google to gather information as well. Interviews are ideally an hour but can be as short as 30 minutes; so that there can be a more strategic discussion both sides must prepare in advance.

At the end of the hiring process when an insurance company recruiting a Network Manager looked at the length of time it took to close the search and found that it took twice as long as other recruiting projects, drilling deeper they realized that it took weeks to go from identifying the candidate to first round interview. The culprit, the hiring manager's administrative assistant gave the recruiter the contact information for the interviewing team and had the recruiter trying to find time on the interviewer's calendar. Based on the process they did not see this as a priority and dates of availability kept slipping out into the future.

As a best practice many companies split the position requirements up amongst the interviewers. Assessment templates with rankings or areas for comment should be distributed to the interviewers in advance and then feedback gathered quickly. The recruiter will be seeking feedback from the candidate at the end of their interview day and the candidate will be expecting a turnaround of a day or two. Managing the recruiting and interview process gives a company a competitive advantage

Figure 1. Integrated talent management acquisition approach

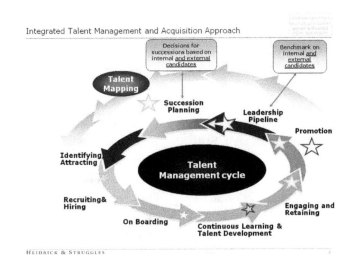

as candidates are likely interviewing with other companies and this initial exposure is the first impression that will stay with them throughout the process.

Assessment and Alignment

The assessment of an IT professional's qualifications and experience can be rather straight forward especially at lower levels where hands-on technical knowledge is required. This would include education such as degrees and certifications; years of experience; functional experience; prior staff and budget responsibility; and business, or industry knowledge. At the management level business acumen goes beyond budget responsibility to include strategic thinking, analyzing, diagnosing, decisiveness, financial acumen and risk taking.

Some of the softer skills include leadership and management behavioral competencies such as being performance driven. That is, being considered to be a self-starter, assertive, goal oriented as well as having tactical planning and tracking abilities. Responsiveness and follow through are measures of one's customer-centric style and personal characteristics such as values, motivation, personality traits and personal style can be more important than technical qualifications and experience. Finally and equally important soft skills include, team leadership and personal effectiveness. This includes the ability to build relationships, listen and be receptive, collaboration, influencing, motivating, developing talent and self development.

A not-for-profit emphasized this aspect of the position specification when recruiting a new Chief Information Officer. Knowing that the organization had such strong cultural values that they knew the successful candidate could only come from an organization with a mission and shared values. Otherwise the ability to build relationships with other C-level executives was going to be difficult and there was added risk in the transition to the new organization.

Just as an organization would assess technical skills by comparing them to the current technology environment (e.g., platforms, operating systems, applications, etc.), interpersonal style and culture fit will be compared to the organization or department's culture and the hiring manager plus peers and possibly the interpersonal style of direct reports. For some organizations articulating culture may not be as straight forward as identifying technical competency. In terms of identifying different cultures, in one example a company grows through the acquisition of other companies and they are at various stages of integration or choose a strategy not to integrate them at all. The result could be multiple cultures within a company. In another scenario, information technology departments that are working off shore whether captive or not are managing through a diverse set of cultures. Assessing a candidate's fit must take this into consideration as well. Still many other organizations have cultures that they are looking to change and therefore are looking for change-agents. Not only will these individuals come from a different organizational culture they will have a demonstrated track record of driving change. On the business and process side these changes may include a move from a decentralized to a centralized structure; the integration or divesture of businesses, and; globalization. On the technology side change may be a move toward more outsourcing or the reverse; SOA, implementation of ITIL or a move from one CMMi level to another and; common enterprise resource planning. Where organizations have gone wrong is when they expect the new hire to be the driver of change without the support of key leaders. Tenure for this individual will likely be short and is referred to by some as "organ rejection". There are many examples of this more at the top of the house, Chief Information Officer or their direct reports than at lower levels. Driving change within your own information technology department has a greater chance of success as the head of IT has direct control of budgets and people. Since information technology touches all business processes the risk increases when the CIO must drive change on the business side where budgets and people naturally report to the head of the business. Here relationship building and influencing skills are critical success factors.

Compensation Management

A good Talent Strategy includes not only an internal comparison of jobs and an alignment of skills

but also market valuations. A decade ago when the Internet bubble was expanding, talent was attracted using equity and salary could be fixed at both the VP and the Manager level. Equity became was variable with Chief Executive Officers taking three to five percent of the outstanding shares and then direct reports to the CEO being offer approximately one to three percent. If the role was Chief Financial Officer and the goal was to go take the company public then having this previous IPO experience would earn the CFO the upper end of the range. As an Internet company the Chief Technology Officer (who may be also managing information technology to run the business) tended to be one of the founders but when the company grew and the role demanded more managerial skills a new CTO could be brought in with both technical and managerial capabilities. Here too the combined skill set would earn the incoming CTO the upper end of the equity percentage range.

In many companies equity was offered not just to vice presidents and managers but to all employees, from the secretaries to programmers. The belief was that this would create a culture of "ownership" resulting in a more committed workforce and had the added affect creating "golden handcuffs" where it would be too expensive for another company to recruit the talent.

It has been almost ten years since the Internet bubble burst and one lasting change in the long term component of a compensation package is a shift from stock options to restricted stock or a mix of both. Depending on level the number of shares may be fixed. If the finalist candidate is leaving some equity on the table then the candidate will look for an off set. Most companies only consider equity that is to vest in the near-term (perhaps one or two years). Black-Scholes (see e.g. Katz & McCormick, 2005) is not a perfect model but a generally accepted way to value the shares. Attempting to keep the candidate "whole" hiring companies may prefer to offer a cash or stock sign on bonus or again it can be a mix of the two. (Note: sign on bonuses generally include a claw-back term (12 months or less) and are pro-rated.) When working with a recruiter it is important to share the range within which the hiring company must work; this is for base salary, annual bonus and equity. Avoiding surprises on both sides is a key goal. An understanding of the prospective candidate's current compensation is done immediately however a full accounting of their equity may take longer as most candidates need to research this information. Three years of history is ideal and W2s should be requested from the finalist candidate at offer. A break out of bonus structure, individual versus company performance, must also be noted as well as when the bonus is earned and when the bonus is paid. These are generally two different dates and candidates will want a hiring company to take their accrued bonus into consideration when structuring an offer. On base salary it is important to know when the candidate last had or expects a review and therefore salary adjustment.

Other aspects of compensation and benefits that the hiring company may consider when trying to "close" the finalist candidate include, accelerating an annual review so that a salary increase might occur sooner, guaranteeing some or all of the first-year's performance bonus (But first agreeing on deliverables, goals and objectives.), and for information technology professionals technical training, telecommuting, ability to attend conferences or participate on standards boards can carry some weight as well.

For example a media company had no internal candidates for a Vice President role within the information technology group and went to market through a search firm. From a technical perspective the specification was very narrow in that the company was looking for experience with an application that is limited to a small industry. As a small industry there was an equally small candidate population and across the candidate slate base salary ranged from the low $200k to the low $300k range. The company stated a

base salary range at the launch of the search and while $300k was beyond that range the company brought those candidates in as well. This gave the hiring manager an opportunity to consider a mix of skills, experience and compensation before making a decision. The finalist's base salary and bonus fit within existing parameters but coming from a private company the internal equity was difficult to value. The CIO worked closely with the information technology group's head of human resources to lay out an equity structure that is easily understood with a value that can be assessed and a plan for future equity. The candidate took a holistic view of the opportunity and accepted.

Always be aware that there are two different base salary figures to keep in mind. One is the current salary and the other is "what it takes" (base salary) to get them to accept the risk of leaving their current company. The first will be within the target range and the second may not. Organizations that recognize the importance of attracting and retaining the best talent will customize an offer or compensation structure to meet the individual's needs. The balance that the hiring manager and human resources professionals need to maintain is parity within the peer group. Of course compensation is only one component. Work environment, potential for career growth and other non-financial factors will be considered by the ideal candidate.

Measuring Outcomes

Measuring outcomes is critical for the success of any human resources organization and this is not simply 'was there or wasn't there a hire.' Other important metrics to track include days to complete the search, number of candidates interviewed, number of days from identification of the candidate until first round interview, and diversity of candidate slate. If internal candidates were considered then they need to have clear feedback as to why they were not selected, the appropriate training and performance management should be put in place to keep them engaged. Financial resources are finite and should be tracked as well. Larger organizations with dedicated internal staffing resources are also maintaining a database of the candidates interviewed. The value-add in the database is when interviewer feedback is captured and stored for future reference. Here again the assessment sheet or template can be saved electronically for future reference. If the candidate was interesting enough to consider for an immediate position there is a good chance that they will be a fit for others positions in the future.

On-Boarding

Once a candidate is hired on-boarding, assimilation and transition support, is critical. New hires have to be introduced to the company and IT department culture, and be informed about their supervisor's management style. Further, pre-hire references should have highlighted areas of development for the individual and support should be provided and progress tracked. The goal is to position everyone for success. A public technology company that did this well began by creating a binder of relevant documentation and providing it to the new hire in advance of the start date. Most candidates must give notice to their current companies but can make time to participate on important conference calls and to review materials. Lastly, organizations operating without an on-boarding program may be losing the opportunity to leverage and secure competencies that the new hire brings to the company.

FUTURE RESEARCH DIRECTIONS

This chapter is a primer for human resource executives supporting information technology organizations as they develop their staffing and talent management capabilities and strategies. Additional research into continuous learning, talent development, retention, promotion and creating a leadership pipeline that provides for better succession planning is warranted. Finally, with many companies growing their internal staffing capabilities a look at the success rates between this model and leveraging external providers would be helpful as both have their pros and cons.

CONCLUSION

The demographics are clear, with the aging population there will be a worker shortage. There may have been a truce in the War for Talent during the recent economic downturn, but combatants on both sides are nearing agreement that the battle has been engaged once again. Combine this with a generally accepted notion that a skills gap remains for entry level workers and that at both middle management and the senior executive level there aren't enough "born leaders" to fill all of the needs and the evidence becomes clear, human resources plays a critical role in the information technology department's talent management value chain. Couple this with a rising demand for a more diverse IT leadership team and human resources should find no shortage of challenges.

One of the lessons learned over the last ten years is that the employees of all companies are easier to identify which of course is the first step in recruiting. It started at the top when companies built their web page and included a list of senior management. Some companies pushed back on this but they soon found themselves fighting a losing battle as social networking sites like LinkedIn expanded rapidly creating a virtual employee directory with biographical and contact information. Couple this with an end to the "one company for life" expectation and IT Human Resources need to make sure they have a visible talent management approach that includes the complete cycle: continuous learning to engaging and retaining to promotion that creates a leadership pipeline and emphasizes succession planning. If not, human resources will find themselves spending more time on recruiting as employees resign to take what they perceive to be companies offering better career growth opportunities.

REFERENCES

Katz, J. O., & McCormick, D. (2005, February 4). Advanced option pricing models.

MacLean, B. (2009, February 13). How to build a talent management strategy – Based on compensation. *Compensation Today.*

ADDITIONAL READING

Hengst, A. (2007). *Talent management FAQ*. HR World.

Kutick, B. (2008). *Who first called it 'Talent Management*. Human Resource Executive.

Ostroff, C., & Judge, T. A. (2009). *Perspectives on organizational fit*. Wiley Periodicals, Inc.

Schein, E. H. (2004). *Organizational culture and leadership*. John Wiley & Sons, Inc.

Watkins, M. (2003). *The first 90 days*. Harvard Business School Publishing.

KEY TERMS AND DEFINITIONS

Assessment: Determine the candidate's fit against the position specification requirements.

Chief Information Officer: The most senior executive responsible for information technology in the company.

Company Culture: A description of the company's style.

Position Specification: Describes the requirements for being qualified for a position and the responsibilities of that position.

Recruiting: The process by which a company attracts talent.

Talent Strategy: A comprehensive approach to managing internal talent and attracting external talent.

Chapter 5
Selection:
The Crux of IT HR Management

Jo Ellen Moore
Southern Illinois University Edwardsville, USA

Clay K. Williams
Southern Illinois University Edwardsville, USA

ABSTRACT

When studying job analysis, recruitment, training, and even retention in IT HR management, an oft-overlooked element of the picture is selection. This chapter acknowledges and models the interplay among these components and then focuses on selection. The general steps in designing an effective selection process are reviewed, and a particularly interesting and useful selection technique is examined: critical incidents (or CI). Data from a CI analysis of the job of IT project manager are used to illustrate how a CI study is conducted and how the output from CI can be used to improve a selection process, as well as inform job analysis and training. The chapter concludes by identifying ways that the examination of selection can extend IT HR research and, ultimately, improve the effectiveness of IT HR management.

INTRODUCTION

You have conducted a thorough job analysis that resulted in an accurate statement of knowledge, skills, abilities and other characteristics (KSAOs) needed for a particular IT position. You designed and implemented a stellar recruitment strategy, so that you have a quality pool of applicants possessing the vital KSAOs. You have effective, targeted

DOI: 10.4018/978-1-60960-535-3.ch005

initial training ready to be deployed. *But if you are unable to identify the best person for the job from the applicant pool, all is for naught.* If selection methods are inadequate or flawed, you are unlikely to identify the individual best qualified on the key KSAOs and, when that happens, you are likely to spend more time on training and coaching the newly placed individual, and on managing job performance issues.

In the research and discussion of job analysis, recruitment, training, retention and other aspects

Figure 1. Selection in HR management

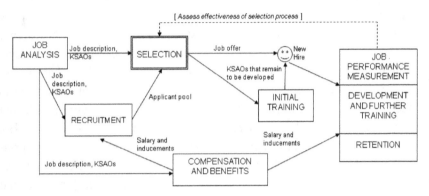

of IT HR management, limited attention has been given to a key element that connects them all: selection. By definition, selection is the process of collecting and evaluating information about individuals for the purpose of extending a job offer. This can be an initial job offer to join an organization in a specific position or an internal offer for promotion or lateral move. Regardless, the resulting selection decision is a pivotal point for the hiring organization. It is a "crossroads" decision, in that a road is chosen and other roads are left behind. In Jim Collins' terminology, you have placed an individual in a seat on your company bus (Collins, 2001).

An understanding of the relationships among components of HR management is necessary for researchers to formulate studies that acknowledge the role and, perhaps most of all, effects of selection. This same understanding can help practitioners optimize the outcomes of IT HR management efforts. Given its importance and the scant IT HR literature on the topic to date, selection is the focus of this chapter.

First, the interplay among selection and other components of HR management is acknowledged and modeled. The general steps in developing a selection process are reviewed, followed by an examination of common assessment devices. This is accompanied by a demonstration of how assessment devices can be applied to a selection process for an IT job.

To ensure a grounded and practical understanding of selection, one particularly useful HR technique is discussed in detail: the critical incident (CI) technique. Data from a CI analysis of the job of IT project manager are examined to illustrate how a CI study is conducted and how the output from CI can be used to improve a selection process, as well as inform other components of IT HR. Finally, suggestions are presented for how to extend IT HR research by considering selection methods, and important recommendations to IT practitioners are provided.

THE ROLE OF SELECTION IN IT HR MANAGEMENT

Practitioners and researchers, particularly those not schooled in HR, may have forgotten or may not be aware of the pivotal role of selection in HR management. Figure 1 models the relationship of selection to other key elements of HR management.

Job analysis is the gathering of information about a job in an organization (Fine & Cronshaw, 1999), typically culminating in a formal job description with identification of knowledge, skills, abilities and other characteristics necessary to perform the job.

This information contributes to recruitment, compensation, and selection. Job analysis outputs serve two purposes in recruitment: to convey to potential applicants the nature and requirements of the job; and, to provide a basis for designing recruitment strategies, i.e., where and how to target potentially qualified candidates. Rynes and Barber (1990) remind us that compensation and benefits also affect the size and qualifications of the applicant pool. Simply stated, the salary and other inducements that the company decides to link to the job (given the job description and KSAOs established through job analysis) can affect recruitment strategies as well as recruitment outcomes. Finally, the job description and identification of KSAOs produced by job analysis provide the foundation needed to design an effective selection process.

The two key inputs to selection are the information produced by job analysis and the pool of applicants generated through execution of the recruitment strategy. Gatewood, Feild, and Barrick (2008) contend that the value of selection to the organization increases as the pool of qualified applicants grows. That is, there is likely to be more well-qualified applicants in a larger pool, so an effective selection process is vital to identifying the well-qualified individuals in that large pool.

On the other hand, if recruitment has produced a small number of applicants, selection may be reduced to what Gatewood and his colleagues refer to as hiring: "…the organization has a need to fill openings within a very short period of time… the organization does little or no evaluation of the applicants… Availability is the critical variable" (2008, p. 4).

Selection is characterized by the systematic collection and evaluation of information about job applicants, and can range from a simple application form and brief interview to a more complex process that utilizes situational structured interviews, simulations, performance tests, and other techniques.

Ideally, the job analysis has differentiated the KSAOs for which training is commonly effective and available from KSAOs that are absolutely required at job entry (Heneman & Judge, 2006). But if not, this classification is completed in the initial stages of selection process design. In essence, the selection process aims to select an applicant who possesses the KSAOs that are not amenable to development through post-hire training.

Once the individual is selected and working in the position, the focus of IT HR management turns to job performance appraisal, employee development and further training, and retention. Measurements from job performance appraisals provide a feedback loop for determining the effectiveness of the selection process and making needed improvements. This data can help to determine how well a particular selection device (for example, having a four-year degree in Information Systems, or performance on a selection interview comprised of situational questions) predicted performance in the job.

Elements of the selection process with high correlation to job performance should be retained, while elements with low correlation to actual job performance may need to be dropped from the selection process.

Employee development includes further training and other mechanisms for growth and advancement. Compensation and inducements continue to play a role as they are exercised to ensure appropriate returns and incentives as the individual progresses within the organization.

The post-hire HR mechanisms (performance appraisal, development, training, compensation and benefits) inherently influence employee retention. Dalton, Todor, and Krackhardt (1982) provided an insightful delineation of "functional turnover" from "dysfunctional turnover." Voluntary turnover of an employee who is negatively evaluated by the organization constitutes functional turnover, because departure of the employee in a sense benefits the company. This is in contrast to dysfunctional turnover (voluntary turnover of a valued employee), which is the assumed form of turnover in nearly all studies and discussions of retention.

Selection relates to retention in that, first, you must have selected an individual that you end up wanting to retain. The more consistently an organization is able to do this, the less time and energy will be spent on employee termination efforts, on correcting or tolerating inadequate performance, and on the crossing of fingers hoping an employee will leave voluntarily, i.e., yearning for functional turnover.

Over the years, researchers in IT HR have examined various elements of the model in Figure 1. For example, Cheney, Hale, and Kasper (1990) conducted a longitudinal study of KSAOs for project managers, systems analysts and designers, and programmers. Agarwal and Ferratt have investigated recruitment practices in their stream of research in IT HR strategy (1999, 2001). Mithas and Krishnan (2008) and Slaughter, Ang, and Boh (2007) provided recent studies regarding compensation of IT professionals. And performance appraisals of Information Systems employees were studied by Igbaria and Baroudi (1995), with an eye toward gender differences.

In the area of employee development, Lee (2002) explored IT professionals' career goals and career management strategies, and Koh, Lee, Yen, and Havelka (2004) examined ways in which IT professionals' technical skill requirements change as they gain experience in an organization. Major, Davis, German, Fletcher, Sanchez-Hucles, and Mann (2007) identified five approaches to on-going training and development that address challenges inherent to IT and IT professionals in organizations. Recognizing the traditional focus on technical skills, Joseph, Ang, Chang and Slaughter (2010) utilized the concept of practical intelligence in developing their Soft Skills of IT (SSIT) inventory to assess IT professionals on non-technical skills such as managing oneself and one's own career.

Finally, voluntary turnover (dysfunctional) has been extensively studied by IT HR researchers. For example, Ferratt, Agarwal, Brown, and Moore (2005) discovered five configurations of IT HR practices that vary in their effects on turnover rates, while Ang and Slaughter (2004) investigated the impact of an organization's internal labor market strategy on the turnover of IT employees, and Joseph, Ng, Koh, and Ang (2007) provided a comprehensive examination of IT turnover through meta-analysis.

Yet, IT HR research examining *selection* is scant. We identified only two empirical studies that have been published. In the first, Witt and Burke (2002) investigated the extent to which two selection factors (general mental ability and personality) were associated with four characteristics of high performance (technical proficiency, relationship management skills, adherence to documentation standards and requirements, and self-initiated professional development) in a sample of 97 IT workers in a service-based firm. More recently, Kynphausen-Aufseß and Vormann (2009) used a policy-capturing experimental design to evaluate how perceptions of applicant fit (person-organization and person-job), competencies (social, personal, subject, method, and entrepreneurial), and social capital influence decisions to hire hypothetical IT job applicants. Although Witt and Burke were unable to breakdown their small sample by IT job classification and Kynphausen-Aufseß and Vormann focused on decision-making elements rather than formulation of the selection process, together these studies give a good indication of the potential for purposefully designed selection processes to enhance the effectiveness of selection decisions in IT.

DESIGNING A SELECTION PROCESS

This section reviews the steps involved in designing a selection process, including the variety of assessment devices that can be incorporated into the process. This is followed by an example that demonstrates how assorted assessment devices can be applied in selection of an IT project manager.

The selection process basically consists of using a set of assessment devices that measure the KSAOs needed for the job. Working from information derived through job analysis, the initial step in designing a selection process is to identify or develop assessment devices to measure KSAOs. If there are KSAOs that can be reasonably developed through initial training, those are given a lower priority in the construction of the selection process. As previously noted, the selection process is designed to select an applicant who possesses the KSAOs that are not amenable to development through post-hire training.

The general categories of assessment devices are:

- Application forms and reference checks
- Selection interviews
- Mental and special abilities tests
- Personality assessment inventories
- Performance and simulation measures.

For each KSAO to be assessed, consideration should be given to whether an assessment device may already exist. HR specialists know where to look for existing assessments and can assist in identifying ones that may be appropriate. The most commonly available assessment devices focus on intelligence, special abilities (e.g., programming), and personality. The GMA (intelligence) and PCI (personality) instruments used by Witt and Burke (2002) are examples of existing assessment devices. Additionally, most organizations have prepared assessment devices that may collect the data needed for a KSAO. These include application forms that are easily refined and reference check forms.

When no existing assessment device is found for a key KSAO, one must be constructed. An HR selection specialist or consultant should be involved in such an effort, to contribute vital expertise in the development and validation of assessment devices, as well as in the technical and legal ramifications associated with selection.

Each assessment device should measure one or more of the targeted KSAOs, and the device should be able to detect variance in the degree of the characteristic possessed by applicants. For example, an assessment device for Java programming skills should produce a rating for a novice Java programmer that differs from the rating an experienced Java programmer would achieve, which differs from a Java guru's rating. An example of an assessment device that commonly *lacks* differentiation is the interview that asks general questions such as what the applicant perceives to be her biggest strength and biggest weakness.

Ultimately, the selection process should be evaluated by comparing the ratings from the selection assessment devices to actual performance of the selected individuals in the job. As previously noted, selection assessment devices with high correlation to job performance should be retained in the selection process for the job, while elements with low correlation to actual job performance should be dropped.

Assessment Devices

Central to an effective selection process is the identification of assessment devices that are valid measures of the KSAOs. Here, the chapter provides additional detail on the types of assessment devices commonly used in selection. Once these are on the table, the chapter continues by applying specific assessment devices to evaluate KSAOs in applicants for the job of IT project manager.

Application forms are used by nearly all companies as a screening device to determine whether the applicant meets minimum requirements for the job. Questions on the application form typically focus on educational background and prior work experience. For example, a question could be designed and included on the application form to provide an initial (screening-level) assessment of the applicant's extent of experience with the SAP ABAP programming language. It is important to work with HR specialists in establishing an application form, particularly because information you may think you want to collect can result in biased and/or discriminatory selection practices. For example, unless a certain age, gender, marital status, or citizenship is directly linked to ability to do the job, the application form should not ask for that information (Gatewood, Feild, & Barrick, 2008). Bottom line, each piece of information collected on the application form should tie to the job description and KSAOs.

Reference checks are used for three purposes: to verify information given by job applicants, e.g., employment and educational background data; to uncover information on applicants, e.g., criminal records and driving records; and to collect further information expected to predict success in the job, e.g., appraisal of an applicant's character and personality (Gatewood, Feild, & Barrick, 2008). In regard to the last objective, research suggests that this type of reference check suffers from leniency errors, as few references provide negative remarks about an applicant (Anderson & Cunningham-Snell, 2000). In the end, reference checks serve chiefly as a basis for detection of the unqualified, rather than identification of the qualified (Lilenthal, 1980).

The *selection interview* is considered a practical and efficient way to assess a number of KSAOs through a single device (the interview). Interviews are commonly viewed as structured or unstructured, with structured being the preferred format for selection (Heneman & Judge, 2006). Structured interviews use predetermined questions that are asked in the same order of all applicants, and predetermined scoring methods and decision rules. Using structured interviews improves the accuracy in assessing KSAOs across applicants. Probing questions, not predetermined, can be asked by the interviewer until enough information is obtained about the topic (Gatewood, Feild, & Barrick, 2008). The validity of structured interview as a selection assessment device is good, when

certain practices are adhered to. Recommendations from Gatewood and his colleagues (2008) include:

- Restrict the use of the interview to the most job-relevant KSAOs
- Use multiple questions for each KSAO
- Use job-related questions
- Apply a formal scoring that allows for the evaluation of each KSAO separately
- Train interviewers in the process of conducting the selection interview.

As structured interviews address the third recommendation (use job-related questions), they become what we call "situation-based" or "behavioral event" or "experience-based" interviews. Going forward, we will use the term *situational* interview to refer to this type of structured interview. Gatewood and Field (1994, p. 534) provide an example of a question that could be used in a situational interview to assess the characteristic of persistence: "Have you ever worked on a project in which it was not clear what exactly should be done or how the project should be completed? If so, please tell me about the situation." A useful tool for developing situational questions such as this is the critical incident (CI) technique (Anderson & Cunningham-Snell, 2000; Gatewood, Feild, & Barrick, 2008), and we discuss this technique later in the chapter.

Mental abilities tests represent another type of assessment device for selection. Standardized mental ability tests exist and can be used to assess general mental ability (as Witt and Burke, 2002, did in using the GMA measure) and specific mental abilities. Specific mental abilities assessed by existing tests include general reasoning, conceptual foresight, and logical evaluation (Gatewood, Feild, & Barrick, 2008). *Special abilities tests* are designed to assess distinct abilities, such as object-oriented programming logic, entity-relationship diagramming, etc. Again, if an abilities test is used as an assessment device in selection, the ability it is measuring should be a KSAO documented as necessary to do the job.

The use of *personality assessment inventories* as a selection assessment device has met with some controversy over the years. While earlier uses of personality inventories in selection were viewed by experts as generally ineffective – according to Guion & Gottier (1966), the best that can be said is that in some situations, for some purposes, some personality measures may be helpful – more recent work in personality theory positions personality inventories to more effectively contribute to selection. The "Big Five" theory (Barrick & Mount, 1991) groups personality characteristics into five broad dimensions: extroversion, agreeableness, conscientiousness, emotional stability, openness to experience. The PCI personality inventory used by Witt and Burke (2002) is based on the Big Five theory. The general thinking today is that personality inventories based on core traits (such as the PCI and other instruments based on Big Five theory) rather than surface traits are more effective as selection assessment devices. A further caveat in the usage of personality inventories in selection is to be sure to use only instruments for which reliability and validity have been established and documented, to indicate that the instrument is a reasonably accurate assessment of the personality traits it purports to measure. And of course, the personality trait should tie to the KSAOs required for the job.

Performance measures assess applicants through testing situations that closely resemble actual parts of the job (Gatewood, Feild, and Barrick, 2008). Performance tests (also called work sample tests) ask the applicant to complete a job activity under structured testing conditions, e.g., requiring applicants to write a computer program to solve a given problem. It comes as no surprise that performance tests are good predictors of job performance (e.g., Cascio & Phillips, 1979; Hunter & Hunter, 1984).

Simulation measures typically involve some form of an assessment center (AC). An AC uses a series of devices (e.g., responding to a sequence of emails, giving a presentation, participating in a leaderless group discussion, etc.) and is administered to a group of individuals (typically 12 to 24) over the course of a day or several days (Heneman & Judge, 2006). The devices (called exercises in the AC) are intended to identify patterns of behavior that represent KSAOs being assessed, and the set of exercises is designed so that candidates have several opportunities to demonstrate each of the KSAOs (Gatewood, Feild, & Barrick, 2008). Trained assessors observe and record the candidates' behaviors in the AC and this information is used when the assessors meet as a group to arrive at assessment of each candidate on each of the KSAOs. Examples of KSAOs frequently measured through an AC are decision making, initiative, tolerance for stress, adaptability, and oral communication (Gatewood, Feild, & Barrick, 2008; Heneman & Judge, 2006).

ACs are also used for employee development within organizations and as a method for identifying candidates to promote to management. Research suggests that ACs are useful in predicting promotions and career development, but are less effective in assessing KSAOs in selection (e.g., Bycio, Alvares, & Hahn, 1987; Gaugler, Rosenthal, Thornton, & Bentson, 1987; Hinrichs, 1978; Klimoski & Brickner, 1987; Sackett & Dreher, 1982). This suggests that the KSAOs being assessed across AC exercises may not be stable, or perhaps assessors are influenced by a halo effect that ends up producing general evaluations of candidates rather than true KSAO-level assessments (Anderson & Cunningham-Snell, 2000). Given the questionable effectiveness of ACs in selection assessments and the fact that they are a costly and time-consuming selection device to implement and administer, many organizations prefer to rely on other methods.

Applying Assessment Devices in a Selection Process

To demonstrate the process of identifying assessment devices for KSAOs, this section begins with a basic job description for the position of IT project manager. O*Net (http://online.onetcenter.org/) is an online resource that provides job requirement information for a very large number of jobs. It is a central reference used by HR professionals and is generally considered the starting point for a job analysis. Each job description includes a summary of the objectives and a listing of the primary responsibilities associated with the job. For our purpose of illustrating the application of assessment devices in selection, we use O*Net's summary description of the job of "Information Technology Project Manager":

Job Description: IT Project Manager

Plan, initiate, and manage Information Technology (IT) projects. Lead and guide the work of technical staff. Serve as liaison between business and technical aspects of projects. Plan project stages and assess business implications for each stage. Monitor progress to assure deadlines, standards, and cost targets are met.

Tasks:

- *Develop and manage work breakdown structure (WBS) of Information Technology projects.*
- *Develop or update project plans for Information Technology projects including information such as project objectives, technologies, systems, information specifications, schedules, funding, and staffing.*
- *Manage project execution to ensure adherence to budget, schedule, and scope.*
- *Prepare project status reports by collecting, analyzing, and summarizing information and trends.*

- *Assign duties, responsibilities, and spans of authority to project personnel.*
- *Coordinate recruitment or selection of project personnel.*
- *Develop and manage annual budgets for Information Technology projects.*
- *Develop implementation plans that include analyses such as cost-benefit or return on investment (ROI).*
- *Direct or coordinate activities of project personnel.*
- *Establish and execute a project communication plan.*

From a job description and task list such as this, the HR specialist works with expert job incumbents and managers of expert job incumbents to identify the KSAOs needed to successfully meet the responsibilities. Gatewood and his colleagues (2008) refer to the extrapolation of job description information to necessary human attributes as an "inferential leap" because it relies on the judgment of HR and job experts. Nonetheless, translating the job description and associated responsibilities into KSAOs needed to do the job is a key step in job analysis.

For illustrative purposes, let's focus on two tasks in the IT project manager job description: Develop and manage the WBS; Manage project execution to ensure adherence to budget, schedule, and scope. For the first of these job responsibilities, we identify two KSAOs we deem necessary to successfully performing it: ability to develop a WBS; knowledge of progressive elaboration and how it applies in managing a WBS. For the first KSAO, we could use performance testing as an assessment device to determine the applicant's ability to develop a reasonable WBS from a brief scope statement. For the second KSAO, we could ask the applicant to explain progressive elaboration (a key concept in developing and managing project plans) and how it can affect the WBS, either in a structured interview or as part of the performance test.

To successfully meet the responsibility of managing a project to adhere to budget, schedule, and scope, we believe that one KSAO the individual needs is the ability to work through problems. Fine and Cronshaw (1999, p. 131) provide an example of a situational interview question (with probes) that assesses this characteristic. With slight modifications to make the question applicable to individuals with or without project management experience, this situational interview question is presented below:

Describe a time when you were managing a project or working with others on a team and things were not going so well. What was the situation? What happened in the team? What role did you play and what did you do? How did you feel at the time? What was the final outcome? What did the team produce as a final result?

Fine and Cronshaw (1999, p. 131) also provide an example of a rating scale that could be applied in scoring applicant responses to this question. A score of 5 represents an outstanding response and a score of 1 indicates a poor response. Scores of 2 and 4 are used to indicate a response that falls between the 1-3-5 anchors:

Score = 5

Remained open to inputs of all team members even if the situation was tense and difficult. Freely shared own expertise with all team members, as it was needed, even if not asked. Remained calm with a professional demeanor. Accommodated to working styles and needs of all members even if this was personally inconvenient or uncomfortable.

Score = 3

Attempted to listen to other team members' concerns and input. Shared own expertise if it was asked for. Recognized needs of other group members and tried to work with them if it was

not too difficult to do so. Felt frustrated but kept his or her "cool."

Score = 1

Became frustrated and angry. Withheld information from team members to increase own power, placate others, or avoid having to take responsibility for making a mistake / offending others. Ignored the inputs and suggestions of others or told them to keep their ideas to themselves. Expected others to work strictly to his or her own style and needs.

This situational measure of an applicant's ability to work through problems is an example of the good things that can come out of critical incident (CI) studies. We next turn our attention to the CI technique, looking at how CI studies are conducted and how the outputs of CI are used in IT HR management.

CRITICAL INCIDENT TECHNIQUE

The sections that follow review the basic steps in conducting a CI study and continue our illustration by utilizing CI data collected from IT project managers. We apply the CI results to demonstrate how situational interview questions can be developed from CI data, and also how the CI data contribute to other IT HR activities such as job analysis and training.

Conducting a Critical Incident Study

The general steps involved in conducting a CI study are (expanded from Lees & Cordery, 2000):

1. Determine the general aim of the study, including the job that is to be examined
2. Specify and plan how the incidents will be collected, including who will serve as the sources of information and the method of

collection (e.g., personal interview, survey instrument, focus group)

3. Collect the data (i.e., execute the plan established in Step 2)

4. Analyze the critical incidents data, including:
   a. Separate incidents into examples of effective vs. ineffective behaviors (both are useful as critical incidents)
   b. Assess the *criticality* (importance to the job) and *generalizability* (extent to which other job experts agree on the effectiveness or ineffectiveness of the behavior) of each incident

5. Use the critical incidents that emerge from the Step 4 analysis as appropriate in selection, job analysis, training, etc.

In a CI study undertaken to collect critical incidents in the job of IT project manager, three IT project manager job incumbents were identified to serve as sources of the incidents. Our job incumbents were from three different companies and each had a minimum of four years experience in the job of IT project manager. An online questionnaire containing the following set of questions was used to collect incident data:

1. Please tell us about a time when an IT project manager encountered a critical work situation. Please describe the situation in as much detail as you can.

2. What specific behavior was exhibited (or what action was taken) by the project manager in this situation?

3. What was the end result of this incident?

4. Do you think the project manager handled the situation in the best way possible, or do you think the project manager should have done something else? (If you're thinking of something specific the project manager should have done, please tell us your thoughts.)

The collected CIs were reviewed by two outside IT project managers (from companies other than those represented in the CI data) for criticality and generalizability. To do this, we provided these two project managers with the CIs and each CI was followed by this set of questions:

1. Is this a critical situation for a project manager? Why or why not?

2. The action taken by the project manager is: (Please check one)
   ____ Clearly an effective action in this situation
   ____ Probably an effective action in this situation
   ____ Probably an ineffective action in this situation
   ____ Clearly an ineffective action in this situation.

3. Please tell us a bit about why you view the action as effective or ineffective. Also, if you view the action to be ineffective, can you describe for us a different action you would suggest a project manager take in this situation?

Three CIs emerged from the analysis as critical and generalizable. Two were determined to be examples of effective behavior of an IT project manager in an important (critical) situation. An additional CI was identified as an example of ineffective behavior of an IT project manager in a critical situation. These three CIs follow.

CRITICAL INCIDENT A

Situation

In 2004, there was a project to install Windows XP on all PCs in "field" locations (about 800 PCs in 45 offices spread throughout the country). The team evaluated two options: do it with our own staff or outsource it. Based upon several factors, including the time it would take to perform the work and the cost of travel, the team recommended that the work be outsourced. Assuming that the estimates from the project team were realistic, the vendor submitted a bid and it was accepted. However, shortly into the project, the vendor and the team both realized that the work was significantly underestimated, thus resulting in a revised cost from the vendor of 20% more than originally bid.

Behavior Exhibited

First the project manager approached his sponsor and explained the situation, stated the facts, and took full responsibility for the mistake in estimating. (The sponsor was not happy about going over budget but was appreciative of the straight-forward communication and candor.)

Secondly, the project manager communicated the situation to the project team. Unfortunately, the team did not seem to take the information seriously, commenting about the extra expenditure that "It's just a drop in the bucket", "That's nothing compared to what other projects overspend", and "They'll still get the work done", etc.

Thirdly, after receiving the comments above, the project manager assembled the team together and explained several things:

1. Every little bit DOES matter; the extra cost was equated to the value of the company bonus and then they realized it was money out of their own pockets!
2. The importance of good estimating because the sponsors are making decisions based on the data we give them; in this case, had our estimates been more realistic, the sponsor may have decided to do the work ourselves instead of outsourcing
3. Not sit back and accept things as they are, but rather, what can we do to streamline the vendor's work so they can get done faster and thus lower the cost of the remaining project?

Result

The team had a better appreciation and understanding of the financial impact of their work on a project. They also stepped it up a bit and came up with improvements to the process that helped the remainder of the project proceed more efficiently.

CRITICAL INCIDENT B

Situation

A project manager was dismissed from our company due to poor performance and an existing project manager took over his remaining work. The main project taken over was completely out of control: no project plan, no timeline, no communication plan, very little documentation and what did exist was not baselined. The assigned resources were left to their own devices and were not communicating with each other in regard to code development and testing. The assigned personnel were assured by their previous Project Manager that "everything is ok".

Behavior Exhibited

Specific behavior exhibited by the assigned personnel was a surprise. The new Project Manager reined in all personnel and instituted a plan of action to complete all outstanding documentation and process requirements. Some assigned resources pushed back or were unresponsive, as the Project Manager attempted to get the project back on track. Specifically some team members said they were assured that "everything is ok" and they did not feel that the previous Project Manager's mistakes should mean make-up work for them. The new Project Manager stood firm to the company SDLC process and used different techniques to hold each resource accountable for their specific deliverables. The new Project

Manager used email, instant messenger, face to face meetings, phone calls and unfortunately escalations to complete all deliverables.

Result

The project deliverables were completed per SDLC process guidelines after 1 month of interaction with assigned team members.

CRITICAL INCIDENT C

Situation

One situation I viewed was a project manager who had a specific personality problem with one of the members on his project team. The PM allowed that conflict to affect how that member was utilized on the team and eventually it affected the overall effectiveness of the team and adversely affected the project itself.

Behavior Exhibited

Because of the personality problems the PM had with the team member, the PM basically alienated the team member from many aspects of the project. The PM refused to talk to the team member directly. Whenever he needed a status update from the project member he would have another member of the team go check on the status for him and report back. The PM would even hold meetings related to the project with the project team but would exclude this team member.

Result

The team member who was being alienated by the PM eventually resigned from the project and took another position. However, by that time, the damage to the project had already been done. The project fell behind schedule and the quality of the work being done on the project was not satisfactory. In fact, the project eventually failed.

In the sections that follow, we apply these CIs to selection for IT project managers, and then to other components of IT HR management.

APPLYING CRITICAL INCIDENTS TO SELECTION

The job description for IT project manager includes these stated responsibilities: Serve as liaison between business and technical aspects of projects; Lead and guide the work of technical staff. We identify two KSAOs we believe are important in performing these duties. The ability to *communicate in a timely and constructive manner with stakeholders and team members* is necessary to meet both responsibilities. Furthermore, to lead and guide staff, the effective IT project manager will possess a characteristic of *taking responsibility*.

The information provided in Critical Incident A makes it a good candidate for development of a situational interview question that can provide an assessment of these two KSAOs. Below is a situational question we developed from Critical Incident A; each part of the two-part question is followed by a basic rating system that could be used to assess applicants on each of the two KSAOs.

Part 1

You are project manager for a project. One of the first things that needs to be determined is whether your team should do "phase 1" of the project in-house, or whether it should be outsourced to your company's preferred vendor. Your team gathers requirements and documents the specifications for the work. You compare estimates of what it would take to complete the work in-house to a bid you receive from your company's vendor. You submit this information to your project sponsor, and she decides this phase of the work will be outsourced to the vendor.

Shortly into the project, the vendor and the team realize that "phase 1" of the project was seriously under-specified. The vendor's revised cost is now 20% more than the original bid. At this point, only you and the project team are aware of the poor specs and the effect they are likely to have on the project cost.

What do you do?

Assessment for KSAO:

Communicate in a timely and constructive manner with stakeholders and team members.

GOOD response:

Go directly to the project sponsor and tell her what has happened and what the present situation is.

POOR response:

Delay in taking the information forward in a timely manner; any effort to try to hide the bad news.

Assessment for KSAO:

Taking responsibility.

GOOD response:

Take full responsibility for the error in documenting requirements.

POOR response:

Blame the error on team members.

Part 2

You call a meeting of the project team to discuss the mistake that was made in documenting require-
ments and the financial impact this is having on the project and the company. The team does not seem to be very concerned about it. You hear comments of "this is just a drop in the bucket" and "this is nothing compared to what other projects overspend."

How do you respond?

Assessment for KSAO:

Communicate in a timely and constructive manner with stakeholders and team members.

GOOD response:

An immediate response in the meeting that uses specific, action-based reasoning to convey the importance of the matter.

POOR response:

No response or a response with any of these characteristics:
  ○ Lacks specific, action-based reasoning
  ○ Is based only on emotional appeal
  ○ Takes an angry or argumentative tone.

Assessment for KSAO:

Taking responsibility.

GOOD response:

Something that shows effort to bring the team members on board with the importance of the matter, i.e., seeing this as a project manager's responsibility. For example, might convey one or more of the following:
  ○ Getting the specs right matters – people are making important decisions based on the belief that our specs and estimates are as accurate

as they can be. If we had been working from accurate specs, the project sponsor might have decided the work should be done in-house instead of outsourced.

○ Every little bit DOES matter – what do you think your annual bonus is based on? Wasting money like this means a lower profit – which also means a lower bonus for you.

○ What can we do now? Aren't there things we can do to streamline the vendor's work so they can get it done faster? If we can help them get it done faster, we can still lower this cost overrun. Let's show them that we're doing what we can to make up for our mistake.

POOR response:

A response that ignores the responsibility to bring team members on board with the importance of the matter.

Next, we focus on two other responsibilities mentioned in the job description and task list: Monitor progress to assure deadlines, standards, and cost targets are met; Manage project execution to ensure adherence to budget, schedule, and scope. These elements of the IT project manager job corroborate the importance of the ability to *communicate in a timely and constructive manner with stakeholders and team members*, while also elucidating the need for *knowledge of established standards and the importance of performing work according to standards*.

The situation in Critical Incident B lends itself to construction of a situational interview question to assess these two KSAOs. Below is a situational interview question we developed from Critical Incident B, followed by a basic rating system that could be used. Because the information collected in Critical Incident B provided less detail about the action taken by the project manager, we presented the situational interview question that we developed to additional project managers asking what they would consider to be a good response and bad response to the situation. We combined their input with the information provided by the originator of Critical Incident B to arrive at the following sample rating system for the situational interview question.

A project manager has been dismissed for poor performance and you are assigned to take over the project she was leading. You find the project is pretty much out of control – no project plan, no timeline, no communication plan, and the work that has been done was not performed according to the company's established standards of practice.

When you meet with the team and explain what needs to be done to establish a plan for the project and to conform to company standards, their reaction surprises you. Some are non-responsive while others push back saying the previous project manager had assured them that "everything is okay" and that they shouldn't have to do more work to make up for mistakes the previous project manager might have made.

What do you do?

Assessment for KSAO:

Communicate in a timely and constructive manner with stakeholders and team members

GOOD response:

Assure the team that they are not being reprimanded for what has happened to this point. But going forward, things must be done differently. Also good to convey a "we're in this together" message, like:

○ You need their assistance in assessing the current state of things and

estimating the remaining work, so you can work to negotiate achievable deadlines with management and stakeholders.
- Together, you will get this project turned around.

POOR response:

Would involve any of:
- Criticizing the former project manager
- Focusing blame on the team ("you should have known better")
- Claiming you are here to save their jobs or "save the day"

Assessment for KSAO:

Knowledge of established standards and the importance of performing work according to standards

GOOD response:

We all – project manager and the project team – are expected to adhere to the company standards. It's part of our job. Acknowledge this means there will be some rework. May also indicate intention to follow up with each team member, making sure each understands assigned tasks and the standards that apply to them.

POOR response:

A response that involves cutting corners on company standards.

This set of examples incorporates two important principles previously mentioned in regard to the design of a selection process, and of structured interviews in particular. One, KSAOs are assessed individually. If an assessment device measures more than one KSAO, such as the situational interview questions developed in this section, separate assessment and scoring systems are formulated for each KSAO. Second, multiple measures of a key KSAO are included in the selection process. Here, the KSAO of "Communicate in a timely and constructive manner with stakeholders and team members" was assessed through two different situational questions.

Applying Critical Incidents to Other IT HR Components

Critical incidents also provide insights for job analysis and training. Consider, for example, Critical Incident C that was viewed as an ineffective behavior exhibited by an IT project manager in a critical situation. While this incident does tie somewhat to tasks identified in the IT project manager job description (Lead and guide the work of technical staff; Direct or coordinate activities of project personnel), it noticeably goes beyond the documented job description. This has implications for both job analysis and training.

The job description that we are working from does not make clear that interpersonal interactions are an important element of the IT project manager job. The fact that our CI study brought this personality conflict situation to light as a critical incident for IT project managers suggests that the job description may need to be revised to indicate the need for interpersonal skills, if they are indeed important in successfully performing the IT project manager job.

What is more, the fact that Critical Incident C reported an ineffective behavior in response to this critical situation elucidates a potential training need. The CI suggests that IT project managers may need more effective training in communication, conflict management, and general interpersonal skills, at least in the organization of the participant who reported this incident.

Finally, as Joseph and his colleagues (2010, p. 153) noted, the documentation of job-based situations accompanied by preferred responses can serve as a "corporate library of best practices." As such, documented situations and preferred responses can contribute directly to the training of IT professionals in an organization, and to the socialization of newly-hired IT professionals into the culture of the organization.

FUTURE RESEARCH DIRECTIONS

We encourage IT HR researchers to uncover or develop selection assessment devices that prove to be valid measures of KSAOs commonly associated with various IT jobs. Assessments of KSAOs may take the form of a mental or special abilities test, a measure of a particular personality characteristic, a detailed work performance test, or a set of situational interview questions. The goal is to bring forward valid measures of KSAOs that are clearly linked to performance of a particular IT job.

Structured interviews will continue to be an integral component of the selection process. The key, then, is to improve the questions used to assess IT job candidates during selection to accurately identify individuals who will demonstrate high performance levels over time. As suggested by Anderson & Cunningham-Snell (2000), organizations need to maximize the true-positive selections (e.g., correctly identifying candidates who become effective performers) and minimize false-negative selections (e.g., incorrectly eliminating candidates who would have become effective performers). Several avenues for future research offer promising opportunities to understand the drivers of selection more deeply and improve selection outcomes.

The first is a broad-based CI study to focus on primary IT jobs that most all companies have – project manager, systems analyst, testing specialist, etc. While differences will exist, the primary responsibilities of these standard jobs are likely to have a good deal of consistency. By compar-

ing the job descriptions for the focal jobs across many organizations, it is possible to identify a common set of key KSAOs. In-depth CI analysis would be applied to develop situational interview questions to assess these KSAOs, resulting in a robust set of questions with behaviorally anchored rating scales that would support more effective assessment of IT applicants during the selection process. Joseph and his colleagues (2010) provide a starting point with their SSIT instrument that assesses some broad managerial skills found to be more manifest in experienced IT professionals than novices.

A closely related opportunity would be to focus explicitly on KSAOs that are critical to performance in team-based environments. The nature of jobs is changing from individually focused responsibilities to work performed interactively by groups and teams (Gatewood, Feild, & Barrick, 2008). This is particularly true in IT where the focus has shifted from work organized on highly specialized technical skills of the individual, to team-based, project work integrating a variety of technical, process and business requirements. The IT HR selection process would benefit by developing a deeper understanding of which team-based KSAOs are most relevant to different IT jobs, and how the importance of KSAOs may shift from technical to team-based depending on the nature of the role and the evolution of projects through the full life-cycle. Stevens and Campion (1994, 1999) have provided a started point for assessing team-based KSAOs through their development of a generic selection test focused on team-based work. The shift to team-based work structures in IT may be complicated by the widespread adoption of highly distributed teams often with international membership. Jobs that involve working in distributed, global teams may require new or different KSAOs and these may need to be assessed in selection, requiring the identification or development of appropriate assessment devices.

The nature of the technical elements of many IT jobs has also changed. Many organizations rely on package software, cloud services and outsourcing rather than internally developed software applications. Many IT jobs may not involve the same technical work task focus traditionally associated with those jobs. Instead of creating a database or writing a software program, the objective of IT in many organizations has shifted towards configuring and integrating packaged software and web services. The key KSAOs, and thus selection assessment devices, may change based on the evolving nature of IT jobs. IT HR researchers could help to refine selection methods to capture these differences.

Ideally, longitudinal study would be conducted that has an organization using technical-work and team-based situational questions and tracking performance of the individuals hired to validate whether the CI-generated items predicted performance. This assessment would permit the refinement of selection questions most important to specific jobs. It would also provide an opportunity to explore relationships between selection and aspects of the HR management process that influence an individual's long-term performance and satisfaction (e.g., performance measurement, training and development, retention strategies, and compensations and benefits). We encourage studies that take into consideration the linkages among the HR components as reflected in our model (Figure 1).

CI analysis is, by definition, a deep exploration of a particular event (e.g., the critical incident) within a specific setting. Researchers in IT are starting to adopt what is called the critical realist approach to conducting research that focuses on identifying specific causes to explain how and why particular events happen (see Mingers 2004, Wynn & Williams 2008). CI analysis is entirely compatible with the critical realist approach. By adopting this approach, researchers could move beyond the linking of behaviors to outcomes to explore why specific KSAOs are important in

particular CIs and to articulate how the particular behaviors lead to the outcomes observed. This offers the potential to bring in contextual cues from the organizational setting that influence the focal behaviors, clarify the specific behaviors that generated the incident outcomes, and permit the creation of more fine-grained selection questions to improve selection decisions.

LESSONS LEARNED

In closing, IT organizations are urged to apply the recommendations outlined in the chapter to conduct a reality check regarding their selection processes. For IT jobs in your organization:

* Are key KSAOs identified and documented?
* Are the KSAOs linked to tasks, duties, and responsibilities noted in the job description?
* Does your selection process target the key KSAOs needed to do the job?
* Are the job description and KSAOs in need of updating – might it be time to revisit them for certain jobs?
* Is there evidence that the selection devices being used are effectively assessing the targeted KSAOs?
* Are more effective assessment devices needed for certain KSAOs?
* Is there evidence that the KSAOs included in the selection process are predictive of job performance?

These are important questions for IT and IT HR managers. Luftman and Kempaiah (2007) identified attracting, developing and retaining IT staff as the second most pressing issue for CIOs, and described an array of skills – "soft" people and business skills as well as "hard" technical ones – that companies need from entry- and mid-level IT employees. Witt and Burke (2002) maintain that in times of pressure the selection of IT employees can fall to "ineffective methods such as self-reported histories of IT experience or applicant responses in hurried unstructured interviews just to get someone to fill the vacancy" (p. 38). While it is understandable that such practices would be adopted in times of a labor market shortage, such practices should not remain in place when the shortage recedes.

The harsh reality is that ineffective or incomplete selection processes can have severe consequences for organizations, as noted by Nash and King (1997) who found that the lack of proper screening, such as skipping background checks, could needlessly expose companies to serious threats from illegal and unethical actions by new employees. And just as importantly, weaknesses in selection will deny an organization a most critical resource – new employees with a high likelihood of performing effectively on the job. Together, the benefits that can be derived from effective selection and the potentially severe consequences that can result from ineffective selection provide a clear indication of the need for IT HR professionals and researchers to focus attention on this core HR management process.

REFERENCES

Agarwal, R., & Ferratt, T. W. (1999). *Coping with labor scarcity in Information Technology: Strategies and practices for effective recruitment and retention.* Cincinnati, OH: Pinnaflex Press.

Agarwal, R., & Ferratt, T. W. (2001). Crafting an HR strategy to meet the need for IT workers. *Communications of the ACM, 44,* 58–64. doi:10.1145/379300.379314

Anderson, N. & Cunningham-Snell. (2000). Personnel selection. In N. Chmiel (Ed.), *Introduction to work and organizational psychology: A European perspective.* Malden, MA: Blackwell Publishers.

Ang, S., & Slaughter, S. (2004). Turnover of Information Technology professionals: The effects of internal labor market strategies. *The Data Base for Advances in Information Systems, 35,* 11–27.

Barrick, M. R., & Mount, M. K. (1991). The big five personality dimensions and job performance: A meta-analysis. *Personnel Psychology, 44,* 1–26. doi:10.1111/j.1744-6570.1991.tb00688.x

Bycio, P., Alvares, K. M., & Hahn, J. (1987). Situational specificity in assessment center ratings: A confirmatory factor analysis. *The Journal of Applied Psychology, 72,* 463–474. doi:10.1037/0021-9010.72.3.463

Cascio, W., & Phillips, N. (1979). Performance testing: A rose among thorns? *Personnel Psychology, 32,* 751–766. doi:10.1111/j.1744-6570.1979.tb02345.x

Cheney, P. H., Hale, D. P., & Kasper, G. M. (1990). Knowledge, skills and abilities of Information Systems professionals: Past, present, and future. *Information & Management, 19,* 237–248. doi:10.1016/0378-7206(90)90033-E

Collins, J. C. (2001). *Good to great: Why some companies make the leap... and others don't.* New York: Harper Collins.

Dalton, D. R., Todor, W. D., & Krackhardt, D. M. (1982). Turnover overstated: The functional taxonomy. *Academy of Management Review, 7,* 117–123. doi:10.2307/257256

Ferratt, T. W., Agarwal, R., Brown, C. V., & Moore, J. E. (2005). IT human resource management configurations and IT turnover: Theoretical synthesis and empirical analysis. *Information Systems Research, 16,* 237–255. doi:10.1287/isre.1050.0057

Fine, S. A., & Cronshaw, S. F. (1999). *Functional job analysis: A foundation for human resources management.* Mahwah, NJ: Lawrence Erlbaum Associates.

Gatewood, R. D., & Feild, H. S. (1994). *Human resource selection* (3rd ed.). Fort Worth, TX: Dryden Press.

Gatewood, R. D., Feild, H. S., & Barrick, M. R. (2008). *Human resource selection* (6th ed.). Mason, OH: Thomson South-Western.

Gaugler, B. B., Rosenthal, D. B., Thornton, G. C. III, & Bentson, C. (1987). Meta-analysis of assessment center validity. *The Journal of Applied Psychology*, *72*, 493–511. doi:10.1037/0021-9010.72.3.493

Guion, R. M., & Gottier, R. F. (1966). Validity of personality measures in personnel selection. *Personnel Psychology*, *18*, 135–164. doi:10.1111/j.1744-6570.1965.tb00273.x

Heneman, H. G. III, & Judge, T. A. (2006). *Staffing organizations*. Middleton, WI: McGraw-Hill.

Hinrichs, J. R. (1978). An eight-year follow-up of a management assessment center. *The Journal of Applied Psychology*, *63*, 596–601. doi:10.1037/0021-9010.63.5.596

Hunter, J. E., & Hunter, R. F. (1984). Validity and utility of alternative predictors of job performance. *Psychological Bulletin*, *96*(1), 72–98. doi:10.1037/0033-2909.96.1.72

Igbaria, M., & Baroudi, J. J. (1995). The impact of job performance evaluations on career advancement prospects: An examination of gender differences in the IS workplace. *Management Information Systems Quarterly*, *19*, 107–123. doi:10.2307/249713

Joseph, D., Ang, S., Chang, R. H. L., & Slaughter, S. A. (2010). Practical intelligence in IT: Assessing soft skill of IT professionals. *Communications of the ACM*, *53*, 149–154. doi:10.1145/1646353.1646391

Joseph, D., Ng, K., Koh, C., & Ang, S. (2007). Turnover of Information Technology professionals: A narrative review, meta-analytic structural equation modeling, and model development. *Management Information Systems Quarterly*, *31*, 547–577.

Klimoski, R. J., & Brickner, M. (1987). Why do assessment centers work? The puzzle of assessment center validity. *Personnel Psychology*, *40*, 243–260. doi:10.1111/j.1744-6570.1987.tb00603.x

Koh, S., Lee, S., Yen, D. C., & Havelka, D. (2004). The relationship between Information Technology professionals' skill requirements and career stage in the e-commerce era: An empirical study. *Journal of Global Information Management*, *12*, 68–82. doi:10.4018/jgim.2004010105

Kynphausen-Aufseß, D., & Vormann, C. (2009). Personnel selection criteria in IT ventures: A policy-capturing analysis. *Zeitschrift für Betriebswirtschaft*, *79*, 213–234. doi:10.1007/s11573-008-0207-8

Lee, P. C. B. (2002). Career goals and career management strategy among Information Technology professionals. *Career Development International*, *7*, 6–13. doi:10.1108/13620430210414829

Lees, C. D., & Cordery, J. L. (2000). Job analysis and design. In Chmiel, N. (Ed.), *Introduction to work and organizational psychology: A European perspective*. Malden, MA: Blackwell Publishers.

Lilenthal, R. A. (1980). *The use of reference checks for selection*. Washington, DC: U.S. Office of Personnel Management.

Luftman, J., & Kempaiah, R. M. (2007). The IS organization of the future: The IT talent challenge. *Information Systems Management*, *24*, 129–138. doi:10.1080/10580530701221023

Major, D. A., Davis, D. D., Germano, L. M., Fletcher, T. D., Sanchez-Hucles, J., & Mann, J. (2007). Managing human resources in Information Technology: Best practices of high performing supervisors. *Human Resource Management, 46*, 411–427. doi:10.1002/hrm.20171

Mingers, J. (2004). Realizing Information Systems: Critical realism as an underpinning philosophy for Information Systems. *Information and Organization, 14*, 87–103. doi:10.1016/j.infoandorg.2003.06.001

Mithas, S., & Krishnan, M. S. (2008). Human capital and institutional effects in the compensation of Information Technology professionals in the United States. *Management Science, 54*, 415–428. doi:10.1287/mnsc.1070.0778

Nash, K. S., & King, J. (1997). IS employers skip background checks. *Computerworld, 31*, 1.

Rynes, S. L., & Barber, A. E. (1990). Applicant attraction strategies: An organizational perspective. *Academy of Management Review, 15*, 286–310. doi:10.2307/258158

Sackett, P. R., & Dreher, G. F. (1982). Constructs and assessment center dimensions: Some troubling empirical findings. *The Journal of Applied Psychology, 67*, 401–410. doi:10.1037/0021-9010.67.4.401

Slaughter, S. A., Ang, S., & Boh, W. F. (2007). Firm-specific human capital and compensation–organizational tenure profiles: An archival analysis of salary data for IT professionals. *Human Resource Management, 46*, 373–394. doi:10.1002/hrm.20169

Stevens, M. J., & Campion, M. A. (1994). The knowledge, skill, and ability requirements for teamwork: Implications for human resource management. *Journal of Management, 20*, 503–530.

Stevens, M. J., & Campion, M. A. (1999). Staffing work teams: Development and validation of a selection test for teamwork settings. *Journal of Management, 25*, 207–228. doi:10.1016/S0149-2063(99)80010-5

Witt, L. A., & Burke, L. A. (2002). Selecting high-performing Information Technology professionals. *Journal of End User Computing, 14*, 37–50. doi:10.4018/joeuc.2002100103

Wynn, D.E. & Williams, C.K. (2008). Critical realism-based explanatory case study research in Information Systems. *ICIS 2008 Proceedings*, Paper 2

Chapter 6
IT Hiring Criteria vs. Valued IT Competencies

Jo Ann Starkweather
Northeastern State University, USA

Deborah H. Stevenson
Northeastern State University, USA

ABSTRACT

Since a significant proportion of IT hiring includes the use of external IT recruiters, opportunities for differing perceptions of the ideal job candidate are introduced. An examination of the steps in the IT recruitment and hiring process suggests many occasions where IT professionals need to take a more active role. The ubiquity of technology throughout a firm ensures that IT professionals interact with a variety of stakeholders in the organization. Pursuant to this, the chapter addresses the relationship between IT recruiters and IT executives in the hiring process from both a conceptual and empirical standpoint.

Following a discussion of best practices for IT recruitment and hiring, an empirical analysis of recent IT recruiter and IT executive data are presented. Solutions to the recruiter/executive gaps are discussed along with the identification of areas for further scholarly research.

INTRODUCTION

Hiring for the IT milieu is both art and science. The number and breadth of competencies desired n the successful applicant necessitate a thorough screening process. Thus, it's incumbent upon the HR professional to identify job candidates with the requisite technical skills in addition to the right mix of soft skills, personality, and attitude. In many instances, the successful IT professional must resemble a chameleon—able to change at a moment's notice. The change might be from discussing IT's role in the company's strategic plan with the CIO, to going over web design options with a company technician, to meeting with an end user, unhappy with the new software installation.

DOI: 10.4018/978-1-60960-535-3.ch006

Hiring a person who can successfully perform all of these roles is a daunting task, yet it's one that an increasing number of HR professionals must face. The material that follows will provide an overview of IT hiring, including a discussion of the hiring process and the screening venue (in-house HR professional versus IT recruiter). After a discussion of the special considerations involved in IT hiring, the results of current scholarship assessing the disparity in valuation of IT hiring criteria used by IT recruiters and the valuation of those criteria by IT executives is presented.

Overview of IT Hiring

The screening/hiring process must be as thorough as the IT environment is complex. Thus the overview will begin with an emphasis on the necessity of performing a job analysis, and will emphasize the utility of the data gathered in this initial phase as input throughout the remainder of the process. An enumeration of the steps in the recruiting process, including new media options available, the pros and cons of using internal versus external recruiters, as well as internal versus external job candidates will be covered. Finally, the import of metrics in the screening stage is discussed.

Anyone who thinks that writing an IT job description is easy, has probably never had to write one. Irrespective of where that position might fall on the IT food chain, it takes a variety of data to craft a description that accurately depicts the knowledge, skills, and abilities needed to facilitate an incumbent's success. If the person writing the job description has not previously held that job or is not intimately familiar with every nuance, then a job analysis must be considered. Despite the availability of standardized job descriptions from the U.S. Dept. of Labor (DOT, Dictionary of Occupational Titles), the operative term "standardized" suggests why conducting an onsite job analysis is preferable. A job analysis (collecting data about the jobs performed in an organization) is conducted to determine the knowledge, skills,

and abilities (KSA's) necessary for successful job performance.

- Knowledge – Specific technical knowledge the incumbent must possess
- Skill – Adequate performance on tasks requiring tools, machinery, and equipment
- Ability – Physical and mental capacities needed

Based on the KSA profile, it should be apparent that there are several types of information that must be collected. Along with an enumeration of any and all types of tools, machinery, and equipment, the job analysis must specify the human skills needed to competently utilize tangible work aids. Depending on the position within IT, the relevant equipment list could be quite lengthy considering the innumerable hardware, software, and network physical layer configurations that might be involved. Finally, the requisite levels and types of knowledge must be stated. Specific to IT, this may include the specification of particular degrees, certifications, training, or experience. Equally important, though, is the enumeration of what might be called, personal characteristics-- such qualities as the ability to communicate at multiple levels, the ability to escalate, flexibility, attitude, and decision-making abilities.

In addition to collecting many different types of data, it is necessary to have multiple measures of each type, i.e., data from several sources (either several persons currently employed in this job or input from multiple persons familiar with the requirements of the job). Information based on just one person's perception runs the risk of being anecdotal and unique. The probability that a single observation or data source would contain some skewness is high and a subsequent job description or screening metric based on these data would be similarly biased. Thus the importance of multiple measures is emphasized.

A final consideration while planning a job analysis rests on how granular the data collection needs to be. When in doubt, err on the more detailed side. If we view the continuum of IT workers using explicit and tacit knowledge as the respective anchors, technical IT staff will be on the left most side of the continuum representing explicit knowledge and anchoring the right side are CIO's/Directors of IT representing the tacit knowledge side of the continuum. Obviously the particulars will be radically different for technicians versus executives; moving from an enumeration of programming languages for the technician to an enumeration of the committees that report to the CIO. After all, this is hiring specifically relevant to IT. Even if the position candidate does not have direct physical layer responsibilities, they will likely need to interface with those folks. Similarly, knowledge of the breadth of interaction with various stakeholders in the business process is essential to hiring the right person as it speaks directly to the need for advanced communication skills. Using the following four levels of analysis as a yardstick, data should be collected at least at the duty level and in many instances at the task level.

- Job – Positions similar enough to be covered by the same job analysis
- Position – All the duties required of one person performing a job
- Duty – Several tasks performed to complete a required work activity
- Task – An identifiable unit of work activity (Anthony et al., 1999)

Once a decision has been made regarding the necessary level of granularity, methods for collecting the data become more apparent. Numerous reliable and valid job analysis instruments are readily available for use. They range from very broad in their potential application (e.g., Common-Metric Questionnaire, Harvey, et al. 1988) to more narrowly define (e.g., Management Position Description Questionnaire, Tornow and Pinto, 1976). While there is no efficiency in reinventing the wheel, it's advisable to resist the temptation

to rely *solely* on prefab questionnaires or other quick, but limited data collection methodologies. Although some aspects of the job analysis may be amenable to an objective survey, many important abilities may be overlooked using this format. Complimentary to survey data, managerial or expert perceptions of critical competencies offer experiential insights on the knowledge, skills and abilities necessary for successful job performance.

This approach focuses on the things a worker does (incidents) that distinguish that person as an effective or ineffective employee. To be considered critical, an incident must occur in a situation in which the intent of the act seems clear to the observer and its consequences leave little doubt about the effects. The data collection process provides descriptions of effective and ineffective job behaviors in critical situations. In addition, they describe behaviors that reflect outstanding versus poor performance on the job. These incident descriptions are examined and put into job dimension categories that characterize particular facets of job performance. (Anthony et al., 1999, p. 216)

Results from the many sources of job analysis data form the basis for both the job description that will be written and a needs assessment test that may be used to screen job candidates.

Having compiled and categorized the requisite knowledge, skills, and abilities indicated by a thorough job analysis, the next step is deciding whether to recruit from within the organization or seek an external candidate. Realistically, the only reason to recruit outside the firm is when the knowledge, skills, and abilities are unavailable (and unattainable) in-house. More specifically, the advantages to in-house recruiting include reduced recruiting and training costs, an intimate knowledge of the incumbent's KSA's and the incumbent's familiarity with the organizational culture. Perhaps more immediately important than familiarity with organizational culture, an in-house IT candidate would also be familiar with aspects of the firm's network, hardware, software applications, and so forth. One further advantage, often overlooked, is the positive impact of internal promotions on overall employee morale. If the firm has historically made professional development of its employees a priority, promoting from within simply takes advantage of that company investment. The primary disadvantage to internal recruiting would have to be the risk of employees' perceptions of the recruitment process as unfair, thus resulting in negative feelings including decreased morale. The process of in-house recruiting is straightforward with opportunities for job postings in organizational print media and all manner of electronic forums via the organizational network/intranet. In addition, candidates may emerge as a result of manager nomination, KSA database searches, or succession planning (Fyock, 2009). Finally, every firm can count on the 'grapevine,' as yet another channel, albeit an informal one, for disseminating news of an open position in the company.

Although clear advantages have been established for in-house recruiting, frequently it is necessary to seek external job candidates. In this situation the traditional print media (newspapers, professional publications) remain available. In addition several digital options may be used to expand the potential audience and eventual candidate pool. Considering that the audience profile is first and foremost an IT audience, it's fair to assume that employers and potential employees are technologically savvy—that they are likely early adherents of the latest technology options in the recruiting/hiring milieu. Thus, along with the monoliths of digital hiring (e.g. Monster.com, CareerBuilder.com, Jobs.com) numerous smaller, specialized venues exist for employers/recruiters to post jobs and candidates to post resumes. Although one might fear being inundated with resumes of unqualified or barely qualified individuals, quite the opposite actually occurs. The ability to elaborate on desired candidate qualifications and all manner of hardware and software experience required allows job seekers to screen them out. The details provided in an online ad facilitate a better understanding of the desired knowledge, skills, and abilities, thus *encouraging* those incumbents most qualified, and realistically *discouraging* those least qualified. Ideally, information for a job ad would be derived from a proprietary job analysis, however other options exist. For example, updated lists of online job ad resources are available through the Riley Guide (http://www.dbm.com/jobbguide/) or Job Hunt (http://www.job-hunt.org/).

Online ads have distinct advantages that include the opportunity to expound on the job, the candidate requirements, and the firm at a significantly lower cost than traditional print ads. Metrics comparing the cost of print ads (newspaper) to online ad costs suggest a 10-1 ratio (Schreyer & McCarter, 1998).

Furthermore, online ads are not limited by column-inch constraints, thereby allowing the company to elaborate on both necessary and desired candidate qualifications, as well as nuances particular to the specific position opening. Similarly, the ability to extol the virtues and visions of the company and the community may be uniquely enhanced with an online advertisement. The latter two areas of interest are particularly important when the potential candidates are not geographically proximate to the company. Specifically, consider a link to the company web site where interested candidates can better acquaint themselves with the organization's vision, mission and goals; or a link to the local Chamber of Commerce where an interested candidate can peruse a wealth of data on local amenities, infrastructure, real estate, and so forth. One can only imagine the impact of an online ad that provides a link to a virtual tour of the corporate headquarters, a local park, or college campus in the firm's community. Finally, if you're convinced that the best candidates are 'happily employed elsewhere,' consider the services of a company like Resume Robot (http://www.resumerobot.com/). This company uses the latest search technologies available to ferret out the 'passive' candidate. This is accomplished by selective searches of web page resumes, curriculum vitae, professional networking sites, virtual communities, and so forth. This is the epitome of the IT environment, it's what IT candidates are familiar with, what they expect, and what successful IT hiring is all about.

Having broached the topic of online recruiting, one of the latest digital recruiting trends is the use of mobile platforms. With the ubiquity of mobile devices approaching 90% of the U.S. population, it was just a matter of time before companies noted the trend from phone calls to SMS (short messaging service), to fully functional recruiting and job search applications via mobile devices. To launch a mobile recruiting campaign using SMS a company provides an avenue for user opt-in by supplying a short text code and number, for example, text "IT PROJ MGT to 12345," and the sender's mobile number is captured and added to a database for future SMS communications. A recent article describing the launch of mobile recruiting by A T & T in early 2009 indicated that the company had 160,000 numbers in its SMS network database by December (Arnold, 2010).

Taking the mobile connection one step further, companies like AutoSearch and Kenexa are on the cutting edge of the mobile recruiting/job search environment with their mobile compatible applications. "Autosearch allows recruiters to find prospective candidates and business leads by typing in key words (such as job title or company name) and targeting a geographic location anywhere… With Kenexa's new mobile platform, corporate recruiters and hiring managers can use their mobile devices to contact job seekers and schedule interviews. Job candidates can apply for job openings with just a few clicks on their mobile devices." (Wright, 2009, pp. 1, 2). Despite the many distinct advantages to keeping the IT recruiting function in-house, situations can arise that exceed HR's human and/or technological experience and expertise.

Remaining within the digital milieu, when used with discretion, ubiquitous social media (such as Facebook and personal blogs), are potential venues for recruiting and hiring. While it may not be as universally subscribed to among the older generation, 96% of Generation Y is reported to have joined a social network (Qualman, 2009). A recent article in PM Network (Smart, 2009) encourages project managers to blog as a means of advancing their careers. It is suggested that thoughtful commentary on accomplishments might get the attention of industry professionals in need of the blogger's expertise.

Undoubtedly every firm could benefit from the organization and expertise of an outside recruiting service from time to time. Whether at the start of a new initiative, when a large number of specialized personnel needed to be on board yesterday, or the anticipated upswing of a seasonal demand, existing in-house human resource professionals may not be equipped to address the immediate IT staffing needs. Fortunately, there are many alternatives available in the external IT recruiter environment. Traditionally, recruiting arrangements/agencies are classified as either contingency or retained. With the former, the recruiter does the recruiting, screening, and initial interviewing and is paid a flat fee or a percentage (20-30%) of the hire's first-year salary after 30 days on the job. The agency generally guarantees the placement for a specified time period (usually several months up to a year). In the case of a retained recruiting agency, "the client company pays a retainer fee to have that (recruiting) company perform a search. One-third of the fee… is paid upfront; one-third is due after 30 days of the search; and the remainder is due at hire, in addition to expenses. The initial retainer fee is paid whether or not a placement/ hire is made," (Frase-Blunt, 2003, p. 1). Of late, some third-party recruiting agencies have created a flexible alternative to contingency and retainer consulting. An array of professional recruiting services is made available with fees accruing per hour spent, rather than per hire. This type of on-demand recruiting service (ODRS) may be more cost-effective for the firm that has the results of a recent job analysis and thus could provide a comprehensive list of required/preferred candidate attributes. Hence, when the firm's HR cannot handle the IT recruiting demands, several external alternatives are available, but it's imperative that someone familiar with the firm's IT milieu be partnered with the recruiting agency throughout the screening process.

As a general rule, recruiting agencies may be a more expedient choice when you're in need of a specialized hire (Adamsky, 2001). If the expertise you're seeking is not available in-house and there isn't time to train a current employee, seek the services of a recruiter for a quick, expert fix. This situation is most likely to occur when you're looking for someone with specific technical expertise. When the person of interest is at the higher levels, a search firm would be the better choice (if the experience and expertise are not apparent within current middle management. In any case, when forced to work with an agency or search firm, ask them to consider providing their services for a flat fee rather than a percentage of the candidate's first year compensation. Under these conditions, the firm controls the cost of the hire and the incentive to show you only the more expensive candidates are removed (Adamsky, 2001).

In the final phase of the recruitment and hiring process, candidate interviews are required and metrics must be gathered on critical competency areas. Once again, if an in-house job analysis was performed, an enumeration of required and desirable skills, knowledge, and abilities is readily available. This list becomes a template for evaluating each of the position finalists. For the straightforward attributes, a simple checklist may be sufficient to verify the incumbent's possession of desired characteristics/training/experience. In other cases, a thorough interview may require greater ingenuity. For example, when contemplating the enumeration of tasks and duties for a project manager position, the issue of granularity is paramount. There are no fewer than 48 competencies listed by the Global Alliance for Project

Performance Standards for project managers (GAPPS, 2007). Since many of these competencies are not readily amenable to objective testing (for example, leadership, conflict resolution, negotiation, success, value management), quickly screening for all 48 is an unreasonable expectation. A practical solution to this dilemma would be the development of cases that tap several of the behavioral or personal attributes. The quality and emphasis of candidate's responses to these scenarios would provide useful insights on the incumbent's personality. IT hiring at the executive level would benefit from cases that emphasize demonstration of an external focus, for example a response that includes consideration of business partners (suppliers, distributors), your competitors, and/or current economic forces. Cases developed for positions at middle or lower IT levels would more appropriately prompt responses that tap a candidate's insights in terms of an internal focus (Andersen, 2002).

Another screening option is a focused interview, group interview, or stress interview. Each of these respective methods yields increasingly different insights on candidate attributes, although requiring successively greater time and human resource commitments. Many firms have determined that using a phone interview to screen candidates is both cost effective and efficient. Within 15-20 minutes you're able to clear up any questions from your review of the resume, ask a handful of structured questions to provide a point of comparison with other candidate phone interviews, and consider the quality of questions the candidate has posed to you.

There is considerable commentary on what one should look for in potential project manager candidates. To some extent, the variety of attributes mentioned and the priority placed on each attribute is understandable when considering the breadth of firms and the scope of projects within firms. Among the preferred attributes mentioned, Yvonne suggests "(t)he best project managers will be solid project mechanics, great communicators, effective influencers, good at building expert networks and able to apply their skills across a variety of subject matter" (2009, p. 1). Research by Ingason and Jonasson (2009) as well as Flannes and Levin (2005) corroborate the importance of interpersonal skills. Indeed, the importance of 'softer' skills may be one of the less obvious competencies critical to project manager success. The cross-functional nature of project management teams coupled with the politically complex environment of the firm at large conspire to test the flexibility and sensitivity of a project manager's communication acumen. This conundrum—whether to hire based on technical expertise or on softer skills such as communication proficiency, is empirically highlighted in the following discussion of recent scholarship on project management hiring.

In an effort to further investigate the relationship between corporate position requirements and recruiter screening criteria, a study was initiated, whereby 375 IT recruiters were sampled nationwide. Validity of the survey instrument was established by first interviewing personal business associates by phone to ascertain consistency and rigor of response. Once content validity was established, the survey was mailed via online survey to 375 IT recruiters from all major geographic areas in the United States, as defined by the U.S. Census Bureau. Each recruiter was asked to identify those characteristics most sought by their clients in hiring IT project managers. Of the 375 recruiters sampled, 32 responded, providing the following list of 15 hiring criteria for IT project managers. (Stevenson & Starkweather, 2010).

As Table 1 indicates, Experience, Education and PMP Certification were identified as the most preferred hiring criteria by respondents in this sample. Interestingly, recruiters indicated Experience and Education to be the most common screening attributes, at 87% and 70% respectively, which might be expected of *general* recruiting requirements rather than particular predictors of successful project managers. Most recruiters

Table 1. Recruiter's hiring criteria (n=32)

Hiring Criteria	Percentage
Experience	87.8%
Education	70.2
PMP Certification	52.6
Technical Expertise	18.7
Leadership	15.6
Length of Prior Engagements	12.5
Work History	9.4
Attitude	6.3
Ability to Escalate	3.1
Ability to Communicate at Multiple Levels	3.1
Ability to Deal with Ambiguity and Change	3.1
Cultural Fit	3.1
Past Team Size	3.1
Verbal Skills	3.1
Written Skills	3.1

agreed that some form of experience, whether general or industry specific, was necessary to be successful as a project manager. There appeared, however, to be a distinction in recruiters' views as to which type of experience was the most preferred, general experience or specific, industry/project experience. Some respondents felt that an applicant was best prepared if they had a broad business background in addition to project management skills. One recruiter specifically states that a general understanding of business issues and problems is necessary to envision technical solutions to those problems:

General professional experience - will help a project manager understand what the basic political requirements are for getting the job done. They will also have an understanding that technology is a tool for solving business problems, and this will help facilitate their ability to develop and implement technical solutions to business problems. They may be less likely to limit their solution of business problems to the limits of their current technology.

In comparing experience to education and certifications, other recruiters state their preferences:

Theory can only teach so much. What one does in their day to day jobs and how they effectively use it for the next assignment is what differentiates quality hands on experience from theoretical experience. Again, certifications are good to have; however, they are primarily a validation of processes and what they do rather than what they are taught.

Experience is very important to a PM's effectiveness. I will always take experience over credentials.

In addition to those who identify the value of general business experience, some recruiters narrowed their scope to those individuals who had specific industry or project experience:

Industry experience is very important because it allows the IT manager to partner with the business professionals in their organization. They speak and understand the same business language and they understand the business problems. This can be overcome, if a manager has a lot of experience in management and in other industries, because there is a bit of universality to the business problems being solved. It takes a lot of experience (and intelligence) to make those correlations.

Greatly, general professional experience helps but most important is industry experience.

It appears, however, that whether recruiters preferred general or specific industry experience, most agreed that the ability to recognize and identify business problems or issues and relate them to technical solutions was critical to the effectiveness of project management and, accordingly, increased a candidate's appeal to their clients.

Education was also viewed as critically important, with 70% of respondents identifying this criterion as a necessary component of a candidate's hiring package. Again, many recruiters focused on the value of education from a business perspective, specifically, in the ability to identify customer's business needs, and then translate those needs to specific technical solutions and project goals.

Business management education is valuable, because as a PM of IT, you are always answering a business need.

While the overall pertinence of this attribute is apparent, recruiters did qualify their perceived value of education as a preferred screening criterion:

Education is important to a PM's effectiveness however its value diminishes over time. I often look for solid business skills when hiring a project manager so it's helpful when a candidate has at least a Bachelors degree.

Education is the backup for the skills learned through firsthand experience. Without the education, you lack the PM skills to manage the data you garner on a project.

While 70% of the respondents in this study identified education as a valid hiring criterion, some recruiters were somewhat cautionary in placing undue value on this requirement:

Education is very important. Not necessarily a degree. I have met a lot of degreed people who cannot manage projects, or even write programs. What is required is the ability to work well with others, even others who are intractable. That isn't taught in school. It takes strong problem-solving skills, and it takes strong technical skills. All IT managers should have programming training and experience. They should also have hardware training of some sort—at least a good overview. They should have organizational, analytical, communications, writing and negotiations training.

The importance and significance of education depends on and varies from company to company. Education like certification is an enhancer not a determinant.

Two of my most successful PMs only have a High School diploma. One of my "C-Player" PMs has an Undergraduate degree. With that said, I do require a minimum of an Associates for my entry-level PM and Bachelor's for my Senior PM positions. I believe that this education level is critical to increasing and maintaining the overall PM maturity level and allowing the organization to implement such concepts as Six Sigma that requires a fair amount of knowledge in the area of Statistics and Quantitative Analysis.

Of particular interest in the list of preferred criteria is the fact that 52% of the recruiters viewed PMP Certification as an important attribute for screening applicants. Gaining in popularity over recent years, the attainment of the PMP Certification from the Project Management Institute is viewed by many as a benchmark in the career preparation of all project managers. The certification process and its valuation by IT executives is the focus of recent scholarship by Starkweather and Stevenson (2010).

They state, "(t)his credentialing process goes beyond mere membership; it purports to signify attainment of a specified set of skills and experiences along with an understanding of a core body of knowledge. We use the term certification to denote mastery of these skills, experiences, and knowledge. The issuance of a certificate by a national or international oversight board is written evidence that the incumbent has met specified requirements. Being certified is similar to being endorsed by the official standards keepers; one might think of it as human (as opposed to product) quality assurance. Given the significance attached to professional certification, it becomes incumbent upon the granting organization to ensure that professional standards and instructional content

reflect best practices within the discipline. This is no small order, as an emerging discipline is, by definition, a work in progress—not easily nor definitively captured. Project management, as a scholarly discipline, has exhibited such growing pains with panoply of perspectives employed to describe and analyze the process. Not surprisingly, the breadth of perspectives and the rapid production of new discipline knowledge create a continual challenge for credentialing organizations" (in press, 2010).

This state of flux within the project management milieu is also evident from the IT recruiters' perspective; that is, they were nearly equally split on the value they attached to the PMP certification criterion. Those that viewed the PMP certification most favorably had the following to say:

In my opinion, I feel it is gives them a formal methodology to follow like making a cake. Projects get completed with less down time, quicker, less money spent and less "hair lost" by executive mgmt over the project. I have been impressed by the PMP certification more than any other.

The PMP certification is valuable and the skills they gain are worth having, especially for upward mobility.

However, respondents in this study had equally moderate or negative opinions about the necessity of requiring the PMP certification as a telling indicator of project management success:

I don't think certification affects a PM's effectiveness. I have worked with several "certified" PMs who didn't know how to do the job—they had the "book learning" but didn't know how to apply it.

PMP is the only certification that I recognize. However, I have had to terminate two PMP certified contractors for non-performance, so having a PMP is no guarantee of effectiveness. Again, it only demonstrates that the candidate has been exposed and understands the minimum PM standards. It does not measure a candidate's ability to apply these concepts in a business environment.

PM certification is basically worthless. There is no correlation between a good pm and certification based on my 15 years of experience.

IT Executives' Valuation of PM Hiring Criteria

With the plethora of IT candidates on the market today, it has become common practice for hiring organizations to foster long standing relationships with recruiters that have provided them with well qualified candidates in the past. The path to the recruiter, however, is sometimes varied. While some companies employ their Human Resources Department as the go-between, other firms prefer the direct contact between Hiring Manager and Recruiter. Through either avenue, however, the recruiter's ability to find the appropriate match between candidate and position is critically dependent on their clients' ability to disseminate position requirements and candidate attributes that are most indicative of project management effectiveness. It is ultimately through this identification of preferred client attributes that a recruiter's success can be determined.

In an attempt to identify and measure the degree to which hiring manager's attributes of project manager effectiveness align with those of front line recruiters, a study was undertaken, where 3,258 IT managers and executives nationwide were sent a questionnaire and asked to identify, on a 7-point Likert scale, which of the 15 recruiters' hiring criteria they found the most important, and hence, most indicative of effective project managers. The sample of IT managers and executives was a subset of data from Dunn and Bradstreet that identified those individuals in mid to large-sized companies, represented by over 750 employees. The timing of this study was unfortunate, in that questionnaire mailings occurred in November of 2008, in the midst of a severe economic downturn, which contributed to a low response rate: Of the 3,258 questionnaires mailed, 84 were returned. It was determined, however, that the 84 respondents were indeed representative of the sampling frame population across a variety of demographics. Of the 84 questionnaires returned, 80 were completed fully and deemed useable.

Demographics and Analysis

In comparing the sample returns to the population, we found a strong alignment in basic demographics such as gender, and position title. 81% of the sample respondents indicated that they were male, as compared to 73% for the original population. An exceedingly strong alignment between the sample and population existed on the position title of "CIO", where 23.8% of the sample indicated they held the title of "CIO", compared to 23% for the population. IT Managers were somewhat underrepresented, however, at 38% for the sample, compared to 56% for the population. Most of the respondents in this survey were employed in Manufacturing, Health Care and Public Administration sectors of the economy.

As the objective of this study was to analyze the relative alignment of recruiters' hiring criteria to IT manager preferences, prior to a comparative analysis of the two, a Cronbach's Alpha was run to determine the level of reliability in the original 15 item list. The resulting statistic of .917 indicated a strong cohesiveness in the ability of all 15 items to effectively measure criteria used in the hiring process.

Upon receipt of the questionnaire, executives were asked to identify which of the 15 hiring criteria were most valued by their organizations, on a 7 point Likert Scale. (It is assumed that attribute preference is directly correlated with those competencies that the executives valued and deemed representative of successful project managers.) Responses ranged on the scale from "Extremely Unimportant" to "Unimportant" to "Somewhat

Unimportant" to "Irrelevant" to "Somewhat Important" to "Important" to "Extremely Important". As the focus of this study was to determine the degree of valuation executives and recruiters placed on hiring attributes, it was appropriate to isolate those characteristics that executives found most important. Therefore, the categories of "Important" and "Extremely Important" were aggregated and ranked by frequency of response. Table 2 presents the results.

As might be expected from what is known about basic management principles, 94.8% of IT executives valued "Leadership" as the most indicative of effective project managers, making this criterion a critical component in IT recruiting. Interestingly, however, the respondents of this study identified "Ability to Communicate at Multiple Levels" as the second most important criterion of the 15, at 93.5%. Most recognize the value of communication in the corporate environment, and, specifically in project management activities, however, this specific type of communication suggests a needed ability to identify and converse with not only team members, but upper level executives as well as project stakeholders. That said, one might expect that this type of communication is more "crisis-based", in that it suggests more of an ability of project managers to advance troubling project issues up the corporate ladder when needed. Yet only 66.3% of executives found "Ability to Escalate" to be a valued characteristics of effective project managers. Clearly, the executives' valuation of the communication criterion in this study needs further investigation.

One of the most surprising results of the executives' responses was the valuation of the "PMP Certification". At 15.4%, this criterion represented the lowest and least important of the 15 hiring criteria, suggesting that this credential, while perhaps complementing other more important candidate skill sets, is by no means an assurance or an effective indicator of a candidate's ability to obtain employment or to be successful, if hired.

Table 2. IT executives hiring criteria preferences

Hiring Criteria	Important + Extremely Important Percentages
Leadership	94.8%
Ability to Communicate at Multiple Levels	93.5
Verbal Skills	87.2
Written Skills	87.1
Attitude	85.3
Ability to Deal with Ambiguity and Change	82.9
Work History	68.9
Experience	67.1
Ability to Escalate	66.3
Cultural Fit	57.2
Technical Expertise	46.1
Education	37.7
Length of Prior Engagements	23.0
Past Team Size	18.0
PMP Certification	15.4

(© 2010, Stevenson & Starkweather. Used with permission.)

In reviewing the data presented in Table 2 in its entirety, it is clear that executives found soft skills to be most preferred among the 15 hiring characteristics. There is a clear distinction between the top six criteria (Leadership, 94.8%; Ability to Communicate at Multiple Levels, 93.5%; Verbal Skills, 87.2%; Written Skills, 87.1%; Attitude, 85.3%; Ability to Deal with Ambiguity and Change, 82.9%), and the remainder of the hiring characteristics. Stevenson and Starkweather (2010) provide further analysis and identify these top six criteria as the "PM Critical Competency Index". In an effort to assess the reliability of these 6 items, a Cronbach's Alpha was calculated, resulting in the statistic of .919, indicating a high degree of reliability for these items. In an effort to further identify the specific association of the 6 soft skills as separate from the 15 item list of hiring criteria, a principal components factor analysis confirmed the validity of these same competencies

Table 3. Rotated factor matrix

Factor	Competency		
	1	**2**	**3**
Ability to Communicate at Multiple Levels	.896	-.028	.027
Leadership	.895	-.085	.064
Verbal Skills	.872	.047	.237
Written Skills	.838	.022	.218
Ability to Deal with Ambiguity and Change	.746	.237	.044
Attitude	.713	.408	-.038
Work History	.686	.344	-.176
Cultural History	.657	.357	-.057
Experience	.597	.381	.299
Ability to Escalate	.543	.490	.071
Technical Expertise	.532	.196	.404
Length of Prior Engagements	.002	.896	.235
Past Team Size	.114	.847	.233
PMP Certification	-.025	.143	.873
Education	.311	.416	.672

as the top 6 variables loading on the first factor were the same 6 variables that executives identified as the most preferable competencies indicative of successful project managers.

Disparate Views of Preferred IT Hiring Criteria

The expectation that IT recruiters' and IT managers' valuation of critical project manager hiring criteria would be complementary seems a reasonable assumption to make, given that both recruiters and managers anchor their positions at either end of the same recruitment continuum. Presumably recruiters and managers work together, one disseminating corporate needs, the other seeking to fulfill them. It is in this light then, that the results provided in Table 4 are so disconcerting.

In viewing the table in its entirety, the reverse weighting of responses between the two groups is apparent, with the top 6 criteria representing the most frequent response for IT executives and the bottom 9 criteria the most preferred by IT recruiters. Of particular note, are the criteria of "Leadership" and "Ability to Communicate at Multiple Levels". Given the expected and almost "common sense" presence of "Leadership" as the most preferred project manager characteristic, it was no surprise that 94.8% of IT managers and executives found this attribute most desirable in a potential IT project manager candidate. The low valuation of this criterion by IT recruiters at 15.6%, while somewhat puzzling, may suggest that those respondents assumed it was implied in the presence of other attributes. The disparity in preference between IT recruiters and managers on the criterion "Ability to communicate at Multiple Levels" is startling; particularly in light of the emphasis that communication has in project management. The ability to communicate with team members, upper management and a variety of stakeholders is critical to the ability of a project manager to drive a project to its completion.

Table 4. Comparison of hiring criteria preferences between IT executives and IT recruiters

Hiring Criteria/Competencies	IT Executive Percentages	IT Recruiter Percentages
Leadership	94.8%	15.6%
Ability to Communicate at Multiple Levels	93.5	3.1
Verbal Skills	87.2	3.1
Written Skills	87.1	3.1
Attitude	85.3	6.3
Ability to Deal with Ambiguity and Change	82.9	3.1
Work History	68.9	9.4
Experience	67.1	87.8
Ability to Escalate	66.3	3.1
Cultural Fit	57.2	3.1
Technical Expertise	46.1	18.7
Education	37.7	70.2
Length of Prior Engagements	23.0	12.5
Past Team Size	18.0	3.1
PMP Certification	15.4	52.6

Another project manager characteristic that was highly valued by IT executives was that of the "Ability to Deal with Ambiguity and Change". Again, a criterion focused on communication and crisis management, this quality points to a candidate being able to handle such issues as project scope changes, changing stakeholder needs, conflicting project objectives, among others. A full 82.9% of IT managers and executives valued this criterion as a preferred soft skill indicative of effective project management, contrasted with a mere 3.1% of IT recruiters.

One of the most disconcerting results of the Stevenson and Starkweather study (2010) is the valuation that each group placed on PMP Certification. IT executives and managers found this criterion to be least important when screening for project manager candidates, at 15.4%. Conversely, IT recruiters ranked "PMP Certification" as their 3rd highest preference at 52.6%, indicating a clear presence of this qualification in their screening process. One possibility that would explain IT managers' low preference for this credential

could be that many of their organizations provide their own in-house training for project manager advancement, given that many IT projects are technology and domain dependent. In any case, the dichotomy of responses to the valuation of "PMP Certification" in this study warrants further investigation.

It is clear from the data in this sample, that IT executives place a higher degree of importance in soft skills such as "Leadership", "Ability to Communicate at Multiple Levels", "Verbal Skills", "Written Skills", "Attitude", and "Ability to Deal with Ambiguity and Change", when screening for effective project managers. IT Recruiters, on the other hand, focus on the more standard "Experience", "Education" and "PMP Certification" criteria for the purpose of screening applicants. It may be, that because of the positioning of the IT recruiters at the front end of the recruitment continuum, their role becomes more of a baseline screening of candidates, or that they simply lack the assessment tools to effectively measure the soft skills that IT managers and executives value.

LESSONS LEARNED

1. Keep the firm involved in every step of the recruitment, assessment, and hiring process.
2. Conduct a job analysis on the most granular level possible. The details will be utilized in every subsequent step—job description, interview questions, case develo9pment, assessment metrics, and so forth.
3. Hire/promote from within whenever possible. The candidate's strengths and weaknesses are known as well as their "fit" within the corporate culture.
4. When you have to recruit outside the organization, use an agency for technical hires; use a search firm for executive hires.
5. Make full use of digital recruiting options including social media.
6. When interviewing, consider not only the answ4rs the candidate's give, but the questions they ask.
7. If two candidates are equally qualified, who fits the culture best? Who would the rest of the Department/team relate to?
8. Pay attention to the candidate's communication skills. The IT Dept. needs communication internally, but also externally with end users.

CONCLUSION

Having empirically demonstrated the mismatch between IT recruiter and IT executive perceptions of PM critical competencies, it's appropriate to return to the best practices discussed at the beginning of this chapter for possible explanations and solutions. One of the key themes in human resource management today is the idea of leveraging company human resources. This suggests a strategy whereby firms act to provide training and professional development for their existing employees rather than hire new persons with extensive training, experience, and so forth.

The advantages to this approach include a lower initial cost per hire, the security of investing in a "known quantity," and the benefit of fostering a positive work environment that openly advocates promotion from within—priceless.

Critical to the success of such a home grown strategy, though, is an investment in HR's technology training and development. The CIO, the IT Director, and the IT professionals need to teach HR how to "speak IT." It may be more cost effective and more results effective to specifically develop IT human resource professionals within the company. If the company is currently paying one third of job candidates' annual salaries to external recruiters, it wouldn't take many of those hiring fees to justify the addition of an in-house recruiter for IT positions. The advantages of this strategy have been amply discussed. Suffice it to say that in this scenario, familiarity brings success.

Whether the recruiters are in-house or external to the firm, they need to be paired with an IT professional well-versed in the specifics of the open position. This is where the thoughtful job analysis discussed earlier becomes the first step on the road to a successful hire. The collective conscience of those who once held such positions and those who now hold those positions provides a valuable blueprint for the specific knowledge, skills, and abilities that need to be addressed in the forthcoming job advertisement. HR professionals know how to write good ad copy and they probably have boilerplate paragraphs to cover an overview of the firm and the community. But an IT professional should take the lead on crafting the list of required and desired candidate attributes. As soon as the list is developed, IT needs to begin working with HR to develop screening metrics that assess these candidate qualities.

The development of reliable and valid screening instruments takes time. Writing a case or scenario that elicits the demonstration of respondent soft skill attributes such as leadership or decision-making abilities is a thoughtful iterative process; one that requires several rounds of collegial feedback and instrument refinement. Once the actual case/scenario creative efforts are completed, agreement must be reached on requirements for the rubric that will be employed to assess the adequacy and appropriateness of responses.

As the resumes come in, someone with IT expertise needs to be involved in the initial screening. Some of these qualifications may be straightforward and therefore relatively easy to confirm, for example, "a Bachelor's degree in Information Systems and 5 years of experience." Other attributes, such as "ability to escalate" or "ability to communicate at multiple levels," are less amenable to quantification or credentialing. At the screening stage, assessment of these skills may require a brief telephone interview with a handful of questions designed to elicit responses that highlight specific candidate attributes. Asking a candidate to describe an IT failure they had to work through or the most recent IT crisis they've had to deal with can be very enlightening. However, hiring candidates who claim no exposure to failure and no involvement in crisis may introduce an unacceptable level of management risk to an organization. Since failure and/or crisis invariably present themselves at some point in the IT environment, the firm may not want to risk the consequences of a new hire's first exposure to such situations. Other questions that seek information on incidents of creativity or critical thinking provide similarly revealing insights on candidate experience and performance. Once again, an IT professional is probably the person best prepared to conduct these interviews—particularly from the standpoint of asking follow up questions or answering candidate questions. Often the simplest questions provide the greatest return. When significant accomplishments are noted on the resume or in the interview, ask "How" they achieved that benchmark. Once the candidate pool has been narrowed to those that will be interviewed, many of the critical soft skills can be demonstrated through a formal presentation and through probing interviews. Other critical attributes, such as leadership or attitude, may be accessed through a battery of objective tests assessing personality traits or cases that emphasize critical thinking, problem solving, and reaction to stress abilities.

While it may seem that an inordinate amount of time is being spent in the hiring process, it's the only way to improve the probability of making a successful hire. The recruiting and hiring process should be guided by the principle of risk avoidance. In the IT recruiting and hiring environment risk avoidance can be enhanced by gathering more of the right candidate information. That is, failure to assess for critical candidate competencies increases the risk of a mediocre hire. If the screening of candidates for IT positions does not include the integral involvement of IT professionals, you're decreasing the probability that this hire will be successful. Simply put, *what they don't know can hurt the firm.*

REFERENCES

Adamsky, H. (2001). *Hiring and retaining top IT professionals*. New York: McGraw-Hill.

Andersen, E. S. (2002). *External or internal focus? A comparison of IT executive and IT project manager roles*. Engineering Management Journal.

Anthony, W. P., Perrewe, P. L. K., & Kacmar, M. (1999). *Human resource management* (3rd ed.). Orlando, FL: Dryden.

Arnold, J. T. (2010). Recruiting on the run. *HR Magazine, 55.* Retrieved February 3, 2010, from http://www.shrm.org/ Publications/hrmagazine/ EditorialContent/Pages/ 0210arnold.aspx

Flannes, S. W., & Levin, G. (2005). *Essential people skills for project managers*. New York: Management Concepts.

Frase-Blunt, M. (2003). Special report on recruiting and staffing. traditional recruiting defined. *HR Magazine, 48,* 4. Retrieved March 2, 2010, from http://www.shrm.org/ Publications/hrmagazine/ EditorialContent/ Pages/0403frase.aspx

Fyock, C. D. (2009). Recruiting internally and externally. *SHRM Online, April.* Retrieved May 2, 2010, from http://www.shrm.org/ Research/ Articles/ Pages/RecruitingInternally andExternally.aspx

GAPPS (Global Alliance for Project Performance Standards). (2007). *A framework for performance based competency standards for global level 1 and 2 project managers.* Retrieved February 26, 2010, from http://www.globalpmstandards.org

Harvey, R. J., Friedman, L., Hakel, M. D., & Cornelius, E. T. III. (1989). Dimensionality of the job element inventory: A simplified worker-oriented job analysis questionnaire. *The Journal of Applied Psychology, 73,* 639–646. doi:10.1037/0021-9010.73.4.639

Ingason, H. T., & Jonasson, H. I. (2009). Contemporary knowledge and skills requirements in project management. *Project Management Journal, 40,* 59–69. doi:10.1002/pmj.20122

Pritchard, K. H. (2010). *Introduction to job analysis.* SHRM White paper. Retrieved February 2, 2010, from http://www.shrm.org/Research /Articles/Articles/Pages /CMS000055.aspx

Qualman, E. (2009, August 11). Statistics show social media is bigger than you think. *Socialnomics.* Retrieved April 14, 2010, from http:// socialnomics.net/ 2009/08/11/ statistics-show-social-media-is-bigger -than-you-think/

Schreyer, R., & McCarter, J. (1998). *The employer's guide to recruiting on the Internet.* Manassas Park, VA: Impact Publications.

Smart, M.P. (2009). Time for an upgrade? *PM Network,* 46-51.

Starkweather, J. A., & Stevenson, D. H. (in press). PMP certification as a core competency: Necessary but not sufficient. *Project Management Journal.*

Stevenson, D. H., & Starkweather, J. A. (in press). PM critical competency index: IT execs prefer soft skills. *International Journal of Project Management.*

Tornow, W. W., & Pinto, P. R. (1976). The development of a managerial taxonomy: A system for describing, classifying, and evaluating executive positions. *The Journal of Applied Psychology, 62,* 410–418. doi:10.1037/0021-9010.61.4.410

Wright, A. D. (2009). Recruiting goes mobile. *SHRM Online, November.* Retrieved February 6, 2010, from http://www.shrm.org/ hrdisciplines/ technology/ Articles/Pages/Recruiting GoesMobile.aspx

Yvonne, K. (2009). Hiring a great project manager. *Helium.* Retrieved October 21, 2009 from http:// www.helium.com/items/1069940-hiring-a-great-project -manager?page=1

Chapter 7
Producing Candidate Separation through Recruiting Technology

Derek J. Sedlack
Nova Southeastern University, USA

ABSTRACT

With millions of potential employment candidates leveraging the Internet to search for jobs (Borstorff et al, 2006) and a massive global economic recession providing increasing availability to otherwise gainfully employed professionals, it is staggering to think that employers cannot find qualified candidates. The number of global candidates is growing, but claims of weak qualifications or poorly drafted resumes that do not appropriately reflect skills or experience leave many positions open. Gallivan et al (2004) found that the technical gap is due to the ease of posting specific technical skills and recruiting for a specialty and the complex, multi-functional modern employee companies now desire. A better method of qualifying and matching candidates with broader skills is required to meet this ever-increasing demand. While no system can incorporate all information, this proposal would provide a modular Information System capable of providing the most relevant information.

INTRODUCTION

With millions of potential employment candidates leveraging the Internet to search for jobs (Borstorff et al, 2006) and a massive global economic recession providing increasing availability to otherwise gainfully employed professionals, it is staggering

to think that employers cannot find qualified candidates. In 2009, the Department of Homeland Security touted a shortage of candidates for 1,000 security-related positions despite the ever-growing numbers of Americans graduating from college with Information Technology or security focused credentials. Searching through job sites in the later part of 2009 resulted in 255,000+ information security jobs at Indeed, 22,000+ at HotJobs,

DOI: 10.4018/978-1-60960-535-3.ch007

over 5,000 (limit) at Monster, nationally and internationally. In October of 2009, the number of Americans without a job topped 15,000,000. While these levels did not approach those of the 1930 depression, 25% of the population, they should provide a more qualified candidate pool than ever before in recent history, but the numbers do not match.

While the focus here is not directly on the recession, it does reflect the significant lack of positions filled during this recession. Normally, economies affect all employment environments, which normally serve the general direction of growth; increased GDP creates jobs that require more candidates. This reveals three trends that deserve further attention: shifts in recruiting, shifts in job searching, and IT utilization. The number of postings remains plentiful despite a purported lack of positions through the media. The national media also declares a lack of qualified candidates to fill key Information Technology positions, but local coverage reports countless highly educated, skilled IT workers remain unemployed. Why such a discrepancy?

IT positions remain open because IT candidates cannot be appropriately qualified through current methods. Rapidly advancing technologies require rapidly adopting recruiters, but this creates a catch-22 scenario: focus on learning new technologies and recruiters identify better candidates, locate more candidates and there is little time to adopt new technologies. Candidates remain on the outside of this conundrum with highly sought after skills, but unable to adequately demonstrate their wares. A more accurate skill assessment method will more accurately identify high demand skills, providing employers with a more focused appraisal tool that aligns with internal specifications instead of relying on 2-page buckshot of job listings.

The number of global candidates is growing, but claims of weak qualifications or poorly drafted resumes that do not appropriately reflect skills or experience leave many positions open. Filling high skill positions is not limited to the rank and file, executives now find their work as highly scrutinized as ever before, perhaps due to the technological infusion of the 1990's that drove gainful increases in productivity. This chapter will look at a technical process to correct what should be the simplest hiring task, entry to mid-level positions that will better position candidates to find long-term, better-suited careers that will provide more valuable, synergistic employment to position the States, again, as the leading nation moving toward a more service-based professional society.

Executive recruiting discussions will encapsulate current, successful methods unrelated to the mid- to entry-level solutions based on inherent tacit skill requirements that differ greatly from explicit, measurable individual contributor skills and will be isolated to better current methods of C-level hiring.

BACKGROUND

There is a wealth of knowledge available on IT skill requirements, available curricula, and longitudinal patterns, but a concise survey that provided relative and absolute rankings of skills was not present. Relative rankings determine how particular skills hold import compared to other skills and while one skill may be deemed vital, over the years its relative ranking may drop. The absolute rankings provide a method of listing the skills required to successfully complete the hired position. Jiang and Klein (1995) studied technical support and analysis positions and concluded that technical skills alone will not sufficiently prepare this type of employee. Niederman (1991) found supporting evidence with jobs moving overseas and Information Systems professionals growing in demand due to explosive industry growth. While the jobs were moving overseas to cut costs, the skills now required by American labor continued to mount. Gallivan et al (2004) found trends in the early 1990s supporting this belief, but through the latter part of the century many technical roles, such as programming, remained highly technical (e.g. evolved toward the next generation language), but analyst roles required more "soft skills" and were requested more by IT hiring managers. Tye, Poon, and Burn (1995) also believed that IT professionals will require more interpersonal and business acumen because of the integration and inundation of technical expertise in all facets of business. These findings are contradictory to the study in Singapore conducted by Lee (2001), even as Lee referenced, but did not cite, a similar U.S. study also concluded the increasing importance of technical skills in such a fast-paced industry. Gallivan et al (2004) found that the technical gap is due to the ease of posting specific technical skills and recruiting for a specialty and the complex, multi-functional modern employee companies now desire. Many technical curricula surveyed by the reviewer: Computer Science, Computer Information Systems, Management Information Systems, and even Computer Engineering degrees have components of management, economics, and communication skills, but a more comprehensive study is required in this area.

The recent acknowledgement of tacit skills as intellectual capital, forces companies to diversify the existing workforce and hire more well-rounded skills that include both highly technical and soft skills (Niederman, 1999). The "curriculum gap" presented by Gallivan et al (2004) is noted throughout the industry, but solutions have been sparse due to the sporadic hiring tendencies created by the DOTCOM boom and bust and innovative integration of technology that transformed the support industry. The DOTCOM area saw recruiting as a defacto requirement as jobs were not only plentiful and high paying, the IT skill requirements were routinely based purely on resumes not lengthy interview cycles. Technological innovations in support led to more robust expert-system infrastructures that led to less qualified technicians who could now find many remedies through software instead of intellectual troubleshooting based on detailed hardware/software knowledge. Stott and

Wood (2001) found disjointed beliefs between critical skill assessment by employers and those skills actually utilized during daily routines. Stott and Wood believe that distributed computing and IT outsourcing have forced both company and employee to re-evaluate those skills vital to long-term survival in the IT field. Wu, Chen, and Chang (2005) found that IT managers decisions were based on strong technical knowledge used to support higher-level competencies, but that each level of management exhibited different skills that reflected a level of focus correlative to their position in the company – as expected. They did mention that companies need to begin addressing those skills with more unilateral awareness to prepare IT managers for any position in the organization regardless of their current capacity, but tendencies do not appear to be heading toward a more qualified candidate, but a more qualified resume.

Shifts in Recruiting

Finding qualified candidates has always been a challenge for corporations or recruiting firms would not exist. Positioning a process to find skilled talent evolved into a systematic process of collecting qualifications and identifying matching skills with posted requirements. As companies began to grow and merge, they required more talent and more methods of talent identification. Hiring managers extended to external recruiting firms, internal growth extended into internal recruiting departments. All competing for the same resource: qualified candidates. Even while scores of diverging paths lead away from efficient job recruiting, studying the issues from an Information Systems perspective provides the following underscoring elements: the recruiter, the hunter, and the landscape.

Recruiting was initially simple: post a position in the town square, broadcast through word-of-mouth, or identify through networking. However, keeping track of candidates and posted positions was a challenge; everything was printed. Information Systems changed the way that recruiters could track candidates and postings without changing the way they did business. Stacking papers or leveraging simple database programs were sufficient when candidate pools, and positions, were in the hundreds or thousands, but with a growing American populous came growing skill requirements. The United States census reported 308 million citizens, 117 million in the civilian labor force and 6.7 billion individuals globally. The costs of transitioning to better Information Systems to process candidates and positions was first a competitive advantage, but quickly devolved into a business requirement. The cost of advertising completely changed the landscape.

Print advertising was sometimes based on letter count, sometimes word count, either way the corporate and the candidate information pools were limited. Modern Information Systems are expansive (global) and only limited by attention span since job descriptions can include company information, benefits, work environments, historical product references, or even work samples along with the requisite job description. While increasing information better informed the client, it also meant trying to match more candidate profile data with more position elements. Company didn't have to decide what was important to list, they could simply list everything. Another modern element rising from reduced or eliminated advertising costs, companies could post positions they were ready to fill, or had no intention of filling, simply to collect candidates as noted through numerous articles in the mainstream media (Dickler, 2009).

Traditional networking transformed into social networking (MySpace, LinkedIn, Facebook, Twitter) where recruiters could instantly broadcast jobs to anyone connected to the Internet. Systems expanded from internal networks to extranets, linking into the information superhighway with lightning pace. Job boards (Craigslist, Monster, The Ladders, BrassRing) expanded in attempt to fill the influx of technically aware job seekers.

What was once a *savvy* or *astute* potential employee utilizing a tool of the future, became the last horse and buggy driver: great for a nostalgic winter-time stroll, but certainly not useful for modern business. With the cost of printing a non-issue on the web, interconnected Information Systems meant recruiting companies could consolidate their postings and candidates and run daily reports pairing key words with position requirements. But does this lead to the best candidate?

The final difficulty facing recruiting is the pace of innovation. After identifying a potential candidate based on key word matching, the recruiter initiates a screening process by telephone. But with technology changing at an accelerating rate, how do recruiters maintain a prevalent understanding of such broad topics as computer software, hardware, programming languages, database design, operating system installation or configuration, security, information security, or specialized computer skills?

To say that technological innovation has handicapped the recruiters and companies would certainly ignore the challenges that candidates currently endure. Local print ads announced positions traditionally reserved for local candidates. The information was limited, but provided a manageable method for job hunting. Scanning through the "want ads" under the relevant sections, even through several papers of local counties, and an individual could determine best matches in a few hours. Then the Internet emerged. Candidates now find methods of accessing the Internet, at work, at home, in the library, even on the go in their automobiles, airplanes, or any number of handheld devices. Anything capable of obtaining an IP address was Internet ready…

Monster claims to have "pioneered the business of digital recruiting in 1994, and today [2010] we are the only online recruitment provider able to service customers on a truly global basis." While online job posting sites allow candidates to list very lengthy descriptions: Monster, The Ladders, Brass Ring; they still do not answer the question candidates want to shout and employers want to hear, "I am special!"

Information Systems have been used to help hiring for decades, but these systems are rarely used to make decisions in the hiring process or to increase the decision-making processes themselves (Tavana, Lee, & Joglekar, 1994). Extejt and Lynn (1988) pointed out that expert systems should only be the penultimate basis for hiring candidates due to a number of unaccountable factors. No expert system can incorporate all relevant information. In a dynamic environment, a company's decision criteria undergo changes over time. The need to update an expert system may become evident only when there is a pattern of conflict between the system's recommendations and the human recruiters' decisions.

Technology-based companies, whether manufacturing or programming, are constantly evolving due to technological advances. Some of these companies, such as Microsoft, Dell, and Citrix, experienced almost exponential growth during the late 20th and early 21st centuries and had to deal with the dynamic environment of personal growth and candidate availability issues, highlighting differences in recruiting efforts over a distinct timeframes. Internally, the people who might have been responsible for creating the recruiting criteria have left or can no longer contend with the demands placed on hiring processes and procedures, in addition to principle duties.

Fishing from the same well for candidates may provide similar backgrounds and qualifications, but hardly enforces a diverse work environment that most employers claim to exalt, or enhances creativity derived from conflict resolution or difference of opinion. Another issue stems from recruiting firms handling sometimes excessive or fluctuating resume inflows that either physically cannot be processed, or cannot adequately qualify candidates in every position they are contracted to fill. It is not possible to replace human recruiting, but establishing an expert system that can qualify the first line of candidates, who statistically job-hop every seven years, would save a multitude of resources, including those of the candidates. A method of ubiquitous, consistent, qualified screening is required, especially in the billion dollar technology industry where diploma mills are spreading unqualified candidates across the globe (Noble, 1998). Both hiring managers and candidate need to begin viewing hiring from an information system perspective.

Shifts in Job Searching

Understanding the shift in technology recruiting has changed the way skilled IT workers hunt for new opportunities. Previous methods were based on individual skills. The Gallivan et al (2004) study demonstrated the importance of highlighting individual skills that focused on some particular job aspect: programming in a language, managing particular projects, or debugging a particular operating system.

As companies posted positioned based on specific need, individuals developed specific skills. While much of this was based on availability, tens of languages vs hundreds in the modern era, individuals could be specialists. It was important to distinguish yourself as an expert in one field with the ability to work in team environments. Simply posting 15 years of COBOL programming expertise landed positions with commiserate compensation and responsibility. The rapid advancement of technology changed the landscape.

Companies no longer know if C# would be the language of choice with any number of object oriented (OO) languages around the corner and job seekers knew this. Resumes changed formats from chronologically skill-based – what languages I used and where – to a much broader business focus that transitioned toward chronological accomplishment-based resumes. Early entrants primary focused on school or trades, but the experienced professional had to demonstrate business impact and broad skills.

As companies required broader skills, resumes started to lose focus. Instead of listing a primary skill (Microsoft Technical Support), candidates had to list related behaviors (Operating System support through relational database manipulation that decreased daily support costs by resolving 15% over quota). Soft skills overtook hard technologies due to the pace of progress to where candidates could no longer isolate themselves with absolute experience, but had to create an environment in which they contributed to the bottom line, without contributing to the bottom line.

As candidates became better skilled at positioning their abilities to match requirements, companies began asking for overlapping, even disjoined characteristics: programmers with excellent presentation skills; truck drivers with strong writing; sales executives experienced in configuring complex systems. Companies pushed candidates for sometimes unattainable, increasing skill demands and candidates simply manufactured them.

Opportunities

The notion of simply moving all recruiting aspects to the Internet is appealing to recruiters and candidates alike due to cost savings and position availability respectively; large segments of industry have already. Consistent with scientific testing and processes for obtaining repeatable results, Dafoulas, Pateli, and Turega (2002, p. 288) found that the Internet should be utilized for conducting employment interviews and while they did not suggest a system to conduct such activities, they did provide the following structure:

- Questions are planned carefully before the interview;
- All candidates are asked the same questions;
- Answers are scored according to agreed rating systems; and

- Questions focus on the attributes and behaviors needed to succeed in the job.

These elements are only currently practiced through human interviewing, not automated systems. Human interview blunders never seem to cover technical details. The key aspect to successful interviewing is tacit knowledge identification through cognitive approaches (Beatty, 2007). Highly desirable: candidate comparison, equivalent rating, and job-relative attributes and behaviors, the business world is in a state of constant flux. Candidate must be agile and embrace change. It is intentional that questions should be misleading, dissimilar in nature, and in every way attempt to deceive all except those fully understanding the discipline in question. Only through continuously updated random question pools will the system remain viable through consistent updates with current technologies and remain elusive to attempts to defraud. Three examples will illustrate how both employer and seasoned professional can further distinguish themselves over skill-based resume sorting that more closely matches human interviewing techniques.

This expert recruiting system builds on the research conducted by Tavana, Lee, and Joglekar (1994); the major difference focused on determining relative expertise based on correct responses to domain-based questioning instead of a branched prediction based on resume information and reference inquiries. Even the most highly qualified candidates may submit inaccurate resume information as revealed by national media attention surrounding highly publicized Notre Dame Head football coach George O'Leary during 2001. While the proposed design, much like the inference tree Tavana et al. system based on degree type, would not have identified such inaccuracies, the proposed system would allow more thorough resume checks by first establishing credibility based on an ability to perform required position skills instead of allowing simple falsehoods to penetrate and defeat the process unchecked. In fact, the Tavana et al.

system would accentuate resume discrepancies. College media outlet typographical errors have also tarnished football and basketball coaches careers (Girard, 2002) and automated expert systems that rely on resume accuracy would be especially vulnerable. Suggestions such as Crow & DeSanto (2004) extraction and recognition-based system can only rely on the information provided by a condensed resume.

The Tavana et al (1994) study was based on accountants recruited directly from college; the proposed system, while allowing immediate college graduates to partake, will emphasize skill assessments from multiple domains extracted through questions answered a varying levels of expertise. Is it more important that a candidate posses a specific college degree, or exhibit the skill set required to expertly perform the job posted? While a majority of the positions filled in the IT sector first scan through resumes for specific qualifiers or skill sets, it is equally possible to discredit a candidate purely based on educational criteria. Highly logical and hard core sciences like physics or mathematics should not be eliminated from consideration unless proven to be likely to yield less qualified candidates than electrical or engineering degreed individuals when programming and networking are based on mathematics and physics.

Most corporate positions require a broad background and diverse abilities to successfully navigate the complex and dynamic environments present in global technology companies today. It is believed that providing a skill-determinant mechanism before resume submission will greatly enhance the overall capture and retention of highly skilled, qualified candidates while reducing expenditures in time and human resources. Additionally, the availability of a web-based system will provide a 24-7, 365 day avenue for continuously pooling qualified talent that can be measured, reported, and enhanced.

One of the most compelling arguments against a resume-based system, whether human designed or automated, is displayed in the Colwell, Brown, and See (July 1999) Intel hiring methods and results that conclude even a consistent, repeatable interview process, grade point average, or degree level cannot predict the future success of a candidate. It is the author's contention that qualified testing before the interview process will provide more information for both interviewer and prospective employee, inducing a more measurable indicator of success prediction.

Let us separate here executive recruitment process from the skilled labor pool based on executive recruiting firms like RIC Executive Search. Differentiation stems from hiring aspects that, like the technical positions of the past, is losing distinction as recruiting becomes more global and technology becomes more infused. How can we successfully impact these two distinct recruiting coteries through technology?

Jason Welch, of RIC, lists the following skills required to fill executive positions: personal contact, an understanding of corporate culture, and coaching. Unlike technical labor, many executive positions are not filled through job board postings, web site listings, or even word of mouth hires. Executive recruiting firms are contacted by corporate presidents or board members through a formal agreement, because these recruiters are skilled at identifying candidate personality, experience, and impact with organizational requirements. Most executives are gainfully employed so the recruiter must convince the candidate in 30 seconds (if the candidate takes the call) there is a better opportunity available and they should consider it. Corporate culture research means the executive recruiter focuses on long-term relationships, not temporary skills. Personal coaches provide the candidate with inside knowledge of successful actions and the company with positive feedback to level set expectations.

This recruiting algorithm would provide the adopting executive recruiting firm with several advantages. Firms would retain searchable criteria based on particular corporate cultural aspects, quantifiable or qualitative. Augmenting tacit expertise with a repeatable method would provide a feedback mechanism for better recruiting. Business expansion would not require timely focused mentorship, instead could begin with understanding match relationships, why candidate are better suited organizationally regardless of their particular expertise (why a distribution executive matched well in the automotive industry). Additional benefits include longitudinal information, data mining to forecast cycles or industry trends, and building segment profiles that would help identify future clientele.

Shifting back toward skilled recruiting, a transformation began from the isolated skill placement found by Gallivan et al (2004), toward including corporate cultural aspects associated with daily team interaction, increasingly on an international level. The following two scenarios will illustrate why a better recruiting method is needed for this candidate sect: the first toward corporate direct recruiting, the second targeting the recruiting firm.

Corporation XYZ is multinational with offices staffed in the United States, Germany, India, and China. XYZ is a service-based company that morphed from simple Microsoft consulting shop into a broad technology company that services several vertical markets including Healthcare, Finance, and Government. We focus here on the knowledge workers, a significant portion of their workforce, traveling remotely to client sites to identify and correct technological issues, both hardware and software. These workers are not only highly skilled technologists, but capable communicators, authors, and negotiators. While highly paid, the sit exposed, often on the front line with financial accountability reaching billions of dollars.

Corporation TTT is a regional technology manufacturing company with products such as plasma televisions, LCD enabled phones, smart devices, and other high-tech equipment. This scenario will focus on the line worker who interacts daily with the products, not the product designer.

TTT demands a high level of product knowledge from their line workers to provide constructive feedback that streamlines the manufacturing process and makes servicing the products more cost effective. We will shortly discuss the similarities modern recruiting has wrought on these two dissimilar candidate pools.

Twenty years ago, these two worker groups were serviced through different educational backgrounds, professional experience, and contrasting want ads for gainful employment. These differing worlds have merged today into a single candidate pool that demands a unified qualification tool because of cost effective advertising and emergent skills employers now demand.

While the consultant requires tactful negotiation skills, technical expertise, and solid writing, our scenario-based line workers are really no different. They contribute to ISO manuals, "best practice" FAQ leveraged throughout the business, and even redesign process efficacies to increase throughput or reduce costs. Consultants are not prodigiously unique in the art of negotiating. Our line workers have the power to halt production based on perceived product quality issues. Describing the problem to management, proper identification techniques, and proposed solutions requires similar tact and thoroughness as an enterprise ERP project. Every employee, according to modern want ads, has Email, files status reports, and probably creates their own personal business goals that lead to raises and/or promotions; requiring deft communication skills and some understanding of SMART goals or quantitative measures.

Modern U.S. workers, knowledge and skilled, no longer have the luxury of owning an isolated skill in a focused tool chest, they must continually adapt to ever-changing, rapidly expanding technologies. Additionally, they must fold neatly into thinning team environments, requiring tact and patience in our supremely litigious society. It isn't enough commanding expert knowledge of a particular product, you have to generate revenue, train outsourced workers, and position executive management with strategic guidance.

While these skills are only required in varying degrees, you better believe that medium- to large-sized businesses are identifying these skills in candidates; at least they want to according to their multi-page ads.

Methodology and Proposal

This expert system model is proposed to provide a more concise, predictable, repeatable method for employers to determine potential new hire candidate confidence levels based on correctly answered questions using the following methods:

- Applied position;
- Multiple domain expertise;
- Relative expertise; and
- Aggregate scoring.

The system is Internet-based yielding maximum availability indicted by research that would reach global candidates with 24-hour accessibility. This Candidate Separation Framework, illustrated in Figure 1, provides individual domain contributions toward an Aggregate Candidate Assessment value with inherent flexibility to accommodate firm customization for optimal suitability.

Providing a qualifying mechanism for candidates before resume screening or human intervention would allow more candidates, specifically qualified for the positions advertised, to provide a quantifiable measurement based on a predetermined confidence level. There are a number of economic and human resource related needs for a better candidate screening system tested through the following hypotheses:

H0: *Candidates qualifying through the proposed expert system will not be distinguishable from those selected by field experts.*

H1: *More qualified candidates will be available for selection based on the proposed expert system.*

H2: *A more consistent method of evaluating previously accepted and proposed resumes based on confidence level will result from the proposed system.*

H3: *The proposed expert system will cost less in total man-hours then manual candidate screening processes.*

Turban, Aronson, and Liang (2005) noted that artificially intelligent systems can only be considered smart when both unseen computer and unseen human experts are indistinguishable by the

Figure 1. Candidate separation framework

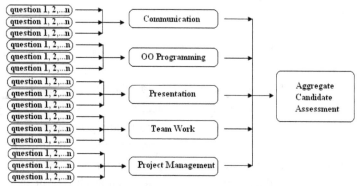

human interviewer. Similarly the author believes that any proposed candidate review system should provide candidates at least as qualified as field experts would select, H0, but will not attempt to replace the interview process, only augment the candidate selection criteria with confidence levels based on relative scoring indicators from multiple domains.

This expert system will eliminate two basic flaws from the human resume candidate selection system; resumes are tailored to desired positions and eliminate potentially important tertiary information, and review timeframes minimize resume perusal to keyword exploration. Resume length is customarily based on perfectly matching requirements posted in a placement ad instead of covering aspects contributing to a more diverse career history.

James Cox, Managing Director at MES Search Company in Smyrna, Georgia notes, "a resume should never be more than 2 pages," "a recruiter is not gauging whether you are a viable candidate for that CFO position at a $200M manufacturing firm based on your first accounts payable position out of school 25 years ago" (ResumeDoctor.com, 2004, P. 1). The researcher argues that a number of vital tasks in the current position leverage experience from that account payable position from 25 years ago. While some extinct skills such as DOS programming may never again be called upon, the aspect of linear programming logic or if/then results will always be applicable in better decision making or designing the next set of policies. Rules based systems that first match degree type might be useful in specialized fields such as legal, accounting, or medical, but in the technical field a psychology or sociology degree might be more applicable to management than a Masters in Science when dealing with personal problems, motivating factors, and personal career development. By increasing the potential candidate pool by first qualifying skills, H0, the proposed system will increase the likelihood of qualified candidates that are interested in the position through initial skill assessment over those with specific qualifications that might only want to increase salary or professional experience made available by degree selection or previous certifications.

Candidate selection is not the only obstacle faced by companies when attempting to fill positions through hiring agencies or posting requisitions on web sites. Bureaucracy can increase decision times that effect candidate availability such as "review more carefully piles" or waiting to schedule a first phone or on-site interview. Potential candidates may have already accepted another offer when located from the stack of candidates. When new resumes are received, what part of the list do they occupy and what criterion determines their positioning, if any? The proposed tool will result in a confidence level based on qualifications questions answered from a number of different domains as they relate to the proposed position and experience level of the candidate. The aspect of integrity will have to be established, whether through timing or signed agreement, but the researcher does not consider that a limiting factor for this information system. Potential employees can easily, upon request, be sorted according to any ratio-based system of sorting most suitable to the employer, or could be based on resume factors in conjunction with the confidence interval, or sorted through a number of other methods once qualifying through the expert system, H2, allowing a more repeatable, accountable method of candidate qualification.

Hiring a recruiting firm can only save part of the financial cost incurred through the hiring process since phone and on-site interviews must take place to ensure interpersonal skills, in addition to technical skills, match the position equally. Replacing the contracted firm would only replace the burden of human resource recruiting back on the organization. The most optimal option would augment a company's current system with more qualified candidates since "an expert system is to be an aid rather than a substitute for human decision making" (Tavana et al, 1994, p.

313) and providing better candidates would yield faster and more qualified interview responses, on-site interview timeframes, and less candidate options – yet more qualified options, H3, resulting in expensive human resources focusing on, arguably, more important tasks. Saving the time of hiring qualifiers and managers (Dafoulas Pateli & Turega, 2002) will result in measurable financial savings and higher quality candidates.

The prospective system here is broken down into four distinct categories: internal qualifications, qualifications per designation or promotable level, candidate scoring based on domain knowledge, and aggregate scoring for corporate extrapolation. The system was left open and vague purposefully: company X may require engineers to support 99.999% uptime conditions with billions of dollars transacting each day through their facility while company Z may simply want someone who can keep their computers running during work hours.

Qualifications per designation are "questions one would ask based on pay grade" and established by each company in the form of simple or complex questions and answers. The researcher suggests posing lower-based pay grades use very straightforward questions such as: define the term multi-threaded; explain how an operating system protects processes; or explain why the data path on a system bus is different sizes. Higher-grade positions can have trick questions that may / may not be accurate or double-barreled questions that require fine analytic skills to determine "best fit" scenarios. This will help devise a method of differentiation between *resume candidates*, those that look good on paper, and *working candidates*, those that look good in the position.

Internal qualifications, or levels, are how a company separates pay grades or role responsibilities. Most familiar systems are numeric-based coupled with a divisional alpha character such as E5 for "Engineering, grade 5" or S9 for "Sales, grade 9". This should provide a solid cross comparison based on pay level and knowledge

requirements matched with role responsibilities. The organization must conduct routine cross-comparison evaluations and external research to determine appropriate compatible skills, compensation, etc if this system were truly functional for the employer; otherwise, the designation is simply an HR label of convenience. The qualifications, regardless of internal structure, serve as a boundary to provide distinct response, or inquiry deltas provisional on an ability to respond. The more qualified the candidate, the more capable of responding appropriately. A distinct advantage provided through this information system over the simple resume format is over qualification. Candidates, based on their own time schedule, a designated timeframe, or the company's approval, can expand their questions into higher grades, if provided, to show advanced knowledge retention. During an interview, it is possible for candidates to demonstrate their quality, but, pre-interview applications were limited to resume exposés or online visual demonstrations, augmented through Flash or another rich media format. Allowing candidates to test beyond the application level may demonstrate a highly qualified candidate with broad skills or someone over qualified that may grow bored and quit within the first year. The applications are reserved and customizable for each implementation.

The aspect of knowledge domains is based on the Gallivan et al (2004) study that found companies are no longer looking for candidates with single digit skills, but those encompassing multiple knowledge domains such as technical skills (in multiple domains), communication, team work, organizational, project management, etc. The questions should rank in difficulty based on the internal relative job structure for that company. Every candidate accumulates skills through personal and professional life. Homemakers balance budgets, juggle schedules, and manage highly complex projects. Does that make them any less qualified than the newly minted PMP with only a college degree to show? If an individual holds an English degree from Cornell, should that preclude them from applying for an engineering position in a software company when they have been programming for 10 years with Perl, Python, and C#? The use of modern Information Systems is nothing more than exclusion- or exclusivity-based systems that "weed out" the "undesired" candidates. Perhaps we are weeding out the most highly qualified, productive candidates based on multi-faceted backgrounds, very broad skill sets, and highly evolved problem solving skills. The key is not sifting through longer, more complex resumes; it is designing a system that accounts for highly evolved job hunters for highly evolved, global corporations. There are no more small companies since everyone is Inter-connected, only small views of employee potential.

Cowling (2003, p. 3) reported that graduating software engineers should have obtained abilities in the following Key Skills:

a. Communication;
b. Information Technology;
c. Application of Numbers;
d. Working with Others;
e. Problem Solving; and
f. Improving Own Learning and Performance.

Technical interviews would probably cover domains b, c, and e unquestionably, but the other 50% is reserved for short on-site interviews, or probationary periods that leave both the company and employee uncomfortably worried about wasted time and expense should things not work out. By questioning candidates with some rudimentary aspects of communication, working with others, and self-improvement, the organization

potentially reveals the candidate's mental and emotional state as well as their technical ability. While the author does not believe this proposed system should replace personal interviews or other professionally developed evaluation methods, it is a cost-effective measure that will allow for better candidate hiring decisions.

The function of i provides each level of knowledge based on questions predicated for that distinct criteria: E1 engineers are only required to understand x% knowledge from the overall set. Each applied question, q, is affording a corresponding correct answer, a. As questions are answered for each level, L, it is important to distinguish advancing levels of difficulty as more important, the higher the knowledge domain, the higher the applied score factor.

Thus, the function of i returns a score based on a particular knowledge domain indicating the candidate strength in that particular field regardless of their college experience, personal exposure to wealth management, or professional experience. Where the function of j represents a mean of the aggregate score, L. All domains required to be completed, t, may or may not be completed by the candidate. If they are not completed, the uncompleted, yet required domains remain included in the summation to provide a more complete candidate score, T.

Finally, it is proposed passing the candidate qualification score through a sigmoid function to provide a more succinct range of comparison between 0 and 1, allowing companies, divisions, or departments, to set their own qualification criteria based on the desired outcome. It is also asserted that candidate qualifications heavily weigh proposed domains in comparison to an-

Figure 2. Function i to determine level-based qualifications

$$f(i) = \left(\frac{a}{q}\right)L$$

Figure 3. Function j to determine domain-based qualifications

$$f(j) = \overline{L}$$

Figure 4. The total score attained by candidates using this information system

$$T = \sum_{\substack{i=1,\\ j=1}}^{t} \frac{f(i)}{f(j)}$$

Figure 5. Candidate distillation process

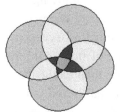

○ Qualified candidates
○ Candidates with skills relative to industry
● Candidates with skills relative to company
◐ Candidates with skills relative to position

swered domains such that each individual has an opportunity to exceed desired qualifications thereby surpassing expectations and distinguishing themselves beyond existing possibilities outside personal contact.

It is important to understand that these scores, by themselves, are meaningless across organizations or even, perhaps, inter-organizationally when the desired traits are not compatible. That is to say that each score is an arbitrate indication of the candidate knowledge expressed at any given time. The idea is not to provide a replacement for human beings, but to augment the existing systems where it is broken, replacing the static resume that clearly has served beyond its capabilities, toward a more dynamic system that reflects our current, more complex environment.

Figure 5 provides a visual example of the candidate distillation process as combined individual tacit skills provide focused benefit to the accompanying industry, organization, and even posted position based on complex requirements.

As candidates complete the sectional evaluation, their score is automatically updated for the hiring managers to retrieve. Candidates falling below established parameters are automatically informed of their disqualification, even if this takes place days, weeks, or months after initial qualification in such an automated system. Figure 6 demonstrates a sample flow of the information system.

FUTURE RESEARCH DIRECTIONS

Understanding the modern integration of Information Systems in nearly every facet of American life, from mobile communications to Internet-enabled refrigerators, creates a new avenue of discovery that should include job hunting and employment postings. No longer should the qualified applicant complete a simple questionnaire and attach a simplified cv to qualify themselves as the optimal candidate for posted positions. Equally, the employer should not settle for just another warm body. As information security becomes an overarching theme for any company connected to the Internet or transacting service-based products, finding more qualified candidates with highly evolved backgrounds will become paramount over filling seats in the industrial complex. More and more candidates can telecommute or complete work remotely, transmitting the results upon completion. It is important that we better understand employee motivational patterns along the lines of W. Edwards Deming (e.g. Maslow and Hertzberg). Identifying explicit skills through direct inspection and tacit skills through problem solving scenarios will identify and perhaps attain the talent, but modern corporations need to inspect retaining employees. Are people working for the paycheck, thus imposing serious information security risk, or do they really care about the companies' success and direct energies toward that end.

Figure 6. Sample ACA information flow

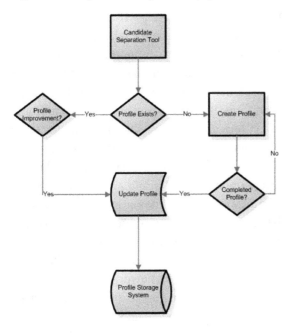

Further developing the propose information system to include salary requirements would be useful in determining if the existing corporate structure cannot attract talent or current outlay is exaggerated. Understanding how total compensation, afforded only the most senior employees currently, could create a more loyal workforce without significantly affecting the bottom line. Ancillary benefits such as dry-cleaning, baby sitting, etc, while afforded by the company, the cost is incurred by the employee. This could enhance factors noted by the 2002 Journal of Accountancy as important to the modern worker. Additional factors worth investigating include incorporating a simple personality profile as another domain. Few companies continue to employ this profile, perhaps because of the length or privacy intrusion. A modified scenario that targeted specific positional traits; accounting, engineering, sales, marketing, may provide a useful domain for inclusion benefiting both sides of employment. Employment has endured decades of study and should continue to rank high to ensure that employees retain the best opportunity to highlight

wares and employers cost benefit for the hiring process is maximized.

LESSONS LEARNED

Corporate superstars and individual contributors have a common element: their unique skill was identified through some hiring process. Unfortunately it has become increasingly difficult to identify those skills due to rapidly advancing technology, diverging business requirements, reduced advertising costs, and a lack of candidate separation. Previous indicators of separation may have been college completion, college branding, corporate branding, or identifiable skill set; however, the global stage now set for employment has increased corporate demands placed on candidates to define and clearly demonstrate uniquely applied characteristics through a 2-dimentional medium.

Posting positions with fewer traits will never reoccur because of population density and exhausting business requirements; however, defining skill requirements important to both firm and function can be isolated with more advanced interviewing techniques.

Personally directing candidates through specialized recruiting firms and executive headhunters will always provide a more intimate link, but properly identifying technical proficiency for the rank and file requires new methods vastly superior to current resume sorting techniques. Companies can either reduce their requirements, thus allowing candidate to match a larger number of requirements, or build a new method of assessment relative to position demands.

Rapid technological innovation will continue from this point forward, increasing both hard and soft skill requirements for sizable business positions, creating a continuing challenge to properly assess hundreds or thousands of resumes. Equally changed are the candidates to adequately position themselves with 1-2 page resumes that are largely accomplishment-based. Reducing requirements or applicants does not appear a likely option.

CONCLUSION

Modern organizations expect their employees to obtain and maintain a wide range of skill sets (Gallivan, Truex, & Kvasny, Summer 2004) and become personally responsible for their own career advancement (Gallivan, 2001), but how do these candidates differentiate themselves from the masses through a simple 1-2 page resume? As candidates become more experienced, it becomes improbable, if not impossible to list every relevant skill or character trait employers are looking for, despite the posted position requirements growing beyond a reasonable level.

This information system, if implemented through recruiting agency or individual corporations, will provide a serious competitive advantage toward identifying long-term talent that can be stylized and customized to match very exacting parameters. Supporting the Extejt and Lynn (1988) criteria:

- No expert system can incorporate all relevant information;
- In a dynamic environment, a company's decision criteria undergo changes over time; and
- The need to update an expert system may become evident only when there is a pattern of conflict between the system's recommendations and the human recruiters' decisions.

While no system can incorporate all information, this proposal would provide a modular information system capable of providing the most relevant information. The proposed information system allows access 24x7, intra- or inter-organizationally and internationally, if so prescribed. Much like the military competency

exams, such an information system directed toward technical recruiting will not only help hiring companies identify better talent, it will provide talented candidates the opportunity to find better matching positions, ultimately resulting in happier workers, higher productivity, and a stronger workforce. It would be possible to determine future skills such as accounting or marketing for small, quick-growth companies where employees must become accustomed to wearing multiple hats. Large organizations would have a more flexible tool to include or exclude particular traits including background information (simply another domain) into the overall score. The proposed modularized approach affords optimal flexibility through a highly structured framework where additional knowledge domains are expanded through the aggregate score. Understanding exactly who you are hiring, or how you are being hired, is the first step toward a more symbiotic workforce in tune with a highly integrated information society that properly leverages technology to grow into a more empowered citizenry.

REFERENCES

Anonymous,. (2002). Hiring smarts. *Journal of Accountancy, 194*(6), 116.

Anonymous,. (2007). Hiring the best and the brightest. *Journal of Accountancy, 204*(2), 27.

Baldiga, N. R. (2005). Opportunity and balance: Is your organization ready to provide both? *Journal of Accountancy, 199*(5), 39–44.

Barron, J. M., Bishop, J., & Dunkelberg, W. C. (1985). Employer search: The interviewing and hiring of new employees. *The Review of Economics and Statistics, 67*(1), 43–52. doi:10.2307/1928433

Beatty, P., & Willis, G. (2007). Research synthesis: The practice of cognitive interviewing. *Public Opinion Quarterly*.

Black, S. E., & Lynch, L. M. (1996). Human-capital investments and productivity. *The American Economic Review, 86*(2), 263–267.

Borstorff, P., Marker, M., & Bennett, D. (2006). Online recruitment: Attitudes and behaviors of job seekers. *Proceedings of Allied Academies International Conference. Academy of Organizational Culture, Communications and Conflict, 11*(2), 9-13.

Colwell, R. P., Brown, G., & See, F. (1999). *Intel's college hiring methods and recent results.* IEEE International Conference on Microelectronic Systems Education, p. 94.

Connet, M., & Bicknese, L. (2001). Basic skills back in demand. *Financial Executive, 17*(5), 44–45.

Cowling, A. J. (2003). *What should graduating software engineers be able to do?* 16th Conference on Software Engineering Education and Training (CSEE&T), p. 88.

Crow, D., & DeSanto, J. (2004). *A hybrid approach to concept extraction and recognition-based matching in the domain of human resources.* 16th IEEE International Conference on Tools with Artificial Intelligence (ICTAI'04), pp. 535-539.

Dafoulas, G. A., Pateli, A. G., & Turega, M. (2002). *Business-to-employee cooperation support through online job interviews.* 13th International Workshop on Database and Expert Systems Applications (DEXA'02), pp. 286-295.

Dickler, J. (2009). The job application black hole. *Money.* Retrieved February 18, 2010, from http://money.cnn.com/ 2010/02/18/news/economy/resume_void/index.htm?hpt=T2

Extejt, M. M., & Lynn, M. P. (1988). Expert systems as human resource management tools. *Journal of Systems Management, 39*(11), 10–15.

Gallivan, M. J. (2001). Meaning to change: How diverse stakeholders interpret organizational communication about change initiatives. *IEEE Transactions on Professional Communication, 44*(4), 243–266. doi:10.1109/47.968107

Gallivan, M. J., Truex, D. P. III, & Kvasny, L. (2004). Changing patterns in IT skill sets 1988-2003: A content analysis of classified advertising. *ACM SIGMIS Database, 35*(3), 64–87. doi:10.1145/1017114.1017121

Giles, C. (2010). Mind the gap. *Financial Times (North American Edition),* 19.

Girard, F. (2002). *Five state college coaches claim unearned degrees.* Retrieved on May 14, 2005, from http://www.detnews.com/ 2002/college/0209/18/ a01-590403.htm

Harris, J. (2009). What's wrong with executive compensation? *Journal of Business Ethics, 85,* 147–156. doi:10.1007/s10551-008-9934-6

Hatzilygeroudis, I. (2004). Integrating rules, neural networks, and cases for knowledge representation. *Expert Systems with Applications, 27*(1), 63–75. doi:10.1016/j.eswa.2003.12.004

Jiang, J. J., & Klein, G. (1995). Requisite technical skills for technical support analysts: A survey. *ACM SIGCPR Computer Personnel, 16*(2), 12–20. doi:10.1145/202896.202899

Lee, P. (2002). *Changes in skill requirements of Information Systems professionals in Singapore.* ACM 35th Annual Hawaii International Conference on System Sciences (HICSS'02), 8, pp. 264-272.

Leitheiser, R. L. (1992). MIS skills for the 1990s: A survey of MIS managers' perceptions. *Journal of Management Information Systems, 9*(1), 69–91.

Leung, Y. W., & Mao, J. Y. (2003). Providing embedded proactive task support for diagnostic jobs: A neural network-based approach. *Expert Systems with Applications, 25*(2), 255–267.

Malhotra, Y. (2001). Expert systems for Knowledge Management: Crossing the chasm between information processing and sense making. *Expert Systems with Applications, 20*(1), 7–16. doi:10.1016/S0957-4174(00)00045-2

Moody, J. W., Will, R. P., & Blanton, J. E. (1996). Enhancing knowledge elicitation using the cognitive interview. *Expert Systems with Applications, 10*(1), 127–133. doi:10.1016/0957-4174(95)00039-9

Niederman, F. (1999). Valuing the IT workforce as intellectual capital. In J. Prasad (Ed.), *Proceedings of the 1999 ACM Special Interest Group Computer Personnel Research Conference*, New Orleans, LA, pp. 174-181.

Niederman, F., Brancheau, J., & Wetherbe, J. (1991). Information Systems management issues for the 1990s. *Management Information Systems Quarterly, 15*(4), 474–500. doi:10.2307/249452

Niederman, F., & Mandviwalla, M. (2004). The evolution of IT (computer) personnel research: More theory, more understanding, more questions. *ACM SIGMIS Database, 35*(3), 6–8. doi:10.1145/1017114.1017117

Noble, D. F. (1998). Perspectives: Digital diploma mills: The automation of higher education. *netWorker, 2*(2), 9–14. doi:10.1145/280449.280454

Ouchi, W. G. (1980). Markets, bureaucracies, and clans. *Administrative Science Quarterly, 25*(1), 129–141. doi:10.2307/2392231

Pilon, S., & Tandberg, D. (1997). Neural network and linear regression models in residency selection. *The American Journal of Emergency Medicine, 15*(4), 361–364. doi:10.1016/S0735-6757(97)90125-X

Poole, W. G. (2003). The softer side of custom software development: Working with the other players. *Proceedings of the 16th Conference on Software Engineering Education and Training (CSEET'03)*, pp. 14-21.

ResumeDoctor.com. (2004). *What recruiters are saying about your resume*. Retrieved on May 14, 2005, from http://www.resumedoctor.com/PP_Artical7_6.htm

Shin, T. (2008). *Working in corporate America: Dynamics of pay at large corporations, 1992-2005*. Unpublished dissertation, University of California, Berkeley, California.

Stott, K., & Wood, W. (2001). What skills do employers require from people who work in the IT client support role? *34th Annual Hawaii International Conference on System Sciences (HICSS-34)*, 8, pp. 8069-8078.

Tavana, M., Lee, P., & Joglekar, P. (1994). The development and validation of a campus recruiting expert system using expert opinions and historical data. *Expert Systems with Applications, 7*(2), 305–321. doi:10.1016/0957-4174(94)90046-9

Tye, E.M., Ng, W., Poon, R.S.K. & Burn, J.M. (1995). Information Systems skills: Achieving alignment between the curriculum and the needs of the IS professionals in the future. *ACM SIGMIS Database, 26*(4).

Waheed, A., & Adeli, H. (2000). A knowledge-based system for evaluation of Superload permit applications. *Expert Systems with Applications, 18*(1), 51–58. doi:10.1016/S0957-4174(99)00050-0

Wu, J.-H., Chen, Y.-C., & Chang, J. (2005). *The IS manager: A study of critical professional activities and skills/knowledge*. 38th Annual Hawaii International Conference on System Sciences (HICSS'05), 8, pp. 266-274.

ADDITIONAL READING

Allen, D. G., Mahto, R. V., & Otondo, R. F. (2007). Web-based recruitment: Effects of information, organizational brand, and attitudes toward a Web site on applicant attraction. *The Journal of Applied Psychology*, *92*(6), 1696–1708. doi:10.1037/0021-9010.92.6.1696

Anderson, N. (2003, June). Applicant and Recruiter Reactions to New Technology in Selection: A Critical Review and Agenda for Future Research. *International Journal of Selection and Assessment*, *11*, 121–136. doi:10.1111/1468-2389.00235

Cable, D. M., & Yu, K. Y. T. (2006). Managing job seekers' organizational image beliefs: The role of media richness and media credibility. *The Journal of Applied Psychology*, *91*(4), 828–840. doi:10.1037/0021-9010.91.4.828

Dineen, B. R., Ling, J., Ash, S. R., & DelVecchio, D. (2007). Aesthetic properties and message customization: Navigating the dark side of web recruitment. *The Journal of Applied Psychology*, *92*(2), 356–372. doi:10.1037/0021-9010.92.2.356

Ehrhart, K. H., & Ziegert, J. C. (2005). Why Are Individuals Attracted to Organizations? *Journal of Management*, *31*(6), 901–919. doi:10.1177/0149206305279759

Gardner, W. L., Reithel, B. J., Foley, R. T., Cogliser, C. C., & Walumbwa, F. O. (2009). Attraction to Organizational Culture Profiles: Effects of Realistic Recruitment and Vertical and Horizontal Individualism—Collectivism. *Management Communication Quarterly*, *22*(3), 437–472. doi:10.1177/0893318908327006

Jones, D. A., Shultz, J. W., & Chapman, D. S. (2006). Recruiting through Job Advertisements: The Effects of Cognitive Elaboration on Decision Making. *International Journal of Selection and Assessment*, *2*(14), 167–179. doi:10.1111/j.1468-2389.2006.00342.x

Kevin, R. M., & Anita, P. T. (2004). The Decisions Job Applicants Must Make: Insights From a Bayesian Perspective. *International Journal of Selection and Assessment*, *12*(1-2), 66–74. doi:10.1111/j.0965-075X.2004.00264.x

Liu, E., & Johnson, S. M. (2006). New Teachers' Experiences of Hiring: Late, Rushed, and Information-Poor. *Educational Administration Quarterly*, *42*(3), 324–360. doi:10.1177/0013161X05282610

Maurer, S. D., & Liu, Y. (2007). Developing effective e-recruiting websites: Insights for managers from marketers. *Business Horizons*, *50*(4), 305–314. doi:10.1016/j.bushor.2007.01.002

Pitariu, A. H., & Ployhart, R. E. (2010). Explaining Change: Theorizing and Testing Dynamic Mediated Longitudinal Relationships. *Journal of Management*, *36*(2), 405–429. doi:10.1177/0149206308331096

Ployhart, R. E. (2006). Staffing in the 21st Century: New Challenges and Strategic Opportunities. *Journal of Management*, *32*(6), 868–897. doi:10.1177/0149206306293625

Ployhart, R. E., Schneider, B., & Schmitt, N. (2006). *Staffing Organizations: Contemporary Practice and Theory*. Mahwah, New Jersey: Lawrence Erlbaum Association, Inc.

Ryan, A. M., & Tippins, N. T. (2004). Attracting and Selecting: What Psychological Research Tells Us. *Human Resource Management*, *43*(4), 305–318. doi:10.1002/hrm.20026

Sally, A. C., & Josephine, W. (2007). Applicant Attraction: The role of recruiter function, work-life balance policies and career salience. *International Journal of Selection and Assessment*, *15*(4), 394–404. doi:10.1111/j.1468-2389.2007.00398.x

Van Hoye, G., & Lievens, F. (2007). Investigating Web-Based Recruitment Sources: Employee Testimonials vs. Word-of-Mouse. *International Journal of Selection and Assessment*, *15*(4), 372–382. doi:10.1111/j.1468-2389.2007.00396.x

Chapter 8
Insourcing vs. Outsourcing:
Critical IT HR Considerations

Anna Frazzetto
Harvey Nash, USA

ABSTRACT

Most discussions of IT outsourcing focus on cost reductions and meeting skills requirements. This chapter focuses on the people considerations and the important role that HR must play to ensure success, especially as it pertains to evaluating the resources and managing the transition. HR must be engaged in monitoring the cost of talent, identifying the required skills, being sensitive to the timing of the requirements, and mitigating the strain on work balance.

INTRODUCTION

When pundits and business experts debate outsourcing versus insourcing, they are often speaking in broad, bottom-line, big-picture strokes. They speak of costs to be saved, skills to be attained, intellectual capital to be protected and standards to be maintained. Many times there is a lot of emotion and judgment in their considerations but sometimes not enough real-world fact. When a business considers whether to outsource or insource an IT project, one of the roles of HR is to help deliver critical workforce facts that help business leaders make the best possible IT sourcing decisions.

Once the decision—insourcing or outsourcing—is made, HR plays a central role throughout the transition by helping to adapt workforce processes to the solution. HR is also responsible for helping internal technology teams transfer knowledge and support the project. The sourcing model selected, as this chapter will show, determines HR's course as each approach requires a different talent support structure. However, the first role HR must embrace in any IT project is that of a strategic

DOI: 10.4018/978-1-60960-535-3.ch008

advisor who helps IT and business leaders as they work to make the right sourcing decisions.

HR'S ROLE IN SOURCING DECISIONS: STRATEGIC ADVISOR

HR has a unique window into the IT organization. The HR team not only has a detailed understanding of the costs associated with internal teams, but also a clear map of the skills and experience across the IT organization. This knowledge is essential in building the best possible business case for project sourcing — be it outsourcing or insourcing. The challenge for HR is to ensure its insights are heard during the sourcing analysis process.

Too many times, IT leaders and managers come to HR for very specific IT workforce data, such as cost to hire, cost to train, and on boarding and recruiting timeframes, but they leave HR out of the rigorous examination to follow. To become a partner in sourcing decisions and elevate the role of HR in organizational planning and operations to a more strategic one, HR teams must be ready to provide rich human capital data, in four core areas:

- Talent Costs
- Skill Roster & Skill Needs
- Timing
- Workload Balance & Strain

However, the goal is not to merely rattle off data or provide a clean report. To become a trusted workforce advisor to the IT organization, HR must deliver substantive data and thoughtful insights across each of these four core areas that give IT and business leaders better visibility into their teams, spending and workforce needs.

Talent Costs

The decision to insource or outsource an IT project or process can sometimes, mistakenly, be seen as merely a financial one. "Is it cheaper to have an expert provider take on the project or process, or can we do it internally for less?" While there are many essential factors that go into an outsourcing decision besides costs (such as resource availability, skill needs and management time), they still remain pivotal to any outsourcing discussion. What will HR be asked to provide in a cost analysis? In most cases, a simple breakdown of team member rates and employment costs (what it costs to pay your team) is required. These costs will be directly compared to the costs coming in from outsourcing and IT services vendors (what it costs to recruit, pay and retain their workers).

To truly provide strong cost information to support business and IT leaders, HR needs to ask questions. What skills and what experience are required? A cost analysis assumes that both teams (internal, contract-based or outsourced) come to the table with equal skills. That, however, is never the case. In some instances, the outsourcing team may need to train its teams to understand the company's internal processes and operation. In an insourcing solution, internal teams may be less skilled in the task at hand, which could mean more time and would likely mean added training costs.

A strong HR partner will also carefully analyze the talent cost breakdowns offered by outsourcing providers. Many times providers may leave off associated costs from their calculation, such as training. When analyzing potential outsourcing firms, it can be helpful to create a cost comparison chart to improve and accelerate the evaluation process.

Skills Needs: Where are They?

The question of skills is not just one of finding out who has the skills. It's also a question of how the business can acquire them. If a business does not have in-house IT talent with the skills needed to execute a project, outsourcing is not automatically the answer. A business can still insource through recruitment, IT staffing or by training internal talent, if timeframes allow. The more important question for HR is this: How critical are these skills to the ongoing success and advancement of the IT and business organization? If these are IT skills that the business needs as part of its internal IT arsenal, HR needs to help business teams consider the best way to begin integrating them into the organization.

Would outsourcing put too great a distance between the project and the internal team that needs to acquire new skills? Or, might outsourcing win the business time to find the right professionals to join the organization while analyzing how an expert provider delivers on the project? In the end, the skills question is a critical one for HR to ensure IT and business leaders consider. In addition, it offers HR the perfect time to sit down with managers and look at how they want their teams to grow. HR must always maintain a strong understanding of the skills that are essential and nonessential to the IT organization's operations. When a question of insourcing or outsourcing arises, HR can use it as a time to ensure the company is continuing to develop mission-critical skills while providing insight into the most cost- and time-efficient way to access and develop the capabilities needed.

Timing

Time is always of the essence and in an IT project, the urgency is often even more intense because clients (internal or external) are clamoring for a solution, or market pressures are driving change or demanding a fix to a problem. Timeframes must be a careful consideration in choosing between insourcing and outsourcing solutions, especially because recruiting could be required by either party.

The insights HR can provide about timing center on recruitment and training. IT HR teams should be able to immediately tap into their IT services networks (trusted staffing and services providers) for solid insight into skill availability. Previous recruiting work will also allow HR to give managers solid insight on how long a full-

blown recruitment process will take. Looking at the urgency of the project and the complexity of the skills required, HR will be able to very quickly advise the business on the best sourcing option from a timing perspective.

Workload Balance & Strain

One important sourcing consideration that is often overlooked in the rush to find a solution is workload balance and organizational strain. HR may likely have insight into how teams are currently managing existing workload. Are teams overwhelmed? Have open jobs remained unfilled due to budget constraints? If so, an IT organization is likely managing overworked and stressed team members.

On the other hand, it's important in an IT organization to also watch for signs of boredom. Technology professionals who are not challenged and curious are famous for moving on and driving up turnover rates and difficulties. If HR has hints that IT teams are eager for new challenges and opportunities, it's important to share those insights as well. All IT resources need to be leveraged to maximum advantage, including talent. Serving as a strategic partner in the measurement and improvement of workforce performance and morale, HR can give IT managers unique insight into resource balance, strain and enthusiasm.

The information HR provides during the sourcing evaluation process is critical to good decision making. The challenge for HR is to get IT leaders and business peers to consider the workforce information they are not asking for — training costs and requirements, the strain on existing teams and recruiting timeframes, etc. The more workforce insight HR can provide in the sourcing analysis phase, the more effective HR will be at supporting the final solution, whether it is an insourcing or outsourcing one.

HR'S ROLE IN SUPPORTING THE SELECTED SOLUTION

Once the sourcing solution is selected, HR will have a number of contributions to make. Most importantly, HR's job is to make certain workforce processes are in place to support the IT teams as they grow and change to meet the demands of the project. However, the lists of HR tasks for each approach do differ.

HR's Outsourcing Role

- Talent & Skill Acquisition Consulting
- Risk Mitigation – Co-Employment
- Cost Oversight
- Change Management & Team Transition
- Training Support
- Performance Management

HR's Insourcing Role

- Recruitment and/or Vendor Selection & Management
- Risk Mitigation – Co-Employment
- On Boarding & Integration
- Training Support
- Performance Management

Outsourcing Role

While many might assume that insourcing puts significantly more demand on HR, outsourcing is equally demanding from an HR perspective. In fact, some might argue outsourcing is more challenging and time consuming because of the change factor. The idea that a company can select a provider, hand over an operation and walk away with little work is nothing short of fantasy. Constant vendor and contract management are a must. For HR, the IT outsourcing work begins with helping to assess the talent resources of potential providers.

- **Talent & Skill Acquisition Consulting:** HR should partner with IT managers as they evaluate potential outsourcing providers to ensure the quality of talent is very high and that recruitment and talent management practices are keeping turnover low and employee satisfaction strong. While in some cases, HR is invited into the outsourcing provider review process, some HR professionals may need to make a little noise to get involved. For HR, it's important to maintain this strategic role to have a constant grasp on the full roster of skills and professionals supporting the IT team. If HR doesn't have a complete understanding of the work being done or what skills are being leveraged by providers, no one in the business does. The danger is that the business is not able to use all skills and resources to maximum advantage or identify true talent requirements and skill gaps. HR also offers strong recruitment assessment capabilities and can help IT teams identify providers that are not upholding topnotch talent acquisition practices.
- **Risk Mitigation – Co-Employment:** Co-employment is a serious legal risk that businesses must be attuned to in any outsourcing or contract staffing engagement. One of the benefits of selecting an outsourcing or staffing partner is legal protection. HR must ensure the outsourcing provider has full supervision of its employees and any employees the company may be transitioning to the outsourcing entity. If there is any risk that the outsourcing organization is taking on only a partial supervisory role, HR must work with the company's legal team to remedy the situation before any engagement work begins.
- **Cost Oversight:** While many executives and IT team members will be carefully monitoring the outsourcing budget, HR needs to make sure they are watching the

talent spending line items with outsourcing providers. They need to work with IT teams to ensure any costs related to outsourced IT teams (training, turnover, etc.) are reported to HR so that a full understanding of hard and soft talent costs can be achieved and monitored.

- **Change Management & Talent Transition:** The people most directly affected by IT outsourcing — internal IT talent teams — need help from HR through the transition. Many HR organizations have established strong change management processes and it's important to apply those to outsourcing engagements as well. Even when just a small piece of IT work is outsourced, there are still internal staff members who become nervous and even disgruntled by the change.

HR's job is to identify which employees will be affected directly by the change, either by assuming new roles in the business or by transitioning over to the outsourced vendor. HR needs to work with IT managers to ensure that the staff members are being guided through the process and given the information they need to successfully continue in their daily jobs.

For large outsourcing engagements, change management will require carefully constructed employee communications as well as internal education. HR needs to support the development and delivery of change management communications and training to ensure that all employees are getting the support and information they need from management, from their teams and from HR.

- **Training Support:** HR will continue to play a role in ensuring internal staff members receive the right training. Internal staff members whose jobs are directly affected by the outsourcing decision may require new business process or skills training. HR can work with hiring managers to see how

job roles are evolving and consider if and when job training, coaching or mentoring would be beneficial.

- **Performance Management:** While HR has traditionally played a key role in monitoring and reporting workforce performance, the performance of the outsourced team will be monitored by the IT team overseeing the engagement. However, workforce performance in one department always has an impact on other departments in one way or another. HR should keep a keen eye on how the work and deliverables of the outsourced organization impact overall workforce performance.

If outsourcing performance lags and it affects employee performance in other areas of IT and the greater business organization, it's important for HR to quantify and report those lapses. The same goes for high performance results. If the outsourcing team's performance is boosting efficiency and performance across IT and the business organization, it's important to measure and share those results so that the company can learn from the success and gain new insights into how to keep the performance momentum strong.

Insourcing Role

Insourcing is a very broad term that refers to an IT project or initiative that is managed on-site by internal IT teams, contract IT staff or a combination of internal talent and contract-based IT professionals. No matter the approach, HR often has a central role in building the teams who deliver an insourced IT solution.

- **Recruitment and/or Vendor Selection & Management**: When the business decides to tackle an IT initiative internally, some recruitment may be involved to fill skill gaps or to help expand a team to handle the added workload. While HR will almost always play a role in recruiting for a direct hire position, HR also often plays a role in vendor selection and management when contract talent is needed. When the IT organization has decided to use contract-based IT consultants to support an insourced project, HR will often partner with procurement and IT teams to determine the best talent vendors. Vendor selection processes differ widely from organization to organization but here are a few critical guidelines to remember:

- *Focus on Service*: Work with staffing and talent vendors that are highly responsive to your needs and concerns.
- *Keep Costs in Perspective*: While costs are a critical factor in vendor selection, don't make them your only consideration. Vendors with the lowest prices are likely to have deficiencies in other areas like service levels and talent quality.
- *Evaluation & Testing*: Testing and interview processes used to recruit and hire internal staff should be leveraged for contract-based talent as well. While timeframes or vendor processes may require alterations to testing and evaluation processes, HR needs to ensure that hiring standards are maintained. It's important to remember that even employees who are temporary can have strong and lasting impact on team performance and results.
- **Risk Mitigation – Co-Employment**: As with outsourcing — as explained in detail above — co-employment is a risk when leveraging a staffing vendor for contract-based and contract-to-hire talent. HR must work in close partnership with the staffing partner to ensure they are taking full, legal supervision of any contract-based talent in order to avoid all potential litigation issues.

- **On Boarding & Integration**: Many businesses make the mistake of creating heavy distinction between internal staff versus contractors. This division can damage teamwork and prevent contractors from truly integrating and successfully contributing to the project(s). HR should work to create mini-on-boarding programs to help contract-based IT talent more successfully integrate into the workplace and more quickly become strong contributors.
- **Training Support**: As with outsourcing, insourcing can also require employee training. In some cases it may be basic training related to internal processes and methodologies. In cases where internal teams are managing the entire initiative, it may be necessary to help IT staff gain new skills or refresh old ones. HR will need to partner with managers to identify when and where job training, coaching or mentoring is needed.
- **Performance Management**: Ongoing performance management processes should continue, covering both internal IT staff members as well as contract-based staff members. HR should watch how integrated teams perform compared with teams made up of only internal staff. Careful performance monitoring and reporting will help the IT organization address immediate performance issues while also providing information that will help the entire insourcing versus outsourcing decision making process better down the road.

LESSONS LEARNED

No HR team should be frightened by the word "outsourcing." After all, HR has been one of the earliest adopters of business process outsourcing when you look at the rapid adoption of outsourced benefits administration. Instead of worrying that increased outsourcing might diminish the role or importance of HR, HR teams must focus on becoming strategic partners that help IT and business leaders make the very best sourcing decisions and build the most effective engagements.

To accomplish this ambitious goal, here are the core lessons HR leaders and team members today can learn:

- **Provide More than Data**. When IT leaders ask you for specific resource or cost advice, go farther. Find out what they need to know and be sure the knowledge you are providing is substantive and unbiased. Give them enough information with enough expertise that they are almost forced to ask, "What do you think?"
- **Support the Evaluation**. Whether the business team is evaluating an insourcing or outsourcing solution (or both), work to have a voice in the discussion. Provide HR data but also insights. Volunteer to get more information and be open to new ideas in how solutions are delivered. The more adaptable HR can be to IT's evolving needs, the more IT will turn to HR for support.
- **Be a Co-Employment & Talent Cost Expert**. Nobody understands better the risks of co-employment or the costs of recruiting, hiring and retaining talent. Use that expertise to your advantage by providing co-employment and cost data to IT managers before they ask for it. A true partner is forthright and eager with information, which is exactly how HR should operate during an insourcing/outsourcing evaluation process.
- **Measure & Report**. Once an insourcing or outsourcing decision has been made or a pilot project begun, do not bow out of the process. Continue to provide performance

data (e.g. training reports and feedback) that will help IT leaders evaluate ongoing success. Ensure that your strategic partnership is an enduring one that business leaders count on, and you can be sure they will invite HR to strategic leadership discussions down the road.

- **Communicate the Change.** Excellence in communication is an important and very visible way for HR to contribute to insourcing and outsourcing initiatives. HR can leverage its change communication expertise to support the migration to insourcing or outsourcing. Best practices to remember include building strong communication timelines that address all audiences — the IT team, employees and management. HR should also incorporate written and verbal one-on-one discussions into communication plans so that everyone affected understands the impact on individuals, groups and the organization. The more communication HR does — and the more strategic it is — the more likely the rest of the company will understand and embrace the workforce change and see HR's role in facilitating and supporting the initiative.

Remember, the more skill, resource, performance and vendor information HR can bring to sourcing decision-making processes, the more business and technology teams will turn to HR to support the planning and execution of these solutions. The goal of HR should not be to protect territory in any solution, but to increase performance, skills and results for IT and the entire business through excellence in human capital support, management and measurement.

Chapter 9
Deliberate Leadership:
Women in IT

Kristen Lamoreaux
SIM Women, USA

Dibi Varghese
Stevens Institute of Technology, USA

ABSTRACT

For decades, societal influences, academic ennui, and corporate resistance to change have contributed toward the reduction of the number of women pursuing the computer science field. Technology innovations have enabled greater workplace flexibility, yet gender schemas and negative stereotypes remain. Human Resources organizations are pivotal in altering negative perceptions and reversing misconceptions. HR has low and no cost options available to them to greatly impact their work environment and subsequent female IT recruitment, development, and retention programs. Organizations that do not deliberately address the talent shortfall within Information Technology will clearly suffer recruitment, retention, and business performance consequences. While the focus of this chapter is women in IT, most of the discussion can also be applied to men.

INTRODUCTION

Women who enter the field of technology know they are entering a historically male dominated field, but their passion drives them to pursue their goal. At the lower ranks, the gender divide is evident, but at the highest leadership levels, men outnumber women 8:1. The women who have fought their way to the top don't need HR to clear the path for them, but they could use a partner in making the hike up the career ladder easier for themselves and the next generation of women leaders.

Female CIOs know what it takes to make it —they've done it against great odds. To retain these talented women an organization needs to acknowledge their value financially certainly, but they also need to game plan their next career move.

DOI: 10.4018/978-1-60960-535-3.ch009

Average CIO tenure is over 4.5 years, based on Luftman 2009 SIM survey. A female CIO is not going to sit idle. She's going to say, "I reached this summit. Now where's my next mountain?"

At the same time, women tend to turn and look behind them to see who they can help by reaching out a hand. Some women may blaze a path to the top via a straight line. Others may stay on previously cleared paths to reach the summit, and yet more may wander along enjoying the views at different stages of their lives and family. It doesn't matter. There's no one right way. The challenge is transferring the confidence and knowledge that female IT leaders have gained downward to those who are coming up the ranks. Human Resources have a tremendous opportunity to combat social influences and negative stereotypes and to positively impact the women inside their IT organizations via both strategic and tactical ways.

BACKGROUND

Societal Influence

At a macro level, a major social disadvantage is the development of products and services that do not include input from half the human population. This results in products and services that may not take into consideration the cognizant needs of half of the consumers in the world. The NCWIT reports that although women influence or control more than 83% of all consumer purchases, and approximately 66% percentage of home computer purchases, they are not involved in the creation of the many products they consume. They also report that spending data from 2003 indicated that women spent $55 billion on consumer electronics, this figure surpassing that of male spending. The lack of explicit inclusion of females in the development of the many of the goods they consume may result in low levels of consumer satisfaction.

Gender Expectations

Gender role expectations result in a boundary created by the social and cultural environment, and this frequently defines limits to women's career choices (Lang, 2007 and Trauth et al., 2008). These gender role expectations are often based on stereotypes. Gender stereotypes define lower expectations for women in fields of technology, science and math, and that women are outsiders in the domain of IT. Gender role expectations define that men have a higher inclination towards technology or computers and goes even as far as stating that men are more competent when it comes to technology (Martin and Wardle, 1999 and Lemons and Parzinger, 2007). This has a negative effect on female self-efficacy levels, achievement and interest in the field.

Panteli et al. (1999) believe that it is the perception of IT being a male-gendered environment that makes the industry exceptionally unattractive to women. This perception is further upheld by the low levels of female representation at management levels of the IT organization. Cultures that do not perceive IT to be male dominated have higher numbers of female students pursuing IT related education. An example from Trauth et al.'s (2008) research is of Asian female students who receive encouragement from their family and society to pursue careers in IT. Another interesting point from their research was that communist or centrally planned societies were more supportive of females pursuing careers in any field, including IT. In comparison to capitalist western cultures, these societies had less stringent gender role expectations. As organizations expand their recruitment practices, HR groups will need to learn how IT is viewed within each culture.

Media Perceptions

The media, specifically advertising, is also responsible for shaping the social values and attitudes of society towards women and IT (Turner, 2001).

Stereotype portrayal of women not confident with technology or not having status or power negatively impact the IT industry and act as a deterrent for women considering IT as a career choice. These kinds of advertisements help create a negative image of the IT industry for women and help reiterate any preconceived stereotyped gender role expectations. This also adversely impacts the women already in the IT workforce as they have to contend with their male counterparts who are influenced by the attitudes of society. An industry which is perceived as being discriminatory is avoided by women, and when women experience negative judgment based on their gender, this leads to dissatisfaction and voluntary turnover.

According to Lang (2007) the inaccurate representation of IT work by the media prevents young women from selecting IT as a future career prospect. IT work is often depicted from a purely technical perspective. Many people view IT work to be deskbound and solitary, with interaction being limited to a computer. Jewel and Maltby (2001) uncovered that boys are more attracted to professions that are lower on people orientation. In contrast, this is what keeps girls away from IT work. They note that the idea that IT work is isolated, lacking in human interaction, sedentary and anti-social as the main reasons that girls prefer to not select IT as a career choice.

The stereotypically low images of IT work makes the choice of a career in IT very unattractive to both genders, but is a stronger deterrent for females (Allen et al., 2006). The stereotypical image of IT is that it is both masculine and 'geeky'. It is also assumed that success in the field requires a level of narrow, obsessive focus on computing. The representations of professions by the media help the general public in conceiving ideas and expectations of specific professions. Most references to IT work in the media focuses on geeky programmers or hackers, usually working in isolation and exhibiting anti-social behavior. The limited and negative exposure has had an adverse impact on the image of the IT workforce. IT work

is seen as being suited for people with limited social and communication skills. IT careers are depicted as geeky and eccentric in nature (Lang, 2007). The image of IT as viewed by society has a negative impact on the employee pipeline.

CORPORATE ORGANIZATIONAL CHALLENGES

Culture

Academic departments in the field of science and technology are known for their weeding out culture; a culture which promotes 'survival of the fittest' and individualist achievement (Martins and Wardle, 1999). Many female students also describe the class classroom environment as being icy and not receptive to their needs (Margolis and Fisher, 2002). The weeding out mentality carries forward into the corporate culture and contributes to a negative work environment.

The continual state of rush/crisis that is characteristic of the IT career is unappealing to many women. Women are traditionally considered to be risk adverse (Armstrong et al., 2007). In contrast IT environments are known to reward heroic behavior and risk taking (Tapia, 2003). This mismatch between needs and the environment can lead to discontented employees.

Gender Schemas & Discrimination

How many men prior to joining a company wonder, "Is this an environment where a man can be successful?" The subtle and not so subtle forms of discrimination women in the IT workforce face often is cited by Teague (2002) and Allen et al. (2006) as one of the key reasons for the high voluntary turnover rates. Although the unconscious biases that women encounter are often unintentional, they have a severe impact on the receiver. When a Connecticut CIO was asked what advice she'd give to her younger self she laughed and said, "Sue. I should have sued. I could be retired by now."

A key root is based in the concept of gender schema has been used by Lemons & Parzinger (2007) to elaborate on the discrimination that women encounter. According to them, women who enter the IT workforce have greater non-traditional gender schemas, while the men in IT have a higher level of traditional schemas. Gender schemas are "mental models that determine the gender role expectations of individuals based on biological sex" (Lemons & Parzinger, 2007, p.92). Schemas are developed from past experience - starting early in childhood. These mental models direct the processing of new information and the retrieval of stored information (Lemons & Parzinger, 2007). Gender schemas make use of behavior and characteristics which are defined by culture to be associated with a particular gender.

Individuals either choose to conform to the expected behaviors of their gender or not. Those that conform to the traditional gender roles have traditional schemas while nonconformists are said to have non-traditional gender schemas. Lemons & Parzinger (2007) further note that people who conform to the traditional gender roles, tend to use these predefined rules in processing and judging the world around them, more than non-conformists. Individuals with traditional gender schemas are said to exhibit more gender stereo-typed behavior i.e. these individuals display the stereotyped behavior assigned to a specific gender. Individuals with high levels of non-traditional gender schemas, have a greater sensitivity to their rights and privileges as they are aware that they are a deviation from the norm/standard (Lemons & Parzinger, 2007). The IT industry is dominated by men and it is their values and norms that apply; women in IT are considered to be an anomaly. Women in IT, as a result of their non-traditional gender schemas are more sensitive to the discrimination and biases they encounter.

Overall, the gender disparity in the IT workforce, "results in loss of opportunity for individuals, loss of talent to the workforce and loss of creativity in shaping the future of the society" – Anita Borg Institute for Women and Technology, 2008. Homogenous hiring practices create hostile work environments for those who are not part of the majority set (Tapia, 2003). Women in IT are scrutinized and judged by stereotyped measures. The Connecticut CIO stated, "In systems what I see more is not discrimination but just the attitude that they don't take you as seriously because I'm a woman - which is surprising that you still run into that. My first boss said, 'I was pleasingly surprised you did as well as the guys.' He thought it was a compliment." Similarly, when she won the Chairman's Award in her company, the Chairman praised her efforts and added, "and she led a department of men!" Women's successes are not always recognized and are frequently attributed to luck rather than competence.

Role Models

In the workplace, the lack of role models, mentors and networking opportunities have been noted as both a barrier to entry and a leading cause of voluntary turnover (Teague, 2002 and Panteli et al., 1999). The shortage of role models also has a negative impact on the perceptions developed about the IT profession (ITAA, 2003). It helps reinforce stereotypes of the field as male dominated and that women are less like to succeed. The lack of female role models and mentors in academic environments significantly hinders efforts to attract and retain female students (Cuny & Aspray, 2000).

Gender stereotypes related to the field of computing and technology reduce girls' interest in pursuing careers in IT (Clayton et al., 2009). As is common with stereotypes, the stereotypes regarding gender and IT are most often developed as a result of a lack of knowledge of the field. Clayton et al. (2009) note that the lack of role models also feeds the negative stereotyping relating to gender and the discipline of IT.

Work Family Conflict

Work family conflict has a direct impact on voluntary turnover in women (Armstrong et al, 2007). Conflict that arises from the pressures that are exerted by the dual roles of family and work is defined as work-family conflict (Armstrong et al, 2007). Although both men and women face work family conflict issues, in a society where the role of homemaker generally remains the responsibility of the woman, more women choose to voluntarily leave the jobs to accommodate family responsibilities (Bartol & Aspray, 2006). Research by Stephan and Levin (2005) uncovered that voluntary turnover as a result of work family conflict is culture and education bound. In the face of work family conflict, they found that women with formal IT education were more likely to remain in the IT workforce than their female counterparts with no formal IT education (They define formal training as holding one or more degrees in IT related fields). They also identified differences between cultures, highlighting that African-American women were more likely to remain in the labor force, i.e. stay with IT or move to a non-IT related profession, than Caucasian females.

Armstrong et al (2007), uncovered that the fear of skills obsolescence and time pressures to commit to the re-skills efforts induced a considerable about of work-related stress for women and in turn voluntary turnover. The constant change in technology resulting in continual learning required to avoid skills obsolescence can be seen as a key deterrent for women. Like in most other occupations, many IT women consider taking time off to bear children. For IT women, transitioning back into the workforce after a maternity break can be difficult due to the pace of change in technology. IT organizations are said to do very little to help returning employees transition back into the workforce. Overall, there is significant dissatisfaction with the lack of support for training and development by IT organizations (Pantelli et al., 1999).

The IT career is characterized by long hours, late nights, after-hour meetings, on-call duty, and a continual state of 'rush' or crisis. (Ahuja, 2002 cited in Armstrong et al., 2007, p142). These IT work characteristics lead to work exhaustion, which is positively correlated with employee voluntary turnover intention (Allen et al., 2009). Though both men and women in IT face work exhaustion, it had a greater impact on female employee's voluntary turnover intentions (Allen et al., 2009).

Flexible work schedules have a positive impact on reducing work family conflict, increasing job satisfaction and increasing women's overall perception of the organizations commitment to them. But, women working on flexible work schedules are perceived to be less committed to their careers and as such have limited opportunities for promotion (Armstrong et al., 2007). Women who are perceived as not being committed to their careers are usually assigned low profile maintenance projects. This causes low levels of job satisfaction as challenging work and job satisfaction are positively correlated. The lack of challenging tasks instigates voluntary turnover (Guthrie et al., 2009). For technical employees job satisfaction is negatively correlated with voluntary turnover intentions (Davis and Kuhn, 2003). Gender schemas also play a role in the allocation of work; employees who are perceived as not being sufficiently competent are allocated less taxing projects.

Hiring Practices

Hiring practices which promote the creation of a homogenous workforce serve as a barrier to entry for women. "Like hires like" and with the majority of the hiring managers being male, HR organizations need to work hard at creating and interviewing diverse candidate slates. Encouraging minority groups, including women, to participate in the IT workforce will ensure maximum use of all potential human resources. As noted by

Trauth et al. (2008), by not addressing the under representation of women in the IT labor force, the US economy is not maximizing the potential of its human capital. Under-representation is not unique to the US, research conducted by Trauth et al. (2008) detailed similar patterns in most developed countries. Furthermore, the exclusion of women from the IT workforce creates a homogenous workforce and limiting the types IT solutions that are implemented.

Gender Technicalities

The unique hierarchy system implemented in IT organizations may also facilitate the creation of a hostile work environment. Technical resources are deemed to be more superior to other roles in the team structure (Fargot et al. 2007). Their unofficial elitism results in the devaluing of many other roles in the team and creating an unwelcoming environment. For the non-technical female resources their exposure to this subculture can be frustrating and deteriorate their interest in the field. Over the last five years there has been a marked increase in demand for technology leaders with strong interpersonal skills, but there remains a bias for those individuals who have a solid technical background as well.

The skill set requirement for the IT workforce is no longer purely technical (Teague, 2002). Although technical understanding is a prerequisite for the IT workforce, globalization, outsourcing, increased understanding of the importance of IT business alignment, have all changed the IT skills landscape. Strategic business alignment depends on effective communication and close relationships between IT and business partners. Relationship management is critical in the new information age; managing relationships between the IT organization and its business partners, and relations between the IT organization and its outsourcing partners are two of the many areas that will be critical in ensuring that technology is leveraged to enable and drive strategic objectives. As

IT employees need to utilize communication and business skills even more so today, less emphasis is placed on an IT employee with purely technical competencies. With this in mind, business and interpersonal skills have been identified as top skill requirements for the current IT workforce (Luftman, 2008). The transition of the skill set requirement to include softer skills such as communication, team management, delegation and negotiation bodes well for greater involvement of other diverse groups.

Some of the varying differences in skills, attitudes and abilities that people posses can arguable be seen across gender lines. A common perception is that women are better at soft skills. Some explanations for this perception refer to their evolving role from gathers to home/care givers - that over time, their circumstances and environment have necessitated the mastering of communication, relationship management, negotiation and a myriad of social skills. These are the very skills that are critical in ensuring the success of the IT organization.

Diversity

The projected shortage of skilled workers provides the impetus for organizations to pursue strategies to attract/retain women within the IT workforce. The majority of female IT leaders believe that diversity initiatives should be championed by the IT executive line versus Human Resources (SIM Women survey, 2008). If an organization has a female CIO or VP IT, that individual should take point because it demonstrates senior level support for the initiative; it also gives permission. Women have spent years demanding equality and trying to prove that we're not different from our male counterparts. When a women's network is established, there can be a hesitancy to participate because women fear co-workers or bosses may perceive the groups as confirming, "We're different" or worse as "We think we're special."

Career Progression

Lack of opportunities for advancement was seen as a reason for voluntary turnover by Allen, et al., (2006). The low numbers of women at the higher echelons of the organization, and the absence of role models and mentors, levels women with the perception that there is no future for them in the field on IT. Women in IT find themselves under pressure to constantly over achieve and prove that the gender stereotypes are incorrect. A CIO at a Fortune 500 company stated, "No one took a chance on me. I was always more than qualified for the next step. I was always the player to be named later. Guys were given stretch positions where women had to prove themselves and then they got the roles." Many women at mid-career level leave the industry because they do not see a career path of progression.

Offshoring vs. Opportunity

Another aspect which causes voluntary turnover is the perceived volatility of the IT environment. Outsourcing and off-shoring have created concerns regarding the employment opportunities for IT workers of both genders. This has been a key deterrent for both males and females. There is a perception that all work will be outsourced to countries with cheaper labor costs. The dot.com debacle and the subsequent job losses have raised concerns about the stability of the IT job market. Many women who lost their jobs during that time have not re-entered the IT workforce. Allen et al. (2006) found that job security and stability are more important for women than men. Therefore an industry that does not appear to be stable will be avoided by women.

On-boarding, Mentoring & Coaching

A senior female IT executive stated she recently changed jobs and was amazed her current company did such a poor job on-boarding her. There was no mentor assigned to her nor was there a female peer group that she could approach for advice. She stated that even at the higher levels women are concerned about getting off to a bad start and not knowing how to course correct.

As women progress up the corporate ladder and their vertical career path shortens, women begin to look outside the company. According to the SIM Women Survey in 2008, fewer than 25% of the IT leaders surveyed saw their next career step inside the company. A key retention practice targeted toward female IT executives is the utilization of an executive coach to explore options beyond the IT career path; unfortunately, few organizations have the budget or mindset necessary to dedicate coaches to well-performing executives.

SUMMARY OF OBSERVATIONS

Cultural and social influences, gender stereotypes and educational environments are key considerations affecting the decisions by many girls to avoid entering the IT workforce. Many women who participate in the IT workforce choose to leave it due to a combination of gender stereotypes, discrimination, and problematic IT occupational culture and work family conflict. No isolated individual factor results in voluntary turnover or avoidance of the industry. The industry and organizations need to develop strategies that will address a combination of the above mentioned factors in order to rectify the current status quo.

Regardless of whether the reason is due to a lack of funds, time, or the fact that so many current IT leaders survived the "initiation by fire" that its simply accepted as the norm, IT leaders and Human Resources professionals cannot ignore the harsh reality approaching: there simply won't be enough IT talent, let alone female IT talent, to achieve corporate goals. How much will saving a dollar today cost you tomorrow?

Solutions & Recommendations

A diverse and well balanced IT workforce is pivotal to the success of the IT organization. Increases in the number of women exiting the industry and decreases in the number of female students graduating with IT related degrees prevent IT organizations from creating well balanced, diverse teams. When developing strategies to minimize the gender disparity in the IT workplace, organizations need to focus on increasing the participation and influence that women have on the IT industry, not just merely increasing the number of recruits.

The lack of parity in the IT workforce has implications for both IT organizations and the greater society. The industry is exposed to a shortage of skills, homogenous work groups that are less effective than diverse ones and the inefficient use of the available talent pool. Society is impacted by an industry which delivers products and services which do not include the perspectives and needs of half the society.

The size of the IT workforce is impacted by both the numbers entering and the number exiting the industry. As noted by Riemenschneider et al. (2006) efforts to recruit women to the IT workforce will be pointless if no effort is made to retain them in the IT workforce. As the challenge of attracting and retaining a gender diverse technology workforce has existed for decades, we cannot anticipate a panacea in the near future; however, we can strive to create an awareness of the issue and to take deliberate steps toward mitigating it.

Incorporate Gender Diversity into the IT Strategy

Commitment from higher levels of the organization ensures the effectiveness and success of strategies. Studies have shown that diversity has a positive impact on the bottom line of IT organizations (Trauth, 2008). Incorporating the goal of gender balance into the IT strategy endorses the organization's commitment to creating a diverse and creative talent pool capable of enabling business objectives. In developing an IT strategy, one component of the internal domain considers the skill and human resource requirements of the IT organization. Strategies to improve and retain the female IT workforce need to be addressed at this level. Tying performance bonuses to maintaining and improving team diversity targets demonstrates the company's commitment toward creating a diverse workforce. Diversity is necessary for better decision making, creativity and innovation (Cox, 1991). Watson et al. (1993), note that diversity in workgroups is critical for exploiting opportunities for creativity and finding alternative ways to working. Panteli et al. (1995) reiterate the importance of diversity in enabling organizations to deliver superior solutions.

It's understood that increasing female employee numbers at the executive level creates role models for new entrants and mid-level female employees. While increasing female representation at various leadership levels throughout the organization is the most effective manner for demonstrating commitment to diversity, it's important to recognize the value in retaining these women as well. An organization may not have a headcount increase or opportunity to hire, but every organization has the responsibility to retain their diverse team members.

Develop a Gender and Diversity Aware Culture

Many female executives cite culture as the driving force for staying inside a company (SIM Women Survey, 2008). A New York IT executive stated that she changed jobs four times in six years until she found a company that was willing to work with her and her family's needs. She is now celebrating her 17th year inside that company. As every woman is different, there's no one successful corporate culture for organizations to mimic. A consistent theme however is one of inclusion and communication - a culture of community (SIM Women Survey, 2008).

Creating awareness of gender and diversity issues in the workplace helps reduce many of the unintentional barriers that women face in the IT workplace (Tapia & Kvasny, 2004). Practices that promote gender awareness reassure potential and existing female employees that the organization is committed to creating a non-discriminatory work environment that values their contribution and is interested in accommodating their needs. Increased awareness of the gender and diversity issues in the IT workplace promotes respect and value for diversity, reduces devaluation of skills, acknowledges the value that different employees add to the organization and creates sensitivity to the issues women face in the IT workplace. A Fortune 500 CIO stated that diversity takes time to build so start now! HR and IT leaders need to make a commitment to the lower levels and take care of them so they stay. Companies can't promote from within if you have no one at the lower levels.

Practices to be employed can include the formation of a diversity committee within HR to actively monitor and promote diversity within the organization. The challenge with diversity is that there is always more that can be done. The first course of action is to establish communication with your female IT executives and ask them how HR can be of assistance in their annual planning as well as in their daily work responsibilities. Focus on the women inside the organization, demonstrate a willingness to address their issues, and then they will become the company's champions in recruiting new women onto the IT team.

Another critical step is clarifying the reason for diversity inside your organization. Ely and Thomas (1996, 2001) identified three diversity paradigms: Discrimination – Fairness paradigm, Access – Legitimacy paradigm, Learning – Integration paradigm. The first two are the most common in business, but each paradigm has different underlying assumptions (1996). The Fairness paradigm is based on the thought that diversity is important because discrimination is unfair (1996). The Legitimacy paradigm is based on the premise that diversity makes good business sense in a multicultural society (1996). The Learning paradigm's core is that diversity enhances all aspects of an organization's work and goals (1996). As HR is initiating conversations with female IT leaders, they should be direct in exploring and assessing which paradigm mirrors their corporate culture. Steps to improve diversity will be dependent upon the reasoning behind the initiative.

Basic training of all employees in gender and diversity issues along with the development of metrics will assist in the management of diversity levels. Depending upon the median age of your employee base, some men may not be aware that endearments can be viewed as contributing toward a hostile work environment. HR needs to educate the workforce to today's standards of conduct and a simple place to start is with basic sexual harassment training. Currently sexual harassment training is only mandated in the state of California, but this has created a host of corporate and vendor resources in that state. Any HR organization can source proven vendors and curriculums to mimic or implement in their own companies. Metrics will demonstrate gender diversity across the company and within IT and will also identify trends in female promotions and attrition. HR needs to partner with the technology organization to gather the data and to game plan solutions. Clear demonstration of the organization's commitment to diversity will retain and attract a diverse workforce

Develop a Mentoring Culture

IT organizations can promote and create a culture of mentoring by rewarding such practices. Acknowledgement of the mentor's efforts can be purely for recognition purposes or included as part of their performance criteria.

Mentoring programs have been cited as the most effective mechanism for employee advancement (Guthrie et al., 2009). Mentors create opportunities and help navigate the organizational ladder. Good mentors provide support to women and help them understand their work environment and improve their levels of self confidence. A female insurance CIO stated that she wished could, "Make myself be more outgoing from the beginning - more self assured. Take some of the confidence I have now and give it to myself earlier. In my first CIO role, I was still looking to tell my boss what I wanted to do and then realized I was the boss and said, 'Okay, here's what I'm going to do.'"

The role of the mentor is more of a supportive figure, in helping with the social aspects of survival in the IT domain and less about imparting technical skills. Mentors play an important role in teaching self awareness and self promotion. Formal mentoring programs where mentors are assigned may not be as successful. According to Guthrie et al. (2009) informal mentoring programs are more effective than formal mentoring programs. Mentoring programs which are not enforced by HR are said to be most successful. Their research subjects who were new to the industry felt that female mentors were more effective than male mentors. They felt that female mentors had a better understanding of the issues they encountered and could offer more applicable insights than their male counterparts. In contrast, male mentors were preferred by those women who had been in the industry for longer.

If one tier of employees is requesting mentoring more than others, HR should consider group mentoring. Peer to peer mentoring, or mentoring circles, can be established with little to no cost. They are facilitated by employees with HR oversight. Groups can be formed based upon job function, community, or career competencies.

At the leadership level, HR may consider "transition teams" (Mahoney, 2010) when a woman is advancing in her career. A female CIO while attending the International Women's Day conference at the UN, raised the concept of "transition teams" where multiple experts come together as a team in order to help a woman execute successfully at the next level (Mahoney, 2010). Each team member focuses on a particular skill or aspect, resulting in a comprehensive overview of the functions, interpersonal demands, and leadership nuances of the role.

A sense of trust and connection is imperative to a successful mentoring relationship. HR should facilitate introductions between potential mentors and those who wish to be mentored. HR can drive mentor participation by tying mentoring goals to executive performance and organizational development metrics. Potential matches conceived should be based upon aligning expectations surrounding time commitment, competency development, and geography if face to face mentoring is expected. Employees need to have ownership of the selection decision to enable empowerment. With HR facilitating the relationship, the mentors volunteering their time, and the employees owning the final decision, it becomes a true partnership on all sides of the equation.

College Recruitment

To further enhance opportunity visibility, create a College Champion program. In today's market many organizations do not have funding for a dedicated college recruitment program; yet if companies want to brand themselves as having a welcoming culture, they'll need to do so by demonstrating their diversity. Guthrie et al. (2009) note that organizations that had minimal high level female representations were viewed as providing little opportunity for advancement and considered by women as an unattractive option as a future employer. Enlist your female IT executives and team leaders to spend one afternoon at their college alma mater. Ideally, your female representative should attend during a college career fair to maximize visibility, but even if they spoke to a series of Computer Science classes with male and female student populations, their presence would augment and solidify to key aspects – women hold IT leadership roles inside your organization and your organization is actively seeking new and fresh perspectives.

Internships

Internships are used by many students to gain exposure to an industry and filter out possible career options. Cohoon (2002)'s recommendation is that academic departments work closely with potential employers to identify opportunities that will provide students with a positive work experience. Effective internship experiences can positively impact retention and persistence levels as they provide access to role models, mentors and an extended support network. It also allows the student to apply their classroom learning to develop something that is of use in the real world. This is very critical for the retention of female students as they place significance on careers that enable them to relate to others and allow them to use their skills and knowledge to solve societal problems (Margolis and Fisher, 2002).

Effective internships provide students with a holistic view of the IT work domain. Many of the internships offered by organizations do attempt to provide students with exposure to as many of the facets of IT work as possible, more organizations need to follow suit and make concerted effort at marketing the well roundedness of the internships programs. When students looking for internships at career fairs or recruitment sites are constantly faced with a flurry of technical job postings, the message that is indirectly being communicated is that all IT work is purely technical and unless one is a 'coding geek', there is no future in the IT field. An industry attempting to attract and retain more women needs to make a concerted effort to communicate the right messages to potential candidates.

Visible Career Paths

HR organizations should review their job descriptions to ensure that big picture context as well as personal attributes and communication patterns are listed along with the technical competencies. More emphasis needs to be placed on communication skills. As noted by Cukier (2003) the current demand for professional with a blend of technical, business and communication skills warrants the need to place more value of communication skills. Women in IT want to know they have a chance to pursue and secure that next step career move. If the only identified gap is a technical skill, then the woman may address that skill via training; however, if descriptions are simply 100% technical, the female employee may feel she has no job options available to her.

Effective retention strategies need to focus on creating opportunities for the upward mobility of female employees. The lack of a predefined career path has been raised as a key reason why many women leave the industry at mid-career level (Allen et al., 2006). A well defined career pathway, augmented by opportunities for skills development and clear evaluation and promotion criteria greatly reduces voluntary turnover in women (Tapia & Kvasny, 2004).

While reviewing your job descriptions, also consider the phrasing of your job advertisements. Do you describe your environment as "fast paced with leading edge technologies"? Are you more focused on listing the specific tools and technologies versus career growth and community? Take the time to create a focus group of non-technical women and have them review your IT job postings. The IT speak is meaningless to them, so they'll be able to validate if the remaining content in the advertisement is attractive to them. Have the focus group provide HR with the company's positive cultural aspects which can also be incorporated into your IT listings.

Managing Risk

An IT leader with 20 years experience stated, "HR should encourage boldness. They should encourage risk." Women are traditionally considered to be risk adverse (Armstrong et al., 2007) and can benefit from the guiding force of HR and any visible successful female IT leaders within the organization.

The concept of risk plays a big part in the development of any leader. Organizations must be prepared to assume a certain level of risk when they expose high potentials to new challenges. The trial by fire career management program is no longer acceptable. A female CIO in New Jersey stated that she came up through the ranks according to the "witch trial theory of IT leadership development." She explained how it often felt like her hands and feet were tied, and she was tossed in a lake. If she didn't drown, she'd be deemed successful. She stated that she learned that having a breadth of IT experience was important, as was the willingness to take risks. She now trains and mentors women in IT to prevent anyone repeating her experience.

A NJ pharmaceutical CIO stated she would "take on risks and run with them." Throughout her career she was challenged to take on additional responsibilities, so that 'next step' career moves were natural and not risks. Many organizations have annual performance reviews and organizational development discussions, but the majority of IT employees get very little structured leadership development.

Leadership Development & Networking

The pace of business demands we look to tomorrow. HR needs to drive that future focus on recruiting and retaining talent via leadership development. Not every woman in IT is seeking leadership development, but those who are should be given a vehicle by which they can get continu-

ous feedback and growth during the course of the year. A promotion may appear a large jump when presented at an annual performance review, but if HR and management have been communicating with the IT employee throughout the year, then the risk is greatly reduced.

A no- to low-cost solution toward building a community of communication and inclusion is the creation of a women's leadership development group. A properly positioned community group is a component of an over-arching leadership development program. Human Resources should advise line IT executives to encourage their female team members' participation. For an initiative to be successful, the participants need to understand this is voluntary and that the potential impact to their careers is only positive.

Networking, understanding the organizational politics and having a sponsor/mentor are noted as critical for successful female IT professionals (Guthrie et al., 2009). It is a simple process to establish a women's leadership network inside your organization. All that's needed is two women. At first the network can truly be a "networking" organization. The company provides a conference room where women are invited to gather together and get to know one another inside the organization. Even if the company offers nothing more than a place to connect, it will be a success. Networking opportunities are critical for retaining female resources as they build social capital which is necessary for advancement and professional development. Ideally, the organization should strive to create networks for women within the organization and make a concerted change existing networks to be less exclusionary.

Everyone wants to have a friend in their workplace. Encouraging a sense of community, arranging for employees to meet one another, and identifying a common bond via which they can open a dialogue is a great first step in retaining your female technologists. As discussed earlier, many job functions inside of technology are compartmentalized. Programmers do their part and networking engineers have their responsibilities and never shall the twain meet. The very nature of technology can encourage a sense of isolation amongst its female members. By having a second community, the first one being their work team, women can connect with other women and combat isolation.

A successful example of a resource group is the Chubb Partnership of Women (CPOW) which was formed in 2002 by two female IT professionals. CPOW's mission is: to encourage, enable and engage women at all levels at Chubb to pursue and practice career development and leadership skills (Marquardt, 2010). As one of their goals is to advance the Chubb's diversity goals, the organization has evolved to include over 652 men and women (7% men/93% women) from all job functions across four sub-business units. They established one page of by-laws to formalize the resource group and its governance in 2004, in order to assure the group's continuity and commitment to fresh perspectives via new board members. The group is led by a seven employees that serve as resource group board members. The resource group is funded by their Diversity office and budgets have run from zero to $14,500 annually based upon program needs. Each year they prepare plan document and budget request where they tie each anticipated program back to both the resource group's and corporate stated diversity goals. They offer employee driven coaching circles, networking events, executive visibility events, as well as educational and enrichment events including financial management (i.e. budgeting/P&L/ROI). CPOW is attributed with multiple job advancement opportunities as women were able to connect and network across job functions. CPOW has designed marketing materials for HR to use in recruitment of new diverse talent (Marquardt, 2010). Chubb's marketing and communications departments have also contributed toward increasing CPOW's visibility though national news and media outlets. They have become the model for other resource groups inside of Chubb to follow (Marquardt, 2010).

Volunteer led communities are also great management development tools. Most programmers don't get to lead projects. Networking engineers aren't typically responsible for planning large corporate meetings. Everyone wants to grow their skill set and stretch their knowledge base, but not every job function offers the opportunity to stretch beyond your job scope. A leadership development program that is volunteer driven affords management an unofficial training ground for future leaders. A manager may not have an opportunity or the risk tolerance that affords a programmer the chance lead a project, but management can create an opportunity for that programmer to project lead an initiative inside the volunteer leadership community. The programmer can secure a speaker for an upcoming meeting or plan an event for the senior executive staff. No one wants to step out on stage and play violin for 10,000 people having had only their first lesson. It's human nature to avoid that level of public failure. If the opportunities to lead are kept finite/smaller in scope, and the programmer understands there is no negative impact to their careers if they fail, management can gain the employee's willingness to take on the project. A failure doesn't hurt the company, but a success helps solidify the women's community and bolsters the confidence of the employee. She will have grown as a person and had that success be visible to her community and the leadership of the organization. According to Marquardt (2010), the greatest benefit of CPOW is the opportunity to "practice" future leadership skills now. In addition, HR is able to see who steps up and demonstrates a natural leadership and then translate those positives to organizational development plans in identification of high potentials. Similarly, HR will get to see who may need additional coaching on being a manager or mentor.

Where a leadership development community within the company is not possible, encouragement and financial support for participation in professional and gender based networks outside the organization will benefit retention efforts.

Women in Technology International (WITI), Women in Technology (WIT), Society for Information Management (SIM) has a vertical: SIM Women, Association for Women in Computing (AWC), National Center for Women & Information Technology (NCWIT), and Network of Women in Computer Technology (NWCT) are all national technology associations.

Work-Life Balance Initiatives

Often cited as the primary reason women are turning away from technology careers, work-life balance has borne the brunt of blame for decades. The unfortunate truth is that societal pressures, cultural influences, organizational ignorance, and self-imposed definitions of success have all contributed to the repeated failure of work-life balance initiatives thought to be the Holy Grail retention solution.

A new focus surrounding the vernacular of work-life balance as well as the deliberate steps taken to ensure success is needed. Cali Williams-Yost, author of Work+Life Fit (2004) "In our quest for big answers, sometimes we forget that simply re-framing how we think about, talk about, and approach an issue can make a big difference. Try this…instead of enduring the ongoing daily frustration of never achieving "work/life balance," focus on optimizing your unique 'work+life fit.'" The definition of balance for a senior executive is far different from that of an individual contributor, and the same individual's needs may alter based upon what's taking place within their lives. Eldercare, a sick family member, an addition to a family, can prompt a woman in IT to review her current situation and require a change. HR needs to foster a culture of openness where a woman feels she can approach HR and partner to find a temporary or longer-term solution.

At the lower levels, the most widely discussed work-life balance initiatives are flexible schedules and telecommuting (work-at home). These initiatives are beneficial to both men and women, but more so for women who culturally are assigned the role of homemaker/caregiver, resulting in dual responsibilities. Work-life balance initiatives promote commitment and loyalty from employees, by communicating a sense of trust extended to the employee by the organization.

At the senior levels women in IT capitalize on technology and make their own work-life accommodations, but at the lower levels women must see visible leadership examples of work-life balance (Finkleman, 2010). If the HR brochure promotes work-life balance, but all leaders work to the contrary, the lower ranks will not take advantage of the benefit offered to them for fear of negative perception (Finkleman, 2010).

The keys to successful work-life balance initiatives are the flexibility and autonomy it provides IT professionals (Davis & Kuhn, 2003). Technology advances empower greater flexibility and those companies that offer options will help ease the burdens of the dual role of homemaker/caregiver and organizational leader experienced by female IT leaders, as well as help reduce work-family conflict.

A final aspect that should not be neglected is succession planning. A female CIO stated her work-life balance came from having a strong team working for her. She didn't have to worry about major initiative deliverables because she could trust her team to perform and had implemented an open communication channel should issues arise. Building a strong organization reduces the work-stress and enables achievable work-life balance.

Flexible Training and Rotational Development

Professional development programs that are flexible and accommodate the needs of female employees are vital in attempts to retain women (Allen et al., 2009 and Panteli et al., 1999). Adaptable and accessible training programs demonstrate the IT organization's commitment to creating opportunities for their human capital. Armstrong et al. (2007) recommend the use of flexible training options such as online-training, self-paced training and paired learning. These approaches can be both useful for current employees who a looking to re-tool and for those re-entering the workforce after a leave of absence. The flexibility that these programs offer greatly reduces work exhaustion and work-family conflict.

If an organization is serious about retaining and developing their female IT leaders, HR and IT should partner to develop rotational job assignments for high potentials. Opportunities for cross-training and job rotation increase retention by helping improve advancement prospects (Alan et al., 2009). A senior IT leader stated that rotational assignments were critical to ensuring a well-rounded professional (Finkelman, 2010).

Funding for development programs, both in terms of monetary fund's and company time allocation further demonstrates the organization's commitment to its employees.

Implement Recognition Programs

The use of recognition programs is a key tool in retaining skilled female IT resources. Consistent throughout motivation literature, non-monetary forms of recognition are just as effective as monetary approaches in reducing turnover intention. In their investigation of the role that gender plays in IT professional attitudes towards technology, Morley et al. (2009) discovered that women place more importance on recognition of their successes while men place more importance on the hedonic relationship they have with technology. The successful female IT professionals stated that the recognition they received assisted in reaffirming their credibility and helped with improving self-efficacy. Recognition programs help improve female IT professionals' self-confidence and commitment to the organization.

The IT leader with over two decades of experienced stated she liked the idea of HR creating or identifying programs for external recognition as well. She shared how outside recognition can augment or shift your co-worker's perception of you or the importance of what you're working on. HR departments should be investigating and soliciting Marketing's assistance with identifying IT industry recognition programs. HR can champion these programs for female IT executives, once again contributing to the branding of the organization.

The IT industry needs to drive initiatives to change its image within society. Changes in societal attitudes and beliefs are necessary to increase the numbers of women in the pipeline. IT organizations are to also demonstrate their commitment to creating a balanced and diverse workforce by implementing strategies that cater to the needs of its talent pool. Training and recognition policies are critical to retaining women. These policies must be gender sensitive and demonstrate the organization's commitment to creating a fair and equal work place for all its employees.

Communicate and Promote IT Careers

Communicating the available opportunities in IT and encouraging students to consider a career in this field will, according to Miliszewska and Sztendur (2009) help attract more female students to IT. Communication is critical to correct many of the misperceptions that girls develop about technology at an early age. Communicating the wide variety of career possibilities, the non-monetary and monetary rewards associated and the opportunities available in the field is bound to kindle interest. This is critical as interest in computing and interest in a career in IT is positively correlated (Miliszewska & Sztendur, 2009).

The negative press surrounding outsourcing and specifically off-shoring has cast a shadow across Information Technology. The general belief is that work is being taken away from the host country; although more cumbersome technical work is sent offshore, new opportunities are created in the host country. The new positions focus on using relationship management skills that are inherent to females. Practices such as the use of virtual teams also drive the need for a new set of communication skills in the IT workforce. HR should be front line evangelists in communicating the "new" face of technology teams.

For the many girls who choose to pursue alternate career options because of the perceived isolated, masculine nature of IT, lack of opportunities and off-shoring trends, information is crucial in attracting them to the field. Academic institutions, industry leaders and professional institutions are responsible for informing students of the assorted career options available in the field. For a generation that has grown up with technology, but refuses to see it as a career option, Beise et al. (2009) recommend the use of technologies, such as wiki, blogs and social networks to reach out. Since females are known to use technology in a more social context, this approach to marketing the message to female students can be very effective.

Visibility through Giveback

Community service opportunities also have the same effect as internships, and may have a greater impact on women. Community service opportunities which demonstrate the usefulness of the technology increase female commitment to the field while validating the career choice of the IT leader.

Another recommendation for raising interest in the IT field is the exposure of young girls to role models. As with a College Champion program, HR can coordinate with female IT leaders to speak at or sponsor local educational institutions. Both academic enrichment programs and career days at schools provide access to roles models in the form of female IT professionals and female faculty members from universities. Role models

may also be in the form of senior female students for middle and junior school kids or university students for high school girls. Interaction with female professionals and other role models gives children a better sense what they can aspire to be. Sandra Brandon, a CIO, volunteers as a mentor to young cadets in the Civil Air Patrol. She stated that her need to giveback is innate and she views serving as a role model as part of her duty to the next generation of leaders. She and her fellow CAP leaders remember when they were cadets and therefore know how the program enriched their lives and their leadership potential (Brandon, 2010). Similarly, SIM Women launched a partnership with a national girl's organization to send female IT leaders to speak to seventh graders about technology. Each of the presenting SIM Women members felt a driving need to give back. This type of interaction helps destroy stereotyped beliefs that IT is not suitable for women, or that it is not possible to succeed in the field of IT. Increased visibility of successful women in IT can elevate the attractiveness of the field and make it a viable career option.

Implementation Issues

Few corporations can champion research toward understanding why young women are not pursuing STEM focused careers, but every company regardless of size can support ongoing research studies via funding or simply information sharing. Associations like the National Center for Women & Information Technology (NCWIT) are focused on encouraging leaders to "undertake institutional change within their organizations, and our work provides them with the tools and support to be change agents" (NCWIT, 2010).

Every strategic change initiative needs to be balanced with practical tactical implementation steps. Human Resources professionals are not interested in communicating Pollyanna positive messages that are seen as false pipedreams. "Research-driven practices provide tangible advice and case studies for recruitment, retention, and educational and institutional reform" (NCWIT, 2010).

When dealing with people, initiatives can fail even with executive backing and the best of intentions. Prior to championing cultural transformation, HR needs to assess the organization's tolerance for change, measure the demand for change as well as the executive leadership's level of commitment. Large scale change requires a great deal of planning, but when dealing with gender related topics, even small changes require attentiveness.

Female Leadership Focus Groups

Human Resources' partnership is critical in negating any "us versus them" mentality when forming a women's resource group. An organization that has a culture of inclusion should not state men cannot attend the women's leadership development workshops. If communication is a key tenet of the focus group, then having a male perspective may be beneficial at times. Also, key male leaders may be seeking insight as to how they can better manage the women on their teams. HR needs to be wary of any male individuals who are antagonistic inside the workshops. Despite the volunteers driving the organization, it is still a corporate event and all professional and respectful communication policies apply. The focus group may wish to limit certain events to a strictly female audience as even the presence of one man changes the dynamic of the group. HR leadership should encourage the focus group members to recognize and appreciate support from every individual. Focus group members may connect with each other on a smaller basis outside of the focus group, but that the focus group meetings will remain open.

Prior to creating a women's leadership group or any diversity focused group, HR needs to be prepared to have an open dialogue with those communities. A women's group may ask HR for changes in environment or policy that HR may not be willing to explore or concede. Again, HR needs to understand the business reasons for diversity within their organization prior to opening the door.

Mentoring Challenges

While mentoring has a great number of tangible and measurable positives, it also has some challenges. If an organization does not have multiple opportunities for women in leadership roles, a woman at the leadership level may be hesitant to mentor someone who could become direct competition. HR needs to look at the career path of both the mentors and those seeking mentorship to ensure each participant has ample growth opportunities inside the organization.

Another concern is that as the mentoring relationship is largely focused on self-awareness and personal and professional growth potential, a high potential employee that's being mentored may realize their next career move should be outside the company. HR should take deliberate steps in identifying and discussing career opportunities with high potentials to avoid those unexpected exit interviews.

Work-Life Balance

Although it allows employees to balance work and personal needs, flexi-time options have been noted to extend the work week of the employee and result in increased levels of stress (Guthrie et al., 2009). Many women on flex-time options have also reported being discriminated against because of the perception that they are not truly committed to their work. Interesting and challenging work is cited as one of the most important factors affecting retention of technical employees (Davis & Kuhn, 2003). Employees with flex-schedules mistakenly allocated repetitive and trivial tasks will lead to voluntary turnover.

Telecommuting reduces office space/logistics costs for the organization and commuting time for the employee. Although many professionals have noted that they are more productive at home, its disadvantages include feeling isolated from the work team and perceptions of lesser commitment to work (Guthrie et al., 2009).

Role Models

It is believed that early education and encouragement followed by visible examples of role models will be imperative to changing the current pattern. Common sense solutions won't be effective if organizations aren't deliberate in their efforts. HR and IT leaders need to make a conscious decision to be that visible role model, to arrange the speaking engagements, to block the time on calendars, and to follow through on the commitment. Too often business demands trump what is seen as a giveback opportunity. It is imperative for HR to encourage their female leaders to sponsor and support diversity initiatives even if they occur during the work day. If HR and IT leaders truly acknowledge the value of diversity in the workplace, then they will contribute to the solution by forming early bonds with girls, increasing visibility of their female IT leaders, and positively branding the company in the process. Perhaps ten years from now we'll all be celebrating the effectiveness of the technology camps and Science, Technology, Engineering, and Math focused programs for young women.

CONCLUSION

Jack Welch stated, "An organization's ability to learn, and translate that learning into action rapidly, is the ultimate competitive advantage."

As with any goal, relying on hope is not a strategic solution. Leadership is defined by action. Societal influences including gender schemas and stereotypes, media portrayals, coupled with discrimination, work-life challenges, and a lack of role models, continue to weigh the scales against industry being able to recruit young women entering the technology workforce, let alone retain

proven female leaders. The challenges present today did not evolve overnight, and we must understand that there is no one guiding solution. Albert Einstein said, "The significant problems we face cannot be solved at the same level of thinking we were at when we created them." New and adaptive thinking needs to be applied to each of the moving parts. It's too easy for HR and IT leaders to dismiss the issues surrounding women in IT as "wicked" (Rittel & Webber, 1973) and opt not to tackle them because "constraints, such as resources and political ramifications, are constantly changing" (Rittel & Webber, 1973).

A key challenge to wicked problems is that "constraints also change because they are generated by numerous interested parties who come and go, change their minds, fail to communicate, or otherwise change the rules by which the problem must be solved" (Rittel & Webber, 1973). We've all experienced this level of frustration with any major corporate initiative, but in this case, HR needs to understand that wicked problems aren't meant to be solved by any one person because generating solutions changes or creates new problems (i.e. launching a women's group may upset other ethnic/gender groups). Wicked problems are resolved through discussion, consensus, iterations, and accepting change as a normal part of the process (Rittel & Webber, 1973). HR needs to work with the women inside the technology organization as well as the IT leaders to define concisely the challenges facing them within their environment. Once the challenges are agreed upon, a course of action can be developed to address the individual components of the larger issue. Everyone needs to be aware that some attempts will fail, but the action itself sends a positive message: We value our female technology leaders and we are going to actively work to retain and develop them. There is no definition of success to a wicked problem, just a sense of improvement. Every effort we can make toward supporting women in technology will contribute toward that sense of improvement. Work to fill tomorrow's diverse candidate pipeline through youth outreach and mentorship today. Assisting women in achieving greater visibility inside the company, and within the technology industry, will have a ripple effect on changing the dynamics at work in greater society. A senior female IT leader stated clearly, "We just have to keep going: Lead & Do, and Do & Lead" (Finkelman, 2010).

REFERENCES

Allen, M. W., Armstrong, D. J., Reid, M. F., & Riemenschneider, C. K. (2009). IT employee retention: Employee expectations and workplace environments. In *Proceedings of the Special interest Group on Management Information System's 47th Annual Conference on Computer Personnel Research* (Limerick, Ireland, May 28 - 30, 2009). (pp. 95-100). SIGMIS-CPR '09. New York: ACM.

Allen, M. W., Armstrong, D. J., Riemenschneider, C. K., & Reid, M. F. (2006). Making sense of the barriers women face in the Information Technology work force: Standpoint theory, self-disclosure, and causal maps. *Sex Roles, 54*(11), 831-844. Retrieved on March 29, 2009, from http://www.springerlink.com/ content/46x01234j8065811/?p=9d820e5af40e47bf8db 7b629f39ad3f2&pi=0

Armstrong, D. J., Riemenschneider, C. K., Allen, M. W., & Reid, M. F. (2007). Advancement, voluntary turnover and women in IT: A cognitive study of work-family conflict. *Information & Management, 44*(2), 142–153. doi:10.1016/j.im.2006.11.005

Barker, L. J., & Aspray, W. (2006). The state of research on girls and IT. In Cohoon, J. M., & Aspray, W. (Eds.), *Women and Information Technology: Research on under representation*. Cambridge, MA: The MIT Press.

Bartol, K. M., & Aspray, W. (2006). The transition of women from the academic world to the IT workplace: A review of the relevant research. In Cohoon, J. M., & Aspray, W. (Eds.), *Women and Information Technology: Research on under representation*. Cambridge, MA: The MIT Press.

Beise, C. M., Robbins, J., Kaiser, K. M., & Niederman, F. (2009). The Information Systems enrollment crisis: Status and strategies. In *Proceedings of the Special interest Group on Management information System's 47th Annual Conference on Computer Personnel Research* (Limerick, Ireland, May 28 - 30, 2009). (pp. 215-216). SIGMIS-CPR '09. New York: ACM.

Buche, M. W. (2008). Influence of gender on IT professional work identity: Outcomes from a PLS study. In *Proceedings of the 2008 ACM SIGMIS CPR Conference on Computer Personnel Doctoral Consortium and Research* (Charlottesville, VA, USA, April 03 - 05, 2008). (pp. 134-140). SIGMIS-CPR '08. New York: ACM.

Bureau of Labor Statistics. (2009). *Computer systems design and related services*. U.S. Department of Labor, career guide to industries, 2008-09 edition. Retrieved on March 27, 2009, from http://www.bls.gov/oco/ cg/cgs033.htm

Clayton, K. L., von Hellens, L. A., & Nielsen, S. H. (2009). Gender stereotypes prevail in ICT: A research review. In *Proceedings of the Special interest Group on Management information System's 47th Annual Conference on Computer Personnel Research* (Limerick, Ireland, May 28 - 30, 2009). (pp. 153-158). SIGMIS-CPR '09. New York: ACM.

Cohoon, J. M., Wu, Z., & Luo, L. (2008). Will they stay or will they go? *SIGCSE Bulletin, 40*, 1. doi:10.1145/1352322.1352273

Cukier, W. (2003). Constructing the IT skills shortage in Canada: The implications of institutional discourse and practices for the participation of women. In *Proceedings of the 2003 SIGMIS Conference on Computer Personnel Research: Freedom in Philadelphia-Leveraging Differences and Diversity in the IT Workforce* (Philadelphia, Pennsylvania, April 10 - 12, 2003). (pp. 24-33). SIGMIS CPR '03. New York: ACM.

Cuny, J., & Aspray, W. (2000). *Recruitment and retention of women graduate students in computer science and engineering: Report of a workshop.* Washington, DC: Computing Research Association. Retrieved on June 1, 2009, from http://www.cra-w.org/ sites/default/files/ r&rwomen.pdf

Davis, J., & Kuhn, S. (2003). What makes Dick and Jane run? Examining the retention of women and men in the software and internet industry. In *Proceedings of the 2003 SIGMIS Conference on Computer Personnel Research: Freedom in Philadelphia-Leveraging Differences and Diversity in the IT Workforce* (Philadelphia, Pennsylvania, April 10 - 12, 2003). (pp. 154-156). SIGMIS CPR '03. New York: ACM.

Ely, R., & Thomas, D. (2001). Cultural diversity at work: The effects of diversity perspectives on work group processes and outcomes. *Administrative Science Quarterly*, 229–273. doi:10.2307/2667087

Fagnot, I. J., Guzman, I. R., & Stanton, J. M. (2007). Toward recruitment and retention strategies based on the early exposure to the IT occupational culture. *AMCIS 2007 Proceedings.* Retrieved on June 29, 2009, from http://aisel.aisnet.org/ amcis2007/199

Finkelman, C. (2010). *Telephone interview*. 27 Feb, 2010.

Franklin, D. (2009). *Gender differences: Recognizing and developing potential in female students.* Washington, DC: Computing Research Association. Retrieved on June 29, 2009, from http://www.cra.org/ CRN/articles/march07/ franklin.html

Freeman, P., & Aspray, W. 1999. *The Supply of Information Technology Workers in the United States.* Washington, DC: Computing Research Association. Available: http://www.cra.org/reports / wits/cra.wits.html [Cited 29 March 2009].

Guthrie, R. A., Soe, L. L., & Yakura, E. (2009). Support structures for women in Information Technology careers. *AMCIS 2009 Proceedings.* Retrieved August 25, 2009, from http://aisel.aisnet.org/ amcis2009/332

Guzman, I. R., Joseph, D., Papamichail, K. N., & Stanton, J. M. (2007). RIP-beliefs about IT culture: Exploring national and gender differences. In *Proceedings of the 2007 ACM SIGMIS CPR Conference on Computer Personnel Research: the Global Information Technology Workforce* (St. Louis, Missouri, USA, April 19 - 21, 2007). (pp. 217-220). SIGMIS-CPR '07. New York: ACM.

ITAA. (2003). *Report of the ITAA blue ribbon panel on IT diversity.* Presentation at the National IT Workforce Convocation, Arlington, VA. Retrieved on March 29, 2009 from http://www.itaa.org/workforce/ docs/03divreport.pdf

Jewell, H., & Maltby, J. R. (2001). *Female involvement in Information Technology degrees: Perception, expectation and enrolment.* ACIS. Retrieved on March 27, 2009, from http:// aisel.aisnet.org/cgi/ viewcontent.cgi?article= 1034&context=acis2001

Katz, S., Aronis, J., Wilson, C., Allbritton, D., & Soffa, M. L. (2006). Traversing the undergraduate curriculum in computer science: Where do students stumble? In Cohoon, J. M., & Aspray, W. (Eds.), *Women and Information Technology: Research on under representation*. Cambridge, MA: MIT Press.

Lamoreaux, K. (2008). *SIM women survey: Separating fact from fiction*. Society for Information Management.

Lang, C. (2007). Twenty-first century Australian women and IT: Exercising the power of choice. *Computer Science Education, 17*(3), 215-226. Retrieved on March 27, 2009, from http://www.emeraldinsight.com/ 0263-5577.htm

Lemons, M. A., & Parzinger, M. (2007). Gender schemas: A cognitive explanation of discrimination of women in technology. *Journal of Business Psychology, 22*, 91-98. Retrieved on April 24, 2009, from http://www.springerlink.com/ content/ b220k15g30220q6h/

Luftman, J. (2008). *Yes, the tech skills shortage is real*. Retrieved on April 5, 2009, from http://www.informationweek.com/ news/global-cio/training/ showArticle.jhtml? articleID=205601557

Margolis, J., & Fisher, A. (2002). *Unlocking the clubhouse: Women in computing*. Cambridge, MA: The MIT Press.

Marquardt, B. (2010). *Telephone interview*. 3 March, 2010

Martin, C. D., & Wardel, D. (1999). Paradigms, pitfalls and the pipeline: Gender issues in the Information Technology workforce. *International Symposium on Women and Technology: Historical, Societal, and Professional Perspectives, 29*(31), 343-346. Retrieved on August 8, 2009, from http://ieeexplore.ieee.org/ stamp/ stamp. jsp?arnumber=00787356

Mathis, S. G. (2008). Introductory course improves retention, especially for women. In *The Proceedings of the Information Systems Education Conference 2008*.

Mckinney, V. R., Wilson, D. D., Brooks, N., O'Leary-Kelly, A., & Hardgrave, B. (2008). Women and men in the IT profession. *Communications of the ACM, 51*(2), 81–84. doi:10.1145/1314215.1340919

Michie, S., & Nelson, D. L. (2006). Barriers women face in Information Technology careers: Self-efficacy, passion and gender biases. [from http://www.proquest.com/]. *Women in Management Review, 21*(1), 10–27. Retrieved on April 24, 2009. doi:10.1108/09649420610643385

Miliszewska, I., & Sztendur, E. M. (2009). Girls from low socioeconomic backgrounds: Factors influencing their interest in ICT study and career. *AMCIS 2009 Proceedings*. Retrieved on July 5, 2009, from http://aisel.aisnet.org/ amcis2009/412

Morley, C., McDonnell, M., & Milon, M. (2009). Gender and the attraction for IT in career paths: A French study. *AMCIS 2009 Proceedings*. Retrieved on August 15, 2009, from http://aisel.aisnet.org /amcis2009/515

Panteli, A., Stack, J., & Ramsey, H. (1999). Gender and profession ethics in the IT industry. *Journal of Business Ethics, 22*, 51–61. doi:10.1023/A:1006156102624

Quesenberry, J. L., & Trauth, E. M. (2007). What do women want? An investigation of career anchors among women in the IT workforce. In *Proceedings of the 2007 ACM SIGMIS CPR Conference on Computer Personnel Research: the Global Information Technology Workforce* (St. Louis, Missouri, USA, April 19 - 21, 2007). (pp. 122-127). SIGMIS-CPR '07. New York: ACM.

Riemenschneider, C. K., Armstrong, D. J., Allen, M. W., & Reid, M. F. (2006). Barriers facing women in the IT work force. *SIGMIS Database, 37*(4), 58–78. doi:10.1145/1185335.1185345

Rittel, H., & Webber, M. (1973). Dilemmas in a general theory of planning. *Policy Sciences, 4*, 155-169. Amsterdam: Elsevier Scientific Publishing Company, Inc. Retrieved on March 5, 2010, from http://www.uctc.net/mwebber/ Rittel+Webber+Dilemmas+ General_Theory_ of_Planning.pdf

Stam, K. R., Guzman, I. R., & Stanton, J. M. (2009). RIP: The use of inoculation theory and online social networking for enhancing attractiveness of IT occupations. In *Proceedings of the Special interest Group on Management information System's 47th Annual Conference on Computer Personnel Research* (Limerick, Ireland, May 28 - 30, 2009). (pp. 139-142). SIGMIS-CPR '09. New York: ACM.

Stephan, P., & Levin, S. (2005). Leaving careers in IT: Gender differences in retention. *The Journal of Technology Transfer, 30*(4), 383-396. Retrieved on April 5, 2009, from http://www.springerlink.com/ content/t512182481151065/

Tapia, A. H. (2003). Hostile_work_environment.com. In *Proceedings of the 2003 SIGMIS Conference on Computer Personnel Research: Freedom in Philadelphia-Leveraging Differences and Diversity in the IT Workforce* (Philadelphia, Pennsylvania, April 10 - 12, 2003). (pp. 64-67). SIGMIS CPR '03. New York: ACM.

Tapia, A. H., & Kvasny, L. (2004). Recruitment is never enough: Retention of women and minorities in the IT workplace. In *Proceedings of the 2004 SIGMIS Conference on Computer Personnel Research: Careers, Culture, and Ethics in A Networked Environment* (Tucson, AZ, USA, April 22 - 24, 2004). (pp. 84-91). SIGMIS CPR '04. New York: ACM.

Teague, J. (2002). Women in computing: What brings them to it, what keeps them in it? *SIGCSE Bulletin, 34*(2), 147–158. doi:10.1145/543812.543849

Thomas, D. & Ely, R. (1996). Making differences matter: A new paradigm for managing diversity. *Harvard Business Journal,* 79-90.

Trauth, E. M., Quesenberry, J. L., & Huang, H. (2008). A multicultural analysis of factors influencing career choice for women in the Information Technology workforce. [from http://www.proquest.com/]. *Journal of Global Information Management, 16*(4), 1–23. Retrieved on April 16, 2009. doi:10.4018/jgim.2008100101

Trauth, E. M., Quesenberry, J. L., & Yeo, B. (2008). Environmental influences on gender in the IT workforce. *SIGMIS Database, 39*(1), 8–32. doi:10.1145/1341971.1341975

Turner, E. (2001). The case for responsibility of the IT industry to promote equality for women in computing. *Science and Engineering Ethics, 7*(2), 247–260. Retrieved on April 5, 2009, from http://www.springerlink.com/ content/ q820q5x41x071202/

Wynekoop, J. L., & Walz, D. B. (1998). Revisiting the perennial question: Are IS people different? *SIGMIS Database, 29*(2), 62–72. doi:10.1145/298752.298759

Section 3
Retaining

Retaining IT personnel is crucial when it comes to developing the respective career building and motivational strategies necessary to maintain the IT workforce. Concerns about turnover have led firms to create formal employee retention programs. These programs are designed to focus on what IT employees are seeking to keep them satisfied and thus avoid the disruption and expense of a high turnover rate.

Chapter 10
Retaining IT Professionals

Gina Pipoli
Universidad del Pacífico, Perú

Rosa María Fuchs
Universidad del Pacífico, Perú

ABSTRACT

Retaining talent is one of the most important issues that HR Managers must address. This chapter discusses the retention practices model applied by IT. In accordance with the model developed by Julia Naggiar in 2001, it analyses six best practices: orientation, training, career development, motivation, compensation, feedback, and evaluation. Additionally, because of their importance, it also deals with turnover rate implications. To find the best retention practices for IT professionals, these variables have been evaluated in an investigation carried out with Latin-American IT professionals and HR Managers to find out which practices IT professionals consider paramount in retaining talent.

INTRODUCTION

Retaining talent is one of the major concerns for HR departments. According to Luftman (2008) and Capelli (2008) recent studies determine that talent management is a top concern for managers. It is common to hear about "The war for talent" and IT industry is no stranger to this trend.

This competitive environment is true during the recession and of course during times of growth. In an industry where Google is considered the best place to work, other factors such as the impending

DOI: 10.4018/978-1-60960-535-3.ch010

retirement of Baby Boomers and the continuous demand for leveraging new technologies, are making companies focus more attention to the retention of the best professionals.

This chapter covers the best practices for keeping people in organizations and analyzes important retention issues. The main focus of the chapter is an elaboration of the thesis on best practices to retain IT employees (An Exploration of retention practices in the IT industry – Julia Naggiar 2001). According to the model, six factors are considered the best for retaining IT people: orientation, training, career development, motivation, compensation and feedback and evaluation.

Two surveys were applied to compare the results with the proposed model, the first one for IT professionals and the second one for HR managers.

The objectives of this chapter are:

- Demonstrate the importance of retaining IT professionals.
- Show the best practices in retaining IT professionals.

A survey for IT professionals and for HR managers have been applied to identify if the six best practices discussed in the Naggiar Model are relevant for IT professionals and for HR managers, and to determine which of the six best practices of the Naggiar Model are the most important for the IT professionals and HR managers.

BACKGROUND

Retention can be understood as an organization's ability to preserve the employees it has hired (Bernthal & Wellings, 2001). According to Phillips and Connell (2003) retention is the percentage of employees that remain in the organization.

Young professionals that begin their career do not expect to stay in their first job for life. They are seeking professional development; therefore, learning opportunities and career development are a must for them.

According to a benchmarking study on retaining talent by Bernthal and Wellings (2001), young employees, especially in technologic fields, are at a high risk of turnover. Turnover is usually calculated comparing the number of worker separations during a given month to the total number of employees at mid month (Bernthal & Wellings, 2001). According to this benchmarking study, the top five factors affecting the employee's decision to stay or leave are: Quality of the relationship with their supervisor or manager, ability to manage work and home life, amount of meaningful work (the feeling of making a difference), level of cooperation with co-workers and level of trust in the workplace.

According to Jenkins (2009) when talking about turnover, costs associated to losing employee knowledge and experience should be considered. Westlund (2007) also emphasizes that if the IT professional leave the company before a project is finished the risk of failure if very high. According to his research the financial damage from failed IS projects is $ 100 billion in the United States.

Griffeth and Hom (2001) indicate that it is important to pay heed to the voluntary turnover rate, which accounts for workers who freely decide to quit their jobs. They present some voluntary causes, being most frequent among them, when employees are leaving the city, getting married, acting upon personal reasons or taking on a new job. Among the voluntary causes, there is functional or dysfunctional turnover. Dysfunctional turnover occurs when effective performers leave a company that does not want to see them go. Dysfunctional turnover can be further divided into avoidable and unavoidable leaves. The latter are those which a company has no control over, such as death, childbirth, family moves, and health problems. In conclusion, the turnover rate that must worry organizations is the one related to voluntary, dysfunctional and avoidable quits.

Exit interviews help to identify the reasons for leaving a company, but sometimes employees may contend to have unavoidable reasons for leaving when the truth is that they do want to quit. It is well known that turnover implies a high cost. The main costs associated with the turnover rate are the ones related to separation, replacement, and training costs. Jenkins (2009) considers direct and indirect costs of turnover. Direct costs are the ones related to recruiting, training, the learning curve. Indirect costs are lower results in organizational climate measurements and problems with customer satisfaction. Turnover must be analyzed because clients might be affected by the departure of a good employee. Sometimes a person who manages to fully comprehend the client's relationship with the company and the personal details involved becomes irreplaceable from the client's point of view. As mentioned before the experience and knowledge from the leaving person will represent and important cost for the company.

Watrous and Pritchard (2006) found that *"turnover is one of the most significant causes of declining productivity and sagging morale in both public and private sectors"* (p.104). They estimated the cost of voluntary and involuntary turnover in American industries in US$ 11 billion annually.

According to Benest (2008) there are some factors that are valued by employees in this competitive time: meaning, challenge, learning, partners in the enterprise and balance. A meaningful job is considered a motivator of behavior, people is looking for being proud of what they do. Finding challenges and learning continuously without overloading people is also useful for retention. If employees are treated as "partners" of the company they also share the risks involved in business and develop commitment. Balance between professional and personal life is critical attribute of the job especially for younger generations. Something negative for an employee may happen, but if factors such as work life balance are being developed in the company, quitting will not be considered the answer to that situation.

Companies are developing several strategies to keep their IT staff comfortable because retaining professionals has become one of the major concerns in the organizations (Dubie, 2007).

Most of the companies consider their employees as value assets. Therefore, they identify employees' requirements, desires and needs to retain their most qualified staff because they are aware that the key factor is to keep employees comfortable and happy (Foote, 1998). In regards to IT companies have to be aware that there are certain benefits that IT professionals value very

much but there are other very important factors which are not related to money (Battey, 2000).

The other factors that IT professionals consider, when they have to decide if they are going to stay in the same company or look for another job, are *"advancement opportunities, job satisfaction, new challenges, leadership, the ability to use new technologies, job security, faith in the organization's financial security, location, retirement plans and bonus plans"* (Luftman, 2007).

MAIN FOCUS OF THE CHAPTER

Organizations have evolved the idea that they had of human capital. Before, companies didn't deem human capital as an important resource for their performance. Now, most companies know that their human resources are their most valuable asset because knowledge and experience are crucial elements to succeed in the labor market. Material resources are important for a company too, but they can be acquired when there is money available. But human knowledge, which is the basis of growth for a company cannot be obtained so easily.

In the last few years, companies have come to grips with a reality that has been steadily growing in importance, that is, the significance of retaining talent. Businesses have made of this issue their number one priority.

Retaining talent is important because a company wants to hold on to the best workers available to achieve their corporate goals and to be considered as one of the best groups in the market (to be not only the best place to work but also one of the best organizations in regard to performance). This reveals that the company has achieved success and its image and reputation have increased. As a consequence, good professionals are likely to apply for jobs and the company will be able to maintain the best talent. Probably, the labor turnover rate would be lower than that of other companies in the industry.

That is why organizations have the incentive to implement retention strategies to keep their staff, lest the competition get some of their work force.

To implement retention strategies, organizations must create a labor culture composed of values and policies. The objective is to ensure that people understand that these elements are essential in the company and the balance between them has to be apparent, so that employees feel comfortable and happy. This culture has to be known and acquired by everyone and at the beginning, the leaders or people in high levels have the task to encourage and practice these values and policies so that employees follow them.

Companies prefer retaining talent rather than recruiting because they can minimize some costs. When a person who has skills and knowledge leaves the company, an important element of the team is gone. Furthermore, the company will assume all the expenses to obtain another employee (Foote, 1998). And there are monetary and non-monetary costs as well, such as spending time in the selection process, training the new worker who does not know about the company operations, losing the experience of the preceding employee, facing low levels of productivity until the new worker becomes fully trained.

Actually, some organizations have not identified very well what the employees want so that is one of the causes why people leave them. Organizations think that they offer good incentives according to a list of priorities but employees may not want those incentives; they have a different list of priorities (Horowitz, 2005; Young, 2008).

When employees and management differ, the former take the initiative to look for other jobs that offer more attractive benefits. The person could go to the competition and this would be disadvantageous for the company.

IT professionals are characterized by innovation because of the continuous changes in technology. These professionals are looking for a training program since their very career demands that

their knowledge be continuously updated (Luftman, 2008). Moreover, IT professionals wish to participate in projects to improve the company's efficiency. They are motivated to learn and executives have to provide them the necessary tools to develop their talent. Otherwise, they probably will not stay in the company for a long time.

As it was observed, IT professionals not only hunt for an above the market salary, they want to be in a company that offers a good labor environment. This could be decisive for them in order to stay or leave (Mill, 2001). If the company creates a great labor environment, IT professionals will probably stay and loyalty will develop between the organization and the employee.

Instead of this, if employees are dissatisfied with the labor environment, they will probably leave because people know that there are more opportunities for IT professionals elsewhere. They could find a better place to work and more benefits (Moore & Burke, 2002).

IT professionals, as all professionals, like to work for an organization where they feel appreciated (Maasland, 1999). There is a list of the best employers, and professionals are motivated to apply for a job in one of those companies. These companies are very important in the market and are very attractive for professionals who are recent graduates (Mazzuckelli, 1999). A person can find career development in these companies.

Considering the war for talent in the IT industry, IT executives have to be creative in order to design some techniques for retaining talent. Sometimes, the awards do not have to be so complicated. Recognition in public or by email is a good way to congratulate someone because sometimes IT professionals yearn for their efforts to be noticed by executives. An awards program will add interest and motivate people to improve their work.

Companies must update their retention programs and evaluate their employees about job satisfaction. This could allow identifying the weaknesses of a particular retention program and being useful to improve certain areas.

RETENTION BEST PRACTICES

Retention Best Practices in the IT Industry

Organization's Perspective

Due to the importance that talent development has today, organizations are aware that retaining professionals is an important issue and therefore has become in a priority for the implementation of their strategies. Naggiar (2001) mentions two factors that have caused this situation:

- **The advent of the twenty-first century:** Good employees have better opportunities in other organizations. Their experience, skills and abilities are appreciated by their companies but they are not prepared to give the workers what they really desire, so they decide to leave in spite of the time spent and the knowledge they have acquired in that company.
- **The cost of high turnover rates:** Some executives say that retaining professionals is cheaper than recruiting them, so that is why employers have decided to implement retention strategies, but it is not only about financial costs but also about non-financial costs. High turnover can affect the area goals and also prevent an organization from achieving its objectives because of the costs that are generated (Moore and Burke, 2002). Some turnover costs that Hansen (2005) has found are: "severance pay, administrative costs, additional overtime and temporary help because of vacancy costs, recruiting, testing, and training costs, and productivity loss during vacancy and transition".

Individual's Perspective

According to Naggiar (2001, there are four factors that have caused the development of the retention practices:

- **Generation X begins to move into the workface:** Generation X (People born between 1965 and 1980) is a group who has different attitudes from people who were born between 1945 and 1964. From that perspective, Generation X is capable of leaving the company more quickly because of not being satisfied with the benefits that the company offers (Thomas, 2006).
- **Globalization of the present economy:** Due to the globalization of the economy, there are more job opportunities for professionals today than there were before. Therefore, it is much more important today than before for an organization to give more benefits to its personnel in order to be attractive for them. The company that has good IT professionals has to implement retention practices in order to keep their most valuable talent (Naggiar, 2001).

Referring to this point, Luftman and Kempaiah (2007) say:, *"domestic IT employment has increased considerably and the market for IT professionals is current the fastest growing sector in the US economy due to advances in technology, government regulation, new opportunities and the retirement of baby-boomers in the U.S"*.

- **Organizational competition for scarce human resources:** The competition among companies that offer more incentives or benefits has increased. Companies are aware that people are a very valuable asset because they will be the ones responsible for implementing the strategies of the company and having good results. Therefore, companies are trying to find the best talent in a market which is scarce, so they compete against each other to get the most qualified professionals.

- **Emergent interest in work-life balance:** IT professionals look for a job that can offer them a balance between work and life. People want to share some time with their family or friends, and want to do other things beside their jobs (Naggiar, 2001)

If IT professionals receive what they desire: *"flexibility in their work schedules, ability to work from home, desirable amenities, greater benefits, and generous vacation and holiday packages" (Luftman, 2008)*, they will probably stay in the company for a long time because they will realize that the company is trying to offer them the best benefits for its more valuable asset (Naggiar, 2001; Wilson, 1998).

Information Technology Organizations

According to Naggiar (2001), there are five factors that have caused an important development in retention practices:

- **Concern about the turnover rates:** Employers know that retention is cheaper than recruitment so they care very much about retaining professionals due to the fact that turnover costs are high (Yablonka, 1999). Therefore, high turnover rates can affect the firm's performance in the long run (Naggiar, 2001; Luftman, 2008).
- **Shifting demographics:** Some companies have retention strategies that were useful for people who were born between 1945 and 1964 but now these strategies have to be evaluated in order to see if they are still effective for younger professionals in the IT industry (Naggiar, 2001).
- **Knowledge economy:** Company culture should focus on the development of social and human capital (Naggiar, 2001). Social

capital refers to the relationship among all the professionals in the organization which can generate a good environment and become an incentive for employees to stay in the company for a long time (Young, 2008).

- **Concerns about "skills gap":** Companies value their IT talent but some organizations cannot offer a good salary and other benefits in order to demonstrate how much they value their employees (Naggiar, 2001; Luftman, 2008). This is the beginning of the lack of qualified talent that some companies have because other organizations possess more attractive instruments with which to develop their professional career (Gibbons, 2006).
- **Non-monetary costs:** Recruitment costs are referred to the time and money that the company spends to hire a new employee and train him (Luftman & Kempaiah, 2007). This is the reason why employers prefer to retain an IT professional instead of recruiting another, and it is not only about the training but also about the employee's knowledge (Luftman & Kempaiah, 2007). These costs can produce low levels of productivity and affect the corporation's goals (Naggiar, 2001).

TURNOVER RATE

Evolution

Phillips and Connell (2003) state that: "It is virtually impossible and undesirable to achieve a continuous zero turnover rate in an organization. Extremely low turnover rates can be dysfunctional and unhealthy particularly when new thinking and fresh ideas are needed". Consequently, it is considered reasonable at least some amount of turnover (Branham, 2001). According to the U.S. Bureau of Labor Statistics, the rate of voluntary

Table 1. Turnover rate 2006-2009

Year	Rate of voluntary quits
2006	23.6
2007	22.6
2008	22.6
2009	16.7

Note: This has been elaborated based on information provided by the Bureau of Labor Statistics, U.S. Department of Labor News release 2009.

turnover has decreased considerably during 2009 after being relatively stable during the past years as shown in Table 1.

The data shown above is referred to the sum of monthly rates. The U.S Bureau of Labor Statistics considers that quits rate is the number of leaves during the entire month as a percent of the total employment, considering that the previous rates are the average of industries quits rates. According to Branhan (2001), turnover rates can vary between industries, companies, geographic areas, departments, job categories and employee characteristics such as age, education and tenure in the organization. In other words, it depends on the way that retaining strategies are being implemented. Therefore, turnover rates can be higher or lower.

Interest in Evaluating Turnover Research

Rosse (1987) found that through time, turnover has been an important issue in the organizational psychology literature. According to this, an important consideration is that the turnover is dysfunctional due to the additional costs generated such as lower productivity and re-staffing requirements. Therefore, companies have been interested in reducing voluntary turnover. According to Naggiar (2001) the literature on employee turnover can be described in three periods of the evolutionary process of turnover research:

- **First period:** Research focuses on the effect of organizational situations on turnover.
- **Second period:** Research focuses on the effect of specific job characteristics on turnover
- **Third and present period:** Employee turnover research focuses on human resources management practices and the effect of best practice retention models on employee turnover. Naggiar (2001) states that: "In the third period organizational turnover research is founded on the premise of self-interest maximization and tied to organizational culture. Organizations that make tangible investments in their employees will achieve increased levels of employee loyalty, since employees seek to maximize self – interest in terms of work experience" (p.27).

Human resources practices played an important role in this research. According to these, the process starts with the selection process and continues with retention strategies (Naggiar, 2001). Knowing exactly what individuals want in terms of their needs can help organizations to design better benefits for them which should be considered as investing in retention.

According to Phillips and Connell (2003), the most important factors to be developed by companies that want to reduce their turnover rates are: Need for a balanced life, need for caring, need for having an adequate environment, need for career development, need for recognition, need for accomplishments and contributions, desire for challenges and challenging work, need for autonomy, flexibility and independence. Therefore, these factors should be included in the strategies for retaining talent in companies.

Turnover rate for IT Professionals

Because of the great competitiveness in the IT industry, finding qualified IT professionals constitutes a great challenge for most of the companies dealing in technology and retaining them is even a greater challenge (Gionfriddo & Dhingra, 1999).

Moore (2000) mentions that there is a continuous growth of information systems and technology. He also argues that the capability of organizations for retaining valuable technological personnel constitutes a very important capacity for achieving the strategic goals of companies, so globalization and the developing of technology through time have made IT professionals very valuable in their organizations. Therefore, special attention for retaining IT Professionals should be developed.

According to Luftman (2008) there is a high demand for IT professionals with suitable skills, in spite of the recession. He also mentions that attracting, developing and retaining IT professionals have become an important concern for IT executives. Luftman (2008) states that turnover costs are not only related to finding a new employee in terms of the selection process; another important cost is the one associated with the productivity of the new member of the company, who will need time to have a high performance.

Consequences of High Turnover Rate

Mitchell, Shaap and Groves (2010) in their research specify that there are two kinds of costs related to turnover rates. The first cost considered is the cost of ending an employee's relationship with an organization. This cost is defined as a separation cost. It includes any severance payment, unemployment tax, exit interviews and other administrative functions. According to Mitchell et al, (2010), these costs may stand between 93% and 200% of an employee's salary. The second cost considered in the research is the cost related with recruiting and training the new employee.

According to Kochanski and Ledford (2001) the cost of turnover for scientific and technical professionals differs from other staff. The difference in the cost of losing a scientific or technical professional can be three to six times the one of losing administrative personnel, therefore the importance of having turnover strategies. Kochanski and Ledford (2001) found that Employee Value Proposition - EVP is the key factor to understand turnover. EVP is the total set of rewards that the company offers the employee; it is an attraction tool that will build the image of the company. The rewards can be classified in five types according to Kochanski and Ledford (2001): Direct financial rewards (all monetary rewards), indirect financial rewards (benefits and perquisites), career rewards, work content and affiliation. Kochanski and Ledford found that in accordance with the technical nature of their professions all five factors were important but work content was uppermost.

According to this study, each one of the reward types has a significant predictor of employee retention. Focusing on work content, predictors are factors that companies could work on for retaining employees: feedback from coworkers and supervisors, job responsibility and skill variety needed in the job. Therefore, money is not the only factor that according to Kochanski and Ledford (2001), will determine if an employee leaves or stays in a company but job enrichment, adequate responsibilities, autonomy and permanent communication with the people of the same area or with the ones that really know about the job performance of the individual.

MOTIVATION TECHNIQUES FOR RETAINING PROFESSIONALS

Motivation

According to Mill (2001), there are some motivation techniques which can be implemented by companies that want to keep their professionals:

- IT professionals feel valued by their companies when executives listen to what they have to say, since they also want to be part of the team projects. Therefore, companies should implement an environment culture in which IT professionals are able to talk and are listened to.

The other important factor for motivating employees is receiving recognition about their work performance (Mill, 2001; Shafer, 2005). Some organizations have recognition programs which generate more incentives for employees so that they do an excellent job and stay in the company. That is what makes the difference with other organizations (Elton, 2005).

- IT employees, as any other professional, want to improve their knowledge and experience. Some companies offer them training programs which constitute an incentive to stay in the company (Mill, 2001).

Nakashima (1999) says there are other benefits that can be useful in order to motivate employees to be loyal to the firm and stay in. Within the package of benefits, there should also be flexibility in the schedules, good lifestyle, good work environment and awards for goal achievement.

Good work environment is referred to an environment full of enthusiasm and energy that start from the employers who are the leaders (Davenport, 2008; Battey, 2000). Leaders should change their management style if necessary because if managers go in a direction which is not backed up by their employees, it can cause a lack of loyalty to the company (Thomas, 2006).

Another motivation technique can be to divide IT professionals according to their work style and give them tasks accordingly. Some of them enjoy what they are already doing; some others would be more motivated if they faced constant challenges, while yet others would feel happier with a different type of activity (LeClaire, 2005).

Motivation techniques are neither difficult nor expensive; the key factor is creativity (Mazzuckelli, 1999). Executives have to find what employees really want besides money. Sometimes, employees are satisfied with just an e-mail recognizing their work.

Compensation

The compensation strategy that a company wants to implement has to be developed according to the labor culture and to what professionals in the IT industry are demanding (Anisa, 1997).

Compensation should not only be referred to financial benefits like salary and bonuses but also to non financial benefits because nowadays, money is not the main concern for employees; although some companies are not aware of that (Walsh, 2005).

Sometimes companies just adjust the salary or bonus in order to remain competitive and to have certain benefits that are better than the ones given by their competitors (Maasland, 1999).

For some people, money compensation is a priority and if the salary is not at market value, IT professionals decide to leave the company (Thomas, 2006). Usually, money compensation is a priority for employees in the lower level positions, who need monetary resources eagerly (Gotcher, 1999).

In some cases, IT professionals are not satisfied with their compensation because they consider that they are not receiving what they deserve (Dubie, 2007).

With respect to bonuses, companies do not have to spend large sums of money because, according to Demers (2002), IT professionals value more a recognition given by their company than a monetary bonus.

According to Gotcher (1997), a monetary bonus program has to be designed very carefully because it can present some problems. For example: If an employee receives a bonus for his high performance in a project once, the next time he will also expect a bonus for the same performance, and if he does not receive a bonus, he will lose his motivation.

In respect to non-financial benefits, Luftman (2008) says that most employees prefer a balance between work and life. Considering this fact, flexibility is an important issue because it gives employees the opportunity to spend some time with others or to work from his/her home when there is an inconvenient to work in the office (Bort, 2000).

When compensation is the problem in the company and there is not enough for employees, there are some barriers that the company has to consider: One of the main barriers can be the conflict between high-level staff and lower-level staff. This situation can occur when the company wants to give a fine work bonus to the whole team but high level staff wants the bonus just for themselves (Mork, Stan & Sovitsky, 1999). According to LeClaire (2005), this situation shows that sometimes compensation is not a good program to be implemented.

Feedback and Evaluation

Feedback and evaluation should be performed at least once a year (Naggiar, 2001). Naggiar (2001) indicated that IT professionals agree with open doors communication because it allows them to present their suggestions and opinions and also to receive opinions from their colleagues. This means that feedback is useful to improve employee's professional development.

If IT professionals do not receive feedback, they will not identify their strengths and weaknesses which is very important in order to improve on their jobs to be better professionally (Melymuka, 1998).

Melymuka (1998) has found fifteen of feedback tips from some managers: *"Accentuate the positive, establish trust, make an example, use customers and peers, strike a balance, be flexible, cut out the middleman, timing is everything, be*

specific, get away from it all, stay on "the job", observe, don't accuse, don't leave 'em bleeding, mentors take the sting out and humor helps".

Establishing trust is the basis for good feedback. Executives have to gain the trust of employees in order to avoid problems after the feedback (Benvenga, 1998). To do so, managers can give some examples of experiences they have had and what they did to solve those particular situations (Benvenga, 1998).

When observing, it is important not to accuse employees but give them the opportunity to explain and see if their explanation is accepted by the manager (Strider, 1998).

Most managers know that it is important to evaluate IT staff but sometimes it is difficult to implement a method of evaluation in accordance with the company (Tinnirello, 1998; Boomer, 2006).

Boomer (2006) has designed an example of IT evaluation form that could be implemented once a year regarding the evaluation about the employees' contribution to the strategic IT plan and the company's strategic plan.

There are different ways to evaluate IT staff. Another way is to appraise technical performance which includes syntactical knowledge and operating knowledge (Tinnirello, 1998).

Orientation

Employee orientation has been defined by Werner and DeSimone as: "the process by which new employees learn important organizational values and norms, establish working relationships, and learn how to function within their jobs" (Werner & DeSimone 2008:10).

Orientation programs seek to facilitate the newcomer adjustment process, so that early turnover will not take place soon after high organizational investment on candidate selection (Naggiar, 2001). Positive work experiences are possible if there is a well-planned employee orientation. Also a well develop employee orientation can help new employees to meet their work expectation quicker (Huang 2006). When a new employee leaves the company a few months after his arrival it is usually due to an expectation problem. Expectations that individuals generate while they were part of the selection process must be addressed by the company. If discussing expectations is not part of the initial meetings in orientation programs there is a high risk of employees quitting because they feel that the real experience in the company is not what they expected.

Orientation is about the organization because all employees should understand certain fundamentals of their organization as what the organization is trying to do, why the organization is doing that and how the particular employee contributes to efforts or goals planned by the organization. Orientations send these messages and provide a framework of where the new employee fits in the organization (Wallace 2009). The company's mission, vision, strategic plan, organizational structure, policies regarding benefits are the usual topics covered in orientation programs.

Sims (2006) found that the orientation process is very important to organizations because it allows employees and organizations time to complete all the paperwork needed according with internal policies and the law. Sims mentions that the orientation period sometimes is understood as the time to fill out forms. However Sims (2006) says that: "new employee orientation is increasingly helping companies to motivate, retain productive loyal employees" (p. 3).

Wallace (2009) argues that attention to personal and social needs helps the new employee to feel welcomed and comfortable in the organization. Considering the new member as part of a new family is a critical aspect for the first days. Organizations must consider the importance of orientation processes in terms of developing a sense of belonging to a new team.

According to Wallace (2009) some of the benefits of an orientation program are making the employee feel as a member of a new family,

decreasing the natural stress of the first days, giving confidence to the new employee, working on personal expectations and giving the right information about the company, and setting the appropriate atmosphere for communication among the members of the organization.

According to Naggiar (2001) a proper orientation helps making new employees feel more comfortable and adjusting to the new environment easily. Adapting to the company's culture is fundamental and a good orientation process helps to accomplish this objective.

Training

Training focuses on changing or improving the knowledge, skills and attitudes of individuals. "Training typically involves providing employees the knowledge and skills needed to perform a particular task or job, though attitude change may also be attempted", according to Werner and DeSimone (2008).

The tools that are used to train employees go beyond using a classroom with a blackboard. Employee's interests and time constraints have given impulse to the use of interactive methods. Sometimes intranets with virtual classes, videos or outdoor training are used. Training can take place inside or outside the company with an internal trainer or with a consultant hired to train employees (Naggiar 2001). It could be considered motivating for an employee to be selected to train his colleagues.

According to Glanz (2001) as you offer your employees excellent training on both the business and the human levels you are not only creating the kind of employees you want in your workplace, but you are also showing that you value them as whole persons (p.182). Glanz also mentions that loyalty can be developed when a company invests in training.

Lockwood and Ansari (1999) proved that training and the opportunity to learn new skills are valued for IT employees and that lifelong training is part of the embedded technological culture and work challenge, and it is also perceived as a means of making oneself more marketable, presumably at a higher salary. Paré and Tremblay (2000) consider that training should be viewed as an essential investment in the intellectual capital of the organization.

Training programs should be developed according to organizational needs. Individual interests must be aligned to the institutional ones. It is also necessary to define which is the behavior that needs to be improved and how is the training going to be delivered. Measuring the results is also an important part of the training process. Companies need to know if the investment was useful or if there is room for improving the program.

Agarwal and Ferratt (1999) state that the amount of training offered is a critical consideration in an IT professional's decision to stay or leave. They include a list of training activities that an organization should follow. Some of them are: finding the right learning and development needs, competency training, and the use of mentors, among others.

As literature has shown, training is an important retention factor but it is necessary to consider it as related to other factors. According to Lockwood and Ansari (1999) training opportunities to learn new, market-valued skills are also related to salary and career advancement factors. Also according to the participants in their study a demonstrable commitment to training was an essential part of retention efforts, but should not be viewed as a substitute for salary parity issues.

Presumably, the more current and marketable the skills, the more opportunities for higher salaries and jobs elsewhere (Lockwood and Ansari, 1999), that is why organizations should be aware and take advantage of the investment they are making in their IT employees. A well prepared employee may leave the company, so the organization should prevent it by designing different tools to try to keep him at least until the investment made in his training has been recovered.

Career Development

McDonald and Hite (2005) present a definition of career development in the following terms: "An ongoing process of planning and directed action toward personal work and life goals. Development means growth, continuous acquisition and application of one's skills."

Career development focuses on employee's career exploration and his or her development as an individual. Naggiar remarks that there is a strong relationship between training and career development and that career plans often develop with, or as a result of, organizational training programs (Naggiar 2001). Career development activities can help employees identify and understand their vocational interests and strengths, plan and implement career goals, and develop themselves. They help employees find who they are, what impression they cause and which the different paths they have within the organization are (Kirk, Downey, Duckett & Woody, 2000).

Career development is an accurate tool to attract the best employees, as well as motivate, develop, and retain the best workers over time. The benefits of a career development system are a better employee-organization fit, a better employee-job fit, better communications between employees and managers and increased employee loyalty (Kirk, Downey, Duckett & Woody, 2000). Some companies dedicate special moments two times a year, as if it were part of the assessment process, to develop conversations about career development between employees and their bosses. In these meetings it becomes clear to the company which the expectations of the employee are and to the employee what he/she can expect for his or her future in the company. It can also be learned which areas should be improved.

The company should create the adequate channels to reach the employee but it is the employee the one interested in growing within the company so he or she must dedicate time to work in career opportunities. It is a shared responsibility to work on career development. According to Watters (2002) good career management practices are initiatives generated at the highest policy-making level that end in the normal relationship between boss and employee. Some practices for developing the career of an employee gives him or her the opportunity to learn more of the business or of different areas of the business. These practices include job rotations, participation in special projects, leading teams, among others.

Having managers connected with their employees in an effort to understand and encourage career development is highly effective in retaining key talent. It is necessary to understand that it will take time and effort to establish this practice; however, it will be worth it. For this reason managers should be coaches of their people. If an organization wants to develop a coaching culture the leaders must be trained. It is not about creating a policy but adopting a new style of managing.

Managers can find alternatives to be in touch with people: time to drink a coffee with an employee, time for having breakfast with a group of people with the same interests can help. The loyalty of employees becomes stronger when they can see that they are valued and that their talents and skills contribute to the success of the organization (Watters, 2003).

As literature has shown, career development could be an important retention tool when planned in accordance with the needs of the organization as well as the individuals'.

METHODOLOGY

In its first phase, the research involved a review of the literature about retention of IT professionals. In the second, an empirical test was performed.

In this phase, an exploratory research was held with surveys applied to IT Professionals of different Latin American countries and to HR managers of the same region.

Data was collected through surveys to be the instrument to collect information used in the questionnaire.

The questionnaires were translated into English and then translated back into Spanish to ensure there were no distortions in the language.

RESULTS

It is interesting to notice that 50% of the IT professionals that answered the survey accepted having being searching for another job last year. 44% of the answers mentioned that they considered quitting at least 1 time during the last year and 22% admitted they considered quitting in more than five occasions last year. This means that although companies are implementing actions to retain their employees, it is still a challenge to keep turnover down.

Motivation, career development and compensation have the most important effect in retention decisions for the IT professionals that answered the survey. These professionals consider that motivation, career development, compensation and training are important retention practices for them.

When asked which of the six best practices for retaining IT talent were implemented in their organizations, IT professionals answered that all of them were. Although career development (66.7%), motivation (61.1%) and training (55.6%) obtained the highest percentages. It was possible to choose more than one option, which is why the percentages do not total 100%.

Orientation practices are mainly being conducted by clarifying who is responsible for which work issues (50%), coaching about the immediate work environment (44%) and by having company processed meetings (39%). It was possible to choose more than one option, which is why the percentages do not total 100%.

Training practices are mainly being implemented by having access to training (44%), availability of the HR manager to answer questions about training (33%), skill development programs (27%) and access to practice labs and other training materials within the company (22%). It was possible to choose more than one option, which is why the percentages do not total 100%.

Career development practices are mainly being implemented by having an open door policy between IT professionals and team leaders (72%), participating in counseling sessions (38%) and by having skills questionnaires (16%). It was possible to choose more than one option, which is why the percentages do not total 100%.

Motivation practices are mainly being implemented by the chance to work on interesting projects that could shape the future market (50%), the diversity of experience gained from working in different projects (38%) and by receiving feedback about their performance (38%). It was possible to choose more than one option, which is why the percentages do not total 100%.

Compensation practices are mainly being implemented by rewards that include performance bonuses (38%), flexible hours for independence (38%), good salaries (33%) and by quality of life benefits (33%). It was possible to choose more than one option, which is why the percentages do not total 100%.

Feedback and evaluation practices are mainly being implemented by receiving feedback about their performance (56%), having the HR manager and team leader's available to answer questions (33%), maintaining the HR manager and team leader's open to receive suggestions for improvement from IT professionals (27%) and by having open communication with the HR managers and their team leaders (27%).

The turnover rate in the organizations of the HR managers that answered the survey is less than 5%. Among the IT employees the turnover rate is less than 5% in two companies and from 5 to 10% in the other one. Two of the HR managers are evaluating their employee's retention strategies.

HR managers consider that the most important of the best practices to retain IT professionals are training, career development, feedback and evaluation and motivation.

Training practices are mainly being implemented by having access to training (100%), by having availability of the HR manager to answer questions about training (66%) and by having skill development programs (66%). It was possible to choose more than one option, which is why the percentages do not total 100%.

Career development practices are mainly being implemented by having an open door policy between IT professionals and team leaders (100%), participating in counseling sessions (33%) and by having skills questionnaires (33%). It was possible to choose more than one option, which is why the percentages do not total 100%.

Feedback and evaluation practices are mainly being implemented by interviews with the boss (100%) and self-evaluation (66%). It was possible to choose more than one option, which is why the percentages do not total 100%.

Motivation practices are mainly being implemented by receiving feedback about their performance (100%) and by the chance to work on interesting projects that could shape the future market (66%). It was possible to choose more than one option, which is why the percentages do not total 100%.

For HR Managers the main barrier to implement retention practices is the limitation of financial resources (100%). Other barriers are disbelief about the usefulness of retention programs (66%) and time constraints (33%). Both, IT professionals and HR managers consider training, career development and motivation the most important practices to retain IT professionals.

LESSONS LEARNED

HR managers consider training, career development, feedback and evaluation and motivation as the most important of the best practices to retain IT professionals and they are working on them. It is interesting to notice that there are coincidences in what is considered important for retention between HR managers and IT professionals.

IT Professionals respond satisfactory to most of the retention practices given to employees but due to their expertise and technical formation, they value a great deal over financial retributions, those that convey the recognition of their companies, because these will demonstrate to them that their work is really appreciated. That is why Recognition Programs are so important for them.

The other facts which IT Professionals value more are those referred to their professional development.

Because their technical specialization, they care very much about being trained and having a well defined career path in their company.

Finally, IT Professionals have special schedules because of the kind of technical job they have so they need flexibility and policies that assure them of having a balance between their life and work in order to feel satisfied with their jobs and willing to continue working in the same company for a long time.

HR managers are developing different options than only pecuniary to retain their key people. Finding out which are the workers' needs is the first step towards developing a retention program or in defining which best practice to prioritize. It seems that creativity will play an important role in the war for IT talent.

CONCLUSION

Retaining IT Professionals is a very important fact nowadays because there is a war for talent in the IT industry. Turnover costs are high and they are not only restricted to the selection process costs but also include the training of the new employee and the learning curve involved in the process. Employees with a long time in the company will have much better performance and will know the clients better.

The six best practices for retaining IT professionals (motivation, career development, compensation, orientation, feedback and evaluation and training) are being implemented in the companies were the survey was applied.

IT professionals consider motivation, career development and compensation as the most effective practices for retention. These professionals are motivated by working in interesting projects and by the diversity they gain working on different projects. Career development practices for IT professionals are mostly related to an open door policy and counseling sessions. IT professionals consider performance bonuses, flexible hours for independence, quality of life benefits and a good salary as effective retention practices.

REFERENCES

Agarwal, R., & Ferratt, T. (1999). *Coping with labor scarcity in Information Technology*. Cincinnati, OH: Pinnaflex Educational Resources.

Anisa, L. (1997, October 20). Combine bonuses with rewards. *InfoWorld*, 119.

Battey, J. (2000, July 24). Retaining your most valuable assets. *InfoWorld*, 46.

Benest, F. (2008). Retaining and growing talent: Strategies to create organizational stickness. *ICMA Public Management, 90*(9).

Benvenga, M. (1998, January 12). How'm I doin'? *Computerworld*, 59.

Bernthal, P., & Wellings, R. (2001). *Retaining talent: A benchmarking study*. Development Dimensions International.

Boomer, G. (2006). Performance evaluations for IT professionals. *Accounting Today*, 27.

Bort, J. (2000, June). Mining for high-tech help. *ColoradoBiz*, 48-56.

Branham, L. (2001). *Keeping the people who keep you in business: 24 ways to hang on to your most valuable talent*. American Management Association Bureau of Labor Statistics. (2009). *March, May, June, July, August, November and December*. US Department of Labor. News release.

Capelli, P. (2008). *Talent on demand. Managing talent in an age of uncertainty*. Boston: Harvard Business Press.

Davenport, T. (2008, April 7). Q&A Thomas O. Davenport. *Computerworld*, 40.

Demers, A. (2002). Solutions and strategies for IT recruitment and retention: A manager's guide. *Public Personnel Management*, 27–35.

Dubie, D. (2007, October 15). What does it take to lure and retain IT talent? *Network-World*, *1*, 14.

Elton, C. (2005). DHL program seeks to hold on to IT staff. *Computerworld*, 43.

Foote, D. (1998, October 12). Recruit with your head, retain with your heart. *Computerworld*, 55–56.

Gibbons, L. (2006, October 30). As IT staff retention takes center stage, get your job titles straight, or lose your best people. *Management & Careers*, 46.

Gionfriddo, J., & Dhingra, L. (1999). Retaining high-tech talent: NIIT case study. *Compensation and Benefits Review*, *31*, 5. doi:10.1177/088636879903100505

Glanz, B. (2002). *Handle with care: Motivating and retaining your employees*. McGraw-Hill.

Gotcher, R. (1997, October 20). Combine bonuses with regards. *InfoWorld*, 119.

Gothcer, R., Steen, M., & Fletcher-Mcdonald, T. (1999, September 27). Building the best workplace. *InfoWorld*, S7.

Griffeth, R., & Hom, P. W. (2001). *Retaining valued employees*. Sage Publications.

Hansen, F. (June 2005). The turnover myth. *Workforce Management*, 38.

Horowitz, A. (2005, September 12). You can't always guess what they want. *Computerworld*, *52*, 55.

Huang, C. (2006). *Needs assessment for new employee orientation at UW-Stout*.

James, K., Downey, B., Duckett, S., & Woody, C. (2000). Name your career development intervention. *Journal of Workplace Learning*, *12*(5), 205. doi:10.1108/13665620010316217

Jenkins, A. (2009). *Keeping the talent: Understanding the needs of engineers and scientists in the defense acquisition workforce*. Defense Acquisition Review Journal.

Kochanski, J., & Ledford, G. (2001). How to keep me: Retaining technical professionals. *Research Technology Management*, *44*, 3.

LeClaire, B. (2005, September 12). You can't always guess what they want. *Computerworld*, *52*, 55.

Lockwood, D. & Ansari, A. (1999). Recruiting and retaining scarce information technology talent: a focus group study. *Industrial Management + Data Systems, 99*(6), 251.

Luftman, J. (2008). Companies can't afford to lose their best IT pros. *Computerworld*, *42*(37), 37.

Luftman, J., & Kempaiah, R. (2007). *The IS organization of the future: The IT talent challenge*. Hoboken, NJ: Stevens Institute of Technology.

Maasland, P. (1999). How to build an employee-centric culture. *Computing Canada*, 33.

Mazzuckelli, K. (1999, June). Be creative in your approach to healthcare IT staffing. *Health Management Technology*, 14–17.

McDonald, K.S. & Hite, L.M. (2005). *Reviving the relevance of career development in human resource development.*

Melymuka, K. (1998, Jan 12). How' m I doin'? *Computerworld*, 58–59.

Mill, S. (2001, Sep 7). Motivating your IT staff. *Computing Canada*, 26.

Mitchell, T., Schaap, J. I., & Groves, M. (2010). Maintaining the integrity of turnover measurements when there are layoffs. *Journal of Business & Economics Research*, *8*(1), 79.

Moore, E., & Burke, L. (2002). How to turn around turnover culture in IT. *Communications of the ACM*, 73–78. doi:10.1145/503124.503126

Moore, J. E. (2000). One road to turnover: An examination of work exhaustion in technology professionals. [Management Information Systems Research Center, University of Minnesota.]. *Management Information Systems Quarterly*, *24*(1), 141–168. doi:10.2307/3250982

Mork, S. & Sovitsky, R. (1999, June). Attracting and retaining IT staff. *InfoTech Update*, 5-6.

Naggiar, J. (2001). *An exploration of retention practices in the IT industry.* Montreal: Concordia University.

Nakashima, J. (1999, April). IT Staffing: Retention is cheaper than recruiting. *Health Management Technology*, 32–34.

Paré, G., & Tremblay, M. (2000). *The measurement and antecedents of turnover intentions among IT professionals.* Ecole des Hautes Etudes Commerciales and CIRANO.

Pawlack, T. (1998). How' m I doin'? *Computerworld*, 59.

Phillips, J. J., & O'Conell, A. (2003). *Managing employee retention: A strategic accountability approach.* Society for Human Resource Management.

Rosse, J. G. (1987). Job-related ability and turnover. *Journal of Business and Psychology*, *1*(4). doi:10.1007/BF01018142

Shafer, M. (2005). DHL program seeks to hold on to IT staff. *Computerworld*, 43.

Sims, D. (2006). Creative new employee orientation programs: Best practices, creative ideas, and activities for energizing your orientation program.

Strider, E. (1998). How' m I doin'? *Computerworld*, 59.

Thomas, P. (2006, May/June). Voluntary employee turnover: Why IT professionals leave. *IT Pro*, 46-48.

Tinnirello, P. (1998, October 2). Does your staff have the right stuff? *PC Week–Strategies*, 86.

Wallace, K. (2009). Creating an effective new employee orientation program. *Library Leadership & Management*, *23*(4), 168–177.

Walsh, G. (2005, September 12). You can't always guess what they want. *Computerworld*, *52*, 55.

Watrous, K., & Pritchard, R. (2006). When co-workers and managers quit: The effects of turnover and shared values on performance. *Journal of Business and Psychology*, *21*(1). doi:10.1007/s10869-005-9021-2

Watters, M. (2002). *Grow employees to raise retention.* Canadian HR Reporter.

Watters, M. (2003). Improving employee retention. *Canadian Printer*, *111*(6), 30–32.

Werner, J. M., & DeSimone, R. L. (2008). *Human resource development* (5th ed.).

Westlund, S. (2007). *Retaining talent: Assessing relationships among project leadership styles, software developer job satisfaction, and turnover intentions.* Unpublished doctoral thesis, Capella University. Proquest Information and Learning Company.

Wilson, T. (1999). How to build an employee-centric culture. *Computing Canada*, 33.

Yablonka, E. (1999, April). IT Staffing: Retention is cheaper than recruiting. *Health Management Technology*, 32–34.

Young, L. (2008, September 22). Disconnect between what IT wants, HR offers. *Canadian HR Reporter*, 7.

APPENDIX A

Objectives of the Survey

The survey objectives were the following:

- To identify if the six best practices discussed in the Naggiar Model are relevant for IT professionals and for HR managers.
- To determine which of the six best practices of the Naggiar Model are the most important for the IT professionals and HR managers?

Some of the questions of the survey were the following:

- From your perspective, how important is each of the following practices to retain IT employees on a 7 point scale (from 1 to 7)? Where 1 is not very much important and 7 very much important. The practices were: orientation, training, career development, motivation, compensation, feedback and evaluation.
- How are the practices being implemented in your organization? There was a question for each of the six practices.
- Which are the barriers to implement retention practices in your organization?

Demographics of the Survey

The survey for IT professionals was answered by 18 IT people. The background of these professionals is shown in table 2.

The survey for HR managers was completed by 3 HR managers. The background of these managers is shown in table 3.

Table 2. IT professionals' background

Educational Background	%
Business Engineering	83.3
MCSE	16.7
Total	100%
Job category	%
R&D	50
Project manager	50
Total	100%
Years of experience	%
Less than 5 years	38.9
From 5 to 10 years	33.3
From 10 to 15 years	16.7
From 15 to 20 years	11.1
More than 20 years	0
Total	100%

This has been elaborated on based on the applied surveys, February 2010.

Table 3. HR Managers Background

Educational Background in IT	%
B.A.; HR diploma	33.3
B.A.; MBA	66.7
Total	100%
Years working in the company	%
Less than 5 years	33.3
5-10 years	66.7
Total	100%
Years working in HR	%
Less than 5 years	33.3
5-10 years	33.3
10-15 years	
15-20 years	
More than 20 years	33.3
Total	100%

This has been elaborated based on the applied surveys. February 2010.

Chapter 11
In the Pipeline:
The New Generations of IT Professionals

Jannie M. Buitenhuis
bITa Center, The Netherlands

ABSTRACT

New generations of Information Technology (IT) professionals are entering and preparing to enter the pipeline for a challenging IT career. This chapter will present their characteristics, compare them to the previous generations, and discuss how the different generations can be effectively deployed in IT organizations. The four key characteristics of the new generations are: First of all, the new generations of IT professionals realize that the globe has become an open and connected system. Their organization should operate as a holistic brain as well, with information-processing as the center. Second, they wonder why Information Technology should stand alone. They want to talk about Community Technology. In other words: all of the technologies needed to support communities. Sharing, creating, and utilizing knowledge in an all-embracing 'space' determined by location and time, is the third aspect that characterizes the new generations. They do not let knowledge flow only virtually, or physically or mentally. They let it flow in all those 'spaces'. Fourth, they want their organization to take care of the planet: their planet. They are non wasteful, and they still keep in mind people and profit. The effective IT department understands the differences in generations and how to adapt and leverage the above characteristics.

INTRODUCTION

Of all the IT resources, the human IT resources are the most significant for the success of IT

departments. It is these IT professionals who decide which technology to use to achieve the business objectives. And even more important: how to leverage that technology. Daily they align IT and the business. They know and understand well the needs (and don't needs) of the business.

DOI: 10.4018/978-1-60960-535-3.ch011

They bring in innovative ideas to the business to support and enhance the business.

Unfortunately this might sound like the perfect IT department with the perfect IT professionals. In reality it seems that the business wants something and IT is tasked with making it happen. There tends to be too little or bad communication between IT and business during the entire life cycle, from strategy to operational support. Too often, when the IT project is finished (delayed and over budget) the business partners are not satisfied.

Where are those perfect IT professionals to create that perfect IT department? There still are not enough of them in the current labor market. Looking into the pipeline does not give us much more hope. Education still focuses on technology and processes. There is frequently too little attention placed on the skills students will need when aligning IT and business.

New generations of Information Technology (IT) professionals are entering and preparing to enter the pipeline for a challenging IT career. They do have characteristics that can help create the perfect IT department; if organizations are prepared and willing to adapt them as the organizational innovators.

What are these characteristics? How will the effective IT department attract and retain these young promising IT professionals?

In this chapter two main questions will be answered:

What are the important characteristics of the new generations of IT professionals, compared to the previous generations?

This question will be supported with the following sub questions:

What is a generation? Which generations can be distinguished?

What is an IT professional?

Which classification of perspectives can be used to sort related values of generations of IT professionals into generation characteristics?

How will the effective IT department attract and retain the new generations of IT professionals?

Among others the Solutions & Recommendations sections in this chapter might inspire CIOs, IT managers, HR managers, education program makers and others to take action. In the Conclusion section four tips will be given to build the pipeline for the new generations of IT professionals. Also four tips will be given to attract and retain these new generations into IT departments.

In the next section the need for awareness of the new generations of IT professionals, and their influence on organizations, will be underpinned.

BACKGROUND

The practical, social, and scientific considerations of becoming aware of the generational characteristics of IT professionals are presented below. CIOs and IT managers work with four kinds of IT resources daily. It is important to begin by explaining what managing human IT resources could mean, and what is understood to be an IT professional.

In the economic sciences the production resources labor, capital, materials, and entrepreneurship are distinguished. In Figure 1 these economic producing resources have been translated into IT resources. IT resources can be subdivided into IT professionals (labor), budget (capital), IT assets like hardware, software, networks, and data (materials), and IT management (entrepreneurship). IT management combines the first three kinds of resources which results into deliverables for the business.

The way production resources are translated into IT resources results into four views on how to look at resources. These views are the human

Figure 1. Managing human IT resources

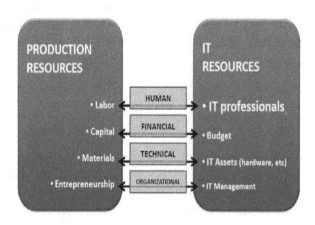

resource view, the financial resource view, the technical resource view, and the organizational resource view. Managing human IT resources is synonymous with managing IT professionals, as Figure 1 shows. But what constitutes an IT professional?

The ideas of Weggeman (2007) about professionals fit the ideas in this chapter regarding IT professionals and business professionals who have to deal with IT. Professionals are persons with knowledge (a profession) who continuously develop their knowledge. According to Weggeman (1997) knowledge includes information, experience, skills, and attitude. Information is the explicit part of knowledge. Experience, skills, and attitude include the implicit part. He denotes this as seen in Figure 2.

These knowledge components can be illustrated by the knowledge of for instance SAP programmers working in the financial market:

Figure 2.

Knowledge = Information x Experience x Skills x Attitude

- **Information:** they have read an article about the new SAP release.
- **Experience:** they have implemented a SAP release before and they know where bottlenecks might appear.
- **Skills:** they have analytic skills, which make them programmers who can find solutions in a complex program environment.
- **Attitude:** they think: "Solving this program error is more important than socializing with my colleagues at the coffee machine".

The scope of professionals working with IT, the IT professionals, is wide. Vertical from a strategic to an operational level refer to professionals, since IT managers use their management knowledge and helpdesk employees use their service support knowledge. Also from the technological to the business perspective, the horizontal axis, refers to IT professionals. A SAP programmer is a software professional, while a systems designer is a professional in translating the business needs into technical requirements.

Practical Considerations

For three groups of people in particular it is relevant to gather more knowledge about the characteristics of the new generations. First the CIOs, since they are responsible for leading and managing the organization of professional IT employees. Second the HR managers who are still exploring the best ways of attracting and retaining IT professionals. The third group is the education program makers. They should run ahead to the business community in preparing candidates for their career.

In several meetings over the past few years of CIOnet International[1], CIOs have been discussing the mismatch in the labor market of IT professionals. 'There is a lack of professional IT employees.' 'We need more business thinking IT professionals, but where can we find them?' We have concerns about the young IT professionals in the pipeline, since education programs and academic research lag behind our own technological and organizational developments.' These are some conclusions that have been made in those CIOnet meetings; as well as other executive forums. Those CIOs belong to the Baby Boom generation and generation X. Are they cognizant of the characteristics of the new generations of IT professionals and the generation gaps? Are they aware enough to attract and assimilate these young IT employees into their IT departments? Without them, the innovative power and existence of the IT department will come into play.

A well performing IT department enables the business to be successful. One of its most important resources is the human IT resources, the IT professionals. From a human resource management perspective it is important to be aware of the new generations. HR managers currently develop themselves into talent scouts to fetch in young professionals. HR managers who recruit IT talent at universities seem more successful in attracting new IT professionals than the HR managers who do not, especially in a tight labor market. But they are still speculating about what the new generations of professionals are looking for. Knowing which values are important to the new generations would help HR managers to build up employer reputation and herewith to attract the best young professionals.

Third, education program makers and lecturers (from universities and training programs) have a challenging job teaching the right knowledge necessary for future IT professionals. CIOs complain about the fact that they have to give in-company training to the just graduated professionals. Is it not the academic world we expect to educate our new professionals? But technological and management developments follow each other quickly. It seems almost impossible for the academic world to implement these developments in their education and research programs. First of all the bureaucratic academic world is less flexible than the business community. Second, academics should be able to look into the future to know what will be going on in IT departments over about four years, so they can start teaching that to IT students right now. Also from a research perspective it is often hard for academics in IT to anticipate the changes. A founded theory first needs an empiric environment.

Social Considerations

Two essential phenomena are occurring in Western society. First is the retirement of the Baby Boom generation[2]. How can that 'retirement gap' be filled in the business community? What role can IT play to enable the new generations to effectively and efficiently pick up the responsibilities currently covered by the retiring generation, let alone work well with these professionals that continue to work? Second is the decreasing interest in IT careers by young people. This is an alarming phenomenon. How can IT be attractive again? Without young people interested in IT careers, how can the growing demands to leverage IT be met?

As the Baby Boom generation (born 1945-1964) starts retiring in larger numbers, the labor market will quickly lose many experienced professionals. As a result, knowledge and experience about IT, business and the industry will leave the business community. Organizations might stagnate if the new generation is not motivated and prepared. From 2001 through 2008 there has been a decline of interest in obtaining a bachelor or a masters degree in Informatics in the Netherlands (Centraal Bureau voor de Statistiek, 2010) and the decline seems consistent in other Western countries as well. Why is IT losing their interest?

The Aging of the Generations

Figure 3 presents the aging of the generations. The Baby Boom generation and generation X (born 1965-1980) are already present in the labor market. Generation Y (born 1981-1999) is starting to enter the IT job market; and generation Z (born 2000-2009) and generation Alpha (born from 2010) are in the future. This chapter will focus on these last three generations; Y, Z and Alpha as ́the new generations ́. Generation Alpha will not be described in-depth since these candidates are just being born and might be a sub generation within generation Z. Around the millennium the first Y-ers started to enter the labor market. The first Baby Boomers started to retire in 2010.

Scientific Considerations

Many people like to give their opinion about 'the older generation' or 'the younger generation'. For example, when an X'er suggests "In the past we had floppy disks with 360K". The Y'er might think "I hope he has heard of Terabytes…". Or when a Y'er sends a Baby Boomer a text message using language that the Baby Boomer does not understand: "Wht@#? Im astnshd! I rlly dnt undrstnd…"

Science does not offer an established generation theory yet (Bontekoning, 2007, p. 59). Aart Bontekoning investigated the differences between generations and their influence on organizations (2007). It seems this has not been done extensively before. He concludes that the function of generation gaps is to renew an organization culture, with an eye on the continuity of an organization. These changes are social evolutionary processes that occur again at every stage of life.

With a short history of scientific research about generations in organizations it seems that no focused scientific research has been done yet about generations of IT professionals. This chapter explores the characteristics of the different generations of IT professionals, based on the existing generation theories, literature study,

Figure 3. The aging of the generations[3]

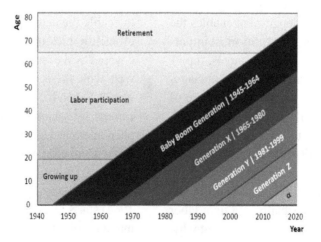

observations and pattern-based understanding of past and present to generate generation behavior futures study.

SUMMARY

This preceding supports the need for an exploration about the new generations of IT professionals. In the business field CIOs and HR managers are struggling with the lack of adequate professional IT employees and how to attract and retain another generation than their own. Education program makers should be able to look into the future to be able to deliver well educated IT graduates but this has not yet been the case.

Now that the Baby Boom generation is retiring, and the interest in IT by younger people decreases, it is even more important for our society to make careers in IT attractive for new generations. Scientifically there is no established generation theory and there is still little empirical research about the differences between generations of IT professionals.

In the next sections four characteristics of the new and the current generations of IT professionals are described. First generations and their origin will be explained.

GENERATIONS DESCRIBED

To be able to understand the characteristics of generations it is important to understand what a generation is, and how a generation is being shaped. In this section the concepts 'generation', 'stages of life', and 'zeitgeist' are defined and explained. Finally an introduction is given to the four main characteristics of generations of IT professionals which are based on the four views on resources. These four views have also been shown in Figure 1.

Figure 3 provides a summary of the generations. The author has conducted extensive litera-

Figure 4.

Generation = Stage of life x Zeitgeist

ture research to apply the most current perspectives on generations in the Western civilization.

A Generation

A generation consists of people who feel connected to peers of the same age; they have experienced the same zeitgeist (Bontekoning, 2008). The zeitgeist appears as a combination of cultural, intellectual, ethical, and political environment. Peers of the same age are in the same stage of life. A generation can be seen as the result of the stage of life and the zeitgeist (Figure 4)

Bontekoning discovered that individuals were not able to tell the characteristics of their generation (personal communication, 2010). He also found that he could explore the characteristics by putting people from the same generations together in one group. Young generations have not learned yet how to go through this process, but with some (perhaps self-made) structure and coaching they will be able to formulate characteristics by cross-pollination with their ideas.

Bontekoning also saw young generations adapting quickly to the older generations, while the elder generations want the younger generations to change (personal communication, 2010). Without the right support they cannot. They need coaching, preferable from people from two generations ahead.

The stages of life are[4]:

- **0 - 15 (Children):** Being raised by a previous generation. They are not aware of the world around them yet.

- **15 – 30 (Youngsters):** Learning and being passive. The basis for the values of a generation is being founded now.
- **30 – 45 (Middle adults):** Starting to get active in society. They are exploring their values and are struggling with the preceding generation and attempting to remove them from power. They try to reform the world and enforcing their innovations to the world.
- **45 – 60 (Late adults):** In a position to use their power and influence in their environments. For example by managing and running organizations. They tend to block the innovations from the younger generations since these innovations might overtake their own innovations, which are implemented in the society by now. They have a big influence on the zeitgeist.
- **60 < (Elderly):** Having the role of the wise experienced person.

Generations in the fourth stage of their life have the biggest influence on the zeitgeist (Strauss and Howe, 1991, 1998).

Although the differences in values of generations are small (Bontekoning, 2008), their effects on organizations can have a significant influence on performance. Bontekoning investigated and proved the relationship between generation gaps and shifts in organizational cultures (2007).

Zeitgeists

As described before, a zeitgeist appears as a combination of cultural, intellectual, ethical, and political environments. These environments are mainly influenced by macro developments. Your children might not have lived without a computer at home. A zeitgeist influences a generation, but is also being influenced by a generation. The zeitgeist in which a generation grows up has a big influence in their values. This is especially true in the ages 15-25 where people are forming their values (Becker, 1992). Parenting and teaching have a big influence on developing values, as do the morals and values of a culture, and historical events like Tsjernobyl and 9/11.

Figure 5 provides a timeline illustrating important events and macro developments. These macro developments and events are sorted according to the DESTEP macro environment factors (also known as PESTEL or PEST analysis).

The current zeitgeist is influenced for a main part by IT. Our society has become dependent on IT. The Kondratiev waves describe a new eco-

Figure 5. Timeline with DESTEP macro developments and events

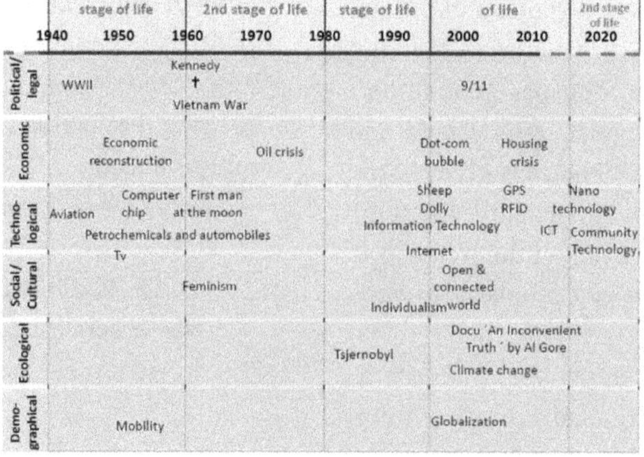

nomic wave every 50-60 years, as a result of the grouping of some basic innovations (Kondratiev, 1928). Since the late eighties the wave of Information Technology has taken over. Ivan Illich also described ideas about the influence of innovations on society (1973). People feel joy and pleasure when they can extend their activities by a new 'tool for conviviality'. For example the first people with a car enjoined their mobility. The first people who started sending e-mails over the Internet had fun by sending a message real time to the other side of the world. However, at a certain point the ′tool′ becomes a commodity and the ′tool′ cannot be thought to be special anymore. People become dependent on the technology. Can you imagine a life without a car, telephone or Internet or an organization without IT?[5] Consider the current impact of social networking tools like Twitter, Facebook, LinkedIn, etc.

According to Nicolas Carr IT will become a commodity, like electricity (2004); this is likely to be true for infrastructure. Developments such as SaaS (Software as a Service), Web 2.0, and cloud computing are signs of IT becoming a commodity. The new generations could see IT as a commodity; albeit how the commoditized infrastructure is leveraged by organizations in innovative ways should be considered an exciting challenging opportunity. The power of groups of individuals working together, without ever having met each other, cannot be underestimated while attracting and retaining the new generations. This phenomenon is underpinned in the book 'Wikinomics' (Tapscott & Williams, 2006). Think for example of Wikipedia, the largest online encyclopedia. Millions of people work on the content to produce and update this enormous online resource; but few of these co-authors have ever met. We could call this Open Source Thinking.

Since Internet connected the world, environments of organizations are changing faster than before. Globalization makes the world more transparent. Hiding information from clients, employees, friends or potential employers has become difficult, since they identify improprieties or unfairness more easily in this new open and connected world. IT has become woven into our daily life. And as a society we have become dependent on IT.

Generation Characteristics and the Four Views of IT Resources

A generation characteristic is a group of related values within a certain perspective by which a generation distinguishes itself from other generations. The values of an individual depend on more than only the characteristics of his generation. For example culture, personal character, and profession play a role in an individual's values.

In this chapter the classification of resource views has been used, consisting of the organizational, technical, human, and financial resource views. The focus now is on IT resources. Generations of IT professionals from the past, present, and future develop values about how IT resources should be considered. Table 1 provides a summary of the characteristics of generations for IT professionals. Each resource view provides a characteristic per generation. These characteristics are based on macro development patterns, and are aspects that can motivate that particular generation.

The first perspective is the organizational resource view. This group considers the following questions. What should the IT department look like, according to the new generations? How do the different generations of IT professionals think about IT management? How do they expect their manager to organize their work environment? The new generations of IT professionals grow up in an open and connected, globalized world. To illustrate these values about organizational design, leadership, and organizational culture Morgan′s images of organization (1997) are applied.

The shifting views of generations of IT professionals regarding technology within IT departments are described from the second view, the technical resource view. The Baby Boom gen-

Table 1. Overview of the generations and their characteristics per resource view

Generation (year of birth)	Resource Views			
	ORGANIZATIONAL	*TECHNICAL*	*HUMAN*	*FINANCIAL*
	Development of paradigms	*Development of technology*	*Development of knowledge creation*	*Development of strategic focus and corporate responsibility*
Baby Boom (1945-1964)	Organizations acting as a machine	Information Technology (IT) & Telecommunication, as engineering	Physical *ba*	Profit
X (1965-1980)	Organizations acting as an organism	Information Technology (IT) & Telecommunication, as engineering	Virtual *ba*	Profit
Y (1981-1999)	Organizations acting as a culture and political system	Information- and Communication Technology (ICT), to support communication	Mental *ba*	People
Z (2000-2009) & Alpha (>2010)	Organizations acting as a brain and flux & transformation	Community Technology, to support communities	All-embracing *ba*	Planet

eration and generation X are used to seeing IT as engineering. Generation Y has started to focus on communications by IT, while generations Z and Alpha will focus on communities supported by IT.

Third, the view IT professionals have on human resources is described. They are the human IT resources themselves. They are knowledge workers. Therefore knowledge and knowledge creation is assumed as the most important aspect an IT professional delivers and works with. This chapter will not elaborate on what that knowledge should be, but will address where this knowledge is coming from, where it develops, and where it is going to. In other words the focus is on the place knowledge is being created.

The fourth view focuses on how IT professionals feel about (financial) investments and the strategic motives of their employer. What kind of corporate responsibility should their organization take? Which strategic decisions should the IT department make? How should IT budget be allocated? The values are linked to the Triple P approach; Profit, People, and Planet. It is an approach for Corporate Social Responsibility (CSR).

Investigating the values of IT professionals is a research challenge. Most IT professionals cannot tell precisely what their generation's values are. Mixed with other generations it cannot be simply observed either. This explorative research has been based on literature study, observations and pattern-based understanding of past and present to generate generation behavior futures study.

Summary

A generation is a collection of people who feel connected to peers of the same age and who have experienced the same zeitgeist. Generations in their fourth stage of life (late adults) have the biggest influence on the zeitgeist although generations in the third stage of life (middle adults) try to be innovative in their zeitgeist. The basis for generation characteristics is made in the second stage of life (youngsters).

A zeitgeist depends on cultural, intellectual, ethic, and political environments. Figure 5 provided a timeline that presents the events and macro that have influenced past zeitgeists.

Table 2. Overview of the generation metaphors

	View from the generation	IT professionals of this generation "My IT department should be…"
Baby Boom	An organization should act as a machine	Organization design: bureaucracy, drawn in a hierarchical organization chart. Leadership: controls by giving clear tasks, hierarchical. Organization culture: efficient, stable, measurable.
X	An organization should act as an organism	Organization design: sets of interacting subsystems. Leadership: internal and external focused. Organization culture: open, informal, together.
Y	An organization should act as a culture, and as a political system	Organization design: democracy. Leadership: conflict solving, natural hero's Organization culture: social interaction
Z/ Alpha	An organization should act as a brain, and as flux & transformation	Organization design: holistic, infinite, decentralized Leadership: strong leader Organization culture: creativity, diversity, self regulating, learning, stories.

Each group of innovations leads to a technological revolution every 50-60 years that will be picked up by industry and commerce. After a certain time the new technology becomes a commodity and makes societies depending on it. The current dominating technology is Information Technology. As a society we have become dependent on IT which influences our current zeitgeist for a main part.

Table 1 provided an overview of the generations and their characteristics per resource view. In the following section the four characteristics of the new generations of IT professionals are described and compared with the previous generations.

CHARACTERISTIC 1: ACTING IN AN OPEN AND CONNECTED WORLD

Important questions to address include the following. How should the company and IT organization be designed according to the different generations? What leadership and management will IT employees demand? What kind of organizational culture will they perform best in? This section describes the characteristics of generations of IT professionals from the organizational resource view.

Organizational paradigms shift from time to time and are strongly related to the zeitgeist and generations. Gareth Morgan described different perspectives by describing 'images' of organizations (1997). Table 2 shows the overview of these images of organization per generation. Each metaphor, or image, is further explained in this section.

The IT Organization as a Machine

Since the industrialization classical management theories have appeared and developed, the scientific management theories prescribe that companies shape an organization by planning, organizing, commanding, coordinating, and controlling. Organizations are designed and operated as if they were machines. Thinking and doing are separated from each other. Efficiency is very important. Everything is measurable, stable, and there is no uncertainty. Employees know exactly what to do because their tasks are described precisely. They are able to accept commands. The organization could be described as a bureaucracy and could be drawn in a hierarchical organization chart. Most of the male Baby Boomers have served the army. The military machine has influenced a main part of the values they developed at their second stage of life.

IT departments are a 'mechanical part' of the organization and are designed and operated by Baby Boomers as if they were machines as well. The set of best practices prescribed in the eight ITIL books supports to shape the perfect efficient IT department.

Another characteristic of the machine IT department is the internal focus. What has been asked by the business will be delivered. ´You ask, we play`, like a jukebox. Demand Management is an unknown term in this machine.

For Baby Boomers their leader needs status that is allowed to control and give clear direction. Their leader must actually lead them in a formal way.

The advantages of the machine IT organization are that tasks and goals are clear and measurable, and that uncertainty of service delivery is strongly reduced. A stable IT department is needed to be able to conform to SLAs.

The IT Department as an Organism

The modern management theories were introduced in the 1950s. This theory was an evolution of the bureaucratic 'machine' organization theories and paradigms. The modern management theories focused on the human aspects of the organization and the organizational environment. The Contingency Theory suggests that organizations should adjust to their environment. Environments like markets change continuously and therefore an organization should change continuously as well. Organizations that fit best will survive, like biologist Charles Darwin described as 'survival of the fittest' (2006), and as Morgan described: "It is possible to identify different species of organization in different kinds of environments. Just as we find polar bears in arctic regions, camels in deserts, and alligators in swamps, we notice that certain species of organization are better 'adapted' to specific environmental conditions than others." (1997, p. 33). In the organization as were it an

organism is balance between the internal organization and the external environment. If necessary, organizations will cooperate with each other, and otherwise they will compete. Contradictions are aligned. Organizations, like organisms, can be conceived of assets of interacting subsystems (Morgan, 1997, p. 43). Information is woven through all these subsystems.

The IT organization as an organism is much more aware of the business demands. Demand Management is growing in attention. Not every IT department should be shaped like ITIL prescribes. New standards have been developed and implemented more often, for example BiSL (the Business Information Services Library).

Generation X is playing a big role in organizations like IT. For example Business Process Management has become noticeable thanks to the hard working independent X'ers. Generation X, also known as the silent generation, is not so visible in organizations. Bontekoning found many executives conveying that their company engaged Baby Boomers and Y'ers, but only a few X'ers. HR statistics shows 1/3 of the employee population are X'ers (personal communication, 2010).

The IT Organization as a Culture and as a Political System

In the eighties the symbolic management theories appeared. To this group of theories two images of Morgan do fit; namely the culture metaphor and the metaphor for organizations as a political system. The names that are related to the culture metaphor are among others Durkheim (collective consciousness), Hofstede (mental programming), Bateson (mind & nature) and Weick (enactment). Hofstede describes a culture is being expressed by values, perceptions and rules (2001). The values are the DNA of an organization. People wonder what the role of generation gaps could mean.

Considering an organization as a culture suggests that an organizational change is a cultural change[6]. A culture means social interaction and is something that cannot be enforced. Meaning and symbols get lots of attention. The organization is comprised of functional groups, ethnic groups, and groups with status. Trust enriches the organization and also the maximum number of people who feel united with the (informal) organizational goals. According to the Dunbar number, the maximum number for a cohesive organization is 148 individuals (Dunbar, 1992)[7].

An organization can be seen as detachable networks of people with different interests; political systems ensue. Power means letting somebody do something for you which they otherwise never would have done. Decision making is based on power, influence, and decisions. Theatre, playing games and metaphors are ways to express symbolism. Where a Baby Boomer just accepted the hierarchical family system, their Y-children might challenge the power position of their parents.

The ideal leader for generation Y is a natural leader who is a great conflict solver. Many Y'ers worldwide would like to work for Google (Universum, 2010). Its founders Larry Page and Sergey Brin might be the ideal leaders for this generation. Google stimulates interaction and continuous changes.

Generation Y understands it is about power games and social interaction between the IT and business organizations. Business IT alignment is still the basic need for a successful IT organization, but with much more attention placed on behavior than previous generations. Just aligning the IT architecture with the enterprise architecture, and shaping business processes is not enough anymore; the focus must be on business value.

Compared to past generations in their second stage of life (youngsters), generation Y is developing a better feeling for (online) social networks. Because of globalization they understand the concept of Open Source. They use Wikipedia as their encyclopedia and YouTube as their television channel. Generation Y develops a feeling for understanding the interests, power and values. This helps them to better understand business

models like Open Source software and 'Cloud Thinking'. Cloud Thinking is thinking from the Cloud, which continues on Cloud Computing. After sharing data space it will become possible to share other computer resources as well, like data and information.

IT governance has been present in IT departments for a while, but generation Y gives this decision making system a new perspective. Values, power, and influence will no longer be seen as something that is part of it, but as the aspects that determine how decisions are made. This will appear in organizations where the new generations are seen as the organizational innovators.

The IT Organization as a Brain and as Flux & Transformation

The post modern management theories made their entry in 1990. The term postmodernism is used to mark a new social era with new types of organizations, management styles, and a new paradigm (Parker, 1990). Herewith fit Morgan´s images of brains, and flux and transformation. A brain is a complex system that makes decisions by itself. It is an information-processor which is able to learn. If the left hemisphere breaks down the right hemisphere will take care of the tasks. The brain acts like playing jazz music: there are no rules, just improvisation. An organization as a brain is a self learning organization, with a strong leader, and where the use of IT inside the organization is a must, no matter what kind of organization.

The organization as flux & transformation relies on the liveliness of the brain metaphor. Flux is constantly moving; one cannot step in the same river twice (because the water has passed you at the time you step in for the second time). Life is like a voyage of discovery. There is no beginning and no end. The organization is holistic; everything is connected to each other. Redundancy is not an issue, because it generates creativity. A story can be more revealing to generation Z and Alpha, than the schemes of the Baby Boomers.

To transform one need to understand the truth, but first an individual needs to understand themselves. Development is complying with the rules of the game; transition is changing the rules of the game. Transformation is changing the rules of the game, but also the game itself. Generation Z and Alpha want to be self regulating, and self learning to be able to be a transformational person.

Generation Z and generation Alpha prefer diversity because this stimulates their creativity. They also prefer decentralization which should result in less hierarchy. These new generations appreciate freedom and openness. In the IT organization they will have great and creative ideas about Business Intelligence. For management it is important to keep in mind that creativity comes together with freedom of thoughts without too much rules.

To generation Z Google might be an attractive employer. Current Google employees get one day a week to spend on inventing their ideas.

Solutions and Recommendations

This section described the metaphors of organizations that fit the different values of the generations, the generation metaphors. The focus has lied on IT departments. It provided insights of the job values that are important for the new generations. The summary of these values are:

- **Organization design:** Generation Y has preference for a democratic designed organization. At the other hand the values of generation Z and generation Alpha will fit to a holistic self learning organization with decentralization and less hierarchy.
- **Leadership:** Managers do control an organization, leaders move organizations forward. Leaders and managers do influence a main part of the motivation of their employees. To motivate the new generations they need responsibilities, not roles or tasks.

Generation Y needs role models and 'reality constructors' as their leaders. A formal leadership position is not decisive. Natural leaders like heroes and people with charisma are important as well. Natural leaders are the ties in the social networks that should be respected.

Generation Z and generation Alpha need strong leadership because one entity should control the information-processing of their holistic organization. The leader should be guiding on results, less on behavior or the process.

- **Organization culture:** Generation Y fits best in an organization culture with shared symbols and values. To keep a cohesive organization culture it is important not to allow the group becoming larger than 148 members (Dunbar, 1992). Generation Z and generation Alpha need self regulation, a learning environment, creativity and diversity.

CHARACTERISTIC 2: OPTIMIZED USE OF COMMUNITY TECHNOLOGY

If the new generations of IT professionals were asked in the future for the definition of Information Technology, they might answer: "Information Technology is part of Community Technology. This technology contributes to Community Technology by supporting information flows through and between communities. Information Technology consists among others of information systems, databases, program software, etc."

In this section the future development of IT is described. This gives an insight into the second important characteristic, based on the technical resource view. Today organizations focus on Information Technology and Telecommunication Technology. Fusing these technologies brings Information- and Communication Technology (ICT). Adding new technologies such as RFID and fingerprint technology will create Community

Table 3. Overview of the generations and their view on information technology

	View from the generation	IT professionals of this generation "The technology I work with is.."
Baby Boom	Automation/ Engineering	IT + Telecom
X	Automation/ Engineering	IT + Telecom
Y	Communication	ICT
Z/ Alpha	Community	Community Technology

Technology. Community Technology is the collection of technologies that support communities. An overview is provided in Table 3.

IT, as eEngineering

The integrated circuit, also known as the computer chip, is one of the most influencing inventions that have impacted on our daily lives. Since its creation in 1958 computer chips are used in computers, cellular phones, TVs, cars, GPS, etc. The fact that the number of transistors on an integrated circuit doubles every two years is a factor in, or a result of, these technological developments. This phenomenon is also called Moore's Law, named after Gordon Moore who predicted this trend already in 1965[8].

In her book 'Inventing the Internet' Abbate wrote: "Between the 1960s and the 1980s computing technology underwent a dramatic transformation: the computer, originally conceived as an isolated calculating device, was reborn as a means of communication (2000, p. 1). Without the developments in Telecommunication (telegraphy, radio, telephony, etc) the predecessor of the Internet, the APRANET, and Internet itself would never have existed.

With the rise of administrative organizations Information Technology (IT) got the chance to develop. Based on computers, but also information systems, and telecommunication, IT provided many opportunities for automation in many kinds of products, services, and processes. The Baby Boom generation and generation X see IT mainly as an engineering of computerization. The primary responsibilities of these IT professionals were to program and learn to think in a systematic way to solve problems.

The Capital C of IT

When people talk about Information Technology (IT) they can mean two different things. First, the technologies and management of Information Systems; second is the technologies and management of Information Systems combined with (Tele) Communication Technology.

In the Netherlands and in Belgium two different words are used for these two different meanings. The first meaning, the Information Systems, is called Information Technology (IT). The second meaning, the Information Systems combined with (Tele) Communication Technology, is called Information- and Communication Technology (ICT). Since technologies got more intertwined ICT would be a better word for IT with the meaning of Information Systems combined with (Tele) Communication Technology. Right now it seems the capital C of IT is missing.

It would be good to realize that when we speak about IT we mean Information- and Communication Technology. It would be even better to start talking about ICT, and also to emphasize the importance of communication. Communications has an important role within IT. Besides the technical side of it (smart phones, wires, VoIP, WiMAX, etc.) the social side of communications within IT has an inestimable value. Since

Internet is opening up many new communication possibilities we have seen just the start of online social communication. Think for example about instant messaging (MSN, Google Chat, etcetera), blogs (as well as micro blogging like Twitter), and online social communities (LinkedIn, Facebook, MySpace, etc.). They are fast in picking up new ways of communications. They do not really seem to desire to put their personal photos online, for example at Facebook.

Generation Y is exploring the communication side of I(C)T and its application possibilities. Both communications and applications should support the business and its individual users. The sociological view on ICT provides a new kind of business IT alignment. New forms of communication to develop ICT are welcome to generation Y. They prefer open source thinking, and thinking from the cloud.

The IT professionals of generation Y would like to be called ICT professionals. Their focus is communication within and without the organization, supported by ICT. They see ICT as a technology with supporting communication as the main purpose, not automation.

Welcome into the Community Age

Once generation Y has started to be the innovators within the IT department with ICT, generation Z starts to arise. How will ICT develop within the next decades?

In the Community Age, which is starting to appear, almost everybody on earth is connected to each other; inside the organization, but also outside the organization. Almost everyone works in an open organization, in a social network. Globalization and the Internet have provided the impetus for this development. Technology is what provides the support to make this community lifestyle possible. A community can be seen as a group of interacting people who are connected to each other and share a similar environment. This environment can be physical (e.g. in a village), but also virtual (e.g. a discussion group at LinkedIn).

New technologies are moving IT into this new stage. Some of these emerging technologies are ID technologies (RFID, iris scan technology, finger-print recognition, DNA, etc) and nano technology. Gps in smartphones is on of the applications of new technology in existing ICT.

IT professionals of generation Z and generation Alpha will appreciate the term Community Technology as the successor of ICT. Community Technology would consist of all technologies that support communities. These technologies are Information Technology, (Tele) Communication Technologies but also new upcoming technologies like ID technologies. Generation Z and generation Alpha see the IT department as the information-processor of the organization as was it a brain. The future IT department will play a direction function, perhaps even with all-round internal directed community managers. Business Intelligence will play an even more important role in the performance of overall organizations.

Solutions and Recommendations

Technological developments will continue to change IT organizations. On the other hand technological developments will influence interests and values of new generations of professionals. To attract and retain these new generations of IT professionals it could help to think and act ahead of technological developments. The focus on IT technologies and methods that could attract and retain the new generations will be:

- **Choices for technologies:** According to generation Y ICT should aim to support communications. Generation Y prefers open source, thinking from the cloud and business IT alignment from a sociological perspective. The technology should support the user. To attract them you should start talking about ICT where you mean IT with the meaning of Information Systems and (Tele) Communication Technology.

Generation Z and generation Alpha see the IT department as one of the most important departments for an overall organization to survive as a brain. They prefer centralizing of data-processing and Business Intelligence. Talking about Community Technology is what they appreciate. The technology should support a community and does not focus at one technology but looks broader.

- **Choices for methods:** Generation Y prefers more overall methods like BiSL above ITIL. They will stimulate a new way of IT Governance with more cultural and political aspects involved. Project Management will get a renewal. Generation Z and generation Alpha prefer methods that support community management. Besides technological and economical insights, sociological insights have to play an important role in community management too.

CHARACTERISTIC 3: OPTIMIZED USE OF *BA*, THE SPACE FOR KNOWLEDGE CREATION

IT professionals are the human IT resources. Since they are knowledge workers, knowledge is the most important indirect human IT resource, carried and distributed by the IT professionals. In the Background section knowledge has been defined as 'Knowledge = Information x Experience x Skills x Attitude' (Weggeman, 1997). This suggests that knowledge must be unique to the individual. Nonaka, Toyama and Konno talk about knowledge assets as 'firm-specific resources that are indispensable to create values for the firm' (2000, p. 20). In the same article they explain the knowledge conversion processes, leadership and *ba* as the components for a unified model of dynamic knowledge creation. The four main knowledge conversion processes move between explicit and tacit knowledge which set up a knowledge creation spiral. These four processes are called Socialization, Externalization, Combination and Internalization (SECI) (Nonaka & Takeuchi, 1995). According to Nonaka and Takeuchi organizational knowledge creation is the input for continuous innovation. And continuous innovation brings competitive advantages (Nonaka & Takeuchi, 1995).

Ba, the Space for Knowledge Creation

This section focuses on *ba*. *Ba* is the shared context in motion for knowledge creation (Nonaka et al, 2000, p. 13). It provides energy, quality and a place to share, create and utilize knowledge. *Ba* is Japanese for 'space'. This 'space' depends on the location and time. Nonaka and Konno distinguish knowledge and information (1998). Knowledge is intangible and residing in *ba*. Information is tangible and independent from *ba*. *Ba* is a place where information is interpreted to become knowledge. It is not bounded to a certain place and time. Therefore its boundary is fluid. It is present around the knowledge conversion processes, at the moments and periods, and places where people interact. For example, if a group of managers get a presentation about the business strategy for the next year, the room they are in and the duration of the presentation define the *ba*.

The knowledge space *ba* appears in three kinds. Knowledge of people who interact can be in the same:

Physical space (e.g. offices)
Virtual space (e.g. e-mail)
Mental space (e.g. shared ideas)

Several combinations are possible. The combination of all three is called in this chapter the all-embracing *ba*. Table 4 provides an overview of the generations and their ideas of what the prior-

Table 4. Overview of the generations and their ideas about the space to create knowledge

	View from the generation	IT professionals of this generation "Knowledge creation should be done in.."
Baby Boom	Physical *ba*	Classes are the best places to gather knowledge
X	Virtual *ba*	Gathering knowledge should be able at any time, independent of a certain physical location
Y	Mental *ba*	They want to share ideas, experiences, feelings
Z/ Alpha	All-embracing *ba*	Gathering knowledge can be done everywhere

ity should be for the space to create knowledge. This is also based on the writing of Bounfour and Grefe who explored the sequences of the three kinds of *ba* (2009).

The IT Organization and its Physical *ba*

The Baby Boom generation is the generation that prioritizes knowledge creation in physical *ba*. They still remember the multiplication tables and memory aids they have been drilled by their teacher at primary school. To develop and learn they want to 'know from the book' (Strauss & Howe, 1991), and want to develop their personal growth by training and education.

In the business community they build offices for employees as the place to be productive with knowledge. It offers places to organize meetings for face to face discussions. For the Baby Boom generation meetings are one of the most important ways to interact, and herewith to create organizational knowledge.

If an IT professional needs new knowledge the Baby Boom manager will send them to a course, workshop, conference, or seminar. The IT professional from the Baby Boom generation expects the same. For internal knowledge creation he prefers considerations and meetings. But could this motivate the new generations as well?

The IT Organization and its Virtual *ba*

The virtual *ba* characterizes generation X. Real time knowledge sharing is not necessary, it can also be done within an interval, and independent of a certain physical location. A book can be written at one time and be read by somebody else at another time. An e-mail can be send at moment A, while it will be read and interpret at moment B. The virtual *ba* can appear with the help of manuals, memos, books but also e-mails and teleconferences. Making the digital virtual *ba* available is the task of IT professionals.

For IT professionals from generation X, externalizing knowledge is important; for their own IT organization and also for the rest of the overall organization. After all, that is the advantage IT can bring to the organization: record and produce traceable information to support business goals.

The IT Organization and its Mental *ba*

As previously described, generation Y uses a culture metaphor to look at organizations. Having the same mental programming as the other organizational members is important to them. They will start looking for another job if they do not feel comfortable with the values of their employer. The mental *ba* is shared in experiences, feelings, emotions and mental models. This mental space becomes bigger when the social links within the organization are stronger. Knowledge in mental spaces is owned by the IT professional. Therefore generation Y believes that the IT professional is the owner of his knowledge, not the employer.

IT professionals from generation Y like to create experiences together. The feeling for team work rises at this generation. This is an important ingredient for renewing project management. Team role management, as Meredith Belbin described for example (1981), is more important in their eyes to succeed a project, than the specialties of each individual group member. Once they give their commitment they will work hard for their employer. A condition is that their authenticity will not come into play.

The IT Organization and its All-Embracing *ba*

Generation Z and generation Alpha will not have a clear preference of where knowledge can be created. They understand knowledge creation is about interaction between people. They are generalists in combining knowledge creation spaces. Social networks are the underlying factor.

IT has become a part of Community Technology by the time generation Z and generation Alpha have entered the labor market. Innovation is very important to achieve competitive advantage. Community Technology can inspire significant innovation. IT professionals of generation Z and generation Alpha combine the physical, virtual, and mental space to generate a well balanced all-embracing *ba*. In this *ba* the SECI knowledge conversion processes are moving fast to deliver innovation to the organization. To achieve this generation Z expects a strong leader who knows how the organizational knowledge should evolve and be leveraged.

Solutions and Recommendations

In this section the concept *ba* is explained. It is the shared context in motion of knowledge creation. *Ba* appears in three kinds of spaces: physical space, virtual space, and mental space. More

insight in *ba* provides more insight of how the new generations of IT professionals think about where knowledge should be created. Their values regarding knowledge creation are:

Knowledge Management

The perspective of knowledge management changes. The knowledge intensive organization, the learning organization and the resource based strategy are the basis for the knowledge creating organization. Generation Y fits best with knowledge management that is not really managed but stimulated. They also see knowledge broader than the previous generations. Being able to find information on the Internet with for example Google or Wolfram Alpha is part of the skills of a knowledge worker as well. Generation Y thinks "As a professional I am the owner of my knowledge. Not my employer." They can use their knowledge with political reasons. To let them share their knowledge you can motivate them by creating a cohesive organization culture to stimulate their mental *ba*. A condition is that they can optimally utilize their authenticity.

Generation Z and generation Alpha would like their employers to find and use their talents. They know they are an important IT resource. You should get the best out of them, like you should with the IT systems. Information-processing is the heart of an organization. Their knowledge, which they develop in the all-embracing *ba*, is decisive in the success of this information-processing. Besides their own unique knowledge they expect having a strong leader who knows what direction the organizational knowledge should move towards.

Interaction & Motivation

Generation Y feels that social interaction cannot be enforced. Motivating their social networking is important. It improves innovation, better knowledge exchange and influence in groups. They are willing to learn from the Baby Boom generation.

For generation Z and generation Alpha a virtual organization works the same as an online social network or community, but with other purposes and other responsibilities.

CHARACTERISTIC 4: TAKING CARE OF THE PLANET

Ideas about the focus of long term direct and indirect financial investments are continuously changing. This section describes the views of the different generations of IT professionals about corporate responsibility and strategical decisions of the IT department. Most IT professionals cannot tell precisely what their ideas about long term IT investments are. It is hidden in their values. To explain these long term values per generation Triple P will be explained. Triple P stands for People, Planet and Profit and is an approach for Corporate Social Responsibility (CSR).

Triple P: Profit, People & Planet

Being a good organization means acting with Corporate Social Responsibility (CSR). This is a self-regulating mechanism of concern and devotion of an organization, aligned with economic performance (Profit), with respect to the social side (People), and within the ecological conditions (Planet). The three Ps Profit, People and Planet are also known as the Triple P approach.

Table 5 provides an overview of the views of the generations, and how IT professionals feel about long term IT investments. In the next section each element of Triple P, related to the responsibility of the IT department, is explored.

Profit and its Demand for Functional Technology

First of all an organization needs to make profit to be able to survive. Without a healthy cash flow on the long term a company will go bankrupt. The production and economic effects of products and services of a company contributes also to the economic welfare. Therefore Profit has been translated by some into Prosperity (Sachs, 2000).

The Baby Boom generation and generation X became mature in a world where profit making was the main goal of an organization. A profit making organization needs functional technology which became the focus of the IT professionals of the Baby Boom generation and generation X. These IT professionals are mainly engineers, as described before. Engineers love the possibilities of technology but are also struggling with translating these possibilities into business cases. This has resulted into for example information systems with the latest functionalities, but with high costs and trouble achieving deadlines, while the business value might not be that high. It is like delivering a new office building without toilets.

People and their Desire for User Friendly Technology

Since organizations are transforming into open organizations, the need for Corporate Social Responsibility has grown. Stakeholder manage-

Table 5. How generations of IT professionals feel about long term IT investments

	View from the generation	IT professionals of this generation "Long term IT investments should.."
Baby Boom	Profit €	Demand for functional technology
X	Profit €	Demand for functional technology
Y	People ,	Desire for user friendly technology
Z/ Alpha	Planet ü	Need for non wasteful technology

ment has become an important aspect in this CSR mechanism.

For a long time shareholders have been seen as the most important stakeholders. But the consciousness has arisen that without customers a company cannot make profit, and without employees and vendors overall organizations cannot even deliver products and services to the customers. Also the indirect stakeholders can be important. Negative news about the company can influence the reputation of your organization, and thereby it can influence your customers, stakeholders, or maybe even a stricter governmental supervisor.

The P of People is about people inside and outside the organization. An organization can contribute to the social well-being inside and outside the overall organization and geography.

Generation Y experiences an open and connected world which makes the world small. Besides making profit, an organization should mean something for the society as well. Corporate social responsibility is changing into a critical success factor for organizations, not only a unique selling point anymore.

IT professionals of this generation are more society and human consideration oriented than the previous generations. They prefer working for companies with a meaning. They want to leave a good footprint, together with their employer. This could affect the Third World, but also the users of their IT solutions. IT professionals of generation Y have a desire for user friendly ICT that still is functional and contributing to profit.

Planet and the Need for Non Wasteful Technology

The third P is Planet. A good company takes care of the consequences of its activities for the environment, and aims to leave a good footprint on earth. The ecological quality is what counts. Demonstrating how the company is taking care of its ecological environment could be seen as strengthening the corporate reputation. The need is growing to act with sustainable results of taking care of natural resources.

The Baby Boom generation, generation X, and generation Y just started discussing the climate change. Generation Z and generation Alpha will be the generations that can really behave as non wasting people who really take care of the planet. They make sure their living environment will stay exist in the future.

Generation Z and generation Alpha grow up and will grow up in a time where fossil fuels will be replaced by 'green' fuels like hydrogen, used by minimal energy consuming vehicles. For these new generations of IT professionals it is very important not to spoil energy and materials. They will give priority to smart non wasting technologies. IT professionals of these generations look for opportunities to save more energy of mainframes. They expect users turning of in case of not using a device; the less devices per user the better. These Green IT solutions will appear soon and make generation Z and generation Alpha having this green value attitude. They expect the IT budget will adapt to this.

Solutions and Recommendations

To attract the new generations of IT professionals even the strategy perspective and intentions of your organization can play a role. The values of the new generations are about being fair and about taking responsibilities. Their opinion about business goals and investments are:

Goals: Your business strategy should contain CSR (Corporate Social Responsibility), by keeping in mind profit, *and* people *and* planet. Generation Y would like you to focus on the People component. Generation Z and generation Alpha expect your company to leave behind a green footprint.

Investments & budget choices: Spend your IT budget to achieve profit for the business, to be valuable for people (your employees but also other stakeholders of the organization and maybe a Third World Country), and spend your budget to take care of the planet what is in your possibilities. Try to combine IT and CSR into social and green IT. Generation Z and generation Alpha are born resource savers.

FUTURE RESEARCH DIRECTIONS

This chapter has been based on an explorative research, build on literature study, observations and pattern-based understanding of past and present to generate generation behavior futures study. The inductive method is used since there currently is no theory about generation differences in organizations, and generation differences of IT professionals in particular (see also the Background section).

It is recommended to further test this explorative research to establish the four characteristics of the new generations of IT professionals. A first step could be a qualitative field research to test the four key characteristics as hypotheses. Longitudinal studies would certainty enrich the establishment of the four characteristics.

This research has generalized generations in Western countries, based on development patterns that are globally present (development in management paradigms, future development of IT, development of knowledge creation and development of corporate responsibility). Nevertheless it could be interesting for further research to investigate differences between nations.

When investigating value differences of generations the best results are given by interacting groups with members from the same generation. Observing blended groups and interviewing individuals will give less significant results, according to Bontekoning (2007, p. 155). Methodologies of social research are recommended. The research method generation behavior futures study has to be further developed.

Besides testing the four characteristics as hypotheses further research can be done to test

the assumptions of the four main developments (used per resource view):

- Further social and economic research to explore the expectations members of the new generations have of their (future) employers.
- Further technological and economic research to explore the possibilities of Community Technology.
- Further empirical social research to establish the theory of *ba*, and the unified model of dynamic knowledge creation.
- Further technological research to explore how IT can become more non wasteful.

CONCLUSION

Every generation has built up its own values that characterize them. These values influence the values in an organization, and herewith its performance. The values of the new generations of IT professionals differ from the values of the previous generations of IT professionals. It is important to recognize that values are invisible and woven throughout culture, and professions.

This chapter is a call for CIOs, IT managers, HR managers, education program makers and academics to become more aware of these generation differences in organizations, and of the characteristics of the new generations of IT professionals in particular. Being aware of this could help to build the pipeline for the new IT professionals, and to become more successful in attracting them to, and retaining them in, IT departments.

In this chapter two main questions have been answered:

What are the important characteristics of the new generations of IT professionals, compared with the previous generations?

How will the effective IT department attract and retain the new generations of IT professionals?

To attract the new IT professionals first a solid pipeline has to be build before they can be attracted into, and retained in IT departments.

Four Characteristics of the New Generations of IT Professionals

Of all kinds of IT resources the human IT resources do affect the success of an IT department the most. The human IT resources are the IT professionals.

The four characteristics of the new generations of IT professionals are:

1. **Acting in an open and connected world:** Generation Y has values that contribute the culture and political system metaphors of organizations and IT departments. The values of generation Z and generation Alpha contribute the brain and flux & transformation metaphor.

2. **Optimized use of Community Technology:** After speaking about IT for years, it is generation Y that is expecting us to start talking about ICT. Generation Z and generation Alpha will have values that support considering Community Technology.

3. **Optimized use of *ba*, the space for knowledge creation:** The values of generation Y encourage using mental spaces for knowledge creation. With this mental space generations have introduced all three kinds of *ba*, namely physical *ba*, virtual *ba* and mental *ba*. The all-embracing *ba* will have the preference of generation Z and generation Alpha.

4. **Taking care of the planet:** Triple P is the approach for taking Corporate Social Responsibility and stands for Profit, People and Planet. The values of generation Y contribute to People and user friendly technology, the values of generation Z and generation Alpha contribute to Planet and non wasteful technology.

4 Tips to Build the Pipeline for the New Generations of IT Professionals

Many CIOs complain about the fact that they have to give in-company training to the just graduated professionals. Is it not the academic world we expect to educate our new professionals? But technological and management developments follow each other quickly. It seems almost impossible for the academic world to implement those developments in their programs. The business community should more support and update the academics because they are inside the developments.

Knowledge exists of Information x Skills x Experience x Attitude. Four tips for education program makers and others to build the pipeline for the new generations of IT professionals:

1. **Building skills by accepting generation gaps:** Strengthen the skills that characterizes the generation of students. Make students of generation Y aware of the sociological phenomena related to IT that have cultural and political characteristics. Their skills will be, amongst others, being pragmatic, social and being team players. Students of generation Z and generation Alpha need more holistic and transformational education. Stimulate their creative, improvising and learning skills.

2. **Information building by seeing new generations as the innovators:** Students of generation Y need to be taught an overview of ICT, Information *and* Communication Technology. Communication deserves focus. Consider social networking, business IT alignment, Wikinomics, Cloud Thinking, IT governance and team role management. Students of generation Z and generation Alpha need to be taught an overview of Community Technology, including emerging technologies like ID technologies. Think

about Business Intelligence. Therefore a discovery has to be started now to explore what Community Technology precisely would contain in the future. The person who knows this the best, are the new generations themselves. To discover Community Technology they need freedom of content, but a structure to work with. Remember the brains of youngster are in development, and that a good framework or structure is necessary for them to gather knowledge.

3. **Experience building by coaching of persons of two generations ahead:** To become an IT professional, students need to be taught how to create knowledge and to interact with others to build up more experiences. Therefore you should concentrate to attend to mental spaces to create knowledge as a way to stimulate students of generation Y. For students of generation Z and generation Alpha you should concentrate at the all-embracing *ba* to create knowledge. Since young generations are just learning how to gather knowledge, they should be supported by a coach, buddy, or mentor. This could be a teacher, but also somebody from the business community. It is preferable to choose a coach from a generation two generations ahead of the person who is being coached.

4. **Attitude building by group interactions:** Attitudes are difficult to teach but by being their example you are able to influence student's attitudes. Students of generation Y should create an attitude that supports the desire for more user friendly Information *and* Communication Technology. Students of generation Z and generation Alpha should create an attitude that supports non wasteful (Community) Technologies. As a teacher you should not tell them this, but moderate an interactive group discussion.

4 Tips to Attract and Retain the New IT Professional from the Pipeline into your IT Organization

Once universities have created our new generations of IT professionals it is the turn of CIOs, IT managers and HR managers to attract and retain them into their IT organizations. If the new generations are given the opportunity to implement their characteristic values, then IT might become more innovative. Four tips to attract and retain the new IT professional:

1. **Create a 'new generation prove' IT organization**: To make your IT organization 'new generation proof' the four resource views of the IT organization, as described in this chapter, give guidelines for changes. These changes should be made especially in the mindsets of executives, managers, and employees. The four ways to change your IT organization in an attractive IT organization are:

   ◦ **Organizational attraction**: To attract generation Y you need to give your overall organization and IT organization characteristics of the culture and political system metaphors. Generation Z and generation Alpha will be attracted by organizations with characteristics of brain and flux & transformation metaphors.

   ◦ **Technical attraction**: IT professionals love technology. But not the 'old fashioned' technology anymore. To attract IT professionals of generation Y demonstrate that IT works with Information *and* Communication Technology (ICT), instead of just IT. To attract IT professionals of generation Z and generation Alpha show that the organization works with Community Technology, which supports communities.

○ **Human attraction**: Show the new IT professional that employees are treated as knowledge workers, and providing all kinds of *ba*, the space for knowledge creation. In particular the mental *ba* to attract generation Y, and the all-embracing *ba* to attract generation Z and generation Alpha.

○ **Financial attraction**: Show IT professionals of generation Y that the organization cares about making profit (and their salary), but also takes care of people inside and outside the company. To attract IT professionals of generation Z and generation Alpha as well show that the organization takes care of the planet by using and developing non wasteful technologies.

2. **Build up a 'new generation proof' corporate image**: To attract the new IT professional an organization needs to show its 'new generation proof' attraction values, as described above. Like HR (but also together with organizations like Marketing and Sales) everyone has the responsibility for the image building of the organization, not only the IT organization. With this image building demonstrate the values of the organization. It is up to HR managers to provide insights about the current values in their organization and to move this up to the values of the new generations.

3. **Use the new generations as the organizational innovators**: To create an effective work environment for the new IT professional and the current IT professional, it is important to see the new generations as the organizational innovators. An IT organization needs to evolve to adapt to the zeitgeist. And the new generations are the ones who make this possible. At least if the current generations let them to their job. This does not mean you can give complete freedom to the new generation. They need direction

because they do not know how to make organizational changes (A.C. Bontekoning, personal communication, April 13, 2010). Merely mixing different generations alone will not suffice. Give the new generations the opportunity to work among themselves. Together they can cross-pollinate new innovative ideas.

4. **Coach the new IT professional by the generation two life stages ahead**: According to Bontekoning (personal communication, April 13, 2010) different generations with one generation between them, fit together effectively. For example a director from the Baby Boom generation can coach a trainee from generation Y better, than when a manager from generation X coaches the trainee. As described in section Generations Described, a generation will naturally block innovations from the generation behind them. The trainee accepts more from the Baby Boomer, while the Baby Boomer would like to share his experiences with the people in their second life stage. Remember they first raised this generation at home as parents, and then they can continue teaching them in their organization as experienced colleagues. The role as coach, buddy or mentor will stimulate the new generations of IT professionals to develop and to stay at the organization.

To make optimal use of the characteristics of the generations let professionals from a the same generation work together in a team, without being mixed up with professionals from other generations (A.C. Bontekoning, personal communication, April 13, 2010); albeit it is also valuable to have diverse teams.

Older generations are fundamental to the shaping of younger generations. They raise them in families, they teach them at schools and universities, they inspire them at work, and they influence the zeitgeist. Let us aim to perfect IT professionals coming out of the pipeline.

REFERENCES

Abbate, J. (2000). *Inventing the Internet*. Massachusetts: MIT Press.

Becker, H. A. (1992). *Generaties en hun kansen*. Amsterdam: Meulenhof.

Becker, H. A. (1997). *De toekomst van de verloren generatie*. Amsterdam: Meulenhof.

Belbin, R. M. (2004). *Management teams: Why they succeed or fail*. Oxford: Elsevier Butterworth-Heinemann.

Bontekoning, A. C. (2007). *Generaties in organisaties. Een onderzoek naar generatieverschillen en de effecten daarvan op de ontwikkeling van organisaties*. Doctoral dissertation, Tilburg University, the Netherlands.

Bontekoning, A.C. (2008). Generatiegolven als vernieuwingsimpuls. *M&O, 1*, 37-51.

Bounfour, A., & Grefe, G. (2009). Designing sequences for knowledge exchange: The Hau-Ba model. In Bounfour, A. (Ed.), *Organisational capital: Modelling, measuring and contextualizing* (pp. 76–108). Oxon, UK: Routledge.

Carr, N. G. (2004). *Does IT matter? Information Technology and the corrosion of competitive advantage*. Boston: Harvard Business School Publishing.

Centraal Bureau voor de Statistiek. Den Haag/Heerlen. (2010). *Bevolking: kerncijfers naar diverse kenmerken*. Retrieved April 16, 2010, from http://statline.cbs.nl / StatWeb/ publication/ ?VW=T&DM= SLNL&PA=37296 ned&D1 =a&D2 =0,10,20,30,40, 50,(1-1)-l&HD =100423-2346& HDR=G1&STB=T

Centraal Bureau voor de Statistiek. Den Haag/Heerlen. (2010). *Hoger onderwijs, eerstejaars studenten naar vooropleiding en studierichting*. Retrieved April 16, 2010, from http://statline.cbs.nl/ StatWeb/publication /?DM=SLNL&PA= 70961ned &D1=0&D 2=1-2&D3= 0&D4= 0,175180&D5=0&D6=0&D7=a&D8=a&HDR= T,G4,G5,G2,G1,G6&STB =G3,G7&V W=T

Centraal Bureau voor de Statistiek. Den Haag/Heerlen. (2010). *Kerncijfers van diverse bevolkingsprognoses en waarneming*. Retrieved April 16, 2010, from http://statline.cbs.nl/ StatWeb/publication/ ?DM=SLNL&PA =70737NED&D1 =8-10&D2 =l&D3 =55,60,65,70,75, 80,85,90,95,l &VW=T

Darwin, C. R. (2006). *On the origin of species: By means of natural selection or the preservation of favoured races in the struggle for life*. New York: Dover Publications.

Dunbar, R. I. M. (1992). Neocortex size as a constraint on group size in primates. *Journal of Human Evolution, 20*, 469–493. doi:10.1016/0047-2484(92)90081-J

Hofstede, G. (2001). *Culture's consequences: Comparing values, behaviors, institutions and organizations across nations*. London: Sage.

Illich, I. (1973). *Tools for conviviality*. New York: Harper & Row.

Kondratiev, N.D. (1928). *The major cycles of the conjuncture*.

Mannheim, K. (1928). Das Problem der Generationen. *Kölner Vierteljahrshefte für Soziologie, 7*(2-3), 157–185.

Marías, J. (1970). *Generations, a historical method*. Alabama: The University of Alabama Press.

Moore, G.E. (1965). Cramming more components onto integrated circuits. *Electronics, 38*(8).

Morgan, G. (1997). *Images of organization*. Thousand Oaks, CA: Sage Publications, Inc.

Nonaka, I., & Konno, N. (1998). The concept of ba: Building a foundation for knowledge creation. *California Management Review, 40*(3), 40–54.

Nonaka, I., & Takeuchi, K. (1995). *The knowledge-creating company: How Japanese companies create the dynamics of innovation*. Oxford: Oxford University Press.

Nonaka, I., Toyama, R., & Konno, N. (2000). SECI, ba and leadership: A unified model of dynamic knowledge creation. *Elsevier Science Ltd, 33*, 5–34.

Parker, M. (1990). *Creating shared vision*. Clarendon Hills, IL: Dialog International.

Sachs, W. (2000). Globalization and sustainability. *Proceedings of the Sixth World Summit 2002*. Johannesburg: Heinrich-Böll.

Strauss, W., & Howe, N. (1991). *Generations: The history of America's future, 1584-2069*. New York: William Morrow.

Strauss, W., & Howe, N. (1998). *The fourth turning*. New York: Broadway Books.

Tapscott, D., & Williams, A. D. (2006). *Wikinomics: How mass collaboration changes everything*. New York: Portfolio.

Universum. (2010). *The Universum student survey*. Retrieved June 11, 2010, from http://universumglobal.com/ IDEAL-Employer-Rankings/ The-National-Editions

Weggeman, M. (1997). *Kennismanagement: Inrichting en besturing van kennisintensieve organisaties*. Schiedam: Scriptum.

Weggeman, M. (2007). *Leiding geven aan professionals? Niet doen! Over kenniswerkers, vakmanschap en innovatie*. Schiedam: Scriptum.

ADDITIONAL READING

Allee, V. (2003). *The Future of Knowledge: Increasing Prosperity Through Value Networks*. Massachusetts: Elsevier Science.

Bakas, A. (2009). *World Megatrends: Toward the Renewal of Humanity*. Oxford: Infinite Ideas Limited.

Bender, L., Burns, S., & David, L. (Producers) & Guggenheim, D. (Director). (2006, May 24). *An Inconvenient Truth*. [Motion Picture]. USA: Paramount Classics.

Carr, N. G. (2004). *Does IT Matter? Information Technology and the corrosion of competitive advantage*. Boston: Harvard Business School Publishing.

Erickson, T. (2008, May 27 2008). Interview with Tammy Erickson by Harvard Business Publishing on Managing Generation Y [Video file]. Retrieved from http://www.youtube.com/ watch?v= rDAdaaupMno

Friedman, T. L. (2006). *The World is Flat: The Globalized World in the Twenty-First Century* (pp. 425–456). London: Penguin Books Ltd.

Gladwell, M. (2008). *Outliers: The Story of Success*. New York: Little, Brown and Company.

Hewlett, S. A. (2009, August 3 2009). Interview with Sylvia Ann Hewlett by Harvard Business Publishing on why generation Y and Boomer employees prefer non-financial incentives [Video file]. Retrieved from http://www.youtube.com/ watch?v=fV Hnug8H1MM& feature=related

Hinssen, P. (2009). *Business/ IT Fusion: How to move beyond Alignment and transform IT in your organization*. Belgium: Mach Media.

Hofstede, G., Hofstede, G. J., & Minkov, M. (2010). *Cultures and Organizations: Software of the Mind*. New York: McGraw-Hill USA.

McDonough, W., & Braungart, M. (2002). *Cradle to Cradle*. New York: North Point Press.

Morgan, G. (1997). *Images of Organization*. Thousand Oaks, California: Sage Publications, Inc.

Nonaka, I., & Takeuchi, K. (1995). *The knowledge-creating company*. Oxford: Oxford University Press.

Nonaka, I., Toyama, R., & Konno, N. (2000). SECI, Ba and Leadership: a Unified Model of Dynamic Knowledge Creation. *Elsevier Science Ltd, 33*, 5–34.

Pijpers, G. G. M. (2010). *Information Overload – A System for Better Managing Every Day Data*. Hoboken, NJ: Wiley US.

Prahalad, C. K. (2004). *The Fortune at the Bottom of the Pyramid*. Pennsylvania: Wharton School Publishing.

Tapscott, D., & Williams, A. D. (2006). *Wikinomics: How Mass Collaboration Changes Everything*. New York: Portfolio.

KEY TERMS AND DEFINITIONS

Ba: The shared context in motion for knowledge creation. Nonaka and Konno wrote: "The concept of ba is used here as 'a shared space for emerging relationships' – space that can be physical, virtual and mental, or any combination" (1998). The combination of all three kinds of ba is called in this chapter the all-embracing ba. Ba provides energy, quality and a place to share, create and utilize knowledge. The 'space' depends on location and time, and has a fluid boundary. It is present around knowledge conversion processes, at the moments and periods, and places where people interact.

Community Technology: Term that encloses all technologies that support communities. These technologies are Information Technology, (Tele) Communication Technology but also new upcoming technologies like ID technologies (RFID, fingerprint recognition, iris scan technology, DNA, etcetera) and nano technology. A community is a group of interacting people who are connected to each other and share a similar environment. This environment can be physical, but also virtual.

Generation: A group consisting of people who feel connected to peers of the same age and who have experienced the same zeitgeist (Bontekoning, 2008). The zeitgeist appears as a combination of cultural, intellectual, ethical and political climates. In this chapter the following generations are distinguished: Baby Boom generation (born 1945-1964), generation X (born 1965-1980), generation Y (born 1981-1999), generation Z (born 2000-2009) and generation Alpha (will be born from 2010).

Generation Behavior Futures Study: A research method that predicts behavior of generations, based on pattern-based understanding of past and present.

Generation Characteristic: A group of related values within a certain perspective by which a generation distinguishes itself from other generations. In this chapter the classification of resource perspectives has been used, consisting of the organizational, technical, human and financial resource perspectives. The values of an individual depend obvious on more than only the characteristics of his generation. For example culture, personal character and also profession play a role in an individual's values.

IT Resources: The components that could support the aims of the IT department. The four kinds of IT resources are: IT professionals (the human IT resources, based on labor and knowledge), IT budget (the financial IT resources, based on capital), IT assets, like hardware, software, networks and data (the technical IT resources, based on ´materials´) and IT management (the organizational IT resources, based on entrepreneurship). Labor, capital, materials and entrepreneurship are the components of the classical economic theory of production resources.

IT Professional: A person with knowledge (a profession) related to IT who continuously develops his knowledge. Knowledge is the product of Information x Experience x Skills x Attitude (Weggeman, 1997). The scope of professionals working with IT goes vertical from strategic to operational, and horizontal from the technological to the business side.

Triple P Approach: Triple P stands for Profit, People and Planet and is an approach for Corporate Social Responsibility (CSR). Corporate Social Responsibility is a self-regulating mechanism of concern and devotion of an organization, aligned with economic performance (Profit), with respect for the social side (People), and within the ecological conditions (Planet).

ENDNOTES

[1] www.cionet.com

[2] The Baby Boom generation is larger than generation X. Dependency ratios will increase in the western world in the next decades. For 2010 the dependency ratio in the Netherlands is 25.1% (Centraal Bureau voor de Statistiek, 2010). This means that for every 100 working persons 25 persons need care (elderly and children). The expectation is that in 2040 the dependency ratio in the Netherlands will be 48.7% (Centraal Bureau voor de Statistiek, 2008). Social care will need much attention, but also the retirement gap that occurs on the labor market. If the retirement gap and the high dependency ratio are not handled properly it can have a negative influence on economy and welfare.

[3] The classification of the generations in years of birth is based on literature study. Chosen is to use a classification that fits most literature and most Western nations. It is not possible to draw a hard line between years of birth. Although demographically the Baby Boom generation can be pointed out clear because the number of birth between 1945 and 1965 has been substantially higher than the years before and after.

[4] This classification is based on the classification that Marias described in 1970 (p. 96). It can be assumed that the stages are evolving into a broader classification.

[5] Illich also includes intangible commodities as 'Tools for Conviviality', like for example education, health, decisions and knowledge (1973).

[6] Older generations should teach younger generations how to handle cultural change. Younger generations seem not have gained insight into cultural changes yet (A.C. Bontekoning, personal communication, April 13, 2010).

[7] Morgan describes the example of Magna International that let clusters of organizations reproduce itself when the size of 200 people is reached (1997, p. 104). This is to avoid becoming impersonal. The Dunbar number of 147.8 is based on the size of the neocortex (a part of the brains) of primates. The larger the neocortex of a primate is, the larger the average size of the groups they live with (Dunbar, 1992).

[8] Moore calculated with data from 1959 till 1965 and predicted till 1975. In 2010 his calculations are still standing.

Chapter 12
Retaining Global IT Talent

Deepak Khazanchi
University of Nebraska at Omaha, USA

Dawn Owens
University of Nebraska at Omaha, USA

ABSTRACT

The general problem of employee retention and the ability of an organization to influence and change actual turnover behavior are of great concern to employers, consultants, and academicians alike. This has been especially true in the IT profession. The growing need for IT professionals, combined with a shrinking labor pool, has made recruitment and retention of IT talent a top priority in many organizations. Forward thinking companies are looking to find and retain qualified IT talent wherever in the world it is available at a reasonable price. This chapter presents research that provides nuggets of wisdom that can be used as best practices for retaining global IT talent.

INTRODUCTION

Information Technology (IT) staffing is a topic that has plagued organizations for many years due to the fluctuating needs for talented IT professionals. During the 1990s, there was a demand for IT staff to support Y2K and the dot com boom. The IT industry could not recruit IT professionals quickly enough. However, with the 2001 recession, the dot-com bust, and the end of Y2K, IT hiring slowed and downsizing/rightsizing became the norm (Luftman & Kempaiah, 2007). More than 100,000 Americans dropped out of the IT labor

market between mid-2002 and late 2004 (Luftman & Kempaiah, 2007). In recent years, an improving economy, growing business confidence, application of IT to new domains like health and biosciences, and the emergence of exciting new technologies have again created a demand for IT professionals. Additional demand for IT professionals in the upcoming years is also likely due to the impending retirement of millions of baby boomers in the United States. According to the American Society of training and development (Gilburg, 2007), over the next two decades 76 million Americans will be retiring and only 46 million will be entering the workplace to replace them. For every two baby boomers who retire in

DOI: 10.4018/978-1-60960-535-3.ch012

the next decade there will only be one college graduate to take their place (op. cit.). In addition, the recent phenomenon of reverse emigration is resulting in skilled foreign IT professionals heading home to attain new opportunities as economies in their home countries are growing because of globalization and stronger economic growth (Bose, 2006). Finally, the downturn of the early 2000s coupled with the media-driven fear that IT jobs are going offshore, has caused a decline in computing enrollment in American universities. This has made it even harder for firms wanting to fill vacant positions (Luftman & Kempaiah, 2007).

Given the pace of change in information technology and businesses, the globalization of organizations, low university enrollments in IT majors, and the impending baby boomer retirement, many believe that there could be an even greater shortage of IT talent in the near future. According to the Bureau of Labor Statistics (USBL, 2005), one out of four new jobs between 2006 and 2012 will be IT related. The U.S. is projected to have a shortage of more than 6 million IT jobs by 2015 (Luftman & Kempaiah, 2007). With the potential for a shortage of IT employees, executives are paying closer attention to their existing IT employees' with the goal of finding ways to reduce turnover. Executives fully realize the importance of retaining talented IT professionals and the enormous cost of employee turnover. Attracting, developing and retaining IT professionals continue to be top-ranked issues for IT executives (e.g. Bernthal and Wellins, 2001; McLean & Luftman, 2004; Luftman, 2005; Luftman et al., 2006; Luftman & Kempaiah 2008; Luftman et al., 2009).

The problem of unfilled positions is aggravated by the difficulty of retaining good IT employees (Bartol & Martin, 1982; Bartol, 1983). Retaining personnel, especially good IT professionals, is an onerous task requiring substantial effort and investment on the part of the organization at many levels.

Businesses long ago learned that having the right people could yield higher financial returns (Bhasin & Cheng, 2001). The U.S. has long been a haven for talented individuals, but now other countries are joining the fight for talent by offering similar or better opportunities for professionals and their families (Bhasin & Cheng, 2001). Companies are competing with each other for IT professionals globally (West & Bogumil, 2001). Asian countries such as India and China, and certain companies in Eastern Europe and Latin America are becoming recognized as suppliers of highly qualified engineering and scientific talent (Lewin, Massini, & Peeters, 2009). The current challenge is that firms are competing for talent globally and not just seeking engineering and science resources in low-cost countries (Belderbos & Heijltjes, 2005; Khanna & Palepu, 2004). Due to globalization, reduced language barriers, the ubiquitous Internet, and availability of stable communication infrastructure, agile companies can hire talent at a reasonable price wherever it is available in the world. Nations are competing globally with visa quotas, working conditions, salaries, benefits, and opportunities to work with cutting-edge technologies (West & Bogumil, 2001).

THE COST OF TURNOVER

Staffing costs take up to 40-50 fifty percent of an IT budget and recruiting and retaining IT professionals is a critical issue for senior management (Argawal et al., 2006; Luftman & Kempaiah, 2007). The cost of employee turnover is expensive and involves both direct and indirect costs. When talented IT personnel leave an organization, costs are incurred with not only the hiring, assimilation and training of new employees, but there are also costs associated with losing an employee's knowledge.

The direct cost of employee turnover is vacant positions and recruitment. Recruitment in general and IT recruitment in particular is challenging and expensive. Initial recruitment costs include advertising, interviews, screening, and recruiter's salary (von Stetten et al., 2008). Additional costs include training and orientation, compensation for interim replacement, and overtime costs paid to current personnel (Scorce 2008).

Indirect or vacancy costs are incurred when employees leave. The indirect costs of employee turnover include productivity losses and loss of knowledge (Scorce, 2008). There is also the potential for delayed projects due to turnover and job errors that may eventually lead to customer dissatisfaction (Scorce, 2008). Organizations may lose customers due to inexperienced replacement workers and lowered quality of work (Scorce, 2008). Employers also need to consider the snowball effect. The departure of one employee could lead to other employees following suit, resulting in mass turnover (Moore & Burke, 2002).

"Talent is an intangible resource embodied in individuals, groups, and social networks, and learning to organize and manage talent globally becomes an idiosyncratic capability that is unobservable and difficult to imitate" (Lewin, Massini, & Peeters, 2009, pg. 30). Companies need talented people with a global mindset, especially in an increasingly unknown future (Jacobs, 2005). Retaining IT professionals on a global scale is a new challenge for many organizations.

Unfortunately, managers and decision-makers in organizations have largely depended on rules-of-thumb and anecdotal evidence rather than scientific means to understand turnover behavior and the psychological reasons for employee turnover. Clearly, "our ability to understand and control employee turnover is strengthened to the degree we can identify the source underlying one's inventions of leaving an organization" (Vandenberg & Nelson, 1999, p. 1334). Thus from a practical standpoint, to the extent one can diagnose the source of employee disaffection, it is possible to improve the probability of retaining employees (op. cit).

The IT workforce has become much more diverse, where IT professionals come from different demographics and cultures. Organizations need to retain their highly skilled IT professionals to remain competitive players in an increasingly global marketplace. Today's IS organization is competing and working in a global marketplace and new skills are needed to manage a workforce that includes a global talent pool (McLean & Luftman, 2004). Organizations need to learn how to leverage offshore talent in conjunction with their local talent, yet managing IT work performed all around the world requires new skills.

Companies are struggling to understand how to identify, develop, engage, and retain talent in global regions such as China, Pacific Asia, India, Middle East, Russia, Eastern Europe, and Brazil. Organizations do not understand the rules of engagement concerning how business is conducted in these foreign regions, let alone factors that motivate behavior of the people native to these regions (Ready, 2009).

Getting the right skills in the right numbers to where they are needed, spreading up-to-date knowledge practices throughout the global enterprise and identifying and developing talent on a global basis are problems that continue to plague employers (Roberts et al., 1998).

"Talent is an integral element of the knowledge base of the firm and consists of a wide range of highly specialized technical skills and knowledge (Lewin, Massini, & Peeters, 2009, pg. 30)". Unplanned, voluntary turnover is most often associated with high labor costs, deficit of skills and company knowledge, low morale, poor customer satisfaction, and financial losses (Hay Group, 2001). As a result, retaining IT professionals is of great concern to organizations.

The primary purpose of this chapter is to use previous research and anecdotal examples to identify a set of best practices for reducing IT turnover and retaining talented global employees.

IT Employee Retention: Challenges and Opportunities

Employee retention is defined as *the effort by an employer to keep desirable workers in order to meet business objectives* (Frank et al., 2004). Employee turnover and retention are closely related. An organization's turnover rate measures the percentage of employees who leave (Agarwal, et al., 2006). Retention rate measures the percentage of employees who remain (Agarwal, et al., 2006). Managers and researchers should focus on practices that affect turnover and retention practices and measure the effectiveness of these practices in terms of a firm's turnover rate or retention rate (Agarwal et al., 2006).

When considering retention factors, employers should note that pay is not as big a motivator as interesting work for most IT workers (Cappelli, 2001). Challenging work, job rotation, mentoring, and work-based support have been cited as important job characteristics (Cappelli, 2001). Specifically, job characteristics such as job autonomy, feedback, task significance, and skill variety are well-established determinants of job satisfaction (Hackman & Oldham, 1975; 1976; 1980) and organizational commitment (Mottaz, 1988; Porter et al., 1976). In this context, the view with respect to job satisfaction is that individuals experience high internal motivation if they (1) perform meaningful work; (2) are responsible for the outcomes of the work; and (3) are informed about the results of the work (Hackman & Oldham, 1976; 1980). Thus, studies in work settings such as hospitals and manufacturing plants have shown that job characteristics such as autonomy and communication quality can influence the safety of a work environment and perceived job worth (Parker et al., 2001; Marchese, 1998; Agho et al., 1993). Other studies have reported that job perception measured in terms of perceived job characteristics has a reciprocal relationship with overall and intrinsic job satisfaction (Wong et al., 1998).

In the IS field, Igbaria and Parasuraman (1994) concluded that the relationship of job characteristics with career expectations and outcomes may be potentially moderated by job involvement. Following their analysis of turnover intentions of IT employees, Igbaria and Greenhaus (1992) contemplated that intrinsic job characteristics "can help explain the impact of demographic characteristics, role stress, and career experiences on the turnover intention of [M]IS employees...". They further concluded, "it is plausible that employee education, age and tenure are associated with perceived job characteristics, which in turn, influence turnover intentions" (p. 47, parenthesis added).

In a 2008 survey conducted by Laumer (2009), two-thirds of those surveyed (728 IT professionals in Western European and U.S. Companies) indicated that an optimal job profile includes creativity in work, working in teams, and an annual monetary or non-monetary reward increase. According to this survey, respondents gave less importance to managerial responsibility and continuous advancement. However, given this data, few employers spend resources to help their IT workers develop and function on the job and most confine their employee management efforts to pay (Cappelli, 2001). Apparently, non-monetary retention practices are more important for reducing an organization's turnover rate and increasing their retention rate than are monetary incentives.

Based on various findings reported in the literature and interviews with two senior IT executives of firms that have a global footprint, we have outlined key best practices and lessons learned for retaining IT employees in a global environment. One of the firms is a global provider of advertising and marketing services. The firm employs over 200 IT professionals in five different countries. The second firm is a provider of management consulting services and studies "human nature and behavior." It has over 40 offices in 27 countries. Their IT staff must interact regularly with global employees. The executives from these firms provided insight into how they

Figure 1. Factors influencing IT employee retention

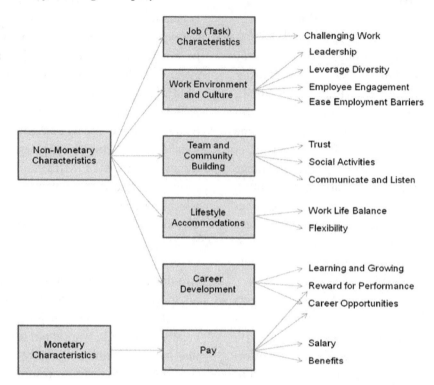

retain their IT staff, both domestically and globally. The following section details some key best practices for retaining IT employees in a global environment.

BEST PRACTICES FOR IT EMPLOYEE RETENTION

To succeed in a globally competitive environment, companies need to attract and retain the best talent worldwide, including both men and women from all nationalities (Adler, et al., 2001). The best method for attracting and retaining IT professionals involves the development of an overall program of economic, social, and technical opportunity (West & Bogumil, 2001). Many of the recommended best practices apply both locally and globally, but some are unique to managing a global IT workforce.

IT employee retention practices are classified into the categories described below and summarized in Figure 1.

Globally oriented employers manage key job characteristics to retain talented IT employees wherever they are located. Here the term job characteristic refers to the tasks assigned and the work being performed by IT employees. Examples of job characteristics that are important to IT professionals include challenging work, job rotation, training, autonomy, and feedback. We provide specific insights into two of these job characteristics that are particularly salient for IT employee retention - challenging work and job rotation.

Challenging work = Engaged employees. Working on varying and challenging projects is important for both global and domestic IT professionals (Laumer, 2009; O'Neal & Gebauer, 2006; Jamrog, 2004; Reff, 2007). The typical IT professional is motivated by being involved with a leading edge technology (Scorce, 2008). IT workers realize what an important asset their resume is and wish to hold positions where they can work with modern and leading edge technologies (West & Bogulmi, 2001). Employers need to stretch their top performers and continually challenge them. Employers do not want to wait until their best people have left to find they were bored. It is also important to provide task variety and create a culture that values intellectual stimulation (Jamrog, 2004; Morgan, 2008). The best employees know they have to be committed to lifelong learning. Employers should consider changing the design of IT jobs, especially programming jobs to reflect their real contribution to the organization (Cappelli, 2001). Providing challenging work has an additional benefit. When an organization does lose good workers, it increases the chance of their return, especially if their new job does not measure up to their old one (Reff, 2007).

Job rotation is one way to challenge employees and keep them engaged. Job rotation is the "lateral transfer of employees between jobs within an organization" (Campion et al, 1994, pg. 1518-9). Job rotation offers many advantages in general and IT jobs in particular. It keeps employees interested in their work and allows them to get hands on experience with different job profiles. It also gives an employee the chance to learn new skills, adding to their portfolio of work. Obviously, providing challenging work is closely tied with job rotation. Part of the value of rotation is that work diversity allows employees to fulfill their full potential. This is particularly critical in some IT jobs that can become routine and mundane. This is also particularly true for top IT graduates from universities who seem to have an expectation that employers will design IT jobs that employ their creative energies while challenging them.

The organizational work environment and culture must be conducive to a variety of differences among employees. The work environment and organizational culture are just as important as the work itself. Organizations should strive for

a climate that is exciting, enjoyable, and fulfilling (Taylor, 2004; Reff, 2007). It is important to create more appealing and welcoming environments for employees (Frank et al., 2004). Global companies need to create a culture where people from all backgrounds and locations feel that their interests and those of the company are much the same (Jacobs, 2005). IT professionals in particular come from different demographics and cultures. Employers need to leverage this diversity. Cultures where people are self-challenged and oriented around a clear purpose are likely to engender committed employees (Jacobs, 2005). Motivation and sense of belonging stem from shared values, doing work that is interesting, challenging and has meaning (Jacobs, 2005). A stable work environment with strong executive leadership is important to employees. Bottom line, *a culture with engaged employees is typically one with higher retention rates.*

Leadership by itself is important, but global leadership skills, global mindset and global knowledge are critical. The role of the front-line leader as the driver of retention has been well-recognized (Frank & Taylor, 2004, Leonard & Dwight, 2004; Society for Human Resource Management, 2000; Buckingham & Coffman, 1999). Organizations need to provide and support front-line and executive leadership (Morgan, 2008; O'Neal & Gebauer, 2006). The role of the front line leader is critical in building employee engagement (Bates, 2004; Gopal, 2004; Grensing-Pophal, 2001; Welbourne, 2003). Employees see the organization as they see their supervisor and they will stay if they have a good relationship with their supervisor (Tross & Egermann, 2004). Therefore, retaining valuable IT employees not only requires an investment in front-line workers, but also an investment in executive leadership. In a growing globally diverse workplace, employers also need to enhance global leadership skills (Adler et al., 2001). Global leadership is not the same as domestic leadership (Adler, 1997; Bartlett & Ghoshal 1989; Dorfman, 1996) and organizations need to understand the difference and train their employees through either formal training or mentoring and coaching.

Global companies and their leadership effectively leverage and celebrate employee diversity in all its forms. Employers need to know their workforce (O'Neal & Gebauer, 2006). This means that employers should be flexible in recognizing, understanding, and adapting to individual needs and views (Morgan, 2008; Taylor, 2004). Global workforces include employees with culturally diverse backgrounds. There are also generational differences that lead to diversity. Employers should leverage this diversity to build engaging teams, but build them carefully. For example, generational tensions can lower morale and increase turnover (Gelston, 2008). There are several different generations currently employed in the IT workforce – Baby Boomers, Generation X, and Generation Y.

Baby Boomers (those born between 1943 and 1960) are known for their commitment to their work. Gen X-ers (born between 1961 and 1981) strive for a work-life balance and Gen Y-ers (those born between 1982 and 2005) are known for their sense of entitlement, outspokenness, inability to take criticism, and technological sophistication (Gilburg, 2007). Sixty-eight percent of Baby Boomers feel younger people do not have as strong a work ethic as they do and that makes doing their work harder (Gelston, 2008). Thirty-two percent of Gen X-ers believe the younger generation lacks a good work ethic and 13 percent of Gen Y-ers say the difference in work ethics across the generations causes friction. Generation Y members are known for their sense of entitlement, outspokenness, inability to take criticism, and technological sophistication (Gilburg, 2007).

Generational clashes are not new. What is new is the extent to which the retirement of the Baby Boomers will leave employers scrambling to recruit and retain the talent they need. Generation Y may be high maintenance, but are also reported to be potentially the most high-performing genera-tion in history because its members are entering the workplace with more information, greater technological acumen and higher expectations of themselves (Fortune, 2007). To attract workers from this talent pool, an organization needs to understand what makes them tick and how to work with its members to bring out their high potential. They demand fast-track career positioning, work-life balance, positive feedback, training, and cutting edge technology (Gilburg, 2007). The millennial generation (generation Y), is technologically sophisticated and highly comfortable with digital communication. They are use to collaborative work environments and can thrive in them. Global mangers need to understand the unique strengths and weaknesses of each generation and manage the points of friction between them (Gelston, 2008).

Effective employee engagement engenders loyalty and trust. Engagement is defined as the willingness and ability to contribute to the organization's success and is measured by the way employees connect to their jobs emotionally and rationally (O'Neal & Gebauer, 2006). According to O'Neal and Gebauer (2006), Mexico has the largest group of engaged employees (40%) with Brazil close behind. In contrast, Asian countries have the lowest level of engagement (O'Neal & Gebauer, 2006). The U.S. has a 21% engagement level and Japan has 2% (O'Neal & Gebauer, 2006). The corporate environment is what engages and retains employees (Jamrog, 2004). Loyalty, engagement, and employee retention are intertwined, and engagement is clearly important for employee retention (Frank, et al., 2004). Loyalty itself does not guarantee engagement or employee retention, it is an influence. Organizations need to monitor retention and pay attention to engagement issues so that preventative measures can be taken before someone leaves or becomes disengaged (Taylor, 2004). Retention and engagement knowledge are necessary to build a committed team (Taylor, 2004). These practices are important for both domestic and global teams. However, it can be more challenging to build loyalty and trust in global virtual teams, a challenge we discuss later.

Develop a work environment that works hard to ease employment barriers for talented individuals in the firm. Hiring the best talent internationally means the employer has to be ready to move people to wherever they are effective in the organization. Easing the pain for international talent to work abroad is critical to achieve this goal (Bhasin & Cheng, 2001). Furthermore, talent should be nurtured and encouraged to rise to the highest ranks of the global firm regardless of their origin. Many examples in global firms such as Pepsi illustrate the success of global migration of executives. Not many examples of IT executives moving from global parts of a company are documented.

Effective team and community building within the global firm engender retention. A strong sense of community offers global employees a "sense of belonging" and is important for not only retaining employees, but also engaging them. Trust, social activities, and an environment that supports communication and listening are important to building a strong community. Using IT tools such as social media to build community networks can allow employees to continually be in touch with each other and feel a strong part of a far-flung firm or team.

Engendering trust in global IT employees is a challenge, but extremely important for retention. Cooperation and trust play a large role in determining employee retention (Bernthal & Wellins, 2001). It is important that employees trust their team members, their supervisor, and the company (Taylor, 2004). Trust and loyalty are closely tied together. Loss of loyalty is the result of loss of trust (Frank et al., 2004). Loyalty starts with trust and trust is on the decline (Frank, et al., 2004). Trust in management continues to fall in many professions (Wall Street Journal Online, 2002). Trust in management continues to fall in many professions (*op. cit*). The increased importance of trust may also reflect the growing

usage of global virtual teams in the IT profession Many organizations are utilizing virtual teams to bring together a distributed workforce. One of the challenges of working in a virtual team is the lack of face-to-face interaction with team members, which is necessary to build trust.

Encouraging informal and formal social activities, helps build a sense of community. Communication between managers and employees through formal and informal interactions is very important to IT professionals. Although IT personnel are known for being independent in character relative to non-IT personnel, communication is important to them (Laumer, 2009). Typically, IT work is characterized by project orientation, and therefore, building a team spirit is important and can be achieved through various social activities (Agarwal et al., 2006). Social activities also help IT workers suffering under stress and burnout to better balance their professional and personal lives (Agarwal & Ferratt, 2002). Such activities provide a basis for trust building among coworkers, which can be important in retaining IT staff (Luftman et al., 2006). Given the project-oriented nature of IT work, mechanisms for sharing information internally can help IT staff see the big picture of where their work fits into the overall organization (Agarwal et al., 2006). Formal social opportunities provide IT staff with opportunities to interact with each other and build a sense of community (Agarwal et al., 2006). This can also help teams succeed in high-pressure deadline situations (Agarwal et al., 2006). Community building not only improves retention, but also has other positive outcomes. It can potentially positively affect productivity and collaboration (Agarwal et al., 2006). Social activities and community building are important to both domestic and global teams. While it may be easier to promote social activities with domestic teams, both synchronous and asynchronous technologies and social media can be used to promote social activities and community building in global teams.

Employers must communicate and listen to employees on a regular basis. Like all employees, IT workers want to be heard and they want to know what is going on in the organization. This is even more vital when employees can feel isolated in globally dispersed organizations. Employees want their supervisors to be the ultimate communicators, people who will provide open and honest information on the organization's mission, policies, systems and practices (Jamrog, 2004). Employers should also communicate effectively to team members regarding retention and engagement issues (Taylor, 2004). Communication and listening builds esteem in team members (Taylor, 2004) and ultimately impacts success. Therefore, it is important that employers spend time both communicating and listening to their employees (Jamrog, 2004; O'Neal & Gebauer, 2006; Taylor, 2004).

Employers must be cognizant of and willing to allow for lifestyle accommodations of employees in globally dispersed organizations. Flexibility and work-life balance are central to the goal of retention (Laumer, 2009; Jamrog, 2004). The importance of this cuts across generations and professions. Quality of life is important for all employees across all cultures. Some cultures emphasize this balance more so than others do. With the large growing global workforce, particularly in IT, it is also important to accommodate the needs of culturally diverse employees. For example, it has been shown that those organizations with large existing immigrant populations providing a natural social support system for new arrivals are more competitive than those that do not (West & Bogumil, 2001; O'Neal & Gebauer, 2006). Organizations today are very likely to use global virtual teams (GVTs) to bring together a geographically dispersed workforce. GVTs can also be used to provide flexible work environments to employees. Using technology within the context of virtual teams allows more team members to work from home (Frank et al., 2004). However, not all the best and the brightest employees are at

the same level of preparedness for an ever changing environment (Jamrog, 2004). There is a small, but growing, group of people who are technologically advanced but socially inept (Jamrog, 2004). Therefore, employers should form these virtual teams carefully. The opportunity to participate in telework programs and policies that allow employees to work flexible hours is particularly important for IT professionals.

IT professionals are no different from other employees in terms of career development. One of the surest ways of retaining and attracting top IT talent is to offer workers ample avenues for furthering their careers and learning new technologies and skills. This includes providing opportunities for learning and growing, rewarding top performers and advancement opportunities.

Career development activities must include ways for employees to learn and grow within the organization. Organizations should develop a culture of learning and growing (O'Neal & Gebauer, 2006; Jamrog, 2004). Such a culture develops and coaches team members to help them grow resulting in greater commitment and loyalty to the organization (Taylor, 2004). This also includes providing mentors and advisors to employees (Reff, 2007). Being a mentor and an advisor is what sets leaders apart from managers (Reff, 2007). Globally dispersed workers require special attention as their sense of isolation can be reduced through opportunities to interact with other employees such as, mentoring, coaching, education and training. Mentors may assist local and remote workers and help them become familiar with the organizational culture and coach them to develop their skills relevant to the firm. Formal and informal training are additional methods for offering employees the ability to learn new skills and grow professionally.

Rewarding performance is a sure fire way of getting the attention of it employees. Applauding a job well done is important for both domestic and global employees (Reff, 2007). Employees will leave a company if they do not feel their work is appreciated (op cit.). Employers should consider creative ways to acknowledge and reward outstanding performs. Such rewards for performance will have to be varied based on generational differences between employees – baby boomers may look for rewards that our different than generation Y. Salary is one of the most obvious elements of competitiveness in any labor market, especially when comparing developed and developing countries (West & Bogumil, 2001; O'Neal and Gebauer, 2006). However, it is important to note that salary is important, but not a driving factor for many employees (op cit.). Additional monetary rewards beyond base salary such as competitive benefits and bonuses and other ad hoc inducements are also important (Agarwal et al., 2006). When using pay to reward performance, increases need to be linked to individual performance (O'Neal & Gebauer, 2006). Employers need to do a better job of measuring performance and tying rewards to performance (Cappelli, 2001). The bottom line about pay is that even though it is not a driving factor, a lack of competitive salary and benefits may cause job dissatisfaction, which in turn can affect job turnover (Igbaria & Greenhaus, 1992). Employers need to offer competitive pay along with competitive benefits.

Employees need to be rewarded for their contributions, but non-monetary rewards are just as important. Motivational fit plays a large role in determining employee retention (Bernthal & Wellins, 2001). It is important to motivate employees in various ways including acknowledging their contributions (Morgan, 2008); global workers may be out of sight but they need to be incentivized in similar ways as collocated workers. High performance and high potential individuals need accelerated development, exposure to different cultures, appropriate rewards and opportunities to keep them learning and growing (Jacobs, 2005). It is also important to recognize contributions of people who are high performers but who will not progress to another role (op cit.).

Attracting and retaining top talent requires employers to offer a diversity of career opportunities. Employers need to provide an abundance of opportunities to their top talent (Reff, 2007). Career advancement opportunities should be clearly communicated to all employers in the global workforce (O'Neal & Gebauer, 2006). This means also providing opportunities for the top IT employees to build not only technical skills but also leadership, managerial and business skills that will enable them to advance in the organization anywhere in the world (Agarwel et al., 2006).

LESSONS LEARNED

Key insights from a thorough analysis of prior academic and practitioner literature and in depth interviews with two IT executives were used to develop best practices and the lessons learned described below.

Tailor job characteristics to IT employees wherever they are located. Providing challenging work and job rotation are important to challenge employees and keep them engaged. Employees rely on immediate supervisors for assignments of tasks, responsibilities, and special projects (Tulgan, 2003). Many employees want their assignments to challenge them while contributing to the success of the organization (Jamrog, 2004). While low pay can lead to dissatisfaction, high pay by itself will not keep people around. The best people are not motivated by and do not stay for money alone. They stay because they are engaged and challenged by their work (Jamrog, 2004).

Offering IT employees the chance to work with new technologies is a way to challenge and in some cases reward IT employees. In fact, one of our interviewees uses technology as a reward for high performing employees. Technologies such as iPhones, iPads, and social networking tools like Twitter and Facebook are seen as status symbols for IT employees within the organization. Job rotation is another mechanism to challenge employees. While job rotation in the IT field is rare (McGilliCuddy, 2007), it is a way to continue to challenge employees and it may provide ancillary benefits to the organization. For example, rotating workers into IT from business operations can strongly align IT with the business. Rotation can also break the silos so often found in IT operations.

Organizational culture should support diversity and encourage global employment. Global leadership skills are critical to retaining IT talent. This includes having global knowledge. Global leadership embraces employee diversity. This includes engendering loyalty and trust. An IT workforce that is happy and engaged is a productive workforce. Offering a culture of flexibility and openness is important where people refer to it like home. One CTO (Chief Technology Officer) of a global firm told us that his IT organization engenders such a culture of openness through a flexible ecosystem that includes direct lines of communication with management using social media and IM and providing flexibility of location. "Many employees feel that the workplace is just like home" stated the CTO.

Encourage team and community building. Encourage informal and formal social activities to develop a sense of community. Communicate and listen to employees on a regular basis. Employees want their supervisors to be the ultimate communicators, people who will provide open and honest information on the organization's mission, policies and practices (Jamrog, 2004). For example, we interviewed a CTO of a globally dispersed IT organization who told us how he encourages freedom of communication with an informal, flat, organizational structure. This structure supports communication at various levels and employees are not limited to hierarchical communication. IM is used to support such communication where employees have direct access to the CTO's phone number. Although employees can communicate to any level the tension between levels does not go away and remains a challenge.

Provide various lifestyle accommodations, particularly, flexibility and work-life balance. Most IT employees these days want a strong balance between managing work, life and family. Many want to pursue interests outside of their work and spend time with their family (Jamrog, 2004). Companies can support this desire by offering technology that allows employees the flexibility to work anywhere anytime through remote access and telecommuting. Technology can provide employees the opportunity to be connected from anywhere at any time. However, this can also present a challenge because it can blur the separation between work and family. In our example firm, this flexible work ecosystem is provided and supported using technologies that included various collaboration tools (SharePoint, WebEx), and a number of communication tools such as IM, email, Facebook cell phone, Twitter and Skype. These are accessible to employees both at work and at home.

Offer a variety of career development/ enhancement activities. Provide opportunities for employees to learn and grow, reward performance, and offer various career opportunities. Star performers are critical for the IT industry and therefore it is important to reward them proportionately. Some companies perform mid-year and end-of-year talent reviews to identify key people for succession planning. This may include setting objectives for employees. Another way to reward performance is to provide rewards. In our example company, the CTO reported that they offer employees various toys and gadgets, which are perceived as status symbols by employees. For example, new technologies such as iPhones and iPads are given to employees as an incentive for delivering on projects. In addition, social networking tools such as Facebook and Twitter are part of the enterprise and are available for all to use. They also offer aggressive training such as online or on-site training and attendance of relevant hardware and software vendor conferences.

FUTURE RESEARCH

Further research is still needed to examine the influence of demographic variables mediated by perceived job (work) characteristics on job satisfaction, organizational commitment, and turnover intentions of IT professionals. Specifically, future research could explore the following issues:

- The relationship of job characteristics with career satisfaction, role stressors, and career performance.
- The differences in the relationships of demographic variables, career performance, career satisfaction, job characteristics, organizational commitment, and turnover intentions between IT and non-IT professionals.

An employee's stated intention of leaving ("turnover intentions") an organization has been identified by many researchers as a much stronger predictor of actual turnover behavior than other affective variables such as job satisfaction and organizational commitment (Vandenberg et al., 1994; Kopelman et al., 1992; Mobley et al. 1978). However, research also shows that the strength of the relationship widely varies across studies (see for example Steel et al., 1990; Lee & Mowday, 1987). Despite this variation in results, researchers continue to use intent to quit an organization as a reasonable surrogate for actual turnover behavior.

On the above basis, researchers have explored the antecedents of IT turnover intentions and produced evidence to show that demographic variables (age, organizational tenure, gender, education), role stressors (role ambiguity, role conflict), career satisfaction, and some career-related variables (salary, perceived promotability, extra organizational career opportunities) have a relationship with job satisfaction and impact turnover intentions directly and through organizational commitment (see e.g., Igbaria & Greenhaus, 1992; Igbaria & Siegel, 1992). There is some evidence in the organizational behavior, psychology and IS literature to indicate that other variables such as intrinsic job characteristics (e.g., skill variety, task identity, task significance, job autonomy, supportive supervisor and feedback or communication quality), personality (e.g., self esteem, locus of control, generalized self-efficacy) and quality of work life (e.g., burnout, social interaction, and work schedule) can also impact organizational commitment, job satisfaction and potentially mediate the influence of demographic variables on an individual's intent to leave their current organization (see for example: Igbaria & Parasuraman, 1994; Igbaria & Guimaraes, 1993; Agho, et al., 1993; Igbaria & Siegel, 1992). However, there has been little further research in the IS/IT field to enhance and evaluate the various antecedents of job satisfaction and turnover intentions developed in the early 1990s.

CONCLUSION

The growing need for IT professionals combined with a shrinking labor pool has made recruitment and retention of IT talent a top priority in many organizations. Forward thinking companies are looking to find and retain qualified IT talent wherever in the world it is available at a reasonable price. The best practices and lessons learned reported in this chapter are derived from various findings reported in the literature and interviews with two senior IT executives of globally oriented firms. They can form the basis for practitioners to develop their own thinking in their particular context.

REFERENCES

Adler, N. J. (1997). Global leadership: Women leaders. *Management International Review*, *37*(1), 135–143.

Adler, N.J., Brody, L.W. & Osland, J.S. (2001). *Going beyond twentieth century leadership: A CEO develops his company's global competitiveness.*

Agarwal, R., Brown, C., Ferratt, T., & Moore, J. (2006). Five mindsets for retaining IT staff. *MIS Quarterly Executive*, *5*(3), 137–150.

Agarwal, R., & Ferratt, T. (2002). Enduring practices for managing IT professionals. *Communications of the ACM*, *45*(9), 73–79. doi:10.1145/567498.567502

Agho, A. O., Mueller, C. W., & Price, J. L. (1993). Determinants for employee job satisfaction: An empirical test of a causal model. *Human Relations*, *46*(8), 1007–1018. doi:10.1177/001872679304600806

Bartlett, C. A., & Ghoshal, S. (1989). *Managing across borders: The transnational solution.* Boston: Harvard Business School Press.

Bartol, K. M. (1983). Turnover among DP personnel: A causal analysis. *Communications of the ACM*, *26*(10), 807–811. doi:10.1145/358413.358433

Bartol, K. M., & Martin, D. C. (1983). Managing Information Systems personnel: A review of the literature and managerial implications. *Management Information Systems Quarterly*, 49–70.

Bates, S. (2004). Getting engaged. *HRMagazine*, *49*(2).

Bernthal, P. R., & Wellins, R. S. (2001). Retaining talent: A benchmarking study. *HR Benchmark Group*, *2*(3), 1–28.

Bhasin, B. B., & Cheng, P. (2001). The fight for global talent: New directions, new competitors–a case study on Singapore. *Career Development International*, *7*(2), 109–114. doi:10.1108/13620430210421632

Bose, A. (2006). *India as a job hub holds its charm for foreign professionals and Indians alike.* Retrieved February 2010, from http://www.assureconsulting.com/articles/rmig.shtml

Buckingham, M., & Coffman, C. (1999). *First break all the rules.* New York: Simon and Schuster.

Campion, M. A., Cheraskin, L., & Stevens, M. J. (1994). Career related antecedents and outcomes of job rotation. *Academy of Management Journal*, *37*(6), 1518–1542. doi:10.2307/256797

Cappelli, P. (2001). Why is it so hard to find information technology workers? *Organizational Dynamics*, *30*(2), 87–99. doi:10.1016/S0090-2616(01)00045-6

Dorfman, P. W. (1996). International and cross-cultural leadership. In Punnett, B. J., & Shenkar, O. (Eds.), *Handbook for international management research* (pp. 267–349). Cambridge, MA: Blackwell.

Frank, F., & Taylor, C. (2004). Talent management: Trends that will shape the future. *Human Resource Planning*, *27*(1), 33–41.

Frank, F. D., Finnegan, R. P., & Taylor, C. R. (2004). The race for talent: Retaining and engaging workers in the 21st century. *Human Resource Planning*, *27*, 12–25.

Gelston, S. (2008). Gen Y, gen X, and the baby boomers: Workplace generation wars. *CIO Magazine*. Retrieved February 2010, from http://www.cio.com/article/178050/Gen_Y_Gen_X_and_the_Baby_Boomers_Workplace_Generation_Wars

Gilburg, D. (2007). Management techniques for bringing out the best in generation Y. *CIO Magazine*. Retrieved February 2010, from http://www.cio.com/article/149053/Management_Techniques_for_Bringing_Out_the_Best_in_Generation_Y

Gopal, A. (2004). *Flawed assumptions can defeat your business*. Gallup Management Journal.

Grensing-Pophal, L. (2001, July). Engaging employees–from A-Z. *HR Magazine*.

Hackman, J. R., & Oldham, G. R. (1975). Development of the job diagnostic survey. *The Journal of Applied Psychology, 60*, 159–170. doi:10.1037/h0076546

Hackman, J. R., & Oldham, G. R. (1976). Motivation through the design of work: Test of a theory. *Organizational Behavior and Human Performance, 16*(2), 250–279. doi:10.1016/0030-5073(76)90016-7

Hackman, J. R., & Oldham, G. R. (1980). *Work redesign*. Reading, MA: Addison Wesley.

Igbaria, M., & Greenhaus, J. H. (1992). Determinants of MIS employees' turnover intentions: A structural equation model. *Communications of the ACM, 35*(2), 35–49. doi:10.1145/129630.129631

Igbaria, M., & Parasuraman, S. (1994). Work experiences, job involvement, and quality of work life among Information Systems personnel. *Information Resources Management, 18*(2), 175–201.

Igbaria, M., & Siegel, S. R. (1992). The reasons for turnover of information systems personnel. *Information & Management, 23*, 321–330. doi:10.1016/0378-7206(92)90014-7

Jacobs, D. (2005). In search of future leaders: Managing the global talent pipeline. *Ivey Business Journal*, 1-5.

Jamrog, J. (2004). The perfect storm: The future of retention and engagement. *Human Resource Planning, 27*, 26–33.

Khanna, T., & Palepu, K. G. (2004). Globalization and convergence in corporate governance: Evidence from Infosys and the Indian software industry. *Journal of International Business Studies, 35*, 484–507. doi:10.1057/palgrave.jibs.8400103

Kopelman, R. E., Rovenpor, J. L., & Millsap, R. (1992). Rationale and construct validity evidence for the job search behavior index: Because intentions (and New Year's resolutions) often come to naught. *Journal of Vocational Behavior, 40*, 269–287. doi:10.1016/0001-8791(92)90051-Z

Laumer, S. (2009). Non-monetary solutions for retaining the IT workforce. *Americas Conference on Information Systems (AMCIS 2009 Proceedings)*, Association for Information Systems, 2009.

Lee, T. W., & Mowday, R. T. (1987). Voluntarily leaving an organization: An empirical investigation of Steers and Mowday's model of turnover. *Academy of Management, 30*, 721–743. doi:10.2307/256157

Leonard, L., & Dwight, S. (2004). Should I stay or should I go? Individual differences between stayers and leavers. In S. Tross & D. Wiechmann (Eds.), *Creative approaches for examining employee retention*. Practitioner Forum, Society for Industrial and Organizational Psychology Annual Conference, April.

Lewin, A. Y., Massini, A., & Peeters, C. (2009). Why are companies offshoring innovation? The emerging global race for talent. *Journal of International Business Studies, 40*(6), 901–925. doi:10.1057/jibs.2008.92

Luftman, J. (2005). Key issues for IT executives 2004. *MIS Quarterly Executive, 4*(2), 269–285.

Luftman, J. (2006). *Proceedings of SIMposium 2006*, Dallas, TX. September 17-20, 2006.

Luftman, J., & Kempaiah, R. (2007). The IS organization of the future: The IT talent challenge. *Information Systems Management, 24*, 129–138. doi:10.1080/10580530701221023

Luftman, J., Kempaiah, R., & Henrique, E. (2009). Key issues for IT executives 2008. *MIS Quarterly Executive, 8*(3), 151–159.

Luftman, J., Kempaiah, R., & Nash, E. (2006). Key issues for IT executives 2005. *MIS Quarterly Executive, 5*(2), 81–99.

Marchese, M. C. (1998). Some factors affecting the relationship between job characteristics and job worth: A job-role interpretation. *The International Journal of Organizational Analysis, 6*(4), 355–369. doi:10.1108/eb028891

McGillicuddy, S. (2007). IT job rotation rare, but critical for business alignment. *Techtarget*. Retrieved June 2010, from http://searchcio-midmarket.techtarget.com/news/article/0,289142,sid183_gci1244573_mem1,00.html

McLean E. & Luftman, J. (2004). Key issues for IT executives. *MIS Quarterly Executive, 3*(2).

Mobley, W. H., Horner, S. O., & Hollingsworth, A. T. (1978). An evaluation of the precursors of hospital employee turnover. *The Journal of Applied Psychology, 63*, 408–414. doi:10.1037/0021-9010.63.4.408

Moore, J., & Burke, L. (2002). How to turn around turnover culture in IT. *Communications of the ACM, 45*(2), 73–78. doi:10.1145/503124.503126

Morgan, H. J. (2008). I hired you, you're perfect…now stay! The top ten list for retaining top talent. *Business Strategy Series, 9*(3), 119–125. doi:10.1108/17515630810873348

Mottaz, C. J. (1988). Determinants of organizational commitment. *Human Relations, 41*(6), 467–482. doi:10.1177/001872678804100604

O'Neal, S. & Gebauer, J. (2006). Talent management in the 21st century: Attracting, retaining, and engaging employees of choice. *WorldatWork Journal,* First Quarter 2006.

Parker, S. K., Axtell, C. M., & Turner, N. (2001). Designing a safer workplace: Importance of job autonomy, communication quality, and supportive supervisors. *Journal of Occupational Health Psychology, 6*(3), 211–228. doi:10.1037/1076-8998.6.3.211

Porter, L. W., Crampon, W. J., & Smith, E. J. (1976). Organizational commitment and managerial turnover: A longitudinal study. *Organizational Behavior and Human Performance, 19*, 87–98. doi:10.1016/0030-5073(76)90030-1

Ready, D. (2009). Forging the new talent compact. *Business Strategy Review,* 5-7.

Reff, D. (2007). Seven strategies for attracting and retaining top IT talent. *CIO Magazine,* Retrieved February 2010, from http://www.cio.com/article/27988/Seven_Strategies_for_Attracting_and_Retaining_Top_IT_Talent3

Roberts, K., Kossek, E., & Ozeki, C. (1998). Managing the global workforce: Challenges and strategies. *The Academy of Management Executive, 12*, 93–106.

Scorce, R. (2008). IT staff management techniques for improved recruiting and retention. *Journal of Business and Public Affairs, 2*(1).

Society for Human Resource Management. (2000). *Retention survey.*

Steel, R. P., Shane, G. S., & Griffith, R. W. (1990). Correcting turnover statistics for comparative analysis. *Academy of Management Journal, 33*, 179–187. doi:10.2307/256357

Taylor, C. (2004). *Retention leadership. T+D Magazine, 58(3)*. Alexandria, VA: ASTD Press.

Tross, S., & Egermann, M. (2004). *Employee-manager relationship duration: Effects on perceived supervisor career development support and voluntary turnover.* Society for Industrial and Organization Psychology Annual Conference, April.

Tulgan, B. (2003). *Generational shift: What we saw at the workplace revolution.*

USBL. (2005). *Career guide to industries* 2004-05. US Bureau of Labor. Retrieved from http://www.bls.gov

Vandenberg, R. J., & Nelson, J. B. (1999). Disaggregating the motives underlying turnover intentions: When do interventions predict turnover behavior? *Human Relations, 52*(10), 1313–1336. doi:10.1177/001872679905201005

Wall Street Journal Online. (2002, November 27). *Truth be told: Survey says Americans are less trusting.*

Welbourne, T. (2003). Employee engagement: Doing it vs. measuring.

West, L., & Bogumil, W. (2001). Immigration and the global IT work force. *Communications of the ACM, 44*(7), 34–38. doi:10.1145/379300.379307

Wong, C.-S., Chun, H., & Law, K. S. (1998). A longitudinal study of the job perception-job satisfaction relationship: A test of the three alternative specifications. *Journal of Occupational Psychology, 71*(2), 127–146.

Chapter 13
Attracting and Retaining ICT Professionals in Brazilian Companies:
Expectancies, Learning, and Gender in the Workplace

Cesar Akira Yokomizo
Fundação Getulio Vargas-EAESP, Brazil & University of São Paulo (USP), Brazil

Lina Eiko Nakata
University of São Paulo (USP), Brazil

ABSTRACT

Although attracting and retaining the best professionals is of utmost importance for Human Resource Management and Information Technology Management in a company, this issue seems to be even more critical in the Information and Communication Technology (ICT) industry because the number of qualified workers is chronically not meeting the needs of this ever growing market.

As a result, it is necessary to deepen the understanding of the expectancies that drive professionals working in ICT companies. Therefore, this chapter focuses on identifying the differences and similarities on expectancies of professionals in ICT (ICTs) and in non-ICT (non-ICTs) Brazilian companies. To attain this goal, a new conceptual model to assess expectancy was developed that is grounded in the literature review. This framework was used to statistically compare proportions of expectancy, learning and development, and gender for ICTs and non-ICTs. Brazil was selected as a target case for the study because it is a dynamic and growing ICT market, both from the domestic and foreign viewpoint. A survey of 550 domestic and multinational companies running business in Brazil was conducted, totaling 142,913 responses (from which 107,464 were valid).

DOI: 10.4018/978-1-60960-535-3.ch013

Results show that ICT professionals consider learning and development the most important expectancy in the workplace, followed by satisfaction and motivation. Women in ICT companies consider the learning and development expectancy much more important than their peers in non-ICT companies, and even more than men in both ICT and non-ICT companies. For HR and IT managers, this chapter provides some insights on what expectancy variables could be better explored and exploited to attract and retain IT professionals.

INTRODUCTION

No matter the industry, attracting and retaining top professionals is a major concern for Human Resources Management (HRM) and Information Technology (IT) Management. This is even truer for IT organizations, which contain perhaps the archetypal *knowledge workers* (Drucker, 1999; Castells, 1999).

Moreover, the IT profession is chronically suffering from a shortage of experienced workers; the number of qualified candidates currently in the marketplace and those being trained in Universities and Technical Schools are not meeting the needs of this huge and growing market. Whenever the demand increases—as was the case during the dot com boom and the Y2K bug—shortage of top IT professionals becomes evident. In this situation, how can IT organizations be capable of attracting and retaining the best talent?

Companies are currently adopting a number of policies and initiatives to attain this goal. However, are these policies and initiatives meeting employees' expectancies? Employees have expectancies regarding the workplace, and these expectancies can or cannot be in line with what the company provides.

Consequently, measuring up to these expectancies must be a desired target for both HRM and IT Management because the higher this fulfillment, the better a company can attract and retain talent. However, how can companies fulfill these expectancies if they do not know how to measure them?

This troublesome challenge is somewhat complicated because, in several occasions, individuals are inhibited from expressing themselves—HRM provides no means of communication, a direct boss has different values, the organizational culture is divergent from their opinions etc., and thus they find it difficult to communicate their expectancies to the organization.

On the one hand, even if some research has been conducted to define expectancy, in general, literature fails to propose an accepted definition. On the other hand, it is not surprising that IT professionals prioritize different expectancies than those not in the IT industry. As a result, it is of utmost importance to identify what these differences are and deepen the discussion on how to fulfill the gap between companies' initiatives and the expectancies of their employees.

In this context, this chapter aims at identifying the differences and similarities between expectancies of IT professionals in Brazilian ICT companies when compared to workers in companies in other industries. One specific expectancy, learning and development, will be further discussed because there is evidence that this is an important expectancy for knowledge workers (Nakata, 2009). Moreover, the gender issue will also be investigated deeper because literature showed that men and women may hold different expectancies (Bruschini, 2000, Scott, 1990).

Empirical research was conducted to comply with these goals because the better ICT companies understand their employees' motivations, the better management can act to fulfill these expectancies.

THEORETICAL BACKGROUND

Expectancy Theory

The expectancy theory focuses on the understanding of attitude and behavior determinants in the workplace (Mitchell, 1974). Although it was developed by Vroom in the 1960's, it was more recently been extended by Porter and Lawler (Bergamini, 1997). It can be considered a cognitive theory, drawn on the economic-rational view. People assume individuals make their decisions when, at a certain time, the alternative seems to be the best. McCormick and Ilgen (1980) affirm that individuals have their own habits and limited rationality. Consequently, the expectancy theory considers not only the cognition in the decision process, but also the way by which the individual processes these elements to decide. This theory claims that there is a relationship between effort and its execution (or work performance) (Borges & Alves Filho, 2001).

There are three main concepts in the theory of expectancies. They include: valence (V), instrumentality (I), and expectancy (E). According to Wagner & Hollenbeck (2000), the first concept, valence, is based on the proposition that, at any time, an individual prefers a certain outcome in detriment to other outcomes. A way to measure it considers the attraction the outcome causes on this individual and the satisfaction he or she aims at obtaining with the outcome. Valence, according to the same authors, can be negative, neutral, or positive: it is positive when an individual prefers attaining a goal, instead of not attaining it.

The second concept, instrumentality, is the result of an individual conviction upon the relation between executing a task and experiencing its outcome. It is also known as *performance-outcome* expectancy. An individual is more likely to do something only when the valence and the instrumentality are high (Wagner & Hollenbeck, 2000). Vroom (1964) proposed the terminology *force*, which meant that people's choices are subjectively rational, since they vary—in terms of direction and magnitude—as a function of valences and expectancies.

According to Wagner and Hollenbeck (2000), expectancies are convictions related to the relationship between exerting effort and achieving a real and good performance. Theoretically, valences and instrumentalities are insufficient to determine an action because someone cannot predict what an individual will do if his expectancies are not known. Vroom (1964, p. 17) states that "when an individual is to choose between alternatives that involve uncertain outcomes, it seems clear that his or her behavior is affected not only by his preferences among these outcomes but also by the degree to which he believes these outcomes to be likely to happen."

The expectancy theory can be applied to a set of different contexts. To attain the goals of this work, we adapted this theory to identify differences and similarities between expectancies of professionals in ICT and non-ICT companies.

Identity

Within the organizational environment, it is essential that people wholeheartedly agree with corporate values, mainly those related to challenges, winning culture, recognition, equity, leadership, career opportunity, training programs, learning environment, and warm ambience (Teixeira, 2002). This is called identity. Bauman (2005) advocates that the demand for identity refers to safety because individuals need to pertain to a group—thus they feel safer. The organizational environment prevents the meaning of an individual's life from being inconsistent: issues related to basic trust sustain ontological safety, so, personal hesitations can be attenuated in the everyday routine (Giddens, 2002). Moreover, high performing mid-aged individuals prioritize identity instead of extrinsic rewards because they seek to reaffirm their own identity (Kanfer & Ackerman, 2004).

Satisfaction and Motivation

Reichers and Scheider (1990) give great importance to the shared perception of how things work in the organizational environment. Are people really happy with what they do in their everyday activities? Satisfaction in the workplace—including interpersonal relationships, management policies and practices—is the main indicator of the majority of organizational climate tools. With the emergence of the human relations theories, motivation has become the core element of the ideal organization (Fischer, 1996).

Bergamini (1997) argues that motivational factors are different from those that lead to satisfaction. Different workers have different motivational factors. They do not only seek different satisfaction, but they can also contribute differently to the organization (Casado, 2002). This means that people in the workplace eagerly seek to meet their needs according to their personal motivations.

Learning and Development

A number of studies highlight the need and importance of creating a favorable learning environment in contemporary organizations (Garvin, 1993; Nonaka & Takeuchi, 1997; Senge, 2002). These organizations offer a morally rewarding environment, where individuals can develop their specialized knowledge as well as their skills (Arruda, Whitaker, & Ramos, 2001). Abbad and Borges-Andrade (2004) affirm that the human being is genuinely oriented toward learning. Eboli (2002) argues that training, development practices and corporate education initiatives must favor a self professional performance, which will generate conditions for creative knowledge development. Also, it happens not only inside a classroom, but everywhere work takes place. Finally, Nakata (2009) suggests the learning and development is the main reason why a person chooses a company as a great place to work.

Leadership

Leadership is a social process by which relationships of influence between people are established (Limongi-França & Arellano, 2002). A leader's performance depends on sharing the results with others (Levek & Malschitzky, 2006). Some authors advocate that the leader can determine the quality of an organization's environment. This is the case when he or she is the main reason to attract and retain a good professional in the company. Rogers (1961), for instance, suggests that the team is more responsible, more creative, more cooperative, and more capable of adapting to new issues when the leader creates a certain microclimate in the organization. According to Schein (1989), leaders embed the group with a sense of commitment because he or she is fair, motivated, and skilled to communicate. And this is the reason why some people would choose their boss as someone to be followed or imitated.

Assessing Learning and Development

Learning is an extremely important psychological process to the development of a human being (Abbad & Borges-Andrade, 2004). Should it not be true, organizations would witness societal efforts to invest in education, companies' initiatives toward training activities, or people aiming at self-development? This is a matter of future perspective!

Literature provides several different definitions of learning; however, in general, it refers to longstanding behavior changes of an individual and it is a result of his or her interaction within a certain context—not only as an outcome of a natural maturation process. It is related to the individual's absorption of new capabilities that will later be reflected in his behavior.

Nonaka and Takeuchi (1997), Drucker (1999) and Patriotta (2006) claim that recent theories on learning are neglecting transfer models, which separate knowledge from practice: they highlight that knowledge depends on the context. This chapter considers that IC workers (an archetype of the knowledge worker) are more dynamic and highly dependent on knowledge, and thus, on learning.

Organizations dependent on knowledge are learning organizations, thus they foster continuous learning. Nevertheless, Garvin (2002) affirms that it is still not possible to precisely define what a learning organization is; even if most academics agree that learning occurs with time and refers to knowledge acquisition and performance, there is still no consensus.

While describing organizational learning, Garvin (2002) provides some of these differences: organizational learning promotes change in the fabric of the organization, new ways of thinking, information processing, insights sharing, organizational routines, memory, failure detection and correction.

Prange (2000) affirms that organizational learning aims at identifying how things are put into practice and at finding the best way to face problems—through ideal methodology and adequate connection. As a consequence, organizational processes can be hidden and that is why they must be revealed for the company.

According to Elkjaer (2001), organizational learning can be understood as a process of situational learning, as a social practice. It can also be understood as a managerial tool deployed to structure organizations. Thus, learning is not based only on the individual, but on the social practice of organizations: it must be interpreted and it is based on personal experiences.

Garvin (2002) affirms that learning can only become effective when it is put into practice. The author claims that it is difficult to describe a learning organization, but it might be the one that is skilled to create, get, interpret, transfer, retain knowledge and deliberately change its behavior to reflect new knowledge and insights.

Similarly, Senge (2002) highlights this differentiated approach in the learning organizations.

According to the Senge, organizations do not merely learn when there is too much information, but when knowledge is a factor that solves problems in a systemic manner. Local solutions only transfer the problem to another department or dimension, and the company does not really get rid of it.

To sum up, organizational learning must favor the creative process of generating value for the company through knowledge. We will next detail some factors that could determine people's learning and development in the workplace.

Professional Growth

Abbad and Borges-Andrade (2004) state that people's potential is better put into practice when they are forced to employ their skills. Professional growth has to do with a more complete set of skills obtained through learning. Learning is based on a system of needs, beliefs, values, and behavior change. An individual makes a decision if he or she believes this decision is the best alternative. Making decision involves the development of a cognition map in which the future will be reached according to his or her personal behavior (Jackson, 1993).

Integration

Senge (2002) also suggests that it is necessary to visualize the entire system to understand more complex issues. Therefore, it is vital to know the work being done by others. Vygotsky (1987) advocates that individuals learn through social relationships. The group's knowledge is determined by the knowledge owned by the one with the highest level of knowledge—after they have interacted. Nonaka and Konno (1998) posit that company knowledge is inside its own shared space; where it is created.

Continuous Learning

Nonaka and Takeuchi (1997) affirm that the creation of knowledge in the organization is a self-growing process that accumulates knowledge generated by employees. This process consolidates this knowledge in the corporate level. Moreover, Garvin (2002) posits that the learning organization generates, acquires, interprets, transfers, and retains knowledge through people.

Outside Knowledge

Terra (2000) argues that the emergence of the knowledge society is no longer questionable. Knowledge, whether inside or outside the company, is vital for dealing with the structural changes of the economy: new technology-intensive industries are being formed and the socio-economic inequality related to education is being widened. Moreover, the *knowledge society* (Drucker, 1999) emphasizes knowledge as the most valuable asset of an organization.

Learning from Supervisor

According to Elkjaer (2001), learning can be used as a managerial tool. One of the most important competencies of a manager is their ability to learn quickly and effectively. This ability will help them to adapt from one situation to another and it will result in the development of the whole team.

Innovative People

Regarding knowledge experts, Drucker (1998) argues that, in the *knowledge society*, it is necessary to convert data into information, goals into actions, and responsibilities into recognition. Fayard (2006) affirms that whenever there is an adequate context, relational situations will energize people and will stimulate them to be more creative in positive and dynamic interactions.

Training opportunities

Meister (1998) and Eboli (2004) explore the corporate education issue in organizations that demand knowledge. People want to be trained and to be more competitive through these self-development initiatives. Martin and Tulgan (2006) explain that young people are those exerting more effort to evolve their education, thus, their own careers.

Gender as a factor that may differentiate perception in the workplace will be further investigated next.

Gender

According to American historian Joan Scott (1990), the concept of *gender* has overcome the terms *sex* and *sexual difference* and established a break in the biological determinism, a historical legacy of the social distinctions between men and women.

At the end of the 1970's and in the beginning of the 1980's, the worldwide economy witnessed a growing number of women in the marketplace, and thus, more and more scientific research about gender was conducted. In Brazil, the concept of gender was more strongly employed at the end of the 1980's. According to Machado (1992), to be more precise, it happened in 1987, when the term women studies shifted to the term gender studies. Since the beginning of the 1990's, the concept of gender was widespread both in academia and in the market, and it was understood in terms of three features: (1) its relational dimension, (2) as a social construction of perceived differences between women and men, and (3) as a fundamental field where power is determined. To comply with the goals of this study, only the first two features will be considered.

Scott (1990) criticizes the use of gender as a descriptive category because even if this term emphasizes that the relations between women and men are social, it holds no relationship on how these relations are built, how they work, and how they change as time passes by. According to Scott, gender means knowing how to respect sexual differences. Because this knowledge is the outcome of cultures and societies, it cannot be absolute; rather, it is always relative. Its uses and meanings emerge from political tensions and they are means by which power relations are built.

Scott's (1990) frame for defining gender as a relational and historical category enabled a new picture on sexual differences and it has also widened its conceptual theory. The author suggests that gender is an extremely useful analytical tool to debate the power and inequality relations between women and men.

Gender is an alternative to the concept of patriarchy, which is often criticized for its essentialism, universalism, and invariable trait (Welzer-Lang, 2004). Yet, it is necessary to locate the concepts of patriarchy in time and space: there are several sorts of patriarchy just as there are different ways that women have confronted masculine domination. Therefore, history and context cannot be taken for granted: they should be considered in every analysis (Sousa, Nakata, & Pádua, 2008).

So, gender relations are the outcome of legitimacy and space delimitations between men and women in society. These relations are made from power relations that involve a wide range of knowledge, and social practices and relations. Accordingly, "[…] we can consider gender a constitutive element of social relations and these relations are grounded in the perceived differences between men and women. This is also a way to provide meaning for power and domination relations, including the workplace." (Cappelle et al., 2007, p. 2).

Since the 1970's the number of women in the workplace is ever growing. Bruschini (2000, p. 14) points out that "when we analyze the Brazilian women workforce in recent years, the first fact that draws our attention is related to its intensity and steady growth." Studies focusing on other economies (see Blum, Field, & Goodman, 1994), conclude that the wider participation of women

in the workplace has its foundations in education and qualifications—because women study more than men do, they are more qualified.

Literature on this subject also points to behavior features that favor women's access to organizational careers. Peters (2004) advocates that women have innate characteristics that let them play a leadership role more effectively than men. They include: (1) connecting employees, instead of ranking them; (2) allowing and favoring interactive and helpful leadership styles; (3) sustaining fruitful cooperation; (4) sharing information; (5) understanding power redistribution not as a defeat, but as a victory; (6) accepting ambiguity with readiness; (7) honoring both intuition and rationality; (8) being flexible; and (9) promoting cultural diversity. Eventually, some of these features match those of the *knowledge workers*.

Homan et al. (2008) demonstrate that men and women perceive work performance differently. As a result, it is quite reasonable to assume that expectancies and ambition in the workplace are different for men and women, and the same can be assumed for learning and development. That is why this study needed to include both learning and gender concepts.

CONCEPTUAL MODEL

In meeting the goals of the research discussed in the Background section of this chapter, identifying the differences and similarities on expectancies of professionals in Brazilian ICT companies when compared to professionals in companies from other industries, the research presented in this chapter considers theories on expectancies, learning and development, and gender.

According to the literature review on expectancy, four categories for assessing expectancy were depicted: (1) identity, (2) satisfaction and motivation, (3) learning and development, and (4) leadership. Each category was set drawn on certain supporting theories and each category led to an affirmative sentence that was used in the resulting questionnaire. The relationship between the created categories, supporting theories, and resulting affirmative sentence is presented in Appendix 1.

Moreover, seven categories to assess the learning and development category were depicted: (1) professional growth, (2) integration, (3) continuous learning, (4) outside knowledge, (5) learning from supervisors, (6) innovative people, and (7) training opportunities. The relationship between the created categories, supporting theories, and resulting affirmative sentence is presented in Appendix 2.

METHODOLOGICAL PROCEDURES

The Brazilian marketplace was selected as the target of the research, because, according to Abes (2009), the Brazilian Association for Software Companies, the IT industry has a total market of USD 29.3 billion, and represents approximately 2% of the world market and 48% of the Latin American (LA) market. Sales of personal computers (PCs) totaled 11.8 million units in 2008, and the country has 44 million Internet users.

Regarding the trends in the IT market, Abes (2009) estimates that Brazil and other LA countries will grow faster than the world average, although there might be a downward trend in future forecasts; the crisis will affect Small and Medium Businesses more adversely than it will in larger companies, but they will keep growing; mergers and acquisitions will keep their pace.

Should this encouraging trend prove true, will the attraction and retention of top professionals in ICT companies be a key factor for these companies' success?

An empirical survey was conducted in April-May 2008 with 142,913 respondents from 550 companies in the Brazilian marketplace. 107,464 responses were valid. Companies within the hardware, software or telecommunications industries are considered ICT companies. Companies in other industries are considered non-ICT companies.

The questionnaire was based on the conceptual model. It was delivered online (using the authors Institution's private platform) and respondents agreed to participate voluntarily, since only aggregate responses would go public.

For expectancy, the questions and options—the respondent could select only one expectancy category—are shown in Appendix 3. For the learning and development category, the questions and options—the respondent could select more than one learning and development category—are also shown in Appendix 3. For gender, only two options were given: male and female.

To compare responses from professionals in ICT companies (ICTs) and those in other industries (non-ICTs), the statistical proportion comparison technique was used. This technique is adequate to determine whether a percentage is higher, equal or lower in one group, even if the number of answers is different between groups. A confidence of 95% was fixed, and thus, considered an error no larger than 5%.

RESULTS AND ANALYSIS

According to the conceptual framework and methodological procedures previously presented, responses to the questionnaire were gathered, and therefore, it was possible to compare expectancy, learning and development, and gender for professionals in ICT and in non-ICT companies. Results will be shown and analyzed next.

Expectancy

Focusing on the expectancy differences of professionals in ICT companies and those in other industries, this research conducted the proportions comparison test for the expectancy categories framework: identity, satisfaction and motivation, learning and development, and leadership. Results

Table 1. Expectancy for professionals in ICT and in non-ICT companies

Expectancy	ICT	non-ICT	Total
Respondents	**9,698**	**97,766**	**107,464**
Identity	18.41%	**24.74%**	24.17%
Satisfaction and motivation	**35.53%**	25.47%	26.38%
Learning and development	39.36%	**40.67%**	40.55%
Leadership	3.86%	**5.53%**	5.38%
None	2.85%	3.60%	3.53%
Total	**100%**	**100%**	**100%**

are presented in Table 1 and the main findings are depicted and analyzed.

Horizontal Analysis

- **Identity**: ICTs show a significantly lower average than non-ICTs for the identity category (18.41% against 24.74%). This difference is an interesting finding of the research and will be further described below.
- **Satisfaction and motivation**: ICTs have a significantly higher average than non-ICTs for the satisfaction and motivation category (35.53% against 25.47%). This difference may reflect a distinguished behavior between ICTs and non-ICTs and that is why it will also be further detailed below.
- **Learning and development**: ICTs show just a slightly lower average than non-ICTs for the learning and development category (39.36% against 40.67%) and, in the practice, there is not much relevance in deepening the study based on such a small difference.
- **Leadership**: ICTs and non-ICTs consider leadership an immaterial expectancy.

Vertical Analysis

Both ICTs and non-ICTs (39.36% and 40.67%) emphasize the learning and development category as being the main reason to consider a company a

great place to work. In ICT companies, the satisfaction and motivation category and the learning and development category together account for approximately 75% of people who agree that these are the two main reasons why a company is recognized as a great place to work. Thus, initiatives that stimulate both categories should be put into practice. Only a few consider leadership the main reason why a company is a great place to work.

Main Findings

The first main finding refers to the significantly lower average of the identity category (18.41% against 24.74%) for ICTs compared to non-ICTs. Corporate objectives, values, and culture are not that important for the *knowledge worker;* perhaps the activities they execute are more important than objectives, value, and culture or, in the case that these are relevant, other categories just appeared to be more attractive as the main reason to consider the company as a great place to work. High levels of turnover in this industry may indicate a relatively weaker liaison between ICT professionals and the organization; as a result, one can depict that these professionals are less loyal to the organization and more activity-driven than organization-driven. This is the case of professionals who leave the company just because they were offered better wages from a competitor. In a specific study on ICT professionals, Gutiérrez-Martinéz (2006) claims that the turnover levels

Table 2. Learning and development for professionals in ICT and in non-ICT companies

Questions	ICT	non-ICT	Total
Respondents	**9,698**	**97,766**	**107,464**
Professional growth	71.35%	**79.06%**	78.36%
Integration	63.43%	**69.10%**	68.59%
Continuous learning	82.06%	**83.18%**	83.08%
Outside knowledge	71.50%	**73.20%**	73.05%
Learning from supervisor	66.66%	**71.06%**	70.66%
Innovative people	70.91%	71.48%	71.43%
Training opportunities	70.97%	**78.32%**	77.66%
Average	**71%**	**75%**	**75%**

reach 25-35%, which is high and supports our finding: ICT professionals show lower identity with the company than non-ICT professionals.

The second important conclusion is the fact that the learning and development category is the most valuable category for professionals in ICT companies—and also for those in non-ICT companies. Accordingly, Nakata (2009) posits that the learning and development category is the main reason why a professional considers a company as a great place to work. Moreover, this can be a result of a highly dynamic and competitive industry that compels professionals to be also more dynamic and competitive, and one concrete way to achieve this is through learning and development. ICT professionals hold this particular profile—continuous learning and development—; as a result, they do not like routine-activities and prefer to be constantly challenged in the workplace. They always welcome new and more difficult challenges, such as discovering how to use a new software feature or posting better answers for technical problems in specialized forums. Specifically for ICT professionals, Stam and Molleman (1999) highlight our finding: one of the main priorities of ICT professionals refers to training and growth.

Third, and maybe the most interesting finding, professionals in ICT companies show a significantly higher average than their peers in non-ICT companies (35.53% against 25.47%) for

the satisfaction and motivation category. Although a conclusive/definitive statement cannot be made based on the research, a guess about this difference would consider professionals in ICT companies and their ever demanding environments: because there is a shortage of good professionals and because it is not easy and fast to train a *knowledge worker*, top professionals are offered better working conditions, better salaries, and better relationships in their day-to-day activities. They may also appreciate untraditional workplaces and flexibility regarding working hours and work clothing. Satisfaction cannot be *separated* from work. This is the reason they have better performance when the working environment meets their needs. It may include sophisticated technological devices, an adequate social fabric, and above-average wages. This is particularly true for ICT professionals, and it was confirmed by Mastracci (2009)'s research. The author also emphasized that ICT professionals are already among those with the highest wages.

Learning and Development

As previously depicted, and confirming to the research assumptions, the learning and development category is the most valuable expectancy category for professionals both in ICT and in non-ICT companies.

According to the conceptual framework, the learning and development category was divided into seven categories: professional growth, integration, continuous learning, outside knowledge, learning from supervisor, innovative people, and training opportunities. Then, these seven categories were compared among professionals in ICT and in non-ICT companies, and the results are presented in Table 2.

Averages for professionals in ICT companies showed statistical differences from averages for professionals in non-ICT companies, except for the innovative people category for which there were no statistical difference.

Horizontal Analysis

ICTs show statistically lower averages than non-ICTs for all learning and development categories.

- **Professional growth**: many excellent technical workers become mediocre managers, mainly because being a manager requires skills different from those of a technical worker. The ideal career for ICTs seems to be different from non-ICTs: becoming a manager is not always what ICTs seek and this may explain why ICTs show lower averages for the professional growth category than non-ICTs. Another way to analyze this difference is considering that becoming a manager in ICT companies can be more difficult because it requires a more complex managerial profile. Professionals with technical profiles appreciate being recognized by their good work and not necessarily by the position they hold in the organization. This is the main reason the Y-career seems to be a must in ICT companies. This point is highlighted by Stam & Molleman (1999) for ICT professionals: the changing demands concern, amongst others, the ability to deal with information technology, business processes and

business strategy issues in an integral way. Accordingly, Enns (2005) adds that ICT professionals have been encouraged to develop basic business competencies and skills so they can relate more effectively with internal business clients.

- **Integration**: ICTs may have more specialized activities than non-ICTs; thus, it is less likely that they need to know their co-workers' activities. Although companies are facing difficulties to interconnect people, systems, and departments, several ICT activities can still be performed individually. While moving toward this more interconnected environment, companies should stimulate more team works, coffee-breaks and lunches with all the staff or team so that experiences could be exchanged. Group working and integration can provide very enriching opportunities to learn and to provide a more holistic view of the company; as a result, fewer conflicts regarding corporate goals should emerge. Enns (2005) posits that ICT professionals are often viewed as being "techno centric" and not interested or able to relate to their counterparts in other areas of the firm. Additionally, Stam and Molleman (1999) advocate that employees should learn from each other and this is a reason to promote integration.

- **Continuous learning and outside knowledge**: surprisingly, ICTs showed lower satisfaction averages than non-ICTs. A reason that may explain this difference is related to the self-learning skill of the vast majority of *knowledge workers*. Although they understand it is important to keep learning, they are not dependent on the company's initiatives to do so. Even when they do not take part in a formal training program, inside or outside the company, they are continually learning from other resources, such as the internet and technical books. Internet has provided easy access to various sources of technical topics and ICT professionals can use this tool to learn new trends and eventually come up with a better solution for their day-to-day activities. Technical profile professionals are known to be very active in specialized forums regarding technical issues. An example of this is the development of open source software, such as the Linux operating system, the Apache webserver and the MySQL database. Both easy access and richness of up-to-date information can result in a weaker liaison between ICT professionals and the organization. Stam and Molleman (1999) point out that every company should seek to become a learning organization: this is the main reason for a company to stimulate workers—and mainly ICT professionals—to search for knowledge inside and outside the organization.

- **Learning from supervisor**: a good reason why ICTs assign less importance on learning from supervisors than non-ICTs may refer to the technical versus non-technical dilemma. Frequently, bosses are required to deepen their knowledge in business issues (or non-technical issues) and this sort of knowledge is less necessary for regular workers, whose knowledge is mainly technical, and may include, programming languages—such as C#,.NET, and Java—, development methodology—such as RUP and XP—, and device-specific hardware—such as interface with printers and bar code readers. Again, technical profile professionals tend to learn alone instead of counting on co-workers or bosses to do so. More critical is to realize that bosses are not required to have deep knowledge on technical issues; on the contrary, they are expected to have a more comprehensive understanding of corporate goals and to provide means by which employees can

reach them. For ICT professionals, Enns (2005, p. 160) posits that "hiring managers should focus on assessing technical as well as business knowledge when interviewing candidates for IT positions. Specifically, gathering evidence about their leadership and interpersonal communication skills would be telling. These business competencies may be just as valuable, if not more valuable, than the technical skills an IT professional brings to the organization."

- **Training opportunities**: ICTs are less satisfied with training opportunities in the company than non-ICTs. The most recognized technical trainings are based on providers' certifications—Cisco network certifications, Java programming certifications, and Microsoft software certifications, just to cite a few—, which are widely accepted. Certificates are not issued for a company; instead, they are issued to the individual. So, this may be the reason why individuals will make every effort to get a certificate, regardless of the company's initiatives. Another way to analyze this difference is considering that ICT companies are not offering these certifications courses in a way to meet employees' demands. It seems obvious that ICT organizations should pay more attention to career development and strategic training and it has direct impact for ICT professionals (Stam & Molleman, 1999).

Vertical Analysis

- As expected, ICTs show the highest satisfaction with the continuous learning category (82.06%) and it may be related to the fact that the market is dynamic and competitive. As a response, ICTs try to improve their competitiveness through learning, both internally and externally. For the reasons already depicted, ICTs show the

Table 3. Expectancy for women and men in ICT and in non-ICT companies

Expectancy and Gender	Women		Men		Total
	ICT	non-ICT	ICT	non-ICT	
Respondents	**3,527**	**32,763**	**6,171**	**65,003**	**107,464**
Identity	16.84%	**21.36%**	19.30%	**26.44%**	24.17%
Satisfaction and motivation	**33.20%**	26.78%	**36.87%**	24.81%	26.38%
Learning and development	42.56%	42.97%	37.53%	**39.51%**	40.55%
Leadership	4.79%	**5.74%**	3.32%	**5.42%**	5.38%
None	2.61%	3.15%	2.98%	3.82%	3.53%
Total	**100%**	**100%**	**100%**	**100%**	**100%**

lowest satisfaction with the learning from supervisors and integration categories (66.66% and 63.43% respectively).

Main Findings

- The main findings refer to the fact that ICTs showed lower averages for all learning and development categories—except for the innovative people category. Two speculative reasons may better explain this discrepancy: (1) ICTs are more exigent than non-ICTs regarding the learning and development categories or (2) ICTs tend to have higher expectancies about the company toward them. For the first case, because ICTs hold a somewhat different background—they are focused more on the hard sciences, instead of on the soft sciences—they may be more tolerant and resilient. For the second case, ICTs may perceive learning as the more concrete way to become a more complete—more valuable, and thus, more well-paid—professional; as a consequence, it is bad idea to wait and see what the company can provide to them.

Gender

Next, a comparison on expectancies that women and men have in ICT and non-ICT companies is shown. Results are presented in Table 3.

All trends depicted in the general expectancy research were maintained when we considered men and women separately. Consequently, some results are only emphasizing a certain trend; they are not creating new ones.

Category learning and development and category satisfaction and motivation continue to be the two most important expectancies men and women have about a top ICT company. Identity is still ranking third and leadership continues to be immaterial.

A first finding that can be depicted when considering gender is related to the satisfaction and motivation category: men in ICT companies hold a higher average (36.87% against 33.20%). What has drawn our attention is that in non-ICT companies the direction is the opposite: women show higher averages for this category than men (26.78% against 24.81%). As a consequence, one can conclude that satisfaction and motivation is very important for men in ICT companies, even if the reason may be pretty much the same from the previous results.

Nevertheless, the most interesting and important finding refers to the fact that women in ICT companies seem to perceive learning and development as more important than men in ICT companies (42.56% against 37.53%). This confirms the literature review since women appear as less privileged than men in terms of positions and wages, mainly in developing economies, which is the Brazilian case (Bruschini, 2000). Another

Table 4. Learning and development for women and men in ICT and in non-ICT companies

Learning and Gender	Women		Men		Total
	ICT	non-ICT	ICT	non-ICT	
Respondents	**3,527**	**32,763**	**6,171**	**65,003**	**107,464**
Professional growth	70.91%	**75.92%**	71.61%	**80.64%**	78.36%
Integration	65.15%	**68.11%**	62.44%	**69.60%**	68.59%
Continuous learning	81.17%	82.16%	82.56%	**83.70%**	83.08%
Outside knowledge	71.11%	**73.06%**	71.72%	**73.27%**	73.05%
Learning from supervisor	67.62%	**70.82%**	66.12%	**71.18%**	70.66%
Innovative people	70.26%	68.95%	71.29%	**72.76%**	71.43%
Training opportunities	72.27%	**78.05%**	70.23%	**78.45%**	77.66%
Average	**71%**	**74%**	**71%**	**76%**	**75%**

reason why women may prefer more learning and development than men is the fact that, normally, women seek more education than men (Bruschini, op.cit.). ICT organizations have been described as largely white, male dominated, anti-social, individualistic, and competitive, which is less favorable for women (Wentling & Thomas, 2009).

On the other hand, women earn significantly fewer undergraduate degrees in computer science and engineering than their representation in the U.S. population (ITAA, 2003). Moreover, only 14% of computer-science undergraduate degree recipients at major research universities were women, and only 1.1% of undergraduate women choose IT-related disciplines as compared to 3.3% of male undergraduates (NCES, 2006).

Regarding the seven learning and development categories, the same tendency for the general picture can be seen now: ICT women and ICT men have lower averages than their peers in non-ICT companies. Results are presented in Table 4.

Each learning and development category is analyzed next:

Professional growth. Men and women in ICT companies show similar averages for the professional growth category. Technical profiles are very similar for both men and women; that is why gender does not seem to be a factor that differentiates ICT professionals regarding professional growth. Women's participation in computer-related occupations is low overall, and it decreases as women climb the corporate ladder (Wentling & Thomas, 2009). Recent exceptions of this include Anne Mulcahy, former chairwoman and CEO at Xerox, Patricia Russo, former chairwoman and CEO at Alcatel-Lucent Technologies, Theresa Gattung, former CEO at Telecom New Zealand Group, Marie Ehrling, former CEO at TeliaSonera Sweden, and Carly Fiorina, former CEO at Hewlett Packard. However, men in non-ICT companies present higher averages than women. It happens because women may perceive that they are offered less opportunities to grow when compared to men and the problem seems to be worse in the ICT industry.

Integration. Compared to men, women in ICT companies have higher averages for the integration category while the opposite occurs in non-ICT companies, where men show higher averages for the integration category. Although there are no previous foundations in the literature, we assume that women in ICT companies are more skilled in interpersonal relationships than men and this is the reason why women show a higher integration average. This is confirmed by Wentling and Thomas (2009) for ICT women professionals: although ICT culture has been described as antisocial, individualistic, and competitive, it was the collaborative and teamwork oriented aspect of the workplace environment and working together on projects and building close relationships with colleagues were in their career development.

Continuous learning. Women in ICT and in non-ICT companies show statistically the same average for the continuous learning category. Men in ICT companies show a slight lower average than men in non-ICT companies. Wentling & Thomas (2009) conclude that the main reason for women being satisfied and liking their careers is constantly learning new things.

Outside knowledge. Both women and men in ICT companies show a slightly lower average than their peers in non-ICT companies, and again, it is not possible to argue that gender causes significant differences in the outside knowledge category.

Learning from supervisor. Both women and men in ICT companies show lower averages than their peers in non-ICT companies, and once more, it is not possible to argue that gender causes significant differences in the learning from supervisor category. Wentling and Thomas (2009) found that the IT culture plays a positive role in the career development of the women: the employee-oriented aspect of the workplace culture and environment provided them with mentoring and challenging work opportunities. In addition, Jepson & Perl (2002) discovered that the implementation of mentoring programs was important for young females and women in IT.

Innovative people. Women in ICT and in non-ICT companies show statistically the same average for the innovative people category. Men in ICT companies show a slight lower average than men in non-ICT companies. Again, it is not possible to argue that gender causes differences in the innovative people category. However, given that IT pervades education, health, entertainment, and other industries, it is essential that women participate in innovating and advancing the IT field (NCWIT, 2007). Additionally, women bring a different life experience and a different perspective to the innovation process and diversity in

innovation leads to the design of products and services that benefit a broader range of consumers as well as business organizations (Wentling & Thomas, 2009).

Training opportunities. Women in ICT companies show higher averages than men in ICT companies, and both show significantly lower averages than their peers in non-ICT companies. Although this difference between women and men in ICT companies is not exorbitant, we suggest that women in ICT companies chase training opportunities because they seek to learn more and overcome the less privileged situation they may face (Nakata, 2009). Moreover, Wentling and Thomas (2009) argue that the IT environment provides women with training and development programs.

To sum up, there is evidence that women in ICT companies seem to seek learning more strongly than men do. The most reasonable ground for this is the recurrent prejudice they suffer in the workplace (Bruschini, 2000) and their will—even their need—to overcome this issue. They may face an everyday battle to prove that they are not only capable of occupying a position or earning a certain wage, but also worthy of being as competitive as men.

LESSONS LEARNED AND IMPLICATIONS FOR MANAGEMENT

According to the research results, three implications for management can be derived.

First, managers should provide better conditions and opportunities for the learning and development category and also for the satisfaction and motivation category because almost 75% of professionals in ICT companies indicate these categories as the two main reasons why a company is considered a good place to work at. This percentage drops to approximately 66% for professionals in non-ICT companies. The learning and development category is, in general, a bit more important than the satisfaction and motivation category; thus, if managers are to focus on only one of these categories, they should focus on the learning and development category. Training, development, and corporate education initiatives should provide means by which knowledge is developed everywhere work takes place. Furthermore, organizations perceive that learning through social interactions in communities of practice is valuable (Wenger & Snyder, 2006).

Second, managers at ICT companies should address learning and development initiatives focused on women. Even if the learning and development category and the satisfaction and motivation category are important reasons why a company is considered a great to work at, they hold different meanings for men and women in ICT companies. Women give much more importance to learning and development than men do. This is the reason why managers should provide special attention to learning and development exclusively for women. Initiatives should include formal and informal processes that promote a learning workplace (Meister, 1998). It is important to highlight that women have their own social and interpersonal abilities and this is the reason they can learn more from relationships with others (Sousa, Nakata, & Araújo), through technology applied to learning (Lévy, 1993), and through communities of practice (Wenger & Snyder, 2006).

Third, managers at ICT companies should focus on four learning and developing initiatives—because they hold the largest average differences between ICTs and non-ICTs—: professional growth, integration, learning from supervisor, and training opportunities. Professional growth refers to one's career and it does not seem to be difficult for HRM or IT Management to provide career definitions and targets to be achieved, even if technical and non-technical careers are considered. Further understanding on this issue may include: more transparent criteria for career plans and the implementation of the Y-Career (technical and non-technical careers). Integration seems to be

the easiest to be implemented because it refers to presenting employees with a holistic view of the company and most HRM already conduct such initiatives—e. g.: corporate presentations, internalization programs, and integration events. On the contrary, learning from supervisor seems to be the toughest to be implemented because it refers to different types of knowledge: employees should master technical issues while supervisors should draw their attention to more business-oriented issues, and it is somewhat difficult—and even unnecessary—to detail non-technical issues to employees. Training opportunities may refer to technical and non-technical subjects and the most important challenge seems to be the definition of the extent to which the company should invest in general technologies rather than in specific ones. Online courses seem to be interesting solutions for this audience, who are already skilled to deal with IT.

Stam & Molleman (1999) has conducted a research in which conclusions drawn from IT companies had implications for IT professionals. This the reason we might extend our conclusions from ICT companies to ICT professionals and from non-ICT companies to non-ICT professionals.

As a result, some recommendations can be given to companies attracting and retaining ICT professionals: (1) introduce corporate education programs or university courses, (2) promote training policies and development programs, and (3) promote coaching and mentoring, mainly for women, to meet the motivational needs of these professionals. This would enable the company to reach higher levels of perceptions regarding learning and development.

Recommendations for ICT professionals in ICT or non-ICT companies include: (1) look for employers who offer conditions for learning, development and satisfaction, (2) negotiate agreements that provide continuous learning and training programs in the workplace, and (3) seek to other factors that may fulfill their expectancies at work.

Overall, this chapter shows that it is important that companies drive efforts in order to capture the expectancies of employees. Knowing these expectancies should result in actions that HRM and IT Management can promote.

FUTURE RESEARCH DIRECTIONS

This research deepens the understanding of expectancies in the workplace regarding the differences between professionals in Brazilian ICT companies and those in non-ICT companies and, by extension, between ICT and non-ICT professionals. Based on the literature review, a conceptual model that divided expectancy into four categories: identity, satisfaction and motivation, learning and development, and leadership was developed. Future research could provide another, or perhaps a better understanding on what expectancy is.

In the same way, the conceptual framework divided the learning and development category into seven categories: professional growth, integration, continuous learning, outside knowledge, learning from supervisor, innovative people, and training opportunities. Again, future research could provide a different and even a more complete definition of what the learning and development category is.

On the one hand, the research explored three concepts that could explain differences between ICT and non-ICT professionals. They include: expectancy, learning and development, and gender. Other concepts should be investigated to provide a deeper understanding of these differences. Examples of such concepts include: HRM model, organizational climate, human performance, financial results, and others.

Another potential pathway for this subject is to deepen the understanding of the explored variables: expectancy, learning and development, and gender. It is of utmost interest to see how these numbers—thus, tendencies—are evolving over time. Extrinsic factors, such as the financial crisis

in 2009, may cause a disruption of a tendency and expose ICT professionals to new realities.

Will they still continue to show the same expectancies in the workplace?

This research covers a quantitative aspect of the differences between ICTs and non-ICTs. Future studies could focus on a qualitative aspect, which may include in-depth interviews with professionals in both industries or with technical and non-technical professionals.

Finally, although the number of respondents was adequate for the purposes of the study, this research focused only on the Brazilian marketplace. Other research should be conducted in other contexts and different numbers could be gathered. Comparing these results with ours may provide valuable insights for country specific HRM and IT Management initiatives.

CONCLUSION

Attracting and retaining the best professionals is a tough challenge that HRM and IT Management face every day in the current knowledge era. This is especially more severe for ICT professionals because traditional HRM and IT initiatives can no longer fit what professionals in this industry require. To identify what could attract and retain ICT professionals in Brazilian companies, we proposed a framework to define expectancy and used this framework to assess occasional differences between ICT and non-ICT professionals.

This research has contributed to the study on expectancies of ICT professionals in two main ways. First, it developed a new conceptual model to define expectancy in the workplace. According to this framework, expectancy is a weighted average of four categories: identity, satisfaction and motivation, learning and development, and leadership. Therefore, it provides a richer discussion on how expectancy could be measured and, thus, assessed. The proposed framework also includes a definition of what learning and development is: a weighted average of seven categories: professional growth, integration, continuous learning, outside knowledge, learning from supervisor, innovative people, and training opportunities. Again, a richer discussion on how learning and development could be measured and assessed was provided.

Second, the results were based on a survey to statistically compare expectancies for both professionals in ICT and non-ICT companies. Results show that most professionals in ICT and non-ICT companies expect leading companies to provide learning and development opportunities. The dynamic and ever competitive ICT market compels professionals in this market to be likewise dynamic and competitive, and a substantial part of this competitiveness comes from learning and development.

The satisfaction and motivation category appears as the second main expectancy in the workplace, followed by identity and leadership. Comparing ICTs and non-ICTs, what draws our attention is the importance ICTs give to satisfaction and motivation; although this category ranks second for both ICTs and non-ICTs, it seems to be much more important for ICTs. Reasons for this may include the shortage of good professionals, due to the fact that it is not easy or fast to train a *knowledge worker*. Therefore, the best professionals are offered better working conditions, better salaries, and better relationships in their day-to-day activities, which may include untraditional workplaces and flexibility regarding working hours and work clothing.

As a result, managers should focus on initiatives that provide not only better learning and development conditions but also satisfaction and motivation conditions. Should managers choose one of them to prioritize, learning and development should be preferred.

Regarding gender, ICT women may give much more importance to learning and development than men. This is the reason why managers should address directed and focused learning and development initiatives for women in ICT companies.

This study has contributed in some ways to the discussion on how to attract and retain ICT professionals. Different expectancies demand different measures; different gender also demands different initiatives. Because we have captured some of these differences, we are delighted to have measured up to the goals of this study and to offer academia and the industry some valuable insights into how to promote better HRM and IT Management.

REFERENCES

Abbad, G. S., & Borges-Andrade, J. E. (2004). Aprendizagem humana em organizações de trabalho. In Zanelli, J. C., Borges-Andrade, J. E., & Bastos, A. V. B. (Eds.), *Psicologia, organizações e trabalho no Brasil*. Porto Alegre: Artmed.

ABES – Associação Brasileira das Empresas de Software. (2009). *Brazilian software market: Scenario and trends, 2009*. São Paulo, Brazil: Câmara Brasileira do Livro.

Arruda, M. C. C., Whitaker, M. C., & Ramos, J. M. R. (2001). *Fundamentos de Ética Empresarial e Econômica*. São Paulo: Atlas.

Bauman, Z. (2005). *Identidade: entrevista a Benedito Vecchi*. Rio de Janeiro: Jorge Zahar.

Bergamini, C. W. (1997). *Motivação nas organizações*. São Paulo, Brazil: Atlas.

Blum, T. C., Fields, D. L., & Goodman, J. S. (1994). Organization-level determinants of women in management. *Academy of Management Journal, 37*(2), 241–269. doi:10.2307/256829

Borges, L. O., & Alves Filho, A. (2001). A mensuração da motivação e do significado do trabalho. *Estudos de Psicologia, 6*(2), 177–194.

Bruschini, C. (2000). Gênero e trabalho no Brasil: Novas conquistas ou persistência da discriminação? In Rocha, M. I. B. (Ed.), *Trabalho e gênero—mudanças, permanências e desafios* (pp. 13–58).

Cappelle, M. C. A., et al. (2007). *A mulher gerente: Um estudo de caso numa companhia mineradora em Belo Horizonte/MG.* Retrieved on October 14, 2007, from http://www.fgvsp.br/iberoamerican/Papers/0429_ACF687.pdf

Casado, T. (2002). A motivação e o trabalho. In Fleury, M. T. F. (Ed.), *As pessoas na organização.* São Paulo: Gente.

Castells, M. (1999). *A sociedade em rede.* São Paulo: Paz e Terra.

Drucker, P. F. (1998). *The coming of the new organization. Harvard Business Review on Knowledge Management* (pp. 1–19). Harvard Business School Press.

Drucker, P. F. (1999). *Administrando em tempos de grandes mudanças.* São Paulo: Pioneira.

Eboli, M. (2002). O desenvolvimento das pessoas e a educação corporativa. In Fleury, M. T. L. (Ed.), *As pessoas na organização.* São Paulo: Gente.

Eboli, M. (2004). *Educação corporativa no Brasil: Mitos e verdades.* São Paulo: Gente.

Elkjaer, B. (2001). Em busca de uma teoria de aprendizagem organizacional. In Easterby-Smith, M., Burgoyne, J., & Araujo, L. (Eds.), *Aprendizagem organizacional e organização de aprendizagem: Desenvolvimento na teoria e na prática.* São Paulo: Atlas.

Enns, H. G. (2005). Do IT professionals need business acumen to build effective partnerships? *The Academy of Management Executive, 19*(2), 159–162.

Fayard, P. (2006). *Le réveil du samouraï: Culture et stratégie japonaise dans la société de la connaissance.* Paris: Dunod.

Fischer, A. L. (1996). *As decisões sobre o método dos diagnósticos organizacionais internos.* CLADEA.

Garvin, D. A. (1993). Building a learning organization. *Harvard Business Review, 71*(4), 78–91.

Garvin, D. A. (2002). *Aprendizagem em ação: um guia para transformar sua empresa em uma learning organization.* Rio de Janeiro: Qualitymark.

Giddens, A. (2002). *Modernidade e Identidade.* Rio de Janeiro: Jorge Zahar.

Gutiérrez-Martínez, I. (2006). L'implication organisationnelle des professionnels de TI. *Revue Française de Gestion, 32*(168/169), 143–156. doi:10.3166/rfg.168-169.143-156

Homan, A. C., Hollenbeck, J. R., Humphrey, S. E., Van Knippenberg, D., Ilgen, D. R., & Van Kleef, G. A. (2008). Facing differences with an open mind: Openness to experience, salience of intragroup differences, and performance of diverse work groups. *Academy of Management Journal, 51*(6), 1204–1222.

Information Technology Association of America (ITAA). (2003). *Report of the ITAA blue ribbon panel on IT diversity.* Arlington, VA.

Jackson, T. (1993). *Organizational behaviour in international management.* Oxford: Butterworth-Heinemann.

Kanfer, R., & Ackerman, P. L. (2004). Aging, adult development, and work motivation. *Academy of Management Review, 29*(3), 440–458. doi:10.2307/20159053

Levek, A. R. H. C., & Malschitzky, N. (2006). *Liderança.* Faculdade São Francisco. Retrieved on May 2, 2006, from http://www.sfrancisco.edu.br/pdf/cap_humano/3.pdf

Lévy, P. (1993) *As tecnologias da inteligência: o futuro do pensamento na era da informática.* Rio de Janeiro: 34.

Limongi-França, A. C., & Arellano, E. B. (2002). Liderança, poder e comportamento organizacional. In Fleury, M. T. F. (Ed.), *As pessoas na organização*. São Paulo: Gente.

Machado, L. Z. (1992). Feminismo, academia e interdisciplinaridade. In A.d.O. Costa & C. Bruschini (Eds.). *Uma questão de gênero.* (pp. 24-39). Rio de Janeiro: Rosa dos Tempos.

Martin, C., & Tulgan, B. (2006). *Managing the generation mix*. HRD Press.

Mastracci, S. H. (2009). Evaluating HR management strategies for recruiting and retaining IT professionals in the U.S. federal government. *Public Personnel Management, 38*(2), 19–34.

McCormick, E. J., & Ilgen, D. (1980). *Industrial and organizational psychology*. Englewood Cliffs, NJ: Prentice-Hall.

Meister, J. C. (1998). *Corporate universities: Lessons in building a world-class work force*. New York: McGraw-Hill.

Mitchell, T. R. (1974). Expectancy models of job satisfaction, occupational choice, and effort: A theoretical, methodological, and empirical appraisal. *Psychological Bulletin, 81*, 1053–1077. doi:10.1037/h0037495

Nakata, L. E. (2009). *As expectativas de aprendizagem nas organizações que buscam se destacar pelo clima organizacional*. Master Thesis, Faculdade de Economia, Administração e Contabilidade, Universidade de São Paulo, São Paulo.

National Center for Education Statistics. (2006). *Report 3, Sisyphus revisited: Participation by minorities in STEM occupations, 1994-2004*. Washington, DC: U.S. Department of Education.

National Center for Women & Information Technology. (2007). *NCWIT scorecard 2007: A report on the status of women in information technology*. Boulder, CO: University of Colorado.

Nonaka, I., & Konno, N. (1998). The concept of ba: Building a foundation for knowledge creation. *California Management Review, 40*(3), 40–54.

Nonaka, I., & Takeuchi, H. (1997). *Criação de conhecimento na empresa: Como as empresas japonesas geram a dinâmica da inovação*. Rio de Janeiro: Campus.

Patriotta, G. (2006). Knowledge-in-the-making: The construction of Fiat's Melfi factory. In Prusak, L., & Matson, E. (Eds.), *Knowledge management and organizational learning*. New York. Oxford.

Peters, T. (2004). *As Mulheres Reinam. HSM Management*. Mar-Apr.

Prange, C. (2000). Aprendizagem organizacional: desesperadamente em busca de teorias? In Easterby-Smith, M., Burgoyne, J., & Araujo, L. (Eds.), *Aprendizagem organizacional e organização de aprendizagem*. São Paulo: Atlas.

Probst, G., Raub, S., & Romhardt, K. (2002). *Gestão do conhecimento*. Porto Alegre: Bookman.

Reichers, A. E., & Schneider, B. (1990). Climate and culture: An evolution of constructs. In Schneider, B. (Ed.), *Organizational climate and culture*. San Francisco: Jossey-Bass.

Rogers, C. (1961). *On becoming a person*. Boston: Houghton Mifflin.

Schein, E. H. (1989). *Organizational culture and leadership: A dynamic view*. San Francisco: Jossey-Bass.

Scott, J. (1990). Gênero: uma categoria útil de análise histórica. *Educação e Realidade, 16*(2), 5–22.

Senge, P. M. (2002). *A quinta disciplina: Arte e prática da organização de aprendizagem*. São Paulo: Best Seller.

Sousa, E. G., Nakata, L. E., & Araujo, A. P. (2008). A emergência do modelo de competências no processo de reorganização da produção: Uma discussão sobre gênero. In *Anais do Enanpad*. Rio de Janeiro: Anpad.

Stam, M., & Molleman, E. (1999). Matching the demand for and supply of IT professionals: Towards a learning organization. *International Journal of Manpower, 20*(6), 375. doi:10.1108/01437729910289729

Teixeira, J. E. (2002). Clima organizacional: Empregados satisfeitos fazem bem aos negócios. In Boog, G., & Boog, M. (Eds.), *Manual de Gestão de pessoas e equipes* (*Vol. 2*). São Paulo: Gente.

Terra, J. C. C. (2000). *Gestão do conhecimento: o grande desafio empresarial*. São Paulo: Negócio.

Veloso, E. F. R., Nakata, L. E., Fischer, A. L., & Dutra, J. S. (2007). Pesquisas de clima organizacional: o uso de categorias na construção metodológica e análise de resultados. In *Anais do Enanpad*. Rio de Janeiro: Anpad.

Vroom, V. H. (1960). *Some personality determinants of the effects of participation. Survey Research Center and Department of Psychology, University of Michigan*. Englewood Cliffs, NJ: Prentice-Hall.

Vroom, V. H. (1964). *Work and motivation*. New York: Wiley.

Vygotsky, L. S. (1987). *A formação social da mente*. São Paulo: Martins Fontes.

Wagner, J. A. III, & Hollenbeck, J. R. (2000). *Comportamento organizacional*. São Paulo, Brazil: Saraiva.

Welzer-Lang, D. (2004). Os homens e o masculino numa perspectiva de relações sociais de sexo. In Schpun, M. R. (Ed.), *Masculinidades* (pp. 107–128). São Paulo: Boitempo Editorial Santa Cruz.

Wenger, E., & Snyder, W. M. (2006). Communities of practice: the organizational frontier. In Prusak, L., & Matson, E. (Eds.), *Knowledge management and organizational learning. New York*. Oxford.

Wentling, R. M., & Thomas, S. (2009). Workplace culture that hinders and assists the career development of women in Information Technology. *Information Technology, Learning and Performance Journal, 25*(1), 25–42.

KEY TERMS AND DEFINITIONS

Human Resources Management (HRM): Rhe way companies manage employees and drive their individual and collective behavior to achieve organizational goals.

Information and Communication Technology (ICT) Companies: Companies pertaining to the telecommunications or computer industries, including both hardware and software.

Expectancy: Conviction related to the relationship between exerting an effort and achieving a real and good performance.

Knowledge Workers: Professionals who use knowledge intensively in their activities.

APPENDIX A: CATEGORIES, CONCEPTS, AND AFFIRMATIVE SENTENCES TO COMPARE EXPECTANCIES AT WORK

Category	Concepts	Affirmative sentence: this category is related to...
Identity	Bauman (2005) advocates that the demand for identity refers to safety because individuals need to belong to a group to feel safe. Moreover, high performing mid-aged individuals prioritize identity related to values instead of extrinsic rewards because they seek to reaffirm their own identity (Kanfer & Ackerman, 2004).	... understanding and agreeing with the company's goals, what the company does for its clients, and what it offers to the society and to the community.
Satisfaction and motivation	Reichers and Scheider (1990) give great importance to the shared perception on how things work in the organizational environment. Are people really happy with what they do in their everyday activities? Different workers have different motivational factors. They do not only seek different satisfaction, but they can also contribute differently to the organization (Casado, 2002).	... being satisfied and motivated with what I do, what I earn, and my day-to-day work routine.
Learning and development	Abbad and Borges-Andrade (2004) affirm that the human being is genuinely oriented toward learning. Nakata (2009) suggests that learning and development is the main reason why a person labels a company as a great place to work. Moreover, the author concludes that offering learning conditions to employees is important for organizations.	... realizing that I am learning more and more at the company and that it provides me the opportunity to grow both as a professional and as a person.
Leadership	Leader's performance depends on sharing the results with others (Levek & Malschitzky, 2006). According to Schein (1989), leaders embed the group with a sense of commitment because he or she is fair, motivated, and skilled to communicate. And this is the reason why some people would choose their boss as someone to be followed or someone to be imitated.	... having bosses I respect, trust, and who provide their team with adequate guidance.

Source: drawn on Veloso et al. (2007).

APPENDIX B: CATEGORIES, CONCEPTS, AND AFFIRMATIVE SENTENCES TO COMPARE LEARNING AND DEVELOPMENT AT WORK

Category	Concepts	Affirmative sentence: this category is related to the fact that...
Professional growth	Abbad and Borges-Andrade (2004) state that people's potential is better put into practice when they are forced to employ their skills. Professional growth has to do with a more complete set of skills obtained through learning.	... I know exactly what I must do for my professional growth.
Integration	Senge (2002) suggests that it is absolutely necessary to visualize the entire system in order to understand more complex issues. Therefore, it is necessary to know the work being done by others.	... the company I work for stimulates me to know what my colleagues do.
Continuous learning	Nonaka and Takeuchi (1997) affirm that the creation of knowledge in the organization is a self-growing process that accumulates knowledge generated by employees and that consolidates them at the corporate level.	... my work allows me to get to know new things.
Outside knowledge	Terra (2000) argues that knowledge, whether inside or outside the company, is vital for dealing with the structural changes of the economy: new technology-intensive industries are being formed and the socio-economic inequality related to education is being widened.	... I feel stimulated to seek new knowledge outside the borders of this company.
Innovative people	Fayard (2006) affirms that whenever there is an adequate context, relational situations will energize people and will stimulate them to be more creative in positive and dynamic interactions.	... people who work in this company are always trying to innovate.
Learning from supervisor	According to Elkjaer (2001), learning can be used as a managerial tool. The younger a person is, the higher the level of effort applied to education and career (Martin & Tulgan, 2006).	... my boss helps me to decide what I should do to learn more.
Training opportunities	Meister (1998) and Eboli (2004) explore the corporate education issues in organizations that demand knowledge.	... everybody in this company has opportunities to take part in training programs.

Source: drawn on Nakata (2009).

APPENDIX C: QUESTIONNAIRE

Questions	Answers
What is the main reason that may distinguish a company that is a great place to work from others?	I understand and agree with the company's goals, what the company does for its clients, and what it offers to the society and to the community;
	I am satisfied and motivated with what I do, what I earn, and my day-to-day work routine;
	I realize that I am learning more and more at the company and that it gives me the opportunity to grow both as a professional and as a person;
	I have bosses I respect, trust, and who provide their team with adequate guidance;
	None.
In a great place to work...	... I know exactly what I must do for my professional growth;
	... the company I work for stimulates me to know what my colleagues do;
	... my work allows me to get to know new things;
	... I feel stimulated to seek new knowledge outside the borders of this company;
	... people who work in this company are always trying to innovate;
	... my boss helps me to decide what I should do to learn more;
	... everybody in this company has opportunities to take part in training programs.

Chapter 14

Present, Past and Future of IT Careers, a Review:
From the Local Pyramid to the "Flat World"

Adrián Hernández-López
Universidad Carlos III Madrid, Spain

Ricardo Colomo-Palacios
Universidad Carlos III Madrid, Spain

Ángel García-Crespo
Universidad Carlos III Madrid, Spain

Fernando Cabezas-Isla
Universidad Carlos III Madrid, Spain

ABSTRACT

Careers have experienced an evolution parallel to society's constant progress. Careers have migrated from hierarchical and unidirectional models within a single organization, to models that provide non-linear or vertical movement within the hierarchy, movement between organizations, changes in employer-employee relationships, etc. Furthermore, careers have transferred responsibility from organizations to individuals. Due to these changes, careers have been transmuted from the organizational pyramid to a globalized, boundaryless, and one-dimensional scheme. In addition, within the IT sector, external factors such as gender, organizational culture, differences in requirements between technical and nontechnical positions, among others, have also impacted career management. This chapter presents a review of the changes that have been undertaken in career management from a general point of view, to the peculiarities of the IT sector, and ultimately encompass some conclusions extracted from research.

INTRODUCTION

The lack of definitions for professional careers in the field of Information Technology (IT) has been highlighted (P. C. B. Lee, 2001). Several studies

recommend making workers responsible for planning their own professional careers (Chesebrough & Davis, 1983), however, significant initiatives such as People-CMM (Curtis, Hefley, & Miller, 2009) point out the importance of establishing

DOI: 10.4018/978-1-60960-535-3.ch014

a professional structure with careers defined, documented and driven by organizations.

In the traditional career system, a career was considered as an upward linear progression in one or two firms or as a stable employment within a profession (Levinson, 1978; Schein, 1978), that Kanter (1991) refers as the bureaucratic career. In the IT field, such career path describes an itinerary from junior programmer to CEO (Chesebrough & Davis, 1983). In this career path, an employee starts programming, works as a technical specialist such as a software or systems engineer, and eventually becomes promoted to senior technical consultant or specialist. Such path will enable programmers to achieve remarkable promotions, wage, and status in an organization while remaining in a technical, non-managerial role (Chesebrough & Davis, 1983). Thus, two broad categories appears: technical and managerial (Ives & Olson, 1981). As a response to this model, a dual ladder approach arises (Ginzberg & Baroudi, 1988). The Dual Career Ladder was created to provide another route for promoting employees exhibiting or possessing particular technical skills and/or education above and beyond the norm of a typical career. A third career ladder is the Protean coined by Hall and Mirvis (1996) and later adopted in IT field by Reich and Kaarst-Brown (1999).

Nevertheless, the present-day scenario is quite different. These traditional views do not reflect the multi-faceted career pattern present in contemporary society (Hall, 2004) transcending organizations boundaries due to globalization and technologies effects, among others. Moreover, current IT workers titles are considered less important; skills and experience are reckoned to be more relevant than titles in determining rank and salary (Evans, 2004). Alexander (1999) supports this viewpoint by arguing that definitions of IT job titles, such as programmer, programmer analyst, systems analyst and project manager, are "fuzzy", varying in a wide manner from one company to another. In this new and exciting scenario, this chapter must address the following

two main questions. Are there opportunities for traditional careers in nowadays IT? And, what are the insights for IT careers in the future? This chapter aims to explore IT career experiences and initiatives from the past and present and tries to depict the opportunities and challenges of IT careers in the future.

The remainder of the chapter is structured as follows: first, IT career concepts from a general viewpoint are introduced; second, IT career issues and solutions are explained; third, the future of IT careers is analyzed; fourth, career opportunities and challenges are assessed; and finally, discussion, conclusions and future works about this chapter are presented.

BACKGROUND

Professionals usually follow the next succession of life stages: school and further education, work and retirement (Elder, 1985; Marshall & Mueller, 2003).

School and Further Education Stage

During the first stage, career development theories suggest that individuals select career fields based on their self-perceptions, values, and beliefs, and these cognitions are developed through experiences in homes, schools and other contexts (Berrios-Allison, 2005; Gottfredson, 1981; Lent, Brown, & Hackett, 1994). In addition, and contrary to the myth, exposure to computers have not proved to be a conclusive factor to attract students towards an IT career; the interest in computers is developed in the same way as other occupations (Messersmith, Garrett, Davis-Kean, Malanchuk, & Eccles, 2008). Nowadays, taking into account the lack of enough prepared professionals in the IT sector, attracting students to shape tomorrow's labor horizon has become a major concern in educational institutions (Garcia-Crespo, Colomo-Palacios, Gomez-Berbis, & Tovar-Caro, 2009).

Previous studies have indicated the imbalance of gender in the profession (Margolis & Fisher, 2002), concluding that gender differences in the computing field lead to negative social, economic, and scientific consequences and must, therefore, be addressed (Papastergiou, 2008). In such scenario, this imbalance is seen as an "input problem" (McKinney, Wilson, Brooks, O'Leary-Kelly, & Hardgrave, 2008). But this is not the only detected problem. Negative media coverage regarding offshoring and outsourcing has resulted in students concerned about their future jobs being shipped outsource (Granger, Dick, Jacobson, & Slyke, 2007), nonetheless, other authors hold that the intention to pursue and IT career does not seemed influenced by IT job availability (Heinze & Hu, 2009) and that offshoring is not undermining the IT job market enough to drive students away from this career, apart from programming and help services (Panko, 2008).

Work Stage

During the second stage, organizations select candidates that match requirements for positions and employer-employee relation starts. Along the selection process and interviews, an study about candidates and careers offered by the organization may be carried to avoid inadequate selections (Granrose & Portwood, 1987; Walker, 1980; Wanous, 1973). Once the selection is finished, organizations manage the hired human resource's knowledge and their learning capabilities (Bird, 1996), mainly due to the knowledge-based intensity of IT positions (Inkson, 2008). During employer-employee relations, employer has to consider employees as a capital resource that requires investment, due to the exclusiveness of competitive advantages when investments are successful, and learning and knowledge expansion are linked with strategic planning (Hill & Jones, 2006). Moreover, career movements complexity is higher at the beginning of the work experience (less than 7 years), and decreases later on (Higgins,

2001; Neal, 1999); for example, a programmer may seek a management position due to a wide mix of factors: wage, challenges, new experiences, dislike of his current programmer task, attraction to customer contact, etc.

Retirement Stage

Once employer-employee relations are about to end, the retirement phase starts. Traditionally, it was assumed that older employees are content to bide their time until retirement and they do not desire a job that requires upgrading their skills and abilities (Rosen & Jerdee, 1990), but these situations depend on personal and organizations factors such as work centrality, learning self-efficacy, perceived organizational support, and respect from coworkers and supervisors (Armstrong-Stassen, 2008). Prior to retirement, both the structural/hierarchical and content/job plateauing may arise (Bardwick, 1986) and have to be correctly managed to employ human capital made up of older employees. For instance, a flat organization chart with four or five levels reduces promotion possibilities and therefore the worker may be doomed to reach a career plateau. Moreover, challenges arising at the beginning for each position will be reduced as the worker gains experience, so the thrilling of the first days will gradually fade.

IT CAREER EVOLUTION

In this section, career related concepts and career models along with career paths are presented with the purpose of establishing a knowledge baseline to address the IT careers future.

Concepts

Prior to presenting different career models and paths, some related concepts such as career, career success, and career commitment are defined.

Definitions

A career can be defined as "the evolving sequence of a person's work experiences over time" (Arthur, Hall, & Lawrence, 1989, p. 8). Consequently, career development may be defined as "the total constellation of psychological, sociological, educational, physical, economic, and chance factors that combine to shape a career of any given individual over their life span" (McDaniels & Gysbers, 1992, p. 138). Hence, in order to understand careers, Van Maanen and Schein (1977) suggest the necessity to consider three interacting perspectives: (1) external vs. internal career, (2) careers over time, and (3) the "career cube".

External Career vs. Internal Career

First, the external career is related to objective elements such as a job title, assignments, a salary, promotions, a status, and has to be managed by organizations, while the internal career is connected to personal progress through their career, and have to be managed by each employee. Moreover, the internal career may be linked with the protean career (Hall & Mirvis, 1996), which is presented afterwards, and the career anchor, defined by Schein (1978) as individual's self-perceived talents, values and motives which mould career decisions. Conflicts between the internal and external career represent an issue that have to be addressed (Seibert, Kraimer, & Liden, 2001). For example, a high performance programmer may seek to promote to a management position due to its higher wage (external career), despite of enjoying his or her current tasks (internal career).

Career Movements

Particularly, and pursuing the goal of this chapter, organizations viewpoint of career over time focuses on movements. These movements were traditionally contemplated as part of the organization and are vertical movements in the ladder.

New movements such as radial and circumferential movements (Schein, 1971) were introduced although employees remain in the organization. Other kind of career movements are those that represent a change in organizations, sometimes without modifying the work outline (Sullivan, 1999). These movements form the inherent organizational career concept. These movements may be produced by four factors: current dissatisfaction, attractive alternatives, obstacles, and confidence to overcome obstacles (Neopolitan, 1980). Another contribution to career movements were the career stages that individuals pass trough during their working life (Dalton, Thompson, & Price, 1977). Despite widening possible movements and the stages knowledge, structural plateau, which represents a low probability of vertical movements and individual no longer challenged by their job or job responsibilities (T. D. Allen, Poteet, & Russell, 1998; Bardwick, 1986), still exists (P. C. B. Lee, 1999). For instance, a technical project manager with ten years of experience may have difficulties to move upward in the organization chart due to his or her eminent experience in technical aspects and his or her modest experience in other areas such as customer relationships or communication skills.

The "Career Cube"

To explain career movements, the "career cube" is represented by three interacting life cycles: (1) the biosocial, (2) the family, and (3) the work/career, and encompass aspects that each individual focus on over his or her life. These aspects are complementary and not (always) exclusive, but as Brooke (2009) argued, there is a hard focus on IT career development on early stages rather than on families. In many cases, career management is focused on changes from technical positions to non technical positions as the worker gains experience and seniority. For example, management positions are seen as high seniority ladder rather than having a specific ladder with multiple input points, including an input point for low experienced workers. In modifying this perspective, organizations may produce a map of career movements within the company, with multiple possible movements in and out of each ladder.

Career Success

Career success is another related factor that has to be taken in consideration when talking about careers. It is defined as the accumulated positive work and psychological outcomes arising from an individual's work experiences (Seibert, et al., 2001). Career success, as career development, has internal and external sides, also known as subjective and objective or intrinsic and extrinsic (Ballout, 2009), and therefore all research have to consider both sides. The internal career success is related to psychological success which emanates from the employee's feeling of pride and personal accomplishment of a variety of goals in life (Hall, 1996), hence it is managed by each employee not by the employer. On the other side, external success is oriented by organizations and involves promotions, recognition and compensations (Hall & Mirvis, 1995).

Career Commitment

Career commitment plays a pivotal role in career management. Career commitment is characterized as "the strength of one's motivation to work in a chosen career role" (Hall, 1971). According to this definition, career commitment implies an individual's approach and a strong presence of personal influences which points to a protean orientation (Hall & Mirvis, 1996). This direction points to a redefinition of experience in IT work, in which individual's career depends on worker's capacity to acquire and apply the most advanced skills rather than accumulate experience. This concept is a predictor of both sides of career success (Ballout, 2009; Poon, 2004). Due to the flattering of organizations and the lack of jobs and

careers, career commitment has become a source of occupational meaning and continuity that facilitate employees to remain focused on their goals (Aryee, Chay, & Tan, 1994; Colarelli & Bishop, 1990). For instance, a programmer-analyst with high technical skills and much experience may seek to stay in the technical ladder because he or she feels committed to it.

IT Career Paths

Once the basic concepts of careers have been defined, traditional and current career models and paths are presented.

Traditional Path

The traditional IT career path consist of three pyramidal levels: (1) starting at programmer/analyst, IT professionals require the development of more "hard" skills; after acquiring some experience and improving some "soft" skills, professionals move up the ladder to (2) system analyst; furthermore, with an important improvement on "soft" skills, professionals may climb the ladder to an IT manager position (C. K. Lee, 2005). During these movements, all skills are considered important, generating a precise viewpoint for IT professionals despite of changes in each skill importance during the climbing of the ladder (Todd, McKeen, & Gallupe, 1995). Regarding the skills required for an IT career, the software development skill is more transferable than other "hard" skills, while "soft" skills, such as communication and interpersonal relationships, are involved in all IT ladder levels (C. K. Lee, 2005). Moreover, the 'normative' age-based career trajectories, which may be defined as the naturalization of age-linked sequences of occupational roles and positions, and the promotion of an employee from technical to management positions along age, may be used as the basic definition of traditional IT careers.

Dual Ladder

Restructuring IT careers trajectories in organizations lead to the creation of another standpoint: the dual ladder in IT careers. These trajectories represent a change from more technical jobs such as programmer to more non-technical ones such as junior project manager, or from analyst to consultant. Establishing a career path in this kind of careers is nearly impossible due to the multidirectional ladder movements that employees may suffer. This career path represents the adaptability of organization and employees to new challenges and changes, and produces a malleable workforce that will face better future changes. Movements using these career trajectories should be guided by the employees' protean orientation or the flexibility requirements of the organization.

Dual ladder represents a way of "advancing" in organizations for technical personnel without requiring managerial responsibilities, nonetheless, it is not a perfect career management considering current boundary less careers (Ginzberg & Baroudi, 1988). In the IT sector, movements of technical to non-technical positions can be conceptualized as transfers of IT knowledge (Reich & Kaarst-Brown, 1999), and are generally produced from technical to non-technical directions due to the status differences (Katz & Allen, 1997). These movements appear to be related to four issues: (1) career expectations and motivations, (2) affiliation with the IT profession, (3) dissatisfaction with the IT job, and (4) preparation for a move out of IT. Nevertheless, they are not always present, (e.g. Reich & Kaarst-Brown, 1999). From the first issue standpoint, IT professionals pursue challenges, thus some of them see the change to non-technical as a challenge. IT professionals have a strong need for growth and personal development, jointly with a high need for learning and a desire to be challenged (Couger, Zawacki, & Opperman, 1973). The second issue is related to the development of careers along their specific career specialization. The third issue is related to subjective items such

as breaks in psychological contracts. Finally, the forth issue is related to obtaining new knowledge from an active viewpoint attitude, setting aside a passive attitude. Once the transition from technical to non-technical position has been completed, there are two factors that have to be managed according to the research carried by Reich and Kaarst-Brown (1999): (1) adjustment periods and initial loss of productivity, and (2) supportive role of mentors and friends during transition. Both factors have to be considered as if the employee was a newcomer in the organization. The first factor includes the time required to acquire the "know-how" and "know-whom" of the new job. The second factor includes supporting adaptation methods such as mentors and welcome guides, along with formal transition programs. In the same research, Reich and Kaarst-Brown (1999) give some recommendations for all the levels included in career development in order to successfully move from technical to non-technical positions:

- For the individual level, being proactive in personal development innovation and assessment and development of skills unconnected to technical positions. For IT management, authors recommend to establish adequate relationships in this line, expose people to business units, develop skills and knowledge to succeed in non-technical positions, raise the idea of movement in the hiring process and provide a fallback strategy to IT professionals who desire to work in non-technical departments.
- For the organization level, it is recommended to establish formal transition programs along with informal ones, and reevaluate compensation systems and job designs in order to be congruent with the ladder movements.

Alpha & Beta

Other concepts that represent career patterns are Alpha and Beta careers (Sullivan & Mainiero, 2007). Both patterns are based on three parameters: (1) authenticity, defined "as being true to oneself in the mindset of the constant interplay between personal development and work and non-work issues"; (2) balance, defined as "making decisions so that the different aspects of one's life, both work and non-work, form a coherent whole"; (3) and challenge, defined as "engaging in activities that permit the individual to demonstrate responsibility, control, and autonomy while learning and growing" (Sullivan & Mainiero, 2007). In the first pattern, the Alpha career begins with an emphasis on challenge early in the career, proceeding to authenticity in the middle of the career, and finishing in a balance late in the career. This pattern is more followed by men (Sullivan & Mainiero, 2007). In the second pattern, the Beta career begins with a focus on challenge early in the career, followed by balance in the middle of the career, and finally authenticity. This other pattern is more followed by women (Sullivan & Mainiero, 2007). These concepts may be used to fit careers on two paths, but according to Keen (1988), IT career paths do not exists; there are only career trajectories because the careers are mould in a state of flux. This conclusion, jointly with the concept of career evolution along life, lead to the conclusion that all career models may exist in order to cover all the career anchors during employee's life (Cohen & Mallon, 1999; McDonald, Brown, & Bradley, 2005; Schein, 1971, 1978).

Kamaleon Career Patterns

A case study that illustrates this alteration of career model over time can be found in the study carried out in Nigeria by Ituma and Simpson (2006), in which they found some career patterns existing at the same time, but represented by different socio-demographic individuals. The first career pattern, called Slow and Steady, represents workers seeking for stability and a traditional career development. The second pattern, named Explorer, represents a rapid development transitioning from project to project and from organization to organization. The third pattern, called Canvasser, emphasizes self-employment based on relationships. The fourth pattern, called Haphazard, represents the mixture of career patterns along with interruptions and work balance with personal life. Finally, Ituma and Simpson (2006) added another career pattern: Kamaleon, which "implies a series of adaptations to modify personal circumstances and social cultural obligations". It should be noted that these patterns are more transitional, representing short term careers, in contrast to the Alpha and Beta careers, which represent all life careers. These patterns are adopted as the worker life changes, both by his/her own changes or by other changes. For example, a worker in pursuit of work life balance fits in Haphazard pattern

Protean Career

In Hall (2004) words "…we need people to have the resources and capability of taking charge of their careers […], as a society, we need for all members to grow, achieve, and contribute to their full potential…". Following this direction, the protean career is described as a career in which a person, not an organization, is in charge, its core values are freedom and growth, and its main success criteria are psychological aspects versus position and salary. According to this definition, a protean careerist is an ongoing learner, always open to new possibilities (Hall & Mirvis, 1996), and has a remarkable level of two "metacompetencies": adaptability and identity (or self-awareness), which have to be jointly developed in order to be a protean careerist (Hall, 2004). Furthermore, Hall states two main factors for measuring the protean orientation: (1) the extent to which a person's career decisions are driven by personal values, and (2) the extent to which a person feels independent and in charge of his or her career. In addition to these factors, the best single predictor for a protean careerist appears to be the number of countries that a person has visited. The development of the protean career has been analyzed from the image violation theory as a source of protean (Sargent & Domberger, 2007). The image violation covers those potential career goals and plans incompatible with individual values or standards. These potential career goals and plans are screened out, and the best alternative is enacted and related to the first protean factor presented above. For example, a worker fond of customer relationships and with a job that does not imply them, most often technical jobs, may search for alternatives in order to promote to a position with customer relationships involvement.

Kaleidoscope Career Model

Similar to the protean career concept is the recently created Kaleidoscope Career Model (KCM) (Mainiero & Sullivan, 2006). This model presents how career patterns shift over time as individual's needs and interests changes, and it is based on three parameters: authenticity, balance and challenge. Authenticity is defined as being true to oneself. This parameter guides people to seek a compatible job with their values. Secondly, the balance parameter alludes to the desire of successfully integrate one's work and non-work fields. Lastly, the challenge includes the desire for responsibility and autonomy, jointly with an interest in growing and learning. All parameters are present at the same time, however, "just as one turns a kaleidoscope to see new patterns, so do career patterns evolve in response to changing life priorities" (Cabrera, 2009), and very similar to protean's ones. Moreover, the switch over time factor has been discovered for protean careers (Briscoe, Hall, & DeMuth, 2006), which makes an approach between both models. Also, both models focus on individual guides of careers, which creates a career guided by individual's own terms,

values and life choices, placing organizations on second stage, that is KCM and protean careers are self-directed (Sullivan & Mainiero, 2007).

Boundaryless Career

Boundaryless may be seen as a liberating model in times of prosperity but also as a mean to arrogate workers' rights by employers (Arthur & Rousseau, 2001), due to a short-term nature of the transactional contract on which is based, a use of performance-based pay, a lower levels of commitment by both parties, and an easy exit from the agreement (Callanan & Greenhaus, 1999). Despite of the benefits of this career type, its expansion is not occurring as extensively as predicted because there are some limitations to boundaryless careers: commitment to organizations (Millward & Hopckins, 1998), "job embeddedness" (Mitchell et al., 2001), investment done in the organization, and loyalty to superiors within the organization (Callanan, 2003). In addition to this limitations, individuals are recommended to remain true to their own interests, values, talents, and life-style preferences (Greenhaus, Callanan, & Godshalk, 2000), and be proactive and self-assertive in how they approach their careers management, establishing a career strategy (Callanan & Greenhaus, 1999). For effectively manage a boundaryless career, an "intelligent" approach have to be undertaken (Arthur, Claman, DeFillippi, & Adams, 1995). This means to manage the seven "knows", that is "know-why", "know-how", "know-whom", "know-what", "know-where" and "know-when", and have "career resilience" (Baruch, 2004; Waterman Jr., Waterman, & Collard, 1994). From an organization standpoint, each employee's career market value has to be considered in order to reduce losses and produce a merited system that reflects goal achievements and results (Yamamoto, 2006).

Boundaryless and protean constructs are related but differ from one another (Baruch, 1998; Briscoe & Finkelstein, 2009; Briscoe, et al., 2006). Both concepts are not negatively related to normative or continuance commitment when development opportunities are perceived, but in case of not perceiving it, boundaryless mindset is negatively related to normative commitment (Briscoe & Finkelstein, 2009). For instance, a software designer working in an organization with old fashioned design techniques may choose to seek a new job if he or she perceives that it may improve his or her designer skills. Furthermore, Schultze and Miller (2004) argued that logotherapy tests "help people ascertain the level of meaning in their lives and will hopefully lead those experiencing the existential vacuum of these meanings discovery" and may be used as a support tool for boundaryless careers.

Symbiotic Career

The "symbiotic career" introduced by Alvarez and Svejenova (2002) as the career trajectory sustained by a couple with a stable, affective, and trusting relationship, who share highly differentiated tasks that are incompatible to be performed by a single person, has to be assessed for IT professionals. In addition, women are less represented in IT workforce (Trauth & Quesenberry, 2007) and, therefore, they may carry the non-IT tasks. In addition to this concept, "joint career" defined by De Bruin and Lewis (2004) as the "unified career path sustained by more than a single individual and which is based on trust and strong ties and ongoing commitments to shared goals that can encompass both the work and family domains", jointly with the inherent concepts of primary and auxiliary careers, which represents core and non-core business tasks, have to be used for IT career research in order to shed some light into broader perspectives that include family business and future blurred business-family dichotomy in career management. For instance, a couple may work in the same organization in different projects; one of them could be working in a management area, whereas the other could be assigned to a technical one.

Portfolio Career

Another alternative and a non-traditional form of work that is emerging is portfolio career (Fenwick, 2006). Workers that have a portfolio work "contract their skills and knowledge to various individuals and organizations, in effect, creating a portfolio of work activity for themselves". This is based on three components: (1) commitment to long-term freelance employment, (2) sense of specialized expertise developed and offered, and (3) sense of unique identity (Fenwick, 2006). This career may be considered as a protean career from a non-organizational employment, in which career anchor is based on development of individual specialization and on knowledge production.

Lee (2001) concluded that organizations could enhance employees' job by rotating them through projects, and also provide opportunities by creating related spin-offs. This conclusion is similar to the one obtained by Allen and Katz (1985), they asserted the existence of a strong preference for project-centered careers, in which employees transit from project to project, rather than climbing up the organization's ladder. Moreover, all presented career paths and models coexist in contemporary organizations. On the one hand, traditional models have not been disused and remain to be a perfect solution in specific cases, while on the other hand, newer models may improve and solve those specific problems. Therefore, both, practitioners and researchers, have to consider the full scope of career models and apply a combination of all them for each specific problem. For example, consider an organization with two main career areas: management and technical. On the one hand, the management career ladder may be more traditionally overseen, with vertical movements based on seniority. On the other hand, technical career ladders may be managed with movements across projects, spiral movements along with positions (i.e. from senior developer to junior analyst). Moreover, movements from the management ladder to technical ladders and vice versa may exist. In this case, both traditional and newer models coexist in the same organization.

IT Career: Issues, Difficulties and Solutions

Once the general concepts about careers have been explained, specific issues and difficulties jointly with some solutions are stated. These issues and difficulties are: gender, race, technical vs. non technical, career responsibility, and mentoring.

Gender

There are a set of themes that influence an IT career (Brooke, 2009). One of the controversial points of careers in IT management lies in the existing gap within the gender parity (Trauth & Quesenberry, 2007). Much research has been done regarding gender factors in IT careers (Adya, 2008; Faulkner, 2000; Trauth & Quesenberry, 2007), and a myriad of macro level theories have been used to analyze these differences. On the one hand, the essentialist theory rests on the assertion of the fixed, unified, and opposite nature of women and men (Wajcman, 1991). This theory suggests a separate dealing for each sex with regard to IT jobs: a female IT workforce and a male IT workforce. On the other hand, social construction theory argues that human performance cannot be fully understood by biological factors, instead it must be explained from a socio-cultural education perspective (Berger & Luckmann, 1966). This theory covers the differences about how men and women as groups receive and response to societal messages in a different way (Trauth & Quesenberry, 2007). Finally, the individual differences theory of gender and IT rejects essentialism and offers refinement of various underexplored areas of the social construction theory (Trauth, 2002). This theory examines personal characteristics and environmental influences that mean that "the focus is on differences within rather than between genders" (Trauth & Quesenberry, 2007).

Considering that differences in representation are not due to a single factor, and the complexity of these factors (Trauth & Quesenberry, 2007), and having a workforce is beneficial for gaining a competitive edge in the market place (Elmuti, 2001), some recommendations have been asserted in order to fill this gap. Examples of these recommendations are assimilating women into IT by helping them to fit into a male domain (Pringle, Nielsen, Hellens, Greenhill, & Parfitt, 2000), creating a more "female domain" in IT (Webster, 1996). This would enable to support structures such as mentors and role models (Cohoon, 2002), and more specifically female mentors and models avoiding stereotypes or generalizations of a holistic group of women (Trauth & Quesenberry, 2007).

To reduce the leak of female talent from IT, traditional career models have to be avoided as norm; instead, models focused on careers' self-direction have to become the standard, jointly with a replacement of the existing culture based on goals and results (Cabrera, 2009).

Race

Along with gender differences, race differences regarding careers have been also analyzed (Alderfer, Alderfer, Tucker, & Tucker, 1980; Brown & Ford, 1977; Greenhaus, Parasuraman, & Wormley, 1990). Race differences influence job performance evaluations in form of a bias rating process, and therefore, objective career outcomes such as promotions and career plateauing (Greenhaus, et al., 1990). Nowadays, race issues have been put aside in order to study more important matters.

Technical vs. Non-Technical

One of the crucial points to be taken in consideration is the requirement of technical vs. non-technical abilities for IT jobs (Bailey & Stefaniak, 1999; Gallivan, Truex III, & Kvasny, 2004; Noll & Wilkins, 2002; Todd, et al., 1995). At the end of the twenty century, organizations looked for professionals with skills in multiple areas (Bird, 1994; Miner & Robinson, 1994). In the IT sector, this issue may be considered from the balance viewpoint between technical and non-technical skills. Technical skills have been, and continue to be, more demanded for early IT careers which typically start with jobs such as programmer rather than non-technical positions (Lash & Sein, 1995; Sumner & Yager, 2004). Along with an IT career, non-technical skills arise as more important assets than the technical ones, as long as individuals are promoted to analysts, IT managers, and further positions (C. K. Lee, 2005). In the last decades, the importance between technical and non-technical skills appears to be reduced (Gallivan, Truex III, & Kvasny, 2002; C. K. Lee, 2005). From "lower" IT jobs, non-technical skills have been defined in job descriptions and advertisements in the last decades, and technical skills continue to be relevant during the IT career of an individual (Gallivan, et al., 2002). As Joshi & Kuhn (2007) recommend, IT curriculums should include soft skills, such as leadership and ability to build relationships, in addition to hard skills such programming or problem solving. Both types of skills should be treated in career management.

In this discussion, these two concepts have been contemplated as career anchors among IT professionals (Crepeau, Crook, Goslar, & McMurtrey, 1992). On the one hand, the technical side is characterized by "hard" skills such as specific programming, critical thinking, troubleshooting, design, analysis, etc. On the other hand, the non-technical side, also known as managerial side, is characterized by "soft" skills such as active listening, coordination, decision making, management of resources, time management, etc. However, from the career anchor standpoint, Creativity, Autonomy, Identity, and Variety, are considered to be more significant for IT professionals than differences between technical and non-technical (Sumner, Yager, & Franke, 2005), but when age average arise, only Variety remains as substantial factor, and the Stability anchor arise (Sumner &

Yager, 2004). Career anchors were introduced by Schein (1978), who defined them as self-perceived talents, motives and values that guide, constrain, stabilize and integrate individual careers. His model consists of five anchors: (1) Managerial Competence, (2) Technical Competence, (3) Security/Stability, (4) Creativity/Entrepreneurship and (5) Autonomy/Independence. Later, DeLong (1982) added three additional career anchors: Identity, Service, and Variety.

Career Responsibility

The responsibility for career management is divided into two: the organization, which is responsible of providing a career planning model, training and resources to employees; and individuals, which are responsible of analyzing career options, deciding development objectives, communicating preferences to the employer (Hall, 1986). From the organization responsibility side, formal career management programs are a part of the human resources strategies, believing that these programs will have outputs such as a better individual performance and development, and an increase employees' commitment (Ginzberg & Baroudi, 1988; Granrose & Portwood, 1987; Schein, 1978). But the institutionalization of this kind of programs does not increase the number of opportunities for career promotion in an organization, and may increase the competitiveness among participants. Also, as people's aspiration rise, fewer or zero satisfying opportunities are likely to be stored for them. On the other hand, the lack of information regarding organizational careers appears to have a positive effect in individuals, tending to rate their prospects with an optimistic bias (Weinstein, 1980). As Granrose and Portwood (1987) noted, career management programs may or may not generate positive outcomes. One of the negative outcomes is the exclusion that an employee may suffer if his career plans are not included in it, and in consequence he or she will look for external alternatives; from the organizational viewpoint, this outcome only has to be considered as negative if it was not part of the desirable outcome (Granrose & Portwood, 1987). As a positive outcome, empirical research has shown that IT professionals whose career orientations matched their job settings and are coherent with their work environment, reported higher satisfaction and career satisfaction (Igbaria, Greenhaus, & Parasuraman, 1991; McKeen & Burke, 1993). In addition, the organization's structure plays a pivotal role in establishing career choices due to its relation with numerous mobility opportunities within the organization, both in job title and functions (Herriot, Gibson, Pemberton, & Pinder, 1993).

From the organizational viewpoint, it is required to plan human resources allocation and keep employees at the organization pace (Walker, 1980). But members of the current workforce demonstrate an increasing willingness to change jobs and even careers if they perceive barriers to attain personal goals (Driver, 1982). This modification in the workforce induces organizations to address the pressure of letting go employees if their expectations about career opportunities are not met. As a result of this will, employees may consider technopreneurial as an alternative for meeting their personal goals (Lee, 2001). Moreover, organizational growth has an influence on plans awareness because individuals may find it easier to identify opportunities in it (Granrose & Portwood, 1987). For example, an organization with new international headquarters may increase the amount of expatriates and therefore the possibility of new challenges and further assignments.

Mentoring

Workplace mentoring provides career promotion (Hunt & Michael, 1983). Moreover, a greater diversity of the individual's overall advice network is positively related to the likelihood of changing careers (Higgins, 2001). This advice network exposes new forms of promotion such as professional networks. Indeed, mentoring and other relational influences represent key resources for protean employees (Gibson, 2004; Higgins, 2001). When considering mentoring as a career development facilitator, factors such as mentor's age and gender impact the outcome of mentoring relationships (Arnold & Johnson, 1997). This gender impact may have a negative influence for women representation in certain IT positions (Adya, 2008; Trauth, Nielsen, & Hellens, 2003). In order to treat this impact, Adya (2008) proposes a self-selection of mentors with the purpose of increasing the support of employees career growth.

FUTURE OF IT CAREERS

To make a solid start point for future practices and research in IT professional's career, and following Inkson's recommendations (2008) about human resources analysis, words used to name these concepts have to be selected with care in order to really represent what is supposed to represent, due to the perception of the world they create. Furthermore, the relationship between career management and career development is considered intricate, also moderating variables, and future studies have to collect feedback from employee and management levels, and compare reports of organizations' programs (Appelbaum, Ayre, & Shapiro, 2002).

Job security based on seniority has been one of the classical pillars of long relationships between employer and employee. This is no longer insured due to modifications in employer-employee contracts associated with the restructuring of organizations and a global economy (Moen, Sweet, & Swisher, 2005). Global-market demands up-to-the-minute skills to meet instantaneous requirements of IT industry in order to increase productivity, which limits career paths security. Extending this limitation, new organizational forms do not facilitate the creation of predictable race maps according to chronological age or seniority (Benner, 2002). Furthermore, possessing valuable skills do not represent insurance for employment and do not completely protect workers against consequences of ageing and lack of demanding skills in IT innovation. In order to cover these limitations, Arthur and Rousseau (2001) recommend adopting a proactive HR management, which promotes opportunities for development inside and outside the organization, improves competencies out of job's assignments, and manages resiliency.

Consistent with Inkson's (2008) recommendation, Callanan (2003) points to a boundaryless philosophy which includes a broader definition of the career success meaning in order to improve the management of their careers and stay true to their beliefs and values; therefore, as Callanan (2003) concluded, a more balanced understanding and measurement of career success is required jointly with a wide research of a boundaryless addressing degree of adoption of this philosophy, and individual and organizational factors influenced by its adoption.

The "flat world" of the IT industry has encourage the redefinition of the actual use of experience based on narrow terms regarding the possession of competitive IT skills, which produces a resetting of the boundary age and a decrease in many IT careers length (Callanan & Greenhaus, 1999). This shortening induces the replacement of older employees with younger ones. According to van Veldhoven and Dorenbosch (2008), older employees are rather inclined to be proactive on the job, and are scarcely different from younger employees in their developmental proactiveness; both types of proactiveness are not considered personality characteristics, they are stated as job behaviors influenced by situational antecedents (Parker, Williams, & Turner, 2006). In addition, they point to an important relevance of being proactive at work for older employees, based on its relation with their psychological capital, hence with their psychological contract (Rousseau, 1989). Thus, these conclusions are oriented to consider different careers management according to employees age, in which on-the-job proactiveness is managed as a value to organizations, consistent with superior career opportunities in younger employees in the IT sector, as it is widely recognized (Brooke, 2009).

One of the basic challenges of IT careers is represented by the reduction of the typical common view of the IT employee as a socially withdrawn male (McConnell, 2004; Wilson, 2003) to a non gender employee in order to attract a broader range of people. This may be achieved emphasizing the cooperative nature of IT, stressing teamwork and group projects (Robertson, Newell, Swan, Mathiassen, & Bjerknes, 2001). Moreover, creating work and life trajectories that bridge the gap between technical and management positions would also be worthwhile (Schmid, 2005). Changing this stereotype, the surplus of three or four men to one in IT positions, and six to one in leadership's positions may be reduced.

In the last 5 years, a marked decrease in IT related enrollments have occurred at colleges in the United Stated and some parts of Europe (Panko, 2008). Meanwhile, the IT industry itself has experienced a consistent growth that is expected to continue at least for 2 more decades. This situation may be considered as a crisis based on ample evidences that support this assertion (Panko, 2008; Zhang, 2007). This crisis has to be considered in the career evolution context due to a future downsizing of the specialized IT workforce.

Another of the most challenging issues that still has not reached a widely accepted solution is prolonging older IT workers careers (Brooke, 2009). Many IT jobs present challenges and new opportunities for development that in many cases are allocated to younger employees while older employees remain aside based on a subjective age criteria. This distribution based on age, produces a counterpart on older employers that may see work until retirement as a time occupation rather than a development opportunity. In order to reduce this plateauing and extend older workers' careers, employers may have to value and respect older employees' contribution, care about them and be committed to them (Armstrong-Stassen, 2008). Moreover, older employees with an underline work centrality, which refers to the overall importance of work in employees' life (Paullay, Alliger, & Stone-Romero, 1994), and learning self-efficacy, which refers to the belief in one's ability to learn and develop new skills (Fletcher, Hansson, & Bailey, 1992; Maurer, Weiss, & Barbeite, 2003), have to be allocated on stimulating and meaningful jobs that provide adequate development opportunities (Armstrong-Stassen, 2008).

Regarding the career success research, it has been identified a lack of focus on how organizational culture and performance in management influences career success (Callanan, 2003), despite of having antecedents of its influence on careers, and the requirement of unbiased systems (Greenhaus, et al., 1990). Furthermore, organizational culture as a moderating variable in relationships between protean and boundaryless career orientation on the one hand, and organizational commitment on the other, are still being untreated (Briscoe & Finkelstein, 2009). This culture may be influenced by newer or less traditional organizational methods such as outsourcing and global software development (GSD). These less traditional methods have some consequences that require being address. On the one hand, they may influence employees' career expectations negatively due to the reduction of available positions inside the organization. On the other hand, they could enable organizations with a specific expertise such as software codification or testing, and offer traditional paths within these expert organizations. Moreover, technologies and methodologies that have remained mainly in research environments, such as artificial intelligence (AI) and reusable component development will arise to large scale markets. These market incomings will produce more jobs and further career opportunities and movements for present and new employees and employers, enabling alternative career paths and new branches in the ladders.

As Cabrera (2009) concluded, organizations require a better adaptation to changes in the environment, recognizing and responding to changes in how work gets done and how careers are built, that is "protean" organizations. In this direction, organizations have to provide opportunities for development and actively manage individual careers in order to increase the retention of talented employees (Herriot & Pemberton, 1996; Millward & Kyriakidou, 2004). Finally, organizational commitment has to be considered as a necessary outcome of future careers research on both sides of job relationships (Briscoe & Finkelstein, 2009). In this context, nowadays organizations need to retain talent in order to become competitive, thus career management should consider an increase of organizational commitment as a way of retaining skilled employees.

FUTURE WORK

Along with the difficulties in the changes presented, studies related to any careers must take into account cultural, social, individual, organizational and time concepts, which further hinders the study of careers and make arduous the creation of universal or general models that cover a wide range of workers and/or organizations. All these difficulties must not lead to a reduction of researches in this area; on the contrary, they must be considered as opportunities to enrich the existing knowledge.

These changes alternate the monolithic careers' view, resulting in a myriad of new options that should enable further researches. Many alternatives in the future research horizon arise. One of them is the study of the focus change of relations employer-employee termination, from contractual to continuous relationships (Arthur & Rousseau, 2001), enabling long-relationships that may be profitable for both parts. Regarding relationships, expatriation and repatriation in the IT sector may be considered for future research, and the hope theory may be used as a construct (Zikic,

Novicevic, Harvey, & Breland, 2006). Another line covers the construction of a general model for career management that encompasses today's issues and solutions. Furthermore, all theories and models may be assessed and contrasted in different "environments" from those that have already been tested, understanding the concept of "environment" as the effect of all variables that affect both, individuals and organizations in career issues. These are some of research lines that may be taking into account for further research, although more research lines may be considered.

LESSONS LEARNED

On the one hand, career research is growing and widening to new knowledge and promising areas such as retirement or work-life balance careers. Regarding retirement, new career paths which enable older workers stay in the workforce are needed in order to reduce the amount of retirees. This is mainly due to the continuous prolongation of life expectation. In addition, IT jobs are not physically demanding but intellectually intense. For this reason, they are perfect for retirement age delay. Following this line, expected retirement age should be increased with the support of new ways of motivation and maybe new positions for older workers in organizations such as mentors, coaches and consultants.

On the other hand, old models seem to be reduced to few cases and are on the verge of disappearing. For instance, pyramidal careers and vertical movements are been replaced for new kind of movements that include moves in and out of organizations, transcending both psychological and psychical boundaries. In this direction, rewards related to vertical promotion have to be reduced and new items such as recognition, employability, job rotations, and cross-functional projects have to be taken into account in HR decisions.

Additionally, the war for talent is present and will continue. So in order to obtain the talent

that cover organization needs, employers have to make efforts to mold HR practices for retaining it. The changes should consider all variables that influence career management which is not an easy task. Inner variable set, work-life balance and generational differences seem to be the most influential ones. In the case of generational differences, the presence of four generation in nowadays workforce complicates career management due to the specific anchors, goals, perceptions and values of each generation.

CONCLUSION

In a current globalized scene with continuous changes, careers are difficult to manage. Job security guarantees of traditional models have led to flexible new models. Careers have changed from a lineal viewpoint, where an employee works for an organization during all his or her life. It has been replaced in a wide number of organizations for different models. Such models enable multidirectional movements and contemplate modifications among organizations. Regarding these changes, the employee is considered the main actor, leaving the organization in the background. This replacement in careers guidance is based on the alteration of career views from a tool for organizational goal achievement to an individual journey guided by the employee personal goals. In addition, delegation or acquisition of such liability further complicates management of careers, due to the fact that there may be no alignment between organizational objectives and individual goals, and there could be differences in perceptions and merits granted (internal vs. external career success).

In addition, an adequate link between talent retention and career management is recommended in order to succeed in the former. Each worker pursues his or her development, a career path and his or her own goals, both work and personal. Regarding this, organizations should be capable of managing this mixture of items as individually as possible without losing the general perspective. In addition, the authors contend that human resources managers should consider a change of name for the term retention. Depending on the cultural context, this term could have negative connotations. Thus, in Spain retention could mean "Preventing something from moving, being removed or eliminated" or "Interrupting or disturbing the normal course of action of something". Hence, more positive terms such as talent care or more general terms such as talent management may contribute to avoid a repressive interpretation of the term.

To sum up, career management is becoming more complex as globalization expands, enabling new opportunities for employees, employers, and researchers. In this complex growth context, some items such as race and career responsibility, which influence in career management is clear enough in today's research literature, are put aside in research. However, new concepts like protean and boundaryless career, and more recently KCM, open new unexplored working lines and research areas and, therefore, both the research of careers and its management becomes globalized too

REFERENCES

Adya, M. P. (2008). Women at work: Differences in IT career experiences and perceptions between South Asian and American women. *Human Resource Management, 47*(3), 601–635. doi:10.1002/hrm.20234

Alderfer, C. P., Alderfer, C. J., Tucker, L., & Tucker, R. (1980). Diagnosing race relations in management. *The Journal of Applied Behavioral Science, 16*(2), 135–166. doi:10.1177/002188638001600202

Alexander, S. (1999). What's in a job title? Less and less, some say. *InfoWorld, 21*(21).

Allen, T. D., Poteet, M. L., & Russell, J. E. A. (1998). Attitudes of managers who are more or less career plateaued. *The Career Development Quarterly, 47*(2), 159–172.

Allen, T. J., & Katz, R. (1985). The dual ladder: Motivational solution or managerial delusion? *R & D Management, 16*(2), 185–197. doi:10.1111/j.1467-9310.1986.tb01171.x

Alvarez, J. L., & Svejenova, S. (2002). Symbiotic careers in movie making: Pedro and Agustin Almodovar. In Pieperl, M., Arthur, M. B., & Anand, N. (Eds.), *Career creativity: Explorations in the re-making of work* (pp. 183–208). New York: Oxford University Press.

Appelbaum, S. H., Ayre, H., & Shapiro, B. T. (2002). Career management in Information Technology: A case study. *Career Development International, 7*(3), 142–158. doi:10.1108/13620430210426123

Armstrong-Stassen, M. (2008). *Factors associated with job content plateauing among older workers.*

Arnold, J., & Johnson, K. (1997). Mentoring in early career. *Human Resource Management Journal, 7*(4), 61–70. doi:10.1111/j.1748-8583.1997.tb00289.x

Arthur, M. B., Claman, P. H., DeFillippi, R. J., & Adams, J. (1995). Intelligent enterprise, intelligent careers. *The Academy of Management Executive, 9*(4), 7–22.

Arthur, M. B., Hall, D. T., & Lawrence, B. S. (1989). *Handbook of career theory*. Cambridge, MA: Cambridge University Press. doi:10.1017/CBO9780511625459

Arthur, M. B., & Rousseau, D. M. (Eds.). (2001). *The boundaryless career: A new employment principle for a new organizational era*. New York: Oxford University Press.

Aryee, S., Chay, Y. W., & Tan, H. H. (1994). An examination of the antecedents of subjective career success among a managerial sample in Singapore. *Human Relations, 47*(5), 487–509. doi:10.1177/001872679404700502

Bailey, J. L., & Stefaniak, G. (1999). Preparing the Information Technology workforce for the new millennium. *SIGCPR Computer Personnel, 20*(4), 4–15. doi:10.1145/571475.571476

Ballout, H. I. (2009). Career commitment and career success: Moderating role of self-efficacy. *Career Development International, 14*(7), 655–670. doi:10.1108/13620430911005708

Bardwick, J. (1986). *The plateauing trap.* New York: Amacon.

Baruch, Y. (1998). The rise and fall of organizational commitment. *Human Systems Management, 17*(2), 135–143.

Baruch, Y. (2004). Transforming careers: From linear to multidirectional career paths. Organizational and individual perspectives. *Career Development International, 9*(1), 58–73. doi:10.1108/13620430410518147

Benner, C. (2002). *Work in the new economy. Flexible labour markets in Silicon Valley* (1st ed.). Malden, MA: Blackwell.

Berger, P. L., & Luckmann, T. (1966). *The social construction of reality: A treatise in the sociology of knowledge.* Garden City, NY: Anchor Books.

Berrios-Allison, A. C. (2005). Family influences on college students' occupational identity. *Journal of Career Assessment, 13*(2), 419–456. doi:10.1177/1069072704270320

Bird, A. (1994). Careers as repositories of knowledge: A new perspective on boundaryless careers. *Journal of Organizational Behavior, 15*(4), 325–344. doi:10.1002/job.4030150404

Bird, A. (1996). Careers as repositories of knowledge: Considerations for boundaryless careers. In Arthur, M. B., & Rousseau, D. M. (Eds.), *The boundaryless career: A new employment principle for a new organizational era* (pp. 150–168). New York: Oxford University Press.

Briscoe, J. P., & Finkelstein, L. M. (2009). The new career and organizational commitment: Do boundaryless and protean attitudes make a difference? *Career Development International, 14*(3), 242–260. doi:10.1108/13620430910966424

Briscoe, J. P., Hall, D. T., & DeMuth, R. I. F. (2006). Protean and boundaryless careers: An empirial exploration. *Journal of Vocational Behavior, 69*(1), 30–47. doi:10.1016/j.jvb.2005.09.003

Brooke, L. (2009). Prolonging the careers of older Information Technology workers: Continuity, exit or retirement transitions? *Ageing and Society, 29*(1), 237–256. doi:10.1017/S0144686X0800768X

Brown, H. A., & Ford, D. L. (1977). An exploratory analysis of discrimination in the employment of black MBA graduates. *The Journal of Applied Psychology, 62*(1), 50–56. doi:10.1037/0021-9010.62.1.50

Cabrera, E. F. (2009). Protean organizations: Reshaping work and careers to retain female talent. *Career Development International, 14*(2), 186–201. doi:10.1108/13620430910950773

Callanan, G. A. (2003). What price career success? *Career Development International, 8*(3), 126–133. doi:10.1108/13620430310471032

Callanan, G. A., & Greenhaus, J. H. (1999). Personal and career development: The best and worst of times. In Kraut, A. I., & Korman, A. K. (Eds.), *Evolving practices in human resources management: Responses to a changing world of work* (pp. 146–171). San Francisco, CA: Jossey-Bass.

Chesebrough, P. H., & Davis, G. B. (1983). Planning a career path in Information Systems. *Journal of Systems Management, 34*(1), 6–13.

Cohen, L., & Mallon, M. (1999). The transition from organisational employmen to portfolio working: Perceptions of boundarylessness. *Work, Employment and Society, 13*(2), 329–352.

Cohoon, J. M. (2002). Recruiting and retining women in undergraduate computing majors. *ACM SIGCSE Bulletin, 34*(2), 48–52. doi:10.1145/543812.543829

Colarelli, S. M., & Bishop, R. C. (1990). Career commitment: Functions, correlates and management. *Group & Orgnization Studies, 15*(2), 158–176. doi:10.1177/105960119001500203

Couger, J. D., Zawacki, R. A., & Opperman, E. B. (1973). Motivation levels of MIS managers versus those of their employees. *Management Information Systems Quarterly, 3*(3), 47–56. doi:10.2307/248788

Crepeau, R. G., Crook, C. W., Goslar, M. D., & McMurtrey, M. E. (1992). Career anchors of Information Systems personnel. *Journal of Management Information Systems, 9*(2), 145–160.

Curtis, B., Hefley, W. E., & Miller, S. A. (2009). *People Capability Maturity Model (P-CMM®) version 2.0. (No. CMU/SEI-2009-TR-003).* Pittsburgh, PA: Software Engineering Institute, Carnegie Mellow University.

Dalton, G. W., Thompson, P. H., & Price, R. L. (1977). The four stages of professional careers: A new look at performance by professionals. *Organizational Dynamics, 6*(1), 19–42. doi:10.1016/0090-2616(77)90033-X

De Bruin, A., & Lewis, K. (2004). Toward enriching united career theory: Familial entrepreneurship and copreneurship. *Career Development International, 9*(7), 638–646. doi:10.1108/13620430410570347

DeLong, T. J. (1982). Reexamining the career anchor model. *Personnel, 59*(3), 50–61.

Driver, M. J. (1982). Career concepts–a new approach to career research. In Katz, R. (Ed.), *Career issues in human resources management* (pp. 23–32). Englewood Cliffs, NJ: Prentice-Hall.

Elder, G. (1985). *Life course dynamics: Trajectories and transitions, 1968–1980.* Ithaca, NY: Cornell University Press.

Elmuti, D. (2001). Preliminary analysis of the relationship between cultural diversity and technology in corporate America. *Equal Opportunities International, 20*(8), 1–16. doi:10.1108/02610150110786642

Evans, N. (2004). The need for an Analysis Body of Knowledge (ABOK)-will the real analyst please stand up? *Issues in Informing Science & Information Technology, 1*(1), 313–330.

Faulkner, W. (2000). Dualisms, hierarchies and gender in engineering. *Social Studies of Science, 30*(5), 759–792. doi:10.1177/030631200030005005

Fenwick, T. J. (2006). Contradictions in portfolio careers: Work design and client relations. *Career Development International, 11*(1), 65–79. doi:10.1108/13620430610642381

Fletcher, W. L., Hansson, R. O., & Bailey, L. (1992). Assessing occupational self-efficacy among middle-aged and older adults. *Journal of Applied Gerontology, 11*(4), 489–501. doi:10.1177/073346489201100408

Gallivan, M. J., Truex, D. P., III, & Kvasny, L. (2002). *An analysis of the changing demand patterns for Information Technology professionals.* Paper presented at the 2002 ACM SIGCPR Conference on Computer Personnel Research.

Gallivan, M. J., Truex, D. P. III, & Kvasny, L. (2004). Changing patterns in IT skill sets 1988-2003: A content analysis of classified advertising. *SIGMIS Database*, *35*(3), 64–87. doi:10.1145/1017114.1017121

Garcia-Crespo, A., Colomo-Palacios, R., Gomez-Berbis, J. M., & Tovar-Caro, E. (2009). IT professionals' competences. *High School Students'. Views*, *8*, 45–57.

Gibson, D. E. (2004). Role models in career development: New directions for theory and research. *Journal of Vocational Behavior*, *65*(1), 134–156. doi:10.1016/S0001-8791(03)00051-4

Ginzberg, M. J., & Baroudi, J. J. (1988). MIS careers-a theoretical perspective. *Communications of the ACM*, *31*(5), 586–594. doi:10.1145/42411.42422

Gottfredson, L. S. (1981). Circumscription and compromise: A development theory of occupational aspirations. *Journal of Counseling Psychology*, *28*(6), 545–579. doi:10.1037/0022-0167.28.6.545

Granger, M. J., Dick, G., Jacobson, C. M., & Slyke, C. V. (2007). Information Systems enrollments: Challenges and strategies. *Journal of Information Systems Education*, *18*(3), 303–311.

Granrose, C. S., & Portwood, J. (1987). Matching individual career plans and organizational career management. *Academy of Management Journal*, *30*(4), 669–720. doi:10.2307/256156

Greenhaus, J. H., Callanan, G. A., & Godshalk, V. M. (2000). *Career management* (3rd ed.). Mason, OH: Thomson-South-Western.

Greenhaus, J. H., Parasuraman, S., & Wormley, W. M. (1990). Effects of race on organizational experiences, job performance evaluations, and career outcomes. *Academy of Management Journal*, *33*(1), 64–86. doi:10.2307/256352

Hall, D. T. (1971). A theoretical model of career subidentity development in organizational settings. *Organizational Behavior and Human Performance*, *6*(1), 50–76. doi:10.1016/0030-5073(71)90005-5

Hall, D. T. (1986). *Career development in organizations*. San Francisco, CA: Jossey-Bass.

Hall, D. T. (1996). Protean career of the 21st century. *The Academy of Management Executive*, *10*(4), 8–16.

Hall, D. T. (2004). The protean career: A quarter-century journey. *Journal of Vocational Behavior*, *65*(1), 1–13. doi:10.1016/j.jvb.2003.10.006

Hall, D. T., & Mirvis, P. H. (1995). The new career contract: Developing the whole person at midlife and beyond. *Journal of Vocational Behavior*, *47*(3), 269–289. doi:10.1006/jvbe.1995.0004

Hall, D. T., & Mirvis, P. H. (1996). The new protean career: Psychological success and the path with a heart. In Hall, D. T. (Ed.), *The career is dead-long live the career* (pp. 15–45). San Francisco, CA: Jossey-Bass.

Heinze, N., & Hu, Q. (2009). Why college undergraduates choose IT: A multi-theoretical perspective. *European Journal of Information Systems*, *18*(5), 462–475. doi:10.1057/ejis.2009.30

Herriot, P., Gibson, G., Pemberton, C., & Pinder, R. (1993). Dashed hopes: Organizational determinants and personal perceptions of managerial careers. *Journal of Occupational and Organizational Psychology*, *66*(2), 115–123.

Herriot, P., & Pemberton, C. (1996). Contracting careers. *Human Relations*, *49*(6), 757–790. doi:10.1177/001872679604900603

Higgins, M. C. (2001). Changing careers: The effects of social context. *Journal of Organizational Behavior*, *22*(6), 595–618. doi:10.1002/job.104

Hill, C. W. L., & Jones, G. R. (2006). *Strategic management: An integrated approach* (7th ed.). Boston: Houghton Mifflin Company.

Hunt, D. M., & Michael, C. (1983). Mentorship: A career training and development tool. *Academy of Management Review, 8*(3), 475–485. doi:10.2307/257836

Igbaria, M., Greenhaus, J. H., & Parasuraman, S. (1991). Career orientations of MIS employees: An empirical analysis. *Management Information Systems Quarterly, 15*(2), 151–169. doi:10.2307/249376

Inkson, K. (2008). Are human resources? *Career Development International, 13*(3), 270–279. doi:10.1108/13620430810870511

Ituma, A., & Simpson, R. (2006). The chameleon career: An exploratory study of the work biography of Information Technology workers in Nigeria. *Career Development International, 11*(1), 48–65. doi:10.1108/13620430610642372

Ives, B., & Olson, M. H. (1981). Manager or technician? Then nature of Information Systems manager's job. *Management Information Systems Quarterly, 5*(4), 49–63. doi:10.2307/249327

Joshi, K. D., & Kuhn, K. M. (2007). What it takes to succeed in Information Technology consulting: Exploring the gender typing of critical attributes. *Information Technology & People, 20*(4), 400–424. doi:10.1108/09593840710839815

Kanter, R. M. (1991). The future of bureaucracy and hierarchy in organizational theory: A report from the field. In Bourdieu, P., & Coleman, J. S. (Eds.), *Social theory for a changing society*. London: Westview Press.

Katz, R., & Allen, T. J. (1997). Managing dual ladder systems in RD&E settings. In Katz, R. (Ed.), *The human side of managing technological innovation* (pp. 47–486). New York: Oxford University Press.

Keen, P. G. W. (1988). Roles and skill base for the IS organization. In Elam, J. J., Ginzberg, M. J., Keen, P. G. W., & Zmud, R. W. (Eds.), *Transforming the IS organization*. Washington, DC: ICIT Press.

Lash, P. B., & Sein, M. K. (1995). *Career paths in a changing IS environment: A theoretical perspective*. Paper presented at the 1995 ACM SIGCPR Conference on Supporting Teams, Groups, and Learning Inside and Outside the IS Function Reinventing IS.

Lee, C. K. (2005). *Transferability of skills over the IT career path*. Paper presented at the 2005 ACM SIGMIS CPR conference on Computer personnel research.

Lee, P. C. B. (1999). Career plateau and professional plateau: Impact on work outcomes of Information Technology professionals. *SIGCPR Computer Personnel, 20*(4), 25–38. doi:10.1145/571475.571478

Lee, P. C. B. (2001). *Technopreneurial inclinations and career management strategy among Information Technology professionals*. Paper presented at the 34th Hawaii International Conference on System Sciences.

Lent, R. W., Brown, S. D., & Hackett, G. (1994). Toward a unifying social cognitive theory of career and academic interest, choice, and performance. *Journal of Vocational Behavior, 45*(1), 79–122. doi:10.1006/jvbe.1994.1027

Levinson, D. J. (1978). *The seasons of a man's life*. New York: Ballantine Books.

Mainiero, L. A., & Sullivan, S. E. (2006). Kaleidoscope careers: An alternate explanation for the opt-out revolution. *The Academy of Management Executive, 19*(1), 106–124.

Margolis, J., & Fisher, A. (2002). *Unlocking the clubhouse: Women in computing*. Cambridge, MA: MIT Press.

Marshall, V. M., & Mueller, M. (2003). Theoretical roots of the life-course perspective. In Heinz, W. R. M. (Ed.), *Social dynamics of the life course: Transitions, institutions and interrelations* (pp. 3–32). New York: Aldine de Gruyter.

Maurer, T. J., Weiss, E. M., & Barbeite, F. G. (2003). A model of involvement in work-related learning and development activity: The effects of individual, situational, motivational, and age variables. *The Journal of Applied Psychology, 88*(4), 707–724. doi:10.1037/0021-9010.88.4.707

McConnell, S. (2004). *Professional software development: Shorter schedules, better projects, superior products, enhanced careers*. Boston: Addison-Wesley.

McDaniels, C., & Gysbers, N. (1992). *Counseling for career development: Theories, resources and practice*. Sam Francisco, CA: Jossey-Bass Publishers.

McDonald, P., Brown, K., & Bradley, L. (2005). Have traditional career paths given way to protean ones? Evidence from senior managers in the Australian public sector. *Career Development International, 10*(2), 109–129. doi:10.1108/13620430510588310

McKeen, C. A., & Burke, R. J. (1993). Use of career strategies by managerial and professional women. *International Journal of Career Management, 5*(4), 19–24. doi:10.1108/09556219310043219

McKinney, V. R., Wilson, D. D., Brooks, N., O'Leary-Kelly, A., & Hardgrave, B. (2008). Women and men in the IT profession. *Communications of the ACM, 51*(2), 81–84. doi:10.1145/1314215.1340919

Messersmith, E. E., Garrett, J. L., Davis-Kean, P. E., Malanchuk, O., & Eccles, J. S. (2008). Career development from adolescence through emerging adulthood: Insights from Information Technology occupations. *Journal of Adolescent Research, 23*(2), 206–227. doi:10.1177/0743558407310723

Millward, L., & Kyriakidou, O. (2004). Linking pre- and post-merger identities through the concept of career. *Career Development International, 9*(1), 12–27. doi:10.1108/13620430410518110

Miner, A. S., & Robinson, D. F. (1994). Organizational and population level learning as engines for career transitions. *Journal of Organizational Behavior, 15*(4), 345–364. doi:10.1002/job.4030150405

Moen, P., Sweet, S., & Swisher, R. (2005). Embedded career clocks: The case of retirement planning. In MacMillan, R. (Ed.), *The structure of the life course: Standardized? Individualized? Differentiated?* (pp. 237–265). New York: Elsevier.

Neal, D. (1999). The complexity of job mobility among young men. *Journal of Labor Economics, 17*(2), 237–261. doi:10.1086/209919

Neopolitan, J. (1980). Occupational change in midcareer: An exploratory investigation. *Journal of Vocational Behavior, 16*(2), 212–225. doi:10.1016/0001-8791(80)90052-4

Noll, C. L., & Wilkins, M. (2002). Critical skills of IS professionals: A model for curriculum development. *Journal of Information Technology Education, 1*(3), 143–156.

Panko, R. (2008). IT employment prospects: Beyond the dotcom bubble. *European Journal of Information Systems, 17*(3), 182–197. doi:10.1057/ejis.2008.19

Papastergiou, M. (2008). Are computer science and Information Technology still masculine fields? High school students' perceptions and career choices. *Computers & Education, 51*(2), 594–608. doi:10.1016/j.compedu.2007.06.009

Parker, S. K., Williams, H. M., & Turner, N. (2006). Modeling the antecedents of proactive behavior at work. *The Journal of Applied Psychology, 91*(3), 636–652. doi:10.1037/0021-9010.91.3.636

Paullay, I. M., Alliger, G. M., & Stone-Romero, E. F. (1994). Construct validation of two instruments designed to measure job involvement and work centrality. *The Journal of Applied Psychology, 79*(2), 224–228. doi:10.1037/0021-9010.79.2.224

Poon, J. M. L. (2004). Career commitment and career success: Moderating role of emotion perception. *Career Development International, 9*(4), 374–390. doi:10.1108/13620430410544337

Pringle, R., Nielsen, S., Hellens, L. V., Greenhill, A., & Parfitt, L. (2000). Net gains: Success strategies of professional women in IT. In Balka, E., & Smith, R. (Eds.), *Women, work and computerization: Charting a course to the future*. Boston: Kluwer Academic Publishers.

Reich, B. H., & Kaarst-Brown, M. L. (1999). Seeding the line: Understanding the transition from IT to non-IT careers. *Management Information Systems Quarterly, 23*(3), 337–364. doi:10.2307/249467

Robertson, M., Newell, S., Swan, J., Mathiassen, L., & Bjerknes, G. (2001). The issue of gender within computing: Reflections from the UK and Scandinavia. *Information Systems Journal, 11*(2), 111–126. doi:10.1046/j.1365-2575.2001.00098.x

Rosen, B., & Jerdee, T. H. (1990). Middle and late career problems: Causes, consequences and research needs. *Human Resource Planning, 13*(1), 59–70.

Rousseau, D. M. (1989). Psychological and implied contracts in organizations. *Employee Responsibilities and Rights Journal, 2*(2), 121–139. doi:10.1007/BF01384942

Sargent, L. D., & Domberger, S. R. (2007). Exploring the development of a protean career orientation: Values and image violations. *Career Development International, 12*(6), 545–564. doi:10.1108/13620430710822010

Schein, E. H. (1971). The individual, the organization, and the career: A conceptual scheme. *The Journal of Applied Behavioral Science, 7*(4), 401–426. doi:10.1177/002188637100700401

Schein, E. H. (1978). *Career dynamics: Matching individual and organizational needs*. Reading, MA: Addison-Wesley.

Schmid, G. (2005). Social risk management through transitional labour markets. *Socio-economic Review, 4*(1), 1–33. doi:10.1093/SER/mwj029

Schultze, G., & Miller, C. (2004). The search for meaning and career development. *Career Development International, 9*(2), 142–152. doi:10.1108/13620430410526184

Seibert, S. E., Kraimer, M. L., & Liden, R. C. (2001). A social capital theory of career sucess. *Academy of Management Journal, 44*(2), 219–237. doi:10.2307/3069452

Sullivan, S. E. (1999). The changing nature of careers: A review and research agenda. *Journal of Management, 25*(3), 457–484. doi:10.1177/014920639902500308

Sullivan, S. E., & Mainiero, L. A. (2007). The changing nature of gender roles, alpha/beta careers and work-life issues. *Career Development International, 12*(3), 238–263. doi:10.1108/13620430710745881

Sumner, M., & Yager, S. (2004). *Career orientation of IT personnel*. Paper presented at the 2004 SIGMIS Conference on Computer personnel research: Careers, culture, and ethics in a networked environment.

Sumner, M., Yager, S., & Franke, D. (2005). *Career orientation and organizational commitment of IT personnel*. Paper presented at the 2005 ACM SIGMIS CPR Conference on Computer personnel research.

Todd, P. A., McKeen, J. D., & Gallupe, R. B. (1995). The evolution of IS job skills: A content analysis of IS job advertisements from 1970 to 1990. *Management Information Systems Quarterly, 19*(1), 1–27. doi:10.2307/249709

Trauth, E. M. (2002). Odd girl out: An individual differences perspective on women in the IT profession. *Information Technology & People, 15*(2), 98–118. doi:10.1108/09593840210430552

Trauth, E. M., Nielsen, S. H., & Hellens, L. A. v. (2003). Explaining the IT gender gap: Australian stories for the new millennium. *Journal of Research and Practice in Information Technology, 35*(1), 7–20.

Trauth, E. M., & Quesenberry, J. L. (2007). Gender and the Information Technology workforce: Issues of theory. In Yoong, P., & Huff, S. L. (Eds.), *Managing IT professionals in the Internet age* (pp. 18–36). Hershey, PA: Idea Group Publishing.

Van Maane, J., & Schein, E. H. (1977). Career development. In Hackman, J. R., & Suttle, J. L. (Eds.), *Improving life at work: Behavioral science approaches to organizational change* (p. 494). Santa Monica, CA: Goodyear.

van Veldhoven, M., & Dorenbosch, L. (2008). Age, proactivity and career development. *Career Development International, 13*(2), 112–131. doi:10.1108/13620430810860530

Wajcman, J. (1991). *Feminism confrots technology*. Philadelphia: Pennsylvania University Press.

Walker, J. W. (1980). *Human resources planning*. New York: McGraw-Hill Book Co.

Wanous, J. P. (1973). Effects of realistic job preview on job acceptance, job attitudes and job survival. *The Journal of Applied Psychology, 58*(3), 327–336. doi:10.1037/h0036305

Waterman, R. H. Jr, Waterman, J. A., & Collard, B. A. (1994). Toward a career-resilient workforce. *Harvard Business Review, 72*(4), 87–95.

Webster, J. (1996). *Shaping women's work: Gender, employmnent and Information Technology*. London: Longman.

Weinstein, N. D. (1980). Unrealistic optimistic about future events. *Journal of Personality and Social Psychology, 39*(5), 327–336. doi:10.1037/0022-3514.39.5.806

Wilson, F. (2003). Can't compute, won't compute: Women's participation in the culture of computing. *New Technology and Employment, 18*(2), 127–142. doi:10.1111/1468-005X.00115

Yamamoto, H. (2006). The relationship between employees' inter-organizational career orientation and their career strategies. *Career Development International, 11*(3), 243–264. doi:10.1108/13620430610661768

Zhang, W. (2007). Why IS: Understanding undergraduate students' intentions to choose an Information System major. *Journal of IS Education, 18*(5), 447–458.

Zikic, J., Novicevic, M. M., Harvey, M., & Breland, J. (2006). Repatriate career exploration: A path to career growth and success. *Career Development International, 11*(7), 633–649. doi:10.1108/13620430610713490

ADDITIONAL READING

Allen, T. J., & Katz, R. (1985). The Dual Ladder: Motivational Solution or Managerial Delusion? *R & D Management, 16*(2), 185–197. doi:10.1111/j.1467-9310.1986.tb01171.x

Arthur, M. B., & Rousseau, D. M. (Eds.). (2001). *The Boundaryless Career: A New Employment Principle for a New Organizational Era*. New York, NY: Oxford University Press.

Bardwick, J. (1986). *The Plateauing Trap*. New York, NY: Amacon.

Baruch, Y. (2004). Transforming careers:from linear to multidirectional career paths: Organizational and individual perspectives. *Career Development International, 9*(1), 58–73. doi:10.1108/13620430410518147

Baruch, Y. (2006). Career development in organizations and beyond: Balancing traditional and contemporary viewpoints. *Human Resource Management Review, 16*(2), 125–138. doi:10.1016/j.hrmr.2006.03.002

Bird, A. (1994). Careers as Repositories of Knowledge: A New Perspective on Boundaryless Careers. *Journal of Organizational Behavior, 15*(4), 325–344. doi:10.1002/job.4030150404

Brooke, L. (2009). Prolonging the careers of older Information Technology workers: continuity, exit or retirement transitions? *Ageing and Society, 29*(1), 237–256. doi:10.1017/S0144686X0800768X

Brotheridge, C. M., & Power, J. L. (2008). Are career centers worthwhile?: Predicting unique variance in career outcomes through career center usage. *Career Development International, 13*(6), 480–496. doi:10.1108/13620430810901651

Cabrera, E. F. (2009). Protean organizations: Reshaping work and careers to retain female talent. *Career Development International, 14*(2), 186–201. doi:10.1108/13620430910950773

Chesebrough, P. H., & Davis, G. B. (1983). Planning a career path in Information Systems. *Journal of Systems Management, 34*(1), 6–13.

Converse, P. D., Oswald, F. L., Gillespie, M. A., Field, K. A., & Bizot, E. B. (2004). Matching Individuals to Occupations Using Abilities and the O*Net. *Personnel Psychology, 57*(2), 451–487. doi:10.1111/j.1744-6570.2004.tb02497.x

Danziger, N., Rachman-Moore, D., & Valency, R. (2008). The construct validity of Schein's career anchors orientation inventory. *Career Development International, 13*(1), 7–19. doi:10.1108/13620430810849506

Defillippi, R. J., & Arthur, M. B. (1994). The Boundaryless Career: A Competency-Based Perspective. *Journal of Organizational Behavior, 15*(4), 307–324. doi:10.1002/job.4030150403

DeLong, T. J. (1982). Reexamining the Career Anchor Model. *Personnel, 59*(3), 50–61.

Gibson, D. E. (2004). Role models in career development: New directions for theory and research. *Journal of Vocational Behavior, 65*(1), 134–156. doi:10.1016/S0001-8791(03)00051-4

Gibson, P. (2004). Where to from here? A narrative approach to career counseling. *Career Development International, 9*(2), 176–189. doi:10.1108/13620430410526201

Gilbert, G. R., Sohi, R. S., & McEachern, A. G. (2008). Measuring work preferences: A multidimensional tool to enhance career self-management. *Career Development International, 13*(1), 56–78. doi:10.1108/13620430810849542

Ginzberg, M. J., & Baroudi, J. J. (1988). MIS careers - a theoretical perspective. *Communications of the ACM, 31*(5), 586–594. doi:10.1145/42411.42422

Granrose, C. S., & Portwood, J. (1987). Matching individual career plans and organizational career management. *Academy of Management Journal, 30*(4), 669–720. doi:10.2307/256156

Greller, M. M. (2006). Hours invested in professional development during late career as a function of career motivation and satisfaction. *Career Development International, 11*(6), 544–559. doi:10.1108/13620430610692944

Hall, D. T. (2004). The protean career: A quarter-century journey. *Journal of Vocational Behavior*, *65*(1), 1–13. doi:10.1016/j.jvb.2003.10.006

Herriot, P., Gibson, G., Pemberton, C., & Pinder, R. (1993). Dashed hopes: Organizational determinants and personal perceptions of managerial careers. *Journal of Occupational and Organizational Psychology*, *66*(2), 115–123.

Higgins, M. C. (2001). Changing Careers: The Effects of Social Context. *Journal of Organizational Behavior*, *22*(6), 595–618. doi:10.1002/job.104

Igbaria, M., Greenhaus, J. H., & Parasuraman, S. (1991). Career Orientations of MIS Employees: An Empirical Analysis. *Management Information Systems Quarterly*, *15*(2), 151–169. doi:10.2307/249376

Ituma, A., & Simpson, R. (2006). The chameleon career: An exploratory study of the work biography of Information Technology workers in Nigeria. *Career Development International*, *11*(1), 48–65. doi:10.1108/13620430610642372

Kanter, R. M. (1991). The future of bureaucracy and hierarchy in organizational theory: a report from the field. In Bourdieu, P., & Coleman, J. S. (Eds.), *Social Theory for a Changing Society*. London: Westview Press.

Kellett, J. B., Humphrey, R. H., & Sleeth, R. G. (2009). Career development, collective efficacy, and individual task performance. *Career Development International*, *14*(6), 534–546. doi:10.1108/13620430910997286

Loogma, K., Ümarik, M., & Vilu, R. (2004). Identification-flexibility dilemma of IT specialists. *Career Development International*, *9*(3), 323–348. doi:10.1108/13620430410535878

Love, M. S. (2007). Security in an insecure world: An examination of individualism-collectivism and psychological sense of community at work. *Career Development International*, *12*(3), 304–320. doi:10.1108/13620430710745917

Mainiero, L. A., & Sullivan, S. E. (2005). Kaleidoscope careers: an alternate explanation for the opt-out revolution. *The Academy of Management Executive*, *19*(1), 106–124.

McDonald, P., Brown, K., & Bradley, L. (2005). Have traditional career paths given way to protean ones?: Evidence from senior managers in the Australian public sector. *Career Development International*, *10*(2), 109–129. doi:10.1108/13620430510588310

Peel, S., & Inkson, K. (2004). Contracting and careers: choosing between self and organ. *Career Development International*, *9*(6), 542–558. doi:10.1108/13620430410559142

Poon, J. M. L. (2004). Career commitment and career success: moderating role of emotion perception. *Career Development International*, *9*(4), 374–390. doi:10.1108/13620430410544337

Rousseau, D. M. (1989). Psychological and implied contracts in organizations. *Employee Responsibilities and Rights Journal*, *2*(2), 121–139. doi:10.1007/BF01384942

Schein, E. H. (1971). The individual, the organization, and the career: A conceptual scheme. *The Journal of Applied Behavioral Science*, *7*(4), 401–426. doi:10.1177/002188637100700401

Schein, E. H. (1978). *Career Dynamics: Matching individual and organizational needs*. Reading, MA: Addison-Wesley.

Skilton, P. F., & Bravo, J. (2008). Do social capital and project type vary across career paths in project-based work?: The case of Hollywood personal assistants. *Career Development International*, *13*(5), 381–401. doi:10.1108/13620430810891437

Trauth, E. M., & Quesenberry, J. L. (2007). Gender and the Information Technology Workforce: Issues of Theory. In Yoong, P., & Huff, S. L. (Eds.), *Managing IT professionals in the Internet age* (pp. 18–36). Hershey, PA: Idea Group Publishing.

Wise, A. J., & Millward, L. J. (2005). The experiences of voluntary career change in 30-somethings and implications for guidance. *Career Development International*, *10*(5), 400–417. doi:10.1108/13620430510615328

Zikic, J., Novicevic, M. M., Harvey, M., & Breland, J. (2006). Repatriate career exploration: a path to career growth and success. *Career Development International*, *11*(7), 633–649. doi:10.1108/13620430610713490

KEY TERMS AND DEFINITIONS

IT Careers: IT specific careers represents a separated notion from the general concept of career in order to focus specific issues and problems of the sector.

Career: Career represents the evolution of an individual along life and comprises all experiences, abilities, knowledge and skills that the individual possess.

Career Development: Career development is the evolution of career over a period of time and using some external sources for achieving the career development goals.

Career Management: Career management represents the management of employees' career development and comprises related practices such as mentoring, sponsorship, and training.

Globalization: Globalization is the phenomenon in which limitation barriers, such as geographical or temporal ones, are reduced or even eliminated.

Career Paths: Career path is the trajectory that an individual will follow in order to achieve some goals.

Boundaryless Career: Boundaryless career represents the globalization of career, that is, individual transcending psychical and psychological boundaries, establishing new career opportunities.

Section 4
Executive Perspectives

In this section of the book, we have an opportunity to hear the experience from IT leaders.

Chapter 15
Building Great Talent and Effective Teams

Marianne Broadbent
EWK International, Australia & Arbiter Leadership Technologies, Australia*

ABSTRACT

A successful IT organization demands having the right talent that works effectively and efficiently together. IT managers must focus on identifying the right people and then continuously build and develop the respective talent, while ensuring the cohesiveness of the team dynamics. The valuable vignettes illustrate the "know and grow" focus of this important chapter.

GREAT CIOS NEED GREAT TEAMS

The era of the 'hero CEO' has now passed, and so should the era of the 'hero CIO'. Great leaders lead great teams. They don't do it on their own. They work with their team, their peer colleagues, and the rest of the executives and CEO to set the vision and identify what it takes to get there. They are dependent on their team members for follow through and dependent on their broader team to exercise leadership that is consistent with the desired culture and values of their organization.

Two areas enable CIOs to build the 'bench strength' that they need. The first is spending time and energy on building their talent; on getting the

right people and developing them well. The second is a genuine focus on improving how those people work together – on taking into account and building real teams, not just a group of direct reports.

This chapter focuses on these two areas. They are interrelated in that great teams are enabled by effective management of talent, as well as focusing on team dynamics and mutual accountabilities.

So what is Talent Management? Why does it matter? How does it help build great teams?

EFFECTIVE TALENT AND TEAM MANAGEMENT IS NOW A 'MUST DO'

Conscientious talent management and succession planning is now a mainstream expectation for all

DOI: 10.4018/978-1-60960-535-3.ch015

executives. Focusing on talent management is no longer something to do when things slow down, but a 'must do' so that you can deal effectively with growth, with changing or shifting demands, be they to contain costs, develop innovative ways to delight customers or integrate a newly acquired business.

But too many executives–and organizations generally–continue to underestimate the risk they place themselves and their organizations in by thinking of talent management, succession planning, and team dynamics as something to focus on next week, next month or next year.

WHAT IF YOU WANT TO TAKE ON A LINE OF BUSINESS ROLE IN YOUR ORGANIZATION?

In conversation with a CIO recently (let's call her Debra) we were discussing her future career options. Debra had terrific experience as an IT professional and manager, including three years working for a respected consulting firm (largely in the IT area), and was now concluding her third year as CIO. While her performance was well regarded in the company, we agreed that if she really wanted to be considered as a potential CEO she needed to have relevant and recent experience managing a line of business and delivering on a P/L. She became very interested in the option of taking on the position of General Manager of one of the company's business lines, a position which was becoming available due to an impending retirement.

My immediate question to Debra was what was the strength of her IT Leadership team? How many potential internal candidates would there be for her CIO position? The question was really about the potential risk she was proposing to her CEO in departing her current position. To what extent could she honestly indicate that the risk was low because she had a very good team

with one or more individuals whom the CEO and his executive peers would be comfortable about seeing 'step up' into the CIO position?

Debra blanched somewhat indicating that she was always going to get around to some serious focus on the whole matter of succession planning, but there were always more urgent priorities. While she had a good team, perhaps she hadn't put the time and effort into careful talent development and management. Two on the team could potentially 'step up', but not just yet. And then there was the problem of the next layer down – the pipeline into the IT Leadership team, which was a bit thin.

The immediate outcome was that Debra did not indicate an interest in the forthcoming business division GM role to her CEO. Instead she indicated that she would be keen to take on such a role in about two years, when her team had the 'bench strength' it needed so that several of her team could be in the candidate pool for a search for a new CIO if she transferred to another position in the company.

GOOD TALENT AND TEAM MANAGEMENT MAXIMIZES ORGANIZATIONAL PERFORMANCE AND MINIMIZES RISK

Debra's experience is not uncommon. If you are a well regarded executive, your CEO and peers want to know that you have managed the company's risk if you want an internal transfer, or if you are unfortunate enough to be in an accident, suffer serious illness or just decide it's time for a 'seachange'. The best compliment any executive can receive is that they have built a sustainable team that is not dependent for its success on one person – you as the leader.

Great talent will go to where it is appreciated, valued, and encouraged to thrive. If you want that talent to be part of your team–and remain part of your team—it requires serious and genuine focus on knowing and growing the capabilities that you have. In the long term, it's much more effective to develop and nurture the talent you have than constantly bringing new people in, especially at a senior level. Sure, you need some turnover to refresh a team, and sometimes to help staff or backfill for new developments, but constantly having to recruit externally through lack of talent development internally demoralizes people. It's just poor management.

GOOD TALENT MANAGEMENT REQUIRES SYSTEMATIC FOCUS ON CAPABILITIES

Good talent management starts with a systematic approach to understanding the real potential of your current talent pool. It's more than ensuring 360 degree reviews and performance appraisals are completed each year, and it's more than sending messages by skewing bonus pools for performance. If done well, these are important sources of (hopefully) critical and constructive feedback to team members. But they usually don't provide an objective and in-depth review of an individual's real capabilities in the context.

Gain objective and actionable insights into your team's—and their team's—technical managerial and leadership capabilities of the potential contribution to your organization.

The essence of good talent management can be summarized into four actions:

1. Gain objective and actionable insights into your team's—and their team's—technical managerial and leadership capabilities
2. Act on those insights, not just once, but constantly, taking a longitudinal and integrated approach to tracking developments over time
3. Identify or create development programs tailored for individuals (and teams) to meet your organization's needs

4. Go external for talent when you have to (and use a well regarded Search firm to assist you)

1. Gain Objective and Actionable Insights into Capabilities

It's hard to develop an individual's capabilities if you don't really understand where they are right now. As leadership consultancy practitioners, EWK International draws on a very grounded Capability Framework built up through working with hundreds of organizations and thousands of individuals globally both through Leadership Capability Assessments and Executive Searches. Other organizations that operate in this area will have their version of this. The purpose here is simply to illustrate where and how these approaches assist executives with the challenges of talent management and succession planning. An outline of the key steps in the usual process is depicted in Figure 1. The actual approach is customized for each organization.

This process is extremely helpful both for the organization and for the individuals themselves. Depending on the objectives and focus we often include as part of the process individual Emotional Intelligence (EI) assessments. This is usually done in an objective way using EI assessment such as those used by the Canadian based MHS group

Depicted below in Figure 2 are the key areas of EI as assessed as part of that exercise which can be completed online by participants. It can be particularly useful for those with a technology background to understand some of their key behaviors and motivators. The learning is often about the combination of attributes of an individual's EI. The process requires too a good facilitator who is able to assist individuals to put their EI in context and to work with the strategies for improvement that usually come with EI individual reports

Janine was a newly appointed Business Technology leader for a consumer goods firm. She

247

Figure 1. Know and grow your team capabilities (©2010, ARBITER Leadership Technologies™ Used with permission.)

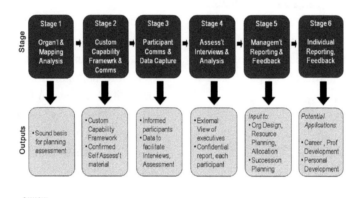

needed to gain a quick understanding of her team. We gave her feedback initially on the organizational and structural changes she was planning to make. When she had settled on the first phase of new organizational arrangements and revised positions, we worked with her staff to develop position descriptions and a role-specific Capability Framework for each. This framework identified the specific leadership, management and techni-

cal requirements for each role. Each member of the team, and then many of their direct reports, was included in a process to understand their track record and potential, particularly in light of the new structure, focus and positions. In the end the new team comprised the majority of the previous incumbents, two from the next level down, and two positions became the subject of an external search due to lack of specific experience and

Figure 2. Understanding your emotional intelligence (©2010, ARBITER Leadership Technologies™ and MHS. Used with permission.)

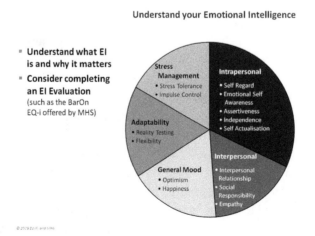

Figure 3. Global Energy Company: Building in agility for new demands and capabilities (©2010,AR-BITER Leadership Technologies™ Used with permission.)

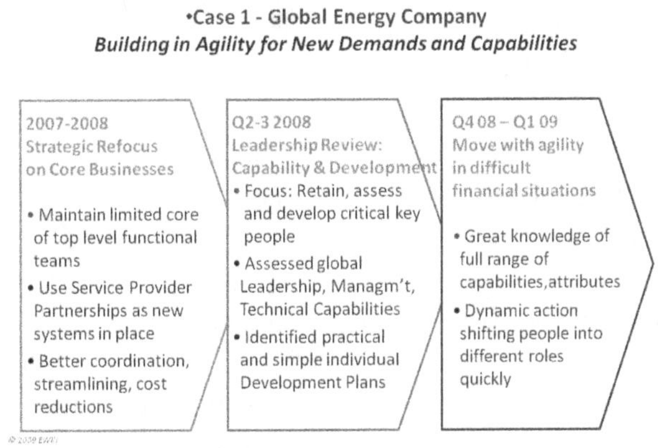

•Case 1 - Global Energy Company
Building in Agility for New Demands and Capabilities

capabilities amongst the top 20 or so in the Business Technology team.

2. Act on Insights and Take a Longitudinal and Integrated Approach to Capability Development

When business technology leaders take on a 'know and grow' approach it is critical to not raise expectations that remain unfulfilled. When leadership capability and development needs assessment are undertaken the results need to be acted on – and in a timely way. A good leader knows there will be some hard decisions to make and will make them.

Our experience is that when a process is transparent and fair people welcome the results and the action. Often you are surfacing what has been simmering under the surface for years in finally recognizing real talent and contribution. It's about making visible and tangible what is often invisible but the source of well founded mutterings. At the same time we find that others are often relieved to have honest and helpful feedback that enables them to make decisions they might have put off for years.

Organizations undertake a capability development assessment for different reasons. We worked

with a global energy company (See Figure 3) when a CEO was appointed and shifted the balance of accountabilities – shifting much more to the business units while retaining a better defined – but smaller - set of services from the headquarters group. This meant that there were higher levels of capability required in the business units as their accountabilities both broadened and deepened. We worked with them to identify the real capabilities and development needs of the technology team at both the whole-of-organization and business unit levels. This enabled them to get a much better understanding of different types of capabilities. While this had an immediate impact on where some staff were deployed, it was also very useful when the Global Financial Crisis hit and they had to work through which staff would be most effective in what locations. Their business performed unevenly across business units and across the globe. A deeper knowledge of the capabilities of team members meant that they were able to match needs with resources much more quickly than they would have been able to do without undertaking the assessment process.

If you want to send a message to your team about what really matters in terms of talent potential and behaviors, it is important to ensure that there is internal consistency in how you assess and develop current staff, how you reward staff and what you look for in new people to join the team. We are currently working with a services provider to complement the talent identification approaches they already have in place. In some ways, they have been more focused on talent management than other firms due to both organic and acquisitive growth. But their efforts in this area comprise a series of separate activities rather than a holistic approach. We are assisting them to integrate their currently disparate and disconnected approaches to assessment for external searches, for talent development and for appraisal.

3. Identify or Create Development Programs Tailored for Individuals (and Teams) to Meet your Organization's Needs

Usually the higher you go in organizations; the more individual and specific development programs need to be for individuals and organizations to really benefit. They might include mentoring, perhaps from an individual with a very different background, perhaps from a colleague on the same level, or perhaps some 'upwards' mentoring

from some Generation Y professionals, especially if your organization works in consumer-related areas. Development programs could include being part of a team in another part of the organization, being seconded for 12 months to a new business, a 'sabbatical' to pursue a 'pet project', or acting as 'chief of staff' for one of the executives. It could include a short course at a national business school, or one located elsewhere. There are many possibilities. The key criterion is what is most likely to further develop the capabilities of the individual to contribute to both their success and the success of the business or organization.

Figure 4 presents on one page a summary of the individual needs of team members (A-J across the top) with the recommended actions. It is also important to act on the fact that this should not be a 'one off' exercise: it needs to be part of a continuum of assessment with a clear set of accountabilities for monitoring the implementation the recommended development programs.

4. Go External for Talent when you have to

Organizations that have a strong focus on developing their internal talent tend to have a much more focused approach when they need to recruit exter-

Figure 4. Sample summary leadership development Matrixes (©2010, ARBITER Leadership Technologies™ Used with permission.)

Sample Leadership Development Summary Matrix

Participant	A	B	C	D	E	F	G	H	I	J
Personal Support										
Coaching	x				x					
Mentoring Support		x	x		x					x
Shadowing							x			
Manager Feedback								x		
Networking	x				x					
Mentoring Others		x	x			x	x			
Role Enrichment/Secondment										
Role Expansion					x					
Line of Business Role					x					x
Secondment Short term										x
Promotional Offer										
Greater Responsibility/ Promotion									x	x
Executive Education										
Short Courses		x	x							
Exec Education			x	x			x			
Skills Development				x					x	

nally. They are in tune with the real capabilities that they need, and with the values and cultural attributes they are seeking in external candidates. Their teams have a better 'shared understanding' of what they want and need in talent that they are seeking to bring into the organization. In short, their external recruitment is likely to entail less risk than those who have not focused so much on internal talent management.

SUCCESSION PLANNING SHOULD NOW BE SEEN AS A BASIC REQUIREMENT

A further evolution of talent management is having an understanding of the talent pool available for succession at multiple levels in the organization. While you can never guarantee who should succeed whom and when, an extension to effective development of your talent is mapping the potential trajectory of professionals, managers and executives against incumbents. The goal is to ensure you have a well developing pool of talent to meet succession needs. That pool of talent becomes smaller the higher you go in the organization, or the more specific and specialized the technical

capabilities. One of the major concerns of some organizations today is the ageing and impending retirement of baby boomers and the expertise and experiences that they will take with them – though the GFC (recent Global Financial Crisis) has deferred the retirement of some of this group due to depletion of their savings. Understanding exactly what stage and age your workforce is at now is a basic requirement, both for managing the workforce today and for managing succession.

Figure 5 depicts some different approaches to looking at the current status and challenges of workforce planning and visualizing the availability of future talent. (drawing on the work of Kerlin, McGaw and Wolf, 2008). For example some organizations we have worked with take a long term view of their talent looking at employee potential and doing age profiles of their workforce. Figure 5 presents this visually - mapping specific roles against the potential of the individuals in those roles and their likely time to retirement. This is particularly important with organizations with 'baby boomer' bulges where they are likely to have significant talent nearing retirement age. Presenting this in a visual form helps them identify their likely talent 'gaps' in the short, medium and longer terms.

Figure 5. Visualizing needs and Potential (Adapted from "Transforming Government: Leadership and Talent," Autumn 2008, © McKinsey & Company. Used with Permission)

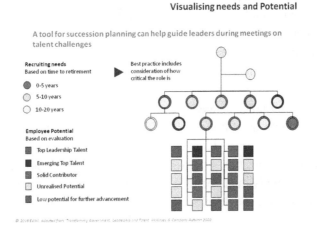

CONSCIENTIOUS TALENT MANAGEMENT IS JUST GOOD MANAGEMENT

The expectations for effective executives will continue to evolve – as they have for the past 50 years. But the talent bar has been elevated. Companies and their boards are seeking to appoint executives who have the acumen to deal with volatile shifts in their competitiveness while concurrently satisfying shareholders and accommodating regulators. Both business and government are increasingly seeking executives who combine multiple sector experience to work through the often conflicting demands for efficiencies, creativity and meeting citizen expectations. Amidst these expectations we are experiencing accelerated change as technology developments fundamentally alter how organizations operate. Some of the fallout from the GFC is a different level of accountability and different set of expectations of those in the private sector. Higher expectations for executives and their teams, and their criticality to the business have raised the profile and importance of talent management and succession planning. There is no readily obtainable pool of great talent to meet all the needs of business, industry and government – no matter what the state of business, global and local economies.

Organizations that want to compete successfully both in their business and in the talent marketplace need to 'know and grow' the capabilities they have. They need to understand what motivates people, and understand the strategically significant leadership, managerial and technical capabilities that they have and that they need. Smart organizations put in place specific strategies to meet the capability and developmental needs of their talent pool and for smooth transitions during successions. They develop programs tailored for individuals to meet the organization's future needs, understanding that if individuals believe their capabilities are continuing to be developed

by their organization, they are less likely to want to go elsewhere.

EFFECTIVE TEAMS ARE CRITICAL TO THE SUCCESS OF CIO'S

While getting the talent gene pool right is important, challenges don't stop there. It is critical for executives and managers to work on creating and nurturing a real team rather than a collection of smart and motivated individuals. This requires hard work and is often underestimated. The key dysfunctions of teams are well described by Lencioni of The Table Group (Lencioni, 2005). It starts with trust: trust amongst team members is the bedrock of effective teams. Without that foundation of trust, it's hard to deal with conflict in a constructive way. Team members don't have the necessary commitment and interpersonal discomfort means that team members won't hold each other accountable.

There is the issue of 'which team am I on'.

This is a hard decision for, say members of the CIO's team – it is that team that should be their primary team. At the same time the CIO's primary team is the executive team of which he or she is a member. The pyramid of team dysfunctions is well depicted in Figure 6.

ACT ON THE FIVE DYSFUNCTIONS OF TEAMS

While developing and sustaining great teams is hard work, the path to achieving these is reasonably clear. There are some simple approaches to tackle each of the five dysfunctions indicated above. These need to be tackled in turn, starting with building trust, where the leader of the team needs to share their concerns and vulnerabilities with the team. Leading by example is critical is at all stages of team building.

Figure 6. The Five Dysfunctions of a Team: A Leadership Fable (Lencioni, 2005; © 2002 Wiley. Reproduced with permission of John Wiley & Sons, Inc.)

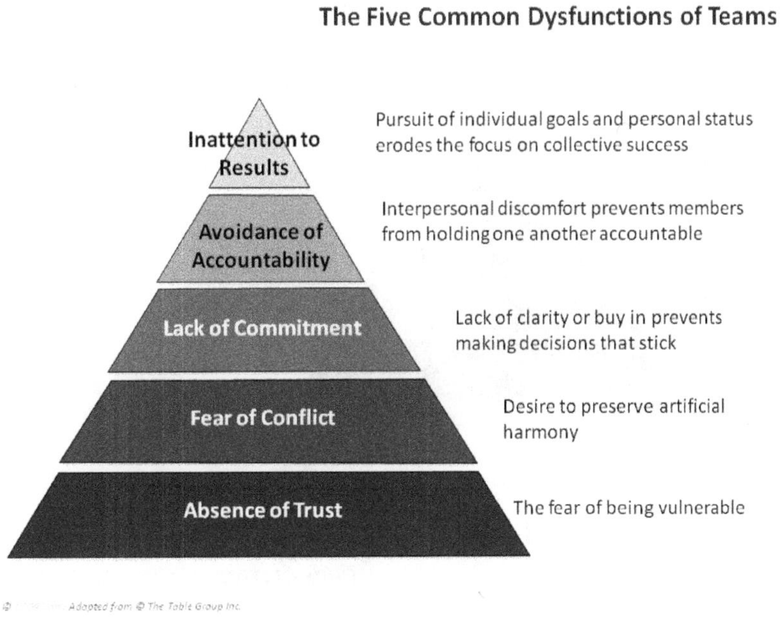

The Five Common Dysfunctions of Teams

Leaders need to mine for conflict, not pretend that it isn't there and achieve a false notion of harmony. Team meetings need to be used carefully to ensure there is open and transparent discussion and there is real clarity and closure of issues. People need to be held accountable – by each other – that is the test of really effective team, that each person feels comfortable about holding their colleagues to account. Difficult issues need to be confronted, dealt with and then the team and the individuals need to move on. Taking collective responsibility shows real team maturity- where the individuals are comfortable with both themselves and with each other. When a CIO has such a team, there are few challenges that can't be effectively tackled.

LESSONS LEARNED

Know and Grow Individual and Team Capabilities

Nurturing great talent and building effective teams is a key objective for most leaders. However not everyone tackles it in a pragmatic, constructive and practical way so that it has real impact on the individuals, the team and business.

From working with executive teams, there are clear lessons that increase the likelihood of real impact:

It's hard to develop your team if you don't really understand the capabilities, aspirations and motivation of each individual. The ability to be an effective *team member* is also now critical While undertaking individual capability and development needs assessment can be seen as confronting (at least initially), it can be done with real engagement and respect. The benefits are real and are appreciated by individuals as well as the team as a whole. It is only when individuals really understand themselves that they are able to reach their full potential as leaders and managers.

The best starting is with the top level executives themselves. There is no substitute for leading by example.

Figure 7. Enabling Teams to be Effective. From The Five Dysfunctions of a Team: A Leadership Fable, (Lencioni, 2005; © 2002 Wiley. Reproduced with permission of John Wiley & Sons, Inc.)

To Keep Talent, Manage it Well

Remember, great talent will go to where it is appreciated, valued, and encouraged to thrive. Effective talent management requires taking thoughtful and considered actions today. It's not something to do next month or next year. By then the 'talent' will have walked and it's very hard to get it back.

REFERENCES

Kerlin, M. D., McGaw, D., & Wolf, W. (2008). Planning for the next generation. *Transforming Government, 3*(Autumn), 8–13.

Lencioni, P. (2005). *Overcoming the five dysfunctions of a team.* San Francisco, CA: Jossey-Bass.

ENDNOTE

*   This research was supported by **ARBITER** Leadership Technologies™, a company wholly owned by EWK International Australia.

Chapter 16
Building IT Capacity for Leadership in a New Age

Mary Jo Greil
Carson Greil Group, LLC, USA

Elaine Millam
WorkWise Coaching and Consulting, USA

ABSTRACT

Throughout society, there is a tremendous need to make the technology changes our world demands. These solutions can only be created by professionals in the technology areas who are willing to step up to leadership roles. All too often these people are overlooked when intentional leadership programs are offered. As HR functions are being scaled back and often outsourced, there is less focus on people development across organizations.

Information Technology professionals have a strong desire to be associated with organizations that provide ongoing development. Professional development becomes the antidote for attracting and retaining the best of the IT community.

Who is responsible for identifying the focus of people development and ensuring that the development of future leaders is being given appropriate attention and support? These authors propose it begins with top management and includes both HR and IT functions in a highly collaborative and integrated fashion. Such collaboration is required for the people development investment to be sustainable.

INTRODUCTION

"Having worked in senior level IT executive search for the past 15 years, I have noticed significant

change. My clients are now asking me to find the IT leaders with strong commercial acumen and strong business skills. They want IT leaders who can chase the revenue, who can use IT commercially, who can create revenue through the

DOI: 10.4018/978-1-60960-535-3.ch016

innovative use of IT. Gone are the days when IT leaders should be highly technically experienced trouble-shooters". – Simon Marcer, Dec. 2009

Effective organizations create a people development culture that directly aligns with its organization and business strategies. Leaders in these effective organizations place a high priority on people development and have an understanding that their competitive advantage is through their people. It is only through energized and engaged people within a resilient learning environment that the possibility is created for innovation to thrive. These same organizational leaders assume responsibility for the development of their people in alignment with the strategic direction of their organization. Typically, they look to HR leadership to assist in this effort. HR leaders must have the strategic insight and organizational savvy to be full partners with top management to impact transformational change.

Recently, however, the impact of the broader economic downturn has created a tendency for organizations and their leaders to pull back from what they have practiced in the past. Often they are scaling back their HR organizations, cutting back on their people development processes, and responding to what they see as pressure to stick to the highest order priorities of keeping the business in survival mode. Indeed, this reflects short-term thinking and can easily dismantle a whole system in the long run.

Meanwhile, every day in the headlines there is a story about some major issue that demands a technology solution or has a technology implication. An amazing number of technical advances addressing human needs have occurred in the 20th century, changing people's lives. These advances began as no more than ideas and dreams, and were brought to reality by passionate pioneers who devoted their lives to the improvement of the human condition. These people were creative

and innovative doers who leveraged their inventions to have massive impact on society. Today, there are fourteen grand issues that have been identified by industry and academia that require technical solutions in the 21st Century, including environmentally friendly power, capturing the carbon dioxide, countermeasures for nitrogen cycle problems, "reverse-engineering" the brain and 10 more (Constable & Somerville, 2008).

We are creatures of habit and any new initiative meets resistance, simply because it is difficult for us to change. It is precisely for this reason why it is imperative that Information Technology professionals become strong leaders; to not only acknowledge the emotional and political aspect of these issues, but to motivate us to move rapidly to the technical solutions for these problems. The future of our country and our world is too important to leave these major decisions to the whims of the uninformed and the special interests that will not immediately benefit from their solutions. It is paradoxical that, in the long run, the major business opportunities will lie precisely in these areas, and hence will influence the well-being of the economy and the public. The sooner they are addressed and solved, the better off economically and socially we will be.

The time is now to recognize the importance of helping professionals in Information Technology (IT) arenas to step up to embrace whatever it takes to assume leadership in a way that has never been the norm in the past. Existing organizational leaders need to take a strong, insightful role in ensuring the resources are there to assist in the people development process, leading the way by being role models for transformational change.

To this end, this chapter proposes how IT, HR and top management can work collaboratively to make the changes that bring about results for IT people as well as business—creating thriving and resilient organizations at the same time. The challenge is to suggest that IT people become strong business leaders, HR people become primary change facilitators and organizational guides focused on development and growth, and top management become models for development, self-awareness, promoting growth and change throughout their organizations. This chapter describes what it might take to create the appropriate culture and accompanying incubator for this development process, bringing forth the potential that is inherent in the IT ranks.

Can you imagine a thriving and resilient organization where employees are continually learning and experiencing a sense of accomplishment? Do you know this type of organization? How prevalent is this in IT? What impact does IT have on the enterprise? What new technical solutions are changing lives beyond the enterprise?

What is meant by being a leader? *Every* person in the organization is capable of being a potential leader. A 'leader' is not about position, but rather about demonstrating skills and capacities that influence others in positive ways in order to reach mutual goals and contribute to a broader picture of the organization. This is about continual learning and experimentation, leading to a sense of accomplishment for the whole organization.

Leadership development does not mean creating a super elite team of leaders with a self-centered focus. Rather, the development process is grounded in clarity of self-awareness and tapping into individual leader's compassion. It is through this deeper understanding of self and others, valuing the importance of knowing the pulse of the people who are working throughout the organization and learning strategies for being effective for the good of the whole system that inspires others into skillful action. This view is not a radical or recent idea. Lao-tzu wrote long ago that "leadership is service, not selfishness. The leader grows more and lasts longer by placing the well-being of all above the well-being of self alone (Lao-tzu, 6th Century BC)."

PLANNING FOR CHANGE

It all begins with a clear intention for key stakeholders (top management, HR, IT, and Board members if possible) to be working collaboratively to prepare the way to develop people for the future. Top management must genuinely believe that the future of the business is dependent upon building strong leadership throughout the organization, particularly in the technical ranks. This more often than not, requires a serious mindset change—not only to collaborate, but also to begin to see the potential for IT professionals to step into leadership roles in the business proposition.

Those HR professionals who play a strategic business role in the organization are key players in facilitating the collaborative process, as well as charting the course for assessing what is needed to awaken the whole organization to what is possible. These professionals need to know what kinds of provocative questions can and should be positioned for the collaborative change team. This team wrestles with them in order to become more reflective and capable of seeing the present organizational mindset and its impact on the business strategy and results. From this place, the team begins to consider what the collective mindset might be if new possibilities for organizational strategy, cultural change, and IT capabilities were the order of the day.

Larry Bossidy, former chairman and CEO of Allied Signal from 1991-1999, is a good example of a CEO who led the company through major transformation focused on building leadership capacity. He was convinced that Allied Signal's success was due in large part to the amount of time and emotional commitment he devoted to leadership development. He reported, "the level of excellence didn't happen by accident. "I devoted what some people considered an inordinate amount of emotional energy and time—perhaps between 30 and 40% of my day for the first two years—to hiring and developing leaders…I knew it was essential (Bossidy, 2001)."

By the time Allied Signal merged with Honeywell in 1999, Larry reports "we had delivered an almost nine-fold return for shareholders, and we had tripled our operating margins. Return on equity stood near 28%....our greatest success was the extraordinary quality of our management group…the best measure of that quality may be the number of top executives who have been recruited in the past three years to lead the organization (Bossidy, 2001, p. 119)."

Other more collaborative examples can be cited in the research over the past couple decades, showing the importance of top management's role in collaboration with HR, to better define leadership and set expectations for a culture of people development and business performance (Heskett, Jones, Loveman, Sasser, & Schlesinger, 1994). Research by the Advanced Practices Council of the Society for Information Management reported that "one of the top four best practices for CIO development is for the top executives in the firm having a strong and visible commitment to CIO development, designing a portfolio of development opportunities that will enhance the capabilities of developing incumbent leaders (Agarwal & Beath, 2007, p. 3)." These authors and others report that a key challenge for CEOs and people growing their businesses is determining whether or not they view people development as an integral part of building a business.

A very important step for change is required from top management, HR and IT working as a collaborative team to clearly determine the collective mindset and organizational beliefs regarding people development as a key driver for the business. Unless the top management group wrestles with its beliefs, assumptions, dreams and visions of possibility, it will be very difficult to change the broader organizational mindsets and promote the possibilities for IT professionals to step up to something that was never expected before. It begins with careful consideration of what is possible and what we expect to be different?

Organizational culture change is not for the faint of heart or the quick-fix approach. Serious change demands serious people along with serious action. Those organizations seeking to adapt in these days of turbulent change need a new kind of leadership capacity to reframe the dilemmas they face, to dialogue on options, and reshape their futures continually. The world is facing rapid and shifting change, everyone knows it. More often these days, top management is frustrated with how to integrate systems, how to collaborate with partners and work cross-functionally to bring about seamless change. Frustrated, they work harder and longer, being unsure of where to take action first.

The days of the heroic leader are over and the "unfolding, emergent realization of leadership as a collective activity is intentional and very, very important (Center for Creative Leadership White Paper, 2009)." A recent CCL study found that the most important capabilities needed by organizations in the future are among the weakest competencies for today's individual leaders—leading people, strategic planning, inspiring commitment and managing change. This same study found that the nature of effective leadership is changing. Approaches focused on flexibility, collaboration, crossing boundaries and collective leadership are more important than the basics of making the numbers (CCL, Changing Nature of Leadership, 2008).

How does one launch organizational change that models these capabilities? Working for Global IT for a Fortune 50 corporation, cross-organization collaboration was witnessed when major data centers were consolidated to the new corporate operation headquarters site. There was a clear goal and adrenalin was high to achieve the stretch objectives. Over the course of three months, three data centers were relocated. However, cross-organization collaboration was short lived. Less than twenty-five percent of the employees from each of the data centers were offered the opportunity to move and decided to relocate. Also, the VP of IT had created an environment of competition among the data centers, which did not inspire consolidation nor collaboration. Out of 500 IT employees, approximately half were new employees and the remaining half were employees moving from the competing data centers. They brought with them different organizational cultures and IT management approaches and practices.

As a first step to bring organizational alignment, the Global IT leadership team conducted a communications survey using the services of an outside consultant who ensured that the results were anonymous. A communications planning team with senior leaders from across Global IT developed a listing of actions that were requested through the communications survey. Then, the CIO, HR and us met with employees in groups of forty to fifty to review with them the actions and, once again, gather their input about the actions that were being proposed. The communications planning team continued overseeing the progress of the actions and describing the results through various communications vehicles (e.g. newsletter, brown-bags with the CIO, quarterly meetings, etc.). Through frequent communications, the results of the actions repeatedly referenced that these actions were requested by the employees through the communications survey. In other words, the employees' viewpoints were being heard, and acted upon, and progress was made.

Managing effective communications was the start of an organization-wide effort to increase the leadership capacity of the IT lead team, shift the decision-making culture that expanded the voice of the employees, and aligned the work, processes, and systems to be more effective. Over the course of three years at least 80% of the strategic plan was accomplished. Additionally Global IT was rated #1 in quality management across the entire corporation for two consecutive years. Employee satisfaction was increased and the management bench strength was expanded.

Key questions early in the cultural mindset change process to ponder might be:

- What is a leader in this organization? What do we want it to be?
- What are the challenges that s/he has to face?
- What is the leadership culture that blends this with our strategic direction?
- What mindsets today are helping forces? Why? What's possible?
- What is IT being called to be for the good of the enterprise?
- What results do we want to see happen? Why? What's possible?
- How do we make it happen?
- What do we want our organization to look like in three years?

INTENTIONALLY CREATING THE CULTURE FOR COLLABORATION AND ENGAGEMENT

Culture is primarily about the meaning that people make of their worlds, the tools they have to deal with in that world, the norms and the organization's DNA. The focus for culture change is about intentionally and proactively building capability for new ways of thinking about the organization and getting the work done. This creates new ways of thinking and behaving that brings about specific outcomes that reflect the organization's vision for success. As business strategies get more complex, so does the complexity of cultural capacity for implementation.

How does an effective organization begin to create a culture for collaboration and engagement that reflects a high value for people development? It is our belief that the term "leadership" needs clarity of understanding. Development of both individual leader capacity and organizational leadership capacity are equally important ingredients to include in the transformation process. Learning must take place in the collective, not just on the part of individuals if organizations are to gain a new perspective. Real breakthroughs can only happen when both are addressed simultaneously. Hence, assessing the culture for individual and/or collective gaps between today's way of being/doing and tomorrow's needs is critically important. Where, how and with whom do we need to collaborate and for what end? Who needs to be engaged and how? Deep, provocative questions about the organizational mindset become part of the rigor of collaborative leadership inquiry and challenge, beginning the organization on a path for transformation in its thinking.

Sharon Parks, in *Leadership Can be Taught,* suggests that "leadership for today's world requires enlarging one's capacity to see the whole board, as in a chess match—to see the complex, often volatile interdependence among the multiple systems that constitute the new commons (Parks, 2005, p.3)." Those leaders who are seeking new ways of thinking and operating are reflecting on the organizational ability to 'see the whole board.' They work with all the players across the board to hear their voices, include their thinking, and challenge the status quo. They recognize this is necessary to understanding mindsets, altering ways of viewing the situation and engaging with a new possibility. They don't pretend to have all of the answers, nor do they suggest there is a one right answer. They model actions that serve to create environments that drive performance and welcome engagement (Hay, 2010).

An example comes from helping executives to lead a significant cultural change at a health services organization over the past four years. The culture of their recent past had been one reflecting entitlement in many areas, lack of accountability and a very bureaucratic style in getting the work done. The majority of the people in the organization were dedicated and caring regarding their clients' needs and interests, hard workers and proud of their contributions to the organization. A fairly new executive group was recently put in place to lead the organization into the future and this group felt a strong desire to do something very innovative that would stimulate new possibilities,

open up the organization to more collaboration across functions/silos, and set new standards for performance. The executives themselves chose to commit to taking on a coach for each individual executive, as well as using a coach for their executive team to shape their plans. The executives began their coaching process, using a 360 feedback instrument that gathered inputs from employees throughout the organization. Each executive was required by the CEO to share their results publicly with their constituent groups, committing to deeper inquiry with these people to put together their 3-4 primary goals for change and improvement over the next year. They asked for support from their constituents to help them in making the necessary changes that were often specific to the individual and some were organizational in scope.

The executives worked hard to demonstrate their integrity with the process, reporting out regularly and including their constituents in their ongoing development process. Many significant changes were made organizationally—more inclusion of employees at all levels, more teams created for process improvements, more all-employee meetings, and new people brought into the organization, replacing some of the less than high performers. Employees were noticing changes, the executive team was genuinely communicating in a two-way process to shape a new vision for the organization, enrolling people in the excitement of what was possible.

After the first year, the executives asked the next level of senior management to follow their lead and begin a 360 feedback process, assisted by a coach, doing the same process with their direct reports. The second year, similar and even more significant shifts were becoming obvious throughout the organization—there was a growing mindset that this health services group was the best organization in California. Recognition of the dramatic change became public as they secured several awards including being rated "a best place to work" in Southern California.

In the next two years, the executives and senior leadership committed to taking on the challenge of building a coaching culture where each leader was enrolled in a series of seminars learning how to become a coaching leader. Slowly the coaching leader practices have been instilled throughout the organization with lots of collegial support for practice and ongoing learning. The organization has increasingly opened up to collaborative work processes, new innovations, and is on its way to achieving its vision. Employees are noticing a remarkable difference and saying loudly, "this is the best organization I have ever worked in. The leaders are authentic and real, willing to be vulnerable and help me be at my best, holding me and others accountable."

Once an organization has clearly assessed the present leadership culture and how it operates, it becomes easier to develop possible plans for change. The organization must then understand the drivers and core capabilities needed for the business strategy, making sure to align the culture of beliefs and leadership logic with that strategy. Giving time and attention to the beliefs that underlie the behavior and decisions, leaders can help the organization gain flexibility and nimbleness for the future. When leaders and teams slow down and are more reflective, they can better address challenges at the root level. Instead of focusing on speed, they are focusing on learning. Many right answers and better solutions are surfaced. Everyone involved is focused on recognizing the underlying assumptions, understanding the problems more clearly and integrating new perspectives that get surfaced. Being reflectives as a learning organization helps to ensure the best ideas are surfaced, conflict becomes easier because we are intentionally asking questions and discovering as a collective. This becomes the model for individual development processes as well.

CREATING AN INCUBATOR FOR DEVELOPING EMERGING LEADERS

Once the senior leadership team, including IT and HR, have begun the culture change assessment, development and actions within the collective, it is time to design the environment and process for development of the potential leaders within the IT ranks, along with other high potential leaders throughout the organization. This becomes the emerging leader program aimed at shaping a process that is multi-pronged and intentionally focused on personal and professional growth and learning.

This proposed incubator becomes the safe, supportive, and hospitable environment for participants to learn, grow, and advance their personal and professional capacity. Initially this incubator might be the pilot testing with a clear intention to mainstream the process within the organization after it has had some gestation time to ensure it leads to thriving, resilient and engaged leaders who are influencing the business success.

First and foremost is the need for senior leadership to take a very active role in shaping the intent of the incubator—expectations, scope, elements that link all components together, mentoring/coaching, and other aspects of the development process. If they leave this important role to others, the incubator process will lose its potency. Everyone in the organization follows the lead of the executive team, so their leadership role in changing the culture, creating a new mindset and shaping the development process for IT people is critical. People take their cue from the leaders at the top. The leaders set the tone, pace and an expectation for what is right and what is wrong—what is acceptable and what is not. When leaders are out in front of what they feel is important, fully engaged and modeling the way, the rest of the organization finds it much easier to follow, stepping into the new expectations.

The whole organizational system becomes the necessary and nourishing container for new leaders to become inspired and step forward to seize their creativity and innovation, while developing an ongoing agenda for their increased leading and learning processes. Unfortunately, when organizations operate as a collection of separate functions, the growth of leaders is limited. Using a systemic approach in managing the organization provides opportunities for breadth and depth in developmental experiences. Inherent in a systems approach is a common language for people development. Having a common language and effective tools for communication serves to accelerate relationship building, collaboration and results.

Facilitating and witnessing mindset change has been part of our consulting experience: Over three years, the senior management teams from nine divisions in a $7 billion sector of a Fortune 50 corporation participated in a sector-wide leadership development process. The leadership team participated first in a four day off-site session followed with classes of 20-60 people that spanned the 6,000 employee sector. During this time, the sector was recognized in the corporation for achieving the best safety record, most effective high performance systems, and improved bottom-line performance. With the direct involvement of the leadership team in learning the language, tools, and expanding their emotional intelligence, they were readily able to benefit from the results—professionally and personally. When the corporate decision was to sell some of the business units at the end of the leadership process, rather than hearing any victim perspective, the attitude from many employees was frequently stated as "I am the CEO of my life."

Having a people development orientation at the senior leadership level means that there is a recognition that transformational change does not occur instantly. Development of emerging leaders involves a planned approach that is intentionally designed to continue growing and strengthening the professional capacity throughout the organization over time. Approaches that produce authentic and sustainable leadership development

are grounded in adult development theory, are strengths based, goal-oriented and engaging. The participants leave the sessions desiring to learn more. Customized development approaches recognize the unique stages of learning and growth for each person and are carefully personalized.

Richard Strozzi-Heckler has been developing leaders among the C-Suite at AT&T, Hewlett Packard, Microsoft, the Navy, the Army and the Marines. He divides leadership into two categories—leadership as a role and leadership as a way of being. His premise is that the 'self' is the leader's primary source of power. "Clearly, intellectual capacity and specific technical skills matter, but alone they do not make a powerful leader. It's the self that is able to mobilize and motivate others, coordinate effectively with them, build trust, and generate positive moods. We have seen time and time again that the value one has as a person, that is, the self that one is, ultimately becomes the deciding factor in success as an exemplary leader (Heckler, 2008, p. 27)."

Significant results have been experienced with that same approach, starting with the 'self awareness' work. Therefore, the recommendations for creating this incubator starts with participants examining themselves first—their present situation, their assessment of who they are as people, what their strengths are, their dreams, their learning style, their life and career history up to this point, and what their contributions have been and might be in the future. All of this initial phase is aimed at building self-awareness, the foundation for their development—a beginning for the "inside-out" process of growth and learning (Millam, 2009; Cashman, 2008; Quinn, 2006).

It seems important to begin early in the process with the participants defining

- What an effective leader is/does;
- What kind of leader has inspired me and how?
- What makes a difference and how do I know?

- What kind of leader do I want to be?
- What are my strengths?
- What have been the patterns and themes in my life history?
- For what purpose do I want to be a leader?

Often, we begin the development process with several key assessment tools, including emotional capacity, 360 feedback tools, learning styles, personality profiles, values, etc. This gives the emerging leader some key data to analyze and use in creating a clear picture of his/her developmental place before s/he begins to define the vision that is pulling them toward becoming the leader s/he idealizes. If the participant has a coach/mentor it is important to enroll them in helping guide the participant to understand how to plan for movement from their starting place to their desired state. Typically, this includes building on the strengths of the individual.

It is helpful to space the various modules out (e.g. at least every two or three months) so that real applications of the leader's development work can be applied and the participant begins to take serious the impact of his/her behavior on those around him/her. From this place, the process expands to incorporating support teams to help the emerging leader with developing his or her leadership plan, with clear milestones and targets over the first year, aiming toward their vision of three years out.

It is the important to be clear about our values, beliefs, and who we were. This shapes our interactions with peers and others throughout the organizations in which we worked. Twenty-five years ago few organizations provided access to leadership development within the organization from employers. The most significant, sustainable development impacting leadership was from the inside-out. It was the individuals own personal and other intensive professional work that focused specifically on helping them to clarify who they are. This included silent retreats, journaling, workshops, readings, etc. In leaving the IT global

organization, one of the greatest compliments was from a peer. When questioning the career change, he said, "You are the soul of IT." This statement affirmed the impact such personal work had on the organization.

The type of leadership development programs that are more sustainable reflect the incubator type of process where participants can clarify their values, beliefs and personal assumptions. Leaders learn how to become more reflective about who they are in a balanced way with what they do, recognizing what is inside-out and what is outside-in. The external (outside-in), such as strategic thinking, systems thinking, organizational change management, can be woven into the participant's experience as long as sufficient time and attention is given to the internal clarification work.

A balance of some outside-in and inside-out pieces that might be considered for the incubator process might include:

- An intentional rotation process that exposes the selected participants to other functional projects or initiatives, giving them a broader perspective of the business;
- An intentional coaching and/or mentoring arrangement for each participant to be paired with someone who is invested in their development process. Ideally having a senior leader as a mentor and a willing guide can be an accelerator for them on their journey;
- Key opportunities to serve on critical cross-functional task teams, change process initiatives, and/or business development initiatives that offer explicit action learning applications;
- Work with a team of peers and superiors who serve as their support team, providing feedback, guidance and opportunities for learning from others' experiences and challenges; and
- Use of learning teams to share successes, challenges and learn from each other, en-

couraging others' growth rather than seeing the other as competition.

Periodic debriefs would be used during each of the above so that deeper reflection is used to understand such questions as:

- What and how am I learning?
- What am I learning about myself?
- How am I taking action?
- How am I showing up?

For example, in a high tech organization, the learning teams take intentional time to do specific debriefs with each other regularly tracking and reporting on their learning as a leader, sharing their progress, seeking feedback and input from their peers, holding themselves accountable tor continued growth and commitment. Often this is tracked against the learning goals they have shared with the group and continue to update in order to stretch themselves. The group acts to hold each other accountable and reinforces each other in taking steps toward more and more conscious leadership actions.

Only by taking this time as a serious learning process do the participants begin to experience themselves as different kinds of leaders, learning from each other in a very intentional way, supporting each other and encouraging risk taking.

DEVELOPING AND IMPLEMENTING THE LEADERSHIP PROCESSES

A transformative and strengths-based emphasis for leadership development means that the design is based on the following attributes:

- It is an obvious, visible priority for senior leadership and they "walk the talk" about their authentic values and practices;
- The focus supports the "interior individual" in working for self mastery as a leader, ac-

knowledging that each participant has his/her own wisdom that needs to be tapped;
- A learning environment is created that deliberately provides for a deep reflective process for the participant who will discover and commit to his/her own developmental journey over time;
- Relevance and balance are critical to development and daily work life through action learning projects—real time application of the learning, testing new practices;
- Support for each participant is provided to design a learning agenda for him/herself for the several years ahead.
- The values of life-long learning and growing employees at all levels are clearly reflected in the organizational culture.

In reviewing the best practices from several organizations, there are some common elements and themes that go beyond these attributes. It is important to consider some of these:

- Design of the leadership process is aligned with business drivers and supported by top management. The best of the models capture the imagination and aspirations of the organization and its leaders.
- Action learning projects and teams tackle significant business problems and projects, using them to build insights and provide a growth challenge.
- Assessment, as discussed earlier in the first phase of the incubator, is a commonly shared element. Assessments can be delivered to individuals, teams, and the culture. Assessment has become a norm for business—the question is how we use the assessment to drive change in our businesses and ourselves (Bennis in Giber, 2008, p. xvi). Often, individual and team coaching accompanies the assessment.
- Talent management systems are in place that ensure the future succession of the

organization is being carefully planned, monitored and ready for implementation. It is important to recognize the need for navigating the pool of talent into the key leadership positions that will arise due to growth, new business opportunities and turnover.

- The voice of the customer and the community are often included in the design of the process.
- The continual use of 360 feedback, and action-oriented individual and team leadership plans. Organizational practices to give and receive feedback are critical to achieving collaboration.
- Constant evaluation metrics are put in place, gaining insight into how to revise and strengthen a program, eliminating barriers to its reinforcement and linking the results to the original goals.
- Active, open participation of key senior leaders, including self-disclosure regarding some of their own leadership challenges and issues.
- HR systems such as selection, succession, compensation and performance reviews are critically important to be linked to the goals of the leadership development process and outcomes.
- Use of organizational forums (large and small) to share success stories and recognize role modeling of the leadership principles.

Specific organizations are known for some of their best practices. Companies like Google, Intel, Cisco Systems, eBay, Nokia, Amazon.com, and Dell are all great examples of their ability to act and react rapidly as a culture. They are avid practitioners of entrepreneurship and innovation, with a demonstrated willingness to take bold risks to create new products, new businesses and new industries (Thompson, Strickland, and Gamble, 2009). They expect their IT people to be about the business, lead the way, and influence information technical know-how in every facet of the business.

A CEO who isn't afraid of taking the lead with people development—Herb Kelleher, from Southwest Airlines, has been an icon for his principles and practices around people management. His senior management team has been in strong agreement that people are their greatest asset. Their thesis is simple—"keep employees happy—they will keep customers happy." The company even changed the personnel department's name to the People Department. Stories are rampant about the whole organization's passion for serving their customers and working collaboratively as leaders at all levels.

Organizations known for the IT development processes include Capital One, where they use their IT group as their competitive advantage. Capital One's "information based strategy" is attracting attention in non-financial quarters, as the company becomes synonymous with mass customization and the "information revolution." Where Wall Street analysts saw a credit card company in 2000, CEO Rich Fairbank saw a technology company. While two-thirds of Capital One's competitors used outsourcing for the IT function, Capital One through their CIO and his developing organization were able to become the back-bone of their information based strategy which has propelled to the forefront in their industry.

IBM Global Business Services (2008) discuss the evolving role of the CIO by drawing on inputs from interviews throughout firms in the U.S. and the UK. They analyze the changes in mindset and approach that a CIO needs to make with respect to the IT organization to evolve beyond a purely IT organization. They conclude that there are three important areas of focus needed in the IT organization for the CIO to be able to evolve his/her role successfully. They are:

- **The intent and style of leadership:** Applied not only in their own IT organi-

Figure 1. Maturity alignment model

		Traditional IT State	Low Maturity	Medium Maturity	High Maturity	Target State – Evolved
Leadership	**Leadership**	Inward, IT focus	Technology inward focused with limited Board interaction	IT is a profit centre; CIO is board member or regular attendee	Responsible for the creation & development of new business services. Enterprisewide change programme accountability	Focus on business service
	Sourcing	Not engaged in sourcing	Ad-hoc approach; point solutions driven solely by cost	Transformation by step changes only; some integration & collaboration with suppliers	Value based commercial models; partnership drive business & IT innovation	Value based
	Organisation structure	Independently dispersed	IT function aligned teams. Centralised management control has IT demand-supply split	Federated IT service lines delivering cross business unit; technology focused centres of excellence	Centralised joint business & IT functions e.g. Process Authority. Federated IT services lines aligned to business services	Business aligned, federated
Processes, Methods, Tools and Capability	**Process, methods & tools**	Locally applied, ad-hoc	Ad-hoc/inconsistent use of processes & tools, non standardised	Processes & tools centralised and standardised including management information & reporting, actively managed asset reuse, benchmarks achieved e.g. CMMI	Continuous improvement. Systematic, enterprise-wide process assurance supported by tooling	Standardised and optimised
	Skills & capabilities	Localised IT skills only	Focus on siloed, IT-aligned skills and frameworks	Growing active communities sharing assets & best practice. Knowledge management in place. Broad skills growth planning in place	Business & IT roles cross pollinate; career paths are flexible. Matrix managed, highly transferrable skills. Integrated business/IT skills. 'T' shaped skills profile	Fully integrated IT and business communities
Culture	**Culture**	Insular, siloed	Project oriented 'them vs us' mentality; risk adverse behaviour	Growing shared values and mutual respect, service provider mentality	Risk sharing. IT, business & suppliers act as equals. Proactive continuous improvement, dynamic business engagement	Full partnership

Source: IBM Global Business Services

zations, but equally to the wider enterprise and beyond it.

- **Capabilities and tools:** Actively building innovative processes, methods and tools used by the IT team, as well as developing skills and capabilities of IT staff.
- **The culture the CIO creates**, both within the IT organization and in the wider enterprise: paying attention to creating the right culture throughout the enterprise to lead—whether part diplomat, part revolutionary and part general, so that s/he is able to touch the intangible, consciously driving many cultural influences into a unified whole.

The transitions made by the more progressive CIOs move away from alignment of IT and business strategies to actually keeping the business running, driving business transformation and enabling business innovation. IBM Global Services have created a maturity model for the three focal areas in the IT organization for CIOs evolving their role (IBM GBS, p. 10):

This type of maturity model becomes another effective assessment tool for use with IT organizations to determine where they are on the continuum and what is required to move to the next level of maturity.

Those CIOs that are using IT strategies to actually keep the business running, carefully keep their

IT leaders focused on the maturity level they are at and where they want to be. A great example of an organization that is doing this is AstraZeneca. The AZ IS Group has interpreted the overall business strategy into an IT strategy to deliver business value. They map the major global initiatives into an IT strategy map using a business performance model. Each initiative has a business sponsor, an AZ IS Lead, defined business value measures and implementation milestones, agreed achievement criteria (measure and metrics), risk management, budget tracking. The progress of each initiative is followed-up quarterly against the defined objectives, baseline and target.

In the Global Drug Development Group, the IS initiatives are measured against business performance perspectives:

Achieve and sustain operational excellence (Business Processes), means do the right things in the right way.

Objective: Provide efficient & effective services, Optimise unit cost structure, Deliver projects & processes to acceptable standards. Exploit Architecture,

Build our skills & leadership at all levels / Create climate for action (People & Growth) means expanding our knowledge and skill and behave in the right way.

Objective: Deliver clear communications, Develop & nurture the talent pool, Share knowledge & learning, Build a performance culture

Change the business (Customer and Partners), means driving the change in the business and being proactive about the role and value of IS.

Objective: Lead and/or respond to business change, deliver agreed improvements in business performance create and make the most of partnerships.

They use a similar maturity model to advance their target state, ensuring they are evolved to be in full partnership in their IT and business communities.

STRATEGIES THAT PROMOTE TRANSFORMATIONAL CHANGE IN IT PEOPLE DEVELOPMENT

Development of key strategies will need to be defined and communicated, and once again, needs full engagement of senior leadership, partnering with HR, and IT leaders.

Some possible areas for consideration include the following:

- Declaring a serious commitment from the executive suite to short and long-term change by adequately committing resources in the form of budget, people (internal and external), time, materials, and necessary space allocations for the process to be visible in the organization.

- Setting expectations from the executive suite for the IT function to become the transformative driver for the business. This means both the collective as well as individual professions, being seen as credible and respected leaders in the organization. Making sure the people development process is clearly linked to business strategies and the vision of the business for the future.

- Executives in the C-suite modeling the leadership behaviors and practices that are expected throughout the organization. This, as stated earlier, paves the way for people development as a priority throughout. Executives set the tone for development of the collective mindset that is about collaboration, engagement and openness to growing bigger minds and stretching one's capacity for new learning.

- HR leadership, partnering with the top management team to ensure supportive structures and people development processes are acquired that are specific to the IT evolutionary role and leadership expertise.

- HR leadership taking a leadership role in linking all HR systems (communications, rewards, recognition, selection, development, compensation, talent management, etc.) with the cultural shifts that the organization intends to position people development as a key ingredient in business operations.
- More organizational visibility for the CIO evolving in his/her new role in driving business transformation and enabling business innovation.
- Development of evaluation metrics and measurement of results of the process, both collectively and individually, communicating openly what is constantly being improved as a learning organization.

All the people development strategies need to be intimately linked to the strategies of the business and communicated in ways that assist everyone to understand the clear connections between growing and learning as a collective with growing the business and achieving business results. Unless the people development proposition is clearly linked to business strategies, it will always be seen as a nice perk instead of a necessary ingredient to business success.

THE JOURNEY: PERSONAL AND COLLECTIVE

The great visionary poet and artist William Blake, whose career spanned the mid-eighteenth to early nineteenth century, was deeply concerned with the idea of transformation. Blake was truly revolutionary in that he believed society needed not just reform but profound change. He didn't believe that political action alone would bring about radical change. He felt the revolution had to come first of all in people's thinking and being. Truly meaningful change would happen only when people awoke to the infinite potential that was inside them.

Blake had an interesting way of talking about the relationship we have with our world around us—the reality we perceive and the view we have of ourselves go together and feedback on each other. He described this relationship as: "they became what they beheld" (Blake, 1965, p. 175). In other words, when we accept the world as it is, we deny our innate ability to see something better, and hence our ability to be something better. We become what we behold. The chains that prison us are "mindset chains." When we accept the present state and name it as "reality," as something that cannot change, then we are complicit with our own enslavement. By the same token, the better world we seek is within us, if only we change our vision (Quinn, 2004, p. 37).Quinn (2004) says, "When we commit to a vision to do something that has never been done before, there is no way to know how to get there. We simply have to build the bridge as we walk on it." If we choose, the future is full of possibility. It means we move forward with great courage and anticipation about what that possibility holds.

While this chapter has laid out some ideas for the journey ahead, it has no doubt fallen short of identifying the full complexity of the journey. That journey is unique to every person and to every organization. It is important to remember to stay present to what is possible, to believe in a future that is full of challenge and excitement, and tap into the voices within that guide and direct us to the infinite potential within, bringing us to the place we intend to go. We have witnessed phenomenal examples in our lifetimes of people and organizations who have chosen to go where no one has been before. It becomes easy once we choose to believe in the possibility and work in a co-creative way with our colleagues to shape the future that serves our stakeholders' needs, interests and common good.

Are you ready for the new hard work?

LESSONS LEARNED

The following are the lessons we have learned over the years of providing leadership development:

- Intentionally working on change is a multi-level process—personal, group, and organizational. All are intimately linked to support each other, making the actions of leadership evident throughout the system.
- Keeping everyone in the system aligned with the business potential creates enthusiasm, ownership and motivation to excel. This shapes and guides the organizational mindset to achieve the impossible.
- Sustainable, long-lasting leadership development is through using an "inside-out" approach.
- Having a community to challenge and support each other with their behavioral change accelerates the development process.
- Having or creating a people development culture in which management walks their talk about people as assets establishes trust for the desired individual and organizational changes.
- Aligning the people development systems and processes with leadership development is through active partnering of senior executives, HR and IT.

CONCLUSION

Companies have no choice but to change these days. The challenges are many and complex. We have addressed what we believe is most critical for making an organization successful in the long run—shaping a culture and a mindset that focuses on their people as the primary asset in getting the organization's work done in the best possible way. Our experience in corporate settings and beyond demonstrate this can work effectively when the top leadership in the organization co-create a mindset, a culture, strategies and actions that tap into the potential of all of its people. These leaders who model the way with authenticity and conscientiousness tend to have great results.

If we believe that the world's future technological problems can be solved, we must take steps to unleash the talent of those people who have the skills and capabilities to make the world a better place. The IT people within organizations can clearly become the catalyst for helping business make the advances that are needed, but they need to be elevated in their stature, developed to their full potential and reinforced by the leadership around them.

We have pointed to key steps that have been taken in some of the best organizations as well as suggesting steps for your organization. In summary, these are the key steps to increase the IT leadership capacity:

- Build a collaborative partnership among top management, HR and IT to prepare the way to develop people for the future of the enterprise.
- As a team, clearly determine the collective mindset and organizational beliefs about people development as a business driver.
- Determine the gap between the current culture and desired future—individual and collective.
- Create an incubator for developing emerging leaders and track its results.
- Spread the effort throughout the enterprise through developing and implementing leadership development processes.
- Incorporate reinforcing elements throughout the organization to ensure its sustainability.

Organizations that have used a similar approach to developing IT people have seen significant and positive business results. In addition, they have created an environment that attracts and retains the best and the brightest. We know it is possible to build the organizations and the individual people who can deliver results for this new age.

REFERENCES

Agarwal, R., & Beath, C. (2007). *Grooming the 2010 CIO*. SIM Advanced Practices Council Report, University of Texas.

Bossidy, L. (2001). The job no CEO should delegate. *Harvard Business Review*.

Bronowski, J. (1965). *William Blake and the age of revolution*. New York: Harper and Row.

Cashman, K. (2008). *Leadership from the inside out*. San Francisco, CA: Berrett Koehler.

Constable, G., & Somerville, B. (2008). *A century of innovation: Twenty engineering achievements that transformed our lives*. Washington, D.C.: Joseph Henry Press.

Fullan, M. (2001). *Leading in a culture of change*. San Francisco: Jossey-Bass.

Giber, D., Carter, L., & Goldsmith, M. (Eds.). (2008). *Linkage, Inc.'s best practices in leadership development handbook*. Linkage Press.

Goffee, R., & Jones, G. (2000). *Why should anyone be led by you?* Leadership Insights in Harvard Business Review.

Heckler, R. S. (2007). *The leadership dojo: Build your future foundation as an exemplary leader*. Frog Books.

Heskett, J.L., Jones, T.O., Loveman, G.W., Sasser, Jr., W.E. & Schlesinger, L.A. (1994). Putting the service-profit chain to work. *Harvard Business Review.*

Lao-tzu. (6th Century BC). *Tao Te Ching*. Vintage Press.

Lash, R. & Huber, C. (2010). *The Hay Group webinar: 2009 best companies for leadership.*

Martin, A. (2008). *The changing nature of leadership*. A CCL Research White Paper. Center for Creative Leadership.

McGuire, J. B., Palus, C. J., Pasmore, W., & Rhodes, G. B. (2009). *Transforming your organization*. Global Organizational Development White Paper Series, Center for Creative Leadership.

Millam, E. (2009). *Women as soul leaders: Integrating the inner and outer*. VDM Verlag.

Parks, S. D. (2005). *Leadership can be taught: A bold approach for a complex world*. Cambridge, MA: Harvard Business School Publishing.

Quinn, R. E. (2004). *Building the bridge as you walk on it*. San Francisco, CA: Jossey-Bass.

Thompson, A. A., Strickland, A. J., & Gamble, J. E. (2009). *Crafting and executing strategy: The quest for competitive advantage: Concepts and cases*. New York: The McGraw-Hill Companies.

Chapter 17
A Players:
High Worth + High Worry

John Stevenson
JG Stevenson Associates, USA

ABSTRACT

The term "A Players" was not a familiar categorization for staff until this author had been leading Information Technology organizations for over twenty five years. "A Players" as well as B, C and D Players is a common term for local charity and Pro-Am golf tournaments where competitively equal golf foursomes are created by balancing the known golf prowess and skills in each group. The "A Player" is the top ranked player in the group and "should" be the "low" or best scorer during play. The "B" Player is the next most skilled and so on. During my youth and mid-adult years, the author pursued other non-golf hobbies and activities such as boating and flying where "A Player" wasn't a common term.

INTRODUCTION

In the early part of the new century I was presented with a new IT executive opportunity by Larry Kittelberger, who at the time was the Chief Information Officer of Lucent Technologies. Larry had previously been the CIO at Allied-Signal where he was an early adopter of ERP packages. We knew each other over the years through sharing our common issues at the business user group of

DOI: 10.4018/978-1-60960-535-3.ch017

one of those large ERP application firms. Lucent had just unfolded a major new corporate strategy where it was going to split the company into three independent businesses: Lucent, Avaya, and Agere Systems. Larry knew I had a lot of consumer business as well as high technology background from my previous IT executive positions and he convinced me to take the inaugural CIO position of the newly formed Avaya Company. As part of this new strategy, each of the Lucent headquarters business segments; human resources, finance, facilities, information technologies and the executive group were expected to divide up their global staffs to go into the three new independent companies.

After the Lucent corporate executives aligned their own future positions with each of the corporations, they wisely decided to have the corporate Human Resources function finish their own split up of staff assignments next. This gave the remainder of the staffing selection process a core group of agents from HR who was focused on creating the best staffing solution for their own new businesses. The process was a lot like a professional sports draft. I presided as the "process owner" for Information Technology for Avaya; my most trusted talent scouts were the Avaya designated human resources leaders assigned to my new IT group.

We needed to select over one thousand information technology staff from the large pool of global resources at Lucent. A key to the potential success of the whole Avaya IT function was going to be the caliber of our choices for top leadership. The three IT group leaders from Lucent, Agere, and Avaya decided to start our selection process by filling our top positions and work down the org chart.

I independently studied the backgrounds and other attributes of the top incumbent vice-president level candidates. When it was time to select the department head for one of the Avaya key IT functions, I thought that either of the current top two highly experienced and very competent appearing execs in that function at Lucent would be good choices to fill the slot. As I was about to firm up my choice, to my surprise, my Avaya designated human resources Director hurriedly called me aside and stated emphatically that there was an "A Player" hidden a bit further down the org chart and that I should pass on the higher two experienced candidates and select that specific lesser experienced individual. When I asked the HR Director what an "A Player" meant, he compared him to a low scoring golfer who would be the one to "win the tournament for my team". Following his guidance, I 'uncomfortably' switched choices and worried that I had given up seasoned talent for this

young "A Player". During the next phase of the selection process, I became guided by my team of HR leaders toward the "A Player" preference style. Of course, the assigned human resource leaders for the other two businesses were savvy to this selection methodology and soon asked if we could all come to consensus as to who each would designate on their A, B and C level staff lists so that we could put one master list A,B and C selection list together. Soon thereafter we were alternating our selections from each of the lists so that all three businesses would have an equal opportunity to get a balanced share of the A, B and C talent.

During the first year of Avaya as a new stand-alone corporation, I soon learned that it was the A Players we selected for the Information Technology group that really pulled the entire organization along to great achievements. I also learned a key priority myself, keep the A Players motivated and satisfied and the whole IT function will thrive.

DEFINITION OF AN A PLAYER

Taking a step back, what is the definition of an A Player when it comes to the Information Technology staff function in a corporation? I found that there isn't a specific prescription or exact set of criteria for an A Players attributes across the broad staff types of an IT function. However, there are some common traits that exist across most of these top contributors.

The first and foremost attribute of an A Player is; when they speak, you 'want' to listen. What they have to say may be on a technical item, or it may be on a project point or just relating a communication that is needed to be heard. The key is, what they say and when and how they say it commands a listener's respect. While this attribute can be learned, often it is innate to the person and their natural style. Later in the chapter we will discuss some ways for an Information Technology executive to nurture that key trait in their current and future A level Players.

Another common trait is knowledge mastery, which can be of a soft skill such as critical meeting leadership or a core IT technical function like databases or networks. I have often found that A Players exhibit effective leadership by utilizing a variety of styles from soft and persuasive to commanding and riveting or sometimes both blended to suit the occasion. Deft use of this style blend can differentiate them from being just a good "leader" or manager. Good leaders or managers often have one style that is effective and they use for all occasions, A Players monitor the situation and adapt to it.

Last on my common attribute list for A Players is that natural capability to get others to perform up to and even beyond their capabilities.

A-Players can have very different personalities and styles. They can be highly technical or exceptionally good leaders or both. They can be young or seasoned. Bottom-line, a savvy CIO will know who an A Player is after they watch, listen and witness them in action.

An example of the impact of an A Player in my group was the need to fill an IT position with someone who had significant telephone "call-center" operations knowledge. This role would help relate what the company's call-center group needed from IT to be both more productive and to achieve higher levels of customer satisfaction when outside customers called our help lines. I initially wanted either a top seasoned leader from that group or one of their key call center technical folks. To become better acquainted with this important IT client, I was asked to join IT and call Center group collaboration meetings. During a couple of those sessions, I observed a young call center supervisor who had a knack for engaging the entire team at the table at just the right time to steer some logical conclusions. I discussed that supervisors habits during those meetings with my IT leaders in attendance and while it would be a gamble we decided to give that person a solid

try at this key relationship leader's role. The top call-center executive was highly relieved that we wanted to borrow such a junior person for our role, and even warned us that it may not work well. We tried the young supervisor out and six months later after witnessing her dramatic impact on the overall alignment between the two groups and the high level of accomplishment getting new capabilities on-line for the call-center, the call-center executive wanted her back, and was going to promote her. When we sat down together and discussed her career future, she chose to stay in IT permanently because we gave her the freedom to pursue the goal of business improvement. Over the next few years her role continued to evolve as she became a liaison for many IT critical interactions with other business groups across the company.

SUPPORTING A PLAYERS

Supporting A Players so that they can thrive and make a strong impact is a significant challenge. It can also be a key to the overall success of IT and the CIO.

One relationship experience I have had to learn (it took a 'number' of repetitions) is to coach your A Players and dialogue with them, not to dictate or overpower their own ability to think and lead. The best thing that an IT executive can do for a truly A Player is to provide the broader strategic guidance they need to effectively operate their area and provide settings where larger area collaboration with their peers and clients can be accomplished.

A-Players almost always thrive under challenging situations. During the two significant economic downturns in the first decade of the twenty first century, the strain of cost and staffing cuts intersected with the high demands placed on IT to accomplish even more. From my attendance at several Society for Information Management annual conferences, I learned that many corporate CIOs recognized that it was their A Players who made it possible for them to navigate difficult times. A Players can carry a workload that exceeds the norm. During the three decades when I have been in senior management assignments, there have been numerous strategic corporate events when critical staff level changes were required that included retain or lay-off staff decisions. These decision points have come when the economy was both at its peak as well as during the downturns. Corporate mergers, acquisitions, business central-izations, decentralization, companies going public and going private are all business events that I have directly faced during my IT career. During many of those difficult required IT staff changes in the 1980s and 1990s, I didn't have the full concept of A Players in my vocabulary or what the final retain versus lay-off criteria should be. However, as I reflect on the names and roles of many of the key staff that I chose to retain when difficult choices had to be made, it was in retrospect, the A Player type individuals who became the shining beacons for everyone in their sphere of influence. New corporate circumstances requiring changes to corporate staffing levels are often difficult to both smoothly relate to your staff and for many of the staff to easily digest. It is the A Players who seem to get by this distraction the quickest and seemingly with the least personal impact.

During one of my earliest CIO assignments, I needed to significantly evolve the IT capability of a corporation during an eight year span where the corporation; bought and merged two equal sized businesses, took the business private, then later took the business public and at the end, sold the business to a larger corporation. This all took place in the span of seven years. Two of my key department leaders consistently asked only the questions needed about each of these significant evolutions of the corporation so that they could rapidly develop plans to support the change and assist our internal and external customers. IT often was prioritizing plans to support these business alterations before the business groups had reacted themselves to the new corporate environment.

It was these two A Players who time after time quickly moved this planning process forward. I noted that they were able to rally a lot of talent around them to make this rapid planning process happen. My main role was to keep all of the com-munication avenues open for them. One skill that both of these individuals developed on their own were both an understanding and an affinity for their business partner peers. They were immediately invited to key sessions where rapid corporate evolution thinking was needed. In private, away from the turmoil of everything going on around them, both of these individuals needed as much attention from me as any of the other leaders and staff members in my group. They had concerns and insightful questions, but in a very different way from their peers in IT, they were able to compartmentalize their own internal thoughts and not let it interfere at all with their ability to focus on the business issues before them and lead. The junior A Player on my team during this era subsequently went on to a highly successful CIO tenure at the same firm after I left.

THE A PLAYER CAREER TRACK

When times are stable or smoothly growing at a corporation, it is often easy for an IT executive to let the staffing function go on "autopilot" for long periods of time. I have found that neglecting IT staffing growth or creating opportunities when not absolutely demanded is the easy way and often does not yield the best long term results. Planning IT staff growth is now a higher continuous objec-tive for both CIOs and their HR counterparts than it was back in the 1980s and 1990s. Identifying individuals who need growth through different job assignments or expansions is now a fairly normal function for executives to manage. The big question here is carefully identifying those who will not accidently reach a Peter Principal type of failure point when a significant assignment change is enacted. This promo to a failure point concern is one of the "High Worry" components of having A Players on staff who need to grow.

Early in my corporate IT management days while I was a young section leader for IT applications, the corporate MIS Director (the top title in those days) called me into his office and succinctly stated that he wanted me to move over and take on the job of running the IT Operations group. This consisted of the mainframe, networks, data entry (in those days), database and operating systems plus 24 hour operations and services. I had never had any previous direct IT Operations experience nor was I considered "technical" when it came to understanding systems and databases. Needless to say this job opportunity was a head spinner for me. I protested politely to the MIS Director that I thought I may be very under qualified for the assignment, plus there were a number of much more experienced leaders already in that area. He mentioned that the current leader of the Operations area was being reassigned and when they both discussed who should be the next group leader and why, my name was high on both of their lists. As it turned out, the top two incumbent section leaders in Operations, while individually talented and knowledgeable in their areas could not agree on very many things and in fact were gradually adding paralysis to the group's ability to change and support the business. The key to my new assignment was to gain their confidence individually and then meld them into a team. It took a lot of time and extensive delicate communications, but after a few months, the performance and customer service aspect of the group improved and soon enough they both took equal credit for the higher customer service grades the group was receiving. However, as I began to learn more about the operations area staff I also discovered several supervisors who were partially hidden A Players. The task of getting the two section leaders to begin to nurture these top supervisors and expand their roles was not natural for them. Eventually I found that if I demonstrated the confidence to trust significant important assignments to them and only lightly coached the outcome, they began to understand the role that they should play in doing the same for these hidden A Player supervisors. While they were not candidates (by style) to become A Players themselves, the section leaders did facilitate the rise and important expansion of the contribution their A Player reports. After less than two years, those emerging A Player supervisors grew to be section leaders and soon thereafter were promoted again to area directors. The role of an IT executive and how they personally approach the style of their own job can often reach down into an organization and even effect the success of the non-A Players among their direct reports. This experience does not mean that it is either good or bad to leave non A Players in critical leadership functions, but sometimes when it is necessary you can still find ways to get good performance from the non- A Player leaders within the group.

THE A PLAYER ADVANTAGE

One of the more difficult staff situations an IT executive faces is when a significant component of the IT function is not co-located in the same set of facilities or nearby geographic area as the executive. Discovering who the A Players may be at those locations and giving them the right support is much more difficult from a distance. However, the payback of having remote leadership that is both self-sufficient and knowledgeable on when and how to effectively communicate with their remote based executive is bigger than even in a centralized site. One method of discovery I have found useful is the "hands-on" approach to gathering 360 degree feedback (as described in Edwards & Ewen, 1996) on all of the remote group leaders and key contributors. Those informal but focused conversations can often give a remotely based executive some solid clues as to who the true A Players at that location may be. It requires careful questioning under the right circumstances to distill who is really an A Player from who is just "popular". This characteristic of popularity is a delicate one to balance. Many A Players (though not all) can have a strong "likeability" attribute which makes it easier for others to both listen to and to follow them. However, not all "likeable" leader/contributors are A Players. Some achieve their popularity by just the force of their personality with ineffective work habits or follow-thru and some are popular but have too limited a set of knowledge to become a strong contributor. Working with corporate HR to develop the right interview ideas and discussion items for these informal 360 degree conversations can be very useful. Also, similar to comments earlier in this chapter, creating workplace opportunities for remote area contributors to demonstrate their capabilities when their area executive is on hand can be very insightful. Remote group key contributors and leaders can be among the highest worry area personnel wise for an IT executive. Corrections for performance gaps could be sporadic and the opportunity for counsel is less frequent and somewhat shallower from a distance. Having a deliberate ongoing remote staff assessment and tracking process can be critical to success at those locations.

During a meet and greet tour of international sites soon after I first joined a global company, I was carefully trying to determine who to select to lead a regional project implementation in Europe. The fan club backing for a particular country IT leader both from his staff and his clients was strong. However, when I looked at the recent history of accomplishments I found that he focused on the popular issues in his business and did not build a sustaining set of IT capabilities that would suit the business as soon as a year or two later. A far less popular leader in another country had the vision and the quiet backing from a few key contributors to smoothly develop a sustainable growth IT platform that was beginning to deliver solid results but had not yet "thrilled" the client or taken pressure off of the IT group to deliver results. Selecting the deliverer of strategic results

over the popular star was difficult to communicate to many of the business and IT leaders on that continent. When the overall plan and key milestone deliveries orchestrated by this assigned leader were achieved below budget and with minimal personnel turnover, the selection of this true A Player proved correct. It took a thorough but informal 360 degree process to decide who to select. I found that it was critical that if a defined A Player existed with the right background that person be given this key role even over voracious objections. As it turns out, the "popular" leader did soon struggle and not long afterward resigned.

During the past decade, budget allocations for staff and management training have been under strain. When corporate IT budgets are pushed hard to handle increasing software and hardware maintenance workloads as well as to create 'new' business efficiencies and business models, budget allocations for training often become an early target for budget cuts. This financially restrictive situation could affect a key component for growth and satisfaction of the A Players. However, I have noticed an interesting phenomenon with this ongoing development gap; A Players on my staff were less concerned for formal training for themselves than the lack of formal training opportunities than their counterparts. Many A Players keenly focus on "getting the tasks at hand accomplished" and are not greatly distracted by personal issues such as limited formal training. However, a CIO cannot just let this developmental gap happen to the key A Players, it must be filled. One year when I faced significant budget cutbacks, we severely cut both managerial and technical skills training. This drastic cut meant that there was no funding for IT applications and technical staff training in newly acquired software that was required to accomplish a group of IT critical upgrades. Everyone on my staff was glum that day. The next morning as I was beginning to prepare a highly revised IT plan for the year, two of my direct reports popped into my office with an emerging plan. These two A Players, one a quieter technical heavy and the other an exceptional relationship developer asked me to hold off on IT planning revisions for 48 hours. They were working on some alternatives. The very next morning I was asked to come to a meeting they organized. There at the meeting were the two regional directors for our new software as well as key representatives of the departments most affected by any delay or change to our IT plan. The vendors spoke first. They were willing to have us do a "Train the Trainer" type of program that was only one tenth the cost of our previously planned vendor training program. In addition, they were willing to delay some software costs to facilitate a zero net budget outcome to us for the "Train the Trainer" program. Next the business department leaders all signed up for their involvement in giving up valuable time by their prospective "trained trainers" to develop and conduct internal training. Not only did the A Players solve this problem, they further ensured that during the project phase the "Trainers" had all of the internal resources needed to carry out this highly effective new training plan. This solved the needed IT technical training gap for the year, but there was also an emerging "management and soft skills" training gap. On their own, these same two A Players armed with some support from others in the group, met with the continuing education director at the local community college. They offered to conduct community college course training themselves in areas of their expertise, in exchange for free course hours for others in the group. The community college director liked the opportunity to reach out to a corporation in a new way and allowed us to develop a two course experiment. Those classes were successful, and we turned this fledgling corporate college alignment over to our HR counterparts to expand across a wider program. Within eighteen months we were caught up on 90 percent of our managerial skills training backlog. The overall cost was less than ten percent of our previous plan and the training program quality was excellent. The biggest concern with both of these A Player developed

initiatives was the added time impact on key staff who was involved in the training and class work. As it turns out, almost everyone was able to fit this new demand into their schedule and still keep up with the rest of their work. Again, this type of impact of A Players on a group has high worth and actually mitigated a lot of worry.

LEVERAGING A PLAYERS FOR YOUR SUCCESS

Hewlett Packard as a top information technology company fully understands the worth of their A Players. In Hewlett Packard's 2009 Annual Shareholders Report where they list the Risk Factors to their future performance they state: "***In order to be successful, we must attract, retain and motivate key employees, and failure todo so could seriously harm us***" (Hewlett Packard, 2009, p. 27). They further defined the high impact roles of some of these key employees as: managerial, technical and skilled solutions providers in the IT support business. This succinct sentence linking company level critical success and failure to key employees including many of the staff components within IT really gives focus to executive's human resources objectives.

When I put together an early outline for this chapter and reflected carefully on lessons learned over my thirty plus years in IT management, I realized that I spent over two decades using only my instincts on how to effectively staff and create leadership within my group. Development of an A Player identification pattern of behaviors has allowed me to be more consistent in positioning the right people who can succeed. I also realized that focusing on coaching and mentoring staff, particularly the A Players, gave very high payback for the effort and time. Often, a tremendous percent of your time can be diverted by managing upward and outward from IT. I recognize this activity is critical to IT group success, but added focus on creating successful venues for the IT A Players can leverage the success.

In summary, IT executives need to develop both the innate sense and the focus to identify their true in house A Players. The added time devoted to mentoring and coaching these critical human resource elements of a department has high payback and leverages the time investment of the executive. It is often difficult to allow significant freedom to subordinates to design and carry out their own workload, but with A Players freedom most often creates the highest overall worth for the group. Are A Players a high worry, "yes" they can be, but creating an effective support environment for them to operate within will mitigate the risk.

Identify, coach and support and the A Players will make you a success.

REFERENCES

Edwards, M. R., & Ewen, A. J. (1996, May). *360 Feedback: The Powerful New Model for Employee Assessment & Performance Improvement.* New York, NY: American Management Association.

Hewlett-Packard Development Company. L.P. (2010, January). *2009 Annual Report.* Palo Alto, CA: HP.

Chapter 18
The Critical Five People Practices of IT Leaders

John N. Oglesby
CIO Services Group, USA

ABSTRACT

The key to an effective IT organization is to hire good people and nurture them. While recognizing that individual people require individual considerations, the five important management practices elaborated in this chapter are fundamental. They are to provide employees (1) interesting and challenging work, (2) the freedom to do it their way, (3) things they can own, (4) an environment in which they can excel, and (5) recognition for their efforts and accomplishments.

INTRODUCTION

When it comes to getting the most from IT people, experience has taught me that there are only a handful of people practices that really matter. They seem to apply regardless of age, level within the organization, gender, or ethnicity. Embed these critical practices in a solid, overall approach to managing people, and you'll have a process that will generate success. But if you don't employ the Critical Five, nothing else you try will be very effective.

It wasn't academic research or a double-blind study that led me to these beliefs, although there is certainly research to support my opinion. Instead, these views were generated from a career spent managing IT people—from infrastructure to development to emerging technologies to major projects to budgeting, purchasing, planning and strategy—a career that's shown me what motivates people. What makes them work their hearts out? What makes them proud? What makes them loyal? What makes them stay?

DOI: 10.4018/978-1-60960-535-3.ch018

THE CRITICAL FIVE

More than anything else, people want to feel needed and to have their work appreciated. Scholars such as Maslow, Alderfer, Wahba, Mitchell, Mellor and others have debated this subject extensively, so I won't repeat those arguments here. Instead, I'll focus on the techniques you can use to fulfill these needs. But, first, let's identify the Critical Five practices that I've found to be so important.

The Critical Five are simple. Just give your people:

1. Interesting and challenging work
2. The freedom to do it their way
3. Things they can "own"
4. An environment in which they can excel
5. Recognition for their efforts and accomplishments

And watch them excel.

AN OVERALL APPROACH

While I've found the Critical Five to be required in unleashing talent, I believe they must be surrounded by three other practices to maximize your success in building and developing a successful IT team. This overall approach is also simple:

A. Hire good people
B. Nurture and develop them
C. Unleash their talent (**The Critical Five**)
D. Take pride in their accomplishments

Now let's explore this overall approach and the critical five practices in more detail.

A. Hire Good People

Every company or team has a specific culture, common practices and core competencies. You want employees with the kind of mind-set, thought-processes, skills, and abilities that will enable them to thrive in that culture. We often refer to this as how people "fit" within an organization.

But while you may look for certain specific characteristics, abilities, and knowledge in your prospective hires, maybe even test for them, finding people who will "fit" is, at best, an imprecise science. I believe it's best to forget about "fit" at first and instead find excellent performers that you can then help "fit" in a way that will maximize their contribution.

So how do you recognize the people who are, or will become, excellent performers? I've discovered that there are key attributes such people have and these are the ones I look for.

The Attributes of Excellent Performers

I've always found that the best performers have an innate intellectual curiosity—a desire to understand why things work or are done a certain way. They also feel a need to improve them. And they're driven to always be learning new things. Just as importantly, they will learn from their experiences and apply those lessons to improving themselves. They have confidence and a sense of purpose. They have a positive attitude and are grounded ethically. They have a sense of humor and are willing to laugh at themselves. And they communicate well.

The good news is that you can search for these attributes in an interview. Ask prospective hires how they would tackle (or have tackled) a project involving unfamiliar technologies or processes. How curious were they about discovering how things worked and what could be improved? Ask what they learned from their experience. Can they generalize those lessons into improvements in their approach? Observe their confidence in answering your questions. Listen to how well they communicate facts and ideas. Do they accentuate the positive or dwell on the negative as they explain how they tackled certain projects or enumerate what's important to them?

Whether and how much a person learns from experience, and whether they are aware of it, is usually a great sign of an excellent performer. If a person actively analyzes their experiences, looking for the reasons certain things worked and others didn't, then they are self-aware about continually trying to improve themselves and this is the kind of person who generally is, or can become, an excellent performer. If a person isn't aware that they're using this approach, but can readily point out what they've learned from an experience and how those lessons will help them the next time, then they're instinctively using the technique and can be trained to consciously and purposefully employ it as a means of improving themselves. I've interviewed some people, however, who seemed unable to either recognize the lessons they should have learned from an experience, or were unable to generalize them into better approaches in the future, or both. I've never hired one of those people.

You'll also find that the best performers take the lead, that they have an ability to influence others, that they're flexible, tenacious, and have a positive energy that conveys excitement about their work and their accomplishments, and they often display a relentless activity. They're also generally upbeat and positive. In truth, I've also seen employees with a negative bias toward work and life who performed well but, really, who would you rather be around?

You'll find that some employees are very ambitious while others may simply be content to do a good job. Some are driven to get things done right now while others may display considerable patience. Some seem like racehorses and others like plodders. Are the ambitious, get-it-done-now racehorses the best, or the most desirable, employees? The answer for you lies in your culture, your needs and the needs of your organization. And most of the time, it's a balance of the two extremes that makes for the best teams. I've found that both types can be excellent employees and I've come to value the contribution of the more patient just as

much as the stars who strive so hard to get ahead. But while the needs of these two extreme types are balanced differently, they're still the same needs. How to fulfill them requires the kind of situational management that has been described by Ken Blanchard, Paul Hersey and others.

A final, rather obscure, indicator of excellent performers in my experience is that they are often either a math or music major or have hobbies related to those subjects. Not that *not* having these degrees or interests is necessarily bad, it's just that I've just observed over the years what seems to me an unlikely number of good IT people with such backgrounds. Perhaps it's simply a curiosity. Or maybe it's an indicator that may one day help spot a star.

Where to Find Good People

So where do you find the best people? Other departments can be an excellent source. Of course, you have to be careful when recruiting from other managers' teams. Managers can be stubborn about giving up good people, even if it's a clear opportunity for their employees to branch out, acquire new skills and grow. After all, their excellent performers are making them look good and for that reason, managers are often reluctant to give them up.

Other companies, especially competitors, can also be good places to look for outstanding performers. The employees of competitors already know your industry and they will have worked with similar products and processes and on projects much like the ones they will encounter with you. Prior successes there are usually a good indicator that they will enjoy success on your team as well.

Employees or contactors who have performed well on key projects may relish the chance to tackle a project of yours. Good project managers possess skills that translate across all kinds of endeavors. If it happens that their successful experience came while working for your company, so much the better. They are either already a part of your culture or know a lot about it.

Recommendations from trusted associates are a great source. But emphasis on 'trusted' is important. Managers have been known to pump up descriptions of employee qualifications and performance when they want to get rid of them. If you don't know the recommending manager well, try to get an honest opinion from someone you know and trust.

Of course, good performers can also be found on college campuses. But be sure to interview for the attributes mentioned above. And look for success both inside and outside the classroom. I've been fortunate to have found several stars among college recruits.

Professional organizations and industry conferences can be target rich environments as well. There you'll find people with interests and objectives similar to yours. Look for high energy, curiosity, and previous accomplishment. And, of course, get recommendations from trusted associates.

There are many other sources you might try, but these are the ones I've used most often.

Recap: Hire Good People

1. Look for these key attributes of excellent performers:
    - Intellectual curiosity
    - Learning from experience
    - Confidence, sense of purpose
    - Positive attitude
    - Communications skill
    - Ethical grounding
    - Sense of honor
    - Shows examples of
        - Leadership
        - Influencing
        - Energy
        - Flexibility
        - Tenacity
    - Two unlikely 'wild card' attributes: math and music majors often make great IT people
2. Look for excellent performers in these places:
    - Other departments
    - Other companies and competitors
    - Good project results
    - Recommendations from others both inside and outside your company
    - College campuses
    - Industry conferences
    - Professional organizations
    - Other organizations

B. Nurture and Develop Them

No matter how you choose your team, it's doubtful they will come to you fully developed as the employees you need. And even if they do, if you've chosen the kind of excellent performers described above, they'll have a restless need to always be growing and learning. You need to nurture their development. So take the time to recognize what they want, give them what they need to grow, and use every opportunity to coach them.

Recognize what they Want

Although different individuals may have slightly different needs, excellent performers as a whole generally require these five things:

1. Challenge
2. Freedom
3. Ownership/accountability and authority
4. A nurturing environment
5. Recognition

You may recognize them as the Critical Five. And while you should consider how much of each one a given individual wants, don't omit any of them, even if it appears that the person doesn't need it, and especially if they say they don't. They do.

We'll talk later about how to get the best performance from your people. Let's focus here on how to best nurture their growth.

Give Them What They Need

While giving each individual their appropriate measure of the critical few, you'll also need to give them your support and confidence, feedback, and as much rope as possible. And you'll have to practice what Ken Blanchard refers to as situational management.

Situational management calls for the application of different management styles to different people at different times, depending upon the individual's (or the team's) maturity in terms of their being able to set goals, take responsibility for them, and have the appropriate knowledge or skill for the task. You may see the need to give more coaching and instruction to one person than to another when they are both doing essentially the same thing. You may also need to give more coaching and instruction to the same person when they tackle something unfamiliar than when they're working within their skills/knowledge domain.

Your stars will run into people issues, resource issues, project management issues, technology issues and other potential roadblocks to success. Some of them will be more capable than others in clearing these obstacles. Give each of them the level of support they need at the point they need it, always encourage them, and display confidence in their ability. Help them push themselves through the challenges. They'll be infinitely better off for having done it themselves than if you'd intervened.

I've often told my staff that I am perfectly willing to watch them make small mistakes if it'll help them learn. But I also tell them that I'll always intervene before they make any big ones.

Use Every Opportunity to Coach

People learn by doing. As they try their wings and develop, let them know how they're doing.

Point out the things they did well and why. Offer suggestions on how to do things better the next time. Relate stories and parables to better illustrate your points.

When something goes wrong and you do need to intervene and show an employee how to do something or prevent a mistake, take the time to point out how the situation got to that point—where mistakes were made, what might have occurred had a different approach been taken, and how to recognize similar situations in the future. And give them techniques they can use in the future to improve results. This is apprenticeship, and it is the best form of learning and growth.

When things go well, point out why. Identify the specific actions that the employee took, and when, that led to their positive results. Tell them why these actions were better than the alternatives. Sometimes employees can get lucky and choose the right option without knowing why it was the right one. Without that knowledge, they might not do so well in the future.

As opportunities arise, you can help employees improve critical skills, like how to confront problems, issues and people. Teach them how to use tools such as personality profiles (Keirsey, Myers-Briggs, etc.) and the Johari window to understand the needs and motivations of others. Show them how to get along with difficult people and how to deal with difficult circumstances. Demonstrate how to prioritize their work and manage their time. And coach them on how to influence others, especially when they have no formal authority over those people.

Early in my career, a manager asked me to lead a fund-raising effort for our department. Now, IT employees are generally not the most outgoing people, and these were no exception. Getting them to do what essentially amounted to sales activities was not an easy task. I floundered. But the manager used this experience as a way to teach me how to uncover what other people wanted and to find a way to help them achieve some of those things by simply doing what I needed them to do.

It worked, and I discovered that people will have a better reason for wanting to participate in your activity or project if there's something in it for them. It was a great lesson, and one that I've used countless times since and have taught to every employee who's ever worked for me.

Another thing I've always done is to insist on "completed staff work." This is an extremely sound practice employed by the military. Teach it to your staff. Help them practice it. Insist that they practice it.

The concept is simple: don't bring me a problem, bring me a solution. Rather than identifying or complaining about a problem, your employee should present you a package that basically says: here's the problem, here are the various ways that I've identified to tackle it, here are the pro's and con's of each option and its likely outcome, and here is the one that I recommend we take. It's then your job as their manager to accept their recommendation or send them back to do more work, pointing out where they might have missed something. The military takes it a step further. Staffers there must take orders to the chief that are ready for signature and that will implement the recommended solution. Until they're ready to stake their reputation and career on having made the right recommendation, and sincerely believe that the chief should sign those orders, their staff work is not complete.

Yet another great coaching tool is the classic Harvard Business Review article "Who's Got the Monkey." It complements the concept of completed staff work by teaching your leaders how to recognize where responsibility for the next action should lie and making sure that's where it stays.

There are countless other tools, techniques and practices that you can employ to coach your people. Use them. Your people need your guidance and experience, and they'll remember and appreciate your efforts, even if they don't always remember some of the specific techniques.

Recap: Nurture and Develop Them

a. Recognize what they want:
   i. Challenge
   ii. Freedom
   iii. Ownership/accountability and authority
   iv. A nurturing environment
   v. Recognition
b. Give them what they need
c. Use every opportunity to coach

C. Unleash Their Talent and Let Them Excel

This is where the Critical Five come in and are so important. Use them to get the best performance from your people.

Give employees the right environment, the right coaching, tools, and training, and the right opportunities to perform, and they will amaze you with what they can and will do. Employees you properly develop, and believe in, will work their hearts out for you as well as for themselves because they understand that the opportunity and the responsibility are shared. And if you allow the spotlight of success to be trained on them, you'll bask in its glow as well.

Getting the best that an employee has to offer is not always easy, it's not fast, and the work is never done. Here's how I've approached providing and using the Critical Five.

1. Give Them Interesting Work

No one wants to be bored. While there are times we all have to perform tasks that we don't enjoy, those times should be the exception and not the norm. Challenging work is interesting work, and it's difficult to get bored when you're facing an obstacle. But if your employees don't enjoy navigating difficult terrain, then the problem is either that you're not challenging them properly, or that you have the wrong employees.

I've found that the number one reason employees hold back is because their work environment punishes failures and doesn't reward experimentation. Finding hard solutions often requires trying different approaches, many of which won't work. If staffers are chastised, looked down upon, or talked about negatively for having tried something that didn't work, then they'll stop trying. And if staffers are treated the same, whether they experiment or not, then why should they run the risk of failure? If you want your people to wade into a swamp full of alligators for you and come out with the ones that are causing problems, then don't criticize them when they get nervous and their first shots go awry. But when they do emerge, dragging a few of the conquered beasts behind them, put those employees on a pedestal and put ribbons on their chest.

It can be tempting to hand out assignments based on skills sets and prior successes, and let those people who best know how to do a particular thing continue to do it, knowing that they'll do it well. Instead, try handing out work to people who haven't done that kind of thing before, but have shown signs that they can handle it. It'll prevent experienced employees who are accustomed to doing such work from becoming bored with repetitive assignments, it'll challenge those who are tackling it for the first time, and it'll build backup skills that you can employ for those tasks in the future. A side benefit may be that the employee new to the work will actually figure out a better way to do it, assuming that you've given them the freedom to try.

2. Give Them the Freedom to do it Their Way

There is almost always more than one way to do a job. Too often, bosses stifle their employees with too much hovering and handing out of directions.

IT managers are especially bad about this because they generally rise through the ranks, moving from masters of a technical discipline into the world of managing others, and most are ill prepared for the change. Before, they were responsible for getting work done. The result was up to them. Then, suddenly, they're thrust into a situation where they must rely upon someone else to get things done, yet they must share the responsibility. Most young managers find that hard to do. They find it hard to let go. Some love the technical challenge and simply can't resist pointing out the "right way" (their way) of getting something done. Others simply can't bear to hand over the authority and the freedom necessary to allow someone else to do a job that they already know how to do. As a result, IT is full of micromanagers who neuter and often alienate their people. They can stubbornly insist that it's their way or the wrong way. Worse, they can threaten that it's their way or the highway.

The managers who excel and grow are the ones who learn to let go, who learn that their way isn't always the best way, who are willing to share responsibility with others, and who are willing to give others the freedom to figure out the solution using their own methods.

Not long after joining my department, Taylor complained that I wasn't giving her enough direction. She didn't know what she was supposed to be doing or how to do it. She said she didn't much like her new job, her new department or her new manager. But I suspected that she'd been working too long for young managers who had told her hourly what to do and how to do it. So in a series of conversations and coaching opportunities, I gave her more (and then gradually less) direction and let her see that it was part of her job to figure out what to do and how to do it. And sometimes I'd let her falter, although never for too long. And, within about six months, she'd blossomed into a much more driven and capable employee who had fallen in love with being given the freedom to chart her own course, knowing that she had my support if she needed it. Later on, she told me privately that she had realized how stifled she had been and that she never wanted to go back to departments whose managers practiced that kind of leadership.

Excellent performers never enjoy being automatons that simply carry out the instructions of others. And even those who say they don't want more responsibility will ultimately appreciate the freedom to figure things out on their own and will immensely enjoy the satisfaction and rewards of doing so.

3. Give Them Things They Can "Own"

People like to be known for a particular expertise or set of knowledge. Give your employees the opportunity to develop special skills, knowledge of certain techniques, or understanding of new technologies. These can help define them as experts in a particular area.

Early in my career, a great manager asked me to read up on and begin becoming the department's expert on microprocessors. It led me to a fundamental understanding of the entire personal computer revolution in a way that I never would have had the opportunity to do otherwise, and also led me into several extremely enjoyable assignments managing them and figuring out how to use them better. As a result, I've given similar assignments to my employees throughout my career. Some embraced the opportunity, others didn't. But the ones who did were always seen as aggressive, actively-learning, high-energy employees who had great potential.

While it's fun to learn things that others don't know, it can be detrimental if the employee who learns it tries to hoard their newfound knowledge and expertise. To prevent this, I've found that it works well if you have newly minted experts do presentations, training sessions, and small joint projects that force them to both use and share their knowledge with their coworkers. Great team building can occur when one employee helps another learn and when the employee who is learning appreciates the effort and expertise of the one helping. So, while you may enable an employee

to "own" knowledge or expertise for a while, if it's important to the success of the organization, make sure that they also share it. If they do, they'll still be acknowledged as the leader, or first-mover, in that area of expertise, plus they'll also be seen as a mentor to others.

People also like to have responsibility for things they can call their own.

Giving an employee the authority and responsibility for a particular process, however small, not only gives them a feeling of ownership, it helps them spread their wings. They will be exposed to conflicts when the process they control is seen by others as being in the way and they'll be forced to learn how to cope. They will have opportunities to see deficiencies in the process and find ways to improve it. How they react to these challenges and opportunities will present interesting coaching and learning moments. They'll feel the weight of responsibility for something small before being faced with larger roles. And, if you do it right, they'll get some needed job satisfaction, praise and recognition for their efforts.

4. Give Them an Environment in Which They Can Excel

Crops won't grow in a desert. Seeds may try to germinate, but they can't survive without water, nutrients and protection from the harsh realities of desert life. Even a desert, though, can be made into a thriving environment for some crops.

Although organizations can sometimes feel like desert environments, managers can create their own small oases where good work can be done and good people can grow. Below are the things I believe are required to enable your employees to grow, thrive and excel.

The Tools and Training they Need to do the Job
Too often, it seems, employees are asked to "do more with less." And while that can sometimes be a corporate reality, neglecting to give your people

the tools and training they need to excel can be the biggest mistake you'll ever make.

People cost is almost always the biggest line item in an IT budget. It's the resource you most need to manage well and to optimize for efficiency. So don't scrimp when it comes to training or acquiring labor-saving tools. It'll pay dividends far into the future.

Poorly trained employees make mistakes. And mistakes cost significantly more to repair than if the work had simply been done right the first time. Multiple studies have shown that the later in a process a given mistake occurs, the more costly it becomes to correct.

Well trained employees don't make many mistakes and, when they do, they usually recognize and catch them early. Plus they are able to recognize when something isn't working as efficiently as it should and find ways to improve it. Well trained employees feel better about themselves and their work. They have confidence in their knowledge and ability and they approach their work with much more enthusiasm.

While tools have prices, and a reasonable cost/benefit analysis should show a positive return on the investment in a given tool and the company's financial status must allow for its acquisition, giving employees tools leverages and multiplies their effectiveness. We've known this truth forever, yet sometimes we act as if we'd never heard it. Give your people tools whenever you can. Both the employee and the organization will benefit from the time and money you invest.

It's also important to give employees training at the point of need and not require training that seems to have no value. One organization I worked with required their employees to take several hours of computer-based or video-based training each year. They could select from a wide variety of titles, but often the things that an employee wanted to learn were not represented in those offerings. So this training requirement came to be viewed as onerous and wasn't valued. And the training that was done didn't provide much of a return.

In another organization, training was only given in connection with a project need. And while this was good for the employees who were on that project, those who weren't and who wanted to get better at certain things didn't have the opportunity.

These lessons have convinced me that training must benefit both the organization and the employee. From an organizational development standpoint, you want to always be improving your biggest asset, your employees, so you should select training programs that meet those broader objectives. But individual employee desires and needs should also come into play. Employees will appreciate being given the tools they believe will help them do their job better and more efficiently, and the organization will benefit.

The Right Reward Systems

What gets rewarded gets done. The book, *GMP: The Greatest Management Principle in the World*, published in 1986 by Michael LeBoeuf, offers this eternally valuable observation: what gets rewarded gets done. Whatever you think of the rest of the book, LeBoeuf's key principle often explains why some things work, others don't, and how organizations and projects can sometimes get so fouled up.

Basically, the GMP principle suggests that if you want a particular thing done, you reward the behavior that leads people to do that thing. It seems simple, but, oh, how we get it wrong.

I knew the Help Desk manager of a $1.5 billion business who wanted to improve his customer satisfaction scores. So he began rewarding his employees for closing calls quickly. But while the number of calls handled went up rapidly, the quality of care provided with each call deteriorated and so did their customer satisfaction ratings.

The CIO of a Fortune 50 firm believed that having his employees evaluate and rate their managers would help those managers improve. But when the employees saw it as an opportunity to criticize without rebuttal (yes, there was more than one problem at work in this organization), the managers who needed most to improve instead found a way to manipulate the evaluations. And when the CIO began using the employee rankings as an indicator of high-potential managers, the level of manipulation often turned into outright intimidation.

And it doesn't stop with IT. The CEO of a major international firm wanted the CIO and a respected business leader to implement standard processes and systems across all the firm's business units. But when the CEO failed to change the way the business unit managers were rewarded, the project was doomed to failure.

What kinds of behavior do you want to encourage in your employees? What kinds do you want to discourage? Put reward systems into place that make it in the employees' best interest to behave that way and they will. But don't stick with any reward system for very long; people will have a tendency to try and manipulate it and that will only cause them to focus on the wrong things.

Provide Fair, Honest, and Timely Feedback
Everyone wants to be treated fairly and to know where they stand.

I'm always a little surprised when I find that some managers of managers feel that their direct reports, as managers and leaders, don't need regular feedback or to be told that they are doing a good job. Often, these upper level managers also seem to shy away from the confrontation needed to point out the shortcomings of their direct reports. It makes me wonder how they ever got so far up in their organization in the first place. In my experience, everyone wants honest feedback on how they're doing. And the behavior you reward with praise, you get more of.

But what if an employee, even a highly-placed manager, isn't doing a good job or isn't doing it as well as you think they should be? Do they want to know that? The answer is yes - An *emphatic* yes.

No one wants to feel like they're letting someone else down. No one wants to be seen as a failure. No one wants to be talked about in unfavorable terms. And all of these things will happen if you don't tell your employees on a timely basis where they're falling down and how they can improve. And help them do it.

Remember to practice situational management even with your leaders. There will be times when they're tackling something for the first time and they need the benefit of your experience. They may even need your support inside the organization in order to get something done that they don't have the organizational clout to pull off. If you don't recognize when they need your help, you might even be an unwitting accomplice to their inability to perform up to the level you expect.

One CIO I knew gave a Director the particularly challenging task of handling IT's relationship with a difficult business manager. But instead of forcing that business manager to deal with the Director, the CIO would instead meet, talk with, and deal with that business manager himself. He not only did it on key projects and issues, but whenever the business manager called or dropped by. This CIO shouldn't have been surprised when his Director was never able to establish the kind of rapport with the business manager that the CIO wanted. The CIO just couldn't see that the Director needed his support. And every time the CIO dealt with the business manager himself, he torpedoed whatever progress the Director had made up to that point.

So did the Director point out to the CIO what he was doing? Yes, but not too forcefully. The CIO was sometimes irascible, and didn't always behave predictably. And since the CIO didn't believe he was doing anything wrong, it was difficult for the Director to get him to see the difficulty that his behavior was causing. This CIO was looking out for himself more than his people—he wanted to be seen as helpful to the business manager more than he wanted to grow his Director. This CIO could have practiced much better situational management.

Another good feedback practice is to not wait until a formal performance evaluation period comes around to communicate to an employee that they're not performing to your level of expectation, or that they've made a mistake. Do it as soon as you observe a bad behavior or result. And certainly do it as soon as you realize that you've formed an opinion that an employee isn't doing as well as they should. You may dread it, not relishing the confrontation, but you'll dislike even more the consequences of not doing it right away. On the other hand, you'll love the results that come from working together with a capable employee to resolve a problem and accomplish what you both want.

Remember that employees are often blind to things that they're close to, or accustomed to, and it can take an outside perspective, another set of eyes, to see that something is amiss or that it can be improved and to call attention to it. This is the foundation of a concept called the Johari Window, which graphically depicts in one of four quadrants those things that an employee knows about themselves that you also know, then in another quadrant those things that you know about them that they don't know. It's here that your outside set of eyes can be invaluable. To get the best from your employees, tell them what they don't know, and sometimes can't know.

Sure, your people want your approval, but they also want your honest feedback on their performance. They want to do well and they want to please you. They need your praise, but they also need your criticism. Everyone knows that there are areas where they have room for improvement, so if you're not pointing them out, they know you're not being honest. And if you never give them praise, this also shows that you're not being honest. Either transgression will cost you respect. Everyone needs praise, even if they claim they don't. Positive feedback is what tells us we're on the right track. And if we don't get it we'll fail.

By the way, the Director I mentioned above failed. But whose failure was it?

Fair but Firm Dealings
Always give your people a fair shake.

Don't play favorites. Don't be overly critical. Don't be gratuitous in your praise. All such actions will be seen as false and insincere.

Don't assume that any criticism or accusation leveled against an employee is true until you've talked to the employee personally and verified it. Hear their side of the story. Then take action accordingly. Always give them the benefit of the doubt and a fair shake. When you do, and when you're consistent about not jumping to conclusions or flying off the handle, they'll come to trust you, even when they know they're at fault.

At the same time, be firm. Establish your expectations for behavior and performance and stick to them. Don't bend to accommodate one person and not do it for another. Don't make arbitrary exceptions. And if you do make an exception, be clear about why you're making it and be sure that it's fair to everyone.

As we've said, if an individual doesn't live up to the expectations you've established, play fair and tell them. Don't surprise them later with something they didn't even know was a shortcoming. Give them a chance to improve. And help them to help themselves wherever you can. But don't do their job for them. Don't take on their monkeys. And if, in the end, an employee is consistently unable to meet the expectations you've established, be fair and tell them that you're going to have to make a change. Help them think about where their skills and abilities can be better utilized, and help them find a suitable position where they can succeed. It's the right thing to do and you both will feel better for having approached it that way.

Always have Their Back
If you want loyalty, give it. You hired them. You're training and developing them. If they fail, or if you allow others to criticize them, it's a reflection on you.

If you've chosen the right people for your team, you know that they have the ability to do the job and do it well and to grow. Don't let others stunt that growth. If someone comes to you with a complaint about one of your people, listen respectively. Make sure you understand the basis of the criticism and ask enough questions to ensure that you do.

If you think a criticism is warranted, ask for help from the complainant in identifying ways to remedy the situation and help the employee improve. And when the situation is corrected and performance has improved, be sure to follow up and let the person who complained know that this has occurred. Ask them to observe for themselves and report back to you whether they agree. You need to get this monkey off your employee's back and there's no better way to do that than to have the person who complained in the first place agree that it's no longer a problem.

If you don't agree that a criticism is warranted, say so. And give sound reasons as to why. Perhaps your argument will win the day. But if it doesn't, find some common ground from which both you and the complainant can move forward. Then develop a plan of action.

Sometimes the criticism of an employee can come from another manager. I've seen some managers defend their employees blindly; I've seen some not do it at all. Managers who react either of these two ways simply don't generate much respect. It's the manager who insists on specifics from the complainant and also insists that they supply recommendations for improvement, who is seen as a leader that employees will follow.

One evening I sat on the top floor of a very nice restaurant after a very expensive meal with all of the top managers of a large firm and listened in amazement as one of them said, "Do you think there's anyone at all in this organization who can think?" Then he went on to characterize the entire workforce (a number of whom were his people) as a bunch of lazy incompetents. Even more amazingly, several other managers joined in and began naming specific employees as good examples of it. And no one defended those employees.

What was this manager thinking? Not only was he criticizing himself and his people, he was also attacking every manager in the room. Why didn't any of the managers defend their people when they were attacked?

Wanton criticism or snide remarks or pigeon-holing of a given individual are marks of weak and dependent personalities, and of people who need to try and push others down in an effort to make themselves stand a little taller. It never works. And over the long term, these kinds of people damage themselves as much as they damage others. But over the short term, they can derail the career of a promising employee and you should never allow that to happen.

In fact, the practice of deriding people can become a cancer inside your organization. I've at times heard people comment that "This place is completely messed up." When pressed for why, they'll usually mention a specific practice that they don't like or an action they don't agree with, but they have broadened their dissatisfaction from there to encompass the whole organization and its leadership. They believe that they are the only enlightened ones. If only they were in control, things would be different. You shouldn't allow your peers or anyone else to level wanton unchallenged criticisms of the organization that you are helping build and lead any more than you should let them criticize your people.

So have your employees' backs. Handle criticisms quickly and wisely. And make sure their mistakes are viewed not as failures, but rather as learning opportunities from which they can grow.

5. Recognize Their Efforts and Their Worth

You can catch more flies with honey than vinegar.

We talked earlier about managers who find it difficult to tell their employees that they're doing a good job. I know one CIO who believes he shouldn't have to tell people that they're doing well at what he hired them to do. He doesn't believe they deserve praise for just doing their jobs; they deserve praise for doing more than their jobs.

Even if I accept that rationale for a moment, I have to ask whether the employees know what "more than the job" is. They don't unless you give them very specific objectives up front. Otherwise, you can always claim after the fact that anything they did was always a part of what you expected--part of the job. Who wants to work for that kind of boss? You'll never be able to please them.

We all want to know what's expected of us. We all want to deliver that. Leaders want to deliver more than what's expected of them and they also want recognition for having done it. That's what takes them to the next level. As their leader, it's up to you to provide what they need: both the direction and the praise that outstanding performers require.

Always give Them Little Pats on the Back: There's no Substitute for the Carrot

I'm not talking about being gratuitous here. So don't overdo it. But when you see someone doing something well, tell them. And from time to time, when there's no special occasion, take the time to just let your people know that you appreciate the work they do.

When the going gets tough on a project, it can be difficult to find something positive to say. Do it anyway. A pat on the back at the right time will do wonders for morale and productivity. Negative criticism, while often necessary, seldom motivates. Balance it with the positive.

Recognize Them Formally at Every Opportunity

Most organizations have meetings that can serve as great opportunities to recognize those who have performed especially well. Sometimes verbal recognition is enough. Sometimes organizations give out certificates or other symbols of accomplishment. Sometimes the reward needs to be financial.

I had an employee named Matt who shied away from public recognition. He wouldn't even show up at an event if he knew he was going to be recognized there. He didn't want to be put on the spot and didn't want to have to say anything in front of a group. A lot of employees are like Matt, although perhaps not to that degree. For many, though, speaking in front of a group can be a fear almost as great as the fear of death.

But people like Matt still need recognition and, by formal, I don't necessarily mean public. An email or a letter to the employee's file, a gift certificate, or a lunch or dinner with a companion can also be effective. A lunch or dinner with you can be even more effective. By taking your time to treat an employee to lunch and getting to know them better personally and listening to their desires and, yes, complaints, you can generate goodwill and loyalty that cannot be claimed in any other way. It will make your employees feel valued and special and a lot more comfortable with you as a leader.

Take an Interest in Them as Individuals and in Their Personal Predilections, Hobbies, and Ideas

Perhaps the most significant form of recognition you can give your people is simply to be interested in them, their families, their hobbies and interests, and their accomplishments outside the office. It's the human thing to do. It recognizes their worth as an individual and shows that you realize they're someone beyond your company's four walls. It recognizes the whole person and not just the part that comes to work. And all of this goes a long way toward making a person feel needed, accepted, and appreciated. Plus it pays rewards far beyond any that are simply work-related.

Recap: Unleash Their Talent and Let Them Excel

1. Give them interesting work
2. Give them the freedom to do it their way
3. Give them things they can "own"
4. Give them an environment in which they can excel
   a. The tools and training to do the job

b. The right reward systems
c. Fair, honest, and timely feedback
d. Fair but firm dealings
e. Always have their back
5. Recognize their efforts and their worth
a. Always give them little pats on the back – there's no substitute for the carrot
b. Recognize them formally at every opportunity
c. Take an interest in them as individuals and in their personal predilections, hobbies, and ideas

D. Take Pride in Their Accomplishments

The secret to your success always lies in the success of the people and the teams that you lead. And your greatest pride as a leader should come from developing leaders that perform even better than you.

So take pride in the accomplishments of your people. Celebrate them. Savor them. They're your accomplishments too, and are a direct reflection of your ability as a leader.

Recognize that your Success and Theirs go Hand in Hand

Know that neither of you can succeed without the other. Your employees need your help, guidance, and coaching. You need them to perform. If you help them succeed, you'll not only get the performance results you want, you'll be recognized as a good leader and developer of talent. Plus you'll have built a stable of loyal employees willing to give of their best when you ask because they know you'll appreciate and reward them. There may come a time when you'll need such a stable of loyal talent.

Brag on Them to your Management

Both you and your employees need the recognition of having turned in a good performance. And no one else is going to brag on your people as much as you. It may be that no one else will brag on them at all. So tell your management how well your people did. Point out their particular skills and abilities. Build an image of your department as being made up of exceptional people. It'll reflect well on your ability to hire, develop, and lead. And it'll reflect well on the performance of your people.

Brag on Them to your Peers

Make sure your peers know that your people are doing good work and that they're accomplishing significant things. It's okay to believe you have the best people. And maybe you do. And perhaps your bragging on your people will have other managers wanting to hire them. But that's a good thing. Good for you and good for your people.

Other managers may not brag about their employees or do a very good job pointing out their accomplishments. Too often, upwardly mobile managers are too busy polishing their own apples to take time to recognize the people who helped them perform, or to even recognize the importance of doing so. But it's difficult for someone to shine the spotlight on themselves, and it's usually seen as self-serving by their employees, other managers, and the boss. Do you think an employee would rather work for a boss who brags on them, or one who takes all the credit themselves? For which one do you think an employee would be motivated to work hardest?

Get Them Good Press and Recognition

Take the time to get stories about your people's accomplishments into company or departmental publications or onto a web site. Recommend them for awards and certificates. Ask the business people for whom they've done good work to submit articles or send emails or present them awards.

Dillon, one employee I rode hard about a shortcoming she had difficulty overcoming, believed that, because I was hard on her, I didn't appreciate her efforts or think that she had the potential to advance. She wore the mantle of my suspected disappointment heavily until I worked with a key business unit head to have her recognized at a major business function. This helped, but it wasn't a complete cure. But she was astounded when the President of the company presented her with a coveted award for which I had sponsored her—an award that had never before been given to an IT employee.

The key was that she deserved it. Yet despite that, she had felt that I was disappointed in her until that moment. Until the fact I was indeed proud of her was so prominently displayed.

Tell Them, Sincerely, that You're Proud of Them

I had told Dillon multiple times that I believed in her, even while I had showed her where and how she could do better. I had patted her on the back whenever I could, although I'm sure it was never enough. After each of her rewards was presented, I told her again that I was proud of her accomplishment. And, finally, it was absolutely obvious that it was true. That's what it took for Dillon to at last throw off the mantle of suspected managerial disappointment.

You never know exactly how your efforts at coaching and trying to help an individual employee to grow will be taken. How your efforts to correct performance and build capabilities will be received. Sometimes, even though your intent is positive, it may be taken in exactly the opposite way. So take the time to praise sincerely. And back it up with action.

Recap: Take Pride in Their Accomplishments

1. Recognize that your success and theirs go hand in hand
2. Brag on them to your management
3. Brag on them to your peers
4. Get them good press and recognition
5. Tell them, sincerely, that you're proud of them

CONCLUSION

Of the people you hire and who make up your team, all want to feel needed. All want to feel important. Just as you do. It's basic to the human condition.

But not everyone is good at the same things or to the same degree. Some are more outgoing and confident; others more introspective and shy. Some are verbal, visual and feelings-oriented; others more analytical. Some may prefer written communications, and demand reason and logic. Others may operate more from the gut. And there's everything in between. Recognizing what your people need, and meeting them at their individual points of need, so that you can develop them and help them realize their goals is the first basic requirement of leadership.

The second is getting the best from them and what they have to offer—both for you and your organization—by unleashing them. Giving them opportunities to excel and making sure that they take advantage of them. Not everyone is ready at the same time or with the same level of proficiency to tackle a given task or project. Recognizing what your people are capable of, or capable of growing into, and giving each of them appropriate, challenging work shows that you have confidence in them and high expectations of them. And good people will always respond.

And when they respond, that reflects positively on you and you both win.

And when you help them by giving them what they need, they will go to the ends of the earth for you. They will have learned to trust you and will know that their efforts will be recognized, appreciated and rewarded.

When you recognize, appreciate, and reward them, they will take pride in their accomplishments, in their team, and in their leader.

When you value them and their successes, they will be fiercely loyal and will work to protect you just as hard as you have worked to protect them.

When you base your success on theirs and take the time to develop them into the leaders they can become, they will go on to bigger and better things, will remember you with fondness, and will emulate you. And that's how you'll know that you have succeeded

REFERENCES

Alderfer, C. P. (1969). An empirical test of a new theory of human need. *Organizational Behavior and Human Performance, 4*(2), 142–175. doi:10.1016/0030-5073(69)90004-X

Alderfer, C. P. (1982). *Existence, relatedness, and growth: Human needs in organizational settings.* Free Press.

Blanchard, K. (1994). *Leadership and the one minute manager.* Harper Collins.

Hersey, P., & Blanchard, K. H. (1977). *Management of organizational behavior 3rd edition–utilizing human resources.* New Jersey/Prentice Hall.

Jung, C. G. (1971). Psychological types. In *Collected works of C.G. Jung, volume 6.* Princeton University Press.

Keirsey, D. (1998). *Please understand me II: Temperament, character, intelligence* (1st ed.). Prometheus Nemesis Book Co.

Luft, J., & Ingham, H. (1955). The Johari window, a graphic model of interpersonal awareness. *Proceedings of the Western Training Laboratory in Group Development* (Los Angeles: UCLA).

Maslow, A. H. (1943). A theory of human motivation. *Psychological Review, 50*(4), 370–396. doi:10.1037/h0054346

Mellora, D., Stokesa, M., Firth, L., Hayashia, Y., & Cummins, R. (2008). Need for belonging, relationship satisfaction, loneliness, and life satisfaction. *Personality and Individual Differences, 45*(3), 213–218. doi:10.1016/j.paid.2008.03.020

Mitchell, V. F., & Moudgill, P. (1976). Measurement of Maslow's need hierarchy. *Organizational Behavior and Human Performance, 16*(2), 334–339. doi:10.1016/0030-5073(76)90020-9

Myers, I. B., & Myers, P. B. (1980, 1995). *Gifts differing: Understanding personality type.* Mountain View, CA: Davies-Black Publishing.

Oncken, W., & Wass, D. (1974). Management time: Who's got the monkey? *Harvard Business Review*, 75–80.

Wahba, M. A., & Bridwell, L. G. (1976). Maslow reconsidered: A review of research on the need hierarchy theory. *Organizational Behavior and Human Performance, 15*(2), 212–240. doi:10.1016/0030-5073(76)90038-6

Chapter 19
Considerations for Organizations and Personnel

Lisa K. Meisenbacher
ADP, USA

ABSTRACT

This recent perspective on IT HR trends discusses the changes in skills required for a successful IT career, while recognizing the dynamics of the changes in demand for IT talent. Fundamental is the need to build and maintain a strong network.

HISTORICAL PERSPECTIVE OF IT

I was fortunate enough during the beginning of my professional career (after college) to be at the right place at the right time. I started working for a pharma firm right out of college before the PC boom emerged in the Fortune 500 workplace. As such, I began my engineering career in a very traditional sense. I started working in pharma as a chemical engineer in a manufacturing environment with every intention of following a traditional engineering career path.

With the emergence of manufacturing automation and instrumentation as well as the PC boom in the workplace, my career aspirations quickly changed. The early nineties served as a cross roads for many professionals like myself interested in the new emerging field of Information Technology and the varied career options that spawned from the maturity and mainstream use of the internet, the dot com boom, and the Y2K frenzy.

CAREERS IN IT

The IT industry has matured and developed tremendously over the past decade so there are almost limitless long-term career opportunities. The greatest barriers to achieving one's immediate IT career aspirations are based on matters of the

DOI: 10.4018/978-1-60960-535-3.ch019

economy and the impacts of increasing numbers of outsourced IT positions.

The recession following 9-11 and the near collapse of financial industry in 2008 have both had tremendous negative impacts on IT opportunities, especially domestically in the US. In retrospect, I feel much of the IT cost containment following both of these significant events was fear based and reactionary. I believe the insatiable need to keep company boards and Wall Street happy continues to drive the seemingly endless number of IT layoffs that have curtailed many IT careers. My observation is that there is not and was not a shortage of work to be done or problems to be solved in the IT industry during these time periods.

As of this writing in 2010, the supply of highly skilled IT professionals outweighs the demand for commensurate IT opportunities. For every open IT position, it's well known the number of available and interested applicants far exceeds the ability of HR organizations to screen manually. Automated screening and online application processes are commonplace today in the IT industry.

HR organizations and recruiting firms alike have been inundated with highly skilled and available applicants. This has created an interesting paradigm shift in the whole recruiting process in the IT industry.

Competition for these scarce open positions has never been greater and the skills and competencies of those professionals in the applicant pool are as diverse as are the hiring managers looking to fill these positions.

Outsourcing and underemployment continue to be common themes in the IT industry. College recruits are competing with "seasoned" and highly skilled hires for entry-level positions. Furthermore, those positions traditionally filled with domestic hires are now going offshore based on the ability to drive down the cost of IT compensation packages for the mid to entry range level IT positions.

The primary economic driving factors I've observed are as follows:

a. Limited IT domestic opportunities
b. Large supply of highly-skilled and available applicants
c. An increasing trend towards outsourcing or underemployment which drives down the total cost of employment

To complicate the process even further, my experience has shown that job descriptions for open positions change many times over during the course of the hiring process due to significant indecision on the part of the hiring managers in terms of what skills and competencies are needed and desired for the open positions.

In short, many times hiring managers don't know what they want or need mainly because they don't know what problem they are trying to solve in their specific organizations. I've lost track of the number of times I've heard recruiters or hiring managers say, "I'll recognize what I need when I see it." I've never found the trial and error approach to be highly effective on either side of the hiring process. I learned very early on in my engineering career that if you can't identify the problem, you'd surely never find the correct solution.

As with other cyclical industries, I believe the IT industry will rebound and will provide ample long-term career opportunities for IT professionals. Overall, the landscape has changed and will continue to change as far as the increasing demands for IT professionals to sharpen their leadership, strategic thinking, problem solving, communication, influencing, relationship management, and interpersonal skills. Contrary to previous time periods, I believe it is no longer sufficient to "hang your hat" on your technical expertise in the IT industry if you want a long lasting and successful career.

A recent article published by the WSJ (5/24/2010) titled "Why CIO's Are Last Among Equals" details the current perceptions and skills that CIO's lack. Although this article focuses on the role of the CIO, I believe it is an easy extrapolation to say these skills are also lacking across the board in the IT industry.

Information Technology will continue to play a vital role in every aspect of the global economy. I'm very optimistic about future career opportunities and will continue to develop my skills to meet and exceed the market demands.

IT PROFESSIONAL ORGANIZATIONS

IT professional organizations will continue to provide the momentum and the "glue" that keeps the IT industry moving forward into future generations. Professional networking groups and organizations have also provided the "silver lining" for IT professionals that were the first to experience the shattering of the "cradle to grave" myth that so many of us were promised when we graduated from college.

Academia has always been at the forefront of promoting peer-to-peer collaboration and information sharing. I believe the popularity of IT professional networking organizations have their origins in the success of many long established academic organizations.

During the past twenty years of my professional experience, professional networking has gone mainstream and is a core competency for anyone that is an IT professional. This skill is not something that was taught to IT professionals that began their careers in the late 80's/ early 90's. Rather, it was spawned out of shear necessity when the "rules of the game" were changed and many IT professionals found themselves out of work for the very first time in their careers.

For those individuals just starting their careers in IT, they are often introduced much earlier on in their careers to the concept of "networking". Many colleges and universities provide internship and networking opportunities so that students can gain these skills before they enter the job market.

For those professionals who are new to networking, there are thousands of IT professional organizations available to participate in. There is something for everyone. Many are free others require an application process and membership fees. Professional networking organizations have become synonymous with sharing business cards, best practices, business opportunities, and building and maintaining professional relationships through social media such as LinkedIn and Twitter.

I believe many of the professional networking organizations provide the breeding ground for developing the very skills that the WSJ highlighted as currently lacking in the IT industry. Professionals learn from each other, develop reciprocal relationships and can at times provide each other with mentor/mentee development opportunities.

I think it's critical that IT organizations fully support the needs of their employees to develop their networking skills and these skills should be formally recognized and promoted by every HR department as a core IT competency.

REFERENCE

Delisi, P. S., Mober, D., & Danielson, R. (2010, May 24). Why CIO's are last among equals. *Wall Street Journal*.

Chapter 20
IT HR and the Perceived Value of Networking Organizations

Donald E. Brown
IT Management Professional, USA

ABSTRACT

The purpose of this chapter is to explore how people and corporations perceive the value of networking organizations and social networking structures. Surveys were used to gather information about how networking organization members and staffing professionals alike view these networks in terms of their effectiveness and general value. This chapter will highlight the issues, controversies, and problems experienced by the modern day worker and staffing professionals, and it will examine the solutions and benefits realized through networking structures and look to the future as the trends uncovered persist. In conclusion, it will be shown that there are synergies in taking advantage of this relatively low investment and low risk way of connecting with communities of experts and corporate opportunities.

INTRODUCTION

The ever changing global business landscape continues to present new challenges for job seekers and employers alike. Global competition and economic pressure have reshaped the way that the workforce thinks about the management of business today. Traditional workforce structures are being compressed, flattened and reorganized

DOI: 10.4018/978-1-60960-535-3.ch020

to take advantage of economies of scales and to eliminate waste and over compensation. A global workforce, very specific required skill sets, larger demands for work-life balance, diversity campaigns, evolving work values by generation and an aging workforce in general are just a few of the variables in the scheme of an ever changing complexity to our workforce. Companies around the globe have no choice but to realize that people are their greatest asset. Hiring and retaining the best talent requires both traditional and non-traditional methods. IT human resources must identify the best available candidates, hire them and retain these professionals if the organization is to be staffed optimally and not be under the pressures of constant employee turnover.

The purpose of this chapter is to explore how corporate IT human resources decision maker perceive the value of networking organizations and similar social networking structures. Surveys will be used to gather information about how networking organization members and staffing professionals alike view these networks in terms of their effectiveness and general value. This chapter will help readers to understand the experiences of the people involved in networking organizations, both internal to their jobs and external, traditional and neo-traditional. This chapter will also present a view of similar concepts from the perspective of the staffing organization and the challenges and benefits that they experience when sourcing through established networking organizations and structures.

NETWORK ORGANIZATION MEMBER INPUTS

The definition of a technology networking organization, in the context of this chapter, is a structure or association through which individuals in the area of technology are drawn together because of common goals or beliefs where knowledge, resources and relationships are leveraged to progress the agenda of the association. Members from various networking organizations were surveyed to find out what their individual experiences as members has been like for them. The first set of people that were surveyed belonged to internal corporate networking organizations and affinity groups and/or members of external volunteer non-profit organizations. The survey responders were of varying ages and degrees of experience, ranging from junior level technology professionals to senior management. The surveys conducted

contained questions that were both multiple choice and open response, based on the focus of the survey question asked. The survey was designed to allow participants to answer as freely and openly as they wished, conducted with the intention of keeping their identity anonymous.

The Networking Value Proposition

The first question asked was to find out whether or not the individual's believe that networking organizations bring value to the company's staffing organization. The question was posed with a yes or no response. As a result, 100% of the people that took the survey said that they do in fact believe that there is value derived by staffing organizations. For IT staffing, this is a strong indication that technology professionals have an expectation that there will be opportunities to seek out new opportunities of employment through membership in networking organizations.

As a direct follow up to the last question, participants were asked how they think that these networking organizations deliver value. The response was designed as an open comment box.

Survey participants shared that they believe that by being involved with networking organizations that individuals in human resources could develop a rapport with professionals through regular interaction. The survey subjects believed that by networking, staffing professionals gain access to highly skilled and experienced individuals, many of which they may have never met. Many of the members of these professional networking organizations do not respond to traditional advertisements for positions. Human Resources may not have otherwise met some of these people because many people that are employed do not search for new opportunities. Networking events and conferences bring people of like interest, skills, etcetera into one venue. This "collection" of individuals would be very expensive and costly in terms of time and effort to get to without networking organizations. The costs to meet, screen and interview these professionals through traditional means greatly outweigh the cost of a membership and participation in the targeted organization.

Also worth mentioning, survey participants shared that referrals by members of other members tend to be taken very seriously. The reason is that by referring someone to their company's staffing organization, the referring individual's judgment and reputation is also on the line. This, according to the survey participants, acts as a candidate screening mechanism or filter for the IT HR professional. The staffing organization can quickly get to the kinds of people that they are looking for. As an example, young, ambitious junior IT associates often seek connections through peer networks. If IT HR can connect themselves with these organizations, they can quickly establish a pool of candidates and referrals with a much narrower focus than staffing could achieve through cold calls and open calls for resumes through other traditional means of advertisement.

Survey participants also shared that they experienced a level of comfort in being a part of an external networking organization because it did not directly affect their performance reviews at work. This allows them to strike out and try new things like becoming a leader in the organization or to learn finance and to serve as members of the Board of Directors for the organization. This too is a benefit to the IT HR person because they are able to reach candidates that have a proven breadth of scope and experience in leading organizations. Others survey participants perceived that networking organizations allowed for informal mentoring and guidance and even with templates, tools and resources to help them in their jobs. They shared that no matter what your title at work is, networking organizations gave them the flexibility to get to needed resources and guidance without concern for their manager's judgment or approval. Participants volunteered that networking organizations gave them an outlet to take risk, exchange ideas, share best practices and also to talk about their likes and dislikes at their jobs and how best to

manage the more negative experiences. For the IT staffing professional, becoming a part of the growth experience of these networking professionals represents an opportunity to know these candidates first hand and to see their work ethic, soft skills and business practices, and to even help to shape some of the candidates' careers and experience.

Do Networking Organizations Work?

Participants were next asked to give their opinions on the value of membership in networking organizations. There were three categories of types of networking organizations in this question. They were the Internal Corporate Organization, the External Networking Organization and the neo-networking or Social Networking Organizations that have found their place because of technology and access through the Internet. Participants were asked to rate the perceived value of these three types of organizations as Not Valuable At All, Somewhat Valuable, Valuable and Very Valuable. 25% of those surveyed shared that internal corporate networking organizations were Somewhat Valuable. 25% also had the experience that virtual or social networking by way of the Internet was Somewhat Valuable. 50% of those surveyed highlighted that external networking organizations were Valuable. To the IT HR professional, these responses would indicate that it makes sense to seek out networking organizations to help deliver some of the value that members are eagerly searching for in the way of new opportunities.

As a follow-up question, survey participants were asked to provide comments to justify why they chose the ratings that they did. In terms of internal networking organizations, participants did not feel comfortable participating heavily in the activities at work, sighting that employees tend not to be as open and honest when involved in company activity. The theme that seemed to come up here was that people are guarded and almost watchful when it comes to internal corporate group activity. Participants shared that on-line social networking is indeed convenient, but it is time consuming and being involved in just social networking does not allow individuals to for any real relationships with one another. Participants that have tried using social networking websites to land interviews, found the sites to be good for perhaps making a phone contact at best. The overwhelming response was that external networking provides the insulated, safe environment that they lack at work, but also allows for the much needed face to face interaction that is lacking with social networking. The take-away here for IT HR is clearly that there is no replacement for one-on-one interaction when trying to establish a rapport with possible candidates.

Survey participants were asked if being a part of a networking organization helped them secure a new position. Of those polled, 33 1/3% said that they did in fact get a new position through networking while 66 2/3% said that they did not.

The next question asked was to find out whether or not the individual's manager or employer supports their being a part of either a company sponsored internal networking organization or an external organization. The question was posed with a yes or no response. As a result, 100% of the people that tool the survey said that their manager or employer does indeed support them as members and participants in member activities.

Economic Factors

Survey participants were then asked to give their opinions on the state of the job market in general. Participants were asked if they were of the opinion that the job market was Frozen, Getting Better, As Good As It Was before the Recession or is it Better Than It Was Before the Recession. Of those polled, 100% said that the market is either frozen or getting better. None of the participants responded that the job market has returned to par since the 2009 recession.

A similar question was asked as related to the job situation for members of networking organizations. For this question, participants were asked if they saw the job market as Not Favorable, Somewhat Favorable, Favorable or Very Favorable for members of networking organization seeking employment. Of those surveyed, 83% replied Somewhat Favorable and 17% replied Favorable.

Networking Trends

Participants were asked about the social networking sites that they used. Of those polled, 90% of them use LinkedIn (http://www.LinkeIn.com). 16% of those polled used Facebook (http://www.facebook.com). No other social networking sites were reported as being a regular part of the participants' on-line activity. The main comment that was included with this question by participants was that it simply takes too much time and effort to manage these social networking sites with any degree of regularity. From an IT HR perspective, it becomes important to realize that candidates are not only looking for an interview, but they are also noting the companies and recruiters that get results in the way of new hires.

Networking Organization Member Thoughts

The final question asked was to share any additional thoughts that people have regarding the value that people derive from being members of networking organizations. Many of the comments hit upon the same themes. Members enjoy inroads with other people from other companies and organizations. They like have the ability to be candid. They feel that networking organizations create a safe environment for feedback, coaching, mentoring and personal growth. They commented on the fact that the successes of individuals within the network become everyone's successes because of association either implied or direct. Credibility is increased for the organization as a whole when this happens creating a value add. Many of the users enjoy the opportunity to help the others. They also find the quid pro quo factor of networking to be a nice currency of exchange. Those polled said that they are able to build a network that will assist them with their personal branding and marketing of their skills. Members also benefit from the confidence that success within the organization fosters in way of leadership positions, public exposure and teamwork.

THE IT STAFFING ORGANIZATION PERSPECTIVE

The second group of individuals surveyed represent IT human resources professionals. The survey responders were of mid level to senior tenure in their HR organizations. These IT HR professionals were surveyed to find out what their individual experiences as human resources personnel working with networking organizations has been like for them. The surveys conducted contained questions that were both multiple choice and open response, based on the focus of the survey question asked. The survey was designed to allow participants to answer as freely and openly as they wished, conducted with the intention of keeping their identity anonymous just as in the member survey.

The Networking Value Proposition for IT HR

The first question asked was to find out whether or not people in human resources believe that networking organizations bring value to the company's staffing organization. The question was posed with a yes or no response. As a result, 100% of the people that took the survey said that they do in fact believe that there connection with networking organizations both internal to the company and external does bring to corporate staffing organizations. The finding further supports the fact that the relationships with networking organizations are usually positive in their returns. As a direct follow up to that question, HR participants were asked how they perceived these networking organizations deliver value. The response was designed as an open comment box. Survey participants all seemed to have a similar response to this question. They all agreed that networking organizations give them an increased level of exposure to candidates that they might not otherwise be able to source. They believed that non-traditional resources of applicants (especially women, minorities and higher caliber referrals). These HR professionals also seemed to believe that they were exposed to highly qualified and highly candidates through networking group referrals because the referring members take their own integrity very seriously before sending candidates.

Participants were next asked to give their opinions on the value of connections with networking organizations. There were three categories of types of networking organizations in this question. They were the Internal Corporate Organization, the External Networking Organization and the neo-networking or Social Networking Organizations. Staffing participants were asked to rate the perceived value of these three types of organizations as Not Valuable At All, Somewhat Valuable, Valuable and Very Valuable. 100% of those surveyed agree that Internal Corporate Networking organizations were Somewhat Valuable. 25% also responded that virtual or Social Networking by way of the Internet was Somewhat Valuable. 50% of those surveyed shared that External Networking organizations were Valuable. The distribution of results shows that with every form of networking organization mentioned, there is indeed a positive value derived. Apparently, current internal networking connections as well as those gained through on-line social networking sites yield a fair return while external peer networks offer a greater return on value.

As a follow-up question, HR survey participants were asked if they could think of anything at all that networking organizations might do or do better to help corporate staffing. Again there was good alignment with the responses in that the participants understood that they needed to provide some insight into what the company in looking for in order that the networking organization might be able to provide or deliver whatever those objectives and goals may be. Items like specific job requirements, the latest core competencies and the latest direction from upper management help to satisfy those descriptions of things that might be needed. The HR participants also stated that without clear objectives and an understanding of the networking organization's value statement, efforts by networking organizations would be hit or miss with IT HR and would surely not be as highly valued as if they were targeted and focused specifically. One final thought was to help the members of networking organizations with basic must have items like strong resumes, continues learning and proper business preparation and presentation. They pointed out that candidates with multiple credentials and certifications frequently come from networking referrals, and they are always a welcome communication. They made it clear that any lead information to good talent was of value to them in their staffing efforts.

Economic Effects on IT HR

Staffing survey participants were then asked to give their opinions on the state of the job market in general. Participants were asked if they were of the opinion that the job market was Frozen, Getting better, as Good as It Was before the Recession or is it Better Than It Was Before the Recession. Of those polled, 100% said that the market is either frozen or getting better. Once again, none of the participants said that the job market has returned to par since the 2009 recession.

A similar question was asked of HR as related to the job situation for members of networking organizations. For this question, participants were asked they said that job market was Not Favorable, Somewhat Favorable, Favorable or Very Favorable

for members of networking organization seeking employment. Of those surveyed, 100% replied somewhat favorable.

The IT Staffing Perspective

The final question asked of the Staffing Professionals in our survey asked for any thoughts or suggestions about how networking organizations might start to develop a relationship with HR. One of the responses was that Human Resources build their network by the people that they call into the inner circle. The face to face interaction is most valuable in that it streamlines the screening and sometimes interview process for them. Other comments circled around the idea that information is the best thing to provide to human resources to start the gears turning on a lasting relationship between corporate HR and a networking organization.

Issues, Controversies, Problems

Based on the feedback from members of networking organizations, the following issues and problems are seen by the individual member in their professional experience where there are no networking outlets:

- There is a lack of a creative environment
- High risk, low reward for exposure to new things
- Lack of the right information when it is needed
- Low interest in the formal mentoring process
- Few referrals for better positions and new experiences
- Less personal satisfaction for helping others
- Established reporting power structure makes it hard to get noticed
- Narrowly and tightly defined roles make new experiences hard to come by

- One-way communication
- Self promotion and exposure is often frowned upon
- Too much control from the top of the organization
- Relatively small circles of influence
- No comfort in candid conversation
- Very little career guidance towards success and success targets
- Lack of clear and honest communication

Based on the feedback from staffing organizations, the following issues and problems are seen by the HR professional when they have a sourcing need:

- Finding skilled, qualified candidates can be hit or miss in this very competitive market
- The costs of recruiting and sourcing are high to IT HR organizations
- Difficult to get to specific kinds of candidates like women, minorities, high caliber candidates through the traditional screening processes which often either screens out good talent or forces the candidate to decide that they want to work in a more progressive environment
- Job requirements are very specific in the skills being sought so sourcing the talent to meet those requirements can be very difficult for the IT staffing organization
- It is hard to get good information on qualified candidates which is why networking organizations offer value in the way of peer referrals to IT HR
- Finding candidates with multiple credentials and skills is often very hard to do through a resume giving credence to interaction by being involved in a networking organization
- Face to face relationship building can be very time consuming, especially when it not done in an informed manner

- Getting the outputs needed to show value like hires, true demographics and graduating students can be a daunting task for the IT HR professional that is not attached to networks with talented and experienced technology professionals
- Creating a stimulating environment through rewards other than money can be a great tool to the staffing team because candidates are able to differentiate between companies that do more to deliver value to their employees
- Retaining and refreshing good talent is always a challenge for IT HR

Solutions and Recommendations

For the employee:

- Find an external source of satisfaction
- Identify lower risk, higher reward opportunities for exposure to new things
- Seek the people that have the information you need
- Seek informal mentors
- Seek outside opportunities
- Find ways to help others externally or internally
- Find noteworthy assignments internally or externally
- Take on a volunteer role that will give you a value added experience
- Find peers outside of work to share with
- Find organizations outside of work to learn from
- Get involved in the community
- Seek informal mentors internally and externally

For the IT Human Resources professional:

- Learn to count on referrals as part of the sourcing process

- Take advantage of free assistance from people and organizations to help meet your IT staffing goals and metrics
- Share job requirements with non-traditional networks because they will find qualified candidates faster and less expensively than IT HR can through traditional means
- Ask direct questions regarding talent when screening candidates
- Look to external and internal groups for referrals because talent comes from many diverse diverse sources, some of which are screened out during the formal screening process
- Join a networking organization to learn who the top talent is in each organization and create a relationship with the people in these networks
- Target and share your sourcing needs and requirements so that eager, talented people can help IT HR find solutions to meet the needs
- Create programs that have good senior sponsorship so that the IT HR relationships formed with these networking organizations remain intact and are not just a flash in the pan
- Develop a rotational program to help mold and guide people through the talent process
- Embrace Flexible Work Arrangements because this alone is huge value to the candidates that end up screen IT HR as they decide if they want to work for the company

CONCLUSION

Based on the research that has led to this point, it is seen that there are indeed synergies that can be obtained between networking organizations and corporate human resources organizations. Most employees simply want the opportunity to grow in a safe environment. They find value in helping others while they are in fact helping more than just one person within their networking organization. The casual worker is looking for inclusion and sense of accomplishment while they gain personal satisfaction from obtaining new skills and trying new roles. The key for networking organizations is to find out what the corporate directives are for any given year and then target larger events, talented people and value based information designed to meet those needs.

Human Resources professionals in IT find it hard to tap into talent through traditional means. Recruiting search firms can cost quite a bit to land even perhaps marginal talent at times. Through information sharing and rapport building with networking organizations, staffing professionals often meet highly qualified and highly skilled talent through personal referrals. These referrals are usually of relatively high quality because the referring employees want to keep a high degree of trust with the HR department. This "pre-screening" can shorten the sourcing process from application, to screening, to first interview, to second interview to hire by eliminating one or more of the intermediate screenings or interviews.

In the end, the staffing organization usually ends up with a larger number of candidates and candidate referrals than they would have gotten through other traditional means.

ADDITIONAL READING

http://www.bdpa.com

http://www.bdpanewjersey.com

http://www.LinkedIn.com

http://www.randalpinkett.com

Section 5
Cases

The successful organization of the future will be the ones with a prepared motivated team. The successful team will be comprised of people with the appropriate balance of skills who have taken charge of their future.

Chapter 21
Influence of the Organizational Culture into IT Department Structure, User Relationships and Motivators:
Brazilian Cases

Ângela F. Brodbeck
Federal University of Rio Grande do Sul (UFRGS), Brazil

Henrique J. Brodbeck
Federal University of Rio Grande do Sul (UFRGS), Brazil

ABSTRACT

This chapter presents two organizational case studies of Brazilian companies: a cutlery multinational with both domestic and international plants, including in the USA, and a public university. The chapter describes their organizational culture and the Information Technology (IT) structure resulting from that culture, how IT responds to business requests, and the main drivers, indicators, and motivators of the IT area. At the end, some questions are raised about organizational and individual culture, how these elements can influence IT personnel, and their attitude towards the problems of users, as well as how they can sometimes change patterns of behavior in the organization.

INTRODUCTION

Organizational or individual culture can affect the structure of a department, how IT staff meets the demands of users as well as to determine the motivators of IT professionals. In the reports presented below were contextualized elements of organizational and individual culture that may affect the relationship of IT staff with the users as

DOI: 10.4018/978-1-60960-535-3.ch021

well as in determining individual and collective patterns of behavior. The cases show that regional and cultural patterns of a particular social group can change the behavior and actions of internal members of an organization. Thus, the individual interests of the IT staff can override the interests of groups and of the whole organization and vice versa. Often IT jargon may be reflected in the way of developing systems and training users, and can affect acceptance of the systems by users and the efficiency of its use. This can be explained through the lens of some organizational theories.

Functionalist theories like the contingency theory or the institutional theory observe organizational actions through the lens of the reactive, adapted, and social behavior, involving social aspects and cultural acceptance. Other theories like the ones that deal with the human behavior displays these actions as individual relations to their environment and to other individuals. For this to happen, societies create symbols, systems, or tools that can change and develop the human behavior. These actions can be noted by attitudes of the individuals in a group, as well as their participation and influence inside an organization (Bruner, 1997; Weber, 1974).

The interests of these individuals (actors of the organization) can be different or can be coexistent among them, for the reason that the social relations between them exalt a social space inside an organizational field. Social practices that are going to be applied inside an objectively structured field are defined through these relations. These social practices can emerge from the interaction, from the perception of mental schemes (collective meanings) and from the interest of the organizational actors. The interaction between the actors of the organizations and the action produced through their mental schemes can lead to a convergence of interests. An actor predicts that the other actor can offer benefits and each one of them has a similar idea about the way this action can be achieved. Such interactions are creating the or-

ganizational culture (Srour, 2005; Weick, 1998; Nizet; Pichault, 1995).

Culture can be defined as a system of beliefs that is essentially comprised of interpretations of the world and of the activities and artifacts that reflect them. The organizational culture can define the form of a department structure or a system or a work team, determined by several elements like (Bourguignon et al., 2004; Mintzberg et al, 2000):

a. **Management type:** there are several possible styles of managers to lead individuals or team members, such as a person-oriented combination of benefits combination as opposed to productivity-oriented benefits. To reward individuals through performance awards, fringe benefits, stock options, and financial compensation may be an important factor in the conduct of individuals or work teams. However, in most cases, this is a decision that depends on the organizational culture and that will also determine the managerial posture towards their teams.

b. **Delegation of power or authority:** individual or team members elect their leader, who is not always the one who holds the authority and power. IT departments work on projects and it is common for individuals or teams receive incentive bonuses for meeting deadlines and project costs. The IT manager should keep in mind what makes a good project leader and should be able to manage people by distributing responsibilities for the activities and tasks to be accomplished to fulfill the project. This leader should have authority enough to keep the members of project teams in line by focusing on the contribution that timely completion of projects will bring to the organization.

c. **Tendency to work in teams:** since IT departments work on projects related to the demands of their business partners, they need to employ work teams. Team work is based on negotiations to solve problems while respecting people and their acts, so it requires that the manager or team leader is sensitive about individual culture (of the members of IT staff) and organizational culture and beliefs (of users).

d. **Organizational or departmental structures:** these structures can vary depending on the type of governmental, industry or multinational organizations. Like other functional organizations IT departments formally assume such structures.

e. **Subordination relations:** IT departments can take the formal reporting structures of the company, but the reporting relationships may have an informal aspect, e.g., based on length of service or even on the inherent leadership that a particular person has on the CIO.

f. **Social demands of the organization:** social demands can affect the internal aspects of the organization, as friendship external to the organization may influence internal conduct or certain features of a town may determine the management conduct and relationship between the individuals of the IT department and other individuals in the organization. Politics and structural influence of the government, where the head today may be the subordinate tomorrow, can also determine relationships and actions among individuals.

g. **Adopted emphasis:** the posture adopted by organizations facing the resolution of problems (or meeting demands) may be of apprenticeship and reward. Usually the individuals in the IT department must adopt an attitude of learning from the problems that arise during the development of their projects or incident support, and with the learning comes the reward – a better relationship between IT staff and users, greater user satisfaction with the service provided, etc. However, the culture of some organizations does not favor this behavior, causing lack of interest by the individuals in learning

or solving problems, affecting mainly the relationship between IT staff and business.

h. **Career plan:** focusing on career planning seems to be a common goal for individuals in organizations. It is therefore in the interest of organizations to retain talent, keeping the turnover low, establishing a good career plan model that gives employees the prospect of professional advancement.

i. **Attitude to external control:** external controls like those exercised by shareholders may be important factors in building the organizational performance and can affect the relationships between business and IT areas. To define and maintain KPIs (Key performance Indicators) for service and support can raise the level of IT services to users, improving the relationship, learning and even linking those KPIs to incentive and bonuses.

j. **Orientation of the organization:** organizations can have a professional or a non-professional orientation. Organizations with professional attitude have rooted in their cultures modern HR management techniques, such as incentive pay for performance and distribution of annual profits, among others. This approach generates in the individuals a competitive spirit, a quest for continuous improvement and constant learning. Organizational culture overrides the individual culture; shareholders interests surpass individual interests.

Organizations with non-professional attitude are typically organizations with a more paternalistic family culture. The business is transferred from father to son and many children of employees follow the footsteps of parents working for the same organization, and this may determine the organizational culture and the attitude of management.

Actions and attitudes between the actors of the organizations reflect the culture that the organization instills among its associates. This way, if the organization has a family-based culture (as in Case 1), with a "visible owner", preserving relations throughout a period of time, then the organization can foster factors such as increased permanence in the respective position, respect for the most experienced and non-existence of a severe performance measurement. Sometimes relationships are more important than results. The opposite happens in organizations with a professional culture, "without an owner" (as in Case 2), where competition for power and good results, replaces relationships and interests. The motivational environments of these organizations differ. The cases presented in this chapter show the influence of some of these aspects of organizational culture and interpersonal relations, on the performance and motivation of Information Technology Departments (IT) professionals.

CASE 1: INDUSTRIAL ENTERPRISE (PRIVATE)

The Organizational Context

This case study is based on a private multinational organization that manufactures cutlery, household utilities, tools, furniture and electric appliances with several plants in Brazil and the USA. This multinational company generates annual revenue of over US$1 billion and has more than 4,300 employees. The company is composed of one holding company (corporation) that manages 10 manufacturing units in Brazil, 2 plants in the USA, 6 Distribution Centers (DC) or warehouses in Brazil and 11 DCs in Latin America, Europe, the Middle East and Australia. Each DC monitors several Sales Offices and a total of more than 500 direct sales representatives in Brazil.

The company preserves the organizational culture which is one of a family-run enterprise, prioritizing people, and product management, according to the group's President. Employees

are rarely made redundant. The Group's Board and the Department Directors believe that sales and profits tend to continuously increase due to this management policy. This management format coupled with the location of almost all of the plants in inland Brazil serve to reinforce the result of low employee turnover. The organizational structure is traditional hierarchical. The power is in the hands of the Group's Board, composed of senior directors, many of them already retired. The IT Department, Controller and Accounting, and Engineering and Marketing departments are the primary organizations of the corporation. However, the Human Resources (HR) Department continues to be spread throughout each and every department, yet focuses on the unique management culture.

Italian and German immigrants make up the majority of the region's population where this company is located; this region is also highly industrialized. This regional culture influences organizational culture and the company is the market leader in this part of the country. The employees usually come from many generations of the same family. As a matter of fact, this is a characteristic typical of many companies in this region, located in the southernmost state of Brazil. This region has one of the highest GDP's in Brazil and also the best education standards in the country. The weather is mild for a tropical country and light snowfall can occur in the winter; a rare occurrence in Brazil. Many IT companies have settled in this region due to a highly skilled workforce, recognized as the best in the country. One of the state's Computer Science Courses is internationally recognized, often hosting foreign students and professors from countries such as Germany, the USA and the UK.

The IT Department

The structure of the IT Department follows the organizational structure of the company. The reduced number of employees' vis-à-vis the number of users and the extensive working experience of IT professionals stand out as key characteristics. The IT counts on 2 CIOs (Chief Information Officers); one responsible for systems applications and the other for the infrastructure. They manage 14 people; 12 working in systems development and support, and 2 in IT infrastructure. Furthermore, each unit (plant or warehouse) counts on a local IT support staff of 2 or 3 people. Despite being a large Brazilian company (with more than 4,000 employees in Brazil and around 1,000 employees abroad) the IT area is quite lean, with about 100 employees distributed between the holding company, factories, warehouses and national and international sales offices. The IT portfolio, IT management rules, systems development patterns, among others, may be compared with that of large companies. The small size of the staff is a relevant factor, because it is distinctive characteristic with a direct connection to the behavior patterns of IT staff affected by local and organizational culture, as described below.

The CIOs report to the Vice President of Operations. There is an IT committee that promotes IT alignment between the business drivers and the IT strategies needed to support them. The committee made up of two CIOs, the Vice President of Operations and an external consultant. Strategic decisions and also some tactical decisions are taken in this Committee. New technologies are absorbed from the subcontractors. The outsourcing contracts include clauses for transfer of technology. All systems are maintained internally. Again, it is noteworthy that this is only possible because of the local and organizational (family) culture already highlighted in the previous section. Another important factor to justify this small structure is the high stability of the personnel. This leads to an increase in skills and competence, as well as greater knowledge of the business.

Systems development, including the central management system (ERP) is done in-house, using relational database technology and an integrated information management model. The systems development group can be divided into two teams; one dedicated to sales, delivery, financial, accounting and HR systems and another responsible for production planning and control systems.

The helpdesk and user support is managed by an incident and work orders system on the web (to be looked at in the next section). The demand for support or office automation systems development is little, as users are experienced and have been well-trained. The service requests comes from about 1,200 users, 800 of whom are very demanding because they own critical processes that can be adjusted following new organizational strategies. It is of great importance that every plant or warehouse unit is supported by one or more key-users, usually a business user, well-trained in some IT areas, who offers direct assistance to other users of his business unit. Sometimes this produces certain conflicts of interest, especially when the factory director has interests that aren't in sync with the IT's technological direction. This IT employee reports to the director of the factory division and does what that director demands. This demand is not always the same as that of the technological direction of the IT. For example, one director from a factory unit bought a warehousing automated system without consulting the IT. Millions were invested in a system that did not integrate in the central management system. The relationship between users and IT were to blame, but the management culture of the company, which gives autonomy to each factory sector, also played an important role in this episode. This is changing at the moment, as the company begins to see itself as a group, but the culture of non-centralized management, with competition between divisions of the same group, is still very strong and is a hindrance at times.

Some services are supplied by third party companies, such as networking setups and the development of specialized systems as automated warehouses and robots programming. All external development is contracted with transfer of technology. The Board decided at a certain moment that the entire information systems development should be done in-house and this policy dictates software development. For 8 years, the two CIOs have counted on the help of an experienced consultant acting as a coach and assisting them on technological directions and special projects. This external assistance helps to promote alignment between the IT projects and actions and also between the business projects and actions. The IT committee has weekly and monthly work meetings to review the strategic planning and execution.

There is no specific HR department within IT, but a HR department for the entire organization, and they are responsible for determining the structure of jobs and salaries and give legal support to other departments within the organization. As the management culture is friendly and protective, employees tend to stay in the organization until retirement. This is also favored by the location of the organization headquarters in a small country town. Progressions of positions are rare but the salaries follow market value. The functional structure of the IT department is formalized by the positions occupied, comprising three levels - CIOs, project manager for the industrial systems and project manager for sales, finance and accounting systems and analysts/programmers. Again, it is worth noting that the family culture of this organization provides this type of structure and HR management in IT. In five years there have been only two resignations, both voluntary. These employees were not at the same pace as others and were naturally feeling excluded. Managers (CIOs) did not stimulate any kind of motivation for personal growth. Technical trainings are supplied only within the context and needs of IT portfolio.

How IT Responds to Business Demands

In 2006 the Board authorized an IT Governance project. The IT Department did not have any formal indications regarding the service satisfac-

tion level of the users, and after some discussion it was decided to conduct a survey. The first round worked as a preview to try to establish the weak and strong points of the relationship and to measure the real gap between IT and users. From these results, corrective procedures were adopted to start the subsequent stages of the survey until it was possible to implement the relationship standards that allowed a constant control through indicators defined by CobiT. SERVQUAL was adapted to the information systems area and used as an instrument (Kettinger and Lee, 1999; Pitt et al., 1995). This instrument was used because it contained questions related to the perception of the users about the IT staff, such as skills, knowledge, empathy, personal presentation, among others. This would allow analyzing the behavior and knowledge of IT staff to meet demands, seeking to improve this relationship between business areas and IT. Another factor which led to the use of this instrument was the possibility of creation of a stimulus bonus for IT employees of IT based on the average satisfaction perceived by users as each demand is met.

The survey participants were selected among the directors, managers and key-users from all of the units located in Brazil. They were chosen due to their frequent contact with the IT staff and the workload they demanded. They were invited to answer the survey by the General Managing Director of the company himself. It is important to mention that the company policy forbids external surveys and that this survey was approved in a Board meeting for strict internal use. These procedures led to a representative sample, limited to 25 directors, 118 factory managers, 8 warehouse managers and 16 key-users, totaling 167 respondents. Something innovative arose, when the same instrument was presented to IT staff to be answered bearing in mind the following question: "How do you think the users will answer?" This encouraged a discussion regarding future improvements.

One of the main motivations of the managers in this survey was the search for the continuous improvement of IT management. The results showed that there were points to be adjusted regarding IT management, especially those related to user interface, meeting deadlines, services and process conformity, and having the help desk closer to user units. Noteworthy is that the executives did not want to eliminate the item that questioned services delivered with errors, as they considered that the comments and perceptions of IT (that were positive, regarding errors) were relevant to corrective actions. However, it was agreed that the word *error* was not used on the results report published on the Intranet, but rather the expression *nonconformity of services and products*. This demonstrates how the culture of this company influences the day-to-day management, including management of staff. CIOs seek to maintain a friendly atmosphere like a normal family. There are no punishments for mistakes but instead search of solutions to the problems. This creates a pleasant working environment, without stress or negative feelings. It is believed that this kind of behavior is supported by the family culture of the city that generates a network of friendship inside and outside the organization.

It is worth noting that some respondents included strong comments in relation to the behavior or skills of some IT employees. However, due to the family-based organizational culture and the people-focused management, these employees have not been laid-off, but relocated. This measure would probably not have been adopted in more professionally-managed companies that look for immediate results from its employees, including IT staff. Some companies in Brazil using indicators of productivity, profitability, among others, individual, usually dismiss employees who fail to meet goals without worrying about the business knowledge they accumulated or if this knowledge could be used better in another activity.

The survey also revealed a backlog of more than 2,000 unanswered trouble tickets or requests.

This generated many comments and complaints by users and dissatisfaction about the behavior and care of IT personnel. This was to be expected, as the IT staff received the requests by phone, in person, at the cafeteria or even outside the company. Most of the requests were lost or simply ignored and forgotten. The backlog was dealt with and the problem that caused it was solved.

Today, users use a requests management system on the web that records each request and places it in a queue managed directly by the corresponding CIO (of systems or infrastructure). The CIO analyses the request, setting a cost and a deadline. The request is sent back to the user for authorization or further detailing. When the user authorizes the request, the CIO designates the person or team responsible for it. When the request is completed and tested by IT, a new warning is generated to the user for approval. If the approval is given immediately and without problems, points are awarded to responsible IT staff.

The original idea was to use this point score to calculate the semester bonus of the IT people. However, the HR department of the company did not adopt this procedure because, due to labor regulations, this procedure would have to be applied to all the company employees. As this is not a common practice for all employees, IT employees cannot receive it. However, the bonus for efficiency project is open to be implemented in the near future.

The IT Drivers, Indicators and Motivators

The main IT driver is system maintenance. Although the consultant hired to advise the CIOs stimulated the internal technological growth, things run slowly. There is a degree of complacency by managers, which might be perceived by the employees. They belong to a community with rooted traditional values and principles related to beliefs and customs from their descendents. On the side of the Italian immigrants, they bring the craftsmanship, family values and respect to the head of the family. From the side of German immigrants, they bring the productivity, quality, and safety afforded to the people within the organization. These leaders overlook technological trends. Although there is an IT committee whose members also attend Strategic Planning meetings, IT is still viewed as an operational / tactical role. Often business directors force some changes in the IT department and this has, on several occasions, generated conflict or impatience on the part of the business division with IT. For example, some time ago a sales director asked for a BlackBerry. IT weren't aware of the functionalities of the device and it took almost a year to implement a new standard for mobile communication. However, this aspect can be explained by a strategic policy of the company – to be the followers, not the innovators or early adopters. The company culture of "seeing is believing" may explain the slow and reactive behavior of CIOs and IT staff in meeting demands that require new technologies.

A bonus policy could be an important motivational factor for the IT staff to move ahead. As this was not implemented, performance-checking indicators are not used. This way, an IT employee is not penalized by the coding errors or failures in software installations of inadequate user training. However, internally, the IT managers show consideration for the effort and good results of the staff with days off and other benefits. Another motivational factor is the proximity between the IT staff and users, the result of the family structure and culture of this company. As a reflection of this relationship of friendship within and outside the company, the employees also seem to be "ashamed" of making mistakes, seeking to solve the problems. Such behavior seems to be a pattern of behavior expected of IT personnel both by CIOs as business managers by the company.

The worst problem noted was the personal relationship. If an employee does not get along with others, this employee is severely criticized. This seems to be an aspect essentially linked to the craftsmanship, family values and respect to culture – everyone knows each other inside and outside the company; everyone belongs to the same "tribe". This can be understood as attitudes and behavior based on the same organizational and regional culture. A typical example of this culture was clear to see during the world financial crisis. The CFO was responsible for high-risk paper investments and the group ended up losing some money. The executive was not laid-off but he resigned due to having felt ashamed of making that mistake.

In a similar vein, one of the IT employees did not behave correctly during a company party. Apparently, he had drunk more than he should have and verbally offended one of the members of the Board. Remember that this organization has fathers and sons working together and most high-ranking directors are friends of the parents of their employees. As a result, the employee was reprimanded by the CIO. However, this employee still had problems regarding his adjustment to the group culture, and was again involved in other inconvenient situations weeks later. Although he was not laid-off, he resigned months later.

SOLUTIONS AND RECOMMENDATIONS

In this case no solutions are presented, but rather improvements areas to be considered. With this in mind, the reader is invited to think about possible improvements in the near future for the IT structure, motivational programs for the CIO and their team, and to create indicators (what would they be, what they control and how to measure them).

A summary of the main features observed in this case where the organizational and individual culture may ultimately determine individual behavior and attitudes of IT managers and individuals are listed below.

Individual Culture can affect Organizational Culture and change management style and the relationship of IT staff with the rest

of the company. A strong friendship, outside the company, among the employees affects the work inside the organization, resulting in individual values and principles to be adopted by the organization. This observation can be supplemented with the following.

The attitude of IT professionals and their relationships with business users affect how the systems are used. IT staff must present new functions and improve the systems in a clear way, without using IT jargon. Since they work in a relatively closed environment, with systems developed in-house, applications are custom-built. The case shows that implementing new work formats, such as viewing information online instead of printed reports may cause some resistance by the users.

An incentive policy through bonus payment or other benefits are motivating elements for the IT staff. In this case, the IT employees still don't receive bonus payment, but most of them said that the bonus payment would make them more proactive when working on the user's requests.

Organizational and individual culture seems to be related to the low turnover of IT staff. Keeping IT staff is important, because the business knowledge base is enriched by its IT employees, improving the system's functions. In this case, the location of the company in a region with unique cultural traits, such as the high appreciation of friendship in and out of work, largely determines the behavior of individuals in the accommodation of IT within the company. Typically, this is the only work of their lives.

CASE 2: EDUCATIONAL ORGANIZATION (PUBLIC)

The Organizational Context

This case study is about a governmental organization that provides college education; undergraduate, postgraduate, research, and extension courses. It is located in the south of Brazil and maintained by the Federal Education Ministry; the Federal Department that coordinates and rules all Universities in the country (both public and private). It is considered as a large institution (one of the three biggest in the country) and comprises 72 divisions (schools and institutes) with more than 132 undergraduate and postgraduate courses. Postgraduate education consists of Master's Degrees and Doctorial Degrees (Ph.D.) courses. This institution has the second biggest annual budget in the state, even when compared to private companies. It has more than 8,000 employees and 38,000 active students. The Organizational Structure is ruled by federal law, having a Chancellor and Vice-Chancellor (voted), Pro-Chancellor (indicated by the chancellor), Unit Chiefs and also Chiefs of Departments inside each unit (voted).

There is a central IT Department that reports to the Chancellor and Vice-Chancellor, with its Director nominated by them. However, because of democratic and bureaucratic policies, some units have kept small IT organizations, which are not centralized. This is currently a problem when a single policy of data protection, database, and other applications are needed to integrate all the systems of the institution, as required by the rules of corporate governance from the Federal Government.

The organizational culture is managed by the national culture of governmental organizations. Admission comes about by public entrance examinations. Once an employee is hired (after the first 3 years that he/she completes the probationary period) the employee acquires job stability; which means that the position is protected by law, and the employee cannot be laid off, unless there are criminal or illegal grounds.

Consequently, the productivity and performance of the public/civil servants vary a lot. For example, if the employee is at his/her desk, or in his/her classroom, but is not being productive, or is not teaching well, there is no HR action, because his job is guaranteed. For this reason, the *turnover* is very low. Nowadays, where jobs are really hard to find, this is a "safe haven" for many people. The exams demand a high level of knowledge from the candidates, which results in a sound intellectual standard amongst the organization's staff. Nowadays, for the candidates to apply for an administrative technician position or IT position they need a Bachelor's Degree and most of them have Master Degree. A substantial number of long-term employees are finishing their studies, which means a good salary raise. Thus, users, business managers, technicians and IT managers have the same level of studies and the same professional level, making the relationship between supervisors and subordinates have a political character, because the boss now can be the subordinate tomorrow. It is noteworthy that the department heads change every four years, either by election or by nomination. This behavior is the opposite of that of private organizations, where higher education does not necessarily imply in a pay rise and the head can remain in office for a long time. Moreover, employment in private companies is not guaranteed and the pressure for individual and team performance is higher and constant.

The organizational structure is hierarchical, as previously mentioned. The power belongs to the presidency office (chancellor) and the orders come from policies called administrative rules. The HR department is centralized and is located in one of the presidency offices, but responds directly to the Education Ministry. The focus of the HR management is determined in each University; however the HR and payroll system is unique.

The region where the University is located is one of the richest regions in the country. The local and regional cultures influence the organizational culture in a superficial way as the governmental culture (of being a public employee) is stronger than the local culture. The staff consists of administrators and professors, with the help of contractors. Some of the University departments maintain close contact and offer exchange programs to students and professors. More than 95%

of the professors have Doctorates. More than 50% of the administrative technicians have a Master's degree or specialization courses (MBA level). As previously stated, one of the biggest motivational factors for a professional development is the functional progression received every 150 hour of lectured classes. Another important factor we have to consider is that the most of the employees are getting old and entering into a retirement phase. After 16 years the government authorized new public entrance exams, resulting in a great disparity of knowledge between new staff and senior employees.

The IT Department (IT)

The structure of the Information Technology Department is in line with the University organizational structure, which means a hierarchical and bureaucratic structure. The key characteristic is the reduced number of employees' vis-à-vis the number of users and also the extensive experience in the job. IT has 1 Director, 1 Vice-Director and 5 Managers; for systems, communications, infrastructure, database and information, and help desk and requests service. They manage an additional 34 people on the operation level – programmers, systems analysts, database administrators, web designers, etc. There are around 15 trainees and scholarship students working on systems and web programming. This is problematic given its constant labor flux (high labor turnover). Furthermore, some University units count on their own IT organization, holding 2 or 3 employees or trainees.

System development is done in-house. The systems are divided into two groups; administrative and educational. In the educational group there are four major applications – undergraduate education, graduate education, research and extension. The applications of the administrative group are developed by the federal development and are the same for all federal universities in the country. Consequently, the IT department only develops and supports applications oriented to education and research management. The database technology is supplied by Oracle and development is based on Visual Basic for desktop applications and PHP for web. There is an attempt to integrate the information systems, but some outdated legacy systems are still in place. Help desk support provided to users is done through an incident and requests management system. The service of incidents is performed for around 45,000 users, culminating in an enrollment period (at the start of each semester). Undergraduate and postgraduate management systems are also run on the web. So, 98% of students, educational professors and technicians, use the service via the web. The rest of them, 2%, is composed of special students or belonging to agreement programs, who are already studying at the University. Few procedures regarding to education are carried out outside the system. However, there are 3 LMS (distance education) platform, the open source Moodle system and two other platforms developed in-house – one by the College of Education, used as an education laboratory and another one by the Business School, for internal use, as this school was a pioneer of distance education in the University. One of the IT projects is the transition of the LMS courses to the Moodle platform. As the University has three LMS platforms, the acceptance of such change is generating a great deal of political and interest's conflict between the users of each platform. The behavior of the IT department with regard to these conflicts is neutral in order not to interfere in relationships. However, they already know in advance that the federal government encourages the use of Moodle in most federal schools and agencies. The behavior of this group in particular is clearly determined by the organizational culture – to let go, do not get involved and do not publicly display their personal vision. Their boat never sinks, sailing in troubled or still water.

There are no IT services provided by third party companies, unless in extraordinary situations. A service or a specialized development can be hired, as for example, employee's time system and document typing. However, there is a project from the Federal Government that intends to leave all IT services to third party companies. This would shut down ITs and the smaller IT units. This decision has been postponed, because this issue involves serious political matters and lots of issues. This policy is being viewed as a threat by IT employee groups because they fear losing their jobs within the department. This reflects the policy of stable employment that generates accommodation in positions throughout the servants' careers within the University, including those of the IT department.

Another factor that leads the IT staff to feel threatened is the fact that the federal government is working on a campaign for the use of a single education and research management information system by all federal universities. This system aims to integrate all data about high education at the national level. But it is something which highly improbable at the moment. Federal Universities located in different areas are less developed than others, nor can they afford the product and services or provide the necessary infrastructure. The Federal Government does not provide enough financial support.

Regardless of such threats, the IT department has worked in educational system seeking improvement. In 2004 the systems which integrate all of the University units were developed based on current database technology and programming language. In 2005 they were put online and several functionalities were deployed at the user level. However, not all features are fully implemented and users sometimes use them incorrectly. This occurs due to the organizational and individual culture, and many times the interests differ. The IT technician wants to pass the work onto the unit's technician, while the latter does not want "more work" and so there is conflict. There are also IT technicians who want to centralize the information and the system functionalities as a way to harness control. A good example of this was the Business

Intelligence (BI) implementation in 2008. There was a specific University center to consolidate information, which would be replaced by the BI system. This resulted in a boycott and problems with the utilization of the BI system. There is no formal IT committee. There are several committees for projects composed by business and IT people. At the end of 2009, the first process of IT Strategic Planning was done. This was a demand of the Federal Government auditing bureau as a requirement to receive financial support for expansions. The IT department was the first unit to develop the strategic plan, showing that possibly the above-mentioned threats may be changing the behavior of individuals – from static and reactive to proactive and interested in learning.

How IT Responds to Business Demands

Since many of the applications are had become web based, IT designed a help desk and Requests Service Office. This office uses an incident and requests management system which is not web based and for the most requests users often call up analysts directly. This results in calls not being recorded by the system. Help desk services for office automation activities and applications are performed directly within each unit. The office productivity software is supplied by Microsoft.

However, in 2008 the Federal Government introduced productivity indicators for the universities. In the first audit, the university received several warnings for nonconformity, among them, help desk and demand indicators. The idea is to control the costs of each help desk service provided. For example, "how much does the help desk service cost per incident and how long does it take for the change of a condition in the enrolment system?"

One of the biggest IT problems is its functional staff. The majority of employees have worked for the institution for 25 years. These employees have a sound understanding and grasp of business

regulations, encapsulated and hard-coded in the systems with documentation being scarce. The sharing of knowledge with new employees rarely occurred. For this reason, IT launched several programs to improve its services. One of them is the "Processes Project" which must document and promote improvements in all automated and non-automated processes in the University. Two projects began at the same time: at the department of academic records (student services) and at IT demand service office (IT specific demand service). These were the offices penalized by the audit, as they offer services to the public. The other one is the "Strategic Project", the implementation of which, is demanded by the federal government of all of the offices, in order to get next year's resources, up to the national standard. Again, the culture of individuals in the IT department demonstrating proactive attitudes when facing new projects reinforce the differences between the individual or group culture with respect to established organizational culture of accommodation.

However, it is noteworthy that the motivating factor for the implementation of these projects was the warning received from the federal audit on processes running so inefficiently that they were burdening taxpayers. Inefficient processes not only occur at this University, but in most Brazilian government agencies. This is a reflection not only of the organizational culture but also of the governmental culture, institutionalized throughout the years. There is no bonus for doing the job, only automatic promotions recognizing educational diplomas when earned. If the personal, team or organization's productivity and performance indicators are not followed or reached, this does not make any difference. What happens to the public/civil servants? Nothing, because they have job stability guaranteed by law. What will happen to the organization? Budget reduction is considered, but this all depends on the negotiations between the University and the Education Ministry.

The new demand service management system should be used only via the web. However, IT will have to face several forces resistant to change. Students prefer to ask by phone and transfer the problem; professors want the offices and units doing the job without interference. Technicians don't want to increase their duties. When the enrollment system was installed via the web, these three groups complained: students wanted to talk to the professor to check if their enrollment was satisfactorily completed, professors needed to close their grades in time which not always was done, generating a lot of complaints; technicians (with old habits) had to learn something new and asked themselves, "Why?...I always did it that way, why should I change?" were the words uttered most often. Again, such response show different attitudes between individuals of the same organization: while the IT department realized the organizational changes initiated by technology and learning of individuals themselves, the user areas still seem to have missed such a change.

The IT Drivers, Indicators and Motivators

With the drivers described above, the IT department has commissioned a strategic planning to an experienced group of the Business School. In the stage of diagnosis of the strategic planning process a survey was conducted with different stakeholders of the University – teachers, technicians and students. The intention was to understand the vision of the stakeholders on the IT department, on the applications and infrastructure and on current and future needs. From the University survey conducted for the strategic planning research, there are clear indicators about the behavior and skills of IT individuals: IT staff that has the knowledge related to the business is in the retirement stage; there is neither formal record nor documentation of the systems, procedures, etc.; and there is also the outsourcing threat. But one of the main indicators of the IT group is the user requests service, which is directly connected to the personal relationship between IT staff and business users. Another aspect

is that the IT wages are not considered compatible with the market, generating turnover, which redefined some department parameters.

Despite the organizational culture, most of the IT technicians are typically interested in new technologies. The communication between them and the Computer Science (Informatics) Institute is frequent. The Institute is responsible for innovations; the Institute owns excellent computer laboratories and has a commercial agreement with several companies like Dell, HP, IBM, Microsoft, Google, etc. Computer Science and Computer Engineering courses were nominated as the best in the country. This culture of one of the units allows a differentiation in IT staff culture. Most of the employees are also part time professors at the Computer Science Institute. In this case the group remains also cohesive, since they have been working together for years, demonstrating convergence of individual behavior and culture that allows teamwork, regardless of reporting or hierarchical relationships – teachers and technicians working together to solve problems and evolve.

In the previous University administration, IT had been given primary importance. This happened because the University as a business had been pressed to reduce the administrative and educational processes costs. Web systems are a result of this.

On the other side, the current performance indicators system still relies upon professors, not upon technicians. University indicators derive from the teachers' production and contribute to position the University in prominence at national and international level. Professors must produce intellectually, lecture classes, and have projects with the industry and community. They have to attend Master's Degree and Doctor's Degree examination board meetings; they have to be member of associations that promote scientific events, to be part of editorial councils, etc. For each activity there is a sum of points accredited to the professor's unit and, by consolidation, to the University. A bonus policy does not exist, only the functional progression rules. Professors' rules are stricter, as they are based on these indicators. This is different from the employee's rules. Therefore, teachers who work in technical activities associated with IT are being burdened with an increased workload, from the academic and technical roles. However, in most cases they stimulate technicians and IT professors to write articles together, raising the level of knowledge of the whole group and increasing the production indicators of the University.

From the IT employee perspective, the IT strengths, which they are most proud, are: a pleasant workplace, homogeneous knowledge about the University "business", technicians' commitment to the services that must be executed and provided and the IT visibility before the academic community. As weak points they mentioned several workmates retirement, outsourcing, an insufficient labor force, weak communication and dissemination of knowledge. Also the lack of reception policy for new workers and scholarship students, resistance to changes and few services being advertised, were also mentioned among others. It is important to state that the group mentioned the strong relationship policies of the IT management as a key factor to success. The administration period of this management lasts 16 years, corresponding to 4 chancellor administrations. This may confirm some of the factors listed by Bourguignon et al., (2004) and Mintzberg et al (2000): the management attitude adopted by this individual is directly reflected in the relationship of trust within the IT department and between IT and business areas; the delegation of authority to the project managers is complete, which reaffirms the established reliability and initiative undertaken by IT teams; the emphasis on the learning opportunity for everyone working with the Computer Science Institute which emerges with innovative research, either calling members to work directly in the IT department or sending members for refresher courses or assisting in research projects.

SOLUTIONS AND RECOMMENDATIONS

In this second case the biggest problem is caused by bureaucratic organizational culture, which, many times blocks the regular development, delaying project and deliveries. It's very hard to have a specific solution since this depends on various factors: external policies, power, resistance and accommodation, among others. The implementation of a set of performance indicators for technical employees could be a solution. However, there are impediments regarding this, because its regulation must occur at national level. Brazil has a very protective labor policy. This results in certain tough positioning on the part of HR management who must respect labor laws. On the other hand, there is a trade union and the vision that the boss always exploits workers. This generates many lawsuits against the employer. And it all seems to be normal for the employee as well as to the employer. This generates some questions: "How does one hold onto good IT workers even with a low market salary?", "Should the government introduce indicators for technical workers?" If so, "How does one provide incentives and not fail? "Can you create at least 3 individual indicators or team indicators and show their structure?" Remember about the cultural, social and political aspects involved.

A summary of the main features observed in this case which also are related to organizational and individual culture as likely determinants of behavior and attitudes of IT managers and individuals is listed below:

- **Organizational Culture is stronger than Individual Culture.** Most employees fit the culture established in the organization. Over the years, IT employees adjust themselves to the cultural elements of Brazilian governmental organizations. Even when their individual behavior is proactive, they adopted a reactive attitude as they begin to work for the University. However, in recent years this attitude has been changed, probably due to the effective reaction of IT management and project managers.

- **Organizational Culture can affect systems development and use.** As can be seen in case report, individual users are not forced to use the systems. Established organizational culture allows that. Despite the advances achieved within the IT department, with new applications and constantly learning about new technologies, IT employees feel no pressure for systems to be put to use and don't strive to convince the users to use the systems, so many features and functions are underused. This can be exemplified by the Business Intelligence (BI) System that is up and running for over four years. However, there is a central administration department that is responsible for the consolidation of information of the entire University. With the BI system implemented, this department ceases to exist. As the department is politically strong, the BI system is not being fully utilized and IT staff does not require its use.

- **Low turnover of IT employees can affect the relationship between IT and business areas.** Retaining IT employees is important, given that the business knowledge base becomes enriched by IT, resulting in more features in the systems. However, this University has a problem because such employees are retiring. In this case, due to low turnover, the University did not prepare for the loss of knowledge of IT staff on business rules and cad lead to difficulties in the department's future relationship with the other business areas, destroying the good relations policy currently in place. In short, failing to plan the renewal of the IT staff the will retire can be cause problems in the long term.

- **External pressures may increase the proactive style of IT employees.** The IT department took a proactive stance with respect to new projects after the federal government auditors identified problems in the implementation of various business processes. Examples are the Process Redesign Project and the Strategic Planning Project, undertaken by the IT department. This led to learning and proactive search for innovations through partnerships with other units of the University, like the Business School and the Computer Science Institute.

FUTURE RESEARCH DIRECTIONS

Organizational culture has been discussed for many years. This subject has been introduced more recently, especially when it deals with IT interventions alongside business (Avgerou, 2002). Organizations tend to mould certain behavioral standards, as individual as well as a group especially when they are working with new information technology. For organizations to have success on reaching their goals, they need to align their technologies to their business operations, organizational structure, beliefs and values of their people. Usually this is seen as alignment of "organizational culture". This alignment might be crucial to the assimilation of new IT. This 'organizational culture' that is passed to members of the organization in a correct way allows a reality vision of the organization (Hofstede and McCrae, 2004).

IT Department members must obtain this true vision of the business model seeking to understand and fulfill better the organizational demands; as such elements can be a crucial factor to their better business comprehension.

This can be seen in both cases, which show that the organizational culture can affect the way in which systems are constructed and used. For example, the University systems remain in a continuous state of initial use and implementation as soon as the IT employees deliver the systems, and the fact that they are not required to be fully used means that users decide its use.

Studies on organizational culture and individual culture can influence relations between IT individuals as the business area individuals, are still in their beginning stage. Ciborra (2002) approached this matter in a more generic way when he studied the relations between several actors throughout the implementation of new information technologies. He described IT as a "guest" many times undesired by an organization or by individual members and explains that the implementation process and later use of new technologies is dynamic involving several actors inside a formative and wide context.

This way, these continuous changes seem to determine a constant implementation state of process and technologies, which means, the guest and host are in constant transaction between alignment stages.

It is one, sharing behavior and knowledge with the other one. This requires flexibility and a larger organizational environment (internal) control unified as one, which can generate resistance of some "orphans" besides unexpected expenses along with the implementation process of these new cultural and behavioral changes.

The appropriation of business knowledge by IT employees was met with resistance on the part of the users. In both cases, the users complained that systems didn't work properly as the IT employees didn't understand the issue. However, after closer examination, the same users failed to pass key information, necessary for the functioning of the system, onto the IT employees. This was due to the former fearing a loss of control related to their job. As was observed, some users preferred to use Access or Excel to perform certain tasks, rather than tell the IT employees the correct way to do the aforementioned. This affected the quality of service provided by the IT division.

This leads us to the understanding that it is necessary to establish new research that deals with this matter. Implementing and assimilating an appropriation of new technologies is something constant in modern organizations. This way, IT Department members should be prepared to take on a more strategic role, seeking to assist the business managers in the discovery of new opportunities and threats through the offer and use of new IT.

The problem isn't always related to the relationship between IT and business. It takes into account the way this new IT is available. IT Department members must comprehend the environment and the culture of the organization to present a new IT. To find the correct way to do this, can guarantee the success of assimilation, motivation and the continuous use of it, providing that the IT actually adds value and competitive advantage to the business. Therefore, IT departments who wish to attain success must be alert to problems of internal relationships in the IT department itself and external relationships with other business areas, should keep multidisciplinary teams that can add value to the projects and bring new ideas, must emphasize the learning and benefits from it, must maintain a proper career plan that adds value to the employee, must seek to retain talent, and must act professionally, respecting the differences among individuals.

CONCLUSION

These two aforementioned cases show aspects that can be analyzed through the lens of the organizational culture elements. By analogy with the organizational studies, we can assume that such elements can influence the structure and organization of the IT department or work team oriented to IT demands service. (Bourguignon et al., 2004; Mintzberg et. a.1, 2000).

Concerning the type of management, Case 1 illustrates a combination of the benefit oriented to people vis-à-vis benefit oriented to productivity. This is clear in the example of the CFO and the IT analyst; organizational culture reflected on department culture. In Case 2, the management style, very often, does not recognize authority. On the other hand, there is no effort regarding productivity recognition. Most of the managers are imposed (appointed) and can stay in office for 4 years, which generates some complacency according to what was declared by interviewers "if I don't like the management, I remain stagnant without involving myself for 4 years". This factor impinges on demand service delays, as nobody is charged or penalized for this. Another important aspect is that the manager can be subordinate of one of its subordinates on future managements. This results in losing the added value which is gained through teamwork continuity.

In Case 1 the tendency for teamwork is found strongly based on the type of management, as it seeks to solve problems respecting people and their acts. Now in case 2, work is very individualized. It's possible to say that some people work it they want to. An example of this is about one systems analyst member of one IT project partnered with a business organization area. When the Director of that business division was replaced, this analyst declared she would resign from that project. The reason given was the incompatibility with the new Director. She left and nothing happened. It is possible that in other organizations (private) this would not happen this way.

It's noted that in both cases an organizational structure oriented towards IT projects seems to work better than a traditional structure. Relations of subordination are ranked, minimizing the discomfort of some members in positioning themselves and sharing their ideas. Examples of this are the members of the committee that can come from the board of directors as well as business operation. In these specific groups, it seems that members do not perceive the hierarchy, they consider themselves equals. Perhaps, the reason is that learning and knowledge seem to have bigger aggregated value while working as a team. Even

without presenting a direct reward system, it is possible to note that the committees "make things happen". Many times they have power to change behavior and aspects of organizational culture placing the IT department in a better position within the organization and providing a better visibility for its members. Both cases reported show that when the intellectual levels of individuals in IT are equal, elements such as internal relationships, learning and trust relationships overlap with elements such as hierarchical structure and relations of power and authority.

Career opportunities are an important aspect to be recognized. It is noted that in Case 2 the extensive studies are made up of functional progressions (as cited in the fourth paragraph of the description of the organizational context of this case – "A substantial number of long-term employees, are finishing their studies, which means a good salary raise). However, more in-depth research should be undertaken in order to understand the impact of this on user's demand services, business understanding and the aggregation value to the organization. Which is the real individual motivation vis-à-vis the organizational expectative of each individual to provide this functional progression mechanism? Would it be only by the salary motivation? Or could it contribute to growth and the organizational culture (assimilation of changes and reduction of resistance)?

Finally, organizations that are more oriented to professionalization make IT members work more in teams and oriented to problem resolution. On the other hand, it seems that the existence of an external control (imposed) also leads to a search for more operational efficiency. Case 2 shows this clearly when they receive the visit of federal auditors. IT only started to work on determinate projects because they were pressured to do so. It is only a matter of time to see if these projects will really be implemented, understood and accepted by the other members of the organization. Apparently, success could depend on cultural and behavioral elements such as the relationship between IT members and the business area members, the way they share and transfer the new know-how, individual and group interest and on institutionalized beliefs and values, amongst others. Over the report of both cases this can be observed. In both cases the IT department was elevated to a strategic level from the moment that CIOs have taken an attitude more managerial and political than technical, changing the form of relationship with the managers of business areas. Likewise, when individuals in the IT departments had higher learning about a technology or on issues related to a new project, his personal interests and attitudes had changed. They adopted a more proactive stance towards the users, either to transfer knowledge, or to encourage the use of full features of the systems implemented or to discuss new ideas or start new projects.

REFERENCES

Avgerou, C. (2002). *Information Systems and global diversity*. London: Oxford Press.

Bourguignon, A., Malleret, V., & Norreklit, H. (2004). *Balanced scorecard versus French tableau de bord: Beyond dispute, a cultural and ideological perspective*. Grenoble, France: Group HEC-Les Cahiers de Resercher.

Bruner, J. (1997). *Atos de Significação. Porto Alegre/RS*. Brazil: Artes Médicas.

Ciborra, C. (2002). *The labyrinths of information: Challenging the wisdom of systems*. London: Oxford.

Hofstede, G., & McCrae, R. R. (2004). Personality and culture revisited: Linking traits and dimensions of culture. *Society of Cross-Culture Research, 38*, 52. doi:10.1177/1069397103259443

Kettinger, W. J., & Lee, C. C. (1999). Replication of measures of Information Systems research: The case of IS SERVQUAL. *Decision Sciences, 3*(30), 893–899. doi:10.1111/j.1540-5915.1999.tb00912.x

Mintzberg, H., Ahlstrand, D., & Lampel, J. (2000). *Safari de Estratégia*. Porto Alegre, Brazil: Editora Bookman.

Nizet, J., & Pichault, F. (1995). *Compreendere Les Organizations: Mintzberg à l'épreuve des fats*. France, Europa: Gaëtan Morin Éditeur.

Pitt, L. F., Watson, R. T., & Kavan, C. B. (1995). Service quality: A measure of Information Systems effectiveness. *Management Information Systems Quarterly, 2*(19), 173–187. doi:10.2307/249687

Srour, R. H. (2005). *Poder, cultura e ética nas organizações: o desafio das formas de gestão*. Rio de Janeiro, Brazil: Elsevier.

Weber, M. (1974). *Economía y sociedad*. Ciudad do México: Fundo de Cultura Económica.

Weick, K. (1998). Substitutes for strategy. In Teece, D. (Ed.), *Technology, organization, and competitiveness: Perspective on industrial and corporate change*. New York: Oxford University Press.

KEY TERMS AND DEFINITIONS

Organizational Culture: Organizational Culture means values and patterns of the organization.

Individual Culture: Individual Culture means values and patterns specific from one person.

IT Culture: IT Culture means some attitude of the IT area like to use technical jargons.

IT Motivators: IT Motivators means some indicators, pressures or relationships that motivates the IT people.

Chapter 22
The Need for a Recruiter 2.0 for Hiring IT Talent:
The Case of a German Software Manufacturer

Andreas Eckhardt
University of Frankfurt a. Main, Germany

Wolfgang Brickwedde
Institute for Competitive Recruiting, Germany

Sven Laumer
University of Bamberg, Germany

Tim Weitzel
University of Bamberg, Germany

ABSTRACT

In times like the current economic downturn, just like when there is growth, companies struggle to meet the challenge of an IT talent shortage as recruitment and HR in general undergo dramatic changes in the methods applied to find suitable candidates and the services provided to internal and external clients. The IT recruiter's job profile has changed dramatically in the Web 2.0 era, as searching for candidates via LinkedIn and Facebook or micro-blogging via Twitter have become part of the recruiter's daily tools. Apart from all the technical and organizational changes involved, it is still unknown how recruiters and their skill sets will be transformed into those of recruiters 2.0.

The purpose of this chapter is to present the case of a German software manufacturer who invented a Recruiter Training Academy to fulfill their IT recruiters' need for new and specific skills.

DOI: 10.4018/978-1-60960-535-3.ch022

INTRODUCTION

Even in times of global financial crisis attracting new IT talent is still one of the key issues for IT executives in the USA (Luftman at al. 2009) as well as in Germany (Bitkom 2009a; Bitkom, 2009b).As the "baby boomers" get older, the proportion of the US population aged 65 or older is projected to increase from 12 percent in 2000 to about 20 percent in 2030 (U.S. Census, 2000). According to Brock's (2003) research, there simply are not enough workers behind the "baby boomers generation" in the labor supply pipeline to fill all open vacancies (Brock, 2003). The situation in Germany is even worse as labor market research has projected that by the year 2028, 71 percent of the German working population will be retirees (Sadin 2003). In addition, one challenge, especially for human-capital orientated firms focusing on attracting, retaining, and developing IT talent on a long-term perspective (Agarwal et al., 2006) continues to be the shortage of highly qualified IT talent on the labor markets, mostly due to demographics and a shrinking total number of IT graduates (Dolan, 2004). Beside the demographic situation (Frank et al., 2004), the history of economic crises like the dotcom bubble and 9/11 shows that after a crisis everybody started hiring again and that those companies who repositioned themselves and their HR function in the crisis were successful (Fernández-Aráoz et al., 2009). The authors also pointed out in the HBR article that even "now, before the recession lifts, our research suggests that most global companies are running into staffing problems in emerging markets, and they are also having a difficult time finding talented younger managers to replace baby boom retirees."

Therefore although the economy is going through tough times, the human resources (HR) function, especially in terms of recruitment, needs to reposition itself to go beyond the traditional ways of thinking. This is necessary to meet the challenge described above as well as the demand for diversity in staff recruitment and the new usage of social media tools among potential employees (Brickwedde, 2010). To help the organization to leverage its potential and flourish, recruiters' skill sets need to shift from focusing solely on processing and compliance to those of long-term strategic thinkers and business partners as they develop into informing consultants (Welbourne, 2009).

IT recruitment is evolving more and more to cope with these problems as the HR profession undergoes a dramatic change (Gueutal, 2009). In general the IT recruiter's job profile has changed dramatically over the past 20 years (Weitzel et al., 2009). New terms and technologies such as Web 2.0 in a changing information society have become part of the recruiter's daily vocabulary and business. New tools such as social networking sites (e.g. LinkedIn or Facebook), blogs, Twitter or rating platforms (e.g. RateMyEmployer) have become a common part of the recruiter's toolset (Kluemper & Rosen, 2009). Several approaches were adopted to investigate how companies could strategically structure and combine their e-recruiting system with these new instruments (Lee, 2007; Eckhardt & Laumer, 2009; Laumer & Eckhardt, 2009) to improve their overall recruitment performance in terms of time and costs per hire. Even though innovative strategies were presented in computer personnel research for attracting IT candidates through online gaming (Laumer et al., 2009), in virtual worlds (Laumer et al., 2008) or via their social network (Eckhardt et al., 2007) there is still no common approach to the way IT recruiters' skill sets could be shifted from mostly administratively orientated ones to those of internal business consultants with diverse knowledge about IT business, culture, marketing or psychology. Therefore the IT HR functions must provide services to groups inside (e.g. hiring managers in operating departments) and outside a company (e.g. applicants) and the mindset of responsible recruiters must be shifted from describing themselves as administrative personnel to accepting that recruiting today is a consultancy business.

This could be summarized by a lesson learned from a case involving Siemens: companies need to transform their IT recruiters into recruiters 2.0 as they will need to know in future how to post job ads on their corporate website and online job boards (e.g. Monster), to use Boolean operators to search in different talent pools, to conduct and evaluate an e-assessment center or to contact potential IT candidates on social networking platforms such as LinkedIn or Facebook. In addition the recruiter 2.0 must consult the internal hiring manger in order to describe the perfect candidate and to learn more about the requirements for a specific job. Therefore the modern recruiter 2.0 must employ different methods for different IT recruitment challenges (Weitzel et al., 2009).

Since a lack of IT talent supply due to a recruiters' inefficiencies could significantly damage a corporation this chapter describes an approach to the way a company could address and cope with the challenge of transforming their recruiters into what this chapter calls the modern recruiters 2.0. The chapter presents the case of a German software manufacturer who recognized at a very early stage that it is fundamental that their IT recruiters' need new and specific skills to perform internal consultancy for hiring managers and the external recruiting of qualified IT candidates successfully. Starting with individual HR development methods on a regional level for the IT recruiters in their headquarters in Germany they finally came up with a Recruiter Training Academy, including a standard skill set for all their recruiters within their corporation worldwide. As HR employees' specific skill sets and their continuous development could represent a strategic advantage for a company, this chapter describes and analyzes in detail how the company developed a company-wide skilling program for their recruiters, the so-called Recruiter Training Academy, and what kind of skills this program implies. Therefore the chapter is structured as follows: After a brief description of the research method applied in this case, a detailed analysis of the company's challenges in IT recruitment is provided. This will be followed by the description of the Recruiter Training Academy and describe both the traditional and 2.0 way of recruiting effectively. The chapter ends with a summary of lessons learned and conclusions. It provides some important considerations for other companies threatened with similar challenges and provides a set of recommendations for raising the current recruiter to the level of a recruiter 2.0.

THE TRANSITION FROM TRADITIONAL TO MODERN RECRUITMENT

Job ads in newspapers were among the first recruiting methods companies used to publish open vacancies (Gannon, 1971). They had the choice of posting these job ads in traditional daily newspapers or specific profession-related magazines (Breaugh, 1981). Companies in Germany also had the option of acquiring personnel procured by the governmental work agencies (Grund, 2006).

Recruitment agencies or headhunters were also used predominately for vacant senior executive positions (Seitz, 2003). In addition job fairs represented a further opportunity to get in touch with potential candidates and to represent their own company as a potential employer (Zottoli & Wanous, 2000). Finally speculative applications also accounted for a distinctive number of the incoming applications although they were not explicitly encouraged by the hiring companies (Breaugh, 1981; Breaugh & Starke, 2000).

The initial transformation of the recruitment function began with the introduction of the internet. Companies began to launch corporate websites and to publish their open vacancies via this complementary channel. In the early post-millennial era internet job boards like Monster. com stepped up and offered the companies the same services as newspapers though with the promise of greater media penetration and lower cost (Cappelli, 2001; Lee, 2007).

The final transformation of the recruitment function then took place in the course of social change over the last five years (Fernández-Aráoz et al., 2009). While the "baby boomer" generation was leaving the work force (Frank et al., 2004), a new generation of young workers emerged, frequently using Web 2.0 tools (O'Reilly, 2007) and actively looking for new job opportunities, a generation frequently communicating via mobile technology and connecting on social network platforms. To attract this new generation of applicants nowadays companies have a broad range of channels (Weitzel et al., 2009). What companies now need to learn is how to use this broad range of channels, especially the opportunities of modern recruitment channels, such as Web 2.0. A necessary precondition is that companies train their recruiters to do so (Weitzel et al., 2009). We therefore present in this chapter the case of a German software manufacturer who managed transform their recruiters into recruiters 2.0.

RESEARCH METHODOLOGY

Due to a lack of theoretical literature on strategies and effective measures about how to improve IT recruiters' skills, a case study was conducted to learn about successful ways in which companies prepare their internal recruiters for the challenge of fighting the battle for IT talent comparing traditional and Web 2.0 ways of recruiting. The interview patterns and procedures used in this case study were adapted from previous case studies in the context of attracting, recruiting and educating IT personnel (Weitzel et al., 2009). Two interviews were carried out for the case; each lasting about two hours. The interviews were conducted using a semi-structured questionnaire especially developed to collect specific information on the company's strategies. The respondent is Senior

Director Recruitment at the software company. The information collected and documented in the interview protocols was enriched by supplementary company documentation (e.g. presentation slides for their Recruiter Training Academy). The interview protocols were transcribed within five days after the interviews and crosschecked for validity by the interview partner. The overall methodology is derived from existing literature on case study research, especially the work of Yin (2003).

TRANSFORMING THE RECRUITER INTO A RECRUITER 2.0

Based on the case study with a German software manufacturer, specific actions are identified which organizations can implement to cope with these challenges.

Challenges in Recruiter Development

In a highly competitive market, like the enterprise software industry, every player needs to present both the excellence of their products and their employees to retain market leadership. This is especially the case for product-related departments (e.g. software development, consulting and service) in the company observed which claimed to represent state-of the-art IT knowledge. However supporting business process functions like HR dragged behind this claim in the past, as HR still operates following the traditional recruiting approach without using the potential of modern methods such as Web 2.0 in staff recruitment. Since the HR function plays the key role in securing the ongoing supply of people for the product-related departments, the company decided to change this situation by raising the HR function (especially for IT recruitment) to a new level to improve their work and skill base. Keim and Weitzel (2006) outlined the importance of specific IT recruitment as IT professionals differ a lot from other candidate groups according to their personal value cluster or application behavior (Keim & Weitzel, 2006).

This idea of enhancing the skill base of their IT recruiters was shared by other major companies in the German market. This is shown by the research results of a market survey within the DAPM[1], a German association for staff recruitment (Brickwedde, 2010). The association includes 90 percent of the largest 50 companies according to annual turnover and number of employees. The Senior Director Recruitment in the company observed emphasizes that, based on the results of that market survey: "It was shown that around 90 per cent of the companies questioned think it is important that their recruiters know and take advantage of Web 2.0 in recruiting and use interactive approaches to attract and contact potential IT candidates. While the companies obviously consider this as important, only 4 per cent stated that it is always practiced within their recruitment departments. In addition, only 16 per cent of the companies surveyed measure the interesting percentage of passive candidates and none of them rewards their recruiters for the successful hire of passive candidates. These candidates remain inactive in the application process and do not contact potential employers directly with an application (Martin et al., 2008, Galanaki, 2002). Moreover they wait for companies to contact them online via social network platforms like LinkedIn or CV databases in major job portals like Monster, or offline via personnel agencies or headhunters (Singh & Finn, 2002). The research by Weitzel et al. (2009) showed that seven out of ten IT workers in Germany publish their CVs on a database where companies can look for qualified IT staff. In addition, nearly half indicated that they prefer being contacted by the company instead of searching for opportunities for themselves. This indicates that passive candidates and active searching companies will be a possible scenario for the future of recruiting IT talent. In general a mind shift is clearly visible since roughly two thirds of the questioned companies have reorganized the

workload of the recruiters in such a way that the recruiter has time for proactive and consulting activities."

A major part of this development was the redefinition of the IT recruiter from an administrative supporter of the business to an equal business partner who consults the hiring managers regarding their talent requirements, supply, and retention. Prior to this, recruiters' attitude towards their applicants was also inappropriate, as candidates were just treated as applicants and not as customers with presumably more than one job offer in their pocket. The Senior Director Recruitment explains the redefinition of the recruiter in the following words: "Our path leads to a pro-active recruiter, who knows how and where s/he can look for qualified personnel, maintains contact with them, introduces them to the company culture, continues pre-selection so as to have them on hand in the case of a vacancy, and does not simply hope that good candidates will apply as the result of an advertisement."

As an IT firm the company has the objective of supporting every internal corporate process using IT so it turned out to be quite important to convince a corporate function like HR to use more of all the current opportunities provided by technology or the Internet. Web 2.0 in particular gained a lot of importance in this context as the Senior Director Recruitment states: "To provide the impetus required for the pro-active creation of talent pipelines it is necessary for our recruiters to be aware of and to use the personnel recruitment opportunities of Web 2.0 in particular".

Renewed Action for Recruiter Development

To cope with this challenge the company decided to start a major training program for all of their internal IT recruiters starting on the regional level in their headquarters and then extending it to all recruiters in the entire corporation worldwide. Additional skills were identified as one of three major determinants for a successful recruiter besides prior work experience and organizational commitment. The reason why the company finally decided to launch a large training initiative was the following: "At our company we generally have large organizational commitment and as prior work experience couldn't be provided, especially for young IT recruiters, we decided to start the Recruiter Training Academy."

The Recruiter Training Academy provides the training for two major skill sets - recruiting and business skills – which the successful IT recruiter needs to have. This is necessary for the two reasons described: First to fight the battle for IT talent on the external labor market and second to consult the operating department. The training is provided by HR executives and external consultants from the two major HR consultancies in Germany who work in close collaboration with the software company. From the company's point of view

recruiting skills must include the competencies needed for the completion of specific activities within the recruiting process (e.g., sourcing skills, candidate assessment skills, interviewing skills) and business skills must include competencies that are not specific to any stage of the recruiting process; rather, business skills can also be applied to any employee outside recruiting (e.g., people management skills, project management skills, salesmanship). Based on the general process perspective of the recruiting process, all competencies of recruiting and business skills are integrated in the Recruiter Training Academy Model in five steps (see Figure 1).

The Recruiter Training Academy Model is based on two building blocks. The first is the recruiting process from the recruitment department's view, from receiving the requisition to closing it. The whole process is subdivided into five steps: requisition, sourcing, pre-screening,

Figure 1. Recruiter training academy

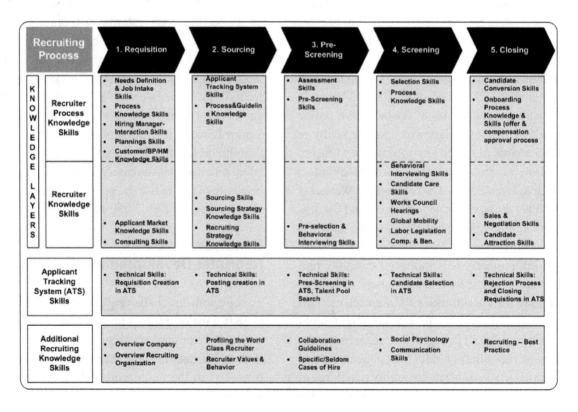

screening and closing. Within the process step "requisition" the recruiter first identifies hiring needs in the operating departments in close collaboration with the hiring manager. Then the job requisition is submitted to the management for approval. After successful approval of the job requisition the job is posted in one of the recruiter's sourcing channels (Lee 2007). In the second step "sourcing" the recruiter conducts the sourcing process by searching actively through various channels like CV databases provided by large job portals, social network platforms like LinkedIn or blogs. The recruiter also awaits incoming applications arising from job postings online on internet job portals, social network platforms or employer rating platforms (for a detailed overview of sourcing actions, see Weitzel et al. 2009). In the third process step "pre-screening" the recruiter needs to remove all unsuitable applications from the total of all incoming applications.

For this purpose the recruiter could use regular offline pre-selection actions like a job interview and manual selection or new online tools like e- or self-assessments (Laumer et al., 2009). Within the "screening" step the recruiter needs to find the candidate with the best match for the open position. Lots of predominately offline selection procedures are available to enable this process step. Procedures testing for math knowledge, the candidate's personality or cognition could be applied both in assessment centers or regular job interviews. For a detailed overview of selection procedures, see Ryan & Ployhart, 2000). Within the final process step "closing" a contract is negotiated and offered to the candidate and after his/her commitment to work for the company the onboarding process starts.

For each of these five process steps the company observed and defined two knowledge layers, consisting of process knowledge skills and recruiter knowledge skills. More technically orientated (e.g. applicant tracking system skills) and more generically orientated skills that could be used over all the process steps building represent the basic part of the required skill set. For each of these modules, training content was developed. In order to explain the content of the modules in the Recruiter Training Academy in more detail, Table 1 describes the recruiting skills identified as a result of the transition from traditional to modern recruitment. A major change within this transition is the redefinition of the recruiter's job profile towards that of an HR business consultant supporting the operating departments in terms of hiring needs, the development of sourcing plans and individual department related recruitment activities. Table 2 thus presents the business skills needed for the new recruiter's job profile in alphabetical order. The design and configuration of all sub-skill sets as well as their integration into the Recruiter Training Academy Model is provided in Figure 1.

After an assessment of the areas in need of most improvement, the company decided to start with training in two modules, consultative recruiting approaches, especially important in the process step "requisition" and sourcing, a major part of the process step "sourcing".

For the module of consultative recruiting the company relied on proven and internally available content for the education of internal and external consultants to educate the recruiters in the required skills: the knowledge, skills, and abilities needed to earn a position in your client's leadership team, allowing you to grow from a delivery partner to a consultative peer. In more detail e.g. client types: how to build trust with a client and to fulfill managerial expectations as well as how to deal with conflicts and to set milestones.

For the sourcing module, since this was crucial to the future success of the recruitment department, a whole new training process needed to be created and established. Sourcing skills are defined by the company observed as follows: the knowledge, skills and abilities needed to survey and understand the labor market and identify candidates from the broad labor market for the company concerned

Table 1. Recruiting skills provided in the recruiter training academy model

Recruiting Skills: Include competencies needed for the completion of specific activities within the recruiting process (e.g., sourcing skills, candidate assessment skills, interviewing skills).		Traditional Recruitment	Modern Recruitment
Applicant Tracking System Skills	Knowledge, skills and abilities relating to using the e-recruiting system properly like: • being able to create and complete requisitions, • ability to create process templates and to assign relevant process template to requisition, • ability to release complete job requisitions	• Whole process conducted manually • No recruiting workflow • Use of Excel sheets to store candidates' personal data. • No templates for requisition, job ad, etc.	• Complex e-recruiting systems • Standardized workflows • Use of several databases to store job profiles, candidate information • Various different templates for job profiles, job ads, requisitions, etc.
Assessment Skills	Knowledge, skills and abilities necessary to assess the quality and skill sets of applicants or candidates	• Assessments in terms of practical job tests • Assessments through job interviews • Assessments though IQ tests • Assessments as part of the final selection procedure	• Regular skill assessments using assessment centers or job interviews combined with various on- and offline procedures testing for math knowledge, candidate's personality and cognition, etc. • Assessments as part of various stages in the entire recruiting process such as the pre-selection and the selection stage
Candidate Care Skills	Knowledge, skills, and abilities associated with maintaining an effective relationship with candidates as they progress through the recruiting value chain	• No regular relationship between candidate and the hiring company • Solely asynchronous communication between candidate and recruiters • No service or candidate care from recruiters	• Recruiters tie relevant candidates to the company at an early stage • Extensive use of candidate relationship management • Candidates are viewed as customers
Candidate Conversion Skills	Knowledge, skills, and abilities needed to understand key candidate conversion factors and persuade them to join the organization. Knowledge of procedure to follow when verbally communicating a job offer to a candidate, reviewing and approving offer for candidate (contract of employment)	• No segmentation between key candidates and regular applicants • Just implicit conversion and persuasion during job interviews	• Comprehensive classification of different candidate groups • Identification of key candidates to develop strategic actions to attract this specific group • Conversion and persuasion of candidates throughout the complete process
Onboarding Process Knowledge Skills	Compensation approval process: negotiate salary and communicate with candidate and if necessary/ together with hiring manager offer approval process: Knowledge of the On-boarding process and Buddy concept	• Salary negotiation within fixed limits and without added components • No particular on-boarding, buddy or mentoring concept	• Salary negotiation with several monetary components (fixed salary + variable bonuses) • Specific on-boarding programs for graduates, young professionals, professionals and executives • Buddy concept for university graduates and young apprentices

continued on following page

Table 1. continued

Hiring Manager Interaction Skills	Knowledge, skills and abilities needed to effectively work, interact, manage and consult with hiring managers: use interview questionnaire for hiring managers (applicant profile) for closer needs definition and faster closing, provide description of the new, recruiting process for hiring manager's ability to develop a recruiting plan (incl. sourcing strategy / requisition/sourcing plan)	• No specific relationship between hiring manager and recruiter • Hiring manager announces open vacancy in his department to recruiting department • No specific applicant profile for ideal candidate • No long-term planning of future hiring needs or sourcing plan	• Close affiliation between hiring manager and recruiter • Recruiter acts as business consultant (see Table 2) supporting the operating departments, helping to define applicant and job profiles, future hiring needs • Recruiter is business and team partner for hiring manager; helping to develop an individual sourcing plan for the department concerned
(Behavioral) Interviewing Skills	Knowledge, skills and abilities needed to conduct interview and extract the most important information from applicants during the interview process, Knowledge of how to conduct first screening of candidates in interviews (telephone or face to-face), Ability to use interview techniques	• Mainly unstructured job interviews as last step of the entire recruitment process to assess applicant's skills • Almost exclusively face-to-face job interviews • Recruiter and applicant(s) located at the same place	• Elaborate methods to acquire information on candidates' individual skills, personality, cultural fit, etc. • Various sorts of job interviews; face-to-face, telephone, desktop and group videoconferencing • Recruiter and applicant(s) located at the same place or in separate locations
Needs Definition/ Job Intake Skills	Knowledge, skills and abilities needed to understand the needs of the hiring managers and translate those needs into the broader labor market display, conceptual understanding of the business sector and relevant job function, Develop competences and lists of representative job activities based on job analysis	• No specific relationship between hiring manager and recruiter • Hiring manager announces open vacancy in his/her department to recruiting department • No specific applicant profile for ideal candidate • Recruiter has no specific knowledge of the processes and related employees in the business departments	• Close affiliation between hiring manager and recruiter • Recruiter acts as business consultant (see Table 2) with profound knowledge of business process, helping to define applicant and job profiles as well as future hiring needs • Recruiter is business and team partner for hiring manager; helping to develop an individual sourcing plan
Selection Skills	Knowledge, skills, and abilities needed to determine which candidates would be most likely to fit, excel in the organization and accept an offer: Knowledge of how to review and rank applications (Pre-Selection guidelines), Ability to determine a candidate's level of interest	• Selection solely within the final job interview but without test for corporate cultural fit • Pre-selection of applications using hard criteria (e.g. final degree of university graduates)	• Test for fit between applicant and corporation throughout the whole recruiting process • Use of self-assessments to support candidates' early self selection • Elaborate interview techniques to acquire information on candidates' individual skills, personality, cultural fit, etc. • Long-lasting selection process with many stages and the inclusion of several different people
Sourcing Skills	Knowledge, skills and abilities needed to survey and understand the labor market and identify candidates from that labor market for the company: Knowledge of sourcing strategies (also including Transfers – internal and international); Knowledge of applicant market and portals / professional sites & forums Knowledge about vendors and the market of external candidates Recruiting knowledge of budget for vendor collaboration & ability to distinguish when vendor collaboration is necessary	• Solely passive search for new candidates with job postings in newspapers or in governmental work agencies • Later on use of internet job boards • No labor market segmentation • No candidate classification • No sourcing strategies	• Mixed approach using both active and passive recruiting methods (see Weitzel et al. 2009) • Several different channels for candidate sourcing • Elaborated sourcing strategies and approaches to find, attract and recruit new candidates

Table 2. Business skills of the recruiter training academy model

Business Skills: Include competencies that are not specific to any stage of the recruiting process; rather, Business Skills can also be applied to any employee outside of recruiting (e.g., people management skills, project management skills, salesmanship).	
Business Acumen Skills	Knowledge, skills, and abilities concerning business fundamentals, business models, the organization's financial goals, business ethics, and competitive analysis
Customer Service Skills	Knowledge, skills, and abilities needed to demonstrate the effectiveness of the organization's products and services and to address customers' requests and complaints
Interpersonal Skills	Knowledge, skills, and abilities concerning communication and cooperation among individuals and groups, including conflict resolution, stress management, diversity awareness, teamwork, and group dynamics
Leadership Skills	Knowledge, skills, and abilities needed to influence and motivate others to achieve the organization's goals, vision, and mission.
People Management Skills	Knowledge, skills, and abilities needed to effectively develop and manage the performance of individual employees or groups of employees
Project Management Skills	Knowledge, skills, and abilities needed to plan, organize, coordinate, execute, track, and evaluate projects
Sales Skills	Knowledge, skills, and abilities needed to influence the purchasing decisions of prospects and customers
Strategic Management	Knowledge, skills, and abilities needed to establish and refine the strategies that drive organizational performance and add value to the business
Technology Skills	Knowledge, skills, and abilities needed to use the equipment, machinery, information technology, and software that create and deliver the organization's products and services
Consultative Skills	Knowledge, skills, and abilities needed to earn a position in your client's leadership team, allowing you to grow from a delivery partner to a consultative peer.

Recruiter Skills are based on research done by the CLC, Corporate Leadership Council

as well as knowledge of the relevant applicant market and portals. One exceptionally important factor was to understand the skill, cultural fit and experience of potential candidates etc. – and the acquisition of knowledge about vendors, partnerships and processes for business and budget approval. In addition to the regular sourcing skills the company observed also tries to improve their recruiters' sourcing strategy knowledge skills. This module also teaches the ability to analyze a position in relation to the market's ability to provide and build a candidate pool and articulate an appropriate sourcing plan. Recruiters will also learn how to build up an internal candidate pool, containing applicants, internal talents, international transfers from foreign dependences or divisions as well as 3rd party candidates (e.g. from mergers in the industry). To enhance the talent pool with more passive candidates the corporate recruiters will

learn how to contact them via direct sourcing, social media recruiting or deep web search.

In order to assess the different levels of already existing sourcing skills among the recruiters a self assessment scheme (Laumer et al., 2009) was developed. Based on the outcome, the recruiters were divided in different subgroups in order to train the recruiters based on their respective level. Senior and more experienced recruiters were used as advisors and trainers.

LESSONS LEARNED

This chapter offer insights from an innovative example showing that a firm which precisely knows their IT talent recruitment needs must help its HR employees to acquire the skills to fulfill these needs. As recruiting IT talent represents a serious challenge for corporations based on this knowledge, firms can focus their recruitment strategies and operations a lot better. With their exclusive approach to training IT recruiters' skills the company also intended to raise the general level of IT recruitment in the IT HR community as the Senior Director Recruitment emphasizes: "With our procedures we wish to raise the level of recruiting and also to improve the image of recruitment within the IT HR community as well as in the whole world of business". In order to guide further companies in the direction of a "recruiter 2.0" the following recommendations arising from the case of the German software company could be outlined:

1. Integrate Recruiters in Business Meetings to Provide Business Process Knowledge

One of the major requirements for a modern recruiter 2.0 is to exactly understand the business' needs and wants regarding labor supply. Therefore recruiters must be able to anticipate potential vacancies within the operating departments in advance. An important precondition for this manpower assessment is a distinctive understanding of the business processes throughout the company, the related employees as well as the executives responsible. Companies could help their recruiters to gain these insights by integrating them in business meetings on a regular basis.

2. Provide Training to Strengthen Recruiters' Technical Knowledge

Within an IT company it is exceptionally important to spread technical knowledge throughout the whole company and all departments. For recruiters in particular, above average IT knowledge is fundamental for two different reasons. First as described above several new IT innovations, especially in the context of Web 2.0, arrived in the recruiting department. To guarantee the adequate

and efficient use of these innovations and their potential for the sourcing process, recruiters need to be skilled in programs such as the Recruiter Training Academy. The second reason for the up-skilling is the modern recruiter's function as "boundary spanner" between business and HR (Eckhardt & Rosenkranz, 2010). While sourcing new candidates the IT recruiter needs to understand the language of the operating departments, including several technical terms and expressions in order to transfer them to a detailed job requirements profile and also to the text of an externally posted job ad and to be able to conduct effective pre-selection for the hiring manager.

3. Provide the Recruiters with Access to Professional Career Networks

After up-skilling the recruiters in using the Web 2.0 adequately it is necessary to ensure that recruiters are provided with access to all potential Web 2.0 channels and networks. Unless the recruiters' fees for premium accounts in LinkedIn or the European equivalent Xing are paid, the entire investment in the recruiters' skill portfolio is almost entirely wasted. In addition, during the vacancy intake meeting, the hiring manager needs to share his/her personal professional network with the recruiter. A major hindrance has also been identified in the restricted access to networks or micro-blogging instruments like Twitter due to corporate policies. Company managements need to take this into account while defining Internet use policies for their employees and incorporating exceptions to their recruiters sourcing in the Web 2.0.

4. Take Time in the Beginning to Save Time Afterwards

In order to increase the quality of pre-selection and save time in the recruiting process, it is paramount that the hiring manager takes time to discuss the vacancy in detail with the recruiter at the beginning of the process. In this way, not only is the profile sharpened, but the hiring manager's satisfaction is also increased.

5. Celebrate Recruiting Success with all Participants of Business and HR

When bringing together different groups after a project terminates, it is always very useful for the management to strengthen the teamwork of the new partners in achieving joint project success. Within the IT integration process during large mergers the joint celebration of stepwise milestones by newly staffed teams and working groups including employees from both sides has been identified as an important lesson learned (Brown et al., 2003). So companies need to provide the opportunity for small celebrations of business and HR when a common recruiting success has been achieved (e.g. an excellent candidate was hired more quickly than the usual time taken to hire or more cheaply than the average cost per hire or the candidate hired represents an extremely scarce resource on the entire labor market, etc.). These celebrations help to build up the relationship between business and the recruiters concerned, to improve their communication and mutual understanding.

CONCLUSION

Finally, regarding the overall objective of hiring IT talent as often as necessary, there is no single silver bullet to overcome the problem but if IT recruiters are capable of analyzing and segmenting the labor market appropriately or developing individual strategies – the competition for talent requires knowing more of and getting closer to the candidates than the competitors – the chances of recruiting success rise dramatically. Proactive approaches in recruiting not only enlarge the total available market of candidates, but increase the quality of hires. General business skills are a must

for conducting business successfully but also a broad range of specific recruiting skills needs to be transferred to the recruiters especially as good knowledge of the recruiting process and the internal applicant tracking system is useless without knowing target groups and the key markets where they could be found. "Only when recruiters know the market, do they also know where the good people are to be found," states the Senior Director Recruitment. So among all these skills, a key to recruiting IT talent still appears to be recognizing talent, that is, knowing the particularities of the IT target groups.

REFERENCES

Agarwal, R., Brown, C., Ferratt, T., & Moore, J. E. (2006). Five mindsets for retaining IT Staff. *MIS Quarterly Executive*, *5*(3), 137–150.

Bitkom. (2009a). *IT-Branche Behauptet Sich in Der Krise*. Retrieved November 6, 2009, from http://www.bitkom.org/de/presse/49896_57979.aspx

Bitkom. (2009b). *45.000 Offene Stellen Im Herbst 2008*. Retrieved November 6, 2009, from http://www.bitkom.org/de/themen/54633_58438.aspx

Breaugh, J. A. (1981). Relationships between recruiting sources and employee performance, absenteeism, and work attitudes. *Academy of Management Journal*, *24*(1), 142–147. doi:10.2307/255829

Breaugh, J. A., & Starke, M. (2000). Research on employee recruitment: So many studies, so many remaining questions. *Journal of Management*, *26*(3), 405–434. doi:10.1177/014920630002600303

Brickwedde, W. (in press). Neue Recruiter braucht das Land: der Recruiter 2.0 – Das Anforderungsprofil fuer den Recruiter von morgen. *Personalmagazin*.

Brock, F. (2003, Oct. 12). Seniority: Who'll sit at the boomers desks? *The New York Times*.

Brown, C., Clancy, G., & Scholer, R. J. (2003). A post-merger IT integration success story: Sallie Mae. *MIS Quarterly Executive*, 2(1), 15–27.

Cappelli, P. (2001). Making the most of online recruiting. *Harvard Business Review*, 79(3), 139–146.

Dolan, A. F. (2004). Recruiting, retaining, and reskilling campus IT professionals. In Hawkins, B. L., Rudy, J. A., & Wallace, W. H. (Eds.), *Technology everywhere: A campus agenda for educating and managing workers in the digital age* (pp. 75–91). Jossey-Bass.

Eckhardt, A., & Laumer, S. (2009). An IT-architecture to align e-recruiting and retention processes. *International Journal of E-Services and Mobile Applications*, 1(2), 38–61. doi:10.4018/jesma.2009040103

Eckhardt, A., & Rosenkranz, C. (2010). Lost in translation?! – The need for a boundary spanner between business and IT. In *Proceedings of the ACM SIGMIS Conference on Computer Personnel Research* 2010: Vancouver, Canada.

Eckhardt, A., Weitzel, T., Koenig, W., & Buschbacher, J. (2007). How to convince people who don't like IT to use IT-a case study on e-recruiting. In *Proceedings of 13th Americas Conference on Information Systems* (AMCIS 2007): Keystone, USA.

Fernández-Aráoz, C., Groysberg, B., & Nohria, N. (2009). The definitive guide to recruiting in good times and bad. *Harvard Business Review*, 87(5), 74–84.

Frank, F. D., Finnegan, R. P., & Taylor, C. R. (2004). The race for talent: Retaining and engaging workers in the 21st century. *Human Resource Planning*, 27(3), 12–25.

Galanaki, E. (2002). The decision to recruit online: A descriptive study. *Career Development International*, 7(4), 243–251. doi:10.1108/13620430210431325

Gannon, M. J. (1971). Sources of referral and employee turnover. *The Journal of Applied Psychology*, 55(3), 226–228. doi:10.1037/h0031151

Grund, C. (2006). Mitarbeiterrekrutierung ueber das Internet – Marktanalyse und empirische Untersuchung von Determinanten und Konsequenzen fuer die Arbeitnehmer. *Zeitschrift fuer Betriebswirtschaft*, 76(5), 451–472. doi:10.1007/s11573-006-0022-z

Gueutal, H. (2009). HR and our virtual business world. *Journal of Managerial Psychology*, 24(6).

Keim, T., & Weitzel, T. (2006) Strategies for hiring IT professionals: An empirical analysis of employer and job seeker behavior on the IT labor market. *Proceedings of the 12th Americas Conference on Information Systems* (AMCIS 2006): Acapulco, Mexico.

Kluemper, D. H., & Rosen, P. A. (2009). Future employment selection methods: Evaluating social networking Web sites. *Journal of Managerial Psychology*, 24(6), 567–580. doi:10.1108/02683940910974134

Laumer, S., & Eckhardt, A. (2009). Help to find the needle in a haystack: Integrating recommender systems in an IT supported staff recruitment system. In *Proceedings of the ACM SIGMIS Conference on Computer Personnel Research* 2009: Limerick, Ireland.

Laumer, S., Eckhardt, A., & Weitzel, T. (2008). Recruiting IT professionals in a virtual world. In *Proceedings of the 12th Pacific Asia Conference on Information Systems* (PACIS 2008): Suzhou, China.

Laumer, S., von Stetten, A., Eckhardt, A., & Weitzel, T. (2009). Online gaming to apply for jobs –the impact of self- and e-assessment on staff recruitment. In *Proceedings of the 42th Hawaiian International Conference on System Sciences (HICSS-42)*: Hawaii, USA.

Lee, I. (2007). The architecture for a next-generation holistic e-recruiting system. *Communications of the ACM, 50*(7), 81–85. doi:10.1145/1272516.1272518

Luftman, J., Kempaiah, R., & Rigoni, E. H. (2009). Key issues for IT executives 2008. *MIS Quarterly Executive, 8*(3), 151–159.

Martin, G., Reddington, M., & Kneafsey, M. B. (2008). *Web 2.0 and HR: A discussion paper*. CIPD Chartered Institute of Personnel and Development, Research Insights, United Kingdom. O`Reilly, T. (2007). What is Web 2.0: Design patterns and business models for the next generation of software. *Communications & Strategies, 65*(1), 16–37.

Ryan, A. M., & Ployhart, R. E. (2000). Applicant perceptions of selection procedures and decisions: A critical review and agenda for the future. *Journal of Management, 26*, 565–606. doi:10.1177/014920630002600308

Sadin, M. (2003, October 6). Computers that care. *Newsweek*.

Seitz, B. (2003). Die Direktansprache und der Schutz unternehmerischer Rechte: Oekonomische Argumente fuer eine rechtliche Problematik. *Schmalenbachs Zeitschrift fuer betriebswirtschaftliche. Forschung, 55*(9), 606–624.

Singh, P., & Finn, D. (2003). The effects of Information Technology on recruitment. *Journal of Labor Research, 24*(3), 395–408. doi:10.1007/s12122-003-1003-4

United States Census Bureau. (2000). *2000 census*. Washington, D.C.: U.S. Department of Commerce.

Weitzel, T., Eckhardt, A., & Laumer, S. (2009). A framework for recruiting IT talent. *MIS Quarterly Executive, 8*(4), 175–189.

Welbourne, T. M. (2009). HRM in tough times. *Human Resource Management, 48*(2), 181–182. doi:10.1002/hrm.20274

Yin, R. K. (2003). *Case study research: Design and methods. London; New Dehli*. Thousand Oaks, CA: Sage Publications Inc.

Zottoli, M. A., & Wanous, J. P. (2000). Recruitment source research: Current status and future directions. *Human Resource Management Review, 10*(4), 353–382. doi:10.1016/S1053-4822(00)00032-2

KEY TERMS AND DEFINITIONS

HR Strategy (Hiring Strategy): The HR strategy is the general strategy of the HR department. It includes the hiring strategy, talent management strategy and retention strategy. The main objective is to engage employees positively and successfully to achieve the company's corporate purpose and strategic goals. For HR strategy being successful it is important that the HR strategy satisfies the business needs, the needs of customers and the needs of employees. An effective HR strategy is an integral part of corporate strategy and is deduced from the general business strategy of a company.

E-Recruiting: E-recruiting (electronic recruiting) means to support the recruitment by the use of electronic media and HR systems. An effective e-recruiting system supports employers as well as job seekers. E-recruiting and its supporting systems represent ideally the entire recruiting workflow. This includes the job requisition, the sourcing, pre-screening and screening procedures and all the communications between companies and candidates until the completion of the application. E-recruiting systems are for example a company's hiring website, an internet job portal or applicant management system.

Recruiting Process: Recruitment is the process of sourcing, screening and selecting people for a job in a specific organization. The main parts of the process are employer branding, sourcing, applicant management, selection (pre-screening and screening) and the final closing. Sourcing involves advertising (posting job ads in newspapers, job portals or the company's website) and recruiting research (searching for candidates in CV databases or social networking platforms). Pre-screening and screening include all activities necessary to select the appropriate candidate. Closing is the last step and involves all activities necessary to sign the contract and to integrate the new employee into the organization.

Sourcing: Candidate attraction is part of the sourcing step of the recruiting process. In contrast to employer branding sourcing has a short-term focus on candidates. In the sourcing phase the recruiter publishes job ads or searches actively for appropriate candidates. Job ads can be published "offline" and "online". Classical offline channels are newspapers or magazines and typical online channels are the company's website or job portals as monster.com. Examples for active search mechanisms are the search in CV databases provided by job portals or in social networking platforms as LinkedIn. The major objectives of sourcing are to find interesting candidates and to generate application

ENDNOTE

[1] Der Arbeitskreis fuer Personalmarketing (DAPM, for more details see www.dapm.org)

Compilation of References

AACSB. (2002). Business schools at risk. *BizEd,* May/June, 48-54.

Abbad, G. S., & Borges-Andrade, J. E. (2004). Aprendizagem humana em organizações de trabalho. In Zanelli, J. C., Borges-Andrade, J. E., & Bastos, A. V. B. (Eds.), *Psicologia, organizações e trabalho no Brasil.* Porto Alegre: Artmed.

Abbate, J. (2000). *Inventing the Internet.* Massachusetts: MIT Press.

ABES – Associação Brasileira das Empresas de Software. (2009). *Brazilian software market: Scenario and trends, 2009.* São Paulo, Brazil: Câmara Brasileira do Livro.

Adamsky, H. (2001). *Hiring and retaining top IT professionals.* New York: McGraw-Hill.

Adler, N. J. (1997). Global leadership: Women leaders. *Management International Review, 37*(1), 135–143.

Adler, N.J., Brody, L.W. & Osland, J.S. (2001). *Going beyond twentieth century leadership: A CEO develops his company's global competitiveness.*

Adya, M. P. (2008). Women at work: Differences in IT career experiences and perceptions between South Asian and American women. *Human Resource Management, 47*(3), 601–635. doi:10.1002/hrm.20234

Agarwal, R., & Ferratt, T. W. (1999). *Coping with labor scarcity in Information Technology: Strategies and practices for effective recruitment and retention.* Cincinnati, OH: Pinnaflex Press.

Agarwal, R., & Ferratt, T. W. (2001). Crafting an HR strategy to meet the need for IT workers. *Communications of the ACM, 44,* 58–64. doi:10.1145/379300.379314

Agarwal, R., Brown, C., Ferratt, T., & Moore, J. (2006). Five mindsets for retaining IT staff. *MIS Quarterly Executive, 5*(3), 137–150.

Agarwal, R., & Ferratt, T. (2002). Enduring practices for managing IT professionals. *Communications of the ACM, 45*(9), 73–79. doi:10.1145/567498.567502

Agarwal, R., & Beath, C. (2007). *Grooming the 2010 CIO.* SIM Advanced Practices Council Report, University of Texas.

Agarwal, R., Brown, C., Ferratt, T., & Moore, J. E. (2006). Five mindsets for retaining IT Staff. *MIS Quarterly Executive, 5*(3), 137–150.

Agho, A. O., Mueller, C. W., & Price, J. L. (1993). Determinants for employee job satisfaction: An empirical test of a causal model. *Human Relations, 46*(8), 1007–1018. doi:10.1177/001872679304600806

Agrawal, V. K. (2005a). From proprietary software to off-the-shelf/ERP solutions: Identifications of critical factors. *National Social Science Journal, 23*(2), 9–32.

Agrawal, V. K. (2005b). Critical factors influencing the requirements of human resources engaged in IT applications. *National Social Science Journal, 24*(1), 1–32.

Agrawal, V. K. (2005c). Implications of environmental and cultural factors on the growth in end-users computing. *National Social Science Journal, 24*(2), 1–14.

Agrawal, V. K. (2005d). Implications of environmental and cultural factors on the trends in usage of various categories of software. *National Social Science Journal, 25*(1), 1–15.

Agrawal, V. K., & Kotcherlakota, V. (2006). Impact of environmental pressures and culture on factors influencing the requirements of human resources engaged in IT applications. *Indian Journal of Business and Economics, 5*(1), 15–40.

Agrawal, V. K., Tenkorang, F., Agrawal, V. K., & Taylor, A. R. (2009). Trends in IT human resources and its impact on curriculum design. *Review of Business Information Systems, 13*(4), 67–78.

Agrawal, V.K., Haleem, A. & Sushil. (2001). Trends in the demand for different categories of software and human resources. *Proceedings of the Annual Conference of Midwest Decision Sciences Institute,* (p. 4).

Alderfer, C. P., Alderfer, C. J., Tucker, L., & Tucker, R. (1980). Diagnosing race relations in management. *The Journal of Applied Behavioral Science, 16*(2), 135–166. doi:10.1177/002188638001600202

Alderfer, C. P. (1969). An empirical test of a new theory of human need. *Organizational Behavior and Human Performance, 4*(2), 142–175. doi:10.1016/0030-5073(69)90004-X

Alderfer, C. P. (1982). *Existence, relatedness, and growth: Human needs in organizational settings*. Free Press.

Alexander, S. (1999). What's in a job title? Less and less, some say. *InfoWorld, 21*(21).

Allen, T. D., Poteet, M. L., & Russell, J. E. A. (1998). Attitudes of managers who are more or less career plateaued. *The Career Development Quarterly, 47*(2), 159–172.

Allen, T. J., & Katz, R. (1985). The dual ladder: Motivational solution or managerial delusion? *R & D Management, 16*(2), 185–197. doi:10.1111/j.1467-9310.1986.tb01171.x

Allen, M. W., Armstrong, D. J., Reid, M. F., & Riemenschneider, C. K. (2009). IT employee retention: Employee expectations and workplace environments. In *Proceedings of the Special interest Group on Management Information System's 47th Annual Conference on Computer Personnel Research* (Limerick, Ireland, May 28 - 30, 2009). (pp. 95-100). SIGMIS-CPR '09. New York: ACM.

Allen, M. W., Armstrong, D. J., Riemenschneider, C. K., & Reid, M. F. (2006). Making sense of the barriers women face in the Information Technology work force: Standpoint theory, self-disclosure, and causal maps. *Sex Roles, 54*(11), 831-844. Retrieved on March 29, 2009, from http://www.springerlink.com/ content/46x01234j8065811/ ?p=9d820e5af40e47bf8db 7b629f39ad3f2&pi=0

Alvarez, J. L., & Svejenova, S. (2002). Symbiotic careers in movie making: Pedro and Agustin Almodovar. In Pieperl, M., Arthur, M. B., & Anand, N. (Eds.), *Career creativity: Explorations in the re-making of work* (pp. 183–208). New York: Oxford University Press.

Ambler, S. (1999). Comprehensive approach cuts project failure. *Computing Canada, 25*(1), 15–16.

Andersen, E. S. (2002). *External or internal focus? A comparison of IT executive and IT project manager roles*. Engineering Management Journal.

Anderson, N. & Cunningham-Snell. (2000). Personnel selection. In N. Chmiel (Ed.), *Introduction to work and organizational psychology: A European perspective*. Malden, MA: Blackwell Publishers.

Ang, S., & Slaughter, S. (2004). Turnover of Information Technology professionals: The effects of internal labor market strategies. *The Data Base for Advances in Information Systems, 35*, 11–27.

Anisa, L. (1997, October 20). Combine bonuses with rewards. *InfoWorld*, 119.

Anonymous,. (2002). Hiring smarts. *Journal of Accountancy, 194*(6), 116.

Anonymous,. (2007). Hiring the best and the brightest. *Journal of Accountancy, 204*(2), 27.

Anthony, W. P., Perrewe, P. L. K., & Kacmar, M. (1999). *Human resource management* (3rd ed.). Orlando, FL: Dryden.

Appelbaum, S. H., Ayre, H., & Shapiro, B. T. (2002). Career management in Information Technology: A case study. *Career Development International, 7*(3), 142–158. doi:10.1108/13620430210426123

Applegate, L. M., Austin, R. D., & McFarlan, F. W. (2007). *Corporate information strategy and management: Text and cases*. New York: McGraw Hill/Irwin.

Armstrong, D. J., Riemenschneider, C. K., Allen, M. W., & Reid, M. F. (2007). Advancement, voluntary turnover and women in IT: A cognitive study of work-family conflict. *Information & Management, 44*(2), 142–153. doi:10.1016/j.im.2006.11.005

Armstrong-Stassen, M. (2008). *Factors associated with job content plateauing among older workers.*

Arnold, J., & Johnson, K. (1997). Mentoring in early career. *Human Resource Management Journal, 7*(4), 61–70. doi:10.1111/j.1748-8583.1997.tb00289.x

Arnold, J. T. (2010). Recruiting on the run. *HR Magazine, 55.* Retrieved February 3, 2010, from http://www.shrm.org/ Publications/hrmagazine/ EditorialContent/Pages/0210arnold.aspx

Arruda, M. C. C., Whitaker, M. C., & Ramos, J. M. R. (2001). *Fundamentos de Ética Empresarial e Econômica.* São Paulo: Atlas.

Arthur, M. B., Claman, P. H., DeFillippi, R. J., & Adams, J. (1995). Intelligent enterprise, intelligent careers. *The Academy of Management Executive, 9*(4), 7–22.

Arthur, M. B., Hall, D. T., & Lawrence, B. S. (1989). *Handbook of career theory.* Cambridge, MA: Cambridge University Press. doi:10.1017/CBO9780511625459

Arthur, M. B., & Rousseau, D. M. (Eds.). (2001). *The boundaryless career: A new employment principle for a new organizational era.* New York: Oxford University Press.

Aryee, S., Chay, Y. W., & Tan, H. H. (1994). An examination of the antecedents of subjective career success among a managerial sample in Singapore. *Human Relations, 47*(5), 487–509. doi:10.1177/001872679404700502

Avgerou, C. (2002). *Information Systems and global diversity.* London: Oxford Press.

Bailey, J. L., & Stefaniak, G. (1999). Preparing the Information Technology workforce for the new millennium. *SIGCPR Computer Personnel, 20*(4), 4–15. doi:10.1145/571475.571476

Baldiga, N. R. (2005). Opportunity and balance: Is your organization ready to provide both? *Journal of Accountancy, 199*(5), 39–44.

Ball, L., & Harris, R. (1982). SMIS members: A membership analysis. *Management Information Systems Quarterly, 61*(1), 19–38. doi:10.2307/248752

Ballout, H. I. (2009). Career commitment and career success: Moderating role of self-efficacy. *Career Development International, 14*(7), 655–670. doi:10.1108/13620430911005708

Bardwick, J. (1986). *The plateauing trap.* New York: Amacon.

Barker, L. J., & Aspray, W. (2006). The state of research on girls and IT. In Cohoon, J. M., & Aspray, W. (Eds.), *Women and Information Technology: Research on under representation.* Cambridge, MA: The MIT Press.

Barrick, M. R., & Mount, M. K. (1991). The big five personality dimensions and job performance: A meta-analysis. *Personnel Psychology, 44*, 1–26. doi:10.1111/j.1744-6570.1991.tb00688.x

Barron, J. M., Bishop, J., & Dunkelberg, W. C. (1985). Employer search: The interviewing and hiring of new employees. *The Review of Economics and Statistics, 67*(1), 43–52. doi:10.2307/1928433

Bartels, A. (2009). *US IT market outlook: Q1 2009. Our bleak alternative view moves closer to reality.* Cambridge, MA: Forrester Research Incorporated.

Bartlett, C. A., & Ghoshal, S. (1989). *Managing across borders: The transnational solution.* Boston: Harvard Business School Press.

Bartol, K. M. (1983). Turnover among DP personnel: A causal analysis. *Communications of the ACM, 26*(10), 807–811. doi:10.1145/358413.358433

Bartol, K. M., & Martin, D. C. (1983). Managing Information Systems personnel: A review of the literature and managerial implications. *Management Information Systems Quarterly*, 49–70.

Bartol, K. M., & Aspray, W. (2006). The transition of women from the academic world to the IT workplace: A review of the relevant research. In Cohoon, J. M., & Aspray, W. (Eds.), *Women and Information Technology: Research on under representation.* Cambridge, MA: The MIT Press.

Baruch, Y. (1998). The rise and fall of organizational commitment. *Human Systems Management, 17*(2), 135–143.

Baruch, Y. (2004). Transforming careers: From linear to multidirectional career paths. Organizational and individual perspectives. *Career Development International, 9*(1), 58–73. doi:10.1108/13620430410518147

Bates, S. (2004). Getting engaged. *HRMagazine, 49*(2).

Battey, J. (2000, July 24). Retaining your most valuable assets. *InfoWorld,* 46.

Bauman, Z. (2005). *Identidade: entrevista a Benedito Vecchi.* Rio de Janeiro: Jorge Zahar.

Beatty, P., & Willis, G. (2007). Research synthesis: The practice of cognitive interviewing. *Public Opinion Quarterly.*

Becker, H. A. (1992). *Generaties en hun kansen.* Amsterdam: Meulenhof.

Becker, H. A. (1997). *De toekomst van de verloren generatie.* Amsterdam: Meulenhof.

Beise, C. M., Robbins, J., Kaiser, K. M., & Niederman, F. (2009). The Information Systems enrollment crisis: Status and strategies. In *Proceedings of the Special interest Group on Management information System's 47th Annual Conference on Computer Personnel Research* (Limerick, Ireland, May 28 - 30, 2009). (pp. 215-216). SIGMIS-CPR '09. New York: ACM.

Belbin, R. M. (2004). *Management teams: Why they succeed or fail.* Oxford: Elsevier Butterworth-Heinemann.

Benest, F. (2008). Retaining and growing talent: Strategies to create organizational stickness. *ICMA Public Management, 90*(9).

Benner, C. (2002). *Work in the new economy. Flexible labour markets in Silicon Valley* (1st ed.). Malden, MA: Blackwell.

Bennis, W. G., & O'Toole, J. (2005). How business schools lost their way. *Harvard Business Review, 83*(5).

Benvenga, M. (1998, January 12). How'm I doin'? *Computerworld,* 59.

Bergamini, C. W. (1997). *Motivação nas organizações.* São Paulo, Brazil: Atlas.

Berger, P. L., & Luckmann, T. (1966). *The social construction of reality: A treatise in the sociology of knowledge.* Garden City, NY: Anchor Books.

Bernthal, P. R., & Wellins, R. S. (2001). Retaining talent: A benchmarking study. *HR Benchmark Group, 2*(3), 1–28.

Berrios-Allison, A. C. (2005). Family influences on college students' occupational identity. *Journal of Career Assessment, 13*(2), 419–456. doi:10.1177/1069072704270320

Bhasin, B. B., & Cheng, P. (2001). The fight for global talent: New directions, new competitors–a case study on Singapore. *Career Development International, 7*(2), 109–114. doi:10.1108/13620430210421632

Bird, A. (1994). Careers as repositories of knowledge: A new perspective on boundaryless careers. *Journal of Organizational Behavior, 15*(4), 325–344. doi:10.1002/job.4030150404

Bird, A. (1996). Careers as repositories of knowledge: Considerations for boundaryless careers. In Arthur, M. B., & Rousseau, D. M. (Eds.), *The boundaryless career: A new employment principle for a new organizational era* (pp. 150–168). New York: Oxford University Press.

Bitkom. (2009a). *IT-Branche Behauptet Sich in Der Krise.* Retrieved November 6, 2009, from http://www.bitkom. org /de / presse /49896_57979.aspx

Bitkom. (2009b). *45.000 Offene Stellen Im Herbst 2008.* Retrieved November 6, 2009, from http://www.bitkom. org/ de / themen/ 54633_58438.aspx

Black, S. E., & Lynch, L. M. (1996). Human-capital investments and productivity. *The American Economic Review, 86*(2), 263–267.

Blanchard, K. (1994). *Leadership and the one minute manager.* Harper Collins.

Blum, T. C., Fields, D. L., & Goodman, J. S. (1994). Organization-level determinants of women in management. *Academy of Management Journal, 37*(2), 241–269. doi:10.2307/256829

Bontekoning, A. C. (2007). *Generaties in organisaties. Een onderzoek naar generatieverschillen en de effecten daarvan op de ontwikkeling van organisaties.* Doctoral dissertation, Tilburg University, the Netherlands.

Bontekoning, A.C. (2008). Generatiegolven als vernieuwingsimpuls. *M&O, 1*, 37-51.

Boomer, G. (2006). Performance evaluations for IT professionals. *Accounting Today*, 27.

Borges, L. O., & Alves Filho, A. (2001). A mensuração da motivação e do significado do trabalho. *Estudos de Psicologia, 6*(2), 177–194.

Borstorff, P., Marker, M., & Bennett, D. (2006). Online recruitment: Attitudes and behaviors of job seekers. *Proceedings of Allied Academies International Conference. Academy of Organizational Culture, Communications and Conflict, 11*(2), 9-13.

Bort, J. (2000, June). Mining for high-tech help. *ColoradoBiz*, 48-56.

Bose, A. (2006). *India as a job hub holds its charm for foreign professionals and Indians alike*. Retrieved February 2010, from http://www.assureconsulting.com/articles/rmig.shtml

Bossidy, L. (2001). The job no CEO should delegate. *Harvard Business Review*.

Bounfour, A., & Grefe, G. (2009). Designing sequences for knowledge exchange: The Hau-Ba model. In Bounfour, A. (Ed.), *Organisational capital: Modelling, measuring and contextualizing* (pp. 76–108). Oxon, UK: Routledge.

Bourguignon, A., Malleret, V., & Norreklit, H. (2004). *Balanced scorecard versus French tableau de bord: Beyond dispute, a cultural and ideological perspective*. Grenoble, France: Group HEC-Les Cahiers de Resercher.

Brancheau, J. C., & Wetherbe, J. C. (1987). Key issues in Information Systems management. *Management Information Systems Quarterly, 11*(1), 23–45. doi:10.2307/248822

Brancheau, J. C., Janz, B. D., & Wetherbe, J. C. (1996). Key issues in Information Systems management: 1994-95, SIM delphi results. *Management Information Systems Quarterly, 20*(2), 225–242. doi:10.2307/249479

Branham, L. (2001). *Keeping the people who keep you in business: 24 ways to hang on to your most valuable talent*. American Management Association Bureau of Labor Statistics. (2009). *March, May, June, July, August, November and December*. US Department of Labor. News release.

Breaugh, J. A. (1981). Relationships between recruiting sources and employee performance, absenteeism, and work attitudes. *Academy of Management Journal, 24*(1), 142–147. doi:10.2307/255829

Breaugh, J. A., & Starke, M. (2000). Research on employee recruitment: So many studies, so many remaining questions. *Journal of Management, 26*(3), 405–434. doi:10.1177/014920630002600303

Brickwedde, W. (in press). Neue Recruiter braucht das Land: der Recruiter 2.0 – Das Anforderungsprofil fuer den Recruiter von morgen. *Personalmagazin*.

Briscoe, J. P., & Finkelstein, L. M. (2009). The new career and organizational commitment: Do boundaryless and protean attitudes make a difference? *Career Development International, 14*(3), 242–260. doi:10.1108/13620430910966424

Briscoe, J. P., Hall, D. T., & DeMuth, R. I. F. (2006). Protean and boundaryless careers: An empirial exploration. *Journal of Vocational Behavior, 69*(1), 30–47. doi:10.1016/j.jvb.2005.09.003

Broadbent, M., & Weil, P. (1997). Management by maxim: How business and IT managers can create IT infrastructures. *Sloan Management Review, 38*(3), 77–92.

Brock, F. (2003, Oct. 12). Seniority: Who'll sit at the boomers desks? *The New York Times*.

Bronowski, J. (1965). *William Blake and the age of revolution*. New York: Harper and Row.

Brooke, L. (2009). Prolonging the careers of older Information Technology workers: Continuity, exit or retirement transitions? *Ageing and Society, 29*(1), 237–256. doi:10.1017/S0144686X0800768X

Brown, H. A., & Ford, D. L. (1977). An exploratory analysis of discrimination in the employment of black MBA graduates. *The Journal of Applied Psychology, 62*(1), 50–56. doi:10.1037/0021-9010.62.1.50

Brown, C., Clancy, G., & Scholer, R. J. (2003). A postmerger IT integration success story: Sallie Mae. *MIS Quarterly Executive, 2*(1), 15–27.

Bruner, J. (1997). *Atos de Significação. Porto Alegre/RS*. Brazil: Artes Médicas.

Bruschini, C. (2000). Gênero e trabalho no Brasil: Novas conquistas ou persistência da discriminação? In Rocha, M. I. B. (Ed.), *Trabalho e gênero–mudanças, permanências e desafios* (pp. 13–58).

Brynjolfsson, E. (1996). The contribution of Information Technology to consumer welfare. *Information Systems Research, 7*(3), 281–300. doi:10.1287/isre.7.3.281

Buche, M. W. (2008). Influence of gender on IT professional work identity: Outcomes from a PLS study. In *Proceedings of the 2008 ACM SIGMIS CPR Conference on Computer Personnel Doctoral Consortium and Research* (Charlottesville, VA, USA, April 03 - 05, 2008). (pp. 134-140). SIGMIS-CPR '08. New York: ACM.

Buckingham, M., & Coffman, C. (1999). *First break all the rules*. New York: Simon and Schuster.

Bullen, C. V., Abraham, T., Gallagher, K., Simon, J. C., & Zwieg, P. (2009). IT workforce trends: Implications for curriculum and hiring. *Communications of the Association for Information Systems, 24*(9).

Bureau of Labor Statistics. (2009). *Computer systems design and related services*. U.S. Department of Labor, career guide to industries, 2008-09 edition. Retrieved on March 27, 2009, from http://www.bls.gov/oco/ cg/ cgs033.htm

Bycio, P., Alvares, K. M., & Hahn, J. (1987). Situational specificity in assessment center ratings: A confirmatory factor analysis. *The Journal of Applied Psychology, 72*, 463–474. doi:10.1037/0021-9010.72.3.463

Cabrera, E. F. (2009). Protean organizations: Reshaping work and careers to retain female talent. *Career Development International, 14*(2), 186–201. doi:10.1108/13620430910950773

Callanan, G. A. (2003). What price career success? *Career Development International, 8*(3), 126–133. doi:10.1108/13620430310471032

Callanan, G. A., & Greenhaus, J. H. (1999). Personal and career development: The best and worst of times. In Kraut, A. I., & Korman, A. K. (Eds.), *Evolving practices in human resources management: Responses to a changing world of work* (pp. 146–171). San Francisco, CA: Jossey-Bass.

Campion, M. A., Cheraskin, L., & Stevens, M. J. (1994). Career related antecedents and outcomes of job rotation. *Academy of Management Journal, 37*(6), 1518–1542. doi:10.2307/256797

Capelli, P. (2008). *Talent on demand. Managing talent in an age of uncertainty*. Boston: Harvard Business Press.

Cappelle, M. C. A., et al. (2007). *A mulher gerente: Um estudo de caso numa companhia mineradora em Belo Horizonte/MG*. Retrieved on October 14, 2007, from http://www.fgvsp.br/iberoamerican/Papers/0429_ACF687.pdf

Cappelli, P. (2001). Why is it so hard to find information technology workers? *Organizational Dynamics, 30*(2), 87–99. doi:10.1016/S0090-2616(01)00045-6

Cappelli, P. (2001). Making the most of online recruiting. *Harvard Business Review, 79*(3), 139–146.

Carr, N. G. (2004). *Does IT matter? Information Technology and the corrosion of competitive advantage*. Boston: Harvard Business School Publishing.

Carr, N.G. (May 2003). IT doesn't matter. *Harvard Business Review*. Boston: Harvard Business School Press.

Casado, T. (2002). A motivação e o trabalho. In Fleury, M. T. F. (Ed.), *As pessoas na organização*. São Paulo: Gente.

Cascio, W., & Phillips, N. (1979). Performance testing: A rose among thorns? *Personnel Psychology, 32*, 751–766. doi:10.1111/j.1744-6570.1979.tb02345.x

Cashman, K. (2008). *Leadership from the inside out*. San Francisco, CA: Berrett Koehler.

Castells, M. (1999). *A sociedade em rede*. São Paulo: Paz e Terra.

Centraal Bureau voor de Statistiek. Den Haag/Heerlen. (2010). *Bevolking: kerncijfers naar diverse kenmerken*. Retrieved April 16, 2010, from http://statline.cbs.nl / StatWeb/ publication/ ?VW=T&DM=SLNL&PA=37296 ned&D1 =a&D2 =0,10,20,30,40, 50,(1-1)-1&HD =100423-2346& HDR=G1&STB=T

Centraal Bureau voor de Statistiek. Den Haag/Heerlen. (2010). *Hoger onderwijs, eerstejaars studenten naar vooropleiding en studierichting.* Retrieved April 16, 2010, from http://statline.cbs.nl/ StatWeb/publication /?DM=SLNL&PA= 70961ned &D1=0&D 2=1-2&D3= 0&D4= 0,175180&D5= 0&D6= 0&D7= a&D8= a&HDR= T,G4,G5,G2,G1,G6&STB =G3,G7&V W=T

Centraal Bureau voor de Statistiek. Den Haag/Heerlen. (2010). *Kerncijfers van diverse bevolkingsprognoses en waarneming.* Retrieved April 16, 2010, from http://statline.cbs.nl/ StatWeb/ publication/ ?DM=SLNL&PA =70737NED&D1 =8-10&D2 =l&D3 =55,60,65,70,75, 80,85,90,95,l &VW=T

Chabrow, E. (2010, April 2). *IT employment gains in first quarter.* Retrieved from http://www.govinfosecurity.com/ articles.php ?art_id =2372

Cheney, P. H., Hale, D. P., & Kasper, G. M. (1990). Knowledge, skills and abilities of Information Systems professionals: Past, present, and future. *Information & Management, 19,* 237–248. doi:10.1016/0378-7206(90)90033-E

Chesebrough, P. H., & Davis, G. B. (1983). Planning a career path in Information Systems. *Journal of Systems Management, 34*(1), 6–13.

Ciborra, C. (2002). *The labyrinths of information: Challenging the wisdom of systems.* London: Oxford.

Clayton, K. L., von Hellens, L. A., & Nielsen, S. H. (2009). Gender stereotypes prevail in ICT: A research review. In *Proceedings of the Special interest Group on Management information System's 47th Annual Conference on Computer Personnel Research* (Limerick, Ireland, May 28 - 30, 2009). (pp. 153-158). SIGMIS-CPR '09. New York: ACM.

Clemons, E. K. (1990). MAC-Philadelphia national banks strategic venture in shared ATM networks. *Journal of Management Information Systems, 7*(1), 5–25.

Clemons, E. K. (1991). Evaluation of strategic investments in Information Technology. *Communications of the ACM, 34*(1), 22–36. doi:10.1145/99977.99985

Clemons, E. K., & Kimbrough, S. O. (1986). Information Systems, telecommunications, and their effects on industrial organizations. In L. Maggi, R. Zmud & J. Wetherbe (Eds.), *Proceedings of the Seventh International Conference on Information Systems,* San Diego, CA, (pp. 99-108).

Cohen, L., & Mallon, M. (1999). The transition from organisational employmen to portfolio working: Perceptions of boundarylessness. *Work, Employment and Society, 13*(2), 329–352.

Cohoon, J. M., Wu, Z., & Luo, L. (2008). Will they stay or will they go? *SIGCSE Bulletin, 40,* 1. doi:10.1145/1352322.1352273

Cohoon, J. M. (2002). Recruiting and retining women in undergraduate computing majors. *ACM SIGCSE Bulletin, 34*(2), 48–52. doi:10.1145/543812.543829

Colarelli, S. M., & Bishop, R. C. (1990). Career commitment: Functions, correlates and management. *Group & Orgnization Studies, 15*(2), 158–176. doi:10.1177/105960119001500203

Collins, J. C. (2001). *Good to great: Why some companies make the leap... and others don't.* New York: Harper Collins.

Colwell, R. P., Brown, G., & See, F. (1999). *Intel's college hiring methods and recent results.* IEEE International Conference on Microelectronic Systems Education, p. 94.

Connet, M., & Bicknese, L. (2001). Basic skills back in demand. *Financial Executive, 17*(5), 44–45.

Constable, G., & Somerville, B. (2008). *A century of innovation: Twenty engineering achievements that transformed our lives.* Washington, D.C.: Joseph Henry Press.

Couger, J. D., Zawacki, R. A., & Opperman, E. B. (1973). Motivation levels of MIS managers versus those of their employees. *Management Information Systems Quarterly, 3*(3), 47–56. doi:10.2307/248788

Cowling, A. J. (2003). *What should graduating software engineers be able to do?* 16th Conference on Software Engineering Education and Training (CSEE&T), p. 88.

Crepeau, R. G., Crook, C. W., Goslar, M. D., & McMurtrey, M. E. (1992). Career anchors of Information Systems personnel. *Journal of Management Information Systems, 9*(2), 145–160.

Crow, D., & DeSanto, J. (2004). *A hybrid approach to concept extraction and recognition-based matching in the domain of human resources.* 16th IEEE International Conference on Tools with Artificial Intelligence (IC-TAI'04), pp. 535-539.

Cukier, W. (2003). Constructing the IT skills shortage in Canada: The implications of institutional discourse and practices for the participation of women. In *Proceedings of the 2003 SIGMIS Conference on Computer Personnel Research: Freedom in Philadelphia-Leveraging Differences and Diversity in the IT Workforce* (Philadelphia, Pennsylvania, April 10 - 12, 2003). (pp. 24-33). SIGMIS CPR '03. New York: ACM.

Cuny, J., & Aspray, W. (2000). *Recruitment and retention of women graduate students in computer science and engineering: Report of a workshop.* Washington, DC: Computing Research Association. Retrieved on June 1, 2009, from http://www.cra-w.org/ sites/default/files/ r&rwomen.pdf

Curtis, B., Hefley, W. E., & Miller, S. A. (2009). *People Capability Maturity Model (P-CMM®) version 2.0. (No. CMU/SEI-2009-TR-003).* Pittsburgh, PA: Software Engineering Institute, Carnegie Mellow University.

Dafoulas, G. A., Pateli, A. G., & Turega, M. (2002). *Business-to-employee cooperation support through online job interviews.* 13th International Workshop on Database and Expert Systems Applications (DEXA'02), pp. 286-295.

Dalton, D. R., Todor, W. D., & Krackhardt, D. M. (1982). Turnover overstated: The functional taxonomy. *Academy of Management Review, 7*, 117–123. doi:10.2307/257256

Dalton, G. W., Thompson, P. H., & Price, R. L. (1977). The four stages of professional careers: A new look at performance by professionals. *Organizational Dynamics, 6*(1), 19–42. doi:10.1016/0090-2616(77)90033-X

Darwin, C. R. (2006). *On the origin of species: By means of natural selection or the preservation of favoured races in the struggle for life.* New York: Dover Publications.

Davenport, T. (2008, April 7). Q&A Thomas O. Davenport. *Computerworld*, 40.

Davis, J., & Kuhn, S. (2003). What makes Dick and Jane run? Examining the retention of women and men in the software and internet industry. In *Proceedings of the 2003 SIGMIS Conference on Computer Personnel Research: Freedom in Philadelphia-Leveraging Differences and Diversity in the IT Workforce* (Philadelphia, Pennsylvania, April 10 - 12, 2003). (pp. 154-156). SIGMIS CPR '03. New York: ACM.

De Bruin, A., & Lewis, K. (2004). Toward enriching united career theory: Familial entrepreneurship and copreneurship. *Career Development International, 9*(7), 638–646. doi:10.1108/13620430410570347

DeLong, T. J. (1982). Reexamining the career anchor model. *Personnel, 59*(3), 50–61.

Demers, A. (2002). Solutions and strategies for IT recruitment and retention: A manager's guide. *Public Personnel Management*, 27–35.

Dickler, J. (2009). The job application black hole. *Money.* Retrieved February 18, 2010, from http://money.cnn. com/ 2010/02/18/news/economy/ resume_void/index. htm?hpt=T2

Dohm, A., & Shniper, L. (2007). Occupational employment projections to 2016, *Monthly Labor Review.* Retrieved on February 12, 2009, from http://www.bls.gov/ opub/mlr/ 2007/11/ art5 full.pdf

Dolan, A. F. (2004). Recruiting, retaining, and reskilling campus IT professionals. In Hawkins, B. L., Rudy, J. A., & Wallace, W. H. (Eds.), *Technology everywhere: A campus agenda for educating and managing workers in the digital age* (pp. 75–91). Jossey-Bass.

Doll, W. J., & Torkzaddeh, G. (1988). The measurement of end-user computing satisfaction. *Management Information Systems Quarterly*, 259–274. doi:10.2307/248851

Dorfman, P. W. (1996). International and cross-cultural leadership. In Punnett, B. J., & Shenkar, O. (Eds.), *Handbook for international management research* (pp. 267–349). Cambridge, MA: Blackwell.

Driver, M. J. (1982). Career concepts–a new approach to career research. In Katz, R. (Ed.), *Career issues in human resources management* (pp. 23–32). Englewood Cliffs, NJ: Prentice-Hall.

Drucker, P. F. (1998). *The coming of the new organization. Harvard Business Review on Knowledge Management* (pp. 1–19). Harvard Business School Press.

Drucker, P. F. (1999). *Administrando em tempos de grandes mudanças*. São Paulo: Pioneira.

Dubie, D. (2007, October 15). What does it take to lure and retain IT talent? *Network-World, 1*, 14.

Dunbar, R. I. M. (1992). Neocortex size as a constraint on group size in primates. *Journal of Human Evolution, 20*, 469–493. doi:10.1016/0047-2484(92)90081-J

Eboli, M. (2004). *Educação corporativa no Brasil: Mitos e verdades*. São Paulo: Gente.

Eboli, M. (2002). O desenvolvimento das pessoas e a educação corporativa. In Fleury, M. T. L. (Ed.), *As pessoas na organização*. São Paulo: Gente.

Eckhardt, A., & Laumer, S. (2009). An IT-architecture to align e-recruiting and retention processes. *International Journal of E-Services and Mobile Applications, 1*(2), 38–61. doi:10.4018/jesma.2009040103

Eckhardt, A., & Rosenkranz, C. (2010). Lost in translation?! – The need for a boundary spanner between business and IT. In *Proceedings of the ACM SIGMIS Conference on Computer Personnel Research 2010*: Vancouver, Canada.

Eckhardt, A., Weitzel, T., Koenig, W., & Buschbacher, J. (2007). How to convince people who don't like IT to use IT-a case study on e-recruiting. In *Proceedings of 13th Americas Conference on Information Systems* (AMCIS 2007): Keystone, USA.

Edberg, D. T., & Bowman, B. J. (1996). User-developed applications: An empirical study of application quality and developer productivity. *Journal of Management Information Systems, 13*(1), 167.

Edwards, M. R., & Ewen, A. J. (1996, May). *360 Feedback: The Powerful New Model for Employee Assessment & Performance Improvement*. New York, NY: American Management Association.

El Sawy, O. A., Malhotra, A., Gosain, S., & Young, K. M. (1999). IT-intensive value innovation in the electronic economy: Insights from Marshall Industries. *Management Information Systems Quarterly, 23*(3), 309–335.

Elder, G. (1985). *Life course dynamics: Trajectories and transitions, 1968–1980*. Ithaca, NY: Cornell University Press.

Elkjaer, B. (2001). Em busca de uma teoria de aprendizagem organizacional. In Easterby-Smith, M., Burgoyne, J., & Araujo, L. (Eds.), *Aprendizagem organizacional e organização de aprendizagem: Desenvolvimento na teoria e na prática*. São Paulo: Atlas.

Elmuti, D. (2001). Preliminary analysis of the relationship between cultural diversity and technology in corporate America. *Equal Opportunities International, 20*(8), 1–16. doi:10.1108/02610150110786642

Elton, C. (2005). DHL program seeks to hold on to IT staff. *Computerworld*, 43.

Ely, R., & Thomas, D. (2001). Cultural diversity at work: The effects of diversity perspectives on work group processes and outcomes. *Administrative Science Quarterly*, 229–273. doi:10.2307/2667087

Emery, J. C. (1990). Misconception about strategic Information Systems. *Management Information Systems Quarterly, 14*(2), vii–viii.

Enns, H. G. (2005). Do IT professionals need business acumen to build effective partnerships? *The Academy of Management Executive, 19*(2), 159–162.

Ettlie, J. E. (1983). Organizational policy and innovation among suppliers to the food processing sector. *Academy of Management Journal, 26*(1), 27–44. doi:10.2307/256133

Evans, N. (2004). The need for an Analysis Body of Knowledge (ABOK)-will the real analyst please stand up? *Issues in Informing Science & Information Technology, 1*(1), 313–330.

Extejt, M. M., & Lynn, M. P. (1988). Expert systems as human resource management tools. *Journal of Systems Management, 39*(11), 10–15.

Fagnot, I. J., Guzman, I. R., & Stanton, J. M. (2007). Toward recruitment and retention strategies based on the early exposure to the IT occupational culture. *AMCIS 2007 Proceedings*. Retrieved on June 29, 2009, from http://aisel.aisnet.org/ amcis2007/199

Faulkner, W. (2000). Dualisms, hierarchies and gender in engineering. *Social Studies of Science, 30*(5), 759–792. doi:10.1177/030631200030005005

Fayard, P. (2006). *Le réveil du samouraï: Culture et stratégie japonaise dans la société de la connaissance.* Paris: Dunod.

Fenwick, T. J. (2006). Contradictions in portfolio careers: Work design and client relations. *Career Development International, 11*(1), 65–79. doi:10.1108/13620430610642381

Fernández-Aráoz, C., Groysberg, B., & Nohria, N. (2009). The definitive guide to recruiting in good times and bad. *Harvard Business Review, 87*(5), 74–84.

Ferratt, T. W., Agarwal, R., Brown, C. V., & Moore, J. E. (2005). IT human resource management configurations and IT turnover: Theoretical synthesis and empirical analysis. *Information Systems Research, 16*, 237–255. doi:10.1287/isre.1050.0057

Fine, S. A., & Cronshaw, S. F. (1999). *Functional job analysis: A foundation for human resources management.* Mahwah, NJ: Lawrence Erlbaum Associates.

Finkelman, C. (2010). *Telephone interview.* 27 Feb, 2010.

Fischer, A. L. (1996). *As decisões sobre o método dos diagnósticos organizacionais internos.* CLADEA.

Flannes, S. W., & Levin, G. (2005). *Essential people skills for project managers.* New York: Management Concepts.

Fleming, D. L. (2008). Building bridges to connect the disconnects: An analysis of business program design processes. *American Journal of Business Education, 1*(2), 21–46.

Fletcher, W. L., Hansson, R. O., & Bailey, L. (1992). Assessing occupational self-efficacy among middle-aged and older adults. *Journal of Applied Gerontology, 11*(4), 489–501. doi:10.1177/073346489201100408

Foote, D. (1998, October 12). Recruit with your head, retain with your heart. *Computerworld*, 55–56.

Frank, F., & Taylor, C. (2004). Talent management: Trends that will shape the future. *Human Resource Planning, 27*(1), 33–41.

Frank, F. D., Finnegan, R. P., & Taylor, C. R. (2004). The race for talent: Retaining and engaging workers in the 21st century. *Human Resource Planning, 27*, 12–25.

Franklin, D. (2009). *Gender differences: Recognizing and developing potential in female students.* Washington, DC: Computing Research Association. Retrieved on June 29, 2009, from http://www.cra.org/ CRN/articles/march07/ franklin.html

Frase-Blunt, M. (2003). Special report on recruiting and staffing. traditional recruiting defined. *HR Magazine, 48*, 4. Retrieved March 2, 2010, from http://www.shrm.org/ Publications/hrmagazine/ EditorialContent/ Pages/0403frase.aspx

Freeman, P., & Aspray, W. 1999. *The Supply of Information Technology Workers in the United States.* Washington, DC: Computing Research Association. Available: http://www.cra.org/reports /wits/cra.wits.html [Cited 29 March 2009].

Fullan, M. (2001). *Leading in a culture of change.* San Francisco: Jossey-Bass.

Fyock, C. D. (2009). Recruiting internally and externally. *SHRM Online, April.* Retrieved May 2, 2010, from http://www.shrm.org/ Research/Articles/ Pages/RecruitingInternally andExternally.aspx

Galanaki, E. (2002). The decision to recruit online: A descriptive study. *Career Development International, 7*(4), 243–251. doi:10.1108/13620430210431325

Gallivan, M. J. (2001). Meaning to change: How diverse stakeholders interpret organizational communication about change initiatives. *IEEE Transactions on Professional Communication, 44*(4), 243–266. doi:10.1109/47.968107

Gallivan, M. J., Truex, D. P. III, & Kvasny, L. (2004). Changing patterns in IT skill sets 1988-2003: A content analysis of classified advertising. *ACM SIGMIS Database, 35*(3), 64–87. doi:10.1145/1017114.1017121

Gallivan, M. J., Truex, D. P., III, & Kvasny, L. (2002). *An analysis of the changing demand patterns for Information Technology professionals.* Paper presented at the 2002 ACM SIGCPR Conference on Computer Personnel Research.

Gannon, M. J. (1971). Sources of referral and employee turnover. *The Journal of Applied Psychology, 55*(3), 226–228. doi:10.1037/h0031151

GAPPS (Global Alliance for Project Performance Standards). (2007). *A framework for performance based competency standards for global level 1 and 2 project managers*. Retrieved February 26, 2010, from http://www.globalpmstandards.org

Garcia-Crespo, A., Colomo-Palacios, R., Gomez-Berbis, J. M., & Tovar-Caro, E. (2009). IT professionals' competences. *High School Students'. Views, 8*, 45–57.

Gartner. (2010). *Gartner says worldwide IT spending to grow 4.6 percent in 2010*. Retrieved from http://www.gartner.com/it/ page.jsp?id= 1284 813

Garvin, D. A. (1993). Building a learning organization. *Harvard Business Review, 71*(4), 78–91.

Garvin, D. A. (2002). *Aprendizagem em ação: um guia para transformar sua empresa em uma learning organization*. Rio de Janeiro: Qualitymark.

Gatewood, R. D., & Feild, H. S. (1994). *Human resource selection* (3rd ed.). Fort Worth, TX: Dryden Press.

Gatewood, R. D., Feild, H. S., & Barrick, M. R. (2008). *Human resource selection* (6th ed.). Mason, OH: Thomson South-Western.

Gaugler, B. B., Rosenthal, D. B., Thornton, G. C. III, & Bentson, C. (1987). Meta-analysis of assessment center validity. *The Journal of Applied Psychology, 72*, 493–511. doi:10.1037/0021-9010.72.3.493

Gelston, S. (2008). Gen Y, gen X, and the baby boomers: Workplace generation wars. *CIO Magazine.* Retrieved February 2010, from http://www.cio.com/article/178050/Gen_Y_Gen_X_and_the_Baby_Boomers_Workplace_Generation_Wars

Gerdes, L. (2005, September 5). B-School with a niche. *Business Week*, 70-72.

Gibbons, L. (2006, October 30). As IT staff retention takes center stage, get your job titles straight, or lose your best people. *Management & Careers*, 46.

Giber, D., Carter, L., & Goldsmith, M. (Eds.). (2008). *Linkage, Inc.'s best practices in leadership development handbook*. Linkage Press.

Gibson, D. E. (2004). Role models in career development: New directions for theory and research. *Journal of Vocational Behavior, 65*(1), 134–156. doi:10.1016/S0001-8791(03)00051-4

Giddens, A. (2002). *Modernidade e Identidade*. Rio de Janeiro: Jorge Zahar.

Gilburg, D. (2007). Management techniques for bringing out the best in generation Y. *CIO Magazine.* Retrieved February 2010, from http://www.cio.com/article/149053/Management_Techniques_for_Bringing_Out_the_Best_in_Generation_Y

Gilder, G. (2002). *Telecosm: The world after bandwidth abundance*. Touchstone.

Giles, C. (2010). Mind the gap. *Financial Times (North American Edition)*, 19.

Ginzberg, M. J., & Baroudi, J. J. (1988). MIS careers-a theoretical perspective. *Communications of the ACM, 31*(5), 586–594. doi:10.1145/42411.42422

Gionfriddo, J., & Dhingra, L. (1999). Retaining high-tech talent: NIIT case study. *Compensation and Benefits Review, 31*, 5. doi:10.1177/088636879903100505

Girard, F. (2002). *Five state college coaches claim unearned degrees*. Retrieved on May 14, 2005, from http://www.detnews.com/ 2002/college/0209/18/ a01-590403.htm

Glanz, B. (2002). *Handle with care: Motivating and retaining your employees*. McGraw-Hill.

Goffee, R., & Jones, G. (2000). *Why should anyone be led by you?* Leadership Insights in Harvard Business Review.

Gopal, A. (2004). *Flawed assumptions can defeat your business*. Gallup Management Journal.

Gotcher, R. (1997, October 20). Combine bonuses with regards. *InfoWorld*, 119.

Gothcer, R., Steen, M., & Fletcher-Mcdonald, T. (1999, September 27). Building the best workplace. *InfoWorld*, S7.

Gottfredson, L. S. (1981). Circumscription and compromise: A development theory of occupational aspirations. *Journal of Counseling Psychology, 28*(6), 545–579. doi:10.1037/0022-0167.28.6.545

Granger, M. J., Dick, G., Jacobson, C. M., & Slyke, C. V. (2007). Information Systems enrollments: Challenges and strategies. *Journal of Information Systems Education, 18*(3), 303–311.

Granrose, C. S., & Portwood, J. (1987). Matching individual career plans and organizational career management. *Academy of Management Journal, 30*(4), 669–720. doi:10.2307/256156

Greenhaus, J. H., Callanan, G. A., & Godshalk, V. M. (2000). *Career management* (3rd ed.). Mason, OH: Thomson-South-Western.

Greenhaus, J. H., Parasuraman, S., & Wormley, W. M. (1990). Effects of race on organizational experiences, job performance evaluations, and career outcomes. *Academy of Management Journal, 33*(1), 64–86. doi:10.2307/256352

Grensing-Pophal, L. (2001, July). Engaging employees–from A-Z. *HR Magazine.*

Griffeth, R., & Hom, P. W. (2001). *Retaining valued employees*. Sage Publications.

Grund, C. (2006). Mitarbeiterrekrutierung ueber das Internet – Marktanalyse und empirische Untersuchung von Determinanten und Konsequenzen fuer die Arbeitnehmer. *Zeitschrift fuer Betriebswirtschaft, 76*(5), 451–472. doi:10.1007/s11573-006-0022-z

Gueutal, H. (2009). HR and our virtual business world. *Journal of Managerial Psychology, 24*(6).

Guion, R. M., & Gottier, R. F. (1966). Validity of personality measures in personnel selection. *Personnel Psychology, 18*, 135–164. doi:10.1111/j.1744-6570.1965.tb00273.x

Guthrie, R. A., Soe, L. L., & Yakura, E. (2009). Support structures for women in Information Technology careers. *AMCIS 2009 Proceedings*. Retrieved August 25, 2009, from http://aisel.aisnet.org/ amcis2009/332

Gutiérrez-Martínez, I. (2006). L'implication organisationnelle des professionnels de TI. *Revue Française de Gestion, 32*(168/169), 143–156. doi:10.3166/rfg.168-169.143-156

Guzman, I. R., Joseph, D., Papamichail, K. N., & Stanton, J. M. (2007). RIP-beliefs about IT culture: Exploring national and gender differences. In *Proceedings of the 2007 ACM SIGMIS CPR Conference on Computer Personnel Research: the Global Information Technology Workforce* (St. Louis, Missouri, USA, April 19 - 21, 2007). (pp. 217-220). SIGMIS-CPR '07. New York: ACM.

Hackman, J. R., & Oldham, G. R. (1975). Development of the job diagnostic survey. *The Journal of Applied Psychology, 60*, 159–170. doi:10.1037/h0076546

Hackman, J. R., & Oldham, G. R. (1976). Motivation through the design of work: Test of a theory. *Organizational Behavior and Human Performance, 16*(2), 250–279. doi:10.1016/0030-5073(76)90016-7

Hackman, J. R., & Oldham, G. R. (1980). *Work redesign*. Reading, MA: Addison Wesley.

Hall, D. T. (1971). A theoretical model of career subidentity development in organizational settings. *Organizational Behavior and Human Performance, 6*(1), 50–76. doi:10.1016/0030-5073(71)90005-5

Hall, D. T. (1986). *Career development in organizations*. San Francisco, CA: Jossey-Bass.

Hall, D. T. (1996). Protean career of the 21st century. *The Academy of Management Executive, 10*(4), 8–16.

Hall, D. T. (2004). The protean career: A quarter-century journey. *Journal of Vocational Behavior, 65*(1), 1–13. doi:10.1016/j.jvb.2003.10.006

Hall, D. T., & Mirvis, P. H. (1995). The new career contract: Developing the whole person at midlife and beyond. *Journal of Vocational Behavior, 47*(3), 269–289. doi:10.1006/jvbe.1995.0004

Hall, D. T., & Mirvis, P. H. (1996). The new protean career: Psychological success and the path with a heart. In Hall, D. T. (Ed.), *The career is dead-long live the career* (pp. 15–45). San Francisco, CA: Jossey-Bass.

Hansen, F. (June 2005). The turnover myth. *Workforce Management*, 38.

Harris, J. (2009). What's wrong with executive compensation? *Journal of Business Ethics, 85*, 147–156. doi:10.1007/s10551-008-9934-6

Harvey, R. J., Friedman, L., Hakel, M. D., & Cornelius, E. T. III. (1989). Dimensionality of the job element inventory: A simplified worker-oriented job analysis questionnaire. *The Journal of Applied Psychology, 73*, 639–646. doi:10.1037/0021-9010.73.4.639

Hatzilygeroudis, I. (2004). Integrating rules, neural networks, and cases for knowledge representation. *Expert Systems with Applications, 27*(1), 63–75. doi:10.1016/j.eswa.2003.12.004

Hayes, F. (1997). Managing user expectation. *Computerworld, 31*(4), 8–9.

He, Z. M., Kusy, K. M., & Zhao, T. (1998). A survey study of the current IS usage in the Chinese manufacturing industry. *Information & Management, 34*, 285–294. doi:10.1016/S0378-7206(98)00063-9

Hecker, D. (2001). Occupational employment projections to 2010. *Monthly Labor Review*, 57-84. Retrieved February 10, 2009, from http://www.bls.gov/opub/mlr/2001/ 11/ art4full.pdf

Hecker, D. (2004). Occupational employment projections to 2012. *Monthly Labor Review*, 80-105. Retrieved February 10, 2009, from http://www.bls.gov/opub/mlr/2004/ 02/art5 full.pdf

Hecker, D. (2006). Occupational employment projections to 2014. *Monthly Labor Review*, 70-101. Retrieved February 10, 2009, from http://www.bls.gov/opub/mlr/2005/ 11/art 5full.pdf

Heckler, R. S. (2007). *The leadership dojo: Build your future foundation as an exemplary leader*. Frog Books.

Heikkilä, J. T., Saarinen, T., & Sääksjärvi, M. (1991). Success of software packages in small businesses: An exploratory study. *European Journal of Information Systems, 1*(3), 159–169. doi:10.1057/ejis.1991.31

Heinze, N., & Hu, Q. (2009). Why college undergraduates choose IT: A multi-theoretical perspective. *European Journal of Information Systems, 18*(5), 462–475. doi:10.1057/ejis.2009.30

Heneman, H. G. III, & Judge, T. A. (2006). *Staffing organizations*. Middleton, WI: McGraw-Hill.

Herriot, P., Gibson, G., Pemberton, C., & Pinder, R. (1993). Dashed hopes: Organizational determinants and personal perceptions of managerial careers. *Journal of Occupational and Organizational Psychology, 66*(2), 115–123.

Herriot, P., & Pemberton, C. (1996). Contracting careers. *Human Relations, 49*(6), 757–790. doi:10.1177/001872679604900603

Hersey, P., & Blanchard, K. H. (1977). *Management of organizational behavior 3rd edition–utilizing human resources*. New Jersey/Prentice Hall.

Heskett, J.L., Jones, T.O., Loveman, G.W., Sasser, Jr., W.E. & Schlesinger, L.A. (1994). Putting the service-profit chain to work. *Harvard Business Review*.

Hewlett-Packard Development Company. L.P. (2010, January). *2009Annual Report*. Palo Alto, CA: HP.

Higgins, M. C. (2001). Changing careers: The effects of social context. *Journal of Organizational Behavior, 22*(6), 595–618. doi:10.1002/job.104

Hill, C. W. L., & Jones, G. R. (2006). *Strategic management: An integrated approach* (7th ed.). Boston: Houghton Mifflin Company.

Hinrichs, J. R. (1978). An eight-year follow-up of a management assessment center. *The Journal of Applied Psychology, 63*, 596–601. doi:10.1037/0021-9010.63.5.596

Hof, R. (2003, August 17). We can't even glimpse the potential. *Business Week*. Retrieved from http://www.businessweek.com/ @@GovuBoUQaQmEPwkA/ magazine/ content/03_34/ b384 6612.htm

Hofstede, G. (2001). *Culture's consequences: Comparing values, behaviors, institutions and organizations across nations*. London: Sage.

Hofstede, G., & McCrae, R. R. (2004). Personality and culture revisited: Linking traits and dimensions of culture. *Society of Cross-Culture Research, 38*, 52. doi:10.1177/1069397103259443

Homan, A. C., Hollenbeck, J. R., Humphrey, S. E., Van Knippenberg, D., Ilgen, D. R., & Van Kleef, G. A. (2008). Facing differences with an open mind: Openness to experience, salience of intragroup differences, and performance of diverse work groups. *Academy of Management Journal, 51*(6), 1204–1222.

Horowitz, A. (2005, September 12). You can't always guess what they want. *Computerworld*, *52*, 55.

Huang, C. (2006). *Needs assessment for new employee orientation at UW-Stout*.

Hunt, D. M., & Michael, C. (1983). Mentorship: A career training and development tool. *Academy of Management Review*, *8*(3), 475–485. doi:10.2307/257836

Hunter, J. E., & Hunter, R. F. (1984). Validity and utility of alternative predictors of job performance. *Psychological Bulletin*, *96*(1), 72–98. doi:10.1037/0033-2909.96.1.72

Igbaria, M., & Baroudi, J. J. (1995). The impact of job performance evaluations on career advancement prospects: An examination of gender differences in the IS workplace. *Management Information Systems Quarterly*, *19*, 107–123. doi:10.2307/249713

Igbaria, M., & Greenhaus, J. H. (1992). Determinants of MIS employees' turnover intentions: A structural equation model. *Communications of the ACM*, *35*(2), 35–49. doi:10.1145/129630.129631

Igbaria, M., & Parasuraman, S. (1994). Work experiences, job involvement, and quality of work life among Information Systems personnel. *Information Resources Management*, *18*(2), 175–201.

Igbaria, M., & Siegel, S. R. (1992). The reasons for turnover of information systems personnel. *Information & Management*, *23*, 321–330. doi:10.1016/0378-7206(92)90014-7

Igbaria, M., Greenhaus, J. H., & Parasuraman, S. (1991). Career orientations of MIS employees: An empirical analysis. *Management Information Systems Quarterly*, *15*(2), 151–169. doi:10.2307/249376

Illich, I. (1973). *Tools for conviviality*. New York: Harper & Row.

Information Technology Association of America (ITAA). (2003). *Report of the ITAA blue ribbon panel on IT diversity*. Arlington, VA.

Ingason, H. T., & Jonasson, H. I. (2009). Contemporary knowledge and skills requirements in project management. *Project Management Journal*, *40*, 59–69. doi:10.1002/pmj.20122

Ingervaldson, P. M. (2008). Top 10 qualities of a great IT shop. *Computerworld*, *42*(50), 17.

Inkson, K. (2008). Are human resources? *Career Development International*, *13*(3), 270–279. doi:10.1108/13620430810870511

ITAA. (2003). *Report of the ITAA blue ribbon panel on IT diversity*. Presentation at the National IT Workforce Convocation, Arlington, VA. Retrieved on March 29, 2009 from http://www.itaa.org/workforce/ docs/03divreport.pdf

Ituma, A., & Simpson, R. (2006). The chameleon career: An exploratory study of the work biography of Information Technology workers in Nigeria. *Career Development International*, *11*(1), 48–65. doi:10.1108/13620430610642372

Ives, B., & Olson, M. H. (1981). Manager or technician? Then nature of Information Systems manager's job. *Management Information Systems Quarterly*, *5*(4), 49–63. doi:10.2307/249327

Jackson, T. (1993). *Organizational behaviour in international management*. Oxford: Butterworth-Heinemann.

Jacobs, D. (2005). In search of future leaders: Managing the global talent pipeline. *Ivey Business Journal*, 1-5.

James, K., Downey, B., Duckett, S., & Woody, C. (2000). Name your career development intervention. *Journal of Workplace Learning*, *12*(5), 205. doi:10.1108/13665620010316217

Jamrog, J. (2004). The perfect storm: The future of retention and engagement. *Human Resource Planning*, *27*, 26–33.

Jenkins, A. (2009). *Keeping the talent: Understanding the needs of engineers and scientists in the defense acquisition workforce*. Defense Acquisition Review Journal.

Jeong, J. J., & Klein, G. (1999). Risks to different aspects of system success. *Information & Management*, *36*, 263–272. doi:10.1016/S0378-7206(99)00024-5

Jewell, H., & Maltby, J. R. (2001). *Female involvement in Information Technology degrees: Perception, expectation and enrolment*. ACIS. Retrieved on March 27, 2009, from http://aisel.aisnet.org/cgi/ viewcontent.cgi?article=1034&context=acis2001

Jiang, J. J., & Klein, G. (1995). Requisite technical skills for technical support analysts: A survey. *ACM SIGCPR Computer Personnel, 16*(2), 12–20. doi:10.1145/202896.202899

Jones, M. (1994). Don't emancipate, exaggerate: Rhetoric, reality and reengineering. In R. Baskerville, S. Smithson, C. Ngwenyama & J.I. DeGross (Eds.), *Transforming organization with Information Technology*. (pp. 357-378). North Holland: Elseiver Science.

Joseph, D., Ang, S., Chang, R. H. L., & Slaughter, S. A. (2010). Practical intelligence in IT: Assessing soft skill of IT professionals. *Communications of the ACM, 53*, 149–154. doi:10.1145/1646353.1646391

Joseph, D., Ng, K., Koh, C., & Ang, S. (2007). Turnover of Information Technology professionals: A narrative review, meta-analytic structural equation modeling, and model development. *Management Information Systems Quarterly, 31*, 547–577.

Joshi, K. D., & Kuhn, K. M. (2007). What it takes to succeed in Information Technology consulting: Exploring the gender typing of critical attributes. *Information Technology & People, 20*(4), 400–424. doi:10.1108/09593840710839815

Jung, C. G. (1971). Psychological types. In *Collected works of C. G. Jung, volume 6*. Princeton University Press.

Kaiser, K.M., Abraham, T., Beath, C., Bullen, C.V., Frampton, K., Gallagher, K.P., et al. (2008). *The Information Technology workforce: IT provider trends and implications 2006-2009*.

Kanfer, R., & Ackerman, P. L. (2004). Aging, adult development, and work motivation. *Academy of Management Review, 29*(3), 440–458. doi:10.2307/20159053

Kanter, R. M. (1991). The future of bureaucracy and hierarchy in organizational theory: A report from the field. In Bourdieu, P., & Coleman, J. S. (Eds.), *Social theory for a changing society*. London: Westview Press.

Kaplan, D. M., & Lerouge, C. (2007). Managing on the edge of change: Human resource management of Information Technology employees. *Human Resource Management, 46*(3), 325–330. doi:10.1002/hrm.20166

Katz, S., Aronis, J., Wilson, C., Allbritton, D., & Soffa, M. L. (2006). Traversing the undergraduate curriculum in computer science: Where do students stumble? In Cohoon, J. M., & Aspray, W. (Eds.), *Women and Information Technology: Research on under representation*. Cambridge, MA: MIT Press.

Katz, R., & Allen, T. J. (1997). Managing dual ladder systems in RD&E settings. In Katz, R. (Ed.), *The human side of managing technological innovation* (pp. 47–486). New York: Oxford University Press.

Katz, J. O., & McCormick, D. (2005, February 4). Advanced option pricing models.

Keen, P. G. W. (1988). Roles and skill base for the IS organization. In Elam, J. J., Ginzberg, M. J., Keen, P. G. W., & Zmud, R. W. (Eds.), *Transforming the IS organization*. Washington, DC: ICIT Press.

Keim, T., & Weitzel, T. (2006) Strategies for hiring IT professionals: An empirical analysis of employer and job seeker behavior on the IT labor market. *Proceedings of the 12th Americas Conference on Information Systems* (AMCIS 2006): Acapulco, Mexico.

Keirsey, D. (1998). *Please understand me II: Temperament, character, intelligence* (1st ed.). Prometheus Nemesis Book Co.

Kemerer, C. F., & Sosa, G. L. (1991). Systems development risks in strategic Information Systems. *Information and Software Technology, 33*(3), 212–223. doi:10.1016/0950-5849(91)90136-Y

Kerlin, M. D., McGaw, D., & Wolf, W. (2008). Planning for the next generation. *Transforming Government, 3*(Autumn), 8–13.

Kettinger, W. J., & Lee, C. C. (1999). Replication of measures of Information Systems research: The case of IS SERVQUAL. *Decision Sciences, 3*(30), 893–899. doi:10.1111/j.1540-5915.1999.tb00912.x

Khanna, T., & Palepu, K. G. (2004). Globalization and convergence in corporate governance: Evidence from Infosys and the Indian software industry. *Journal of International Business Studies, 35*, 484–507. doi:10.1057/palgrave.jibs.8400103

King, J. (2008, February 19). Career paths you never dreamed of. *ComputerWorld*.

Klepper, R., & Jones, W. O. (1998). *Outsourcing Information Technology, systems, & services*. Upper Saddle River, NJ: Prentice Hall.

Klimoski, R. J., & Brickner, M. (1987). Why do assessment centers work? The puzzle of assessment center validity. *Personnel Psychology, 40*, 243–260. doi:10.1111/j.1744-6570.1987.tb00603.x

Kluemper, D. H., & Rosen, P. A. (2009). Future employment selection methods: Evaluating social networking Web sites. *Journal of Managerial Psychology, 24*(6), 567–580. doi:10.1108/02683940910974134

Kochanski, J., & Ledford, G. (2001). How to keep me: Retaining technical professionals. *Research Technology Management, 44*, 3.

Koh, S., Lee, S., Yen, D. C., & Havelka, D. (2004). The relationship between Information Technology professionals' skill requirements and career stage in the e-commerce era: An empirical study. *Journal of Global Information Management, 12*, 68–82. doi:10.4018/jgim.2004010105

Kondratiev, N.D. (1928). *The major cycles of the conjuncture*.

Kopelman, R. E., Rovenpor, J. L., & Millsap, R. (1992). Rationale and construct validity evidence for the job search behavior index: Because intentions (and New Year's resolutions) often come to naught. *Journal of Vocational Behavior, 40*, 269–287. doi:10.1016/0001-8791(92)90051-Z

Kynphausen-Aufseß, D., & Vormann, C. (2009). Personnel selection criteria in IT ventures: A policy-capturing analysis. *Zeitschrift für Betriebswirtschaft, 79*, 213–234. doi:10.1007/s11573-008-0207-8

Lamoreaux, K. (2008). *SIM women survey: Separating fact from fiction*. Society for Information Management.

Lang, C. (2007). Twenty-first century Australian women and IT: Exercising the power of choice. *Computer Science Education, 17*(3), 215-226. Retrieved on March 27, 2009, from http://www.emeraldinsight.com/ 0263-5577.htm

Lao-tzu. (6th Century BC). *Tao Te Ching*. Vintage Press.

Lash, P. B., & Sein, M. K. (1995). *Career paths in a changing IS environment: A theoretical perspective*. Paper presented at the 1995 ACM SIGCPR Conference on Supporting Teams, Groups, and Learning Inside and Outside the IS Function Reinventing IS.

Lash, R. & Huber, C. (2010). *The Hay Group webinar: 2009 best companies for leadership*.

Laudon, K. C., & Laudon, J. P. (1999). *Essentials of management Information Systems: Transforming business and management*. Upper Saddle River, NJ: Prentice Hall.

Laumer, S. (2009). Non-monetary solutions for retaining the IT workforce. *Americas Conference on Information Systems (AMCIS 2009 Proceedings)*, Association for Information Systems, 2009.

Laumer, S., & Eckhardt, A. (2009). Help to find the needle in a haystack: Integrating recommender systems in an IT supported staff recruitment system. In *Proceedings of the ACM SIGMIS Conference on Computer Personnel Research* 2009: Limerick, Ireland.

Laumer, S., Eckhardt, A., & Weitzel, T. (2008). Recruiting IT professionals in a virtual world. In *Proceedings of the 12th Pacific Asia Conference on Information Systems* (PACIS 2008): Suzhou, China.

Laumer, S., von Stetten, A., Eckhardt, A., & Weitzel, T. (2009). Online gaming to apply for jobs –the impact of self- and e-assessment on staff recruitment. In *Proceedings of the 42th Hawaiian International Conference on System Sciences* (HICSS-42): Hawaii, USA.

Lazowska, E. (2008, July 11). Computer Science enrollment: The real news. *Computer Community Consortium*. Retrieved from http://www.cccblog.org/ 2008/07/11/computer-science-enroll ment-the-real-news/

LeClaire, B. (2005, September 12). You can't always guess what they want. *Computerworld, 52*, 55.

Lee, P. C. B. (2002). Career goals and career management strategy among Information Technology professionals. *Career Development International, 7*, 6–13. doi:10.1108/13620430210414829

Lee, T. W., & Mowday, R. T. (1987). Voluntarily leaving an organization: An empirical investigation of Steers and Mowday's model of turnover. *Academy of Management, 30*, 721–743. doi:10.2307/256157

Lee, P. C. B. (1999). Career plateau and professional plateau: Impact on work outcomes of Information Technology professionals. *SIGCPR Computer Personnel, 20*(4), 25–38. doi:10.1145/571475.571478

Lee, I. (2007). The architecture for a next-generation holistic e-recruiting system. *Communications of the ACM, 50*(7), 81–85. doi:10.1145/1272516.1272518

Lee, C. K. (2005). *Transferability of skills over the IT career path*. Paper presented at the 2005 ACM SIGMIS CPR conference on Computer personnel research.

Lee, P. (2002). *Changes in skill requirements of Information Systems professionals in Singapore*. ACM 35th Annual Hawaii International Conference on System Sciences (HICSS'02), 8, pp. 264-272.

Lee, P. C. B. (2001). *Technopreneurial inclinations and career management strategy among Information Technology professionals*. Paper presented at the 34th Hawaii International Conference on System Sciences.

Lees, C. D., & Cordery, J. L. (2000). Job analysis and design. In Chmiel, N. (Ed.), *Introduction to work and organizational psychology: A European perspective*. Malden, MA: Blackwell Publishers.

Leitheiser, R. L. (1992). MIS skills for the 1990s: A survey of MIS managers' perceptions. *Journal of Management Information Systems, 9*(1), 69–91.

Lemons, M. A., & Parzinger, M. (2007). Gender schemas: A cognitive explanation of discrimination of women in technology. *Journal of Business Psychology, 22*, 91-98. Retrieved on April 24, 2009, from http://www.springerlink.com/ content/b220k15g30220q6h/

Lencioni, P. (2005). *Overcoming the five dysfunctions of a team*. San Francisco, CA: Jossey-Bass.

Lent, R. W., Brown, S. D., & Hackett, G. (1994). Toward a unifying social cognitive theory of career and academic interest, choice, and performance. *Journal of Vocational Behavior, 45*(1), 79–122. doi:10.1006/jvbe.1994.1027

Leonard, L., & Dwight, S. (2004). Should I stay or should I go? Individual differences between stayers and leavers. In S. Tross & D. Wiechmann (Eds.), *Creative approaches for examining employee retention*. Practitioner Forum, Society for Industrial and Organizational Psychology Annual Conference, April.

Leung, Y. W., & Mao, J. Y. (2003). Providing embedded proactive task support for diagnostic jobs: A neural network-based approach. *Expert Systems with Applications, 25*(2), 255–267.

Levek, A. R. H. C., & Malschitzky, N. (2006). *Liderança*. Faculdade São Francisco. Retrieved on May 2, 2006, from http://www. sfrancisco.edu.br/pdf/cap_humano/3.pdf

Levinson, D. J. (1978). *The seasons of a man's life*. New York: Ballantine Books.

Lévy, P. (1993) *As tecnologias da inteligência: o futuro do pensamento na era da informática*. Rio de Janeiro: 34.

Lewin, S. G., Lewin, S. L., & Meisel, J. B. (1987). A dynamic analysis of the adoption of a new technology: The case of optical scanners. *The Review of Economics and Statistics, 69*(1), 12–17. doi:10.2307/1937895

Lewin, A. Y., Massini, A., & Peeters, C. (2009). Why are companies offshoring innovation? The emerging global race for talent. *Journal of International Business Studies, 40*(6), 901–925. doi:10.1057/jibs.2008.92

Li, M. F., & Ye, R. L. (1999). Information Technology and firm performance: Linking with environmental strategic managerial contexts. *Information & Management, 35*, 53–51. doi:10.1016/S0378-7206(98)00075-5

Lilenthal, R. A. (1980). *The use of reference checks for selection*. Washington, DC: U.S. Office of Personnel Management.

Limongi-França, A. C., & Arellano, E. B. (2002). Liderança, poder e comportamento organizacional. In Fleury, M. T. F. (Ed.), *As pessoas na organização*. São Paulo: Gente.

Lockwood, D. & Ansari, A. (1999). Recruiting and retaining scarce information technology talent: a focus group study. *Industrial Management + Data Systems, 99*(6), 251.

Lucas, H. C. (2000). *Information Technology for management* (7th ed.). New York: McGraw-Hill, Inc.

Luft, J., & Ingham, H. (1955). The Johari window, a graphic model of interpersonal awareness. *Proceedings of the Western Training Laboratory in Group Development* (Los Angeles: UCLA).

Luftman, J., & Kempaiah, R. M. (2007). The IS organization of the future: The IT talent challenge. *Information Systems Management*, *24*, 129–138. doi:10.1080/10580530701221023

Luftman, J. (2008). Companies can't afford to lose their best IT pros. *Computerworld*, *42*(37), 37.

Luftman, J. (2005). Key issues for IT executives 2004. *MIS Quarterly Executive*, *4*(2), 269–285.

Luftman, J., Kempaiah, R., & Henrique, E. (2009). Key issues for IT executives 2008. *MIS Quarterly Executive*, *8*(3), 151–159.

Luftman, J., Kempaiah, R., & Nash, E. (2006). Key issues for IT executives 2005. *MIS Quarterly Executive*, *5*(2), 81–99.

Luftman, J. & Kempaiah, R. (2008). Key issues for IT executives 2007. *MIS Quarterly Executive, 7*(2).

Luftman, J. (2006). *Proceedings of SIMposium 2006*, Dallas, TX. September 17-20, 2006.

Luftman, J. (2008). *Yes, the tech skills shortage is real.* Retrieved on April 5, 2009, from http://www.informationweek.com/ news/global-cio/training/ showArticle.jhtml? articleID=205601557

Maasland, P. (1999). How to build an employee-centric culture. *Computing Canada*, 33.

Machado, L. Z. (1992). Feminismo, academia e interdisciplinaridade. In A.d.O. Costa & C. Bruschini (Eds.). *Uma questão de gênero.* (pp. 24-39). Rio de Janeiro: Rosa dos Tempos.

MacLean, B. (2009, February 13). How to build a talent management strategy – Based on compensation. *Compensation Today.*

Mahmood, M. A., & Mann, G. (1993). Measuring the organizational impact of Information Technology investment: An exploratory study. *Journal of Management Information Systems*, *10*(1), 97–122.

Mainiero, L. A., & Sullivan, S. E. (2006). Kaleidoscope careers: An alternate explanation for the opt-out revolution. *The Academy of Management Executive*, *19*(1), 106–124.

Major, D. A., Davis, D. D., Germano, L. M., Fletcher, T. D., Sanchez-Hucles, J., & Mann, J. (2007). Managing human resources in Information Technology: Best practices of high performing supervisors. *Human Resource Management*, *46*, 411–427. doi:10.1002/hrm.20171

Malhotra, Y. (2001). Expert systems for Knowledge Management: Crossing the chasm between information processing and sense making. *Expert Systems with Applications*, *20*(1), 7–16. doi:10.1016/S0957-4174(00)00045-2

Mann, J. (2010, February 2). Obama requests $80 billion in IT spending for 2011. *ExecutiveGov*. Retrieved from http://www.executivegov.com/2010/02/ obama-requests-80-billion-in- it-spending- for-2011/

Mannheim, K. (1928). Das Problem der Generationen. *Kölner Vierteljahrshefte für Soziologie*, *7*(2-3), 157–185.

Marchese, M. C. (1998). Some factors affecting the relationship between job characteristics and job worth: A job-role interpretation. *The International Journal of Organizational Analysis*, *6*(4), 355–369. doi:10.1108/eb028891

Margolis, J., & Fisher, A. (2002). *Unlocking the clubhouse: Women in computing*. Cambridge, MA: The MIT Press.

Marías, J. (1970). *Generations, a historical method*. Alabama: The University of Alabama Press.

Marquardt, B. (2010). *Telephone interview*. 3 March, 2010

Marshall, V. M., & Mueller, M. (2003). Theoretical roots of the life-course perspective. In Heinz, W. R. M. (Ed.), *Social dynamics of the life course: Transitions, institutions and interrelations* (pp. 3–32). New York: Aldine de Gruyter.

Martin, C., & Tulgan, B. (2006). *Managing the generation mix*. HRD Press.

Martin, G., Reddington, M., & Kneafsey, M. B. (2008). *Web 2.0 and HR: A discussion paper*. CIPD Chartered Institute of Personnel and Development, Research Insights, United Kingdom. O`Reilly, T. (2007). What is Web 2.0: Design patterns and business models for the next generation of software. *Communications & Strategies*, *65*(1), 16–37.

Martin, A. (2008). *The changing nature of leadership.* A CCL Research White Paper. Center for Creative Leadership.

Martin, C. D., & Wardel, D. (1999). Paradigms, pitfalls and the pipeline: Gender issues in the Information Technology workforce. *International Symposium on Women and Technology: Historical, Societal, and Professional Perspectives, 29*(31), 343-346. Retrieved on August 8, 2009, from http://ieeexplore.ieee.org/ stamp/ stamp.jsp?arnumber=00787356

Maslow, A. H. (1943). A theory of human motivation. *Psychological Review, 50*(4), 370–396. doi:10.1037/h0054346

Mastracci, S. H. (2009). Evaluating HR management strategies for recruiting and retaining IT professionals in the U.S. federal government. *Public Personnel Management, 38*(2), 19–34.

Matheson, L., & Tarjan, R. (1998). Culturally induced information impactedness: A prescription for failure in software ventures. *Journal of Management Information Systems, 15*(2).

Mathis, S. G. (2008). Introductory course improves retention, especially for women. In *The Proceedings of the Information Systems Education Conference 2008.*

Maurer, T. J., Weiss, E. M., & Barbeite, F. G. (2003). A model of involvement in work-related learning and development activity: The effects of individual, situational, motivational, and age variables. *The Journal of Applied Psychology, 88*(4), 707–724. doi:10.1037/0021-9010.88.4.707

Mazzuckelli, K. (1999, June). Be creative in your approach to healthcare IT staffing. *Health Management Technology,* 14–17.

McConnell, S. (2004). *Professional software development: Shorter schedules, better projects, superior products, enhanced careers.* Boston: Addison-Wesley.

McCormick, E. J., & Ilgen, D. (1980). *Industrial and organizational psychology.* Englewood Cliffs, NJ: Prentice-Hall.

McDaniels, C., & Gysbers, N. (1992). *Counseling for career development: Theories, resources and practice.* Sam Francisco, CA: Jossey-Bass Publishers.

McDonald, P., Brown, K., & Bradley, L. (2005). Have traditional career paths given way to protean ones? Evidence from senior managers in the Australian public sector. *Career Development International, 10*(2), 109–129. doi:10.1108/13620430510588310

McDonald, K.S. & Hite, L.M. (2005). *Reviving the relevance of career development in human resource development.*

McGillicuddy, S. (2007). IT job rotation rare, but critical for business alignment. *Techtarget.* Retrieved June 2010, from http://searchcio-midmarket.techtarget.com/news/article/0,289142,sid183_gci1244573_mem1,00.html

McGuire, J. B., Palus, C. J., Pasmore, W., & Rhodes, G. B. (2009). *Transforming your organization.* Global Organizational Development White Paper Series, Center for Creative Leadership.

McKeen, C. A., & Burke, R. J. (1993). Use of career strategies by managerial and professional women. *International Journal of Career Management, 5*(4), 19–24. doi:10.1108/09556219310043219

McKenna, J. F., Cotton, C. C., & Van Auken, S. (1995). Business school emphasis on teaching, research, and service to industry: Does where you sit determine where you stand? *Journal of Organizational Change Management, 8*(2), 3–16. doi:10.1108/09534819510084319

Mckinney, V. R., Wilson, D. D., Brooks, N., O'Leary-Kelly, A., & Hardgrave, B. (2008). Women and men in the IT profession. *Communications of the ACM, 51*(2), 81–84. doi:10.1145/1314215.1340919

McLean, E. R., Kappelman, L. A., & Thompson, J. P. (1993). Converging end-user computing and corporate computing. *Communications of the ACM, 36*(12), 79–92. doi:10.1145/163298.163314

McLean E. & Luftman, J. (2004). Key issues for IT executives. *MIS Quarterly Executive, 3*(2).

McNamara, D. E. (2006). The relevance of business school education, what do you think? *Journal of College Teaching & Learning, 3*(11), 1–14.

McNurlin, B. (Ed.). (1991). *Trends in Information Technology.* Chicago: Anderson Consulting.

Meister, J. C. (1998). *Corporate universities: Lessons in building a world-class work force.* New York: McGraw-Hill.

Mellora, D., Stokesa, M., Firth, L., Hayashia, Y., & Cummins, R. (2008). Need for belonging, relationship satisfaction, loneliness, and life satisfaction. *Personality and Individual Differences, 45*(3), 213–218. doi:10.1016/j.paid.2008.03.020

Melymuka, K. (1998, Jan 12). How' m I doin'? *Computerworld,* 58–59.

Messersmith, E. E., Garrett, J. L., Davis-Kean, P. E., Malanchuk, O., & Eccles, J. S. (2008). Career development from adolescence through emerging adulthood: Insights from Information Technology occupations. *Journal of Adolescent Research, 23*(2), 206–227. doi:10.1177/0743558407310723

Michie, S., & Nelson, D. L. (2006). Barriers women face in Information Technology careers: Self-efficacy, passion and gender biases. [from http://www.proquest.com/]. *Women in Management Review, 21*(1), 10–27. Retrieved on April 24, 2009. doi:10.1108/09649420610643385

Miliszewska, I., & Sztendur, E. M. (2009). Girls from low socioeconomic backgrounds: Factors influencing their interest in ICT study and career. *AMCIS 2009 Proceedings.* Retrieved on July 5, 2009, from http://aisel.aisnet.org/ amcis2009/412

Mill, S. (2001, Sep 7). Motivating your IT staff. *Computing Canada,* 26.

Millam, E. (2009). *Women as soul leaders: Integrating the inner and outer.* VDM Verlag.

Millward, L., & Kyriakidou, O. (2004). Linking pre- and post-merger identities through the concept of career. *Career Development International, 9*(1), 12–27. doi:10.1108/13620430410518110

Miner, A. S., & Robinson, D. F. (1994). Organizational and population level learning as engines for career transitions. *Journal of Organizational Behavior, 15*(4), 345–364. doi:10.1002/job.4030150405

Mingers, J. (2004). Realizing Information Systems: Critical realism as an underpinning philosophy for Information Systems. *Information and Organization, 14,* 87–103. doi:10.1016/j.infoandorg.2003.06.001

Mintzberg, H. (2004). *Managers not MBAs: A hard look at the soft practice of managing and management development.* San Francisco: Berrett-Koehler.

Mintzberg, H., Ahlstrand, D., & Lampel, J. (2000). *Safari de Estratégia.* Porto Alegre, Brazil: Editora Bookman.

Mitchell, T., Schaap, J. I., & Groves, M. (2010). Maintaining the integrity of turnover measurements when there are layoffs. *Journal of Business & Economics Research, 8*(1), 79.

Mitchell, T. R. (1974). Expectancy models of job satisfaction, occupational choice, and effort: A theoretical, methodological, and empirical appraisal. *Psychological Bulletin, 81,* 1053–1077. doi:10.1037/h0037495

Mitchell, V. F., & Moudgill, P. (1976). Measurement of Maslow's need hierarchy. *Organizational Behavior and Human Performance, 16*(2), 334–339. doi:10.1016/0030-5073(76)90020-9

Mithas, S., & Krishnan, M. S. (2008). Human capital and institutional effects in the compensation of Information Technology professionals in the United States. *Management Science, 54,* 415–428. doi:10.1287/mnsc.1070.0778

Mobley, W. H., Horner, S. O., & Hollingsworth, A. T. (1978). An evaluation of the precursors of hospital employee turnover. *The Journal of Applied Psychology, 63,* 408–414. doi:10.1037/0021-9010.63.4.408

Moen, P., Sweet, S., & Swisher, R. (2005). Embedded career clocks: The case of retirement planning. In MacMillan, R. (Ed.), *The structure of the life course: Standardized? Individualized? Differentiated?* (pp. 237–265). New York: Elsevier.

Moody, J. W., Will, R. P., & Blanton, J. E. (1996). Enhancing knowledge elicitation using the cognitive interview. *Expert Systems with Applications, 10*(1), 127–133. doi:10.1016/0957-4174(95)00039-9

Moore, E., & Burke, L. (2002). How to turn around turnover culture in IT. *Communications of the ACM,* 73–78. doi:10.1145/503124.503126

Moore, J. E. (2000). One road to turnover: An examination of work exhaustion in technology professionals. [Management Information Systems Research Center, University of Minnesota.]. *Management Information Systems Quarterly, 24*(1), 141–168. doi:10.2307/3250982

Moore, J., & Burke, L. (2002). How to turn around turnover culture in IT. *Communications of the ACM, 45*(2), 73–78. doi:10.1145/503124.503126

Moore, G.E. (1965). Cramming more components onto integrated circuits. *Electronics, 38*(8).

Morgan, G. (1997). *Images of organization.* Thousand Oaks, CA: Sage Publications, Inc.

Morgan, H. J. (2008). I hired you, you're perfect...now stay! The top ten list for retaining top talent. *Business Strategy Series, 9*(3), 119–125. doi:10.1108/17515630810873348

Mork, S. & Sovitsky, R. (1999, June). Attracting and retaining IT staff. *InfoTech Update*, 5-6.

Morley, C., McDonnell, M., & Milon, M. (2009). Gender and the attraction for IT in career paths: A French study. *AMCIS 2009 Proceedings.* Retrieved on August 15, 2009, from http://aisel.aisnet.org /amcis2009/515

Mottaz, C. J. (1988). Determinants of organizational commitment. *Human Relations, 41*(6), 467–482. doi:10.1177/001872678804100604

Myers, I. B., & Myers, P. B. (1980, 1995). *Gifts differing: Understanding personality type.* Mountain View, CA: Davies-Black Publishing.

Naggiar, J. (2001). *An exploration of retention practices in the IT industry.* Montreal: Concordia University.

Nakashima, J. (1999, April). IT Staffing: Retention is cheaper than recruiting. *Health Management Technology*, 32–34.

Nakata, L. E. (2009). *As expectativas de aprendizagem nas organizações que buscam se destacar pelo clima organizacional.* Master Thesis, Faculdade de Economia, Administração e Contabilidade, Universidade de São Paulo, São Paulo.

Nash, K. S., & King, J. (1997). IS employers skip background checks. *Computerworld, 31*, 1.

National Center for Education Statistics. (2006). *Report 3, Sisyphus revisited: Participation by minorities in STEM occupations, 1994-2004.* Washington, DC: U.S. Department of Education.

National Center for Women & Information Technology. (2007). *NCWIT scorecard 2007: A report on the status of women in information technology.* Boulder, CO: University of Colorado.

Neal, D. (1999). The complexity of job mobility among young men. *Journal of Labor Economics, 17*(2), 237–261. doi:10.1086/209919

Neiderman, F., & Mandviwall, M. (2004). The evolution of IT (computer) personnel research: More theory, more understanding, more questions. *ACM SIGMIS, 35*(3), 6–8.

Neopolitan, J. (1980). Occupational change in midcareer: An exploratory investigation. *Journal of Vocational Behavior, 16*(2), 212–225. doi:10.1016/0001-8791(80)90052-4

Network World. (2009). IT spending as a percentage of corporate revenue. *New World (New Orleans, La.), 26*(1), 27.

Nidumolu, S. R., & Knotts, G. W. (1998). The effect of customizability and reusability on perceived process and competitive performance of software firms. *Management Information Systems Quarterly*, 105–137. doi:10.2307/249392

Niederman, F., Brancheau, J., & Wetherbe, J. (1991). Information Systems management issues for the 1990s. *Management Information Systems Quarterly, 15*(4), 474–500. doi:10.2307/249452

Niederman, F., & Mandviwalla, M. (2004). The evolution of IT (computer) personnel research: More theory, more understanding, more questions. *ACM SIGMIS Database, 35*(3), 6–8. doi:10.1145/1017114.1017117

Niederman, F. (1999). Valuing the IT workforce as intellectual capital. In J. Prasad (Ed.), *Proceedings of the 1999 ACM Special Interest Group Computer Personnel Research Conference*, New Orleans, LA, pp. 174-181.

Nizet, J., & Pichault, F. (1995). *Compreendere Les Organizations: Mintzberg à l'épreuve des fats.* France, Europa: Gaëtan Morin Éditeur.

Noble, D. F. (1998). Perspectives: Digital diploma mills: The automation of higher education. *netWorker, 2*(2), 9–14. doi:10.1145/280449.280454

Noll, C. L., & Wilkins, M. (2002). Critical skills of IS professionals: A model for curriculum development. *Journal of Information Technology Education*, *1*(3), 143–156.

Nonaka, I., & Konno, N. (1998). The concept of ba: Building a foundation for knowledge creation. *California Management Review*, *40*(3), 40–54.

Nonaka, I., & Takeuchi, K. (1995). *The knowledge-creating company: How Japanese companies create the dynamics of innovation*. Oxford: Oxford University Press.

Nonaka, I., Toyama, R., & Konno, N. (2000). SECI, ba and leadership: A unified model of dynamic knowledge creation. *Elsevier Science Ltd*, *33*, 5–34.

Nonaka, I., & Konno, N. (1998). The concept of ba: Building a foundation for knowledge creation. *California Management Review*, *40*(3), 40–54.

Nonaka, I., & Takeuchi, H. (1997). *Criação de conhecimento na empresa: Como as empresas japonesas geram a dinâmica da inovação*. Rio de Janeiro: Campus.

O'Neal, S. & Gebauer, J. (2006). Talent management in the 21st century: Attracting, retaining, and engaging employees of choice. *WorldatWork Journal,* First Quarter 2006.

Oncken, W., & Wass, D. (1974). Management time: Who's got the monkey? *Harvard Business Review*, 75–80.

Ouchi, W. G. (1980). Markets, bureaucracies, and clans. *Administrative Science Quarterly*, *25*(1), 129–141. doi:10.2307/2392231

Panko, R. (2008). IT employment prospects: Beyond the dotcom bubble. *European Journal of Information Systems*, *17*(3), 182–197. doi:10.1057/ejis.2008.19

Panteli, A., Stack, J., & Ramsey, H. (1999). Gender and profession ethics in the IT industry. *Journal of Business Ethics*, *22*, 51–61. doi:10.1023/A:1006156102624

Papastergiou, M. (2008). Are computer science and Information Technology still masculine fields? High school students' perceptions and career choices. *Computers & Education*, *51*(2), 594–608. doi:10.1016/j.compedu.2007.06.009

Paré, G., & Tremblay, M. (2000). *The measurement and antecedents of turnover intentions among IT professionals*. Ecole des Hautes Etudes Commerciales and CIRANO.

Parker, M. (1990). *Creating shared vision*. Clarendon Hills, IL: Dialog International.

Parker, S. K., Axtell, C. M., & Turner, N. (2001). Designing a safer workplace: Importance of job autonomy, communication quality, and supportive supervisors. *Journal of Occupational Health Psychology*, *6*(3), 211–228. doi:10.1037/1076-8998.6.3.211

Parker, S. K., Williams, H. M., & Turner, N. (2006). Modeling the antecedents of proactive behavior at work. *The Journal of Applied Psychology*, *91*(3), 636–652. doi:10.1037/0021-9010.91.3.636

Parks, S. D. (2005). *Leadership can be taught: A bold approach for a complex world*. Cambridge, MA: Harvard Business School Publishing.

Patriotta, G. (2006). Knowledge-in-the-making: The construction of Fiat's Melfi factory. In Prusak, L., & Matson, E. (Eds.), *Knowledge management and organizational learning*. New York. Oxford.

Paullay, I. M., Alliger, G. M., & Stone-Romero, E. F. (1994). Construct validation of two instruments designed to measure job involvement and work centrality. *The Journal of Applied Psychology*, *79*(2), 224–228. doi:10.1037/0021-9010.79.2.224

Pawlack, T. (1998). How'm I doin'? *Computerworld*, 59.

Peters, T. (2004). *As Mulheres Reinam. HSM Management*. Mar-Apr.

Phillips, J. J., & O'Conell, A. (2003). *Managing employee retention: A strategic accountability approach*. Society for Human Resource Management.

Pilon, S., & Tandberg, D. (1997). Neural network and linear regression models in residency selection. *The American Journal of Emergency Medicine*, *15*(4), 361–364. doi:10.1016/S0735-6757(97)90125-X

Pitt, L. F., Watson, R. T., & Kavan, C. B. (1995). Service quality: A measure of Information Systems effectiveness. *Management Information Systems Quarterly*, *2*(19), 173–187. doi:10.2307/249687

Poole, W. G. (2003). The softer side of custom software development: Working with the other players. *Proceedings of the 16th Conference on Software Engineering Education and Training (CSEET'03)*, pp. 14-21.

Poon, J. M. L. (2004). Career commitment and career success: Moderating role of emotion perception. *Career Development International, 9*(4), 374–390. doi:10.1108/13620430410544337

Porter, M. (1980). *Competitive strategy*. New York: Free Press.

Porter, M. E. (1996). *What is a strategy? Harvard Business Review*. November/December.

Porter, L. W., Crampon, W. J., & Smith, E. J. (1976). Organizational commitment and managerial turnover: A longitudinal study. *Organizational Behavior and Human Performance, 19*, 87–98. doi:10.1016/0030-5073(76)90030-1

Porter, M.E. (2001). Strategy and the Internet. *Harvard Business Review*.

Prange, C. (2000). Aprendizagem organizacional: desesperadamente em busca de teorias? In Easterby-Smith, M., Burgoyne, J., & Araujo, L. (Eds.), *Aprendizagem organizacional e organização de aprendizagem*. São Paulo: Atlas.

Pringle, R., Nielsen, S., Hellens, L. V., Greenhill, A., & Parfitt, L. (2000). Net gains: Success strategies of professional women in IT. In Balka, E., & Smith, R. (Eds.), *Women, work and computerization: Charting a course to the future*. Boston: Kluwer Academic Publishers.

Pritchard, K. H. (2010). *Introduction to job analysis*. SHRM White paper. Retrieved February 2, 2010, from http://www.shrm.org/Research /Articles/Articles/Pages /CMS000055.aspx

Probst, G., Raub, S., & Romhardt, K. (2002). *Gestão do conhecimento*. Porto Alegre: Bookman.

Qualman, E. (2009, August 11). Statistics show social media is bigger than you think. *Socialnomics*. Retrieved April 14, 2010, from http://socialnomics.net/ 2009/08/11/ statistics-show-social-media-is-bigger -than-you-think/

Quesenberry, J. L., & Trauth, E. M. (2007). What do women want? An investigation of career anchors among women in the IT workforce. In *Proceedings of the 2007 ACM SIGMIS CPR Conference on Computer Personnel Research: the Global Information Technology Workforce* (St. Louis, Missouri, USA, April 19 - 21, 2007). (pp. 122-127). SIGMIS-CPR '07. New York: ACM.

Quinn, R. E. (2004). *Building the bridge as you walk on it*. San Francisco, CA: Jossey-Bass.

Ready, D. (2009). Forging the new talent compact. *Business Strategy Review,* 5-7.

Reff, D. (2007). Seven strategies for attracting and retaining top IT talent. *CIO Magazine,* Retrieved February 2010, from http://www.cio.com/article/27988/Seven_Strategies_for_Attracting_and_Retaining_Top_IT_Talent3

Reich, B. H., & Kaarst-Brown, M. L. (1999). Seeding the line: Understanding the transition from IT to non-IT careers. *Management Information Systems Quarterly, 23*(3), 337–364. doi:10.2307/249467

Reichers, A. E., & Schneider, B. (1990). Climate and culture: An evolution of constructs. In Schneider, B. (Ed.), *Organizational climate and culture*. San Francisco: Jossey-Bass.

ResumeDoctor.com. (2004). *What recruiters are saying about your resume*. Retrieved on May 14, 2005, from http://www.resumedoctor.com/ PP_Artical7_6.htm

Riemenschneider, C. K., Armstrong, D. J., Allen, M. W., & Reid, M. F. (2006). Barriers facing women in the IT work force. *SIGMIS Database, 37*(4), 58–78. doi:10.1145/1185335.1185345

Rittel, H., & Webber, M. (1973). Dilemmas in a general theory of planning. *Policy Sciences, 4*, 155-169. Amsterdam: Elsevier Scientific Publishing Company, Inc. Retrieved on March 5, 2010, from http://www.uctc.net/ mwebber/ Rittel+Webber+Dilemmas+ General_Theory_of_Planning.pdf

Roberts, K., Kossek, E., & Ozeki, C. (1998). Managing the global workforce: Challenges and strategies. *The Academy of Management Executive, 12*, 93–106.

Robertson, M., Newell, S., Swan, J., Mathiassen, L., & Bjerknes, G. (2001). The issue of gender within computing: Reflections from the UK and Scandinavia. *Information Systems Journal, 11*(2), 111–126. doi:10.1046/j.1365-2575.2001.00098.x

Rogers, C. (1961). *On becoming a person*. Boston: Houghton Mifflin.

Rosen, B., & Jerdee, T. H. (1990). Middle and late career problems: Causes, consequences and research needs. *Human Resource Planning, 13*(1), 59–70.

Rosse, J. G. (1987). Job-related ability and turnover. *Journal of Business and Psychology, 1*(4). doi:10.1007/BF01018142

Rousseau, D. M. (1989). Psychological and implied contracts in organizations. *Employee Responsibilities and Rights Journal, 2*(2), 121–139. doi:10.1007/BF01384942

Ryan, A. M., & Ployhart, R. E. (2000). Applicant perceptions of selection procedures and decisions: A critical review and agenda for the future. *Journal of Management, 26*, 565–606. doi:10.1177/014920630002600308

Rynes, S. L., & Barber, A. E. (1990). Applicant attraction strategies: An organizational perspective. *Academy of Management Review, 15*, 286–310. doi:10.2307/258158

Sachs, W. (2000). Globalization and sustainability. *Proceedings of the Sixth World Summit 2002*. Johannesburg: Heinrich-Böll.

Sackett, P. R., & Dreher, G. F. (1982). Constructs and assessment center dimensions: Some troubling empirical findings. *The Journal of Applied Psychology, 67*, 401–410. doi:10.1037/0021-9010.67.4.401

Sadahiro, I., Checkley, D., & Trivedi, M. (2001, August). REFLICS: Real-time flow imaging and classification system. *Machine Vision and Applications, 13*(1).

Sadin, M. (2003, October 6). Computers that care. *Newsweek.*

Sargent, L. D., & Domberger, S. R. (2007). Exploring the development of a protean career orientation: Values and image violations. *Career Development International, 12*(6), 545–564. doi:10.1108/13620430710822010

Sawyer, S., & Williams, B. (2003). *Using Information Technology: A practical introduction to computers and communications* (5th ed.). New York: McGraw-Hill.

Schein, E. H. (1989). *Organizational culture and leadership: A dynamic view*. San Francisco: Jossey-Bass.

Schein, E. H. (1971). The individual, the organization, and the career: A conceptual scheme. *The Journal of Applied Behavioral Science, 7*(4), 401–426. doi:10.1177/002188637100700401

Schein, E. H. (1978). *Career dynamics: Matching individual and organizational needs*. Reading, MA: Addison-Wesley.

Schmid, G. (2005). Social risk management through transitional labour markets. *Socio-economic Review, 4*(1), 1–33. doi:10.1093/SER/mwj029

Schreyer, R., & McCarter, J. (1998). *The employer's guide to recruiting on the Internet*. Manassas Park, VA: Impact Publications.

Schultze, G., & Miller, C. (2004). The search for meaning and career development. *Career Development International, 9*(2), 142–152. doi:10.1108/13620430410526184

Scorce, R. (2008). IT staff management techniques for improved recruiting and retention. *Journal of Business and Public Affairs, 2*(1).

Scott, J. (1990). Gênero: uma categoria útil de análise histórica. *Educação e Realidade, 16*(2), 5–22.

Scott Morton, M. S. (1991). *The corporation of the 1990s: Information Technology and organizational transformation*. Oxford University Press.

Seibert, S. E., Kraimer, M. L., & Liden, R. C. (2001). A social capital theory of career sucess. *Academy of Management Journal, 44*(2), 219–237. doi:10.2307/3069452

Seitz, B. (2003). Die Direktansprache und der Schutz unternehmerischer Rechte: Oekonomische Argumente fuer eine rechtliche Problematik. *Schmalenbachs Zeitschrift fuer betriebswirtschaftliche. Forschung, 55*(9), 606–624.

Senge, P. M. (2002). *A quinta disciplina: Arte e prática da organização de aprendizagem*. São Paulo: Best Seller.

Shafer, M. (2005). DHL program seeks to hold on to IT staff. *Computerworld*, 43.

Shin, T. (2008). *Working in corporate America: Dynamics of pay at large corporations, 1992--2005*. Unpublished dissertation, University of California, Berkeley, California.

Sims, D. (2006). Creative new employee orientation programs: Best practices, creative ideas, and activities for energizing your orientation program.

Singh, P., & Finn, D. (2003). The effects of Information Technology on recruitment. *Journal of Labor Research, 24*(3), 395–408. doi:10.1007/s12122-003-1003-4

Slaughter, S. A., Ang, S., & Boh, W. F. (2007). Firm-specific human capital and compensation–organizational tenure profiles: An archival analysis of salary data for IT professionals. *Human Resource Management, 46,* 373–394. doi:10.1002/hrm.20169

Smart, M.P. (2009). Time for an upgrade? *PM Network,* 46-51.

Society for Human Resource Management. (2000). *Retention survey.*

Sousa, E. G., Nakata, L. E., & Araujo, A. P. (2008). A emergência do modelo de competências no processo de reorganização da produção: Uma discussão sobre gênero. In *Anais do Enanpad.* Rio de Janeiro: Anpad.

Srour, R. H. (2005). *Poder, cultura e ética nas organizações: o desafio das formas de gestão.* Rio de Janeiro, Brazil: Elsevier.

Stam, M., & Molleman, E. (1999). Matching the demand for and supply of IT professionals: Towards a learning organization. *International Journal of Manpower, 20*(6), 375. doi:10.1108/01437729910289729

Stam, K. R., Guzman, I. R., & Stanton, J. M. (2009). RIP: The use of inoculation theory and online social networking for enhancing attractiveness of IT occupations. In *Proceedings of the Special interest Group on Management information System's 47th Annual Conference on Computer Personnel Research* (Limerick, Ireland, May 28 - 30, 2009). (pp. 139-142). SIGMIS-CPR '09. New York: ACM.

Starkweather, J. A., & Stevenson, D. H. (in press). PMP certification as a core competency: Necessary but not sufficient. *Project Management Journal.*

Steel, R. P., Shane, G. S., & Griffith, R. W. (1990). Correcting turnover statistics for comparative analysis. *Academy of Management Journal, 33,* 179–187. doi:10.2307/256357

Stephan, P., & Levin, S. (2005). Leaving careers in IT: Gender differences in retention. *The Journal of Technology Transfer, 30*(4), 383-396. Retrieved on April 5, 2009, from http://www.springerlink.com/ content/ t512182481151065/

Stevens, M. J., & Campion, M. A. (1994). The knowledge, skill, and ability requirements for teamwork: Implications for human resource management. *Journal of Management, 20,* 503–530.

Stevens, M. J., & Campion, M. A. (1999). Staffing work teams: Development and validation of a selection test for teamwork settings. *Journal of Management, 25,* 207–228. doi:10.1016/S0149-2063(99)80010-5

Stevenson, D. H., & Starkweather, J. A. (in press). PM critical competency index: IT execs prefer soft skills. *International Journal of Project Management.*

Stott, K., & Wood, W. (2001). What skills do employers require from people who work in the IT client support role? *34th Annual Hawaii International Conference on System Sciences (HICSS-34),* 8, pp. 8069-8078.

Strauss, W., & Howe, N. (1991). *Generations: The history of America's future, 1584-2069.* New York: William Morrow.

Strauss, W., & Howe, N. (1998). *The fourth turning.* New York: Broadway Books.

Strider, E. (1998). How' m I doin'? *Computerworld,* 59.

Sullivan, S. E. (1999). The changing nature of careers: A review and research agenda. *Journal of Management, 25*(3), 457–484. doi:10.1177/014920639902500308

Sullivan, S. E., & Mainiero, L. A. (2007). The changing nature of gender roles, alpha/beta careers and work-life issues. *Career Development International, 12*(3), 238–263. doi:10.1108/13620430710745881

Sumner, M., & Yager, S. (2004). *Career orientation of IT personnel.* Paper presented at the 2004 SIGMIS Conference on Computer personnel research: Careers, culture, and ethics in a networked environment.

Sumner, M., Yager, S., & Franke, D. (2005). *Career orientation and organizational commitment of IT personnel.* Paper presented at the 2005 ACM SIGMIS CPR Conference on Computer personnel research.

Tapia, A. H. (2003). Hostile_work_environment.com. In *Proceedings of the 2003 SIGMIS Conference on Computer Personnel Research: Freedom in Philadelphia-Leveraging Differences and Diversity in the IT Workforce* (Philadelphia, Pennsylvania, April 10 - 12, 2003). (pp. 64-67). SIGMIS CPR '03. New York: ACM.

Tapia, A. H., & Kvasny, L. (2004). Recruitment is never enough: Retention of women and minorities in the IT workplace. In *Proceedings of the 2004 SIGMIS Conference on Computer Personnel Research: Careers, Culture, and Ethics in A Networked Environment* (Tucson, AZ, USA, April 22 - 24, 2004). (pp. 84-91). SIGMIS CPR '04. New York: ACM.

Tapscott, D., & Williams, A. D. (2006). *Wikinomics: How mass collaboration changes everything*. New York: Portfolio.

Tavana, M., Lee, P., & Joglekar, P. (1994). The development and validation of a campus recruiting expert system using expert opinions and historical data. *Expert Systems with Applications*, 7(2), 305–321. doi:10.1016/0957-4174(94)90046-9

Taylor, C. (2004). *Retention leadership. T+D Magazine, 58(3)*. Alexandria, VA: ASTD Press.

Teague, J. (2002). Women in computing: What brings them to it, what keeps them in it? *SIGCSE Bulletin*, 34(2), 147–158. doi:10.1145/543812.543849

Teixeira, J. E. (2002). Clima organizacional: Empregados satisfeitos fazem bem aos negócios. In Boog, G., & Boog, M. (Eds.), *Manual de Gestão de pessoas e equipes (Vol. 2)*. São Paulo: Gente.

Terra, J. C. C. (2000). *Gestão do conhecimento: o grande desafio empresarial*. São Paulo: Negócio.

Thomas, D. & Ely, R. (1996). Making differences matter: A new paradigm for managing diversity. *Harvard Business Journal*, 79-90.

Thomas, P. (2006, May/June). Voluntary employee turnover: Why IT professionals leave. *IT Pro*, 46-48.

Thompson, A. A., Strickland, A. J., & Gamble, J. E. (2009). *Crafting and executing strategy: The quest for competitive advantage: Concepts and cases*. New York: The McGraw-Hill Companies.

Tinnirello, P. (1998, October 2). Does your staff have the right stuff? *PC Week–Strategies*, 86.

Todd, P. A., McKeen, J. D., & Gallupe, R. B. (1995). The evolution of IS job skills: A content analysis of IS job advertisements from 1970 to 1990. *Management Information Systems Quarterly*, 19(1), 1–27. doi:10.2307/249709

Tornow, W. W., & Pinto, P. R. (1976). The development of a managerial taxonomy: A system for describing, classifying, and evaluating executive positions. *The Journal of Applied Psychology*, 62, 410–418. doi:10.1037/0021-9010.61.4.410

Trauth, E. M., Quesenberry, J. L., & Huang, H. (2008). A multicultural analysis of factors influencing career choice for women in the Information Technology workforce. [from http://www.proquest.com/]. *Journal of Global Information Management*, 16(4), 1–23. Retrieved on April 16, 2009. doi:10.4018/jgim.2008100101

Trauth, E. M., Quesenberry, J. L., & Yeo, B. (2008). Environmental influences on gender in the IT workforce. *SIGMIS Database*, 39(1), 8–32. doi:10.1145/1341971.1341975

Trauth, E. M. (2002). Odd girl out: An individual differences perspective on women in the IT profession. *Information Technology & People*, 15(2), 98–118. doi:10.1108/09593840210430552

Trauth, E. M., Nielsen, S. H., & Hellens, L. A. v. (2003). Explaining the IT gender gap: Australian stories for the new millennium. *Journal of Research and Practice in Information Technology*, 35(1), 7–20.

Trauth, E. M., & Quesenberry, J. L. (2007). Gender and the Information Technology workforce: Issues of theory. In Yoong, P., & Huff, S. L. (Eds.), *Managing IT professionals in the Internet age* (pp. 18–36). Hershey, PA: Idea Group Publishing.

Tross, S., & Egermann, M. (2004). *Employee-manager relationship duration: Effects on perceived supervisor career development support and voluntary turnover*. Society for Industrial and Organization Psychology Annual Conference, April.

Tulgan, B. (2003). *Generational shift: What we saw at the workplace revolution*.

Turban, E., McLean, E., & Whetherbe, J. (2001). *Information Technology for management: Making connections for strategic advantages* (2nd ed.). New York: John Wiley and Sons, Inc.

Turner, E. (2001). The case for responsibility of the IT industry to promote equality for women in computing. *Science and Engineering Ethics, 7*(2), 247–260. Retrieved on April 5, 2009, from http://www.springerlink.com/content/q820q5x41x071202/

Tye, E.M., Ng, W., Poon, R.S.K. & Burn, J.M. (1995). Information Systems skills: Achieving alignment between the curriculum and the needs of the IS professionals in the future. *ACM SIGMIS Database, 26*(4).

United States Census Bureau. (2000). *2000 census*. Washington, D.C.: U.S. Department of Commerce.

Universum. (2010). *The Universum student survey*. Retrieved June 11, 2010, from http://universumglobal.com/IDEAL-Employer-Rankings/The-National-Editions

USBL. (2005). *Career guide to industries* 2004-05. US Bureau of Labor. Retrieved from http://www.bls.gov

Van Maane, J., & Schein, E. H. (1977). Career development. In Hackman, J. R., & Suttle, J. L. (Eds.), *Improving life at work: Behavioral science approaches to organizational change* (p. 494). Santa Monica, CA: Goodyear.

van Veldhoven, M., & Dorenbosch, L. (2008). Age, proactivity and career development. *Career Development International, 13*(2), 112–131. doi:10.1108/13620430810860530

Vandenberg, R. J., & Nelson, J. B. (1999). Disaggregating the motives underlying turnover intentions: When do interventions predict turnover behavior? *Human Relations, 52*(10), 1313–1336. doi:10.1177/001872679905201005

Veloso, E. F. R., Nakata, L. E., Fischer, A. L., & Dutra, J. S. (2007). Pesquisas de clima organizacional: o uso de categorias na construção metodológica e análise de resultados. In *Anais do Enanpad*. Rio de Janeiro: Anpad.

Vroom, V. H. (1960). *Some personality determinants of the effects of participation. Survey Research Center and Department of Psychology, University of Michigan*. Englewood Cliffs, NJ: Prentice-Hall.

Vroom, V. H. (1964). *Work and motivation*. New York: Wiley.

Vygotsky, L. S. (1987). *A formação social da mente*. São Paulo: Martins Fontes.

Wagner, J. A. III, & Hollenbeck, J. R. (2000). *Comportamento organizacional*. São Paulo, Brazil: Saraiva.

Wahba, M. A., & Bridwell, L. G. (1976). Maslow reconsidered: A review of research on the need hierarchy theory. *Organizational Behavior and Human Performance, 15*(2), 212–240. doi:10.1016/0030-5073(76)90038-6

Waheed, A., & Adeli, H. (2000). A knowledge-based system for evaluation of Superload permit applications. *Expert Systems with Applications, 18*(1), 51–58. doi:10.1016/S0957-4174(99)00050-0

Wailgum, T. (October 2007). How Wal-Mart lost its technology edge. *CIO*. Retrieved February 10, 2009, from http://www.cio.com/ article /print / 143451

Wajcman, J. (1991). *Feminism confrots technology*. Philadelphia: Pennsylvania University Press.

Walker, J. W. (1980). *Human resources planning*. New York: McGraw-Hill Book Co.

Wall Street Journal Online. (2002, November 27). *Truth be told: Survey says Americans are less trusting*.

Wallace, K. (2009). Creating an effective new employee orientation program. *Library Leadership & Management, 23*(4), 168–177.

Walsh, G. (2005, September 12). You can't always guess what they want. *Computerworld, 52*, 55.

Wanous, J. P. (1973). Effects of realistic job preview on job acceptance, job attitudes and job survival. *The Journal of Applied Psychology, 58*(3), 327–336. doi:10.1037/h0036305

Waterman, R. H. Jr, Waterman, J. A., & Collard, B. A. (1994). Toward a career-resilient workforce. *Harvard Business Review, 72*(4), 87–95.

Watrous, K., & Pritchard, R. (2006). When coworkers and managers quit: The effects of turnover and shared values on performance. *Journal of Business and Psychology, 21*(1). doi:10.1007/s10869-005-9021-2

Watters, M. (2002). *Grow employees to raise retention*. Canadian HR Reporter.

Watters, M. (2003). Improving employee retention. *Canadian Printer, 111*(6), 30–32.

Weber, M. (1974). *Economía y sociedad.* Ciudad do México: Fundo de Cultura Económica.

Webster, J. (1996). *Shaping women's work: Gender, employmnent and Information Technology.* London: Longman.

Weggeman, M. (1997). *Kennismanagement: Inrichting en besturing van kennisintensieve organisaties.* Schiedam: Scriptum.

Weggeman, M. (2007). *Leiding geven aan professionals? Niet doen! Over kenniswerkers, vakmanschap en innovatie.* Schiedam: Scriptum.

Weick, K. (1998). Substitutes for strategy. In Teece, D. (Ed.), *Technology, organization, and competitiveness: Perspective on industrial and corporate change.* New York: Oxford University Press.

Weinstein, N. D. (1980). Unrealistic optimistic about future events. *Journal of Personality and Social Psychology, 39*(5), 327–336. doi:10.1037/0022-3514.39.5.806

Weitzel, T., Eckhardt, A., & Laumer, S. (2009). A framework for recruiting IT talent. *MIS Quarterly Executive, 8*(4), 175–189.

Welbourne, T. M. (2009). HRM in tough times. *Human Resource Management, 48*(2), 181–182. doi:10.1002/hrm.20274

Welbourne, T. (2003). Employee engagement: Doing it vs. measuring.

Welzer-Lang, D. (2004). Os homens e o masculino numa perspectiva de relações sociais de sexo. In Schpun, M. R. (Ed.), *Masculinidades* (pp. 107–128). São Paulo: Boitempo Editorial Santa Cruz.

Wenger, E., & Snyder, W. M. (2006). Communities of practice: the organizational frontier. In Prusak, L., & Matson, E. (Eds.), *Knowledge management and organizational learning. New York.* Oxford.

Wentling, R. M., & Thomas, S. (2009). Workplace culture that hinders and assists the career development of women in Information Technology. *Information Technology, Learning and Performance Journal, 25*(1), 25–42.

Werner, J. M., & DeSimone, R. L. (2008). *Human resource development* (5th ed.).

West, L., & Bogumil, W. (2001). Immigration and the global IT work force. *Communications of the ACM, 44*(7), 34–38. doi:10.1145/379300.379307

Westlund, S. (2007). *Retaining talent: Assessing relationships among project leadership styles, software developer job satisfaction, and turnover intentions.* Unpublished doctoral thesis, Capella University. Proquest Information and Learning Company.

Wilson, F. (2003). Can't compute, won't compute: Women's participation in the culture of computing. *New Technology and Employment, 18*(2), 127–142. doi:10.1111/1468-005X.00115

Wilson, T. (1999). How to build an employee-centric culture. *Computing Canada*, 33.

Winter, S. J., Chudoba, K. M., & Gutek, B. A. (1997). Misplaced resources? Factors associated with computer literacy among end-users. *Information & Management, 32*, 29–42. doi:10.1016/S0378-7206(96)01086-5

Witt, L. A., & Burke, L. A. (2002). Selecting high-performing Information Technology professionals. *Journal of End User Computing, 14*, 37–50. doi:10.4018/joeuc.2002100103

Wong, C.-S., Chun, H., & Law, K. S. (1998). A longitudinal study of the job perception-job satisfaction relationship: A test of the three alternative specifications. *Journal of Occupational Psychology, 71*(2), 127–146.

Wright, A. D. (2009). Recruiting goes mobile. *SHRM Online, November.* Retrieved February 6, 2010, from http://www.shrm.org/hrdisciplines/technology/Articles/Pages/Recruiting GoesMobile.aspx

Wu, J.-H., Chen, Y.-C., & Chang, J. (2005). *The IS manager: A study of critical professional activities and skills/knowledge.* 38th Annual Hawaii International Conference on System Sciences (HICSS'05), 8, pp. 266-274.

Wynekoop, J. L., & Walz, D. B. (1998). Revisiting the perennial question: Are IS people different? *SIGMIS Database, 29*(2), 62–72. doi:10.1145/298752.298759

Wynn, D.E. & Williams, C.K. (2008). Critical realism-based explanatory case study research in Information Systems. *ICIS 2008 Proceedings*, Paper 2

Yablonka, E. (1999, April). IT Staffing: Retention is cheaper than recruiting. *Health Management Technology*, 32–34.

Yamamoto, H. (2006). The relationship between employees' inter-organizational career orientation and their career strategies. *Career Development International*, *11*(3), 243–264. doi:10.1108/13620430610661768

Yin, R. K. (2003). *Case study research: Design and methods. London; New Dehli*. Thousand Oaks, CA: Sage Publications Inc.

Young, L. (2008, September 22). Disconnect between what IT wants, HR offers. *Canadian HR Reporter*, 7.

Yvonne, K. (2009). Hiring a great project manager. *Helium*. Retrieved October 21, 2009 from http://www.helium.com/items/1069940-hiring-a-great-project-manager?page=1

Zhang, W. (2007). Why IS: Understanding undergraduate students' intentions to choose an Information System major. *Journal of IS Education*, *18*(5), 447–458.

Zikic, J., Novicevic, M. M., Harvey, M., & Breland, J. (2006). Repatriate career exploration: A path to career growth and success. *Career Development International*, *11*(7), 633–649. doi:10.1108/13620430610713490

Zottoli, M. A., & Wanous, J. P. (2000). Recruitment source research: Current status and future directions. *Human Resource Management Review*, *10*(4), 353–382. doi:10.1016/S1053-4822(00)00032-2

Zweig, P., Kaiser, K.M., Beath, C.M., Bullen, C.V., Gallgher, K., Goles, T., et al. (2006). The Information Technology workforce: Trends and implications 2005-2008. *MIS Quarterly Executive, 5*(2).

About the Contributors

Jerry Luftman is a Professor at the Wesley J. Howe School of Technology Management of Stevens Institute of Technology. He also serves as Executive Director, for Information Systems Programs at Stevens. After a notable twenty-three year career with IBM, and over fifteen years at Stevens, Dr. Luftman's experience combines the strengths of practitioner, consultant, and academic. His career with IBM included strategic positions in management (IT and consulting), management consulting, Information Systems, marketing, and executive education. As a practitioner, he held several positions in IT, including a CIO. Dr. Luftman is frequently called upon as an executive mentor and coach. He has authored or co-authored over a fourteen books and dozens of articles that address areas for improving IT resources.

* * *

Thomas Abraham is a professor and chair of the Department of Management at Kean University. He received his PGDM (MBA) from the Indian Institute of Management, Bangalore and his PhD from the University of Massachusetts. He is a member of the New Jersey Chapter of the Society for Information Management (SIM) and the Association for Information Systems (AIS). His research interests include global Information Technology (IT) sourcing, sustainable development through Information Technology, and MIS education. He has been a consultant at various companies including Sony and BMG in the US and an analyst for companies in India including Motor Industries Co. His research has appeared in several peer-reviewed journals including MIS Quarterly Executive, Communications of the AIS and the Journal of Electronic Commerce in Organizations. He has received the Bright Idea Award, awarded by Seton Hall University and New Jersey Business and Industry Association, for Information Technology research in successive years in 2007 and 2008.

Vijay K. Agrawal is an Associate Professor of Management Information Systems in the College of Business and Technology at the University of Nebraska at Kearney. His areas of interest are management Information Systems, operations management, and accounting. He received his B.S. in mechanical engineering from the University of Indore, MBA from the University of Toledo, and M.S. in computer science from Bowling Green State University. He received his PhD from Jamia Millia Islamia (University of Millia Islamia), New Delhi, India. Since 2003, he has been an Assistant Professor at California State University at Fullerton. In addition, he was Visiting Assistant Professor at the University of Texas at Austin for the 2006-2007 academic year. His research has been published in journals such as The

Quarterly Review of Economics and Finance and has been presented at various conferences such as the Financial Management Association and National Decision Sciences Institute.

Vipin K. Agrawal, after receiving his undergraduate degree (in Electronics and Communications Engineering), went to Texas A&M University for his M.S. (Finance), and the University of Texas at Austin for his PhD (Finance). Since 2003, he has been an Assistant Professor at California State, University at Fullerton. In addition, he was Visiting Assistant Professor at the University of Texas at Austin for the 2006-2007 academic year. His research has been published in journals such as The Quarterly Review of Economics and Finance and has been presented at various conferences such as the Financial Management Association and National Decision Sciences Institute.

Wolfgang Brickwedde is the founder of the Institute for Competitive Recruiting (ICR), Heidelberg. The Institute for Competitive Recruiting (ICR) consults companies on recruitment performance management and acts as a platform for improving the recruitment function in Germany. Before founding the ICR, he held management positions at SAP and Royal Philips Electronics in the areas of Employer Branding and Recruitment for various regions and countries. Wolfgang Brickwedde has a background in banking and holds a masters degree in Business Administration from the University of Hamburg. He served as the speaker of the board of the DAPM (Association of Direct Employers in Germany) from 2007-2009 and as a board member of the HR-Alliance from 2008-2009. Wolfgang Brickwedde is a well known speaker on the topics recruitment, employer branding and talent management at various occasions and organizations.

Marianne Broadbent is a Senior Partner at the innovative global leadership consultancy and executive search firm, EWK International, where she has both global and regional responsibilities. She is an executive advisor, specialist in leadership and executive capabilities, international speaker, facilitator, and author. Her career has blended senior executive corporate roles, academic leadership, and consulting roles. Her senior executive roles have included Senior Vice President, New Product Development for Gartner Inc globally, and Group Vice President for Gartner's CIO Executive Programs, where she also founded Gartner's CIO Academy. In academia, she has been Associate Dean (and Chair of Management) at Melbourne Business School, University of Melbourne, a senior academic at RMIT University and visiting researcher at Boston University. Marianne is co-author of two Harvard Business School Press best sellers, The New CIO Leader (with Ellen Kitzis) and Leveraging The New Infrastructure (with Peter Weill). Her insights and research have been published in many genres from regular columns about leadership and management in CIO Insight and CIO Magazine, Sloan Management Review articles, commentaries in The Financial Times (UK) and the Australian Financial Review, through to major 'A' list academic journals. She is a Director of CAVAL Ltd and is a Fellow of the Australian Institute of Company Directors.

Angela Freitag Brodbeck, UFRGS/EA/PPGA, Brazil. PhD in Business Administration (Information Systems), Associate Professor at UFRGS and consultant for many multinational companies. She is an active researcher in strategic alignment, business process management, business intelligence and data mining techniques, and she studies the impact of new technologies in the organization, using qualitative and interpretative research methods. Besides authoring many papers and books in the area, her career includes strategic positions as a member of the board of directors of Brodbeck Consultores Ltda, management consulting in Information Systems, member of IT Committees and coordinator of BPM projects in governmental universities.

Henrique Jorge Brodbeck is an Associate Professor at the Computer Science Institute, UFRGS, Brazil and teaches as a visiting professor in graduate courses at other universities in the country. With a Masters degree in Civil Engineering, and a background of almost 40 years in the Information Technology scene, he is founder and director of Brodbeck Consultores Ltda, a leading consulting company in southern Brazil with a significant record of projects in large clients of all market segments. His interests include strategic planning of Information Technology, selection, acquisition, and implementation of ERP, CRM, business intelligence, e-commerce, knowledge management, and enterprise portals. Prof. Brodbeck also develops projects in process management, IT governance, and IT management, besides acting as coach and mentor of many CIOs.

Donald Brown has over fifteen years of experience in Information Technology and has been with Prudential for 10 years. He is now a Systems Manager. Donald holds a Master of Science in Information Systems degree from Steven Institute of Technology. In his work with Prudential, Donald has provided enterprise solutions which have saved Prudential several millions of dollars. Donald recently was selected to participate in a divisional rotational program to further share his knowledge within other departments. Donald has continued involvement with several internal company and community initiatives. He has been involved with National Black Data Processing Associates for more than five years, filling leadership roles on both on the National and Local levels.

Jannie Buitenhuis investigates the origin of the appearance of generations, and the differences and the similarities between the different generations. Her research focuses on how the different generations can strengthen each other. During her career within the IT management market, Buitenhuis has advised organizations from around the globe. She understands what IT organizations and IT professionals require, and what a perfect IT department with the perfect IT professionals should be. With her analytic skills, and her strong ability to detect what organizations will require in the future, she creates refreshing organizational perspectives and visions. Buitenhuis' background is grounded in organization sciences, industrial management, and IT management. Her expertise includes generations in organization, strategy, business IT alignment, organizational culture, knowledge creation management, and marketing. She has earned her credentials as research director, university teacher, event director, researcher, and consultant. Nowadays she works for her company, NOTIF, as an independent researcher and consultant within the generation- and organization sciences.

Christine Bullen, Industry Professor at the Howe School of Management, Stevens Institute of Technology, is the director of the four-course concentration/major in IT Outsourcing in the MSIS and MBA programs and the coordinator of the capstone course in strategic issues in IT. She is currently conducting research on the IT workforce as part of a team of academics under the sponsorship of the Society for Information Management (SIM). She is developing an IT Workforce Decision Model looking at the impact of sourcing strategy on the in-house needs for IT skills. She earned her PhD from Stevens Institute and her MS from MIT, where she served as the Assistant Director of the MIT Center for Information

Systems Research (CISR) for 17 years. She is an active member of AIS, the New York Chapter of SIM, INFORMS, and the IAOP. Dr. Bullen is currently serving as a reviewer for U.S. Department of Commerce National Telecommunications and Information Administration on BTOP (Broadband Technology Opportunities Program), which is an essential component of President Obama's broadband strategy. Dr. Bullen has co-authored and contributed to eight books and numerous articles in the areas of impacts of outsourcing on the IT workforce, computer-supported cooperative work, electronic communications, critical success factors, managing the I/S function, in a variety of journals, including CAIS, MIS Quarterly, IBM Systems Journal, Harvard Business Review, Auerbach Publications, and MIT CISR working papers.

Fernando Cabezas-Isla is a Research Assistant and a PhD candidate of the Computer Science Department at Universidad Carlos III de Madrid. He holds an MSc in Computer Science from Universidad Carlos III de Madrid. He has been involved in several research projects as Software Engineer and Software Engineering consultant.

Ricardo Colomo-Palacios is an Associate Professor at the Computer Science Department of the Universidad Carlos III de Madrid. His research interests include applied research in Information Systems, software project management, people in software projects, and social and Semantic Web. He received his PhD in Computer Science from the Universidad Politécnica of Madrid (2005). He also holds a MBA from the Instituto de Empresa (2002). He has been working as software engineer, project manager and software engineering consultant in several companies including Spanish IT leader INDRA. He is also an Editorial Board Member and Associate Editor for several international journals and conferences and Editor in Chief of International Journal of Human Capital and Information Technology Professionals.

Andreas Eckhardt is a postdoctoral researcher at the Institute of Information Systems of Goethe University Frankfurt and a member of the "Centre of Human Resources Information Systems," a research cooperation project of two German Universities. Prior to this, he received his PhD from Goethe University Frankfurt and worked as an HR project manager at Daimler AG in Taiwan. His research interests include social influence in IT adoption, IT resistance, user personality, and computer personnel-related issues like recruiting, retaining and skilling the IT workforce. He has published numerous articles in journals including Journal of Information Technology, MIS Quarterly Executive, Information Systems Frontiers, Business Process Management Journal, and Business & Information Systems Engineering and is the author of one book and several book chapters.

Anna Frazzetto, Vice President of Technology Solutions for Harvey Nash USA, is a seasoned IT executive who has architected and implemented application development, managed services and outsourcing/offshoring initiatives for Global 1000 business, as well as mid- to small-sized companies. Frazzetto began her career in Information Systems as a Systems Engineer with IBM. She later joined Syncsort as a Product Developer and was responsible for managing quality assurance for new software development. In 1983, she moved to MHT Software and had strategic responsibility for software development, capacity planning, and production support teams. In 1993, she joined Spherion and was a key driver in expanding their managed service line of business from $30 million to $120 million. Prior to joining Spherion, she was an Integration Manager with Comdisco Computing Services, where she developed and implemented their remote computing service and initiated a help desk practice. Recently named to the HDI Strategic Advisory Board, and also a member of HDI's Support Center Leadership Certification Standards Committee, Frazzetto's professional affiliations include leading IT industry groups such as Support Services, Xephon and The Gartner Group. She holds a bachelor's in computer science and mathematics from New York University.

Rosa María Fuchs is Bachelor in Business Administration from Universidad del Pacífico in Lima-Peru, International MBA from IE Business School (Madrid, Spain), with studies of concentration in Strategy and Human Resources and certified Leader Coach by The Coaching Project - Canada. She is professor of Introduction to Business, People Management, Organizational Behavior, Coaching and Managing Change at Universidad del Pacífico. She has served as advisor on the development of business plans for entrepreneurs at Universidad del Pacífico. Prof. Fuchs is currently involved in the "10,000 Women" joint project with Thunderbird School of Global Management and Goldman Sachs with the goal of training entrepreneurial women in the whole country. During her 12 years at Universidad del Pacífico she has obtained experience as project manager. She has been Head of the President Staff, Vice Dean of the Business Administration School and Assistant Manager of the Graduate School, among other positions within the institution. As a consultant she has conducted various recruitment processes and strategic plans. She is member of the Research Center of Universidad del Pacífico. Her research interests are related to people management issues: measurement of human potential, talent retention strategies, and gender diversity in the corporate workplace.

Angel García-Crespo is the Head of the SofLab Group at the Computer Science Department in the Universidad Carlos III de Madrid and the Head of the Institute for promotion of Innovation Pedro Juan de Lastanosa. He holds a PhD in Industrial Engineering from the Universidad Politécnica de Madrid (Award from the Instituto J.A. Artigas to the best thesis) and received an Executive MBA from the Instituto de Empresa. Professor García-Crespo has led and actively contributed to large European projects of the FP V and VI, and also in many business co-operations. He is the author of more than a hundred publications in conferences, journals, and books, both Spanish and international.

Mary Jo Greil, EdD, is a certified executive coach and president of the Carson Greil Group, LLC, since 2002. Her company helps leaders become more effective individually and helps organizations become more engaged collectively. She draws upon over 20 years of broad business management experience from a startup business, midcap, and a Fortune 50 company in a diverse set of industries including steel manufacturing, forest and specialty products, and healthcare. Nationally, her work has been recognized for pioneering large-scale business change efforts across North America and Europe, and for many years she has been a speaker at international and national business conferences. She has a doctoral degree and two masters degrees. Mary Jo has a unique blend of solid experience in leadership development, organizational engagement, and business management. Her certifications in Appreciative Inquiry, Somatic Leadership Coaching, Systems Thinking, and Leadership and Adult Development inform her consulting services. She was one of the founding members of the Memphis Chapter of the Society for Information Management and has served on the SIM-International Board as well as other non-profit boards. In 2007, she launched a community initiative and was recognized as one of the Top 50 Women Who Make a Difference by the Women's News of the Mid South.

Deepak Khazanchi is Associate Dean for Academic Affairs and Professor of Information Systems and Quantitative Analysis in the College of Information Science & Technology at the University of Nebraska in Omaha. Deepak's research has been published in various peer-reviewed professional and academic journals including *IEEE IT Professional, Electronic Markets, Decision Support Systems, Information Systems Management, Marketing Research, Journal of the Association for Information Systems, Decision Support Systems, Information Systems Management, and ACM's DATA BASE for Advances in Information Systems.* Deepak served as the President of the Midwest Association of Information Systems, AMCIS representative member of the Association for Information Systems (AIS) Council, and the AMCIS Site Advisory committee. Deepak was the founding chair of the AIS Special Interest Group for IT Project Management in 2006. He served as the conference co-chair of the 2005 Americas Conference in Information Systems (AMCIS) held in Omaha. He has also served as the VP of Programs for the Project Management Institute's (PMI) Heartland Chapter. Dr. Khazanchi received the PhD degree with a specialization in Management Information Systems from Texas Tech University. Prior to this, he completed the MBA degree from Southern Illinois University at Carbondale and obtained an undergraduate degree in Civil Engineering from the Indian Institute of Technology (IIT), Kharagpur (India).

Benn R. Konsynski is the George S. Craft Distinguished University Professor of Business Administration for Information Systems and Operations Management at Emory University. He arrived at the Goizueta Business School in 1992. He currently teaches in the Executive MBA, Doctoral IS, and, MBA programs. Prior to Goizueta, he spent 7 years on the faculty at the Harvard Business School. While at Harvard, he taught in the MBA and Executive MBA Programs. Prior to Harvard, he was a Professor at the University of Arizona, where he helped build the MIS Department and the group-decision support laboratory. He holds a PhD in Computer Science from Purdue University. He was also named Baxter Research Fellow at Harvard, and Hewlett Fellow at The Carter Center. Professor Konsynski specializes in issues of digital commerce, extended enterprise, and Information Technology in transformation of relationships across organizations. This work involves extensive domestic and international on inter-organizational systems, information partnerships, and the digital marketplace. He has strong interests in virtual worlds, immersion technologies and gesture-based navigation-reducing cognitive load in immersive environments.

Kristen Lamoreaux, President of Lamoreaux Search LLC has over 13 years experience in information technology executive search. Prior to launching Lamoreaux Search LLC, Kristen was a Senior Director with Jarvis Walker Executive Search, and held Talent Acquisition roles within Automatic Data Processing, Inc. She began her career in executive search with a boutique retained search firm, Dupont, White & Stone. Kristen is also the Founder of SIM Women – a networking organization for female CIOs and their direct reports that is focused on promoting communication, mentorship, leadership and career development of women within information technology. SIM Women has over 400 members across the US and Canada. Programs Kristen created within SIM Women include: Ladies Who Lunch, 1:1 Mentoring, and Call a Coach. In addition to SIM Women, Kristen is an active member of SIM Philadelphia supporting the Members in Transition organization and Teen Tech Camp initiative. Kristen previously held several SIM New Jersey board roles and served as a Director for the NJ SIM Foundation when she lived in New Jersey. Kristen has a Bachelors Degree in English from Rutgers University and enjoys contributing industry related articles to CIO Magazine.

Sven Laumer is doctoral student at the department for Information Systems and Services. He is part of the research project "Centre of Human Resources Information Systems" and interested in the support of Information Systems for HR tasks in organizations. His research results about human resources Information Systems, IT adoption and usage, IT resistance, social influence and IT, and the IT workforce have been published among others in Journal of Information Technology, Information Systems Frontiers, Wirtschaftsinformatik (Business & Information Systems Engineering) and MIS Quarterly Executive as well as in the proceedings of various conferences (including HICSS, ECIS and WI). He also serves as a consultant investigating organizational recruiting processes and gives talks at congresses and seminars about the usage of IT in recruiting.

Adrián Hernández López is a PhD student at the Computer Science Department of the Universidad Carlos III de Madrid in Spain. His research interests include applied research in people in IT, human aspects in IT and software process improvement. He finished his Bachelor's degree in Computer Science in 2007 and his Master's degree in IT Science specialized on Software Engineering in 2009 at the Universidad Carlos III de Madrid. He has been working as software engineer in several companies including Telefónica and INDRA.

Lisa Meisenbacher is currently an IT Director at ADP located in Roseland, NJ. Prior to joining ADP, Dr. Meisenbacher served in various leadership roles of increasing responsibility in the pharmaceutical, high-tech, financial, and consulting industries. Dr. Meisenbacher's broad and in-depth IT expertise includes more than twenty years of experience in software development, state –of- the- art Web technologies, SaaS architectures, project and program management, strategic planning, portfolio management, client relationship management, quality assurance, business process improvement, infrastructure engineering, and the successful delivery of complex, large-scale IT solutions that increase business value. Dr. Meisenbacher holds a Bachelors degree in Chemical Engineering from the University of Rochester, and Master's and Doctoral degrees in Electrical and Computer Engineering from Stevens Institute of Technology. She is published in the area of Requirements Engineering and has presented as a keynote guest speaker at both the "Software Process Symposium" and the "IEEE International Requirements Engineering" conferences. She is also an active member of WITI, AWC, PMI, TENG, ETP, MIS, and the SIM networking organizations.

Elaine Millam is a senior consultant, a master coach (ICF Certified) and an educator/facilitator specializing in leadership development, executive coaching, strategic planning and organizational effectiveness, and change management. Her career includes strategic positions in management (Human Resources, Organizational Effectiveness, Leader Effectiveness, Executive Education and OD consulting) and she has served as an adjunct professor in graduate studies in leadership at several institutions, including the University of Minnesota, University of St. Thomas and Argosy University. After an eighteen year career with Honeywell, and over fifteen years teaching at the graduate level, Dr. Millam's experience combines the strengths of leader, practitioner, consultant, and academic. She created and teaches a series of leadership courses for Engineering Professionals seeking their Master's degrees in various technical backgrounds, including IT Resources. She is presently publishing a book aimed at helping technical and engineering professionals step into leadership roles. She is the author of Women as Soul Leaders, published in 2008. Her executive coaching clients include several from J & J, Saint Gobain,

Agilent, 3M, Parker, Goodrich and many more global organizations. She is actively involved with the OD Network, a member of Human Resource Professional Society and other professional organizations.

Jo Ellen Moore is a Professor in the Department of Computer Management and Information Systems at Southern Illinois University Edwardsville. She holds a PhD in organizational behavior and HR management from Indiana University, a master's degree in psychology from Illinois State University, and a B.A. in mathematics from Millikin University. In the corporate environment, Jo Ellen worked as an IT manager, project manager, systems programmer, and applications programmer. She teaches project management in the SIUE curriculum and in workshops offered through the School of Business Executive Education. As a researcher, Jo Ellen is interested in the management of IT professionals and technology. Her work has been published in both academic and applied outlets such as *Information Systems Research, MIS Quarterly, Academy of Management Review, MIS Quarterly Executive, Communications of the ACM, Human Resource Management Review, HR Magazine* and *Cutter Benchmark Review*.

Lina Nakata is a PhD candidate in Business Administration at the School of Economics, Business Administration and Accountancy (FEA), University of São Paulo (USP, Brazil). She received her bachelor's and master's degree in Business Administration at the same university. Her career includes research and consultancy in Human Resources Management, particularly in Organizational Climate, Learning and Careers. Lina Nakata is a lecturer at Escola Superior de Administração de Gestão (Esags), responsible for the Human Resources Management classes. She is also a project manager at the Great Place to Work Institute (Brazil), a consulting institute specialized in promoting improvements in the workplace.

John Oglesby is Director, IT planning and Governance at Buckman Laboratories International, co-founder of the CIO Services Group, and an Executive in Residence at the University of Memphis. His 42 years experience in Information Technology spans all aspects of operations and management and crosses industries such as aerospace, financial services, manufacturing, consumer services, healthcare, and education. He is a multiple past president of SIM-Memphis, serves on the University of Memphis MIS Advisory Board, and is a founder of the innovative and highly-acclaimed Teen Tech Camp, sponsored yearly by SIM Memphis and the Memphis Public Library. He has sponsored and led a number of innovative industry programs and research efforts, including the development of a practical methodology for I.T. strategic planning, the TPR™—Technology Performance Rating system, as well as an academic research project to determine whether and how TPR scores are related to corporate performance and IT satisfaction. John holds a bachelor's degree in aerospace engineering and an MBA from Georgia Tech, and currently serves on several corporate boards. He has published numerous technical articles, has been a contributor to industry publications, is widely traveled, having visited all seven continents, and has written several novels and short stories.

Dawn Owens is a PhD student in the College of Information Science and Technology at the University of Nebraska at Omaha specializing in Information Technology. Her professional experience in Information Systems, executive management, leadership, quality assurance, and software development provide a foundation for her continuing educational pursuits and research interests. She is also an assistant professor at Bellevue University. Her research interests include project management, virtual teams, software quality assurance, and utilizing technology to enhance trust in virtual teams. She has published in such journals as Journal of the Association for Information Systems, Data Base for Advances in Information Systems and IEEE IT Professional. Her master's and undergraduate degrees are in Management Information Systems.

Gina Pipoli de Azambuja PhD (c) works as Principal Professor and researcher in Marketing at Universidad del Pacífico in Lima, Perú. She has an MBA with a major in Marketing, a title in Business Administration and a title in Accounting. Nowadays she is finishing her Doctoral Thesis for obtaining her Doctoral Degree in Economics and Management at Deusto University in Spain. As international professor, she has given several courses, seminars, and conferences abroad, and has published ten books. Her teaching and research areas are: marketing management, branding, customer relationship management, loyalty marketing, strategy and development of new products. She is also Project Faculty in the Wharton Global Consulting Practicum of Wharton Business School since 2003 and works as international Marketing Consultant and Advisor. She has been Associate Dean of the Graduate Business School, Vice Dean of the School of Business Administration and Accounting, Head of the Business Department, Director of the Language Center, among other responsibilities held at Universidad del Pacifico. Her professional activity is based on more than 25 years of experience, during which she has worked in important companies such as: Cosapi Data S.A., Cosapi S.A., The Chase Manhattan Bank and Xerox.

Phil Schneidermeyer is a Partner in the New York office of Heidrick & Struggles specializing in the recruitment of Chief Information and Chief Technology Officers across all industry sectors. Previously, Phil led the CIO Practice for Highland Partners and founded an Information Technology and engineering boutique executive search firm. Earlier, Phil was a managing director at another global executive search firm, where he served as the Chief Information Officer Practice leader and a member of the firm's Advanced Technology Practice. He also sat on the Americas Operating Group and served as chairman of Information Technology Committee. Prior to his executive search career, Phil was an economist with a Hartford-based consulting firm focused on the Connecticut economy and commercial real estate markets. Phil currently serves on the Advisory Board for Year Up New York City, an organization providing young urban adults with professional skills, technical training and corporate apprenticeships. Phil earned his BA in business administration and was awarded a Master's degree in public affairs from the University of Connecticut.

Derek J. Sedlack is the President and CEO of Blueskin Technologies, LLC a CyberSecurity consulting organization and a doctoral candidate at Nova Southeastern University's Graduate School of Computer and Information Sciences, Davie, Florida, with a focus on information security. His career includes strategic positions in technology (including CTO), management consulting, and strategic investment guidance. Mr. Sedlack is a multiple individual U.S. patent award recipient and designed innovative infrastructure solutions for Fortune 100 clients that revolutionized custom computer ordering and manufacturing. After a notable fifteen year career traveling internationally with global IT corporations including IBM, Dell, HP, and Citrix, Mr. Sedlack is leveraging his combined strengths as practitioner and academic serving as adjunct faculty in the topics of information security. His developing framework for assessing IT-business incongruity will help organizations around the world understand, define, and scope appropriate strategic direction, driving profitability through enhanced information security. Active memberships include a board position with Experience.com, continued involvement with Junior Achievement of South Florida, and frequent requests as a technology consultant.

Jo Ann Starkweather is a Professor in the Department of Information Systems & Technology at Northeastern State University. She has 10 years of experience as a Social Research Consultant in Washington, D.C. and 25 years devoted to teaching and scholarship. She holds an MA from George Mason University and a PhD from Cornell University.

Deborah H. Stevenson is an Associate Professor in the Department of Information Systems & Technology at Northeastern State University. Having recently returned to academia, she has 15 years of project management experience in various industries, most recently in telecommunications. She holds BS and MBA degrees from Florida Institute of Technology, and a PhD from Clemson University

John G. Stevenson is a former Chief Information Officer with over 25 years of senior Information Technology executive experience. His broad experience includes key executive assignments in large corporations spanning high technology, consumer goods, pharmaceuticals, and manufacturing industries. John's most recent assignment was as Vice President and Chief Information Officer at Sharp Electronics Corporation of the Americas, a maker of consumer and business electronics. John previously served as Chief Information Officer at Avaya Communications, an $8 billion manufacturer of voice and data switching equipment, he was also the Chief Information Officer at Lennox International, the number two global heating and air conditioner equipment manufacturer. During the 1990's, John was the top information executive for the Bristol-Myers-Squibb $16 billion Pharmaceutical Group and for over eight years prior to that, he was the top information executive at Dr Pepper/Seven-Up Corporation. John presently serves as Vice Chairman of the Board of The Barton Corporation, a global mining and abrasives manufacturer. He also recently served on the board of GridApp Software Corporation and on the Advisory Board of the University of North Texas. John presently has his own IT executive consulting practice which specializes in leadership analysis, strategy and sourcing alternatives.

Allen Ross Taylor is an Assistant Professor of Management Information Systems in the College of Business and Technology at the University of Nebraska at Kearney. His areas of interest are computer-aided decision making, rural economic development, and social media. He received his PhD from the University of Arkansas. His research has been published in journals such as European Journal of Operations Research and Journal of Behavioral Studies in Business.

Frank A. Tenkorang was born in Accra, Ghana. In 1996, he received his Bachelor's degree from the University of Ghana, in Legon, Ghana. Frank joined the Health Economics unit of the Institute of Statistical, Social and Economic Research (ISSER) of University of Ghana as a research assistant a year later. The University of Wyoming in Laramie conferred upon him the Master of Science in Agricultural Economics in 2002. Then he joined the graduate program at Purdue University and graduated in May 2006 with his PhD in Agricultural Economics. Currently, Dr. Tenkorang is on the faculty of the College of Business and Technology, University of Nebraska at Kearney, Nebraska, USA where he teaches economics and agribusiness courses. Some of his research studies focused on fertilizer demand forecasting, agricultural commodities prices forecasting, profitability of remote sensing in agriculture, and demand for Information Technology professionals.

Dibi Varghese is a graduate of the Master of Science in Information Systems (MSIS) program from Stevens Institute of Technology and recipient of the program's Outstanding Academic Achievement Award. She holds an undergraduate degree in Information Systems from University of the Witwatersrand (South Africa), and a Honors degree in Informatics from University of Pretoria (South Africa) where she received an award for her research project. Prior to starting her master's degree, Dibi spent over 9 years in the South African financial industry working on various IT projects. She is currently employed by Credit Suisse and is a member of the Technology Analyst program. She is also a member of the Golden Key International Honor Society.

Tim Weitzel is Full Professor and Chair of Information Systems at Bamberg University, Germany. Tim's research on IT management and alignment, IT adoption, standards, outsourcing, e-finance and e-HR has been published in journals including MIS Quarterly, MIS Quarterly Executive, Journal of Information Technology and Decision Support Systems. Tim is director of the "Centre of Human Resources Information Systems (CHRIS)" that he founded at Goethe University Frankfurt in 2002 to analyze the role and opportunities of Information Systems in the HR process. He serves as Associate Editor for the Journal of the Association for Information Systems and the European Journal of Information System

Clay K. Williams is an Assistant Professor in the Department of Computer Management and Information Systems at Southern Illinois University Edwardsville. He holds a PhD in management Information Systems from the University of Georgia, and a master of science in management and a bachelor of electrical engineering from Georgia Tech. Dr. Williams has over 18 years professional experience in consulting and project management in the areas of business process reengineering and IS implementations. He managed a consulting practice and co-founded a (short lived) dot com start-up. Dr. Williams teaches IS in Business courses for both MBAs and undergraduates. His research deals with the role of coordination and governance in achieving organizational outcomes with IS, the role of self efficacy in the use of IS, and applying the critical realism research paradigm to improve theoretical explanations and the practical relevance of IS academic research. Dr. Williams has presented his research at the International Conference for Information Systems (ICIS) and the Academy of Management.

Cesar Yokomizo has a Master of Science degree and is currently a Ph. D. candidate in Business Administration (Information Systems) at the São Paulo Business Administration School (EAESP), Fundação Getulio Vargas (FGV, Brazil). He also has a Master of Science degree and is currently a PhD candidate in Business Administration (Strategy & Innovation) at the School of Economics, Business Administration and Accountancy (FEA), University of São Paulo (USP, Brazil). He has a specialist degree in Networking Engineering and Telecommunications Systems from the National Institute of Telecommunications (Inatel, Brazil) and received bachelor's degrees in Computing Engineering and Economics from USP. He is currently a graduate lecturer at Fundação Instituto de Administração (FIA, Brazil), Serviço Nacional de Aprendizagem Comercial (Senac, Brazil), and conducts research for FGV and Serasa Experian. His main research interests include: strategy & innovation, organizational intelligence, Information and Communication Technologies for development, and Information Technology professionals and careers. A unique aspect of his research is his focus on cases from developing countries, especially those from Brazil. His work experience includes research and consultancy projects at A.T. Kearney (Brazil), Portugal Telecom Inovação (Portugal and Brazil) and in universities in France and Germany.

Index

Printed in the USA
CPSIA information can be obtained
at www.ICGtesting.com
LVHW080304260124
769949LV00050B/36